Handbook of Research on Foundations and Applications of Intelligent Business Analytics

Zhaohao Sun
Papua New Guinea University of Technology, Papua New Guinea

Zhiyou Wu
Chongqing Normal University, China

A volume in the Advances in Business Information Systems and Analytics (ABISA) Book Series

Published in the United States of America by
  IGI Global
  Business Science Reference (an imprint of IGI Global)
  701 E. Chocolate Avenue
  Hershey PA, USA 17033
  Tel: 717-533-8845
  Fax: 717-533-8661
  E-mail: cust@igi-global.com
  Web site: http://www.igi-global.com

Library of Congress Cataloging-in-Publication Data

Names: Sun, Zhaohao, editor. | Wu, Zhiyou, 1967- editor.
Title: Handbook of research on foundations and applications of intelligent
  business analytics / Zhaohao Sun, and Zhiyou Wu, editor.
Description: Hershey, PA : Business Science Reference, [2022] | Includes
  bibliographical references and index. | Summary: "This book addresses
  research issues by investigating into foundations, technologies, and
  applications of intelligent business analytics, offering theoretical
  foundations, technologies, methodologies, and applications of
  intelligent business analytics in an integrated way"-- Provided by
  publisher.
Identifiers: LCCN 2021037619 (print) | LCCN 2021037620 (ebook) | ISBN
  9781799890164 (hardcover) | ISBN 9781799890188 (ebook)
Subjects: LCSH: Management--Data processing. | Big data. | Business
  planning--Statistical methods.
Classification: LCC HD30.2 .H364256 2022 (print) | LCC HD30.2 (ebook) |
  DDC 658/.0557--dc23
LC record available at https://lccn.loc.gov/2021037619
LC ebook record available at https://lccn.loc.gov/2021037620

This book is published in the IGI Global book series Advances in Business Information Systems and Analytics (ABISA) (ISSN: 2327-3275; eISSN: 2327-3283)

British Cataloguing in Publication Data
A Cataloguing in Publication record for this book is available from the British Library.

All work contributed to this book is new, previously-unpublished material. The views expressed in this book are those of the authors, but not necessarily of the publisher.

For electronic access to this publication, please contact: eresources@igi-global.com.

Advances in Business Information Systems and Analytics (ABISA) Book Series

Madjid Tavana
La Salle University, USA

ISSN:2327-3275
EISSN:2327-3283

MISSION

The successful development and management of information systems and business analytics is crucial to the success of an organization. New technological developments and methods for data analysis have allowed organizations to not only improve their processes and allow for greater productivity, but have also provided businesses with a venue through which to cut costs, plan for the future, and maintain competitive advantage in the information age.

The **Advances in Business Information Systems and Analytics (ABISA) Book Series** aims to present diverse and timely research in the development, deployment, and management of business information systems and business analytics for continued organizational development and improved business value.

COVERAGE

- Business Information Security
- Data Governance
- Business Process Management
- Forecasting
- Legal information systems
- Data Strategy
- Management Information Systems
- Business Models
- Data Analytics
- Business Decision Making

IGI Global is currently accepting manuscripts for publication within this series. To submit a proposal for a volume in this series, please contact our Acquisition Editors at Acquisitions@igi-global.com or visit: http://www.igi-global.com/publish/.

Titles in this Series

For a list of additional titles in this series, please visit: www.igi-global.com/book-series/advances-business-information-systems-analytics/37155

Utilizing Blockchain Technologies in Manufacturing and Logistics Management
S. B. Goyal (City University, Malaysia) Nijalingappa Pradeep (Bapuji Institute of Engineering and Technology, India) Piyush Kumar Shukla (University Institute of Technology RGPV, India) Mangesh M. Ghonge (Sandip Institute of Technology and Research Centre, India) and Renjith V. Ravi (MEA Engineering College, India)
Business Science Reference • © 2022 • 290pp • H/C (ISBN: 9781799886976) • US $225.00

Business Applications in Social Media Analytics
Himani Bansal (Jaypee University, Solan, India) and Gulshan Shrivastava (National Institute of Technology, Patna, India)
Business Science Reference • © 2022 • 330pp • H/C (ISBN: 9781799850465) • US $195.00

Achieving Organizational Agility, Intelligence, and Resilience Through Information Systems
Hakikur Rahman (Ansted University Sustainability Research Institute, Malaysia)
Business Science Reference • © 2022 • 350pp • H/C (ISBN: 9781799847991) • US $195.00

Handbook of Research on Applied Data Science and Artificial Intelligence in Business and Industry
Valentina Chkoniya (University of Aveiro, Portugal)
Engineering Science Reference • © 2021 • 653pp • H/C (ISBN: 9781799869856) • US $425.00

Using Strategy Analytics to Measure Corporate Performance and Business Value Creation
Sandeep Kautish (Lord Buddha Education Foundation, Nepal)
Business Science Reference • © 2021 • 287pp • H/C (ISBN: 9781799877165) • US $225.00

Adapting and Mitigating Environmental, Social, and Governance Risk in Business
Magdalena Ziolo (University of Szczecin, Poland)
Business Science Reference • © 2021 • 313pp • H/C (ISBN: 9781799867883) • US $195.00

Innovative and Agile Contracting for Digital Transformation and Industry 4.0
Mohammad Ali Shalan (Aqarat Real Estate Development Company, Saudi Arabia) and Mohammed Ayedh Algarni (Information and Documents Center, Institute of Public Administration, Saudi Arabia)
Business Science Reference • © 2021 • 415pp • H/C (ISBN: 9781799845010) • US $225.00

701 East Chocolate Avenue, Hershey, PA 17033, USA
Tel: 717-533-8845 x100 • Fax: 717-533-8661
E-Mail: cust@igi-global.com • www.igi-global.com

List of Contributors

A., D. N. Sarma / *Centre for Good Governance, India* 21

Akila, Djebbar / *Badji Mokhtar University, Algeria* 113

Aljarrah, Emran Mahmoud / *Jadara University, Jordan* 189

Alomari, Saleh Ali / *Jadara University, Jordan* 189

Alqaraleh, Muhyeeddin Kamel / *Jadara University, Jordan* 189

Alzboon, Mowafaq Salem / *Jadara University, Jordan* 189

Anthonyraj, Selvakumar / *Ayya Nadar Janaki Ammal College, India* 142

Bick, Markus / *ESCP Business School Berlin, Germany* 238

Bouguettaya, Abdelmalek / *Research Centre in Industrial Technologies (CRTI), Algeria* 166

Chen, Li / *University of the District of Columbia, USA* 273

Chiu, Dickson K. W. / *The University of Hong Kong, Hong Kong* 301, 320

Farida, Merouani Hayet / *Badji Mokhtar University, Algeria* 113

Giebe, Carsten / *MATE Hungarian University of Agriculture and Life Sciences, Hungary* 350

He, Zhixuan / *The University of Hong Kong, Hong Kong* 320

Ho, Kevin K. W. / *University of Guam, Guam* 288, 301, 320

Kechida, Ahmed / *Research Centre in Industrial Technologies (CRTI), Algeria* 166

Khan, Muhammad Haseeb / *University of Tsukuba, Japan* 288

Matheus, Ricardo / *Delft University of Technology, Netherlands* 71

Narongou, Desmond / *National Airports Corporation, Papua New Guinea* 216

Pambel, Francisca / *Papua New Guinea University of Technology, Papua New Guinea* 1

Paramasivam, Isakki Alias Devi / *Ayya Nadar Janaki Ammal College, India* 142

Pinheiro, Luiz / *Positivo University, Brazil* 71

Rai, Shivanand / *ESCP Business School Berlin, Germany* 238

Ryjov, Alexander P. / *Lomonosov Moscow State University, Russia* 47

Safa, Gasmi / *Badji Mokhtar University, Algeria* 113

Stranieri, Andrew / *Federation University, Australia* 96

Sun, Zhaohao / *Papua New Guinea University of Technology, Papua New Guinea* 1, 96, 216

Taberkit, Amine Mohammed / *Research Centre in Industrial Technologies (CRTI), Algeria* 166

Wakabayashi, Kei / *University of Tsukuba, Japan* 288

Wang, Bingnan / *The University of Hong Kong, Hong Kong* 301

Wu, Zhiyou / *Chongqing Normal University, China* 1

Ye, Shaoyu / *University of Tsukuba, Japan* 288

Zarzour, Hafed / *University of Souk Ahras, Algeria* 166

Table of Contents

Preface..xvii

Acknowledgment...xxvii

Section 1
Foundations of Intelligent Business Analytics

Chapter 1

The Elements of Intelligent Business Analytics: Principles, Techniques, and Tools............................1

Zhaohao Sun, Papua New Guinea University of Technology, Papua New Guinea
Francisca Pambel, Papua New Guinea University of Technology, Papua New Guinea
Zhiyou Wu, Chongqing Normal University, China

Chapter 2

Intelligent Business Analytics: Need, Functioning, Challenges, and Implications............................21

D. N. Sarma A., Centre for Good Governance, India

Chapter 3

Principles of a Hybrid Intelligence Framework for Augmented Analytics............................47

Alexander P. Ryjov, Lomonosov Moscow State University, Russia

Chapter 4

Designing Business Analytics Projects (BAP): A Five-Step Dashboarding Cycle............................71

Luiz Pinheiro, Positivo University, Brazil
Ricardo Matheus, Delft University of Technology, Netherlands

Section 2
Technologies for Intelligent Business Analytics

Chapter 5

A Process-Oriented Framework for Regulating Artificial Intelligence Systems............................96

Andrew Stranieri, Federation University, Australia
Zhaohao Sun, Papua New Guinea University of Technology, Papua New Guinea

Chapter 6

A Survey on Hybrid Case-Based Reasoning and Deep Learning Systems for Medical Data
Classification.. 113
    Gasmi Safa, Badji Mokhtar University, Algeria
    Djebbar Akila, Badji Mokhtar University, Algeria
    Merouani Hayet Farida, Badji Mokhtar University, Algeria

Chapter 7

Big Data Analytics for Search Engine Optimization in Intelligent Business 142
    Isakki Alias Devi Paramasivam, Ayya Nadar Janaki Ammal College, India
    Selvakumar Anthonyraj, Ayya Nadar Janaki Ammal College, India

Chapter 8

Machine Learning and Deep Learning as New Tools for Business Analytics..................... 166
    Abdelmalek Bouguettaya, Research Centre in Industrial Technologies (CRTI), Algeria
    Hafed Zarzour, University of Souk Ahras, Algeria
    Ahmed Kechida, Research Centre in Industrial Technologies (CRTI), Algeria
    Amine Mohammed Taberkit, Research Centre in Industrial Technologies (CRTI), Algeria

Chapter 9

Semantic Image Analysis on Social Networks and Data Processing: Review and Future Directions 189
    Mowafaq Salem Alzboon, Jadara University, Jordan
    Muhyeeddin Kamel Alqaraleh, Jadara University, Jordan
    Emran Mahmoud Aljarrah, Jadara University, Jordan
    Saleh Ali Alomari, Jadara University, Jordan

Section 3
Applications of Intelligent Business Analytics

Chapter 10

Applying Intelligent Big Data Analytics in a Smart Airport Business: Value, Adoption, and
Challenges... 216
    Desmond Narongou, National Airports Corporation, Papua New Guinea
    Zhaohao Sun, Papua New Guinea University of Technology, Papua New Guinea

Chapter 11

Immunize Your Organization: A People Analytics Exploration of the Change in Employee
Priorities After the COVID-19 Lockdown... 238
    Shivanand Rai, ESCP Business School Berlin, Germany
    Markus Bick, ESCP Business School Berlin, Germany

Chapter 12

Undergraduate Computer Science Capstone Projects: Experiences and Examples in Data Science . 273
    Li Chen, University of the District of Columbia, USA

Chapter 13
The Relationships Between Users' Negative Tweets, Topic Choices, and Subjective Well-Being in
Japan 288
  Shaoyu Ye, University of Tsukuba, Japan
  Kei Wakabayashi, University of Tsukuba, Japan
  Kevin K. W. Ho, University of Guam, Guam
  Muhammad Haseeb Khan, University of Tsukuba, Japan

Chapter 14
A Comparison of Deep Learning Models in Time Series Forecasting of Web Traffic Data From
Kaggle 301
  Bingnan Wang, The University of Hong Kong, Hong Kong
  Dickson K. W. Chiu, The University of Hong Kong, Hong Kong
  Kevin K. W. Ho, University of Guam, Guam

Chapter 15
Weibo Analysis on Chinese Cultural Knowledge for Gaming 320
  Zhixuan He, The University of Hong Kong, Hong Kong
  Dickson K. W. Chiu, The University of Hong Kong, Hong Kong
  Kevin K. W. Ho, University of Guam, Guam

Chapter 16
Big Data Analytics and the Discovery of the Hidden Data Treasure From Savings Banks in
Germany 350
  Carsten Giebe, MATE Hungarian University of Agriculture and Life Sciences, Hungary

Compilation of References 374

About the Contributors 416

Index 422

Detailed Table of Contents

Preface.. xvii

Acknowledgment xxvii

Section 1
Foundations of Intelligent Business Analytics

Chapter 1

The Elements of Intelligent Business Analytics: Principles, Techniques, and Tools 1

Zhaohao Sun, Papua New Guinea University of Technology, Papua New Guinea
Francisca Pambel, Papua New Guinea University of Technology, Papua New Guinea
Zhiyou Wu, Chongqing Normal University, China

This chapter explores the elements of intelligent business analytics and addresses the following research questions: What are the elements, principles, technologies, and tools of intelligent business analytics? How can one incorporate the latest intelligent technologies into business analytics? This research highlights that big data and big DIKIW are the elements for intelligent business analytics; big data analytics and intelligent big data analytics and big DIKIW and intelligent big DIKIW analytics are the foundation of intelligent business analytics; the principles, technologies, and tools of intelligent business analytics are emerging strategic sources for organizations and individuals in the competitive global environment. This chapter presents a framework for DIKIW-driven intelligent business analytics through incorporating DIKIW analytics into intelligent business analytics. The proposed approach might facilitate research and development of intelligent business, big data analytics, business intelligence, AI, and data science.

Chapter 2

Intelligent Business Analytics: Need, Functioning, Challenges, and Implications 21

D. N. Sarma A., Centre for Good Governance, India

This chapter begins with a brief introduction to the evolution of the data analytics ecosystem and its role. The terms such as data, insight, and action are defined in the context of business analytics. The authors explain briefly about analytics, business analytics (BA), business intelligence, and intelligent BA. They mention the need for intelligent analytics for the organizations in a digital world. The latest innovations in AI, big data, and analytics together result in a new branch known as intelligent big data analytics, in short, intelligent BA. Further, intelligent BA becomes an important tool for the organizations for intelligent decision making. The key components of intelligent BA are presented and explained. Additionally, various applications of intelligent BA are presented, and a few challenges for implementing the system are mentioned. Finally, possible future directions of research for the development of intelligent BA are discussed.

Chapter 3

Principles of a Hybrid Intelligence Framework for Augmented Analytics 47
Alexander P. Ryjov, Lomonosov Moscow State University, Russia

Analytics is a key success factor for any business in the competitive and fast-changing world. Using good analytics, people, business, social, and government organizations become capable of making good decisions. With augmented analytics, human expertise actually becomes more crucial than ever. This chapter aims to introduce the hybrid intelligence approach by focusing on its unique analytical capabilities. The state-of-the-art in hybrid intelligence, symbiosis and cooperative interaction between human intelligence and artificial intelligence in solving a wide range of practical tasks, and one of the hybrid intelligence frameworks, a human-centered approach for evaluation and monitoring of complex processes, have been considered in this chapter. The chapter could be interesting for analysts and researchers who desire to do analytics with more intelligence.

Chapter 4

Designing Business Analytics Projects (BAP): A Five-Step Dashboarding Cycle 71
Luiz Pinheiro, Positivo University, Brazil
Ricardo Matheus, Delft University of Technology, Netherlands

Private and public organizations have been using data for decision-making. However, these organizations have been struggling in putting into practice the design data analytics projects. In this sense, this chapter aims to present a proposal of a designing business analytics projects with a practical five steps dashboarding cycle. The first step, Business Questions, deals with the scope of a data analytics project creating problem-based questions. The second step, Data Sources, details which are the data sources to be collected. The third step, Extraction, Transform, and Loading (ETL), sets up data source routines of what, where, and when to collect data. The fourth step, Data Warehouse, creates a data repository where data is stored and treated after ETL process. The fifth step, Data Visualization, designs a web dashboard with interactive features such as tables and graphs. This chapter ends with three practical examples in both public and private organizations.

Section 2
Technologies for Intelligent Business Analytics

Chapter 5

A Process-Oriented Framework for Regulating Artificial Intelligence Systems 96
Andrew Stranieri, Federation University, Australia
Zhaohao Sun, Papua New Guinea University of Technology, Papua New Guinea

Frameworks for the regulation of artificial intelligence (AI) systems are emerging; some are based on regulation theories; others are more technologically focused. Regulation of AI systems is likely to emerge in an ad-hoc, unstructured, and uncoordinated fashion that renders high level frameworks philosophically interesting but of limited benefit in practice. In this paper, the task of arriving at a collection of interventions that regulate an AI system is taken to be a process-oriented problem. It presents a process-oriented framework for the design of regulating systems by deliberating groups. It also discusses regulations of

AI systems and responsibility, mechanisms and institutions, key elements for regulating AI systems. The proposed approach might facilitate research and development of responsible AI, explainable AI, and ethical AI for an ethical and inclusive digitized society. It also has implications for the development of e-business, e-services, and e-society.

Chapter 6

A Survey on Hybrid Case-Based Reasoning and Deep Learning Systems for Medical Data Classification..113

Gasmi Safa, Badji Mokhtar University, Algeria
Djebbar Akila, Badji Mokhtar University, Algeria
Merouani Hayet Farida, Badji Mokhtar University, Algeria

Several artificial intelligence approaches, particularly case-based reasoning (CBR), which is analogous to the context of human reasoning for problem resolution, have demonstrated their efficiency and reliability in the medical field. In recent years, deep learning represents the latest iteration of an advance in artificial intelligence technologies in medicine to aid in data classification, diagnosis of new diseases, and complex decision-making. Although these two independent approaches have good results in the medical field, the latter is still a complex field. This chapter reviews the available literature on CBR systems, deep learning systems, and CBR deep learning systems in medicine. The methods used and results obtained are discussed, and key findings are highlighted. Further, in the light of this review, some directions for future research are given. This chapter presents the proposed approach, which helps to make the retrieval phase of the CBR cycle more reliable and robust.

Chapter 7

Big Data Analytics for Search Engine Optimization in Intelligent Business 142

Isakki Alias Devi Paramasivam, Ayya Nadar Janaki Ammal College, India
Selvakumar Anthonyraj, Ayya Nadar Janaki Ammal College, India

Big data has a massive impact on the world today, publicly and in the business province. SEO (Search Engine Optimization) is one of the areas of intelligent business marketing that is continuously affected by the insights. Big data makes it easier for search engines to analyze the content and deliver results that are relevant to user needs. Search engine optimization takes into account how search engines work, the computer-programmed algorithms that govern look search engine behavior, what users search for, and the actual search keywords submitted into search engines. Search engines are always preferred by their targeted audience. Big data analytics is obliging to increase website traffic. This really helps to apply intelligence in business areas. This chapter deals with big data analytics for SEO in intelligent business.

Chapter 8

Machine Learning and Deep Learning as New Tools for Business Analytics....................................166

Abdelmalek Bouguettaya, Research Centre in Industrial Technologies (CRTI), Algeria
Hafed Zarzour, University of Souk Ahras, Algeria
Ahmed Kechida, Research Centre in Industrial Technologies (CRTI), Algeria
Amine Mohammed Taberkit, Research Centre in Industrial Technologies (CRTI), Algeria

Data scientists need to develop accurate and effective tools and techniques to handle a huge amount of data. Therefore, machine learning and deep learning algorithms have come to the life, especially with the impressive advances in both hardware and software fields. Many impressive existing services are helping us in our daily lives, such as Google Assistant, Uber, Alexa, and Siri, which are based on big data, machine learning, and deep learning. Although intelligent algorithms and big data have been adopted in many modern business intelligence and analytics applications, in this chapter, the authors aim to present the basics of machine learning and deep learning concepts and their utilization in the field of business intelligence. As concrete examples, with the high spread of the COVID-19 pandemic, Tesla and Amazon achieved the biggest revenue ever, where many other companies suffer. These high revenues could be due to the strategic decisions of their leaders, which are based especially on artificial intelligence.

Chapter 9

Semantic Image Analysis on Social Networks and Data Processing: Review and Future Directions 189
Mowafaq Salem Alzboon, Jadara University, Jordan
Muhyeeddin Kamel Alqaraleh, Jadara University, Jordan
Emran Mahmoud Aljarrah, Jadara University, Jordan
Saleh Ali Alomari, Jadara University, Jordan

In the last decade, a significant number of people have become active social network users. People utilize Twitter, Facebook, LinkedIn, and Google+. Facebook users generate a lot of data. Photos can teach people a lot. Image analysis has traditionally focused on audience emotions. Photographic emotions are essentially subjective and vary among observers. There are numerous uses for its most popular feature. People, on the other hand, use social media and applications. They handle noise, dynamics, and size. Shared text, pictures, and videos were also a focus of network analysis study. Statistic, rules, and trend analysis are all available in massive datasets. You may use them for data manipulation and retrieval, mathematical modeling, and data pre-processing and interpretation. This chapter examines social networks, basic concepts, and social network analysis components. A further study topic is picture usage in social networks. Next, a novel method for analyzing social networks, namely semantic networks, is presented. Finally, themes and routes are defined.

Section 3
Applications of Intelligent Business Analytics

Chapter 10

Applying Intelligent Big Data Analytics in a Smart Airport Business: Value, Adoption, and Challenges 216
Desmond Narongou, National Airports Corporation, Papua New Guinea
Zhaohao Sun, Papua New Guinea University of Technology, Papua New Guinea

Airports have always been one of the biggest contributors of big data to the aviation ecosystem. With the abundance of data available, big data analytics can help transform the airports to smart ones. This chapter examines airport analytics from a business process viewpoint. It explores the value of applying intelligent big data analytics in an airport from an operations perspective and strategic differentiation perspective. This chapter also discusses the challenges faced when adopting intelligent big data analytics in a smart airport paradigm from the perspective of PNG's National Airports Corporation (NAC). This chapter then looks at how these challenges can be overcome to realize the true value of applying intelligent big data analytics in an airport. The approach proposed in this chapter might contribute to expediting research of future development of intelligent big data analytics solutions that are customizable to an airport to recognize the real value of intelligent big data analytics in all facets of its operations.

Chapter 11

Immunize Your Organization: A People Analytics Exploration of the Change in Employee
Priorities After the COVID-19 Lockdown..238

Shivanand Rai, ESCP Business School Berlin, Germany
Markus Bick, ESCP Business School Berlin, Germany

The pandemic has changed the world immensely and provided a natural experiment for the field of people analytics. Herein, the authors analyze how this has changed employees' priorities, what the future might look like, and how corporations can respond. This is the first study of its kind to examine the entire construct of Glassdoor and map the changes it reveals during the pandemic, using machine-learning and NLP techniques. Individual ratings were used to create a model of satisfaction that would provide us with a framework to see which factors drive employee satisfaction and what changed during the pandemic. The results show that culture and management are the most critical organizational factors in a time of crisis, with career reducing in importance. Culture appears to be the vaccine that immunizes against tough times. Although actual compensation did not increase, its rating did so during the pandemic, showing that career and compensation are rated more on external factors. Most employees pointed to the bureaucracy and silo mentalities of banks as the nexus complicating their lives.

Chapter 12

Undergraduate Computer Science Capstone Projects: Experiences and Examples in Data Science . 273

Li Chen, University of the District of Columbia, USA

The CS&IT senior capstone project at the University of the District of Columbia has three components: 1) Senior Seminar, 2) Senior Project I, and 3) Senior Project II. The purpose of Senior Seminar (one credit) is to expand the students' scope of knowledge through reading cutting-edge materials in CS&IT. Students in the class often learn from each other, while the instructor organizes talks given by professors at the university as well as industry professionals. Students give formal presentations as their final exam. The main purpose of Senior Project I (two credits) is to teach students how to start a research project. Students are asked to complete a simple research proposal after doing background research to select a research project. The final report is a short report. In Senior Project II (three credits), many students choose to continue the project Senior Project I. For this course, students complete a well-written report ranging from 20 to 25 pages. This paper explains how we teach these courses and include five examples in data science.

Chapter 13

The Relationships Between Users' Negative Tweets, Topic Choices, and Subjective Well-Being in
Japan 288

Shaoyu Ye, University of Tsukuba, Japan
Kei Wakabayashi, University of Tsukuba, Japan
Kevin K. W. Ho, University of Guam, Guam
Muhammad Haseeb Khan, University of Tsukuba, Japan

This study examined the relationships between expressions in Tweets, topic choices, and subjective well-being among undergraduates in Japan. The authors conducted a survey with 304 college students and analyzed their Twitter posts using natural language processing (NLP). Based on those who posted over 50 tweets, the authors found that (1) users with higher levels of social skills had fewer negative tweets and higher levels of subjective well-being; (2) frequent users posted both positive and negative tweets but posted more negative than positive tweets; (3) users with fewer negative tweets or with more positive tweets had higher levels of subjective well-being; and (4) "safe" topics such as social events and personal interests had a positive correlation with the users' subjective well-being, while debatable topics such as politics and social issues had a negative correlation with the users' subjective well-being. The findings of this study provide the foundation for applying NLP to analyze the social media posts for businesses and services to understand their consumers' sentiments.

Chapter 14

A Comparison of Deep Learning Models in Time Series Forecasting of Web Traffic Data From Kaggle 301

Bingnan Wang, The University of Hong Kong, Hong Kong
Dickson K. W. Chiu, The University of Hong Kong, Hong Kong
Kevin K. W. Ho, University of Guam, Guam

In recent years, time series forecasting has attracted more attention from academia and industry. This research used raw data from the "Web Traffic Forecasting" competition on the Kaggle platform to test the prediction accuracy of different time series models, especially the generalization performance of various deep learning models. The experiments used historical traffic data from 145,063 web pages from Wikipedia from 2015-07-01 to 2017-11-13. Traffic data from 2015-07-01 to 2017-09-10 was used to forecast traffic from 2017-09-13 to 2017-11-13, a total of 62 days. The experimental results showed that almost all deep learning models predicted far more effectively than statistical and machine learning models, showing that deep learning models have great potential for time series forecasting problems.

Chapter 15

Weibo Analysis on Chinese Cultural Knowledge for Gaming 320

Zhixuan He, The University of Hong Kong, Hong Kong
Dickson K. W. Chiu, The University of Hong Kong, Hong Kong
Kevin K. W. Ho, University of Guam, Guam

This chapter analyzes the current situation of video games with Chinese cultural knowledge in China's game market by analyzing Weibo messages of five selected video games developed based on Chinese culture to explore their relationships with Chinese culture. The authors then summarize the results from comments, likes, word cloud, and clustering analysis to provide practical suggestions. As a new industry, video games and e-sports are gaining popularity worldwide. However, scant research has focused on video games developed based on Chinese culture in the current market, mainly because they started much later than their Western counterparts. Therefore, the findings of this research can help game developers better understand these markets and customer preferences while protecting and spreading Chinese culture through gaming and e-sports activities in this digital era.

Chapter 16

Big Data Analytics and the Discovery of the Hidden Data Treasure From Savings Banks in Germany 350

Carsten Giebe, MATE Hungarian University of Agriculture and Life Sciences, Hungary

The banking sector in Germany is undergoing a massive change. The reasons are digitalization, changing customer behaviour, and low interest rates. The focus of this research is on the savings banks in Germany. Savings banks could miss the boat in the age of digital transformation. On the one hand, savings banks are demonstrably forced to take drastic measures, such as mergers, branch closures, and staff reductions. On the other hand, savings banks possess more data about their customers than other industries. Savings banks can order a big data analytics solution called "Sparkassen-DataAnalytics" (aka savings banks data analytics). Sparkassen-DataAnalytics could be used to offer customers tailormade banking products from the information obtained. It is an open secret that costs can be reduced through a higher degree of automation. The main purpose of this research is to discuss to what extent big data analytics could be a lifeline for German savings banks. Research methods are a literature review and subsequent discussion on the use of big data analytics in the German banking market.

Compilation of References 374

About the Contributors 416

Index 422

Preface

Intelligent business analytics is an emerging paradigm in the age of big data, analytics, and artificial intelligence (AI) (Sun, 2020). Intelligent business analytics is an integration intelligence that integrates artificial intelligence, business intelligence, business analytics, data, information, knowledge, intelligence, and wisdom using advanced ICT computing to provide smart services for improving business, management, and governance. Intelligent business analytics is an emerging intelligent technology and becomes a mainstream market adopted broadly across industries, organizations, and geographic regions and among individuals to facilitate big data-driven decision-making for businesses and individuals to achieve desired business performance (Ali, 2016; Vesset et al., 2013; Sun, 2021). Intelligent business analytics is a crucial part of intelligent analytics for business and management. Augmented analytics and advanced analytics for business are examples of intelligent business analytics (Howson et al., 2019; Sun & Stranieri, 2021).

Intelligent business analytics has been revolutionizing our work, lives, business, marketing, management, and organization as well as healthcare, finance, e-commerce, and web services. It becomes disruptive technology for service computing, cloud computing, the Internet of Everything (IoE), and social networking computing.

Intelligent business analytics is based on data analytics. Data analytics is at the heart of any business, management, and its corresponding decision-making, just as data analysis is at the heart of decision-making in all business applications (Azvine et al., 2003). Intelligent business and decision-making depend not only on big data, but also on big information, big knowledge, and big wisdom. Therefore, intelligent business analytics depends not only on big data analytics, but also on big information analytics, big knowledge analytics, and big wisdom analytics to facilitate intelligent business and intelligent decision-making. At least only data analytics is not enough to realize intelligent business analytics (Azvine et al., 2003; Sun & Stranieri, 2021).

Briefly, intelligent business analytics is a kind of applied intelligent analytics, that is, intelligent analytics for business and management. Intelligent business analytics as a tool or a platform to build decision support systems for e-businesses was studied by Azvine et al. (2003). They proposed an intelligent business analytics platform and then looked at soft computing as an intelligent technology suitable for incorporation into business analytics applications to model hidden patterns in data and to explain such patterns automatically. Intelligent business analytics has been considered a system and a service since then (Sun, 2019).

Google search engine for "intelligent business analytics" shows about 20,700 results (retrieved on December 6, 2021). Several companies have used intelligent business analytics as their marketing mission. For example, Exigy has promoted intelligent business analytics as a cutting-edge technology that can digitally transform business and solve business challenges through providing "accurate insights, on-demand everywhere" (https://www.exigy.com/intelligent-business-analytics/). However, Google Scholar (https://scholar.google.com.au/) search for "intelligent business analytics" (retrieved on December 6, 2021) found only 91 results. We first analyze the titles of the 91 found document results (based on the ranking of Google Scholar) in terms of "intelligent business analytics". Among the 91 mentioned results, only 8 publications have used "intelligent business analytics" as a keyword in their titles. 40 mentioned results include "intelligent business analytics" in either titles or contents. Among them, intelligent business analytics also includes intelligent business analytics systems, intelligent business analytics platforms (Azvine et al., 2003), intelligent business analytics services, intelligent business process analytics, intelligent human resource analytics, intelligent marketing analytics, business analytics intelligence, intelligent business analytics tools, advanced intelligent business analytics, intelligent customer analytics, intelligent process analytics, each of them has appeared in the 40 mentioned results. Furthermore, Google Scholar search for "intelligent analytics" (December 8, 2021) found about 1,390 results and showed that intelligent traffic analytics, intelligent data analytics, intelligent health data analytics, intelligent big data analytics have drawn some attention in academia.

The above big data-driven small data analysis (Sun & Huo, 2021) demonstrates that intelligent business analytics is still an emerging discipline in academia although artificial intelligence and business analytics have become a hotspot in academia and industries over the past decade. Many theoretical, technological, and application issues surrounding the development and implementation of intelligent business analytics remain unsolved. For example: What is the foundation of intelligent business analytics? What are the elements of intelligent business analytics? What is the nature of intelligent business analytics? What are the relationships between intelligent business analytics and big data analytics? How can we incorporate the latest intelligent techniques into business analytics applications? How can we apply intelligent business analytics to improve intelligent business, healthcare, mobile commerce, digital services, cloud services, and digital transformation? What are the implications of intelligent business analytics on intelligent business and management, IoT, blockchain, service, and society? What are the real big characteristics of intelligent business analytics? All these challenges should be addressed through theoretical, technological, and methodological development of intelligent business analytics to meet the social, economic, marketing, managerial, scientific, and technological demands from different parties or individuals for intelligent business analytics. As a follow-up to two books titled *Intelligent Analytics with Advanced Multi-Industry Applications* (Sun, 2021) *and Managerial Perspectives on Intelligent Big Data Analytics* (Sun, 2019), this book addresses the above-mentioned issues by exploring the cutting-edge theories, technologies, and methodologies of intelligent business analytics with applications, and highlights the integration of artificial intelligence, business intelligence, intelligent business, analytics intelligence, intelligent analytics including intelligent big data analytics from a perspective of computing, business, service, and management. This book also provides an original and innovative understanding of and insight into how the proposed theories, technologies, and methodologies of intelligent business analytics can improve e-SMACS (electronic, social, mobile, analytics, cloud, and service) business and services, healthcare, IoE (the Internet of everything), sharing economy, blockchain, 5G technology, cybersecurity, robotic automation, and Industry 4.0 in the real world. This book highlights: 1. Not only big data but also big information, big knowledge, and big wisdom are important for intelligent business and decision-making. 2. Intelligent business analytics is not only a science and technology of integrating artificial intelligence, business intelligence, and business analytics, it is also business analytics intelligence that can embody what customers are eagerly expecting in the digital age. 3. Intelligent business analytics is an emerging paradigm that digitally transforms business to intelligent business, decision-making to intelligent decision-making under the ever-increasing complexity of businesses and business processes. The proposed approaches will facilitate research and development of intelligent business, intelligent business analytics, intelligent analytics, big data analytics, data science, digital transformation, e-business, digital service, service computing, cloud computing, and social computing, and more.

Intelligent business analytics is science and technology about collecting, organizing, and analyzing big data, big information, big knowledge, and big intelligence as well as big wisdom to discover and visualize patterns, knowledge, and intelligence as well as other information within the big data, information, knowledge, and intelligence based on big business analytics, AI, and intelligent systems (Sun & Stranieri, 2021). Intelligent business analytics at least includes intelligent data analytics, intelligent information analytics, intelligent knowledge analytics, and intelligent wisdom analytics for business and business decision-making, all of them are technologically underpinned by intelligent statistical modeling, machine learning, intelligent visualization, and intelligent optimization. Intelligent data analytics further includes big data, intelligent big data analytics, intelligent data analysis, intelligent data warehousing, intelligent data mining, and intelligent data visualization (Sun, 2019). Intelligent information analytics at least includes big information, intelligent information analysis, intelligent information warehousing, intelligent information retrieval, and intelligent information visualization. Intelligent knowledge analytics at least includes big knowledge, intelligent knowledge analysis and engineering, intelligent knowledge systems, intelligent knowledge retrieval and warehousing, and intelligent knowledge visualization. Intelligent wisdom analytics at least includes big wisdom, intelligent wisdom analysis and engineering, intelligent wisdom systems, intelligent wisdom retrieval, and intelligent wisdom visualization (Sun, 2021).

Currently, intelligent business analytics can be classified into intelligent business descriptive analytics, intelligent business diagnostic analytics, intelligent business predictive analytics, and intelligent business prescriptive analytics for big data, information, knowledge, intelligence, and wisdom (Sun & Stranieri, 2021; Sharda et al., 2018). Intelligent big data analytics has made remarkable achievements thanks to the dramatic development of big data and big data analytics. Intelligent information analytics, intelligent knowledge analytics, and intelligent wisdom analytics have not yet drawn significant attention in academia and industry, because we are still indulged in the age of big data, and ignore the dawning age of big information, big knowledge, big intelligence, and big wisdom. Big data is a foundation of big information, big knowledge, and big intelligence or wisdom. Therefore, we are still at the foundational stage and scare about the emerging age of big information, big knowledge, big intelligence, and big wisdom. This is also the reason why intelligent business analytics has not drawn significant attention in academia.

Intelligent techniques that are used to incorporate in business analytics include soft computing, fuzzy logic, neuro-fuzzy systems, neural networks, evolutionary computation, machine learning and deep learning, case-based reasoning, decision trees, probabilistic computing and models (Russell & Norvig, 2020; Azvine et al., 2003; Sun & Stranieri, 2021).

There are no books on "Intelligent business analytics" available based on Amazon.com search although there are hundreds of books for "business analytics", and three books for "intelligent analytics" (retrieved on December 6, 2021). All the books on intelligent analytics can be considered as applications of intelligent analytics in the Internet of Things (IoT). This is the first book titled "Intelligent business analytics" which focuses on intelligent business, intelligent business analytics, intelligent analytics including intelligent big data analytics in the age of big data, analytics, and artificial intelligence. This book titled "Foundations and Application of Intelligent Business Analytics" is the first book to reveal the cutting-edge theory, technologies, methodologies, and applications of intelligent business analytics in the emerging age of intelligent analytics in an integrated way. This is also the first book demonstrating that intelligent business analytics is at the center of intelligent business, intelligent decision-making, intelligent management, digital transformation, governance, and services in the digital age.

This book covers foundations, technologies, and applications of intelligent business analytics. The foundations of intelligent business analytics mainly include core foundations and supporting foundations. The core foundations include intelligent warehouses, intelligent mining, intelligent statistical modeling, machine learning including deep learning, intelligent reporting, intelligent visualization, and optimization for big data, information, knowledge, intelligence, and wisdom. The supporting foundations include artificial intelligence (AI), explainable AI, BI, machine learning, natural language processing, mathematics and statistics, data science, and optimization, domain sciences including business, management, and service science. The topics for this part include fundamental concepts, models/architectures, frameworks/schemes, or foundations for planning, designing, building, operating or evaluating, managing intelligent business analytics.

Technologies of intelligent business analytics in this book include intelligent technology, computational technology, web technology, Internet technology, social networking technology, cloud technology, intelligent business technology, management technology, big data technology, and IoE technology, to name a few. The topics for this section include all the mentioned cutting-edge technologies and tools for developing intelligent business analytics as a service/tool/app/system/platform.

Applications of intelligent business analytics in this book cover all the applications and case studies of intelligent business analytics in business and management, e-commerce, social networking, big data, digital transformation, e-SMACS business, IoT, 5G systems, intelligent drones, healthcare, smart cities, and other real-world problem-solving. The topics for this part include cases and applications for using foundations and technologies in Sections 1 and 2 for planning, designing, building, managing, and operating or evaluating intelligent business analytics in the various domains such as digital transformation, e-SMACS computing, commerce, and services, financial services, legal services, healthcare services, educational services, and military services taking into account intelligent descriptive, diagnostic, predictive, and prescriptive analytics for business and management. This book also includes emerging cutting-edge technologies, methodologies, and applications for intelligent business analytics.

To develop this book, we released the Call for book chapter (CFP) with a large number of topics for foundations, technologies, applications at the website of IGI-Global (https://www.igi-global.com/publish/call-for-papers/call-details/5211), wikiCFP (http://wikicfp.com/cfp/servlet/event.showcfp?eventid=128907&copyownerid=49462), AIS world (aisworld@lists.aisnet.org), and Researchgate (https://www.researchgate.net/project/Foundations-and-Applications-of-Intelligent-Business-Analytics) to appeal to the worldwide scholars for contributions. We also released the CFP at international conferences including ACSW/HIKM 2021, and I3E2021 as well as more with the help of the advisory editorial board (AEB). We received 29+ book proposals based on CFP and 21 full book chapter manuscripts' submissions. Based on the double-blinded peer review, 16 book chapters out of them are selected from the book chapter manuscripts' submission, and published in this book, each of them aligns with one or a few of the mentioned topics. In what follows, we will overview each of the chapters published in this book.

SECTION 1: FOUNDATIONS OF INTELLIGENT BUSINESS ANALYTICS

Section 1 consists of the following four chapters.

Chapter 1, contributed by Zhaohao Sun, Francisca Pambel, and Zhiyou Wu, titled "The Elements of Intelligent Business Analytics: Principles, Techniques, and Tools," addresses the following two research questions: What are the elements, principles, technologies, and tools of intelligent business analytics and their interrelationships? How can we incorporate the latest intelligent technologies into business analytics? It highlights three points and investigates each of them: First, not only big data but also big DIKIW (i.e., data, information, knowledge, intelligence, and wisdom) are the most important elements for intelligent business analytics. Second, not only big data analytics and intelligent big data analytics but also big DIKIW and intelligent big DIKIW analytics are the foundation of intelligent business analytics. Third, the principles, technologies, and tools of intelligent business analytics are emerging strategic sources for organizations and individuals in the ever-increasing competitive global environment. This chapter presents a framework for DIKIW-driven intelligent business analytics through incorporating DIKIW analytics into intelligent business analytics. Finally, this chapter examines the theoretical and technical implications of intelligent business analytics.

Chapter 2, contributed by A.D.N. Sarma, titled "Intelligent Big Data Analytics: Need, Challenges, Opportunities, and Implications," looks at the evolution of the data analytics ecosystem and its role. It defines data, insight, and action in the context of business analytics. This chapter briefly explains analytics, business analytics (BA), business intelligence, and intelligent BA. It analyses the need for intelligent analytics for organizations in a digital world. The research shows that a paradigm shifts from data analytics to intelligent big data analytics because of the recent technological advances in AI resulting in analytics applications to learn intelligence from the data. The research highlights that intelligent BA becomes an important tool for organizations for intelligent decision-making. This chapter presents various applications of intelligent BA, a few challenges for implementing the system, and possible future directions of research for the development of intelligent BA.

Chapter 3, contributed by Alexander Ryjov, titled "Principles of Hybrid Intelligence Framework for Augmented Analytics," claims that analytics is a crucial success factor for any business in the competitive and fast-changing world; people, business, social, and government organizations can use good analytics to make good decisions. This chapter looks at the hybrid intelligence approach by focusing on its unique analytical capabilities. The state-of-the-art hybrid intelligence is the symbiosis and cooperative interaction between human intelligence and artificial intelligence in solving a wide range of practical tasks. This chapter presents a human-centered hybrid intelligence framework for evaluating and monitoring complex processes. The chapter could appeal to analysts and researchers who have an interest in intelligent analytics.

Chapter 4, contributed by Ricardo Matheus and Luiz P. Pinheiro, titled "Designing Business Analytics Projects (BAP): A Five Steps Dashboarding Cycle," presents a proposal of designing business analytics projects with a practical five steps dashboarding cycle. The first step: Business questions deals with the scope of a data analytics project creating problem-based questions. The second step: Data sources details which are the data sources to be collected. The third step: Extraction, transform, and loading (ETL) sets up data source routines of what, where, and, when collecting data. The fourth step: Data warehouse creates a data repository where data is stored and treated after the ETL process. The fifth step: Data visualization designs a web dashboard with interactive features such as tables and graphs. This chapter ends with three practical examples in both public and private organizations.

SECTION 2: TECHNOLOGIES FOR INTELLIGENT BUSINESS ANALYTICS

Section 2 consists of the following five chapters.

Chapter 5, contributed by Andrew Stranieri and Zhaohao Sun, titled "A Process-Oriented Framework for Regulating Artificial Intelligence Systems," claims that frameworks for the regulation of artificial intelligence (AI) systems are emerging; some are based on regulation theories; others are more technologically focused. The task of arriving at a collection of interventions that regulate an AI system is taken to be a process-oriented problem. This chapter presents a process-oriented framework for the design of regulating systems by deliberating groups. It also discusses regulations of AI systems and responsibility, mechanisms and institutions, key elements for regulating AI systems. The proposed approach might facilitate research and development of responsible AI, explainable AI, and ethical AI for an ethical and inclusive digitized society.

Chapter 6, contributed by Safa Gasmi, Akila Djebbar, Merouani Hayet Farida, titled "A Survey on Hybrid Case-Based Reasoning and Deep Learning Systems for Medical Data Classification," reviews the available literature on CBR systems, deep learning systems as well as CBR deep learning systems in medicine. This chapter discusses the methods used and results obtained and highlights key findings. This chapter also gives some directions for future research. The proposed approach in this chapter might help make the retrieval phase of the CBR cycle more reliable and robust.

Chapter 7, contributed by Isakki Alias Devi Paramasivam and Selvakumar Anthonyraj, titled "Big Data Analytics for Search Engine Optimization in Intelligent Business," deals with big data analytics for search engine optimization in intelligent business. The chapter demonstrates that search engine optimization takes into account how search engines work, the computer-programmed algorithms that govern looking at search engine behavior, what users search for, and the actual search keywords submitted into search engines. Search engines are always preferred by the targeted audience. Big data analytics is obliging to increase website traffic. This helps apply intelligence in business areas.

Chapter 8, contributed by Abdelmalek Bouguettaya, Hafed Zarzour, Ahmed Kechida, and Amine Mohammed Taberkit, titled "Machine Learning and Deep Learning as New Tools for Business Analytics," aims to present the basics of machine learning and deep learning concepts and their utilization in the field of business intelligence. As concrete examples of this research, with the high spread of the COVID-19 pandemic, Tesla and Amazon achieved the biggest revenue ever, where many other companies suffer. These high revenues could be due to the strategic decision of their leaders, which is based especially on artificial intelligence.

Chapter 9, contributed by Mowafaq S. Alzboon, Muhyeeddin K. Alqaraleh, Emran M. Aljarrah, and Saleh A. Alomari, titled "Semantic Image Analysis on Social Networks and Data Processing," examines social networks, basic concepts, and social network analysis components. It also looks at picture usage in social networks. This chapter presents a novel method for analyzing social networks, namely semantic networks.

SECTION 3: APPLICATIONS OF INTELLIGENT BUSINESS ANALYTICS

Section 3 consists of the following seven chapters.

Chapter 10, contributed by Desmond Narongou and Zhaohao Sun, titled "Applying Intelligent Big Data Analytics in a Smart Airport: Business Value, Adoption, and Challenges," explores the value of applying intelligent big data analytics in an airport from an operations perspective to strategic differentiation viewpoints. This chapter also discusses the challenges faced when adopting intelligent big data analytics in a smart airport paradigm from the perspective of Papua New Guinea's National Airport Corporation. This chapter further explores how these challenges can be overcome to realize the true value of applying intelligent big data analytics in an airport. The approach proposed in this chapter might contribute to expediting research of future development of intelligent big data analytics solutions that are customizable to an airport to recognize the real value of intelligent big data analytics in all facets of operations in an airport.

Chapter 11, contributed by Shivanand Rai and Markus Bick, titled "Immunize Your Organization: A People Analytics Exploration of the Change in Employee Priorities After the COVID-19 Lockdown," points out that the pandemic has changed the world immensely and provided a natural experiment for the field of people analytics. Herein, this chapter analyzes how this has changed employees' priorities, what the future might look like, and how corporations can respond, and examines the entire construct of Glassdoor, and maps the changes revealed during the pandemic, using machine learning and NLP techniques. This chapter provides a framework to determine which factors drive employee satisfaction and what changed during the pandemic. The research shows that culture and management are the most critical organizational factors in a time of crisis. Culture appears to be the vaccine that immunizes against tough times.

Chapter 12, contributed by Li Chen, titled "Undergraduate Computer Science Capstone Projects: Experiences and Examples in Data Science," classifies the capstone project at the University of the District of Columbia into three components: 1) Senior Seminar, 2) Senior Project I, and 3) Senior Project II. The Senior Seminar aims to expand the students' scope of knowledge through reading cutting-edge materials in computer science and IT. Students in the class often learn from each other, while the instructor organizes talks given by professors at the university as well as industry professionals. Students give formal presentations as their final exam. The main purpose of Senior Project I is to teach students how to start a research project. Students are asked to complete a simple research proposal after doing background research to select a research project. The final report is a short report. In Senior Project II, many students choose to continue the project Senior Project I. For this course, students complete a well-written report ranging from 20 to 25 pages. This chapter explains how the author teaches these courses with five examples in data science.

Chapter 13, contributed by Shaoyu Ye, Kei Wakabayashi, Kevin K.W. Ho, and Muhammad Haseeb Khan, titled "The Relationships Between Users' Negative Tweets, Topic Choices, and Subjective Well-Being in Japan," examines the relationships between expressions in Tweets, topic choices, and subjective well-being among undergraduates in Japan. The authors surveyed 304 college students, and analyzed their Twitter posts using natural language processing (NLP). Based on those who posted over 50 tweets, this research found that: (a) users with higher levels of social skills had fewer negative tweets and higher levels of subjective well-being; (b) frequent users posted both positive and negative tweets but posted more negative than positive tweets; (c) users with fewer negative tweets or with more positive tweets had higher levels of subjective well-being; and (d) "safe" topics such as social events and personal interests had a positive correlation with the users' subjective well-being, while debatable topics such as politics and social issues had a negative correlation with the users' subjective well-being. The findings of this study provide the foundation for applying NLP to analyze the social media posts for businesses and services to understand their consumers' sentiment.

Chapter 14, contributed by Bingnan Wang, Davison Chiu, and Kevin K. W. Ho, titled "A Comparison of Deep Learning Models in Time Series Forecasting of Web Traffic Data From Kaggle," used raw data from the "Web Traffic Forecasting" competition on the Kaggle platform to test the prediction accuracy of different time series models, especially the generalization performance of various deep learning models. The experiments in the research used historical traffic data from 145,063 web pages from Wikipedia from July 1, 2015, to November 13, 2017. Traffic data from July 1, 2015, to September 10, 2017, was used to forecast traffic from September 13, 2017, to November 13, 2017, a total of 62 days. The experimental results showed that almost all deep learning models predicted far more effectively than statistical and machine learning models, and, therefore, deep learning models have great potential for time series forecasting problems.

Chapter 15, contributed by Zhixuan He, Davison Chiu, and Kevin K. W. Ho, titled "Weibo Analysis on Chinese Culture Knowledge for Gaming," looks at the current situation of video games with Chinese cultural knowledge in China's game market by analyzing Weibo messages. The research collected data related to five selected video games based on Chinese cultures and analyzed the collected data to explore the relationships between these video games and Chinese culture. It then summarized the results from comments and likes, word cloud, and clustering analysis and provided practical suggestions. The findings of this research can help game developers better understand these markets and customer preferences while protecting and spreading Chinese culture through gaming and e-sports activities in this digital era.

Chapter 16 contributed by Carsten Giebe, titled "Big Data and Analytics and the Hunt for the Hidden Data Treasure of Savings Banks in Germany," shows that the banking sector in Germany is undergoing massive change. The reasons are digitalization, changing customer behavior, and low-interest rates, etc. The focus of this chapter is on the savings banks in Germany. Savings banks could miss the boat in the age of digital transformation. On the one hand, savings banks are demonstrably forced to take drastic measures, such as mergers, branch closures, and staff reductions. On the other hand, savings banks possess more data about their customers than other industries. Savings banks can order a big data analytics solution called "Sparkassen-DataAnalytics" (aka savings banks data analytics). Sparkassen-DataAnalytics could be used to offer customers tailor-made banking products from the information obtained. It is an open secret that costs can be reduced through a higher degree of automation. The main purpose of this research is to discuss to what extent big data analytics could be a lifeline for German savings banks. Research methods are a literature review and subsequent discussion on the use of big data analytics in the German banking market.

It is certainly impossible for a book to cover each of these topics, although the editors have tried to do their best to use various media and research social networking platforms.

This book's primary aim is to convey the foundations, technologies, thoughts, and methods of intelligent business analytics with applications to scientists, engineers, educators and university students, business, service, and management professionals, policymakers, decision-makers, and others who have an interest in big data, intelligent business, intelligent management, intelligent business analytics, AI, digital transformation, e-SMACS business and intelligence, commerce, service and data science. Primary audiences for this book are undergraduate, postgraduate students, and a variety of professionals in the fields of big data, intelligent business analytics, intelligent business and management, data science, information science and technology, knowledge technology and engineering, intelligence science, analytics, AI, ICT, computing, commerce, business, services, management, and government. The variety of readers in the fields of government, consulting, marketing, business, and trade, as well as the readers from all the social strata, can also be benefited from this book to improve understanding of the cutting-edge theory, technologies, methodologies of intelligent business analytics with applications in the digital age.

Zhaohao Sun
Papua New Guinea University of Technology, Papua New Guinea

Zhiyou Wu
Chongqing Normal University, China
December 2021

REFERENCES

Ali, Z. (2016). *New IDC MarketScape Provides a Vendor Assessment of the Worldwide Business Analytics Consulting and Systems Integration Services for 2016.* Retrieved from IDC: https://www.idc.com/getdoc.jsp?containerId=prUS41224416

Azvine, B., Nauck, D., & Ho, C. (2003). Intelligent Business Analytics— A Tool to Build Decision-Support Systems for eBusinesses. *BT Technology Journal, 21*(4), 65–71. doi:10.1023/A:1027379403688

Howson, C., Richardson, J., Sallam, R., & Kronz, A. (2019). *Magic Quadrant for Analytics and Business Intelligence Platforms.* Retrieved 7 7, 2019, from Gartner: https://cadran-analytics.nl/wp-content/uploads/2019/02/2019-Gartner-Magic-Quadrant-for-Analytics-and-Business-Intelligence-Platforms.pdf

Russell, S., & Norvig, P. (2020). *Artificial Intelligence: A Modern Approach* (4th ed.). Prentice Hall.

Sharda, R., Delen, D., Turban, E., & King, D. (2018). *Business Intelligence, Analytics, and Data Science: A Managerial Perspective* (4th ed.). Pearson.

Sun, Z. (2019). Intelligent Big Data Analytics: A Managerial Perspective. In Z. Sun (Ed.), *Managerial Perspectives on Intelligent Big Data Analytics* (pp. 1–19). IGI-Global. doi:10.4018/978-1-5225-7277-0.ch001

Sun, Z. (2020). *Business Analytics Intelligence: An Emerging Frontier for Innovation and Productivity.* Retrieved February 3, 2021, from https://www.researchgate.net/profile/Zhaohao_Sun/publication/343876626_Business_Analytics_Intelligence_An_Emerging_Frontier_for_Innovation_and_Productivity

Sun, Z. (2021). *Intelligent Analytics with Advanced Multi-Industry Applications.* IGI-Global. doi:10.4018/978-1-7998-4963-6

Sun, Z. (2021). *An Introduction to Intelligent Business Analytics.* doi:10.13140/RG.2.2.19361.94562

Sun, Z., & Huo, Y. (2021). The spectrum of big data analytics. *Journal of Computer Information Systems, 61*(2), 154–162. doi:10.1080/08874417.2019.1571456

Sun, Z., & Stranieri, A. (2021). The Nature of Intelligent Analytics. In Z. Sun (Ed.), *Intelligent Analytics with Advanced Multi-industry Applications. I* (pp. 1–22). IGI-Global. doi:10.4018/978-1-7998-4963-6.ch001

Vesset, D., McDonough, B., Schubmehl, D., & Wardley, M. (2013). *Worldwide Business Analytics Software 2013–2017 Forecast and 2012 Vendor Shares* (Doc # 241689). Retrieved 6 28, 2014, from https://www.idc.com/getdoc.jsp?containerId=241689

Acknowledgment

The publication of this book titled *Handbook of Research on Foundations and Applications of Intelligent Business Analytics* reflects the integration of intelligence, wisdom, and perseverance of many researchers and friends worldwide. We would like to express our sincere gratitude to all the members of the Editorial Advisory Board (EAB) for their erudite comments and guidance. We heartily thank all the contributors for their time and submission of manuscripts, they have made this book possible and transformed our initiatives into reality. We would also like to thank all the contributors who have submitted book chapter proposals, drafts, and ideas to this book although the proposals have not been changed into accepted book chapters for publication because of the worldwide coronavirus pandemic and other reasons. Our special thanks go to the international team of reviewers for blindly reviewing the book chapters and submitting review reports on the paper selflessly, timely, and professionally, of them, Dr. Selena (Sally) Firmin, Federation University, Australia and Dr. Dickson K.W. Chiu, University of Hong Kong, China are recognized as the best reviewers for this book. These review reports include their erudite comments on the book chapters included in this book. Without such selfless and professional contributions, most books in general and this book in particular would not have been published. We must express our sincere thanks to PNG University of Technology, Chongqing Normal University, and Hebei University of Science and Technology for their excellent research environment that we have used to develop our ideas, books, and research papers effectively. We express extreme thanks to WikiCFP, ResearchGate, IS World, and other social networking platforms for their timely and tirelessly sharing our CFP on the platform. Our hearty thanks also go to researchers for accessing WikiCFP, ResearchGate, and IS World, and caring for our CFP. Our sincerest thanks go to my excellent friends Ms. Maria Rohde, Ms. Angelina Olivas, Ms. Rowan Rumbaugh, Ms. Jan Travers, and Ms. Crystal Moyer of IGI-Global for their outstanding and continuous support and patience throughout the book development process. Finally, Zhaohao would like to express his deepest appreciation for the support and encouragement of his wife, Dr. Yanxia (Monica) Huo. Without her lasting support and patience as well as academic comments, authoring and editing this book would not have been possible.

Zhaohao Sun
Papua New Guinea University of Technology, Papua New Guinea

Zhiyou Wu
Chongqing Normal University, China
December 2021

Section 1
Foundations of Intelligent Business Analytics

Chapter 1
The Elements of Intelligent Business Analytics:
Principles, Techniques, and Tools

Zhaohao Sun

https://orcid.org/0000-0003-0780-3271

Papua New Guinea University of Technology, Papua New Guinea

Francisca Pambel

Papua New Guinea University of Technology, Papua New Guinea

Zhiyou Wu

Chongqing Normal University, China

ABSTRACT

This chapter explores the elements of intelligent business analytics and addresses the following research questions: What are the elements, principles, technologies, and tools of intelligent business analytics? How can one incorporate the latest intelligent technologies into business analytics? This research highlights that big data and big DIKIW are the elements for intelligent business analytics; big data analytics and intelligent big data analytics and big DIKIW and intelligent big DIKIW analytics are the foundation of intelligent business analytics; the principles, technologies, and tools of intelligent business analytics are emerging strategic sources for organizations and individuals in the competitive global environment. This chapter presents a framework for DIKIW-driven intelligent business analytics through incorporating DIKIW analytics into intelligent business analytics. The proposed approach might facilitate research and development of intelligent business, big data analytics, business intelligence, AI, and data science.

INTRODUCTION

Intelligent business analytics has drawn increasing attention in industries. Google search engine for "intelligent business analytics" shows about 36,700 results (retrieved on August 26, 2021). Some companies

DOI: 10.4018/978-1-7998-9016-4.ch001

have used intelligent business analytics as their marketing mission. For example, Exigy has promoted intelligent business analytics as a cutting-edge technology that can digitally transform business and solve business challenges through providing "accurate insights, on-demand everywhere" (https://www.exigy.com/intelligent-business-analytics/).

Artificial intelligence (AI) and business intelligence (BI) have been already applied in business analytics for decades (Eiloart, 2018; Richardson, Schlegel, Sallam, Kronz, & Sun, 2021). Gartner predicts that 30% of new revenue growth from industry-specific solutions will include AI technology in 2021 (Laney & Jain, 2017). AI-derived business value is forecasted to increase from $US1.2 trillion in 2018 to $US3.9 trillion in 2022 (Pettey & van der Meulen, 2018). International Data Corporation (IDC) forecasts that big data and business analytics revenue will increase to $274.3 billion by 2022 with a five-year compound annual growth rate (CAGR) of 13.2% from 2018 (IDC, 2019).

Furthermore, a Google Scholar search for "intelligent business analytics" (August 27, 2021) found only 89 results. This implies that intelligent business analytics is still an emerging research area in academia although business analytics has been around us for decades (Davenport, December 2013; Delena & Demirkanb, 2013) and drawn increasing attention in the past decade (Sun Z., 2020). The following are still pressing issues for the academia, industries, and governments, based on our preliminary analysis:

1. What are the elements, principles, techniques, and tools of intelligent business analytics and their interrelationships?
2. What is the relationship between intelligent big data analytics and intelligent business analytics?
3. How can we incorporate the latest intelligent techniques into business analytics applications?

This research addresses the above-mentioned research issues. More specifically, this chapter identifies and explores the elements, principles, technologies, and tools of intelligent business analytics through an investigation into the state-of-the-art scholars' publications and market analysis of advanced analytics. It examines intelligent business analytics as integration of AI, other intelligent techniques, and business big data analytics. This research demonstrates that not only big data and big data analytics but also DIKIW (data, information, knowledge, intelligence, wisdom) and DIKIW analytics constitute the foundation of intelligent business analytics. The chapter presents a framework for DIKIW-driven intelligent business analytics through incorporating DIKIW analytics into intelligent business analytics.

The remainder of this chapter is organized as follows: Section 2 identifies and looks at the elements of intelligent business analytics. Section 3 examines the principles of intelligent business analytics. Sections 4 and 5 discuss the technologies and tools for intelligent business analytics. Section 6 provides discussion and implications as well as future research directions of this research. The final section ends this chapter with some concluding remarks and future work.

From a viewpoint of research methodology, this chapter uses a multidisciplinary approach consisting of business, logical, algebraic, systematic methods, research as a search, and big data-driven small data analysis methods. For example, the backgrounds are based on the principle of "research as a search" and big data-driven small data analysis (Sun & Huo, 2021). This chapter uses Google Scholar indexed publications search, which reflects the state-of-the-art research of the scholars on intelligent analytics and intelligent business analytics worldwide. It uses the market analysis provided by Gartner (Richardson, Schlegel, Sallam, Kronz, & Sun, 2021), which reflects the state-of-the-art research and development of the tools for intelligent business analytics. Both are a complement to each other for understanding state-of-the-art intelligent big data analytics. This chapter also uses business, logical, and systemic approaches to examine intelligent business analytics as to the incorporation of KIDIW analytics with AI and other intelligent techniques and proposes the technologies and tools for intelligent business analytics.

It should be noted that throughout this research, we use at least three perspectives on intelligent as a term: First, we use intelligent from an AI perspective (Russell & Norvig, 2010) to denote intelligent business analytics as integrating business analytics, business big data analytics, and AI-driven latest intelligent technologies (Sun & Stranieri, 2021; Azvine, Nauck, & Ho, 2003). Second, we use intelligent as a term from a BI perspective (Sun, Sun, & Strang, 2018; Sharda R., Delen, Turban, & King, 2018), to indicate that intelligent business analytics is about integrating business analytics and BI. Finally, we consider intelligent an entity that is not only used in AI and BI but can be applied elsewhere. For example, we consider intelligent a representation of what we eagerly expect. Intelligent can also be used as an operation of algebra, which is an abstraction of operations within an intelligent system (Sun & Wang, 2017).

THE ELEMENTS OF INTELLIGENT BUSINESS ANALYTICS

The elements of intelligent business analytics include data, data analytics, big data analytics, and intelligent big data analytics from a computing perspective. Correspondingly, from a business perspective, the elements of intelligent business analytics also include business data, business data analytics, business big data analytics, and business intelligent big data analytics. We will look at each of them below.

Analytics: The Most General Definition

We are in the age of analytics (Henke & Bughin, 2016). Analytics has become the new queen of science and technology (Ghavami, 2020). Millions of analytics form a web of analytics around us based on a Google Scholar search. This section will present the most general definition for analytics. One can consider all the analytics in the web of analytics such as data analytics, enterprise analytics, organization analytics as to the special cases of the proposed definition.

Data analytics can be defined as a set of methods, processes, and disciplines that extract, analyze, and transform data into meaningful sight, new discovery, and knowledge to make more effective decisions (Ghavami, 2020, p. 1). This definition of data analytics can be generalized as follows:

$$x \text{ analytics is about analytically transforming } x \text{ into } y \text{ to } z, \text{ where } x, y, \text{ and } z \text{ are variables.} \qquad (1)$$

If x = data, y = meaningful insight, z = support decision making, then formula (1) is changed into that data analytics is about analytically transforming data into meaningful insight to support decision making. This basically reflects the meaning of the above-mentioned definition of data analytics. We use "analytically transform" to replace related parts in the definition to differentiate our definition from other similar definitions. For example, an information system can be defined as a system that transforms data into information (Laudon & Laudon, 2020).

Furthermore, data analytics can be defined as the "art of examining, summarizing, and drawing conclusions from data" from a data processing viewpoint (Norusis, 1997). This definition of data analytics can be generalized as follows:

x analytics is the "art of examining, summarizing, and drawing conclusions from x."   (2)

Where x is a variable.

Data analytics can also be defined as a method that "uses data to learn, describe, and predict something" (Turban & Volonino, 2011, p. 341). This definition of analytics can be generalized below.

x analytics is a method that "uses x to z"   (3)

Combining (2) and (3), the following formula holds.

x analytics is the art of examining, summarizing, and drawing conclusions from x to z (4)

If $x = \text{data}$, then x analytics = data analytics. Similarly, if x is an element of {big data, intelligent big data}, we have big data analytics and intelligent big data analytics. If x is an element of {Google, enterprise, organization}, we have Google (data) analytics, enterprise (data) analytics, and organization (data) analytics. Therefore, we provide a most general definition for analytics. (1) and (4) will be interchangeably throughout this chapter. Any special analytics mentioned in this chapter can be defined using this most general definition, if it is not defined in other ways.

Data and Data Analytics

Data are raw, unorganized, and unprocessed materials such as facts, numbers, figures, signals, assertions, perceptions, or observations that represent the properties of objects and events (Rowley, 2007; Wang Y., 2015). Data usually are devoid of meaning, context, content, and value (Sabherwal & Becerra-Fernandez, 2011). Data are considered the input of information systems, data analytics, and many other data systems (Coronel, Morris, & Rob, 2020; Laudon & Laudon, 2020).

Briefly, data analytics can be represented below:

$$\text{Data analytics} = \text{data} + \text{analytics} \tag{5}$$

Hereafter, + can be explained as "and". From an algebraic viewpoint, data analytics is a system. equation (5) implies that data is the set of the system; analytics is the operation performing over the dataset (Davenport, December 2013; Norusis, 1997).

Data analytics can be classified into descriptive analytics, diagnostic analytics, predictive analytics, and prescriptive analytics (Sun & Stranieri, 2021; Sharda R., Delen, Turban, & King, 2018).

Data has become the new oil and gold of the 21st century. Data analytics mines the data for new knowledge and meaningful insights (Ghavami, 2020). Data analytics is at the heart of business and decision making (Sharda, Delen, & Turba, 2018), just as data analysis is at the heart of decision making in almost real-world problems solving (Azvine, Nauck, & Ho, 2003).

Big Data and Big Data Analytics

Big data has become a strategic asset for an organization and even a nation (Sun & Stranieri, 2021; Tu, 2015). Big data analytics is a science and technology about organizing and analyzing big data, and discovering knowledge, insights, and intelligence from big data, visualizing and reporting the discovered knowledge and insights for assisting decision making (Sun, Sun, & Strang, 2018). Briefly, big data analytics can be represented below using big as an operation over both sides of (5)

$$\text{Big data analytics} = \text{Big data} + \text{Big analytics} \tag{6}$$

Big data is the set of big data analytics as a system. Big analytics is the operation performing over the big data set (Davenport, December 2013).

The main components of big data analytics include big data descriptive analytics, diagnostic analytics, predictive analytics, and prescriptive analytics (Sun & Stranieri, 2021; Sharda R., Delen, Turban, & King, 2018).

Big data and big data analytics have become one of the most important research frontiers in academia and industries (Sun & Stranieri, 2021; Ghavami, 2020; Richardson, Schlegel, Sallam, Kronz, & Sun, 2021).

Intelligent Big Data Analytics

Intelligent big data analytics has become a disruptive technology for effective innovation and decision-making in the digital age (Sun & Stranieri, 2021; Holsapple, Lee-Postb, & Pakath, 2014). Intelligent big data analytics as an intelligent system can aid managers by extracting useful patterns of information, capturing, and discovering knowledge, and generating solutions to problems encountered in decision-making, delegating authority, and assigning responsibility (Sun & Huo, 2019).

Briefly, intelligent big data analytics can be represented as

$$\text{Intelligent big data analytics} = \text{Intelligent} + \text{Big data analytics} \tag{7}$$

Intelligent in equation (7) means AI if one works in computing. It means BI, marketing intelligence, organization intelligence, and enterprise intelligence if one works in the corresponding fields. Therefore, intelligent as a term can be understood differently by different people. Even so, big data, analytics, AI, and their integration are at the frontier for revolutionizing our work, life, business, management, and organization (Sun & Huo, 2019; Henke & Bughin, 2016; Laney & Jain, 2017).

Intelligent big data analytics can be also represented as

$$\text{Intelligent big data analytics} = \text{Intelligent} + \text{Big data} + \text{Analytics} \tag{8}$$

Equation (8) at least means that intelligent big data analytics includes big data, analytics, and AI and their integration (Sun Z., 2019a; Wang F.-Y., 2012).

Intelligent big data analytics consists of intelligent big data descriptive analytics, intelligent big data diagnostic analytics, intelligent big data predictive analytics, and intelligent big data prescriptive analytics (Sun & Stranieri, 2021).

- Intelligent big data descriptive analytics is intelligent descriptive analytics for big data (Delena & Demirkanb, 2013; Kantardzic, 2011) (Sun, Sun, & Strang, 2018). It is used to discover new, nontrivial information based on AI techniques (Kantardzic, 2011, p. 2), and explain the characteristics of entities and relationships among entities within the existing big descriptive data (Coronel, Morris, & Rob, 2020). It addresses the problems such as what and when happened, and what is happening (Delena & Demirkanb, 2013; LaPlante, 2019). For example, intelligent business reports with dashboards for the global COVID-19 pandemic are a result of intelligent big data descriptive analytics on big data of the global COVID-19.
- Intelligent big data diagnostic analytics is intelligent diagnostic analytics for big data (Sun, Sun, & Strang, 2018). It is used to examine data or content to answer the question "Why did it happen?", from the historical and current diagnostic data based on AI techniques such as drill-down, data discovery, data mining, and correlations (Gartner-diagnostic analytics, 2020). For example, diagnostic analytics available on the cloud belongs to intelligent big data diagnostic analytics.
- Intelligent big data predictive analytics is intelligent predictive analytics for big data (Sun, Zou, & Strang, 2015). It focuses on forecasting future trends by addressing the problems such as: what will happen next? what is going to happen? what is likely to happen? and why it will happen? based on historical and current big data (LaPlante, 2019; Kumar, 2015). Intelligent big data predictive analytics uses techniques of predictive mining, statistical modeling, mathematics, and AI to create intelligent models to predict future outcomes or events (Sun & Stranieri, 2021; Delena & Demirkanb, 2013). For example, intelligent big data predictive analytics can be used to predict where might be the next exposure site of COVID-19.
- Intelligent big data prescriptive analytics is intelligent prescriptive analytics for big data (Sun, Zou, & Strang, 2015). It addresses the problems such as what we should do, why we should do and what should happen with the best outcome under uncertainty (Delena & Demirkanb, 2013; LaPlante, 2019). Intelligent big data prescriptive analytics uses intelligent algorithms to determine optimal decisions for future actions (Delena & Demirkanb, 2013). For example, intelligent big data prescriptive analytics can be used to provide an optimal marketing strategy for an e-commerce company.

Business Analytics and Intelligent Business Analytics

Using the most general definition of analytics provided in Section 2.1, we can define business analytics, business big data analytics, intelligent business big data analytics, and intelligent business analytics as follows.

Business data analytics is the art of examining, summarizing, and drawing conclusions from business data to learn, describe, and predict something. The business data can be defined as "flows of events or transactions captured by an organization's systems that are useful for transacting but little else" (Laudon & Laudon, 2020, p. 455). Business data analytics and business analytics are used interchangeably.

Business big data analytics is the art of examining, summarizing, and drawing conclusions from business big data to learn, describe, and predict something.

Intelligent business big data analytics is the art of examining, summarizing, and drawing conclusions from business big data to learn, describe, and predict something using AI and other intelligent techniques.

Intelligent business analytics is the art of examining, summarizing, and drawing conclusions from business data and other sources to learn, describe, and predict something using AI and other intelligent techniques. Briefly,

$$\text{Intelligent business analytics} = \text{AI} + \text{other intelligent techniques} + \text{business analytics} \qquad (9)$$

Currently, intelligent business analytics can be classified into intelligent business descriptive analytics, intelligent business diagnostic analytics, intelligent business predictive analytics, and intelligent business prescriptive analytics (Sun Z., 2019a).

DIKIW and DIKIW Analytics

All digital things seem to be data, but much of it is not really "data" outside the big data world (Williams, 2016, p. 34). In the age of big data, analytics, and AI (Sun Z., 2019a; Minelli, Chambers, & Dhiraj, 2013), most people have flattened the hierarchical structure from data via information, knowledge, and intelligence up to wisdom to data level, so that wisdom as data, intelligence as data, knowledge as data, and information as data become popular. In fact, information, knowledge, intelligence, and wisdom have played the same significant role as data in computing and ICT, business and management, and many other fields in the past few decades (Sun & Huo, 2020). All science in the digital age is like a tree of which five elements, namely, data, information, knowledge, intelligence, and wisdom, are the roots, mathematics and computing the trunk, and all the other sciences the branches that grow out of this trunk (Sun & Stranieri, 2021). This section looks at data, information, knowledge, intelligence, and wisdom in a unified way. It reveals that data, information, knowledge, intelligence, and wisdom (for short, DIKIW) are not only the elements of AI (Weber, 2020, pp. 22-27). DIKIW and its corresponding analytics are also the elements of intelligent business analytics.

DIKIW forms a hierarchical structure (Sun & Huo, 2020; Liew, 2013; Rowley, 2007), as shown in Figure 1. DIKIW is an updated form with the reverse pyramid of DIKW (Sun & Huo, 2020; Liew, 2013; Rowley, 2007) and DIKEW (Sun & Huo, 2020).

$$\text{DIKIW} = \text{data} + \text{information} + \text{knowledge} + \text{intelligence} + \text{wisdom}. \qquad (10)$$

Information is processed data with the usefulness, content, relevance, purpose, background, and value (Ackoff, 1992; Sabherwal & Becerra-Fernandez, 2011) (Tu, 2015). For example, the reorganization of raw data into categories of understanding as a data processing is to obtain more meaningful information on the trend for daily sales (Laudon & Laudon, 2020, p. 455).

Knowledge is processed, organized, or structured information with the insight of experts and certain rules (Laudon & Laudon, 2020) (Liew, 2013) (Tu, 2015). Knowledge is one of the central concepts in intelligent systems (Sun & Huo, 2020; Russell & Norvig, 2010). Knowledge is usually defined as the beliefs, objects, concepts, and relationships that are assumed to exist in some areas of interest (Sabherwal & Becerra-Fernandez, 2011), for example, knowledge discovery from a large database (Sun & Huo, 2020).

Figure 1. The pyramid of DIKIW and DIKIW analytics

Intelligence is the ability to learn, think, and understand" (Oxford, 2008). These three abilities are the core of basic human intelligence. Intelligence is also a consequence of big data-driven smart services for human beings (Tu, 2015, p. 363). However, only learning, thinking, and understanding are not enough in modern society, connecting should be another component of human intelligence. Advanced communication technologies and tools such as mail, telephone, email, and information sharing on the Web aim to develop the skill of connecting (communication) as a form of intelligence, hyperintelligence. Hyperintelligence is a kind of intelligence that has been developed with hypertexting and connecting in social networking. For example, social networking services such as Facebook, LinkedIn, and WeChat have developed one's skill of hyperintelligence as a part of human intelligence (Laudon & Laudon, 2020).

Wisdom is defined as "the ability to make sensible decisions and give good advice because of experience and knowledge that one has" (Oxford, 2008; Liew, 2013). Wisdom can be defined as the ability to increase effectiveness through processing data, information, knowledge, and intelligence, and all together (Ackoff, 1992). Wisdom adds value through appropriate judgments and creative ideas (Rowley, 2007). For example, the key idea in PageRank of Google is wisdom (Sun & Huo, 2020). The business model of Uber is also a business wisdom. Wisdom usually consists of revolutionary ideas that can bring big decisions and value for an individual or an organization. A question for wisdom is as follows: Why has only David pointed out such wisdom in our big organization? Therefore, wisdom is closest to innovation, creativity, and ingenuity, compared with knowledge and intelligence, although the latter can be used for producing wisdom.

In the DIKIW pyramid, information is defined in terms of data (Rowley, 2007), knowledge in terms of data and information (Sabherwal & Becerra-Fernandez, 2011), intelligence in terms of data, information, and knowledge (Sun & Huo, 2020); wisdom in terms of data, information, knowledge, and intelligence. This is the reason why the reverse pyramid has been used to model the DIKIW, as shown in Figure 1.

If x is an element of {information, knowledge, intelligence, and wisdom}, we have information analytics, knowledge analytics, intelligence analytics, and wisdom analytics, based on equation (1) or (4) in Section 2.1. These analytics can be called analytics (Sun & Stranieri, 2021), that is,

$$\text{Analytics} := \text{data analytics} + \text{information analytics}$$
$$+ \text{knowledge analytics} + \text{intelligence analytics} + \text{wisdom analytics} \tag{11}$$

Apply analytics as an operation on both sides of equation (10), we have

$$\text{DIKIW analytics} = \text{data analytics} + \textit{i}\text{nformation analytics} \\ +\text{knowledge analytics} + \text{intelligence analytics} + \text{wisdom analytics} \tag{12}$$

From equations (11) and (12), analytics can be defined as DIKIW analytics consisting of data analytics, information analytics, knowledge analytics, and wisdom analytics, corresponding to data, information, knowledge, intelligence, and wisdom respectively, as shown in Figure 1.

DIKIW analytics are the important elements of intelligent business analytics, taking into account DIKIW and its implications on big data, data science, and AI (Sun & Huo, 2020; Weber, 2020). The above discussion demonstrates that data analytics is not a unique form of analytics. DIKIW analytics is a more inclusive representation of analytics.

Applying big as an operation (Sun & Wang, 2017) to both sides of equation (10), we have

$$\text{Big DIKIW} = \text{big data} + \text{big information} + \text{big knowledge} + \text{big intelligence} + \text{big wisdom} \tag{13}$$

As well-known, big data is significant for innovation, competition, and productivity in the digital age (McKinsey, 2011), then big information, big knowledge, big intelligence, and big wisdom are also significant for effective management, decision making, and innovation for the development of economy, society, and even nation because many governments and organizations have carried out a number of initiatives on development of information industry (e.g. China), knowledge economy (e.g. Australia) and wisdom cities (e.g. China) (Sun & Stranieri, 2021). Big intelligence is a characteristic of big data (Sun, Strang, & Li, 2018). Tu considers that we are living in the big wisdom age (Tu, 2015).

Combing equations (12) and (13), we have

$$\text{Big DIKIW analytics} = \text{big data analytics} + \text{big information analytics} \\ +\text{big knowledge analytics} + \text{big intelligence analytics} + \text{big wisdom analytics} \tag{14}$$

This implies that big DIKIW analytics should have played the same significant role as that of big data analytics, nevertheless, some academia, industries, and governments have technically ignored them.

Now, apply intelligent as an operation to both sides of equation (14), we have

$$\text{Intelligent big DIKIW analytics} = \textit{I}\text{ntelligent big data analytics} \\ +\text{intelligent big information analytics} + \text{intelligent big knowledge analytics} \\ +\text{intelligent big intelligence analytics} + \text{intelligent big wisdom analytics.} \tag{15}$$

Equations (11) to (15) forms a unified approach to integrating DIKIW, DIKIW analytics, big DIKIW, big DIKIW analytics, and intelligent big DIKIW analytics. This is an important complement to the current hotspots of big data, big data analytics, and intelligent big data analytics (Sun Z., 2019a). DIKIW, DIKIW analytics, big DIKIW, big DIKIW analytics, and intelligent big DIKIW analytics are elements of intelligent business analytics because DIKIW is fundamental for business and management decision making (Laudon & Laudon, 2020). Big DIKIW analytics and intelligent big DIKIW analytics can be represented as big analytics and intelligent big analytics respectively (Sun, Strang, & Li, 2018) and

Figure 2. A framework for DIKIW-driven intelligent business analytics

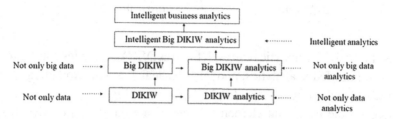

$$\text{Intelligent analytics} = \text{intelligent DIKIW analytics} + \text{intelligent big DIKIW analytics} \qquad (16)$$

Based on (16) intelligent business analytics, as an application of intelligent analytics, at least includes intelligent business big data analytics, intelligent business big information analytics, intelligent business big knowledge analytics, and intelligent business big wisdom analytics.

Currently, intelligent business analytics can be classified into intelligent business descriptive analytics, intelligent business diagnostic analytics, intelligent business predictive analytics, and intelligent business prescriptive analytics for big data, information, knowledge, intelligence, and wisdom (Sun & Stranieri, 2021; Sharda R., Delen, Turban, & King, 2018). Intelligent business big data analytics has made remarkable achievements thanks to the dramatic development of big data and big data analytics (Sun & Stranieri, 2021). Intelligent business big information/knowledge/wisdom analytics have not yet drawn significant attention in academia and industry, because we are still indulged in the age of big data. Big data is a foundation of big information, big knowledge, big intelligence, and big wisdom. Therefore, we are still at the foundational stage (see Figure 1) and scare about the emerging age of big information, big knowledge, big intelligence, and big wisdom.

PRINCIPLES OF INTELLIGENT BUSINESS ANALYTICS

The principles of intelligent business analytics are laws, rules, models, and theories that it is based on. Most parts of the previous section belong to the principles of intelligent business analytics. Even so, this section presents a framework for DIKIW-driven intelligent business analytics, as illustrated in Figure 2.

In Figure 2, DIKIW, big DIKIW, DIKIW analytics, and big DIKIW analytics are the solutions to that not only data, big data, data analytics, and big data analytics are important for intelligent business analytics. In other words, DIKIW, big DIKIW, DIKIW analytics, and big DIKIW analytics play a fundamentally important role in developing intelligent business analytics.

Intelligent big DIKIW analytics is the further development of big DIKIW technology and big DIKIW analytics and the technological foundation for developing intelligent business analytics.

Therefore, Figure 2 is not only a framework for DIKIW-driven intelligent business analytics, it is also a spectrum of elements of intelligent business analytics (Sun & Huo, 2021).

Figure 3. Macro, meso, and microtechnologies for intelligent business analytics

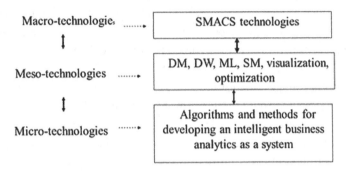

TECHNOLOGIES FOR INTELLIGENT BUSINESS ANALYTICS

Technologies for intelligent business analytics at least include macro-technologies, meso-technologies, and micro-technologies, illustrated as in Figure 3. Macro-technologies dominate a society of humans in a few decades. For example, SMACS (social, mobile, analytics, cloud, and service) technologies have dominated our digital age with SMACS products and services over the past decade. Meso-technologies work together with other technologies to facilitate and promote the development of analytics to align with the market and social environment provided by the macro-technologies. Meso-technologies are also called techniques (Ghavami, 2020; Sharda, Delen, & Turba, 2018). Micro-technologies include all the algorithms and methods for developing intelligent business analytics as a system or service. This section only looks at meso-technologies for intelligent business analytics, due to space limitations.

The meso-technologies for intelligent big data analytics encompass a wide range of mathematical, statistical, modeling, and algorithm technologies (Coronel, Morris, & Rob, 2020) (Sun Z., 2018), and intelligent technologies such as soft computing, fuzzy logic, neuro-fuzzy systems, OLAP, neural networks, evolutionary computation, probabilistic computing and models (Sun & Stranieri, 2021; Azvine, Nauck, & Ho, 2003). Intelligent big data analytics always involves historical or current data and data visualization (LaPlante, 2019). This requires intelligent big data analytics to use data mining (DM) to discover knowledge from a data warehouse (DW) to support decision-making (Ghavami, 2020). Therefore, we look at only six of them below in some detail.

Data warehousing (DW) is a process of creating data warehouses using intelligent data techniques. A data warehouse is a collection of integrated, subject-oriented databases designed to support decision-making, where each unit of data is non-volatile and relevant to some moment in time (Sharda, Delen, & Turba, 2018). Briefly, a data warehouse is a collection of integrated databases. Avanced data warehousing has been incorporated within BI and advanced business analytics (Richardson, Schlegel, Sallam, Kronz, & Sun, 2021). DW extracts and obtains the data from operational databases and external open sources, providing a more comprehensive data pool (Coronel, Morris, & Rob, 2020; Holsapple, Lee-Postb, & Pakath, 2014). The current leading DW providers include Amazon Redshift, Snowflake, Google BigQuery, and Microsoft Azure Synapse (EM360 Tech, 2020). Not only warehousing data, how to warehouse information, knowledge, intelligence, and wisdom is a big issue for developing intelligent big data analytics. In other words, DIKIW warehousing is of significance for intelligent business analytics.

Data mining (DM) is a process of discovering novel patterns, knowledge from a large database or data warehouse, or the web to support intelligent business analytics and managerial decision making.

(Ghavami, 2020). Traditionally, data mining is knowledge discovery from a large database (Laudon & Laudon, 2020). DM employs advanced statistical and analytical tools to analyze the big data available through DWs and other sources to identify possible relationships, patterns, and anomalies and discover information or knowledge for business decision making (Delena & Demirkanb, 2013; Kantardzic, 2011). In DM, regression and classification are usually used for prediction, predictive mining and analytics, while clustering and association are used for description or descriptive mining, and analytics (Fan, Lau, & Zhao, 2015). Currently, advanced data mining aims to discover and generate insights, intelligence, and wisdom to support decision-making (Richardson, Schlegel, Sallam, Kronz, & Sun, 2021). DM is one of the top intelligent technologies for business analytics, business big data analytics, and intelligent business analytics. Not only mining data is a future trend in the age of big analytics and AI. In other words, DIKIW mining is future-oriented mining technology for intelligent business analytics. For example, knowledge mining, intelligence mining, and wisdom mining as a part of DIKIW mining have become a social demand for business people and analytics professionals.

Machine learning (ML) is a branch of AI that is concerned with making machines learn from data (Ghavami, 2020, p. 25). Machine learning has become vital for big data analytics (Weber, 2020, p. 33). Recently, advanced machine learning includes deep learning based on artificial neural networks (Ghavami, 2020, p. 97). Deep learning involves multiple hidden layers of non-linear processing for extraction, transformation, pattern recognition, and classification (Weber, 2020, pp. 26-33; Ghavami, 2020). Machine learning including deep learning aims to automate the ability of human learning through "improving the performance on future tasks after making observations about the world" (Russell & Norvig, 2010, p. 693). Case-based reasoning (CBR) is a kind of machine learning (Weber, 2020, p. 35). CBR is based on the similarity principle of "similar problems have similar solutions" (Sun & Finnie, 2004; 2010). Case retrieval, reuse, revision, retention, and repartition are the cyclic reasoning process of CBR. CBR has successful applications in healthcare and medical diagnosis (Weber, 2020, p. 35), e-commerce, e-services, recommendation, and customer segmentations. CBR is useful for developing big data reasoning and intelligence, which is the basis for big data analytics in general and intelligent business analytics in particular.

Statistical modeling (SM) **and analysis.** Statistics is the science of collecting and organizing data and drawing meaningful and interpretable knowledge, intelligence, and wisdom from the datasets (Kantardzic, 2011, p. 140). Statistics includes statistical inference and statistical modeling. Statistical inference at least includes Bayesian inference, predictive regression, and logistic regression (Kantardzic, 2011). Statistical modeling is about discovering knowledge through statistical analysis (Sun, Sun, & Strang, 2018). Statistical analysis includes descriptive analysis and predictive analysis. Descriptive analysis and predictive analysis lead to descriptive data mining and predictive data mining (Kantardzic, 2011, p. 2). The latter further brings forth descriptive analytics and predictive analytics (Ghavami, 2020, p. 97). More generally, not only statistical modeling technology, other modeling technologies have a significant impact on big data, intelligence, and analytics with applications. For example, knowledge modeling technology includes decision trees and the analytic hierarchy processes (Sharda R., Delen, Turban, & King, 2018, p. 352).

Visualization is a technology for presenting the results, generated insights, intelligence, and wisdom, typically in graphical dashboards, scorecards, and charts (Ghavami, 2020, p. 31). Visualization technologies at least include DIKIW visualization, for example, information visualization deals with abstract, information such as text, hierarchies, and statistical data (Kantardzic, 2011, p. 450). In other words, data visualization is not a unique visualization technology. Visualization technologies including display technologies make knowledge patterns and information for decision making in a form of figures or tables or multimedia. Data visualization is an important part of business big data analytics and supports highly interactive dashboards and the exploration of data through the manipulation of chart images (Richardson, Schlegel, Sallam, Kronz, & Sun, 2021).

Optimization is a technology that enables effective decisions or predictions in a variety of contexts from database management and big data management to knowledge discovery to intelligent systems. Historically, optimization technology is a part of operations research, which includes linear, nonlinear programming models, and other mathematical programming models (Sharda, Delen, & Turba, 2018, pp. 362-370). The optimization principle is "everything can be improved" to meet the ever-increasing demand of humans and society. Optimization technology has been used in almost every discipline or area in academia and industry because finding a better solution or the best solution from a large number of alternatives using a step-by-step improvement process and intelligent business analytics is always a pressing demand from any decision-makers and organizations. Optimization technology can be used for developing and improving intelligent business analytics as a system, as a metric, and as a service (Sun Z., 2019a).

In summary, intelligent business analytics can facilitate business decision making and improve the competitive advantages of an organization through analyzing existing DIKIW and future trends, creating predictive models to forecast future threats and opportunities, and optimizing business processes to enhance organizational performance using (Delena & Demirkanb, 2013; Chen, Chiang, & Storey, 2012).

TOOLS FOR INTELLIGENT BUSINESS ANALYTICS

There are various intelligent business analytics tools available in the market. The tools are not only for analytics developers but also for end-users. Gartner's magic quadrant for analytics and BI platforms (Richardson, Schlegel, Sallam, Kronz, & Sun, 2021) includes state-of-the-art tools for intelligent business analytics in the global market. These tools targets business people and data analysts, analytics developers, and other analytics consumers. This section explores the tools for intelligent business analytics in the market worldwide based on our early analysis (Sun & Stranieri, 2021) and the latest research of Gartner (Richardson, Schlegel, Sallam, Kronz, & Sun, 2021).

Gartner's magic quadrant classifies the related software vendors into four categories: leaders, challengers, visionaries, and niche players. In 2021's magic quadrant the leaders were Microsoft, Tableau, Qlik whereas the leaders were Microsoft, Tableau, ThoughtSpot, Qlik in 2019's magic quadrant. The challenger was MicroStrategy, Google (Looker), and Domo, increasing to three challengers in 2021 from one in 2019, it was MicroStrategy as the challenger in 2019's magic quadrant (Sun & Stranieri, 2021). In 2021's magic quadrant, the niche players include Amazon's Web Services, IBM, Alibaba Cloud, Pyramid Analytics, Board, Infor, Information Builders; the visionaries include ORACLE, ThoughtSpot, Sisense, SAP, SAS, and Yellowfin. In what follows, we review the tools offered by the three leaders in some detail due to space limitations.

Microsoft offers data preparation, visual-based data discovery, interactive dashboards, and augmented analytics in Power BI as an intelligent business analytics tool (Richardson, Schlegel, Sallam, Kronz, & Sun, 2021). Power BI is available as a SaaS option running in the Azure cloud or as an on-premises option in Power BI Report Server. The Power BI cloud service is extremely rich in its capabilities that include a set of augmented analytics and automated ML capabilities. Power BI Desktop can be used as a stand-alone, free personal analysis tool. Power BI also offers AI-powered services, such as text, sentiment, and image analytics.

Qlik. Qlik's lead solution to intelligent business analytics is Qlik Sense (Richardson, Schlegel, Sallam, Kronz, & Sun, 2021). Qlik Sense enables one to create interactive reports and dashboards with excellent charts and graphs (Qlik, 2021). It simplifies data analysis and helps one make effective decisions faster than ever before. Qlik Sense runs on the unique Qlik Associative Engine. Qlik's Cognitive Engine adds AI/ML-driven intelligent functionality to the product and works (Richardson, Schlegel, Sallam, Kronz, & Sun, 2021). Qlik's Associative Engine offers context-aware insight suggestions and augmentation of analysis. Qlik has built on its augmented analytics vision, with key elements based on its Cognitive Engine. It provides intelligent analytics services such as data preparation, search-based visual analytics, conversational analytics, associative insights, and accelerated creation.

Tableau Tableau's visual analytics platform is transforming the way people use data to solve problems (Tableau, 2021). It offers a visual-based exploration experience that enables business users to access, prepare, analyze, and present findings in their data (Richardson, Schlegel, Sallam, Kronz, & Sun, 2021). Tableau's vision is to help people see and understand data (Tableau, 2021).

However, all the above tools' providers still focus on data analytics and technically ignore the importance of information, knowledge, intelligence, and wisdom, although the real focus of AI is how to transform knowledge into intelligence (Russell & Norvig, 2010). This is also the reason why we emphasize that not only data and data analytics play an ever-increasing role in developing intelligent business analytics and its services.

DISCUSSION AND IMPLICATIONS

We have mentioned a number of scholarly researches on intelligent business analytics. This section will discuss the related work, based on the principle of research as a search and big data-driven analysis (Sun & Huo, 2021), and examine theoretical and technical implications of this research as well as limitations and future research directions.

Discussion

A Google search for "The elements of" showed about 113,000,000 results (retrieved on August 28, 2021). This indicates that the elements are big interests for almost every discipline. However, a Google search for "the elements of intelligent business analytics" found no research results except our early work. This motivates us to develop the elements of intelligent business analytics.

A Google Scholar (https://scholar.google.com.au/) search for "intelligent business analytics" (27 August 2021) found 89 results. We first analyze the titles of the found results (based on the ranking of Google Scholar) in terms of "intelligent business analytics".

Among the 89 found results, only 3 publications have used "intelligent business analytics" as a keyword in their titles. 40 mentioned results include "intelligent business analytics" in either titles or contents. Among them, intelligent business analytics also includes intelligent business analytics systems, intelligent business analytics as a tool to build decision-support systems for e-businesses (Azvine, Nauck, & Ho, 2003), intelligent business analytics services, intelligent business analytics for supply chain, intelligent business process analytics, intelligent human resource analytics, intelligent marketing analytics, business analytics intelligence, intelligent business analytics tools, advanced intelligent business analytics, analytics as a decision discipline in intelligent business, intelligent customer analytics, and intelligent process analytics. This preliminary analysis shows that intelligent business analytics has been applied in the business areas including intelligent business, decision-support, supply chain, e-business, business process, human resources, customer services, although the applications are still scattered to some extent. All the above-mentioned terms can be examined under one roof of intelligent business analytics. The preliminary analysis also demonstrates that Azvine et al first coined intelligent business analytics as a term (Azvine, Nauck, & Ho, 2003). Their research focuses on intelligent business analytics as a tool to build decision-support systems for e-businesses. It is this research that provides unified research on intelligent business analytics in terms of elements, principles, technologies, and tools.

Furthermore, a Google Scholar search for "intelligent analytics" (August 27, 2021) found about 1,300 results and showed that intelligent traffic analytics, intelligent data analytics, intelligent big data analytics, and intelligent health data analytics have drawn some attention in academia. This implies that intelligent analytics has been applied in business areas including traffic, big data, and health. This analysis demonstrates that intelligent business analytics and intelligent analytics are still emerging disciplines although AI, big data, and business analytics have drawn increasing attention in academia and industries over the past decade.

Gartner uses analytics and BI (ABI) to do research and release an annual report on ABI platforms in the market (Richardson, Schlegel, Sallam, Kronz, & Sun, 2021). The difference between ABI and intelligent business analytics is that the former is a loose and simple collection of analytics and BI without scientific and systemic investigation; the latter is a logical and systemic treatment based on intelligent analytics, DIKIW analytics, and their applications in business. Therefore, intelligent business analytics is a more scientific term for the development of analytics, big data, intelligence, and intelligent business.

Theoretical and Technical Implications

The theoretical implication of this research is that it provides a unified solution to that 1. not only data, big data, data analytics, big data analytics, and intelligent big data analytics underpin the development of intelligent business analytics. 2. not only AI-driven intelligent techniques have played a significant role in the development of intelligent business analytics. The research demonstrated that intelligent business analytics consists of intelligent business big data analytics, intelligent business big information analytics, intelligent business big knowledge analytics, and intelligent business big wisdom analytics. This approach will pave a new way for developing intelligent business analytics with principles, technologies, tools, and applications.

The technical implication of this research is that the proposed approach on intelligent business analytics in general and intelligent business DIKIW analytics in specific can appeal to more researchers and practitioners to undertake the research and application of intelligent business analytics for more effective decision making, taking into account the proposed DIKIW framework for intelligent business analytics.

LIMITATIONS

A limitation of this research is that it should consider intelligent business descriptive, predictive, and prescriptive analytics as one dimension, and the technologies of intelligent business analytics as another dimension. Therefore, one of the future research directions is to provide matrix analysis for intelligent business analytics.

FUTURE RESEARCH DIRECTIONS

Intelligent business analytics is an application of intelligent analytics in business to promote intelligent business, improve business performance, and support business decision-making (Sun & Stranieri, 2021). Intelligent business analytics is an analytics paradigm of integrating big DIKIW, AI, and other intelligent technologies, analytics intelligence, and intelligent analytics. Therefore, one of the future research directions is to address systems integration among intelligent analytics, modern analytics, and intelligent business to realize intelligent business analytics for supporting decision making (Howson, Sallam, & Richa, 2018).

As mentioned earlier, intelligent business analytics is an emerging frontier for intelligent business. Many fundamental theoretical, technological, and managerial issues surrounding the development and implementation of intelligent business analytics remain unsolved. For example, how can we apply intelligent business analytics to improve intelligent business, healthcare, mobile commerce, web services, cloud services, and digital transformation? What are the implications of intelligent business analytics on intelligent business and management, IoT, blockchain, service, and society? These should be addressed as a future research direction to meet the social, economic, marketing, managerial, scientific, and technological demands from different parties or individuals for intelligent business analytics with applications.

CONCLUSION

This chapter explored the elements of intelligent business analytics. This mainly consists of the principles, technologies, techniques, and tools of intelligent business analytics. This chapter highlights 1). not only data, big data, data analytics, and big data analytics underpin the development of intelligent business analytics. 2). not only AI-driven intelligent techniques have played a significant role in the development of intelligent business analytics. The main three contributions of this research consist 1). Intelligent business analytics is a science and technology of digitally transforming data and big data into big information, knowledge, intelligence, and wisdom for enhancing business performance and decision making. 2). DIKIW, big DIKIW, DIKIW analytics, and big DIKIW analytics as elements will play a significant role in the development of intelligent business analytics. 3). Both AI and other intelligent technologies are promoting the development of intelligent business analytics. Therefore, intelligent business analytics is an emerging paradigm that analytically transforms a business into intelligent business, big data to big wisdom, and decision making to intelligent decision making under the ever-increasing complexity of businesses and business processes for developing intelligent business, improving business performance, and supporting decision making. The proposed approach in this chapter might facilitate research and development of intelligent business, big data analytics, business analytics, enterprise analytics, business intelligence, AI, and data science.

In future work, as a part of future research directions, we will investigate matrix (2D) analysis for big data, big information, big knowledge, and big wisdom as a dimension, and descriptive analytics, diagnostic analytics, predictive analytics, and prescriptive analytics as another dimension based on AI and machine learning to form a unified framework of intelligent business analytics. We will also develop a unified theory for business analytics thinking and business analytics intelligence.

REFERENCES

Ackoff, R. (1992). *From Data to Wisdom.* http://faculty.ung.edu/kmelton/Documents/DataWisdom.pdf

Azvine, B., Nauck, D., & Ho, C. (2003). Intelligent Business Analytics— A Tool to Build Decision-Support Systems for eBusinesses. *BT Technology Journal, 21*(4), 65–71. doi:10.1023/A:1027379403688

Chen, H., Chiang, R., & Storey, V. (2012, December). Business intelligence and analytics: From big data to big impact. *Management Information Systems Quarterly, 36*(4), 1165–1188. doi:10.2307/41703503

Coronel, C., Morris, S., & Rob, P. (2020). *Database Systems: Design, Implementation, and Management* (14th ed.). Course Technology, Cengage Learning.

Davenport, T. H. (2013, December). Analytics 3.0. *Harvard Business Review*, 65–72.

Delena, D., & Demirkanb, H. (2013). Data, information and analytics as services. *Decision Support Systems, 55*(1), 359–363. doi:10.1016/j.dss.2012.05.044

EM360 Tech. (2020, September 18). *Top 10 Cloud Data Warehouse Solution Providers.* Retrieved August 25, 2021, from https://em360tech.com/data_management/tech-features-featuredtech-news/top-10-cloud-data-warehouse-solution-providers

Eiloart, J. (2018, December 2). *Top five business analytics intelligence trends for 2019.* Retrieved from https://www.information-age.com/business-analytics-intelligence-123477004/

Fan, S., Lau, R. Y., & Zhao, J. L. (2015). Demystifying Big Data Analytics for Business Intelligence Through the Lens of Marketing Mix. *Big Data Research, 2*(1), 28–32. doi:10.1016/j.bdr.2015.02.006

Gartner-diagnostic analytics. (2020). *Diagnostic Analytics.* Retrieved August 12, 2020, from Gartner: https://www.gartner.com/en/information-technology/glossary/diagnostic-analytics

Ghavami, P. (2020). Big Data Analytics Methods: Analytics Techniques in Data Mining, Deep Learning and Natural Language Processing (2nd ed.). de Gruyter.

Henke, N., & Bughin, J. (2016, December). *The Age of Analytics: Competing in a Data-Driven World.* McKinsey Global Institute.

Holsapple, C., Lee-Postb, A., & Pakath, R. (2014). A unified foundation for business analytics. *Decision Support Systems, 64*, 130–141. doi:10.1016/j.dss.2014.05.013

Howson, C., Sallam, R. L., & Richa, J. L. (2018, Feb 26). *Magic Quadrant for Analytics and Business Intelligence Platforms.* Retrieved Aug 16, 2018, from Gartner: www.gartner.com

IDC. (2019). *IDC Forecasts Revenues for Big Data and Business Analytics Solutions will Reach $189.1 Billion This Year with Double-Digit Annual Growth Through 2022.* Retrieved 1 23, 2020, from IDC: https://www.idc.com/getdoc.jsp?containerId=prUS44998419

Kantardzic, M. (2011). *Data Mining: Concepts, Models, Methods, and Algorithms*. Wiley & IEEE Press. doi:10.1002/9781118029145

Kumar, G. B. (2015). An encyclopedic overview of 'Big Data' Analytics. *International Journal of Applied Engineering Research: IJAER, 10*(3), 5681–5705.

Laney, D., & Jain, A. (2017, June 20). *100 Data and Analytics Predictions Through*. Retrieved August 04, 2018, from Gartner: https://www.gartner.com/events-na/data-analytics/wp-content/uploads/sites/5/2017/10/Data-and-Analytics-Predictions.pdf

LaPlante, A. (2019). *What Is Augmented Analytics? Powering Your Data with AI*. Boston: O' Realy. Retrieved from https://go.oracle.com/LP=84622

Laudon, K. G., & Laudon, K. C. (2020). *Management Information Systems: Managing the Digital Firm* (16th ed.). Pearson.

Liew, A. (2013). DIKIW: Data, Information, Knowledge, Intelligence, Wisdom and their Interrelationships. *Psychology (Irvine, Calif.)*.

McKinsey. (2011, May). *Big data: The next frontier for innovation, competition, and productivity*. Retrieved from McKinsey Global Institute: https://www.mckinsey.com/business-functions/business-technology/our-insights/big-data-the-next-frontier-for-innovation

Minelli, M., Chambers, M., & Dhiraj, A. (2013). *Big Data, Big Analytics: Emerging Business Intelligence and Analytic Trends for Today's Businesses* (Chinese Edition 2014). Wiley & Sons. doi:10.1002/9781118562260

Norusis, M. J. (1997). *SPSS: SPSS 7.5 Guide to Data Analytics*. Prentice Hall.

Oxford. (2008). *Oxford Advanced Learner's English Dictionary* (7th ed.). Oxford University Press.

Pettey, C., & van der Meulen, R. (2018, April 25). *Gartner Says Global Artificial Intelligence Business Value to Reach $1.2 Trillion in 2018*. Retrieved August 04, 2018, from Gartner: https://www.gartner.com/newsroom/id/3872933

Qlik. (2021). Retrieved August 28, 2021, from https://www.qlik.com/us

Richardson, J., Schlegel, K., Sallam, R., Kronz, A., & Sun, J. (2021, February 15). *Magic Quadrant for Analytics and Business Intelligence Platforms*. Retrieved March 6, 2021, from Gartner: https://www.gartner.com/doc/reprints?id=1-254T1IQX&ct=210202&st=sb

Rowley, J. (2007). The wisdom hierarchy: Representations of the DIKW hierarchy. *Journal of Information and Communication Science, 33*(2), 163–180. doi:10.1177/0165551506070706

Russell, S., & Norvig, P. (2010). *Artificial Intelligence: A Modern Approach* (3rd ed.). Prentice Hall.

Sabherwal, R., & Becerra-Fernandez, I. (2011). *Business Intelligence: Practices, Technologies, and Management*. John Wiley & Sons, Inc.

Sharda, R., Delen, D., & Turba, E. (2018). *Business Intelligence and Analytics: Systems for Decision Support* (10th ed.). Pearson.

Sharda, R., Delen, D., Turban, E., & King, D. (2018). *Business Intelligence, Analytics, and Data Science: A Managerial Perspective* (4th ed.). Pearson.

Sun, Z. (2018). Intelligent Big Data Analytics: Foundations and Applications. *PNG UoT BAIS, 3*(4), 1–8. doi:10.13140/RG.2.2.11037.41441

Sun, Z. (2019a). Intelligent Big Data Analytics: A Managerial Perspective. In Z. Sun (Ed.), *Managerial Perspectives on Intelligent Big Data Analytics* (pp. 1–19). IGI-Global. doi:10.4018/978-1-5225-7277-0.ch001

Sun, Z. (2020). *Business Analytics Intelligence: An Emerging Frontier for Innovation and Productivity*. Retrieved February 3, 2021, from https://www.researchgate.net/profile/Zhaohao_Sun/publication/343876626_Business_Analytics_Intelligence_An_Emerging_Frontier_for_Innovation_and_Productivity

Sun, Z., & Finnie, G. (2010). Intelligent Techniques in E-Commerce: A Case-based Reasoning Perspective. Springer-Verlag.

Sun, Z., & Huo, Y. (2019). A Managerial Framework for Intelligent Big Data Analytics. In *Proceedings of ICBDSC 2019*. Bali, Indonesia: ACM.

Sun, Z., & Huo, Y. (2020). Intelligence without Data. *Global Journal of Computer Science and Technology C, 20*(1), 25–35. doi:10.34257/GJCSTCVOL20IS1PG25

Sun, Z., & Huo, Y. (2021). The spectrum of big data analytics. *Journal of Computer Information Systems*. doi:10.1080/08874417.2019.1571456

Sun, Z., Strang, K., & Li, R. (2018). Big data with ten big characteristics. *Proceedings of 2018 The 2nd Intl Conf. on Big Data Research (ICBDR 2018), October 27-29* (pp. 56-61). Weihai, China: ACM.

Sun, Z., & Stranieri, A. (2021). The Nature of Intelligent Analytics. In Z. Sun (Ed.), *Intelligent Analytics with Advanced Multi-industry Applications* (pp. 1–22). IGI-Global. doi:10.4018/978-1-7998-4963-6.ch001

Sun, Z., Sun, L., & Strang, K. (2018). Big Data Analytics Services for Enhancing Business Intelligence. *Journal of Computer Information Systems, 58*(2), 162–169. doi:10.1080/08874417.2016.1220239

Sun, Z., & Wang, P. P. (2017). A Mathematical Foundation of Big Data. *Journal of New Mathematics and Natural Computation, 13*(2), 8–24.

Sun, Z., Zou, H., & Strang, K. (2015). *Big Data Analytics as a Service for Business Intelligence. In I3E2015, LNCS 9373*. Springer.

Tableau. (2021, August 25). Retrieved August 25, 2021, from https://www.tableau.com/

Tu, Z. (2015). *The Big Data Revolution 3.0*. Guanxi Normal University Press. (in Chinese)

Turban, E., & Volonino, L. (2011). *Information Technology for Management: Improving Performance in the Digital Economy* (8th ed.). John Wiley & Sons.

Wang, F.-Y. (2012). A big-data perspective on AI: Newton, Merton, and Analytics Intelligence. *IEEE Intelligent Systems, 27*(5), 2-4.

Wang, Y. (2015, June). Formal Cognitive Models of Data, Information, Knowledge, and Intelligence. *WSEAS Transactions on Computers*, *14*, 770–781.

Weber, H. (2020). Big Data and Artificial Intelligence: Complete Guide to Data Science, AI, Big Data, and Machine Learning. ICGtesting.

Williams, S. (2016). *Business Intelligence Strategy and Big Data Analytics: A General Management Perspective*. Morgan Kaufmann.

KEY TERMS AND DEFINITIONS

Artificial Intelligence (AI): Science and technology concerned with understand, imitate, extend, augment, and automate intelligent behaviors of human beings and others including machines.

Big Data: Data with at least one of the ten big characteristics consisting of big volume, big velocity, big variety, big veracity, big intelligence, big analytics, big infrastructure, big service, big value, and big market.

Data Mining: A process of discovering various models, summaries, and derived values, knowledge from a given collection of data. Alternatively, it is the process of using statistical, mathematical, logical, AI methods and tools to extract useful information, knowledge, and intelligence from large database.

DIKIW: An abbreviation of data, information, knowledge, intelligence, and wisdom. The latter are the elements of many disciplines such as computing, AI, business, and management.

Intelligent Analytics: science and technology about collecting, organizing, and analyzing big data, big information, big knowledge, and big wisdom to transform them into intelligent information, intelligent knowledge, and intelligent wisdom based on artificial intelligence and analytical algorithms and technologies. Intelligent analytics consists of big DIKIW analytics and intelligent big DIKIW analytics.

Intelligent Big Data Analytics: Science and technology about collecting, organizing, and analyzing big data to discover patterns, knowledge, and intelligence as well as other information within the big data based on artificial intelligence and intelligent systems.

Machine Learning: Concerned about how computer can adapt to new circumstances and to detect and extrapolate patterns.

SMACS Technology: Includes social technology, mobile technology, analytics technology, cloud technology, and service technology.

Chapter 2
Intelligent Business Analytics:
Need, Functioning, Challenges, and Implications

D. N. Sarma A.
Centre for Good Governance, India

ABSTRACT

This chapter begins with a brief introduction to the evolution of the data analytics ecosystem and its role. The terms such as data, insight, and action are defined in the context of business analytics. The authors explain briefly about analytics, business analytics (BA), business intelligence, and intelligent BA. They mention the need for intelligent analytics for the organizations in a digital world. The latest innovations in AI, big data, and analytics together result in a new branch known as intelligent big data analytics, in short, intelligent BA. Further, intelligent BA becomes an important tool for the organizations for intelligent decision making. The key components of intelligent BA are presented and explained. Additionally, various applications of intelligent BA are presented, and a few challenges for implementing the system are mentioned. Finally, possible future directions of research for the development of intelligent BA are discussed.

INTRODUCTION

Data science is one of the hottest subjects for more than a decade in all most all the organizations including industrial, businesses, and government and non-governments, which continue its demand for a few more decades. In the past few years, organizations are generating a lot of data and get started focusing on data to gain more meaningful insights to make innovative and intelligent decisions for not only the growth of the business but also to improve the business performance. Most commonly, the data generated by the organizations includes information about their customers, suppliers, marketing, sales, accounts, finance, and operations. In a digital world, organizations are transforming digitally and generating larger volumes of data. Now the challenge is to make use of the data. Thus, organizations are focusing on data analysis in order to get insights from the data because of changing business functioning. According to

DOI: 10.4018/978-1-7998-9016-4.ch002

the Oxford dictionary, the term analysis refers to "the detailed study or examination of something to understand more about it" whereas analytics refers to "a careful and complete analysis of data using a model, usually performed by a computer". The term analytics referring to data analytics which finds variety of applications in business; thus, it is also commonly referred as business data analytics. In the business, analytics applications include but not limited to market analysis, sales analysis, market forecasting, strategic planning and financial analysis, customer analytics. The goal of this chapter is to present the need, functioning, challenges, opportunities, and implications of Intelligent Big Data Analytics in a digital world.

Business Intelligence (BI) solution can combine data from multiple sources and analysing a business's data and allows organization to see the big picture and facilitate better business decisions. Organizations adopt BI and analytics tools majorly to benefit the organization in terms of better business decisions at strategic levels, including but not limited to the financial planning, marketing, sales, understanding customers, and operational efficiency. In the early days, BI was available in offline mode which is accessible to limited strategic users mainly for decision-making. The later version of BI was evolved as Operational BI this extends insights from data to all the levels of users in the organization, including strategic, tactical, and operational users for their decision-making. Additionally, organizations have been leveraging the use of Operational BI (Sarma, 2018) for their strategic, tactical use and proliferating into low level decision making for smooth running of business operations.

The need and usage of BI systems for operational decision making has significantly increased for a timely decision to all users in the organisations. Further, an Operational BI is not merely a simple combination of operational and BI systems, but this constitutes the whole complex set of components that cover overall functionalities from the storage, process, monitor, visualize, and delivery of information to form an operational BI ecosystem. Besides, Operational BI is a unified business information system that provides a real-time decision-making information to all the users in the organization including operational, tactical, and strategic. According to a study (Sarma, 2021), an Operational BI ecosystem consists of five key components namely Business Process Monitoring (BPM), Event Monitoring and Notification (EMN), Operational Analytics (OA), Operational Reporting (OR), and Portal. BPM provides configuring and measuring performance of various operational, business and process parameters, while the EMN component delivers the right message to the right person at the right time. The component, OA will provide analytical functionalities such as extraction of knowledge and updates the available knowledge repositories, whereas OR present information in real-time to the users that describes what is happening at the present time.

In the 21st century the use of Artificial Intelligence (AI), Machine Learning (ML), Big Data and Cloud computing technologies are greatly increased, and organizations are moving towards digitization at a faster pace and automation of more and more business and industrial processes for better control and monitoring to improve the efficiency of organization functioning. Nowadays, AI has been playing a major role in business analytics and BI domains which enables organizations to get the advantage of intelligent analytics. Besides, this result in the evolution of a new kind of the analytics known as Intelligent BA. Furthermore, organizations are focusing on the data generated by itself as well as generated by external means like social media and news for instant insights for improved decision-making. Thus, the future BA could consist of more and more automated processes and simpler to use. Additionally, it works for any volume, variety, and varsity of data on a real-time basis with in-depth insights to make an actionable result. Further, Intelligent BA extracts knowledge, even from complex data objects such as text, image, audio, and videos.

Figure 1. Evolution of data analytics ecosystem

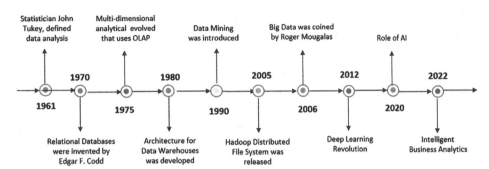

Evolution of Analytics Ecosystem

In 1961, statistician John Tukey defined data analysis. From this point onwards, data analytics has the long history with its technological evolution, development of database concepts, and tools which continues to appear. Figure 1 shows the various stages in the evolution of the data analytics ecosystem. In 1970, relational databases were invented by Edgar F. Codd, who is popularly known as the father of the relational database. In 1975, the concept of multi-dimensional analysis evolved which is popularly known as Online Analytical Processing (OLAP) wherein the aggregate values are stored in the cube of various combinations of the dimensions. Furthermore, these cubes allow the user to view the data in multiple views, and the most common dimensions are time, location (or geography), departments and product category.

Data Warehouses architecture was developed in the 1980s, which mainly store large amounts of the operational data in a well-organized manner. Besides storage, data warehouse enables a vital role in transforming operational data into a decision-making perspective. Though the term Business Intelligence (BI) was first used in 1865, which was later adapted by Howard Dresner at Gartner in 1989. In 1990, the concept of data mining was evolved which is recognized as a sub-process of Knowledge Discovery in Databases (KDD). The term data mining refers to a process of extracting and discovering patterns in large data sets, whereas KDD comprises a sequence of steps such as selection, preprocessing, transformation, data mining and evaluation. The term data mining is defined as a process of extracting and discovering patterns in large data sets. In 2005, Hadoop Distributed File System was released that acts as a core layer of data storage in a distributed file system that provides high-throughput access to application data. Multiple versions of Hadoop have been released from its inception. In June 2021, Apache Hadoop 3.3.1 was released which is the first stable release this comprises of four modules such as Hadoop Common, Hadoop Distributed File System (HDFS), YARN and MapReduce. Hadoop Common - the common utilities that support the other Hadoop modules. Hadoop Distributed File System (HDFS) - a distributed file system that provides high throughput access to the application data. Hadoop YARN is a framework that provides allocating system resources to the various applications for job scheduling and cluster nodes management whereas Hadoop MapReduce is a system that helps for parallel processing of large datasets.

In the year 2013, data science has come to light because of extensive use of Machine Learning (ML) and Deep Learning (DL) and Natural Language Processing (NLP) techniques become a widespread across the domains in all businesses and non-business applications, which are sub-sets of Artificial Intelligence

(AI). Early 2020, the role of AI has started and steadily increasing its presence in all most all major applications. Further, AI is revolutionizing the world by its availability as one of the highly matured technology footprints of several independent service providers, open systems and finding its applications in all business, industry, and government. Nowadays, organizations are so keen to develop new products and services based on AI to provide value addition to their customers. Further, few organizations are already adopted AI tools and techniques for automation of the existing business processes to gain the benefits of AI. A continuously evolving process of AI methods, tools and techniques in analytics can help organizations to discover the knowledge from the data. Further, organization can use the extracted knowledge for informed decision making which in turn results the effective functioning as well to run businesses intelligently. Additionally, AI, Big data and Analytics together, result an evolution of a new system known as Intelligent BA. Besides, the use of Intelligent BA will continue not only in the business, but also equally in the government and other industry verticals. Further, Intelligent BA transforms functioning of an organization from a process driven to a data driven.

Definitions of Analytics and BA, BI and BIA

Most commonly, analytics are used in the business even though it has been used in many other areas. The term 'analytics' is broadly coined with business, then it is referred to as 'business analytics' when is combined with data, then it is known as 'data analytics'. Sometimes it may be combined with both business as well as data, then it is known as 'business data analytics'. In general, data analytics is more of a general description of an analytics process, whereas business analytics refers to in the context of business, which is mainly applied for operations, marketing, finance, and strategic planning among other functions in the organizations. The ability to use data effectively to drive rapid, precise, and profitable decisions has been a critical strategic advantage for organizations.

According to an online material related to business analytics product info of (Oracle, n.d.) the term business analytics refers to taking in and processing historical business data; analysing that data to identify trends, patterns, and root causes; making data-driven business decisions based on those insights.

According to the study (Bichler et.al, 2017) the terms Business Analytics is stated as ''evidence-based problem recognition and solving that happen within the context of business situations''.

According to the Institute for Operations Research and Management Science (INFORMS, 2015) the term "Analytics is the scientific process of transforming data into insight for making better decisions". Additionally, define business analytics as "it facilitates the realization of business objectives through reporting of data to analyze trends, creating predictive models for forecasting, and optimizing business processes for enhanced performance".

According to online material of Gartner's glossary of information technology (Gartner, n.d.) the term business analytics is comprised of solutions used to build analysis models and simulations to create scenarios, understand realities and predict future states. Business analytics includes data mining, predictive analytics, applied analytics and statistics, and is delivered as an application suitable for a business user. Generally, these analytics solutions often come with a prebuilt industry content that is targeted at an industry business process. For example, claims, underwriting or a specific regulatory requirement.

According to the study (Yin & Fernandez, 2020) business analytics is a system that enabled by machine learning techniques aiming at promoting the efficiency and performance of an organization by supporting the decision-making process.

According to Bhatt (2014), business analytics refers to "the skills, technologies, applications and practices for continuous iterative exploration and investigation of past business performance to gain insight and drive business planning".

According to an online source (TechTarget, n.d.) the term Business Analytics (BA) is the iterative, methodical exploration of an organization's data, with an emphasis on statistical analysis. Business analytics are used by companies that use data-driven techniques for decision-making.

Business Analytics (BA) and Business Intelligence (BI) applications are used in organizations for some, or other purpose related to business analysis and planning. At a broader level, the terms BA and BI look like similar meaning, but there is an underlying difference in their functioning. BA analyses the past data to analyze the current scenarios and mainly help the organizations in the future business, whereas BI system analyses both past and present data and provides insights to the current business needs. In a nutshell, the term business analytics can define as "the process that uses statistical methods and technologies for analysing historical data to gain new insights". In other words, the application of data analysis in the context of business to discover hidden patterns and findings in the data that helps organizations to solve most of the business problems. Alternatively, the ways in which enterprises such as business, non-profit organizations, and governments can use data to gain insights and make better informed decisions for their use. The term BI is defined as "a set of processes, architecture and technologies that converts both historical data and present data into a meaningful insight. In summary, BI transforms data into intelligence and provides reports, graphs, charts, dashboards to the user for easy decision making.

According to the authors (LIM et al., 2013), Business intelligence and analytics (BIA) is about the development of technologies, systems, practices, and applications to analyze critical business data so as to gain new insights about business and markets. The new insights can be used for improving products and services, achieving better operational efficiency, and fostering customer relationships.

What Is Data, Insight, and Action?

According to the Merriam-Webster, the term data refers to "factual information (such as measurements or statistics) used as a basis for reasoning, discussion, or calculation"; or "information in digital format that can be transmitted or processed". Few examples of data are prices of food items, age of employees in an organization, professional experience details of employees, and rates of various types of cars. Data are the basic form of information which is available either in digital or non-digital formats. Most commonly, the term data are referred to as digital data only when transforming from its source form. The nature of the data may be structured, semi-structured or unstructured or qualitative or quantitative. The quantitative data may be either discrete or continuous. Further, the data may be either audio, images, or text or it may be a combination of all these. In statistics, there are four different data measurement scales such as nominal, ordinal, interval, and ratio, which are subcategories of different data types. Nominal and ordinal data scales fall into qualitative or categorical whereas interval and ratio data scales will fall into quantitative or numerical data types.

In analytic terminology, when data and analytics are combined, analytics discover not only hidden patterns present in the data, but also the relationship between the variables present in the data, which is commonly referred to as insight. Figure 2 shows a flow of data to insight and actions in a typical analytics system. Nowadays, organizations are generating a lot of data on a daily basis because of digitization of various processes, and there is a need to know more about this data that requires better understanding the data which is performed by data exploration process. Once the understanding of the data is completed,

Figure 2. Data, insights, and action flow in a typical analytics system

Data   Insight   Actions

then it needs to be analysed by applying a process of cleaning, transforming, and modelling with a goal of discovering useful information (Brown, 2014). By applying various methods, techniques, processes of analytics on the data, it will be a well-known insight about the data. The term insight refers to the knowledge that is gained from the data with the aid of analytics. According to an online source, a recent study which describes insights-to-action journey (Deloitte, 2021) as data-gathering and analysis in turn will make better people decisions that drive business outcomes. The various use cases of data insights, in multiple business organizations, are (a) Employee acquisition cost which includes the amounts spent by employers on a new employee for recruiting, tracking, and interviewing, onboarding, and training in an organization. (b) Customer acquisition costs which refers the cost spent by an organization for gaining a new customer in a marketing company. (c) Customer buying patterns in a specific season or segment or over a period in an e-commerce industry. (d) Identification of fraudulent transactions (e) optimal physician scheduling in the health care industry.

What Is an Intelligent BA?

In recent years, BA gained an increased amount of interest among industry, business, government, researchers, and practitioners due to many success cases that have reported tremendous improvements in business performance. Business analytics provide a process of turning raw data into information needed to guide informed business decision making, whereas Intelligent BA is a superset of BA, but it provides the users for decision-making with the aid of machine leaning models, techniques, and tools to provide insights from all sorts of the data. The various types of data that include relational and multimedia. Multimedia data refers to data that consists of various types like text, images, audio, video, and animation. Additionally, it provides insights for streaming data. In Intelligent BA, more and more business processes of an organization are automated compared with traditional and modern BA. The most commonly used techniques for analytics are regression, classification, decision tree, and clustering for solving various business problems. These techniques will learn, discover, and infer from the data in intelligent way by the use of ML and DL techniques. Further, the results are present with a suitable visualization to the users for decision making.

How Does Intelligent Analytics Help Business?

In recent years, the field of data analytics has grown significantly and now there is a need for intelligent analytics for organizations to plan the operations and functioning of business in more intelligent way at the same time to handle large data. Further, intelligent analytics can be used for any industries irrespective of its size and operation that enables a wide range of business applications to gain intelligent insights from the data. Further, these insights can help the users to make efficient decisions to run business on a daily basis. Moreover, it brings insight from other data objects such as text, images, audio, and video besides numerical data. Additionally, it brings new business opportunities from the uncovered market space for further expansion of products and services. Moreover, it increases the operational efficiency of the business and reduce costs.

Market Size and Growth of AI, Big Data, and Business Analytics

According to a report (Marc et al., 2014), the global big data and business analytics (BDA) market was valued at 168.8 billion U.S. dollars in 2018 and is forecast to grow to 215.7 billion U.S. dollars by 2021. In 2021, more than half of BDA spending will go towards services. IT services is projected to make up around 85 billion U.S. dollars, and business services will account for the remainder. Big data is characterized as high volume, high velocity and high variety and the kind of data sets that are too large or too complex for traditional data processing applications. Fast-growing mobile data traffic, cloud computing traffic, as well as the rapid development of technologies such as AI and the Internet of Things (IoT) all contribute to the increasing volume and complexity of data sets. For example, connected IoT devices are projected to generate 79.4 ZBs of data in 2025. Business analytics - Advanced analytics tools, such as predictive analytics and data mining, help to extract value from the data and generate business insights. The size of the business intelligence and analytics software application market is forecast to reach around 16.5 billion U.S. dollars in 2022. Growth in this market is driven by a focus on digital transformation, a demand for data visualization dashboards, and an increased adoption of cloud.

According to the latest release of International Data Corporation (IDC) report (IDC, 2021) worldwide revenues for the AI market, including software, hardware, and services, are forecast to grow 16.4% year over year in 2021 to $327.5 billion. By 2024, the market is expected to break the $500 billion mark with a five-year Compound Annual Growth Rate (CAGR) of 17.5% and total revenues reaching an impressive $554.3 billion.

According to a report (Markets and markets, 2021), the global big data market size to grow from USD 138.9 billion in 2020 to USD 229.4 billion by 2025, at a CAGR of 10.6% during the forecast period. The major growth factors of the big data market include the increasing awareness of Internet of Things (IoT) devices among organizations, increasing availability of data across the organization to gain deeper insights to remain competitive, and increasing government investments in various regions for enhancing digital technologies.

According to a report (Market Research Future, Nov 2020) predicts the global data analytics market size to reach USD 132,903.8 million at a 28.9% CAGR from 2016 to 2026. Additionally, the global data analytics industry has been segmented based on type, solution, application, deployment, organization size, function, and vertical. By type, the global market has been segregated into predictive analytics, prescriptive analytics, customer analytics, descriptive analytics, and others. By solution, the global market has been segregated into data management, data mining, fraud and security intelligence, and data monitoring. Based on application, the global market has been segregated into enterprise resource planning, database management, supply chain management, human resource management, and others. By deployment, the global market has been segregated into cloud and on-premises. By organization size, the global market has been segregated into large enterprises and small and medium enterprises. By function, the data analytics market has been segregated into marketing analytics, sales analytics, operational analytics, accounting and finance analytics, HR analytics, and others. By vertical, the global market has been segregated into BFSI, IT and Telecom, manufacturing, retail and e-commerce, energy and power, healthcare, transport and logistics, media and entertainment, and others. The Banking, Financial Services, and Insurance (BFSI) segment earned the largest market share of 22.3% in 2019, with a market value of USD 5.127.7 million, and is projected to have the highest CAGR of 30.9% in the assessment period. The IT & Telecom segment was valued at USD 4.444.9 million in 2019 and is expected to have a CAGR of 30.6%. The key players in the global data analytics market are IBM Corporation, Microsoft, Oracle, SAP, Amazon Web Services, Inc., Tableau Software, SiSense Inc, Zoho Corporation, ThoughtSpot, Inc, Mu Sigma, Looker Data Sciences, Inc., Datameer, Inc., Alteryx, Inc, Dell Inc., SAS Institute Inc.

At the end of the chapter, an additional reading material is provided in the reference section. This covers various studies on AI, Big Data, Frameworks, Architectures, Use Cases, and papers that explore BA, BI and Operational BI in greater depth.

NEED FOR INTELLIGENT BA

In this section, the need for Intelligent BA in a data-driven digital business world is presented.

Growth of Data

More than a decade, the growth of data has been rapidly increasing in all most all the organizations including government, public and private. Further, the importance of data has been gaining steadily for all organizations and its growth is continuing at a fast face which continue further. The volume of data generated by organizations has tremendously increased in the recent past compared to previous years because of multiple channels of data sources including social network, news, multimedia, forums to name a few. For example, an airbus generates 10 TB of data every 30 minutes, and a self-driving car will generate 2 Petabyte of data every year. In the 21st century, businesses, government, and organizations have been living in a data-democratic world. Thus, data are pivotal and continue its growth at a rapid face for functioning of business in more efficient ways. For effective functioning of organization requires a good insight from the data generated by the organization itself as well data generated by external sources. The external data includes social media, and news, channels. Similarly, data generated by the competitors for offering similar kind of products and services including flyers, brochures, price list, infographics, sales quantities, and reports as that of the organization. Therefore, data is like a gold mine which requires efficient tools to extract patterns, insights from the data and make it useful for not only to improve the performance of business but also the economic value of an organization. Additionally, this information should be made available to next generation that will become the digital asset to the organization. According to a report on data growth (Arne Holst, 2021) the total amount of data created, captured, copied, and consumed globally is forecast to increase rapidly, reaching 64.2 zettabytes in 2020. Figure 1 shows the total volume of that is data created from 2010 to 2025, which includes forecast period from 2021 to 2025. From the graph it is seen that the data volume is increasing stately from 2010 to 2015, whereas from 2016 onwards there is a rapid increase which continue to increase further. It is shown that in 2020, the volume of data was 64.2 Zettabyte. A Zettabyte is equivalent to a trillion gigabytes; One Zettabyte is equal to one sextillion bytes or 1021 bytes. By 2025 it is estimated to reach 181 Zettabytes.

Big data usually include data sets with sizes beyond the ability of commonly used software tools to capture, curate, manage, and process data within a tolerable elapsed time. The size of data ranges from a few dozen terabytes to many petabytes of data and even into Zeta bytes. In other words, big data is

Figure 3. Growth of data
(source: Arne Holst, 2021)

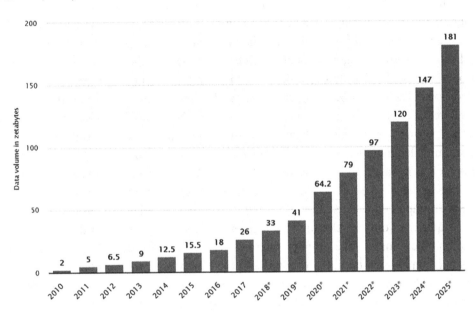

defined as a set of techniques and technologies that require new forms of integration to uncover large hidden values from large datasets that are diverse, complex, and of a massive scale. Additionally, Big data refers to data sets that are not only big but also high in velocity, volume, and variety of data, which makes them difficult to handle using traditional tools and techniques. In order to effectively handle such a humongous volume of data requires a big data system. Moreover, these systems require efficient handling of large file systems for capturing, storing, and processing of data. This results to evolution of Big Data systems and new files systems such as Hadoop, and Spark. Besides, more and more organizations are adopting digital transformation, with this resulting availability of organizational omnipresence. As a result of this, organizations demand the use of predictive analytics for obtaining insights from continuously generated data by the organizations. Applications that use Intelligent Analytics must use a combination of data, statistical algorithms, machine learning, deep learning techniques to predict, prevent, or relay significant risks, opportunities, and general information. According to online news source (CISION PR Newswire, Jun 2021), data emerged as the new wealth creator and big data solutions are expected to gain an increasing role in organizations expansion. Additionally, organizations have always had access to data, but only limited capabilities in accessing and processing data for meaningful insights. In addition, Big data solutions can enable organizations to overcome these challenges. The efficiency of big data solutions largely depends on the compatibility of analytics solution. Moreover, big data does not require further data processing steps, thereby simplifying data storage and analysis.

Adaption of New Technologies and Algorithms

According to the UN Data Revolution report (IEAG, 2014), new technologies are leading to an exponential increase in the volume and types of data available, creating unprecedented possibilities for informing and transforming society and protecting the environment. Governments, companies, researchers, and citizen groups are in a ferment of experimentation, innovation, fand adaptation to the new world of data, a world in which data are bigger, faster, and more detailed than ever before. This is epitomized as the data revolution. Thus, the evolution of new technologies such as AI, Machine Learning (ML), Deep Learning (DL), Cloud computing are changing the landscape of the application architecture, providing improved process automation, and resulting higher accuracy. Additionally, these technologies can provide not only high scalability, but also deeper insight into the data which results more actions for intelligent decisions. The data processing capabilities of earlier technologies are limited to relational data, i.e., structure data only, whereas the present technologies ML and DL can leverage processing both structure, semi-structured, unstructured datasets which include image, audio, text more efficiently using Python programming language because of the availability of its richest libraries. Moreover, new technology platforms such as Keras, Kurl, Pycale, Tensorflow, and PyTorch are simplifying the approaches for handling and processing of complex image and audio datasets more efficiently in terms of extraction of knowledge with improved understanding. Further, these technologies offer better data visualization to the users for quick actions. Furthermore, DL algorithms provides to get a detailed understanding even from the complex images like graphs, diagrams, flowcharts, illustrations, organizational charts, weather maps that contain substantial information. In the similar way, the new age of technologies such as Amazon Kinesis, Apache Storm, Azure Stream Analytics, Google Cloud DataFlow, IBM Streaming Analytics, Striim, StreamSQL that support features of analytics for steaming data which resulting instant understanding from data in a real time which is one of the important characteristics of Intelligent BA. Moreover, the recent advances made in data pipeline architecture such as Kafka, Spark, Spark, Elastic Block Storage (EBS) and Simple Storage Services of Amazon Web Services that provides better organizing raw from disparate sources, movement of the data to a destination for storing, reporting, filtering, analytics, and visualization.

Analytics for All

Traditional BI systems are historic, limited access to strategic users in the organization that uses mainly OLTP system. Modern BI systems support analytics on real time which is known as Operational BI or Real Time BI systems which extends use of BI services to tactical and operational levels. The use of Operational BI in the organizations results improved decision-making support to all the levels of users in the organization which not only improves the decision-making capacity of individual but also results in improving the performance of the organization.

To Increase Decision Certainty

In today's world, business operations have become not only riskier but also involve a more volatile, uncertain, complex, and ambiguous (VUCA) environment. Now there is a paradigm shift from traditional practices of VUCA environment to Agile practises in current business functioning of the modern business world. Apparently, organizations are adopting transformation at a rapid pace to reshape their ecosystem to cope with a data-driven decision-making approaches for a sustainable new business model for improving decision certainty. These changes not only result in the VUCA change from volatility into vision, uncertainty into understanding, complexity into clarity and ambiguity into agility as envisaged by (Nathan Bennett, & G. James Lemoine, 2014). The emphasis on data using proper tools and techniques for extraction of knowledge that helps organizations for timely expansion of business in the growing areas, the feedback analysis will facilitate to improve better ways of customer satisfaction through which business expansion. At the same time, it also helps the white gaps for further expansion of business in new areas.

According to a report (UN IEAG, 2014) data is characterized as the lifeblood of decision-making and the raw material for accountability. Without high-quality data providing the right information on the right things at the right time, designing, monitoring, and evaluating effective policies becomes almost impossible. In the modern business environment, there is a great need for Intelligent BA to the business leader for innovating new business models and timely data-driven decision making. Thus, effective implementation of Intelligent BA in the organization result not only helps the organization in better understanding from data but also helps monetization for the growth of the organization.

Digital transformation is enabled by big data, automation of business process, as well as in enabling new business models. While businesses can analyze data at hand, it becomes ineffective unless the analysis provides meaningful insights, based on which organizations can make strategic decisions (CISION PR Newswire, 2021).

Decision Intelligence and Insight for All Sorts of Data

Decision intelligence is a new branch of analytics which is steadily evolving and continue its grown in next two decades and this can be applied for all branches of science, engineering, and management. The advantage of decision intelligence is that it provides both experienced and non-experienced users for taking decision logic without any complexity.

According to a study (TechTarget, n.d.), decision intelligence is going as a field includes a range of decision-making techniques. Gartner describes it as a domain that encompasses applications like complex adaptive systems that combine multiple traditional and advanced disciplines. The biggest advantage of decision intelligence is that it provides a framework that brings together traditional techniques like rules-based approaches, together with advanced techniques like AI and ML. This enables non-technical users to alter decision logic without involving programmers.

Power of External Data

Nowadays organizations are not only interested in data generated internally within the firm but also data generated externally because the insights extracted from external data brings lot visibility in functioning of organizations as well to understand the services and delivery of their products from the whole sum of customers as well competitors. The external data typically one or more of the following - stock marketing, geospatial and satellite, weather, public data which include macroeconomic indicators, news, patent filings, research journals. Overlooking such external data is a missed opportunity. Many companies have made great strides in collecting and utilizing data from their own activities. A well-structured plan for using external data will provide a competitive edge to the organizations (KDnuggets, 2019). Organizations that stay abreast of the expanding external-data ecosystem and successfully integrate a broad spectrum of external data into their operations can outperform other companies by unlocking improvements in growth, productivity, and risk management.

Above all, it seems that organizations in great need of Intelligent BA for efficient business operational not only for planning, monitoring, and but also for controlling the functions of the business in more intelligent way.

Figure 4. Types of data analytics

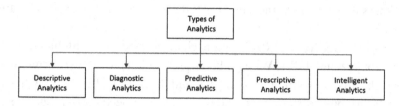

TYPES OF ANALYTICS, FUNCTIONING OF INTELLIGENT BA

In this section we present various types of analytics and explain the same. Moreover, presented the key components of an Intelligent BA and briefly explain its functioning.

Types of Analytics

In general, analytics applications are classified based on techniques which they used for analysis of data and based on the value of decision-making information extracted from the data. Figure 4 shows the most common types of analytics. The value of decision information that is available to the organizations increases from descriptive to intelligent analytics at the same time, the complexity of the analytics also increases greatly. The reader is advised to refer (Sarma, 2021) for more detail study on various types of analytics and the key software components that are associated to each type of analytics and its functioning of each component.

- **Descriptive Analytics:** It mainly provides better understanding of the system from the data in terms of what has happened. This analytics technique provides very basic understanding of how the business is performed with the aid of simple graphs, reports, and charts which mainly describe the systems in terms of basic information. Most of the organizations use descriptive analytics to understand the business in terms of its size, volumes, quantity, and ratios.
- **Diagnostic Analytics:** It is one type of the analytics technique in which the data can be interpreted and analysed to get the information that mainly refers to why it happened. Thus, this kind of analytic techniques are mainly used for the root cause of the problems and cause and effect relations. This analysis technique mainly helps individuals and practitioners for developing solutions to root cause problems and the relationship between two things from the case and effect problems.
- **Predictive Analytics:** This type of analytics provides prediction related information from the data which means it provides information refer to what could happen or what will happen. Data mining is mainly used for predictive analytics techniques that incudes data classification, clustering. The data classification technique mainly predicts the category or grouping of the data whereas clustering techniques extracts grouping or categories from the data. This kind of analytics technique mainly helps for forecasting etc.,
- **Prescriptive Analytics:** This It includes the features of descriptive and predictive analytics, which describes what should we do. It uses AI tools and optimisation algorithms in order to provides advise on possible outcomes.

Figure 5. A conceptual view of intelligent business analytics system

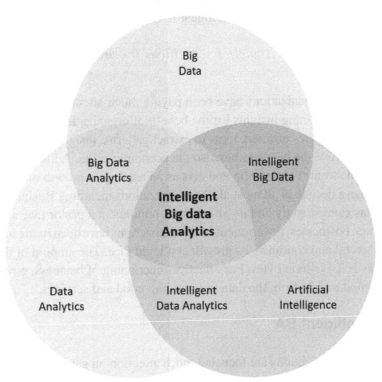

- **Intelligent Analytics:** This uses the power of Artificial Intelligence including Machine Learning, Deep learning, Natural Language Processing and advanced optimization algorithms to prescriptive analytics, and extract insights intelligently that helps for intelligent actions. Sometimes this is also known as cognitive analytics. Additionally, the process is more automated using AI Tools and techniques.

Conceptual View of Intelligent BA

A conceptual view of Intelligent BA is shown in figure 5, which is a result of AI, Big Data and Data Analytics. The intelligent BA can be described as a set of analytical programs that assist in solving daily business problems via various models of ML and DL techniques.

Intelligent Analytics is a combination of data, statistical algorithms, and machine learning techniques to predict, prevent, or relay significant risks, opportunities, and general information. This type of predictive software requires AI. The AI used in the most intelligent programs can learn, infer, discovery, and visualization on both a large and small scale. There are many ways that this can help organizations primarily related to improving business value. The combination of big data and data analytics leads to a new branch which is known as big data analytics, whereas the combination of big data and AI is known as intelligent big data which means the big data become more intelligent enough that include the features of AI. Similarly, the combination of AI and data analytics results, a new branch of analytics known as intelligent data analytics; this performs data analytics functionality in a more intelligent way but is limited to small size data. Further, the combination of big data, data analytics and AI results into a new branch of intelligence which is known as intelligent big data analytics, which finds the most commonly use in the business. In short this is also known as Intelligent BA.

$$Intelligent\ BA = Big\ Data + Data\ Analytics + Artificial\ Intelligence \tag{1}$$

For more than a decade, organizations have been paying much attention on the generated data and trying to best use of it for obtaining insights for the benefit of organization economic value. Now data is like a gold mine which requires efficient tools to extract patterns, insights from the data and make it useful for not only to improve the business but also the economic value. Additionally, this information should be made available to next generation and acts as an asset. The growth of data has been rapidly increasing for more than a decade in all most all the organizations including Business, Government, the importance of data has gaining study end its growth is continuing at a pastor face and continue further also. In the 21st century, businesses, government, and organizations have been living in a data-democratic world. Now data is pivotal and continues its growth at a rapid face. The amount of data generated by a driverless car in a day is 2.4 trillion bytes. For effective functioning of business, government and organizations requires a good insight from the data in providing good and services.

Functioning of Intelligent BA

For more than a decade, organizations are focusing much attention on generated data and trying to best use of it for obtaining insights for the benefit of organization economic and business values. The functioning of businesses in digital democratic world is greatly differ from the traditional business approaches and further trying to understand more and more from the data for efficient functioning of business. In order to know insights from the organizational data requires good understanding on the functioning of analytics systems specially Intelligent BA. The functioning of any analytics systems is based on top-down approach. The major functioning of an Intelligent BA can be stated as accessing, storing, validating, aggregating, analysing, interpreting, and visualizing the results. At a broader level, a typical Intelligent BA comprise of three major building blocks namely the first building blocks is data, the second is analysis and the third is action which drives decision making.

Figure 6 shows the anatomy of Intelligent BA system. From the definition of the term analytics as presented in the introduction section, it is clear that it has three fundamental components known as data, model and a computer. Nowadays, the data is obtained from multiple sources such as social media platforms such as Facebook, Twitter, YouTube, Instagram, IoT sensors, Internet platforms and other multimedia channel which generates humongous volumes of data contents in terms of videos, audios, images, news, chats, blogs just to name a few. Further, data may be either internal or external to an organization. The model is designed by an individual or data scientist who analyses a specific business problem(s) and extract more insight from the data. The model here acts a bridge for transforming the data into knowledge. Most commonly, the model may be either one of the following: statistical model or machine learning model or a combination of these. The two steps for modelling are formulation and solution.

A statistical model is the use of statistics to build a representation of the data and then conduct analysis to infer any relationships between variables or discover insights whereas machine learning is the use of mathematical and or statistical models to obtain a general understanding of the data to make predic-

Figure 6. Anatomy of intelligent business analytics system

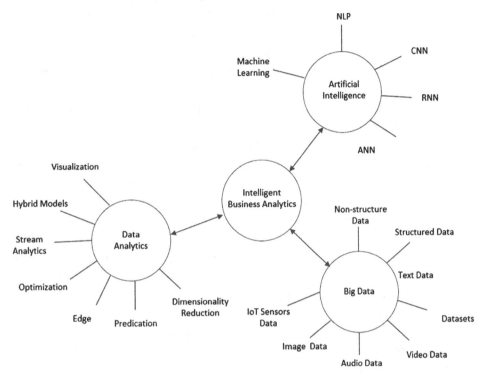

tions (KDnuggets, 2019). Further, statistical modelling is a method of mathematically approximating the world which contains variables that can be used to explain relationships between other variables. Making inferences and validating hypothesis using hypothesis testing, and confidence intervals. A statistical model will have sampling, probability spaces, assumptions, and diagnostics to make inferences. Machine Learning predictions are assessed differently depending on its type: 'Classification', 'Regression', 'Clustering' or 'Supervised' and 'Unsupervised'.

ADVANTAGES, APPLICATIONS, CHALLENGES, IMPLICATIONS OF INTELLIGENT BA

Advantages

Several research studies and reports have revealed that the application of analytics will greatly increase when coined with the new age of technologies such as Big data, ML, DL and NLP. The advantage of Intelligent BA includes, but not limited to value creation, eliminates cognitive and personal biases from decision making, gaining advantage from the semi and unstructured data for insight and actions, cost reduction, faster and better decision making, and new products and services.

Value creation - Over the past decade, BI and Analytics (BI&A) have been identified for promoting to deliver competitive value gains to the organizations. Previous studies have identified the role of BI&A mainly for value creation to the customer relationship, organizational learning, business process improvement and organizational efficiency. The subsequent studies have identified the results of a meaningful transformation of BI&A insights into knowledge. These insights emerge as additional value to operational and strategic BI capabilities. According to the study (Katerina et. al., 2019), the value creation from BI&A has identified as an absorptive capacity, which is generated in the process of raw data transformation into valuable knowledge, BI&A triggered insights, for action taking and decision-making. This study envisages that organizations should develop higher order dynamic capabilities to allow the continuous acquisition, search and management of knowledge which is from BI&A resources and lower order knowledge capabilities.

According to the study (SAS, 2014) revealed that the three big benefits of big data analytics are cost reduction, faster and better decision making, and new products and services. Organizations such as Google, eBay and LinkedIn were among the first to experiment with big data. They developed proof of concept and small-scale projects to learn their analytical model and found real results and expanding their efforts to encompass more data and models. Further, it is observed that the use of Big data technologies like Hadoop and cloud-based analytics can provide substantial cost advantages compared to traditional architectures like data warehouses and marts. Besides, better, and faster decision making - analytics has always involved attempts to improve decision making, and big data does not change that. Now, Organizations are seeking both faster and better decisions with big data which are driven by the speed of Hadoop and in-memory, whereas better decision is trying to achieve analysing new source of data. Additionally, the most interesting use of big data analytics is to create new products and services for customers.

Additionally, the knowledge generated from Intelligent BA is free from cognitive and personal biases because ML and DL algorithms can learn on their own from the data. Hence, there is no room for cognitive or personal biases in Intelligent BA. Besides, Intelligent BA generates knowledge not only from the structured data but also from semi-structured and unstructured data objects such as text, images, audio and videos, and further, it can support streaming of data.

Applications

Several researchers (have reported real word applications on new age of technologies such as AI Sanjeev et. al., 202), (Gacanin, 2021), Machine learning and Deep Learning (Rahul Rai et al., 2021), (Sarker, 2021), BI and Analytics (LIM et al., 2013), and Big Data (Amit et al., 2021). The use of AI techniques in data analytics not only transforms into intelligent analytics, but also brings more insights from the data. Further, AI can automate repeated tasks performed manually and improve decision-making to the users compared to traditional methods of analytics. Intelligent Analytics has immense potential can find many applications in the marketing, e-Commerce, manufacturing, banking and finance, security, telecommunications, agriculture, education, medical, transport to name a few.

Market Analytics

According to the authors (Sanjeev et at., 2021) the use of AI in marketing majorly in the areas of the strategy and planning, product management, price, place, and promotion management. The major activities of strategy and planning in the marketing includes segmentation, targeting and positioning. Text mining techniques and ML algorithms can be applied to identify profitable customer segments. By applying a combination of the data optimization, ML and causal forests can further narrow down the target customers. The major activities of product management are to gauge the suitability of the product design to the customer needs and satisfaction. Preference weight assigned to product attributes during the product search help the marketers to understand product recommender system. Price management on the real-time variation of fluctuating demand based on multi-armed bandit algorithm. Further, the use of Bayesian inference in ML algorithm can quickly adjust the price points to match the competitor's price. By offering collaborative robot, in short cobots, for packing of products, use of drones for delivery not only mainly help for product tracking but also delivery status which helps to handle technical issues related to the place management. Personalization and customization of messages as per the customer profiles can help promotion management activities.

E-Commerce

According to the study (Sarker, 2021), product recommendation is one of the most well-known and widely used applications in the e-commerce portal. ML technique can assist in analysing the order history of the customer and make customized product suggestions for their next purchase based on their behaviour and preferences. Further, customer buying patterns can be extracted by the use of ML techniques on the customer's order history data such as peak days and non-peak days, holiday, and non-holidays and festival season. Similarly, customer buying patterns from a specific geographical location can be studied. Further corelations analysis, if any, between the specific buying pattern(s). Moreover, customer buying patterns by similar types of customers from different geographical locations can be studied.

Manufacturing and Industry 4.0

According to a study (Rahul et al., 2021), Industry 4.0 has given rise to an emerging sector in manufacturing is known as smart manufacturing that opens doors for intelligent analytics in the industry. ML techniques enable the generation of actionable intelligence by processing the collected data to increase manufacturing efficiency without significantly changing the required resources. Besides, the use of intelligent analytics in the manufacturing sector can amplify the growth to improve assembly line efficiency, improved customer experience through personalization and individualized value, inventory management with real time insights, and visibility in the inventory along the supply lines. Reduced errors and corrections during product development and improve products quality by the use of analytics backed simulations and product modelling. Further, ML techniques provide predictive insights in the form of complex patterns of manufacturing which offers a pathway for an intelligent decision support system in a variety of manufacturing activities including but not limited to, intelligent and continuous inspection, predictive maintenance, quality improvements, process optimization, supply chain management, and task scheduling.

Healthcare

In the new age of data, the combinations of Big data with machine learning find good number of applications in healthcare (Amit, 2021) which includes the usage of the data generated through sensors such as MRI, eye, Fitbit helping the doctors to address diseases like diabetic Mellitus, cardiovascular diseases. The other application is the use of patients' consuming the data in the form of chatbots on a particular disease or even the doctors accessing the electronic health care records, diagnosing the complex diseases quickly and making the prescription of the medicines.

Challenges of Intelligent BA

The following are a few challenges for implementation of Intelligent BA.

Challenges in Big Data

Most commonly, big data are referred to its V's that are called its dimensions. The initial version of big data focused only on the three V's, known as volume, velocity, and variety of data. The volume indicates its size, whereas velocity refers to the speed in which data is generated which is getting generated by human or machines. The variety refers to the nature of data that is structured, semi structure and unstructured. Additionally, the big data definition includes two more V's. The fourth V is known as veracity; this refers to the accuracy or truthfulness or trustworthiness of a data, whereas the fifth V refers to the value which is the desired outcome of big data processing. Most importantly, big data has come up with the several challenges for processing of data as well when combined with ML as discussed by several researchers (Heureux et al., 2017), (García et al., 2016) because of the nature of its dimensions known as volume, velocity, and variety. These challenges include but not limited to the processing, modularity, class in balance, curse of dimensionality, feature engineering, non-linearity, bias and variance, data locality, heterogeneity, and noisy data.

1. Processing performance - In big data, the volume of data is high which adds computational complexity. Generally, Machine Learning (ML) algorithms are computationally expense because it has both training and verification phases. Thus, computational complexity increases exponentially with increasing data size. Additionally, as data size increases the performance of algorithms will depend on the architecture used to store and move data.

2. Curse of modularity – Most of the learning algorithms are based on the assumptions that the data being processed can help entirely in memory or in a single file on a disk. As data size increases, the storage of the entire data in memory assumption will fail. This challenge is known as the cure of modularity.

3. Class imbalance - The dataset gets larger; the assumption is that the data are uniformly distributed across all classes often fails; this leads to a challenge referred to as class imbalance. The performance of ML algorithms can be negatively affected when datasets contain data from classes with various probabilities of occurrence. Algorithms such as decision trees, neural networks, and support vector machines are highly sensitive to class imbalance.

4. Curse of dimensionality –The term dimension describes the number of features or attributes predictor variables or the number of instances or present in the dataset. As the dimensionality of the data increases, the predictability and effectiveness of algorithm decreases drastically. Further, dimensionality affects processing performance. In many ML algorithms, time complexity is polynomial in the number of dimensions.

5. Feature Engineering - Feature engineering is the process of using domain knowledge to extract features from raw data. This may use either feature selection or feature extraction. Feature selection is simply selecting and excluding given features without changing them, whereas feature extraction techniques for data reduction dimensionality reduction transforms features into a lower dimension. As the data set grows, both horizontally and vertically so it is difficult in finding new features as well as highly relevant features. Few examples of feature extraction techniques are

Polynomial Expansion that expands the set of features into a polynomial space, Vector Assembler that combines a set of features into a single vector column. Single Value Decomposition (SVD) is matrix factorization method that transform a real/complex matrix M (m x n) into a factorized matrix A. Principal component analysis (PCA) tries to find a rotation such that the set of possibly correlated features transforms into a set of linearly uncorrelated features. The various methods of feature selection are Vector Slicer that the user selects manually a subset of features, R Formula that selects features specified by an R model formula and Chi-Squared selector that orders categorical features using a Chi-Squared test of independence from the class.

6. Non-linearity - The relationship between two or more variables is described by its correlation coefficient, which is referred to as linearity. The value of the correlation coefficient is significant when a linear relationship exists between the variables. Thus, non-linear relationship between variables can affect the performance of ML algorithms. The challenge of non-linearity in Big Data also stems from the difficulties associated with evaluating linearity, Further, the linearity is often evaluated using graphical techniques such as scatter plots.

7. Variance and bias – The term variance describes the consistency of a learner's ability to predict random things, whereas bias describes the ability of a learner to learn the wrong thing. Ideally, both the variance and bias error should be minimized to obtain an accurate output. However, as the volume of data increases, the linearity may become too closely biased to the training set and may be unable to generalized adequately for new data.

8. Regularization is a technique that adds information to a model which aims to improve generalization and reduce overfitting of the model. This technique is well established in ML, but further investigation is needed with respect to the efficiency with big data.

9. Data locality - In traditional ML, the assumption is that the total data get loaded into memory in order to increase the performance of model execution, which is not the case in the context of ML and big data. In big data, transfer of data to memory would result in processing latency and could cause massive network traffic. A new approach was developed that provides moving computation closer to the data instead of moving large data to computation. This approach is especially prominent with Big Data which is known as data locality. In short it refers to the use of data elements within relatively close storage locations. Additionally, the use of data locality in big data not only minimizes network congestion, but also increases the overall throughput. In Hadoop, the logic of Map Reduce is used to implement data locality which map tasks and execute on the nodes. Further, MapReduce-based approaches encounter difficulties when working with highly iterative algorithms. Thus, data locality is a paramount challenge that must be addressed in any successful way.

10. Data heterogeneity – Big data analytics is often involves integrating multiple types of data sources. These data sources are diverse in terms of data types, format, data model and semantic. In general, there are two types of data heterogeneity such as syntactic and semantic. Syntactic heterogeneity refers to diversity in data types, file formats, data encoding, data model, whereas semantic heterogeneity refers to differences in meanings and interpretations.

The following table shows a mapping between various approaches of machine learning techniques with the identified challenges of big data. The symbol '✓' indicates high degree of remedy whereas '*' represents partial resolution.

According to a recent study on the challenges of big data (Uthayasankar et at., 2017) can be grouped into three main categories, based on the data life cycle: (i) data, (ii) process, and (iii) management chal-

Table 1. Machine learning approaches that addresses various challenges of big data.

		Volume								Variety			Velocity				Veracity		
Approaches ↓ / Challenges →		Process performance	Curse of Modularity	Class Imbalance	Curse of dimensionality	Feature Engineering	Non-linearity	Bonferroni Principle	Variance & Bias	Data Locality	Data Heterogeneity	Dirty & noisy data	Data Availability	Real-time process/ Streaming	Concept drift	Iid	Data Provenance	Data Uncertainty	Dirty & Noisy Data
Manipulation	Dimensionality reduction	✓			✓														
	Instance Selection	✓	✓																
	Data Cleaning											✓							✓
	Vertical Scaling	✓															*		
	Horizontal Scaling — Batch oriented	✓	✓							✓							*		
	Horizontal Scaling — Stream oriented	✓	✓							✓			✓	✓			*		
	Algorithm modification	✓	*		*					✓				✓					
	Algorithm modification with new paradigm	✓	*		*									✓					
Learning Paradigm	Deep learning					✓	✓			✓	*							*	*
	Online learning		✓	*						✓		*	✓	✓	*	✓			*
	Local learning	✓	✓	✓					✓	✓									
	Transfer learning		✓						✓	✓	*							*	*
	Lifelong learning	✓	✓							✓	*		✓	✓	*			*	*
	Essential learning	✓	✓												✓				

Source: (Heureux et al., 2017)

lenges. The data challenges are mainly related to the characteristics of the data itself, for example data volume, variety, velocity, veracity, volatility, quality, discovery, and dogmatism. The process challenges are related to series of how techniques: how to capture data, how to integrate data, how to transform data, how to select the right model for analysis and how to provide the results. A few examples of management challenges are privacy, security, governance, and ethical aspects.

Regulatory Compliances and Cultural Shift

The first requirement of analytics is the data. So, it is mandatory that organizations follow regulations to ensure the sensitive data. Further, organizations adopt a possesses to organize, stored, and manage the data to protect against loss, corruption, theft, and misuse. Additionally, organizations follow standard approaches for the data being maintained and used for analytics applications to bring transparency, auditability, and security. Industries such as Pharma, Drug, Healthcare and Banking, and insurance shall comply regulations for the data and knowledge specific to that industry from time to time. For example, modelling of Artificial Neural Network (ANN) is not only complex, but also opaque and the algorithms being used in ANN are black boxes. Therefore, it is limits organizations in using advanced algorithms for extraction of knowledge or insights from the data and at the same time bringing transparency of the extraction process.

Cultural shift in the organization from the process driven to data (or knowledge) driven decisions requires a paradigm shift of employees in the organization in terms of digital perspective and adoption of new digital systems this may also have a significant impact on the use of analytics in the organizations. This has become one of the biggest challenges to turn into a data organization because of their geographical presence, different maturity levels of process automation, and different categories of teams at different capacities, which generally creates heavy impediment on the organizations for the effective use of digital analytics and decision-making process.

Data Intensive and Computationally Intensive

Big data applications, the size of data ranging from a few dozen terabytes to many petabytes of data. In a few cases even, it may be higher as many zettabytes. To process such a large volume of data requires parallel computing techniques which require high volumes of computational resources such as computation for manipulation of data, main memory storage and processing time to I/O. In addition, machine learning and deep learning tasks are computationally intensive. Further, the number of layers used in a deep learning particullarly in neural networks have increased to several thousand layers, and each layer requires high-end computational resources. Additionally, in deep-learning networks, each layer of nodes is trained on a distinct set of features based on the previous layer's output.

Generalization of Models

In analytics environment, model is a simplified description of a system or process to assist calculations and predictions. Thus, the models that are designed for one domain may not be the best fit to other domains because generalization rules will vary from domain to domain. For example, a model that is developed for the risk management application in the finance domain will greatly differ from the model being developed for the drug processing in pharma. This is resulting one of the major challenges in implanting a generalized model for implementing Intelligent BA which further demands domain specific knowledge.

Hybrid Data Model

For many times, there is a need to combine the results of several models or multiple models into a single model for better prediction which is commonly referred as ensembling or hybrid modelling. For example, the models such as Random forest, gradient boosting, XGBoost and super learners are combined with one another. Thus, it is understood that there is an improvement in the performance of the prediction levels by the use of hybrid modelling.

Implications of Intelligent BA

The following are a few implications of intelligent business intelligence in the organizations.

Operationalization of Intelligent BA

In the recent past, the organization's investments are significantly increased in the business analytics mainly because of increased business demands of businesses to discover intelligent insights from the data which is generated by the organization itself as well as external. The main sources of external data are from news, social media and the product catalogues of competitors. The use of analytics in the organizations, mainly depends on the level of digital transformation of the business processes in the organization. According to the usage of BA, organizations can be broadly classified into three categories known as matured, moderate and entry levels. There are few organizations, mainly startups may choose limited digital transformation of their business processes. This limits the use of the analytics in such organizations for their decision-making purposes, so such organizations may fall under the entry-level category. Apparently, data that is not available for analytics to discover insights that will greatly influence and limit critical decisions to be made by an organization, which is one of the major implications of using Intelligent BA in organizations. Similarly, organizations that have a clear roadmap for use of analytics need to be transformed digitally first and then leverage analytics. In such cases the implications for using Intelligent BA for their decision-making does not leads to any issues. Organizations that are using analytics moderately may enhance digital transformation of the existing processes and then move to the next level to leverage the features of Intelligent BA. Further, organizations that are using analytics at a matured level can focus towards optimizing the existing processes and systems to leverage Intelligent BA more effectively at all the levels, so they turn into a data driven organization.

FUTURE DIRECTIONS OF RESEARCH ON INTELLIGENT BA

This section presents the need for the future development trends of Intelligent BA analytics in the following aspects, namely the (i) Data originality, (ii) Spurious correlation, and (iii) Benchmarking of data generalization.

Dataset Originality

In data analysis, dataset, in short data, is the building block, which is put into the model, which processes the data and generates output that consists of hidden patterns and trends present in the data which is known as insights. Once modelling is done, then the results obtained from the model, either from small or large data, are truly dependent on the data. One of the important points here is that the originality of the dataset is most essential in intelligent analytics because the results (or actionable insights) which are generated from the model depends on the source data feed to the model. Here, the assumption is that the model works ideal, which means the results generated by the model are highly accurate. Alternatively, the errors produced by the model are significantly lower, so it does not alter the decision. If there is any change in the dataset in terms of appending or eliminating or adding of new columns or modifying the existing data, then the results obtained from model will adversely affect. Subsequently, the discovered insights from the data can significantly vary from the true results. Therefore, there is a great need to check the originality of dataset, whether it is tampered with or not before being utilized the dataset for processing. Thus, one of the interesting future directions of work in Intelligent BA is to evaluate the originality of the most power datasets that are available in the market. At the same time, whenever a new dataset is generated and get ready to publish for public or restricted access, then the source system shall automatically validate and ensure that entrusting of the dataset. Thus, data is the basis for discovering insights which are performed by the model in data analysis. Therefore, it is essential to check the originality of data or the dataset before beginning to analyze in Intelligent BA.

Spurious Correlation

In order to find a specific type of incident or event with a certain amount of data, the likelihood for finding of that event is high. In the Statistics, this phenomenon is referred as spurious correlation. However, the presence of the event in the overall dataset does not constitute any significance, but meaningless event instances exist within the dataset. As the size of data increases, the presence of a specific event interest can create a causal relationship with one or more events or variables due to this it generates wrong results. Therefore, there is a need for devising a mechanism to minimize this phenomenon in large datasets such as big data, especially in intelligent analytics, because this may generate wrong insights from smaller instances of data.

Benchmarking of Model Generalization

Model generalization is one of the common approaches to improve the performance of learning algorithms. The performance of a single model is low. In order to increase the performance of learning algorithm requires ensembling of models or to combine multiple types of models, this process is commonly known as hybrid modelling, which is commonly used in DL models. The choice of hybrid modelling can vary with respect to the application. In general, no two analytics applications can have identical hybrid modelling requirements because the accuracy of the model changes with respect to the purpose, such as classification, clustering, prediction, and the nature of the data. More particularly, it differs from domain to domain. Thus, model generalization in ML and DL can become one of the challenging tasks. Therefore, there is a great need to develop standards and benchmarking for model generalization for analytics and data science applications because they find application in multiple domains including banking, finance, insurance, health, pharma, media, trade, travel, manufacturing, to name a few. The other direction of research of Intelligent BA is to develop benchmarking scales for model generalization for every domain. The developed benchmarking standards of model generalization can act as a tool for assessing and comparing performance of models to achieve continuous improvement in intelligent business analytics.

CONCLUSION

In this chapter, the evolution of the data analytics is briefly explained. Further, the most commonly used terms in the business analytics such as data, insight and action are defined in a lucid manner with examples. Moreover, explained in simple terms what is Analytics, BA, BI, and Intelligent BA. In addition, explained the need for Intelligent BA in today's digital business world. Besides, briefly explained different types of data analytics and their working. Furthermore, presented the conceptual view of Intelligent BA and explained its functioning. The major applications, challenges, and implications of Intelligent BA are briefly presented. Finally, discussed the further research directions of Intelligent BA in the three aspects like dataset originality, spurious correlation, and benchmarking of the model generalization.

REFERENCES

Bhatt, C., Shah, T., & Ganatra, A. (2014). Business Analytics -Applications and Practices for Continuous Iterative Exploration. *CSI Communications, 38,* 10–13.

Bichler, M., Heinzl, A., & van der Aalst, W. M. P. (2017). Business Analytics and Data Science: Once Again? *Business & Information Systems Engineering, 59*(2), 77–79. doi:10.100712599-016-0461-1

Božič, K., & Dimovski, V. (2019). Business intelligence and analytics for value creation: The role of absorptive capacity. *International Journal of Information Management, 46,* 93-103. doi:10.1016/j.ijinfomgt.2018.11.020

Brown, M. (2014). *Transforming Unstructured Data into Useful Information, Big Data, Mining, and Analytics.* Auerbach Publication. doi:10.1201/b16666

CISION PR Newswire. (2021). *Big Data - Global Market Trajectory & Analytics.* https://www.prnewswire.com/news-releases/global-big-data-market-to-reach-234-6-billion-by-2026--301322252.html

Davenport, S. A. S. (2014). *Three big benefits of big data analytics.* http://book.itep.ru/depository/big_data/AST-0147176_Three_Big_Benefits_of_Big_Data_Analytics.pdf

Deloitte. (2021). *The Insights-to-Action journey Using data and analytics to make better people decisions and drive business outcomes.* https://www2.deloitte.com/content/dam/Deloitte/us/Documents/human-capital/us-insights-to-action-journey-2021.pdf

Gacanin, H., & Wagner, M. (2019). Artificial Intelligence Paradigm for Customer Experience Management in Next-Generation Networks: Challenges and Perspectives. *IEEE Network, 33*(2), 188–194. doi:10.1109/MNET.2019.1800015

García, S., Ramírez-Gallego, S., & Luengo, J. (2016). Big data preprocessing: methods and prospects. *Big Data Analytics, 1*(9), 1-22. doi:10.1186/s41044-016-0014-0

Gartner. (n.d.). *Gartner Glossary for the term Business Analytics.* https://www.gartner.com/en/information-technology/glossary/business-analytics

Harvard Business Review. (2014). *What VUCA Really Means for You.* https://hbr.org/2014/01/what-vuca-really-means-for-you

Holst, A. (2021). *Volume of data/information created, captured, copied, and consumed worldwide from 2010 to 2025.* https://www.statista.com/statistics/871513/worldwide-data-created/

IDC. (2021). *IDC Forecasts Improved Growth for Global AI Market in 2021.* https://www.idc.com/getdoc.jsp?containerId=prUS47482321

INFORMS. (2015). *Best definition of analytics.* https://www.informs.org/About-INFORMS/News-Room/O.R.-and-Analytics-in-the-News/Best-definition-of-analytics

KDnuggets. (2019). *Statistical Modelling vs Machine Learning.* https://www.kdnuggets.com/2019/08/statistical-modelling-vs-machine-learning.html

Kushwaha, A. K., Kar, A. K., & Dwivedi, Y. K. (2021). Applications of big data in emerging management disciplines: A literature review using text mining. *International Journal of Information Management Data Insights*, *1*(2). doi:10.1016/j.jjimei.2021.100017

L'Heureux, A., Grolinger, K., Elyamany, H. F., & Capretz, M. A. M. (2017). Machine Learning With Big Data: Challenges and Approaches. *IEEE Access: Practical Innovations, Open Solutions*, *5*, 7776–7797. doi:10.1109/ACCESS.2017.2696365

Lim, Chen, & Chen. (2013). Business intelligence and analytics: Research directions. *ACM Transactions on Management Information Systems*, *3*(4), 1-10. https://ink.library.smu.edu.sg/sis_research/1966

Marketresearchfuture. (2020). *Data Analytics Market Research Report*. https://www.marketresearchfuture.com/reports/data-analytics-market-1689

Markets and markets. Big Data Market. (2021). https://www.marketsandmarkets.com/Market-Reports/big-data-market-1068.html

Rai, R., Tiwari, M. K., Ivanov, D., & Dolgui, A. (2021). Machine learning in manufacturing and industry 4.0 applications. *International Journal of Production Research*, *59*(16), 4773–4778. doi:10.1080/0020 7543.2021.1956675

Sarker, I. H. (2021). Machine Learning: Algorithms, Real-World Applications and Research Directions. *SN Computer Science, 2*(3), 1-21. doi:10.1007/s42979-021-00592-x

Sarma, A. D. N. (2018). A Generic Functional Architecture for Operational BI System. *International Journal of Business Intelligence Research*, *9*, 64–77. doi:10.4018/IJBIR.2018010105

Sarma, A. D. N. (2021). The five key components for building an operational business intelligence ecosystem, *Int. J. Business Intelligence and Data Mining*, *19*(3), 343–370.

Schniederjans, M. J., Schniederjans, D. G., & Starkey, C. M. (2014). *Business Analytics Principles, Concepts, and Applications What, Why, and How*. Pearson FT Press.

Sivarajah, U., Kamal, M. M., Irani, Z., & Weerakkody, V. (2017). Critical analysis of Big Data challenges and analytical methods. *Journal of Business Research*, *70*, 263–286. https://dx.doi.org/10.1016/j.jbusres.2016.08.001

TechTarget. (n.d.). *Definition for Business Analytics*. https://searchbusinessanalytics.techtarget.com/definition/business-analytics-BA

UN IEAG. (2014). *A world that counts mobilizing the data revolution for sustainable development*. https://www.undatarevolution.org/wp-content/uploads/2014/11/A-World-That-Counts.pdf

Verma, S., Sharma, R., Deb, S., & Maitra, D. (2021). Artificial intelligence in marketing: Systematic review and future research direction. *International Journal of Information Management Data Insights*, *1*(1). https://www.sciencedirect.com/science/article/pii/S2667096820300021

What is Business Analytics? (n.d.). https://www.oracle.com/in/business-analytics/what-is-business-analytics/

Yin, J., & Fernandez, V. (2020). A systematic review on business analytics. *Journal of Industrial Engineering and Management, 13*(2), 283–295. doi:10.3926/jiem.3030

ADDITIONAL READING

Ajah, I. A., & Nweke, H. F. (2019). Big Data and Business Analytics: Trends, Platforms, Success Factors and Applications. *Big Data and Cognitive Computing, 3*(2), 32. doi:10.3390/bdcc3020032

Chapter 3
Principles of a Hybrid Intelligence Framework for Augmented Analytics

Alexander P. Ryjov

Lomonosov Moscow State University, Russia

ABSTRACT

Analytics is a key success factor for any business in the competitive and fast-changing world. Using good analytics, people, business, social, and government organizations become capable of making good decisions. With augmented analytics, human expertise actually becomes more crucial than ever. This chapter aims to introduce the hybrid intelligence approach by focusing on its unique analytical capabilities. The state-of-the-art in hybrid intelligence, symbiosis and cooperative interaction between human intelligence and artificial intelligence in solving a wide range of practical tasks, and one of the hybrid intelligence frameworks, a human-centered approach for evaluation and monitoring of complex processes, have been considered in this chapter. The chapter could be interesting for analysts and researchers who desire to do analytics with more intelligence.

INTRODUCTION

Analytics has become ubiquitous in our day-to-day life. Why do people spend time and effort on analytics? People want to make good decisions based on sound analytics. One of the latest data and analytics trends that has gained considerable traction these days is Augmented Analytics. Gartner coined the term in 2017: "Augmented analytics is the use of enabling technologies such as machine learning and AI to assist with data preparation, insight generation, and insight explanation to augment how people explore and analyze data in analytics and BI platforms. It also augments the expert and citizen data scientists by automating many aspects of data science, machine learning, and AI model development, management, and deployment" (Gartner, 2017).

Big Data, Machine Learning, Artificial Intelligence, and other technologies allow improved analytics for making more good decisions, it is true. However, the complexity and volume of data every business

DOI: 10.4018/978-1-7998-9016-4.ch003

accumulates is a common challenge for those that need to make decisions. Data is a continuous and constantly growing asset, and it can be particularly challenging for decision-makers.

With Augmented Analytics, human expertise becomes more crucial than ever. The following comment good enough describes the situation "Analytics is at a critical inflection point. Businesspeople are awash with data yet struggle to determine what's most important and the best actions to take. Augmented analytics addresses this growing challenge, using AI and machine learning techniques to augment human intelligence to present to businesspeople the insights most important to them, and drive data-driven decisions". (ThoughtSpot, 2021).

The author agrees with the vision "Ultimately, Augmented Analytics will strip out the dull, robotic processes involved in BI and empower employees to focus on being human" (MHR, 2021).

This chapter focuses on when a person (analyst or decision-makers) is at the center of the analytics framework and collaborates with computer analytics tools. This situation is typical for many organizations and is not so well-studied, like analytics based on Big Data, Machine Learning, Artificial Intelligence.

An example of such a situation could be project management. There is usually a measurable project goal and tools for collecting various metrics describing the current situation with resources, time, and scope. Based on such metrics, the project's current status is analyzed, and measures are developed to achieve the project goal in the best way. Within the framework of the proposed approach, these processes (evaluation of the project's current status and the choice of measures for optimal achievement of the goal or expected status) are solved in an automated way. Additional examples are discussed in the HYBRID INTELLIGENCE FRAMEWORK FOR AUGMENTED ANALYTICS section.

BACKGROUND

Collaboration of human and computer intelligence in solving practical tasks is not a new idea. This vision was first proposed in the 1950-s and 1960-s by cybernetics and early computer pioneers. The term Amplifying intelligence was introduced by William Ross Ashby in his classical work (Ashby, W.R., 1956, p. 271). At the end of his fantastic book, he wrote: *"Intellectual power, like physical power, can be amplified. Let no one say that it cannot be done, for the gene-patterns do it every time they form a brain that grows up to be something better than the gene-pattern could have specified in detail. What is new is that we can now do it synthetically, consciously, deliberately."* (Ashby, 1956, p. 272). The idea of a symbiosis of human and computer was formulated by psychologist and computer scientist Joseph Carl Robnett Licklider: *"Man-computer symbiosis is an expected development in cooperative interaction between men and electronic computers. It will involve very close coupling between the human and the electronic members of the partnership. The main aims are 1) to let computers facilitate formulative thinking as they now facilitate the solution of formulated problems, and 2) to enable men and computers to cooperate in making decisions and controlling complex situations without inflexible dependence on predetermined programs. In the anticipated symbiotic partnership, men will set the goals, formulate the hypothesis, determine the criteria, and perform the evaluations. Computing machines will do the routinizable work that must be done to prepare the way for insights and decisions in technical and scientific thinking. Preliminary analyses indicate that the symbiotic partnership will perform intellectual operations much more effectively than man alone can perform them."* (Licklider, 1960, p. 4). This idea was specified and studied by Douglas Carl Engelbart: *"By "augmenting human intellect" we mean increasing the capability of a man to approach a complex problem situation, to gain comprehension to suit his par-*

ticular needs, and to derive solutions to problems. Increased capability in this respect is taken to mean a mixture of the following: more-rapid comprehension, better comprehension, the possibility of gaining a useful degree of comprehension in a situation that previously was too complex, speedier solutions, better solutions, and the possibility of finding solutions to problems that before seemed insoluble. And by "complex situations" we include the professional problems of diplomats, executives, social scientists, life scientists, physical scientists, attorneys, designers—whether the problem situation exists for twenty minutes or twenty years. We do not speak of isolated clever tricks that help in particular situations. We refer to a way of life in an integrated domain where hunches, cut-and-try, intangibles, and the human "feel for a situation" usefully co-exist with powerful concepts, streamlined terminology and notation, sophisticated methods, and high-powered electronic aids." (Engelbart, 1962).

After this romantic period, we had tens of years of stagnation for human-computer systems. One of the fundamental problems from the author's point of view was a vast difference between perception, manipulation of information, reasoning, etc., for a human being and a computer. Boolean 0/1 logic is natural for computers but very artificial for people; work with uncertain information is natural for people but very complicated for computers. How can we organize the symbiosis of such two completely different subsystems?

A mathematical tool capable of being an interface between human beings and computers - fuzzy logic - was introduced by Lotfi Zadeh (Zadeh, 1965). In (Zadeh, 1975, p. 200), he wrote: *"The main applications of the linguistic approach lie in the realm of humanistic systems-especially in the fields of artificial intelligence, linguistics, human decision processes, pattern recognition, psychology, law, medical diagnosis, information retrieval, economics and related areas"*. His definition of the humanistic system is: *"By a humanistic system we mean a system whose behavior is strongly influenced by human judgement, perception or emotions. Examples of humanistic systems are: economic systems, political systems, legal systems, educational systems, etc. A single individual and his thought processes may also be viewed as a humanistic system"* (Zadeh, 1975, p. 200). Fuzzy logic allows us to use perception-based descriptions of objects and manipulate them in a human-like reasoning manner in computer models. It is a base for cognitive computing and Augmented Intelligence as defined by IBM (2018): *"At IBM, we are guided by the term "augmented intelligence" rather than "artificial intelligence". It is the critical difference between systems that enhance and scale human expertise rather than those that attempt to replicate all of human intelligence. We focus on building practical AI applications that assist people with well-defined tasks, and in the process, expose a range of generalized AI services on a platform to support a wide range of new applications"*.

The chapter's mission is to discuss the mathematical foundations and analytical capabilities of a hybrid (human + computer) intelligence. A subclass of hybrid systems - human-computer systems for evaluating the status and monitoring of complex processes' progress (Ryjov, 2013) is discussed in detail. These systems allow "assist people with well-defined tasks" in managing of complex processes in a partnership manner. In an ideal case, it becomes possible to combine the strengths of a human being (for example, intuition) and a computer (for example, computation power) in an optimal way.

From a business perspective, these systems are close to the "Automation of knowledge work" set of technologies in McKinsey Global Institute terms (McKinsey Global Institute, 2013, p. 41): *"These capabilities not only extend computing into new realms ..., but also create new relationships between knowledge workers and machines. It is increasingly possible to interact with a machine the way one would with a coworker"*. McKinsey estimated potential economic impact across sized applications in 2025 from $5.2 trillion to $6.7 trillion per year (McKinsey Global Institute, 2013, p. 44).

Figure 1. s-function example.

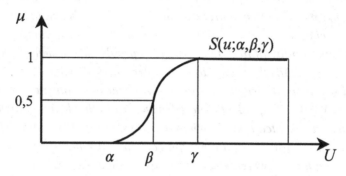

MATHEMATICAL FOUNDATIONS OF HYBRID INTELLIGENCE

The concept of a fuzzy set, introduced by Zadeh (1965). A fuzzy set is intuitively clear, but it refers to the basic concept of mathematics - the concept of a set and therefore is at the same time conceptual.

The formal definition of a fuzzy set is as follows.

Let a universal set U of elements u and $\mu_A : U \to [0,1]$ be given. *A fuzzy set* A in U is the graph of the map μ_A, that is, a set of the form $\left\{ \left(u, \mu_A \left(u \right) \right) : u \in U \right\}$; in this case, the value $\mu_A \left(u \right)$ is called the membership function of u to A.

Thus, specifying a fuzzy set A in U is equivalent to specifying its membership function $\mu_A \left(u \right)$).

In practical tasks, various implementations of such membership functions were used. Here are some of them. Historically, the first to use and study the so-called s- and π-functions, defined as follows:

$$S\left(u;\alpha,\beta,\gamma\right) = \begin{cases} 0 & 4;O \quad u \le \alpha \\ 2\left(\dfrac{u-\alpha}{\gamma-\alpha}\right)^2 & 4;O \quad \alpha \le u \le \beta \\ 1-2\left(\dfrac{u-\gamma}{\gamma-\alpha}\right)^2 & 4;O \quad \beta \le u \le \gamma \\ 1 & 4;O \quad u \ge \gamma \end{cases}$$

$$\pi\left(u;\beta,\gamma\right) = \begin{cases} S\left(u;\gamma-\beta,\gamma-\dfrac{\beta}{2},\gamma\right) & 4;O \quad u \le \gamma \\ S\left(u;\gamma,\gamma+\dfrac{\beta}{2},\gamma+\beta\right) & 4;O \quad u \ge \gamma \end{cases}$$

Their graphs are shown in Figures 1 and 2, respectively.

Using this kind of formalization, we can describe concepts such as "old man" or "high stock value" (in the form of s-functions) or " medium-size" (in the form of π-functions). Such description is natu-

Figure 2. π-function example.

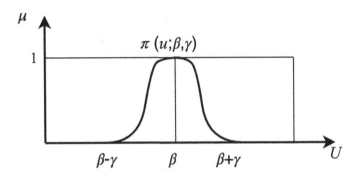

ral for human perception and language on the one hand and is available for subsequent computer processing on the other.

A *fuzzy variable* is a triplet $\langle \alpha, U, G \rangle$, where α is the name of a fuzzy variable; U - universal set (domain of definition); G - restrictions on possible values (meaning) of the variable α presented in the form $\mu_\alpha(U)$).

Thus, a fuzzy variable is a named fuzzy set.

A *linguistic variable* is a five $A, T(A), U, V, M$, where A is the name of the linguistic variable; $T(A)$ - term-set of the linguistic variable A, that is, the set of its linguistic meanings; U is a universal set in which the values of the linguistic variable A are determined; V is a syntactic rule that generates the values of the linguistic variable A (often in the form of a formal grammar); M is a semantic rule that assigns each element of $T(A)$ its "meaning" as a fuzzy subset of U. An example of a linguistic variable is shown in Figure 3.

Note that within the framework of the concept of a linguistic variable, the semantics (membership function) of a term depends on the context. Consider the term-set T_2 of the linguistic variable "Age" containing 2 values "Young" and "Old" with membership functions $\mu_1(u)$ and $\mu_2(u)$, respectively (Fig. 4). Now let us consider the term-set T_3 with three values, which differs from T_2 by the value "Middle-aged" with the membership function $\mu_3(u)$. Such a change in T_2 leads to a modification of

Figure 3. An example of the linguistic variable "Age".

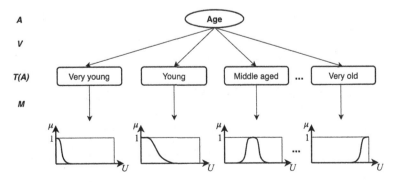

Figure 4. Modification of membership functions.

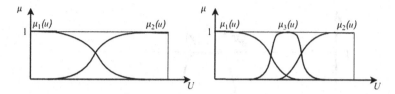

the membership functions (Figure 4). Thus, the membership functions $\mu_1(u)$ and $\mu_2(u)$ in the context of T_2 differ from the membership functions $\mu_1(u)$ and $\mu_2(u)$ in the context of T_3. It turns out that understanding the membership functions without specifying the context generally does not make sense.

A special case of a linguistic variable, free from this drawback and having a wide range of practical applications, may be a set of fuzzy variables describing a certain concept (that is, a linguistic variable with a fixed term-set). Such structures can be interpreted, in particular, as a set of linguistic meanings that describe the possibility of implementing certain processes; in the pattern recognition theory, this can be interpreted as a set of values of a qualitative attribute.

Consider t fuzzy variables named $a_1, a_2, .., a_t$, given on one universal set (Figure 5). We will call such a collection *the semantic space* s_t.

Thus, the semantic space is a collection of fuzzy variables $s_t = \left\{ \alpha_1, U, G_1, \cdots, \alpha_t, U, G_t \right\}$ defined in one universal set. Different semantic spaces may exist for the same linguistic variable A:

$$s_2 = \left\{ \alpha_1, U, G_1, \alpha_2, U, G_2 \right\}, \ ..., \ s_k = \left\{ \alpha_1, U, G_1, \cdots, \alpha_k, U, G_k \right\}.$$

Below we will consider not all semantic spaces but only their important subclass - complete orthogonal semantic spaces.

Let us introduce a system of limitations for the membership functions of the fuzzy variables comprising s_t. For the sake of simplicity, we shall designate the membership function a_j as μ_j. We shall consider that:

1. $\forall \mu_j \left(1 \leq j \leq t \right) \exists U_j^1 \neq \varnothing$ where $U_j^1 = \left\{ u \in U : \mu_j(u) = 1 \right\}$ is an interval or a point;

Figure 5. An example of a sematic space.

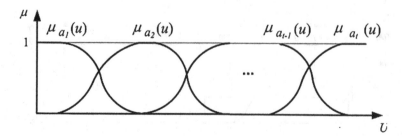

2. $\forall j \left(1 \leq j \leq t\right) \mu_j$ does not decrease on the left of U_j^1 and does not increase on the right of U_j^1 (since, according to 1, U_j^1 is an interval or a point, the concepts "on the left" and "on the right" are determined unambiguously).

Henceforth, we shall need to use the characteristic functions as well as the membership functions, and so we shall need to fulfill the following technical condition:

3. $\forall j \left(1 \leq j \leq t\right) \mu_j$ has no more than two points of discontinuity of the first kind.

For simplicity, let us designate the requirements 1-3 as L.

Let us also introduce a system of limitations for the sets of membership functions of fuzzy variables comprising s_t. Thus, we may consider that:

4. $\forall u \in U \exists j \left(1 \leq j \leq t\right) : \mu_j \left(u\right) > 0$;

5. $\forall u \in U \sum_{j=1}^{t} \mu_j \left(u\right) = 1$.

For simplicity, we shall designate requirements 4 and 5 as G.

We will call a semantic space consisting of fuzzy variables whose membership functions satisfy requirements 1-3 and their populations - requirements 4 and 5 a *complete orthogonal semantic space* and denote it by $G\left(L\right)$.

For $s_t \subset G\left(L\right)$ it is possible to determine the degree of fuzziness (the measure of uncertainty) as follows.

Let there be a certain population of t membership functions $s_t \in G\left(L\right)$. Let $s_t = \left\{\mu_1, \cdots, \mu_t\right\}$. Let us designate the population of t characteristic functions $\hat{s}_t = \left\{h_1, \cdots, h_t\right\}$ as *the most similar population of characteristic functions*, if $\forall j \left(1 \leq j \leq t\right)$

$$h_j \left(u\right) = \begin{cases} 1 & , \quad if \ \mu_j \left(u\right) = 1 \\ 0 & , \quad otherwise \end{cases}$$

It is not difficult to see that if the complete orthogonal semantic space consists not of membership functions but characteristic functions, then no uncertainty will arise when describing objects. The expert unambiguously chooses the term a_j if the object is in the universal set's corresponding region. Some experts describe the same object with the same term. This situation may be illustrated as follows. Let us assume that we have scales of certain accuracy, and we have the opportunity to weigh a certain material. Moreover, we have agreed that, if the material's weight falls within a certain range, it belongs to one of the categories. Then we shall have the situation accurately described. The problem lies in the fact that there are no such scales for our task, nor do we have the opportunity to weigh on them the objects of interest to us.

However, we can assume that, of the two semantic spaces, the one having the least uncertainty will be most "similar" to the space consisting of the populations of characteristic functions. In mathematics, distance can be a degree of similarity. Is it possible to introduce distance among semantic spaces? For complete orthogonal semantic spaces, it is possible.

First of all, note that the set of functions L is a subset of integrable functions on an interval so that we can enter the distance in L, for example,

$$\rho(f,g) = \int_U |f(u) - g(u)| du, \ f \in L, g \in L.$$

Let consider two population of t membership functions $s_t = \{\mu_1, \cdots, \mu_t\}$ and $s_t' = \{\mu_1', \cdots, \mu_t'\}$. The following lemma holds (Ryjov, 1988).

Lemma 1. Let $s_t \in G(L)$, $s_t' \in G(L)$, $\rho(f,g)$ - some distance in L. Then $(s_t, s_t') = \sum_{j=1}^t \rho(\mu_j, \mu_j')$ is a distance in $G(L)$.

The semantic statements formulated above may be formalized as follows.

Let $s_t \in G(L)$. For the measure of uncertainty of s_t, we shall take the value of a functional $\xi(s_t)$, determined by the elements of $G(L)$ and assuming the values in $[0,1]$ (i.e., $\xi(s_t): G(L) \to [0,1]$), satisfying the following conditions (axioms):

A1. $\xi(s_t) = 0$, if s_t is a set of characteristic functions.

A2. Let $s_t, s_{t'}' \in G(L)$, t and t' may be equal or not equal to each other. Then $\xi(s_t) \leq \xi(s_{t'}')$, if $d(s_t, \hat{s}_t) \leq d(s_{t'}', \hat{s}_{t'}')$.

Does such functional exist? The answer to this question is given by the following theorem (Ryjov, 1988).

Theorem 1 (theorem of existence). Let $s_t \in G(L)$. Then the functional

$$\xi(s_t) = \frac{1}{|U|} \int_U f\left(\mu_{i_1^*}(u) - \mu_{i_2^*}(u)\right) du,$$

where

$$\mu_{i_1^*}(u) = \max_{1 \leq j \leq t} \mu_j(u), \ \mu_{i_2^*}(u) = \max_{1 \leq j \leq t, j \neq i_1^*} \mu_j(u),$$

f satisfies the following conditions:

F1: $f(0) = 1$, $f(1) = 0$; F2: f does not increase – is a measure of uncertainty of s_t.

There are many functional satisfying the conditions of Theorem 1. They are described in sufficient detail in (Ryjov, 1988). The simplest of them is the functional in which the function f is linear. It is not difficult to see that conditions F1 and F2 are satisfied by the sole linear function $f(x) = 1 - x$. Substi-

Figure 6. Interpretation of degree of fuzziness of $s_t \in G\left(L\right)$

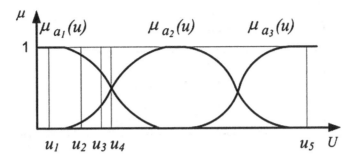

tuting it in $\xi\left(s_t\right)$, we obtain the following simplest measure of uncertainty of the complete orthogonal semantic space:

$$\xi\left(s_t\right) = \frac{1}{|U|} \int_U \left(1 - \left(\mu_{i_1^*}\left(u\right) - \mu_{i_2^*}\left(u\right)\right)\right) du.$$

We can provide the following interpretation of the simplest measure of uncertainty (Ryjov, 1988). Let us consider the process of a description of real objects by a person. We do not have any uncertainty in providing a linguistic description of an object with the ''physical'' value of the attribute u_1 (Figure 6).

We attribute it to term a_1 with complete certainty. We can repeat this statement about an object whose "physical" value of the attribute is u_5. We choose the term a_3 for its description without fluctuations. We begin to experience difficulties in choosing a suitable linguistic significance in describing an object with the physical value of attribute u_2. These difficulties grow (u_3) and reach the maximal significance for an object with the physical value of attribute u_4: for such objects, both linguistic significances (a_1 and a_2) are equal. If we consider the significance of the integrand function

$$\eta\left(s_t, u\right) = 1 - \left(\mu_{i_1^*}\left(u\right) - \mu_{i_2^*}\left(u\right)\right)$$

in these points, we can say, that

$$0 = \eta\left(s_t, u_5\right) = \eta\left(s_t, u_1\right) < \eta\left(s_t, u_2\right) < \eta\left(s_t, u_3\right) < \eta\left(s_t, u_4\right) = 1.$$

Thus, the integral $\xi\left(s_t\right)$ value can be interpreted as an average degree of human doubt while describing some real object.

It is also proved that the functional has natural and good properties for fuzziness degree (Ryjov, 1988).

Finally, we present the results of our model's analysis, when the membership functions that are members of a given collection of fuzzy sets are not given with absolute precision, but with some inac-

Figure 7. Presentation of $G^\delta\left(L\right)$.

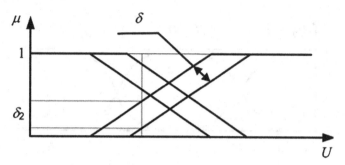

curacy not exceeding δ (Figure 7). Let us call this particular situation the δ - *model* and denote it by $G^\delta\left(L\right)$.

In this situation, we can calculate the top ($\overline{\xi}\left(s_t\right)$) and the bottom ($\underline{\xi}\left(s_t\right)$) valuations of the degree of fuzziness $\xi\left(s_t\right)$. The following theorem holds (Ryjov, 1988).

Theorem 2. Let $s_t \in G^\delta\left(L\right)$. Then

$$\underline{\xi}\left(s_t\right) = \left(1 - \delta_2\right)^2 \xi\left(s_t\right), \ \overline{\xi}\left(s_t\right) = \left(1 + 2\delta_2\right)\xi\left(s_t\right).$$

Therefore, we can use our estimation technique of the degree of fuzziness in practical tasks since we have shown it to be robust.

HYBRID INTELLIGENCE FRAMEWORK FOR AUGMENTED ANALYTICS

Many organizations and specialists are trying to achieve their goals in a complex environment using some understanding of a current status (where are we?) and possible ways to achieve the expected level or the objective (where would we like to be?). There are many different types of processes (a journey from current status to the expected one), from well-defined (for example, manufacturing processes) to very uncertain (for example, political processes). Many people and institutions are involved in understanding these processes and finding actions that allow achieving the goal via some acceptable (or optimal in the ideal case) path.

The evaluation and monitoring task includes evaluating some process' current status and modeling possible ways of its development based on real information. System for Evaluation and Monitoring (SEM) is a human-computer system that provides a solution to the evaluation and monitoring task. There are many evaluations and monitoring tasks in business (marketing, management, strategic planning, etc.), politics (elections, control of bilateral and multilateral agreements, terrorism, etc.), and many other areas of our life. A significant share of analysts focuses on evaluation and monitoring tasks, and SEM is a tool for automation of their work.

Human-Centric Systems for Evaluation of the Status and Monitoring the Progress of Complex Processes

From the systems point of view, SEM relates to a class of hierarchical fuzzy discrete dynamical systems. The theoretical base for this class of systems is provided by the fuzzy sets theory, discrete mathematics, methods of the analysis of hierarchies, which was developed in works of L.A. Zadeh (1965, 1975), M.D. Mesarovich et al. (1970), T.L. Saaty (1980), and others. The analytic hierarchy process (AHP) was developed in the 1980s by (Saaty, 1980). It is a systematic decision-making method that includes both qualitative and quantitative techniques. It has been widely used in many fields for a long time. J.J. Buckley (1985) incorporated the fuzziness into the AHP, called the FAHP. Hierarchical fuzzy systems have attracted considerable attention in recent years. V. Torra (2002) summarized the related recent research work in this domain. A detailed FAHP literature review is also presented in (Anvary et al., 2012).

SEM allows uniformly process diverse, multi-level, fragmentary, unreliable, and varying in time information about some processes. Based on this type of information, SEM can monitor the process's status evaluation and work out strategic plans for process development. These capabilities open a broad area of applications in business (for example, (Ryjov, 2004)), politics (Ryjov et al., 1998; Ryjov, 2014a), health care (Ahkmedzhanov et al., 2003), engineering (Lebedev, 2009), social systems (Ryjov, 2014a).

There is a growing interest in such systems (The Economic Times, 2016). These systems could be one of the automation of knowledge work technologies defined by McKinsey as a disruptive technology number 2 (McKinsey Global Institute, 2013). This chapter could help people who work in this extremely exciting and important area of development of optimal systems.

Basic Elements of SEM

Let's name a task of evaluating a current state of the process and elaborating the forecasts of its evolution as an evaluation and monitoring task, and human-computer systems are ensuring support of a similar sort of information tasks – systems for evaluation and monitoring.

Basic elements of SEM at the top level are the process, the information space, in which information about the state of the process circulates, and analysts, working with this information and making conclusions about the state of the process and forecasts of its progress. Basic elements of IMS and their interaction are presented in Figure 8.

The *information image* represents a set of various information elements, which can be characterized as follows:

- Diversity of the information carriers, i.e., presentation of the information in articles, newspapers, electronic documents, audio-, and video- data, etc.;
- Fragmentary. The information most often related to any fragment of a problem, and the different fragments may be differently "covered" with the information;
- Multi-levelled. The information can concern the whole problem, some of its parts, or a particular element of the process;
- Various degrees of reliability. The information can contain data points with various degrees of reliability, indirect data, results of conclusions on the basis of reliable information or indirect conclusions;

Figure 8. Basic elements of SEM and their interaction

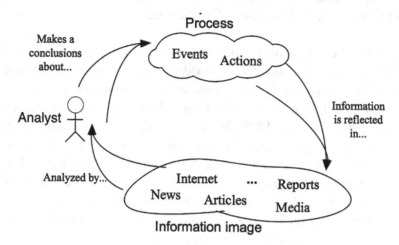

- Possible discrepancy. The information from various sources can coincide, differ slightly or be contradictory;
- Varying in time. The process develops over time; therefore, the information about the same element can be different between two different moments in time;
- Possible bias. The information reflects the specific interests of the source of information; therefore, it can have a tendentious character.

The *analysts* are an active element of the monitoring system. They observe and study pieces of the information space and make conclusions about the state of the process and prospects of its development while considering the information space's above-listed properties.

Basic Principles of Technology for Evaluation and Monitoring of Complex Processes

Taking into account the given features of the information and specific methods of its processing is possible to declare the main features of the technology for evaluation and monitoring of complex processes as follows:

- The system provides the facility for taking into account data conveyed by different information vehicles (journals, video clips, newspapers, documents in electronic form, etc.). Such a facility is provided through storage in a database of references to an evaluated piece of information if it is not a document in electronic form. If the information is a document in electronic form, then both the evaluated information (or part thereof) and a reference thereto are stored in the system. Thus, the system makes it possible to consider and use in analysis all pieces of information, which have a relationship to the subject area, irrespective of the information vehicle.
- The system makes it possible to process fragmentary and/or multi-level information. For this purpose, a considerable part of the model is represented in the form of a tree or graph (Figure 9).

Figure 9. Typical structure of a model for SEM

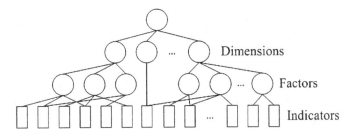

- Information with different degrees of reliability, possibly biased, can be processed in the system. This is achieved by assessing the influence of a particular piece of information on the model's elements' status using fuzzy linguistic values.
- Time is one of the parameters of the system. This makes it possible to have a complete picture of the variation of the model's status with time.

SEM workflow is presented in Figure 10.

Thus, the systems constructed based on this technology allow having the model of the process developing in time. It is supported by the references to all information materials chosen by the analysts, with general and separate evaluations of the process's status. Using time as one of the system's parameters allows the retrospective analysis and building the forecasts of the development of the process. There is the opportunity to allocate "critical points", i.e., element(s) of the model for which a small change can cause significant changes in the whole process's status. The knowledge of such elements has immense practical significance. It allows to reveal "critical points" of the process, work out the measures on blocking out undesirable situations or promote the desirable ones, i.e., somewhat guide the development of the process in time in the desirable direction.

Figure 10. SEM workflow

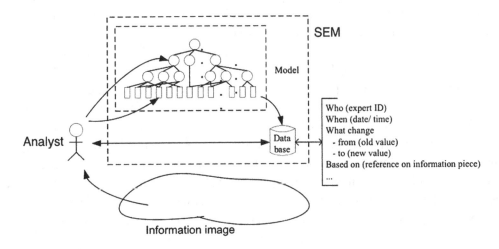

Theoretical Base of SEM

To effectively apply the proposed technological solutions, it is necessary to tackle a series of theoretical problems.

It is assumed that the expert describes the degree of inconsistency of the obtained information (for example, the readiness or potential for the readiness of certain processes in a country (Ryjov et al., 1998)) in the form of linguistic values. The subjective degree of convenience of such a description depends on the selection and the composition of such linguistic values (Ryjov, 2003).

It is assumed that the system tracks the development of the problem, i.e., its variation with time. It is also assumed that it integrates the evaluations of several different experts. This means that different experts may describe one object. Therefore, it is desirable to have assurances that the different experts describe the same object in the most "uniform" way.

Based on the above, we may formulate the first problem as follows:

Problem 1 (perception-based descriptions of physical objects). Is it possible, considering certain features of the man's perception of objects of the real world and their description, to formulate a rule for selecting the optimum set of values of characteristics based on which these objects may be described? Two optimality criteria are possible:

Criterion 1. We regard as optimum those sets of values through which one experiences the minimum uncertainty in describing objects.

Criterion 2. If a certain number of experts describes the object, then we regard as optimum those sets of values that provide the minimum degree of divergence of the descriptions.

It is shown that we can formulate a method of selecting the optimum set of values of qualitative indications (scale values). Moreover, it is shown that such a method is robust, i.e., the natural small errors that may occur in constructing the membership functions do not significantly influence the selection of the optimum set of values. The sets which are optimal according to criteria 1 and 2 coincide. The results obtained are described in (Ryjov, 1988). Following this method, we may describe objects with minimum possible uncertainty, i.e., guarantee optimum operation of the systems for evaluation and monitoring from this point of view.

Below we shortly describe the main ideas of formalization and a summary of the method's main results.

The model of estimating real object's properties by a person as a procedure of measuring in fuzzy linguistic scale (FLS) has been described in (Ryjov, 2003). The set of scale values of some FLS is a collection of fuzzy sets defined on the same universum. Below we will assume that the set of scale values of the FLS forms a complete orthogonal semantic space.

Requirements 1 and 2 are quite natural for membership functions of concepts forming scale values set of an FLS. The first one signifies that at least one object for any concept is used in the universal set, which is standard for the given concept. If there are many such standards, they are positioned in a series and are not "scattered" around the universe. The second requirement signifies that, if the objects are "similar" in the metrics sense in a universal set, they are also "similar" in the sense of FLS.

Requirements 4 and 5 also have quite a natural interpretation. Requirement 4, designated the completeness requirement, signifies that for any object from the universal set, there exists at least one concept of FLS to which it may belong. This means that in our scale values set, and there are no "holes". Requirement 5, designated the orthogonality requirement, signifies that we do not permit the use of semantically similar concepts or synonyms, and we require sufficient distinction of the concepts used. Note also that this requirement is often fulfilled or not fulfilled depending on the method used for constructing the membership functions of the concepts forming the scale values set of a FLS (Ryjov, 2003).

Different FLS have a different degree of internal uncertainty. Let us explain this in a model example.

Example. Let it be required to evaluate the height of a man. Let us consider two extreme situations.

Situation 1. It is permitted to use only two values: "short" and "tall".

Situation 2. It is permitted to use many values: "very short", "not very tall", ..., "not short and not tall", ..., "very tall".

Situation 1 is inconvenient. In fact, for many men, both the permitted values may be unsuitable, and, in describing them, we select between two "bad" values.

Situation 2 is also inconvenient. In fact, in describing the height of men, several of the permitted values may be suitable. We again experience a problem, but now due to the fact that we are forced to select between two or more "good" values.

Is it possible to measure this degree of uncertainty? For complete orthogonal FLS, the answer to this question is positive – it is $\xi\left(s_t\right)$.

Based on the properties of $\xi\left(s_t\right)$ (interpretation, Theorem 2), we can propose the following method for selection of the optimum set of values of characteristics:

1. All the "reasonable" sets of linguistic values are formulated;
2. Each of such sets is represented in the form of $G\left(L\right)$;
3. For each set, the measure of uncertainty $\xi\left(s_t\right)$ is calculated;
4. As the optimum set minimizes both the uncertainty in the description of objects and the degree of divergence of users' opinions, we select the one with minimal uncertainty.

Following this method, we can describe objects with minimum possible uncertainty, i.e., guarantee that different users will describe the objects for SEM in the most unified manner possible (see Criterion 2 in Problem 1). This means that the number of situations when one real object has more than one image in SEM, or different real objects have the same image in SEM, will be minimal. Accordingly, we will have maximal possible adequacy of the SEM as a model of the real world from this point of view. Robustness of the measure of uncertainty (Theorem 2) allows us to use this method in practical applications.

Evaluation and monitoring technology assumes the storage of information (or references to it) and its linguistic evaluations in a system database. In this connection, the following problem arises.

Problem 2 (information retrieval for perception-based descriptions). Is it possible to define metrics of quality of information retrieval in fuzzy (linguistic) databases and formulate a rule for selecting such a set of linguistic values that would maximize information retrieval quality?

It is shown (Ryjov, 2004) that it is possible to introduce such quality metrics of information retrieval in fuzzy (linguistic) databases and formalize them. It is possible to formulate a method of selecting the optimum set of values of qualitative indications, which maximizes the quality metric of information retrieval. Moreover, it is shown that such a method is robust, i.e., the natural small errors in the construction of the membership functions do not significantly affect the selection of the optimum set of values. The results obtained are shown in (Ryjov, 2004; Ryjov, 2012). It ensures that the offered methods can be used in practical tasks and guarantees optimal systems for evaluation and monitoring of complex processes.

Like for Problem 1, below, we shortly describe main ideas of formalization and summarize the main facts for Problem 2. As well as in analysis of Problem 1, we shall consider that the set of the linguistic meanings can be submitted as $G(L)$.

In our study of the process of information searches in databases whose objects have a linguistic description, we introduced the concepts of information loss ($IL_X(U)$) and information noise ($IN_X(U)$). These concepts apply to information searches in these databases, whose attributes have a set of values X, which are modeled by the fuzzy sets in s_t. The meaning of these concepts can informally be described as follows. While interacting with the system, a user formulates his query for objects satisfying certain linguistic characteristics and gets an answer according to his search request. If he knows the real (not the linguistic) values of the characteristics, he would probably delete some of the objects returned by the system (information noise), and he would probably add some others from the database, not returned by the system (information losses). Information noise and information losses have their origin in the fuzziness of the linguistic descriptions of the characteristics.

These concepts can be formalized as follows (Ryjov, 2004):

$$IL_X(U) = IN_X(U) = \frac{1}{|U|} \sum_{j=1}^{t-1} (p_j + p_{j+1}) \int_U \mu_j(u) \mu_{j+1}(u) N(u) du,$$

where $X = \{a_1, \cdots, a_t\}$, $p_i(i = 1,2,\cdots,t)$ - the probability of request offering in i- meaning of the characteristic X, $N(u)$ is the number of objects, the descriptions of which are stored in the database, that possess a real (physical, not linguistic) value equal to u.

The following theorems hold (Ryjov, 2004; Ryjov, 2012).

Theorem 3. Let

$$s_t \in G(L),\ N(u) = N = Const,\ p_i = \frac{1}{t}(i = 1,2,\cdots,t).$$

Then

$$IL_X(U) = IN_X(U) = \frac{c}{t} \xi(s_t),$$

where c is a constant with depends on N only.

This theorem shows that the volumes of information losses and information noise arising when searching for information in SEM are proportional to the degree of uncertainty of objects' description. It means that by optimally describing objects (concerning minimizing the degree of uncertainty), we also provide the optimal search of information in SEM.

Similarly to the analysis of Problem 1, we can construct the top ($\overline{IL_X}(U) = \overline{IN_X}(U)$) and the bottom ($\underline{IL_X}(U) = \underline{IN_X}(U)$) valuations of the $IL_X(U)$ and $IN_X(U)$.

Theorem 4. Let

$$s_t \in G^{\delta}\left(L\right),\ N\left(u\right) = N = Const,\ p_i = \frac{1}{t}\left(i = 1, 2, \cdots, t\right).$$

Then

$$\underline{IL}_X\left(U\right) = \underline{IN}_X\left(U\right) = \frac{c}{t}\left(1 - \delta_2\right)\underline{\xi}\left(s_t\right),$$

$$\overline{IL}_X\left(U\right) = \overline{IN}_X\left(U\right) = \frac{c}{t\left(1 + 2\delta_2\right)}\left(\frac{\left(1 - \delta_2\right)^3}{3} + 2\delta_2\right)\overline{\xi}\left(s_t\right).$$

This theorem shows us that for small significances δ our model of information retrieval's main laws is preserved. Therefore, we can use our estimation technique of the degree of uncertainty and our model of information retrieval in fuzzy (linguistic) databases in practical tasks since we have shown it to be robust.

Since we model processes as hierarchical structures (see Figure 3), choosing and selecting (tuning) of aggregation operators for the nodes of the model is another important issue in the development of SEM. We may formulate this problem as follows:

Problem 3. (aggregation in fuzzy hierarchical dynamic systems) Is it possible to find the operators of information aggregation in fuzzy hierarchical dynamic systems that allow us to minimize contradictoriness in the model of process in SEM?

It is shown that it is possible to propose the following approaches based on different interpretations of aggregation operators: geometrical, logical, and learning-based. The latter includes learning based on genetic algorithms and learning based on neural networks. These approaches are described in detail in (Ryjov, 2001).

Analytical Capabilities of SEM

Having set up an SEM, we can solve two types of problems: direct and inverse.

The direct problem is to find all "critical ways" of the process. It means to reveal those process elements, the small change of which status may qualitatively change the process's status as a whole. For a significant class of aggregation operators, we can calculate the degree of criticality for any element of the model; for all aggregation operators, we can use universal algorithms (like backtracking algorithms) to calculate the degree of criticality for any model element. That means that we can understand and measure the strengths and weaknesses of any element of the current process. This understanding is a base for developing a strategic plan for optimally controlling the process.

The inverse problem is finding elements of the model, which must be changed for reaching some given status of the model's target element. For example, we can understand how we can reach a maximal effect for a given budget or reach a given effect for a minimal budget.

We can formalize this in the following way. Let's use notations:

N – number of nodes in the Model;

m_i – number of values for node i;

Figure 11. Example of the Model

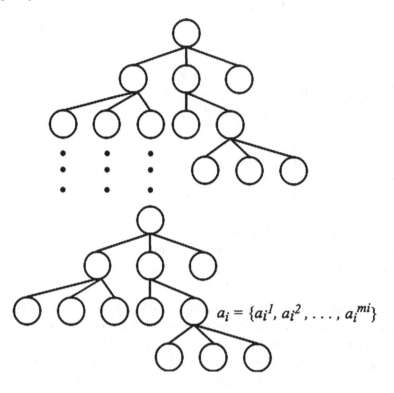

$a_i = \{a_i^1, a_i^2, \ldots, a_i^{mi}\}$

$a_i = \left\{a_i^1, a_i^2, \cdots, a_i^{m_i}\right\}$ – values for node i ($i = 0, 1, \cdots, N-1$) – see Figure 11;

X – budget;

c_i – cost of changing for node i ($a_i^k \rightarrow a_i^{k+1}, k = 1, \cdots, m_i - 1$); for simplicity assume that c_i is the same for all k;

Δa_i - the "power of changing" for node i; $\Delta a_i = q$ for changing $a_i^k \rightarrow a_i^{k+q}$.

Task 1. To find a set of nodes $\left\{a_{i_1}, a_{i_2}, \cdots, a_{i_n}\right\}$: $\Delta a_0 \rightarrow \max, \sum_{j=1}^{N-1} c_{i_j} \leq X$.

It is a task to reach the maximal effect for a given budget.

We can also formulate a dual task:

Task 2. To find a set of nodes $\left\{a_{i_1}, a_{i_2}, \cdots, a_{i_n}\right\}$: $\sum_{j=1}^{N-1} c_{i_j} \rightarrow \min, \Delta a_0 \geq q$.

It is a task to reach the given effect for a minimal budget.

Examples of such tasks could be evaluation and increasing capitalization for startups, increasing an investment's attractiveness for companies and/or regions, increasing the sustainability of a business, etc.

We can solve these tasks if we have the model (structure and tuned aggregation functions), the nodes' actual status, i.e., a working system for evaluation and monitoring of the process. Comparison analysis of these capabilities with other analytical tools is presented in Figure 12.

The current level of almost all companies – Excel/ SQL or OLAP Analytics; only a few companies use Big Data Analytics; analytical tools of systems of evaluation and monitoring used in selected international and governmental organizations, and large international high-tech business. The use of analytical

Figure 12. Analytical capabilities of SEM

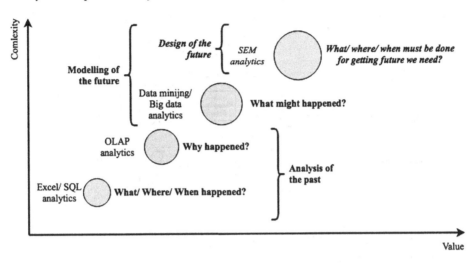

systems capabilities of SEM is a natural evolutionary stage in the development of analytical tools and frameworks for the Automation of knowledge work.

SOLUTIONS AND RECOMMENDATIONS

SEMs can solve the task of evaluation and monitoring, allow user input of all available information in a "natural manner", and capable of:

- saving the history of process development,
- evaluating the current status,
- modeling the future of process development.

SEMs are effective when:

- we do not have (cannot develop) a mathematical model of the process in the form of equations, automata, etc.
- we have experts who perform the monitoring task.

- We can develop SEM with minimal requirements for the task when:

- it is possible to develop a "semantic model" of the process in the form of a set of concepts and their inter-dependencies
- we work with real information (we can learn or tune the system)

We can develop an optimal system in terms of:

Figure 13. Task-driven information granulation
(Ryjov, 2015)

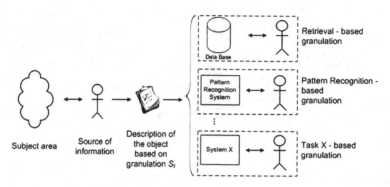

- how easy it is for the user to input information
- coordination of estimations of users
- information support of processes of input information and modeling.

Based on the methods described above, several systems for evaluation and monitoring were developed: a system for evaluation and monitoring of peaceful nuclear activities (DISNA) for the department of Safeguards International Atomic Energy Agency (Ryjov, et al., 1998), a system for evaluation and monitoring of risks of cardiovascular disease for Federal State Institution "National Research Center for Preventive Medicine" of the Ministry of Healthcare of the Russian Federation (Ahkmedzhanov et al., 2003), a system for evaluation and monitoring design team capability and project progress in microelectronics for Cadence Design Systems (Lebedev, 2009) and others.

Analytical capabilities of SEM allow us not only to analyze the past, even not only to model the future like Big Data analytics, but they also allow us to design the future and answer questions like "What, where and when we need to change to get the future we need?".

FUTURE RESEARCH DIRECTIONS

Because we have solved fundamental theoretical problems needed to develop human-centric systems to evaluate the status and monitor the progress of complex processes, we see future research directions in an expansion into new application areas.

For problem 1, we see perspectives in the personalization of a person's interaction with the digital world. The digital world - social networks, e-government, digital services, etc. - has become an essential part of our everyday life. However, our interaction with it is still not so comfortable and personalized as with the physical world. The first steps in this direction are described in (Ryjov, 2014b).

The generalizationn of problem 2 is task-driven information granulation. When solving this problem, we have proposed an optimal and robust information granulation for information retrieval. Can we do the same for other tasks like pattern recognition, data mining, reasoning, etc.? The general picture for this direction is presented in Figure 13 (Ryjov, 2015).

The technology of evaluation and monitoring of complex processes is a framework for a big part of the automation of knowledge work tasks. Many analysts work every day in this paradigm (Figure 2), and automating their work based on the described results will dramatically increase their effectiveness and efficiency.

Fuzzy logic is a natural mathematical foundation for Hybrid Intelligence. Described solutions for problems 1-3 are the solution of fundamental issues for developing optimal Hybrid Intelligence systems.

CONCLUSION

A big part of "tasks that rely on complex analysis, subtle judgments, and creative problem solving" (McKinsey Global Institute, 2013, p. 41) is evaluation of the status and monitoring the progress of processes in business, economy, society, etc. Modeling and control for these processes are very different from physical and technical ones. These processes are unique in the physical sense – a series of independent experiments is not possible; we cannot measure parameters like in physics – "measuring device" is a human being; we do not have adequate models like heat transfer equation – processes are described in natural language or the form of parametric dependencies, etc. As a result, we can conclude that classical mathematics is unsuitable for describing and modeling socio-economic processes due to colossal complexity, uncertainty, vagueness. Only the right mixes of computer intelligence and human intelligence can solve these problems.

ACKNOWLEDGMENT

The author would like to express his deep appreciation to professors V.B. Kudrjavtcev and A.S. Stogalov from Lomonosov Moscow State University (Russia); professors N.M. Ahkmedzhanov and R.G. Oganov from Federal State Institution "National Research Center for Preventive Medicine" of the Ministry of Healthcare of the Russian Federation (Russia); professor L.A. Zadeh from Berkeley, California (USA); professors E. Kerre and G. de Cooman from Gent University (Belgium); professor Y. Nishiwaki from Osaka University (Japan); Mr. A. Fattah from IAEA (Austria); Mr. W.-E. Matzke from Cadence Design Systems (Germany) for fruitful work on projects based on technology to evaluate and monitor complex processes.

REFERENCES

Ahkmedzhanov, N. M., Zhukotcky, A. V., Kudrjavtcev, V. B., Oganov, R. G., Rastorguev, V. V., Ryjov, A. P., & Stogalov, A. S. (2003). System for evaluation and monitoring of risks of cardiovascular disease. *Intelligent Systems*, *7*, 5–38.

Ashby, W. R. (1956). *An Introduction to Cybernetics*. Chapman and Hall. doi:10.5962/bhl.title.5851

Buckley, J. J. (1985). Fuzzy hierarchical analysis. *Fuzzy Sets and Systems*, *17*(3), 233–247. doi:10.1016/0165-0114(85)90090-9

Engelbart, D. C. (1962). *Augmenting human intellect: A conceptual framework*. Retrieved from http://www.dougengelbart.org/pubs/augment-3906.html

Gartner. (2017). *Glossary. Information Technology Glossary. Augmented Analytics.* Retrieved from https://www.gartner.com/en/information-technology/glossary/augmented-analytics

IBM. (2018). *Cognitive computing. Preparing for the Future of Artificial Intelligence.* Retrieved from https://research.ibm.com/cognitive-computing/ostp/rfi-response.shtml

Lebedev, A. A., & Ryjov, A. P. (2009). Design team capability and project progress evaluation based on information monitoring technology. In *Proceedings of the 5th International Conference on Soft Computing, Computing with Words and Perceptions in System Analysis, Decision and Control.* IEEE. 10.1109/ICSCCW.2009.5379492

Licklider, J. C. R. (1960). Man-Computer Symbiosis. *IRE Transactions on Human Factors in Electronics, HFE-1,* 4-11. Retrieved from http://groups.csail.mit.edu/medg/people/psz/Licklider.html

McKinsey Global Institute. (2013). *Disruptive technologies: Advances that will transform life, business, and the global economy.* Retrieved from https://www.mckinsey.com/insights/business_technology/disruptive_technologies

Mesarovich, M. D., Macko, D., & Takahara, Y. (1970). *Theory of hierarchical multilevel systems.* Academic Press.

MHR. (2021). *Augmented analytics: The new face of BI & Analytics. A Future with Augmented Analytics.* Retrieved from https://www.mhranalytics.com/blog/augmented-analytics-the-new-face-of-bi-analytics/

Rostamy, A. A. A., Meysam, S., Behnam, A., & Bakhshi, T. F. (2012). Using fuzzy analytical hierarchy process to evaluate main dimensions of business process reengineering. *Journal of Applied Operational Research, 4*(2), 69–77.

Ryjov, A. (1988). *The principles of fuzzy set theory and measurement of fuzziness.* Dialog-MSU Publishing.

Ryjov, A. (2001). On information aggregation in fuzzy hierarchical systems. *Intelligent Systems, 6,* 341–364.

Ryjov, A. (2003). Fuzzy Linguistic Scales: Definition, Properties and Applications. In L. Reznik & V. Kreinovich (Eds.), *Soft Computing in Measurement and Information Acquisition* (pp. 23–38). Springer. doi:10.1007/978-3-540-36216-6_3

Ryjov, A. (2004). *Models of information retrieval in a fuzzy environment.* MSU Publishing.

Ryjov, A. (2004). Information Monitoring Systems as a Tool for Strategic Analysis and Simulation in Business. In *Proceeding of the International Conference on Fuzzy Sets and Soft Computing in Economics and Finance.* RFSA.

Ryjov, A. (2012). Modeling and Optimization of Information Retrieval for Perception-Based Information. In F. Zanzotto, S. Tsumoto, N. Taatgen, & Y.Y. Yao (Eds), *Proceedings of the International Conference on Brain Informatics 2012 (Macau, China)* (pp. 140-149). Springer. 10.1007/978-3-642-35139-6_14

Ryjov, A. (2013). Systems for evaluation and monitoring of complex processes and their applications [in Russian]. *Intelligent Systems, 17*(1-4), 104–117.

Ryjov, A. (2014a). Human-centric systems for evaluating the status and monitoring the progress for socio-political processes. In *Proceedings of the 8th International Conference on Theory and Practice of Electronic Governance*. ACM Conference Publications. 10.1145/2691195.2691285

Ryjov, A. (2014b). Personalization of Social Networks: Adaptive Semantic Layer Approach. In W. Pedrycz & S.-M. Chen (Eds.), *Social Networks: A Framework of Computational Intelligence* (pp. 21–40). Springer International Publishing Switzerland. doi:10.1007/978-3-319-02993-1_2

Ryjov, A. (2015). Towards an optimal task-driven information granulation. In W. Pedrycz & S.-M. Chen (Eds.), *Information Granularity, Big Data, and Computational Intelligence* (pp. 191–208). Springer International Publishing Switzerland.

Ryjov, A., Belenki, A., Hooper, R., Pouchkarev, V., Fattah, A., & Zadeh, L. A. (1998). Development of an Intelligent System for Monitoring and Evaluation of Peaceful Nuclear Activities (DISNA), Vienna: IAEA, STR-310.

Saaty, T. L. (1980). *The analytic hierarchy process*. McGraw-Hill.

The Economic Times. (2016). *Human-machine super-intelligence may tackle world's problems*. Retrieved from http://articles.economictimes.indiatimes.com/2016-01-01/news/69448299_1_systems-hci-problems

ThoughtSpot. (2021) *Gartner. Augmented Analytics is the Future of Analytics*. Retrieved from https://go.thoughtspot.com/analyst-report-gartner-augmented-analytics.html

Torra, V. (2002). A review of the construction of hierarchical fuzzy systems. *International Journal of Intelligent Systems*, *17*(5), 531–543. doi:10.1002/int.10036

Zadeh, L. A. (1965). Fuzzy set. *Information and Control*, *8*(3), 338–353. doi:10.1016/S0019-9958(65)90241-X

Zadeh, L. A. (1975). The concept of a linguistic variable and its application to approximate reasoning. Part 1,2,3, Information Sciences, 8, 199-249. doi:10.1016/0020-0255(75)90036-5

ADDITIONAL READING

IBM. (2017). Augmented Intelligence, NOT Artificial Intelligence! Retrieved from https://www.ibm.com/blogs/collaboration-solutions/2017/01/31/augmented-intelligence-not-artificial-intelligence/

Padmanabhan, G. (2018). Industry-Specific Augmented Intelligence: A Catalyst For AI In The Enterprise. *Forbes*. Retrieved from https://www.forbes.com/sites/forbestechcouncil/2018/01/04/industry-specific-augmented-intelligence-a-catalyst-for-ai-in-the-enterprise/#31d1eac31748

Technologies, D. (2017). Dell Technologies 2018 Predictions – Entering the Next Era of Human Machine Partnerships. Retrieved from https://www.delltechnologies.com/en-us/perspectives/dell-technologies-2018-predictions-entering-the-next-era-of-human-machine-partnerships/

Zadeh, L. A. (1999). From computing with numbers to computing with words. From manipulation of measurements to manipulation of perceptions. *IEEE Transactions on Circuits and Systems. I, Fundamental Theory and Applications*, *46*(1), 105–119. doi:10.1109/81.739259

Zadeh, L. A. (2012a). *Computing with Words: Principal Concepts and Ideas*. Springer Publishing Company. doi:10.1007/978-3-642-27473-2

Zadeh, L. A. (2012b). Fuzzy logic-a personal perspective. *Fuzzy Sets and Systems*, *281*, 4–20. doi:10.1016/j.fss.2015.05.009

Zadeh, L. A. (2015). The Information Principle. *Information Sciences*, *294*, 540–549. doi:10.1016/j.ins.2014.09.026

KEY TERMS AND DEFINITIONS

Artificial Intelligence (AI): AI is the simulation of human intelligence processes by computer systems. Particular applications of AI include text and speech recognition, machine vision, learning by examples, etc.

Augmented Intelligence: Human-computer systems allow us to combine human intelligence strengths (for example, intuition) and computer's computational power. Augmented intelligence enhances and scales human expertise; AI systems attempt to replicate human intelligence.

Evaluation and Monitoring: It is a process that helps improve performance and achieve results for particular processes. Its goal is to improve current and future management of outputs, outcomes, and impact. It establishes links between the past, present, and future actions.

Fuzzy Logic: Fuzzy Logic is a form of mathematical logic in which the truth values of variables may be any real number between 0 and 1. It is employed to handle the concept of partial truth, where the truth value may range between completely true and completely false. By contrast, in Boolean logic, the truth values of variables may only be the integer values 0 or 1.

Fuzzy Sets: It is a set of elements that have no strict boundaries. Examples of such sets are sets of "young people", "expensive cars", "successful companies", etc.

Hierarchical Systems: It is a special type of systems where elements (objects, names, values, categories, etc.) are represented as being "above", "below", or "at the same level as" one another. A hierarchy can link elements either directly or indirectly, and either vertically or diagonally.

Measurement: Measurement is the assignment of a value (number, symbol, etc.) to a characteristic of an object or event, which can be compared with other objects or events.

Chapter 4
Designing Business Analytics Projects (BAP):
A Five–Step Dashboarding Cycle

Luiz Pinheiro
Positivo University, Brazil

Ricardo Matheus
Delft University of Technology, Netherlands

ABSTRACT

Private and public organizations have been using data for decision-making. However, these organizations have been struggling in putting into practice the design data analytics projects. In this sense, this chapter aims to present a proposal of a designing business analytics projects with a practical five steps dashboarding cycle. The first step, Business Questions, deals with the scope of a data analytics project creating problem-based questions. The second step, Data Sources, details which are the data sources to be collected. The third step, Extraction, Transform, and Loading (ETL), sets up data source routines of what, where, and when to collect data. The fourth step, Data Warehouse, creates a data repository where data is stored and treated after ETL process. The fifth step, Data Visualization, designs a web dashboard with interactive features such as tables and graphs. This chapter ends with three practical examples in both public and private organizations.

INTRODUCTION

The use of data in business analytics projects (BAPs) has been used since organizations' information could be computerized or digitized. In a brief historical search, it is possible to identify that business analytics (B&A) and Business Intelligence (BI) concepts were described by Devens (1868) in his work at Cyclopaedia of Commercial and Business Anecdotes. This document is the first known document explaining how business can extract 'intelligence' from data analysis, giving advantages and benefits in strategic level.

DOI: 10.4018/978-1-7998-9016-4.ch004

A century later Devens's work, the IBM computer scientist Luhn (1958) publishes a paper titled "A Business Intelligence System" in the IBM magazine. This publication aimed to show how data is used to enhance the decision-making in organizations. Luhn is one of the oldest practitioners in organizing scientifically how data can be organized and used for strategic level besides the common storage practice.

Few decades later Luhn's publication, Dresner (1989) conceptualized data use in organizations. Dresner was a Gartner researcher and Digital Equipment Corporation (DEC) professional. In his paper, Dresner points out that BI plays a key role and describes a set of tools, methods and techniques to improve decision-making in modern business models. Later, this BI description purposed by Dresner was sharpened and have been used as an official concept in all publications and studies conducted by Gartner.

Recently, Davenport (2006); Davenport and Harris (2017) are some of the most recent authors in the BI field, in special conducting research among re-engineering processes after innovative needs during the 1990 decade. These studies conducted by Davenport have a focus on what he defined as "competitive analytics", in summary, organizations using data analysis to allow competitive advantage over competitors.

More recent studies have been published on the use of BAPs in in sectors such as human resources (Margherita, 2021), supply chain (Boehmke et al., 2020), finance (Dincer, et al., 2019), healthcare and public health (Mosavi & Santos, 2020), manufacturing (Park et al., 2019), marketing (Liu & Burns, 2018), small and medium enterprises (Lu et al., 2020), Enterprise Information Systems (Sun et al., 2017) and, public sector (Matheus, Janssen, & Maheshwari, 2018). However, these studies present different models, frameworks according to the specific needs of each sector. After analyzing this literature, this chapter presents the three research questions:

- How can we develop an applied cycle for BAPs in organizations?
- Is it possible to designing the BAP projects into steps?
- What are the most relevant steps and tools used in BAP projects?

To answer these questions, this chapter aims to present a proposal for a designing business analytics projects with a practical five steps dashboarding cycle. In this text we propose to go forward and contribute with literature about business analytics projects (BAPs) and propose an applied framework for organizations. The expected audience for this chapter is diffuse and ranging from operational data analysts to managers in charge of strategic decision-making in organizations.

This chapter is structured in five sections as follows. The first section introduces this chapter and its objectives. The second section has a non-exhaustive literature review is presented regarding data and analytics supporting theoretical and scientific evidences to be included in the BAP proposal, in special the most common expected benefits and challenges. In the third section, the BAP five steps are presented exploring tasks, and recommendations of methods and techniques to create dashboards in practice.

The fourth section provides a benchmarking of tools to assemble web/online dashboards, including a diversity of paid and free options. Has three examples of dashboards using the BAP five steps dashboarding cycle proposed. The five section presents conclusions of this chapter with a summary of limitations and future research discussion, and a potential agenda of topics and gaps for following practical and scientific publications.

LITERATURE REVIEW

In this chapter we build a literature review to theoretically support this theme. Searches were performed in the Google Scholar database looking for articles related to the topic of business analytics projects. The keywords were used: "analytics" or "dashboard" and "finance"; "marketing"; "human resources"; "manufacturing"; "health"; "supply chain"; "small firms"; and "public sector". In these searches, we identified two or three articles with the highest number of citations in each theme, we carried out a complete reading of them to use as seminal references in the following paragraphs.

Currently, the easy access of advanced information and communication technologies such as smartphones, sensors, robust data servers and telecom infrastructure enabled a phenomenon classified as "digitalization of the world" (Lycett, 2013; Matheus, Janssen, & Janowski, 2021). This digitalization simplified the collection and use of huge amount of data with a small budget investment by organizations. These recent changes impacted organizations in how they create and improve strategic decision-making process (Davenport & Harris, 2017). Apart from these changes and impacts on organizations, there is in the scientific literature a debate about the value brought by data collection enabled by digitalization of the world and the true potential of data analytics for decision-making or leading innovation in internal processes and new products (Iansiti, 2021; Sun, 2020).

Besides these chances and discussions, organizations have been creating dashboards as a way to visualize data analysis in an easy and simple way. In accordance with Martins, Martins, and Brandão (2022), BAPs are becoming more and more used in organizations to reduce information asymmetry between departments aiming to a fast and proper decision-making. Lepenioti, Bousdekis, Apostolou, and Mentzas (2020) proposes that BAPs can be divided in four approaches: Descriptive, Diagnostic, Predictive, and, Prescriptive. These approaches are better described in the follow section.

However, to develop BAPs and data analysis behind dashboards organizations should respect some requirements such as rapid access to good data quality, friendly graphical interface of dashboards, and flexible functionalities tools for visualization when prototyping new analysis for new research questions (Martins et al., 2022). Following these requirements, BAPs have positive impacts in several sectors such as human resources (Margherita, 2021), supply chain (Boehmke, Hazen, Boone, & Robinson, 2020), finance (Dincer, Hacioglu, Tatoglu, & Delen, 2019), healthcare and public health (Mosavi & Santos, 2020), manufacturing (Park, Ko, Lee, Cho, & Witherell, 2019), marketing (Liu & Burns, 2018), small and medium enterprises (SME) (Lu, Cairns, & Smith, 2020), and, public sector (Matheus, Janssen, & Maheshwari, 2018).

Margherita (2021) conducted a literature review regarding how data can contribute to manage people and its professional development. In accordance with Margherita (2021) analysing human resources in an organization is a modern method to follow individual or collective performance, besides of diagnose and prescribe improvements helping managers in charge of people. Combined with artificial intelligence (AI) and machine learning (ML) algorithms, this field of study is also called as "people analytics" by others researchers such as Bodie, Cherry, McCormick, and Tang (2017) and Tursunbayeva, Di Lauro, and Pagliari (2018).

In the supply chain field, Boehmke et al. (2020) point out that data analysis can show and predict supply demand to all organizations involved in the supply chain. Instead of using analytical methods of problem-solving and decision-making, also known as "Operations research (OR)", Boehmke et al. (2020) explains organizations can visualize all the supply chain in graphical and visual ways using dashboards. Combined with Internet of Things (IoT) technologies, these dashboards in supply chain can also use data in real-time or near real-time, enabling higher quality and faster decision-making processes (Hopkins & Hawking, 2018).

Aiming to reduce costs and increase operational efficiency, banks and the financial system use dashboards with data analysis in some activities, such as fraud detection (Kovach & Ruggiero, 2011), clustering clients (Soukal & Hedvicakova, 2011), churn behaviour of bank customers (Prasad & Madhavi, 2012), and, efficiency of bank deposits (Dincer et al., 2019).

Another sector benefited by datafication is healthcare and public health. The huge amount of data from sensors and automated reports of patients helped healthcare professionals to improve models and give efficiency when dealing with decision-making (Mosavi & Santos, 2020). Using big data and wearable technologies such as smart watches (e.g., Apple Watch, Xiaomi Amazfit), it is possible to monitor patients with a decent precision and predict when patients should contact their physicians (Chakraborty, Bhatt, Chakravorty, & Technology, 2020). Similar approach can also be used to monitor diseases (Bansal, Chowell, Simonsen, Vespignani, & Viboud, 2016), and, prevention of adverse effects of pharmaceuticals using pharmacovigilance methods (Salathé, 2016). However, some discussions around health surveillance is made regarding some privacy issues (Nguyen et al., 2020) in special after national and supranational legislations such as General Data Protection Regulation (GDPR) in Europe (European_Union, 2021).

It is also possible to use dashboards combined with data analysis to manufacturing industry and improve product quality, avoid machine failures and bullwhip effects in the mass production. Park et al. (2019) conducted three case studies in manufacturing industry and compared five dimensions of these organizations: value, decision making, analysis, data and sources. An analytical model was created to bring evidences of how manufacturing industry performance was affected and how much could be improved in terms of operations management. Besides that, dashboards can help manufacturing sector to predict when machines in charge of producing its products demand maintenance and preventing machines complete failures (Gordon, Burnak, Onel, & Pistikopoulos, 2020).

Another relevant use of BAPs in the goods-producing industries is the prediction of sales forecasting aiming to avoid bullwhip effects in the mass production (Fu, Ionescu, Aghezzaf, De Keyser, & Engineering, 2014). Furthermore, the use of dashboards, data science and open data transparency is a low-cost alternative described by Coleman (2016). Open data transparency is a movement led by public sector organizations providing free and open access data collected and processed by governments or any other public agencies (Matheus & Janssen, 2019).

Dashboards and BAPs are also useful to marketing field (Liu & Burns, 2018). Organizations desire to understand what happened in the past, monitor the present, and, predict the future. Combining descriptive statistics, the past and present can be graphically visualized instead of static spreadsheets or printed tables with statistical results, while AI and ML algorithms can lead to predictive and prescriptive discoveries in useful and interactive dashboards.

This dashboard and data science approach enables marketing sector several opportunities such as: create automated marketing campaigns using automated chat robots and Natural Language Processing (NLP) (Hafaiedh, Rhouma, Chargui, Haouas, & Kerkeni, 2020); reducing risks to the brand and company image anticipating issues and proposing ready solutions analysing in real-time what are the customers' reactions in social media (e.g., Instagram, Twitter, Facebook) (Kauffmann et al., 2019); improve user experience when searching for products and services using Search Engine Optimization (SEO) (Matošević, Dobša, & Mladenić, 2021); create personalized engagement marketing to audience (Kumar, Rajan, Venkatesan, & Lecinski, 2019); monitor customer retention (churn analysis) of products and services (Coussement

& Van den Poel, 2008); Customer segmentation analysis in sportswear industry (Ko et al., 2012); and, develop new products and services tailored to determined segments of customers (Liu & Burns, 2018).

Although the use of dashboards, huge amount of data in good quality, top-level sensors and AI/ML algorithms look like a trend in high-tech and big companies, literature shows that SME can also profit from the use of BAP approach. Lu et al. (2020) demonstrated how SME can enhance its sales strategy and fund raising. BAPs can also be used to improve sales of SMEs using social media such as Instagram and e-marketplaces. Purwandari, Otmen, and Kumaralalita (2019) showed that SMEs using social media analytics during COVID-19 pandemics grew up in terms of sales amount due the closure of physical stores during lockdowns and the consequent physical stores sales reduction.

Literature also shows that dashboards and modern data science technologies are used in the public sector as well (Matheus et al., 2018). Major part of these dashboards and data science projects have been happening in part due the transparency of open government data (Janssen, Matheus, Longo, & Weerakkody, 2017). Examples of this approach used in the public sector are COVID-19 real-time monitoring (Mitra, Soman, & Singh, 2021); Smart energy and urban mobility enhancements (Janssen, Matheus, & Zuiderwijk, 2015); Public services delivery during big events World Cup 2014 and Olympics 2016 (Matheus, Vaz, & Ribeiro, 2014); social aid for families in risk (Lo, Wei, Chuang, Yin, & Hsieh10, 2017), and, management efficiency of public administrations (Corbu, Edelhauser, & Lupu-Dima, 2019).

After reading all these paper, we can identify that some papers present relevant cases of dashboards use and data science algorithms. Some of these papers have models and others have high-level design principles. However, none of these papers found had a combination of empirical guidelines based on scientific and theoretical foundation. This gap in the literature, besides the need of a proper guideline with technical recommendations in our data analytics and data science lecturers led us to propose the BAP five steps approach presented in the next section. The BAP proposed can help at same time managers in charge of data analytics and data science teams, as well, technical people in charge of delivering data products in meaningful, useful, and, interactive visualizations.

Business Analytics Projects (BAP)

After all, '**What are Business Analytics Projects (BAP)?**' The aforementioned authors show that business analytics projects are projects using data and analysis to enhance decision-making in organizations. The projects mentioned by authors have some elementary constructs such as: data, methods, techniques, tools, and, skilled people. A similar summary of this constructs is provided by Gartner (2014) in Figure 1. Data is usually acquired from structured Information Technology (IT) systems, relational databases, regular spreadsheets and text document. Recently, the introduction of cloud technology and big data non-relational databases helped to increase the range and type of options when retrieving data for analysis. Besides data, methods and techniques for data analysis have been evolving, in special connected with the huge amount of data and the evolution of tools for analysis (e.g., see section 3 list). Last, skilled people using data and conducting analysis became a bottleneck for organizations when creating data analytics teams. Initially, these positions were labelled as "BI analyst" or "data analysts" but after data science boom, positions such data scientists, data engineers, machine learning engineers became usual in LinkedIn job descriptions.

In accordance with Gartner (2014) perspective, BAP can be divided in two level of capabilities and four types of projects analysis. The elementary constructs are data, selecting the type of analytics, deciding the level of human input (and non-human input), decision, and action (or decision-making). While

Figure 1. Business Analytics Projects (BAPs) and capability
Source: Adapted from Gartner (2014)

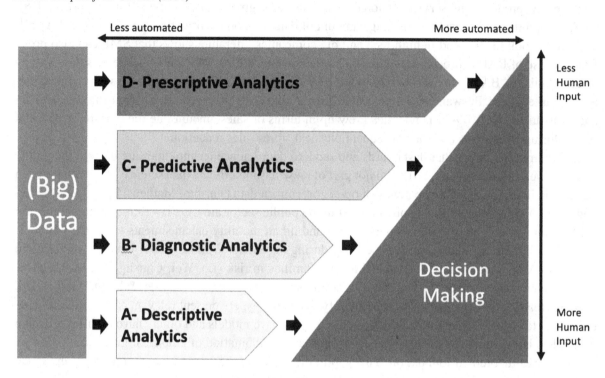

the two level of capabilities are human and non-human input, there are four types of BAP projects: 1) Descriptive; 2) Diagnostic; 3) Predictive; and, 4) Prescriptive.

The BAP type 1 'Descriptive' aims to describe the past in organizations. It means collecting history registers and make sense of them in a diverse of tables, graphs and dashboards. Usually, these descriptive analysis have descriptive statistical analysis such as frequency, average, and, mean. Descriptive is the simplest type of BAP, however, authors plea for readers do not compare or rank these four types. The ideal scenario is to select the best BAP type taking into consideration the business question (see section 2.1). A key question to describe BAP type 1 Descriptive is: *"What happened in my organization?"*

The BAP type 2 'Diagnostic' aims to diagnose the past in organizations combining present data (history + current data). Some organizations cannot rely only on history data (e.g., 1 month, 1 year ago) and when combine descriptive statistical analysis with basic statistics methods such as hypothesis testing, linear and multilinear regression analysis, ANOVA, T-test, aiming to identify trends, associations and correlations. Similar visualizations methods employed in descriptive type can be used in diagnostic type to enhance daily decision-making in organizations, supported by statistical models (hypothesis testing). A key question to describe BAP type 2 Diagnostic is: *"Why did it happen in my organization?"*

The BAP type 3 'Predictive' aims to predict the future using past and present data. It means more complex statistical methods should be employed such as Machine Learning (ML) and Artificial Intelligence (AI) algorithms. Some examples of ML and AI algorithms are linear and logistic regression, Random Forest, Decision Tree. A key question to describe BAP type 3 Predictive is: *"What will happen in my organization?"*.

Figure 2. Benefits and challenges to put BAP in practice[1]

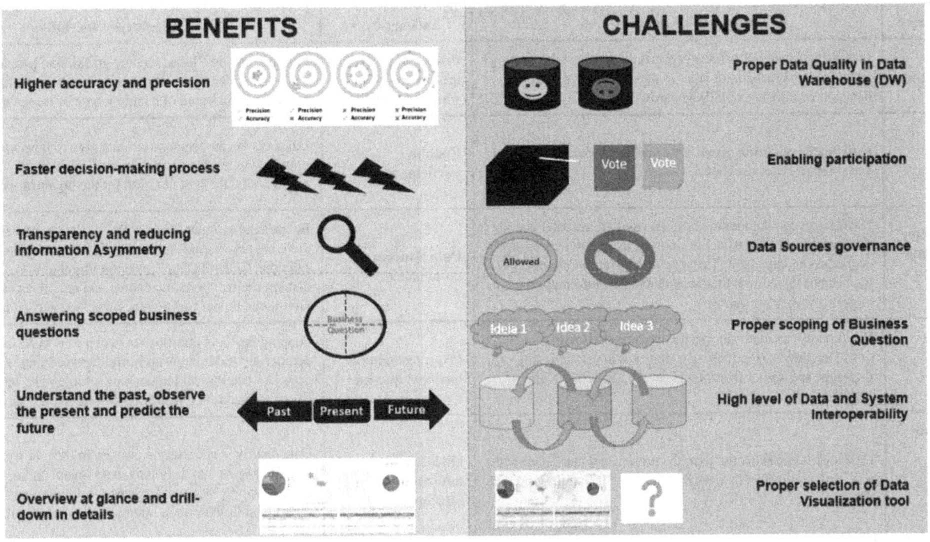

The BAP type 4 'Prescriptive' aims to reduce the human input and interaction needed in all three other types of BAP combining ML, AI and automation of processes. This automation can also be designed using Robotic Process Automation (RPA) software such as UiPath and Automation Anywhere, or, using scripts written in programming languages (e.g., Python, Java, R). Usually, the prescriptive project needs a combination of all statistical methods and techniques described in the other three types of projects, and, more complex ML and AI techniques such as Gradient Boosting (GB) and Artificial Neural Networks (ANN). A key question to describe BAP type 4 is: *"How can we make it happen automatically?"*

Benefits and Challenges to Put BAP in Practice

This section shows example and descriptions of the most common benefits and challenges in BAP extracted from literature review presented in the previous section. The summary is presented in Table 1 and Figure 2 in a way to capture common benefits and challenges when creating BAPs, influencing the BAP five steps dashboarding cycle proposed in the follow section.

METHOD

This section explains what is a dashboard and how to design and deploy a functional dashboard in five steps. The five steps are: 1) Step 1- Business Question; 2) Step 2- Data Sources; 3) Step 3- ETL; 4) Step 4- Data Warehouse; and, 5) Step 5 - Data Visualization. Since this is a cycle, after step five, it is possible to re-start this cycle from step 1 again with new insights and business questions. Figure 3 below graphically shows the five Steps Dashboarding Cycle.

In accordance with Matheus, Janssen, and Maheshwari (2018, p. 1) dashboards are digital panels to visualize a consolidated dataset for a certain purpose which enables users to see what is happening and

Table 1. Benefits and challenges to put BAP in practice

#	Benefit Name	Benefit Description	Challenge Name	Challenge Description
1	Higher accuracy and precision	Increasing data quality allow organizations to have higher accuracy and precision in order to make faster and better decision-making through dashboards.	Proper data quality in data warehouse (DW)	Investments in IT infrastructure and skilled people to deal with data quality can avoid data quality issues. Sometimes is better to not have data instead of having wrong or biased data sets.
2	Faster decision-making process	Dashboards can bring efficiency to decision-making process and produce faster decisions.	Enabling participation	Dashboards can democratize data access, however, if there are no proper channels for people involved participate, faster decisions might not be the best decision for the organization.
3	Transparency and reducing information asymmetry	Dashboards can democratize the data and information access to all people and departments involved in determined service or product supply chain. This data transparency created by dashboards reduces internal and external information asymmetry in organizations.	Data Sources governance	Besides the technical perspective of data governance, currently, there are new legislations might influence data sources. As an example, General Data Protection Regulation (GDPR) in Europe demands a treatment in personal and sensitive collected data. Giving the proper transparency level to users is mandatory.
4	Answering scoped business questions	Dashboards can focus on specific and targeted business questions. Answering these questions might reduce losing the scope and aim of determined people, department and organizations.	Proper scoping of business question	Scoping business questions is not an easy task. Including democratic and bottom-up approaches can increase participation, however, filtering and organizing all ideas and needs is hard. A balance when ranking and scoping these questions is needed.
5	Understand the past, observe the present and predict the future	Dashboards can show the past, the present and combined with artificial intelligence and machine learning techniques, predict the future.	High level of data and system interoperability	Data quality is necessary, however, in the real world, there are legacy systems and dirty data in an organization. To simplify the cleansing process, it is necessary investments to create interoperability between internal and external data and system.
6	Overview at glance and drill-down in details	Dashboards can use a diverse of data visualizations features. These features allow us to customize to each user a different configuration, since overview at glance, or, drill down in details.	Proper selection of data visualization tool	Some users do not have technical skills to decide or explain what they would like to have in a dashboard. It is an IT task to help these users to select the proper data visualization tools and features.

to initiate actions. These digital panels can have static or dynamic tables, graphs, maps, and simulations of a huge number of datasets and databases, connected or not connected.

Examples of dashboards are present in all fields such as health, government, education, finances, and, accountancy. Besides the use in both public and private organizations, several machines we use daily have dashboards as an example automobile panel showing how much gas we still have or alerting us the need for specific maintenance. Figure 4[REMOVED REF FIELD] provides an example of Type 1 BAP regarding accidents and fatalities in workplace (Safety and Health) in Parana State (Brazil), using real open government data.

These dashboards can support managers and decision-makers to understand the past, making decisions in the real time, or, predicting and planning the future. However, to design and maintain a dashboard is not easy in practice. As already seen in section 1.1, there is a need of proper data to keep this dashboard reliable besides well scoped business question to provide to users the needed answers. Section 2 provides a dashboard cycle to readers design and deploy their own dashboard following five steps.

Step 1 - Business Question

The Step 1 'Business Question' aims to define and scope proper business questions to each user of this dashboard. If necessary, many dashboards should be built to a diverse of departments in the organizations and roles of these users (operational, tactical, strategic). While logistic department might be interested in the number of products sold, marketing department would be interested in the margin profit or sales by vendors. Another example is given in Table 2.

To facilitate the definition and scope process we encourage leaders to follow collaborative and rapid prototyping methodologies. As an example, Knapp, Zeratsky, and Kowitz (2016) has the Scrum meth-

Figure 3. Five steps Dashboarding Cycle[2]

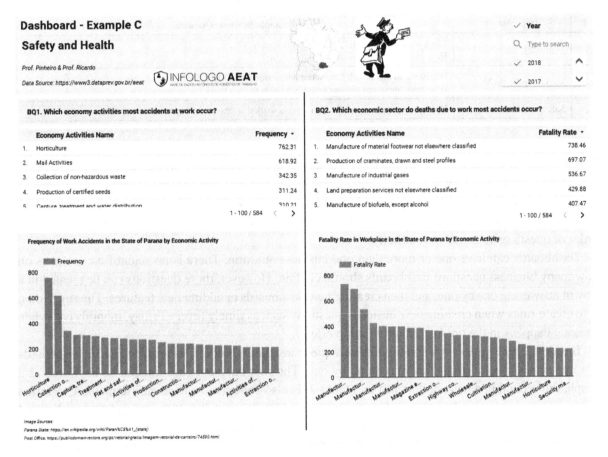

odology of defining and scoping business questions in a collaborative approach. Be careful, this step can

Figure 4. Dashboard example A – Accidents and Fatalities in Workplace

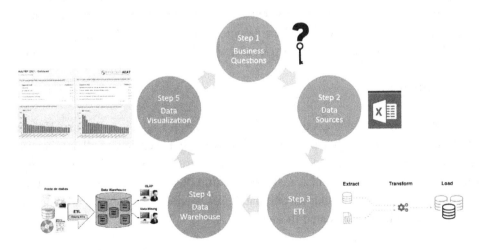

Table 2. Business question examples

#	Department	Example Business Question
A	Marketing Sales	What is the gross monthly revenue of company X? How many cars did vendor A sell this month?
B	Marketing Social Media	Which social media will have more interaction for product x? How many mentions did our brand X have in the last week?
C	Safety and Health	How many people did suffer accidents at work this year in the organization X?

look simples, however, as Rose, Fischer, and Perspective (2011) recommends in 'garbage-in / garbage-out' theory for data quality, if business questions are not properly defined, the higher is the chance of failures in the end of having a useless dashboard. Besides these methodologies, the low hanging-fruit approach (Conklin, 2006) might be useful to select which is the most relevant and easier to rank the order of questions to be answered firstly.

Dashboards can have one or more than one business question. There is no scientific consensus on how many business questions dashboards should contain. However, these questions can be created in a way of answering one by one, and then creating new dashboards or adding new features. The suggestion is to create rules when creating new business questions such as timely (every Friday, monthly) or, when an issue happens in the organization (bullwhip effect).

Besides defining rules for when creating new questions, the answers can be materialized in dashboards at same time or included and answered one by one. The first business question can be answered as a graph, the second in a map, and a third in a table. It is also common, as in scientific method, to refine the business questions in later stages. Due these reasons data sources should have good data quality and prepared for interconnection, as well systems interoperability (see this effect in step 2, step 3 and step 4).

In this step 1, we recommend the use of collaborative ideation tools, methods, and techniques (e.g., Design SPRINT, Forced relationships, Mind maps, Canvas, Brainstorming meetings, internal and external surveys or interviews) to create business questions. A recommended structure of this collaborative sessions uses a bottom-up approach, since group of work, department, up to the whole organization. These business questions should be transparently public. As an example, creating and sharing open access documents (e.g., Google Docs) or using online collaborative platforms (e.g., Miro).

Another approach to create business questions is based on the logic of creating business questions taking into consideration products or services that are built or delivered using several different departments or organizations. These processes can be conducted every week, or after the presentation of results (see step five). The inputs collected here can start a new dashboard or an update of old ones.

Step 2 - Data Sources

In order to answer the selected business questions created in step 1 data is necessary. Before discussing which data is necessary to answer all questions, we should have an overview of all data sources presented in the organization and also potential data sources external to the organization. This overview can be created through a data inventory action. A task force within all departments in the organization asking for a generic description of all data sources and databases is enough to identify all potentially relevant data to answer business questions created in section 1.

Table 3. Data sources examples

#	Data Sources	Department	Example Business Question
A	Legacy Systems (ERP)	Marketing Sales	What is the gross monthly revenue of company X? How many cars did vendor A sell this month?
B	Social Media Facebook, Instagram, Twitter	Marketing Social Media	Which social media will have more interaction for product x? How many mentions did our brand X have in the last week?
C	Open Data regarding Injuries, Illnesses, and Fatalities	Occupational Safety and Health Administration	How many people did suffer accidents at work this year in the organization X?

These data sources and databases can be Word Documents (.doc), Excel Spreadsheets (.xls), Relational Databases (SQL), Big Data Social Media, Legacy Systems (e.g., Enterprise Resource Planning ERP) and any other source of data relevant to answer business questions. This overview turns into a list of data sources and databases, usually summarized in an online spreadsheet. If more details are needed, later processes can be conducted, in special during step 3 ETL. Examples of updates needed are who has access to this data? Is there any legal issue in sharing this data? What should be anonymized? Is this data updated? and other several questions to help data scientists and people in charge of dashboards to have a deep level of knowledge about data sources without having access to them. Table 3 presents data sources examples following similar examples used in Table 2.

Step 3 - Extract, Transform and Load (ETL)

ETL is the acronym for Extract, Transform and Load. ETL can be conceptualized as a diverse of software tools aiming to extract data from different sources to answer the business question loaded in a dashboard Gartner (2020). The ETL process is related to data sources identified in the Step 2. Part, or the whole data sources, will help to answer the selected business questions in Step 1. Some questions can help to decide what to prioritize in the Extraction part: What do I need to extract? What are these data source structures?

Regarding Transforming part, the typical question emerged is "Do I need to convert or transform these data sources?". Usually, organizations have multiple data sources and data might be in a diverse of formats. A common example when transforming data is applying rules to data variables (columns): Instead of having (1) Woman or (2) Man, we might want to transform this variable into (F) Female or (M) Male, aiming to have similar structure of other data sources. All of them explain which gender a person is, however, if multiple data sources cannot be combined, this might create later problems when analysing data or creating new dashboards to answer new business questions.

The last part of ETL is Loading. Loading is the process that deals with the frequency and flow of these data sources into the data warehouse (step 4) or directly to the dashboard (step five), depending on the architecture selected by the organization. It is also in the Loading part that other data routines are configured, as well cleansing processes. Examples of these Extract and Transforming are presented in Table 4.

Potential ETL tools are given by Gartner (2020): Informatica - Power Center or IBM - Data Stage. When selecting the ETL tool, it is recommended to check if this selected tool can be easily connected

Table 4. ETL processes examples

#	Example Business Question	Data Sources	Extract (E)	Transform (T)	Loading (L)
A	What is the gross monthly revenue of company X? How many cars did vendor A sell this month?	Legacy Systems (ERP)	Car sales	Vender, intermediary, e-commerce	Daily
B	Which social media will have more interaction for product x? How many mentions did our brand X have in the last week?	Social Media Facebook, IG, etc.	Interactions	Like, share, view multiple channel	Hourly
C	How many people did suffer accidents at work this year in the organization X?	Open Data about accidents	Number of Accidents	Standardize multiple industries	Weekly

with tools in the next steps Data warehouse and Data visualization. If not, we do recommend to have tools in the same environment or have data engineers able to set up connections between these tools.

Step 4 - Data Warehouse

Data warehouse (DW) is known as a huge data repository aiming to store data collected, transformed, and, prepared to be loaded in analytical tools or end-users graphical dashboards where business questions should be answered (Ravat, Teste, & Zurfluh, 1999). The main difference between databases and data warehouse is the structure logic of organization. While databases use relational logic, DW are configured by thematic. These groups of themes are also called as "Data Marts" (DM) (see examples in Figure 5).

Besides this difference of logic, DW centralizes all data and information regarding the core business of your organization and simplifying the process to answer the business questions created in Step 1. A recommendations when structuring the DW is to start with DMs, and then, centralize all DMs in a DW as the main repository of all DMs. This structure helps to create a synergy and alignment between business teams and IT teams. This structure allows businesspeople to have a big picture of all data sources and data scientists easily use these data sources to answer business questions.

Figure 5. Data warehouse example

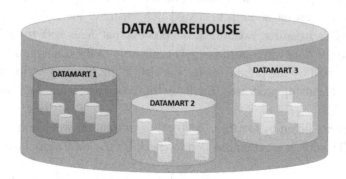

Figure 6. Association examples bar chart and scatterplot

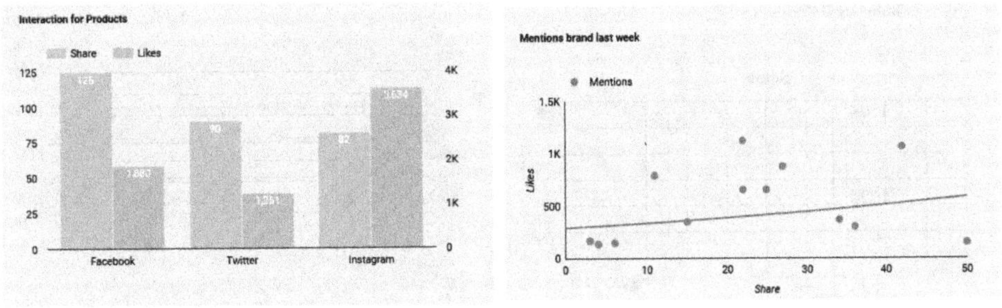

Step 5 - Data Visualization

The Step Five - Data Visualization (DV) is the last step to create dashboards. Step five is the materialization of dashboards through graphs, tables, maps and other digital features using data found in step 2, properly extracted, transformed and loaded in Step 2, and, structured in step 4 in a Data warehouse to answer the business questions created in step 1.

This book chapter focus in three most common types of graphical visualization techniques: association, trend lines and clustering. There are several data mining techniques available such as data cleaning, tracking patterns, outlier detection, geographical maps and others. Marketing professionals are valuable in the step five, contributing to the best choice of techniques and graphical features to be selected, as well, the KPIs to be shown in the dashboards. Besides data scientists, data journalists or professionals in charge of storytelling are also useful to increase transparency and reduce information asymmetry.

The first graphical visualization technique is association. Association is the data analysis technique aiming to link occurrences to an event (e.g., Supermarket purchase, when customers buy French fries and a Coca-Cola. This association can be graphically visualized in a bar chart (see for Figure 6 examples).

The second graphical visualization technique is a trend line. Trend line is a technique that fits data analysis where time series is an important aspect, and you aim to compare two or more variables during a certain period of time (see Figure 7). An example is house construction. Usually, if people buy a house, there is 45% of chance to buy an oven within a month.

The third technique is clustering. Clustering aims to aggregate certain types of individuals divided in determined characteristics (see Figure 8). As an example, we could cluster customers, dividing them by region, gender or income. Find customer characteristics and determine which types of promotions will be most effective. Obviously, the preview will run as per the demand of the business question.

BENCHMARKING TOOLS - POWEBI, TABLEAU, AND, GOOGLE DATA STUDIO

BAP does need the use of a tool to use and explore data. This BAP market has several tools that might adapt to each type of use. Gartner (2021) aims to rank all tools considering some classification in terms of Leaders, Visionaries, Challengers and Niche players. This rank is created after a survey of 1000 top big tech IT managers around the world. Table 5 is the result of a not scientific perception of authors. We strongly recommend readers to test themselves all tools and select what best fit in your organization.

Figure 7. Time series example

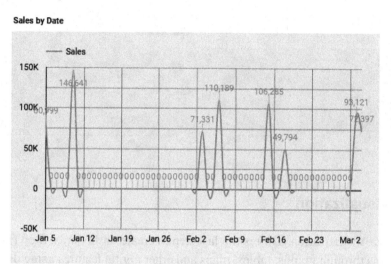

All tools presented in Table 5 can be used in step five. However, pay attention in positive and limitations of all tools to properly select where your organization will deploy the dashboard. As an example, part of organization has been in early stage of data analytics and might uses rapid prototyping approach. Low cost and easy to use tools are proper for this scenario. Google Data Studio has a web/cloud version where dashboards can be designed and integrated with free services from Google family (e.g., Google Drive, Google Analytics).

On the other hand, part of organizations use big tech family software. The Microsoft Power BI is paid, but if all other departments and business partners use Microsoft, this might be the best choice to avoid any interoperability issues when creating data warehouses or using the data in the dashboards. Besides these approaches, Tableau has limited cost and has fashion and easy to use characteristics, similar of what happens in Qlik View and Qlik Sense. Cognos, Microstrategy, Oracle, NetWeaver are more

Figure 8. Clustering example

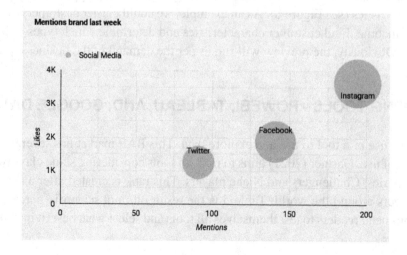

Table 5. Business analytics tools

#	Tool	Gartner Rank	Positive Aspects	Limitations and Observations
1	Google Data Studio	-	Free, Self-service, diverse of features, proper community and support, and, easy to use.	Recommended in rapid prototyping cases with low budget.
2	IBM Cognos	Niche Players	Integrated with IBM family software, Cognos is able to deal with big data scenario. Community and support is proper.	Management and graphical interface are old fashion but stable with limited features.
3	Microstrategy	Challengers	Low-cost management, specialized IT support provided by Microstrategy.	Management and graphical interface are old-fashion but stable with limited features.
4	Microsoft Power BI	Leaders	Integrated with Microsoft family, self-service approach, dynamic and easy to use. Proper support and community.	Recommended in rapid prototyping cases with limited budget and organization using Microsoft family.
5	Oracle	Visionaries	Integrated with Oracle family, it deals well with other Oracle relational databases and big data technologies.	Management and graphical interface are old-fashion but stable with limited features.
6	Pentaho	-	Free, deals well with big data technologies.	Certain level of programming skills is needed, but community is friendly.
7	QlikView/ Sense	Leaders	Free, Self-service, diverse of features, proper community and support, and, easy to use.	Recommended in rapid prototyping cases with limited budget
8	SAP NetWeaver	Visionaries	Integrated with SAP family, deals well with big data technologies.	Management and graphical interface are old-fashion but stable with limited features.
9	Tableau	Leaders	Self-service, diverse of features, proper community and support, and, easy to use.	Recommended in rapid prototyping cases with limited budget with certain level of programming and database skills.

traditional and robust tools and combined with its family databases, mainframes and ERPs organization might increase efficiency and reduce other costs with ETL. Nonetheless, Pentaho is an open source, however, the biggest barrier is the certain programming skills needed to configure and create dashboards. However, Pentaho community is friendly and easy to learn if data scientists or other professionals have basic programming skills.

Examples of Dashboards Using BAP Five Steps Dashboarding Cycle in Google Data Studio

This section has three dashboards using as source Table 2 - Business Question Examples. Links and descriptions below:

Dashboard A – https://datastudio.google.com/reporting/7baf90c1-edbe-4fa0-9d36-158ad2d30f76

The Dashboard A presents a BAP regarding marketing sales of automobiles. We analyze data in terms of gross revenue, and, sale by vendors.

Dashboard B – https://datastudio.google.com/reporting/84620efd-1fb2-4800-8d43-da473fc1318d

The Dashboard B has a marketing analytics of determined product performance in social media. This marketing analysis shows customer interactions with products and mentions in social media (e.g., Instagram, Facebook, Twitter).

Figure 9a. Example Dashboard A

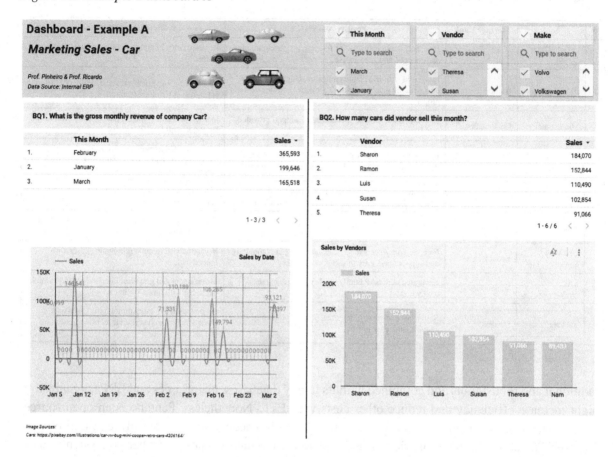

Dashboard C – https://datastudio.google.com/reporting/e8b7af53-f0d0-4d08-87ec-a69ea5ad88a6

The Dashboard C uses open government data regarding safety and health, aiming to identify labor accidents and deaths. These graphs and tables in Dashboard C can help policy managers in charge of public policies to reduce or eradicate these accidents and deaths.

CONCLUSION

This book chapter aimed to explain "How to design a business analytics projects with a five steps dashboarding cycle". This is demonstrated in the five steps dashboarding cycle proposed. All these steps have common questions to be observed and some tools or techniques that might help when selecting, designing, and, creating dashboards.

This dashboarding cycle emerged from a gap seen in a non-extensive literature review. The literature review presented empirical and scientific studies in the follow sectors: human resources, supply chain, finance, healthcare and public health, manufacturing, marketing, small and medium enterprises, and, public sector. After literature review, we extracted from selected papers some benefits and challenges to put dashboards into practice. This section also helped to identify most common challenges that BAP

Figure 9b. Example Dashboard B

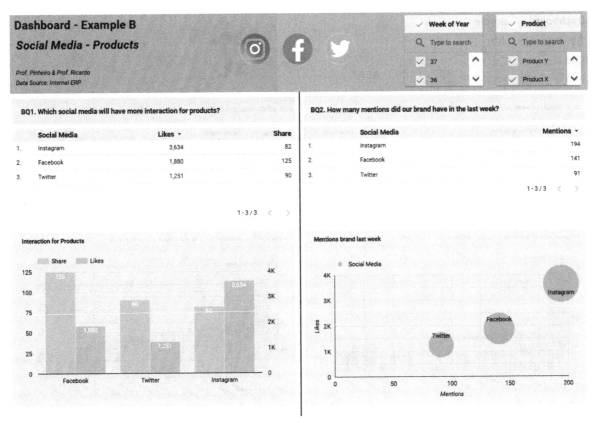

five steps dashboarding cycle should have, as well, the most common expected benefits of people in charge to select, design, build, and, maintain dashboards.

As result of these literature review analysis aforementioned to support managers and academics in the construction of BAPs, we created five steps that are relevant for data analysis, namely: business question, data sources, ETL, data warehouse and data visualization. After presenting the five steps dashboarding cycle, we benchmarked well-known tools that enable creating dashboards for people in charge to buy, design, or, build dashboards easily compare and judge best options.

In the end, we present three examples of dashboards in different sectors. These dashboards were created following the five steps dashboarding cycle, aiming to contribute to a diverse of professionals such as academics, data science teams in both public and private organizations, and, data journalists.

Research Limitations and Future Research Directions

We identified four limitations in this study and explored future research directions for them:

1.   Level of Generalizability of Five Steps Dashboarding Cycle

Figure 9c. Example Dashboard C

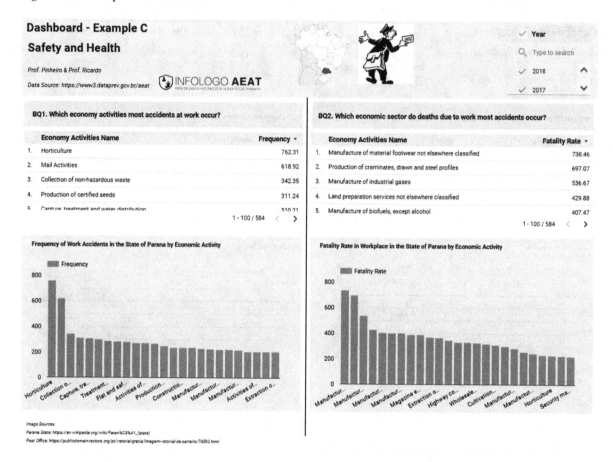

There is no scientific validation of the five steps dashboarding cycle. The level of generalizability and the application of the approach in multiple organizations cases are one of the limitations and recommendations for future research. We suggest researchers, entrepreneurs and executives use this approach in order to explore their limitations and contribute to BAP empirical and scientific development. One of the specific directions might be design principles when creating dashboards, UI and UX studies, the acceptance of this approach and technology in determined sectors, as well, cases studies showing how much efficiency employees could have using BAP five steps dashboarding cycle.

2.   Non-Exhaustive Literature Review of Dashboards

The literature review conducted in this book chapter is non-exhaustive. Researchers could explore this limitation of this research. As an example, a paper conducting an exhaustive literature review in the marketing sector, finding new tasks or details that change the proposed BAP five steps dashboarding cycle. As well, finding other examples and comparing results between different approaches.

3.   Combining Data Science Methods and Techniques (AI and ML)

There are several technological drivers not included in the scope of this work. As an example, artificial intelligence and machine learning techniques were not used in the dashboards examples. As well, potential developments of robotic process automation (RPA) when automatizing some functions in a dashboards might reduce the need of human interaction and accelerate tasks.

4. Low-Code and No-Code Solutions for Dashboards

Besides that, we also highlight the new low-code and no-code applications helping designers and data scientists to create dashboards. This will facilitate when designing and creating dashboards but learning basic skills of some programming languages and databases (SQL and NOSQL) might increase chances of reduce interoperability issues and allowing data science teams to create a diverse of dashboards tailored for specific business needs.

REFERENCES

Bansal, S., Chowell, G., Simonsen, L., Vespignani, A., & Viboud, C. (2016). *Big data for infectious disease surveillance and modeling.* Academic Press.

Bodie, M. T., Cherry, M. A., McCormick, M. L., & Tang, J. (2017). *The law and policy of people analytics.* Academic Press.

Boehmke, B., Hazen, B., Boone, C. A., & Robinson, J. (2020). *A data science and open source software approach to analytics for strategic sourcing.* Academic Press.

Chakraborty, S., Bhatt, V., Chakravorty, T. (2020). *Big-data, iot wearable and mhealth cloud platform integration triads-a logical way to patient-health monitoring.* Academic Press.

Coleman, S. Y. (2016). *Data-mining opportunities for small and medium enterprises with official statistics in the UK.* Academic Press.

Conklin, M. S. (2006). *Beyond low-hanging fruit: Seeking the next generation in floss data mining.* Paper presented at the IFIP International Conference on Open Source Systems. 10.1007/0-387-34226-5_5

Corbu, E. C., Edelhauser, E., & Lupu-Dima, L. (2019). *Analytic Dashboard, a Solution for Increasing Efficiency in Management of the Public Administration.* Academic Press.

Coussement, K., & Van den Poel, D. (2008). *Churn prediction in subscription services: An application of support vector machines while comparing two parameter-selection techniques.* Academic Press.

Davenport, T., & Harris, J. (2017). *Competing on analytics: Updated, with a new introduction: The new science of winning.* Harvard Business Press.

Dincer, H., Hacioglu, U., Tatoglu, E., & Delen, D. (2019). *Developing a hybrid analytics approach to measure the efficiency of deposit banks.* Academic Press.

Fu, D., Ionescu, C. M., Aghezzaf, E.-H., De Keyser, R. (2014). *Decentralized and centralized model predictive control to reduce the bullwhip effect in supply chain management.* Academic Press.

Gartner. (2020). *Magic Quadrant for Data Integration Tools*. Retrieved from https://www.gartner.com/en/documents/3989223/magic-quadrant-for-data-integration-tools

Gartner. (2021). *Analytics and Business Intelligence Platforms Reviews and Ratings*. Retrieved from https://www.gartner.com/reviews/market/analytics-business-intelligence-platforms

Gordon, C. A. K., Burnak, B., Onel, M., & Pistikopoulos, E. (2020). Data-Driven Prescriptive Maintenance. *Failure Prediction Using Ensemble Support Vector Classification for Optimal Process and Maintenance Scheduling, 59*(44), 19607–19622.

Hafaiedh, K., Rhouma, M. B., Chargui, F., Haouas, Y., & Kerkeni, A. (2020). AdRobot: a smart segmentation application for automated & personalized marketing campaigns. *Proceedings of the 2nd International Conference on Digital Tools & Uses Congress*. 10.1145/3423603.3424052

Hopkins, J., & Hawking, P. (2018). *Big Data Analytics and IoT in logistics: a case study*. Academic Press.

Iansiti, M. (2021). *The Value of Data and Its Impact on Competition*. Academic Press.

Janssen, M., Matheus, R., Longo, J., & Weerakkody, V. (2017). Transparency-by-design as a foundation for open government. *Transforming Government: People, Process and Policy, 11*(1).

Janssen, M., Matheus, R., & Zuiderwijk, A. (2015). Big and Open Linked Data (BOLD) to Create Smart Cities and Citizens: Insights from Smart Energy and Mobility Cases. In E. Tambouris, M. Janssen, H. J. Scholl, M. A. Wimmer, K. Tarabanis, M. Gascó, B. Klievink, I. Lindgren, & P. Parycek (Eds.), *Electronic Government* (Vol. 9248, pp. 79–90). Springer International Publishing. doi:10.1007/978-3-319-22479-4_6

Kauffmann, E., Peral, J., Gil, D., Ferrández, A., Sellers, R., & Mora, H. (2019). *Managing marketing decision-making with sentiment analysis: An evaluation of the main product features using text data mining*. Academic Press.

Knapp, J., Zeratsky, J., & Kowitz, B. (2016). *Sprint: How to solve big problems and test new ideas in just five days*. Simon and Schuster.

Ko, E., Taylor, C. R., Sung, H., Lee, J., Wagner, U., Navarro, D. M.-C., & Wang, F. (2012). *Global marketing segmentation usefulness in the sportswear industry*. Academic Press.

Kovach, S., & Ruggiero, W. V. (2011). Online banking fraud detection based on local and global behavior. *Proc. of the Fifth International Conference on Digital Society*.

Kumar, V., Rajan, B., Venkatesan, R., & Lecinski, J. (2019). *Understanding the role of artificial intelligence in personalized engagement marketing*. Academic Press.

Lepenioti, K., Bousdekis, A., Apostolou, D., & Mentzas, G. (2020). *Prescriptive analytics: Literature review and research challenges*. Academic Press.

Liu, X., & Burns, A. (2018). *Designing a marketing analytics course for the digital age*. Academic Press.

Lo, S.-Y. J., Wei, H., Chuang, C., & Yin, C.-Y., & Hsieh10, J. (2017). *Applying data science for social good in nonprofit organization with troubled family risk profiling r dashboard application*. Paper presented at the The R User Conference, useR!, Brussels, Belgium.

Lu, J., Cairns, L., & Smith, L. (2020). *Data science in the business environment: customer analytics case studies in SMEs*. Academic Press.

Lycett, M. (2013). *'Datafication': Making sense of (big) data in a complex world*. Taylor & Francis.

Margherita, A. (2021). *Human resources analytics: A systematization of research topics and directions for future research*. Academic Press.

Martins, N., Martins, S., & Brandão, D. (2022). Design Principles in the Development of Dashboards for Business Management. In *Perspectives on Design II* (pp. 353–365). Springer. doi:10.1007/978-3-030-79879-6_26

Matheus, R., & Janssen, M. (2019). *A systematic literature study to unravel transparency enabled by open government data: The Window Theory. In Public Performance & Management Review*. PPMR.

Matheus, R., Janssen, M., & Janowski, T. (2021). *Design principles for creating digital transparency in government*. Academic Press.

Matheus, R., Janssen, M., & Maheshwari, D. (2018). Data science empowering the public: Data-driven dashboards for transparent and accountable decision-making in smart cities. *Government Information Quarterly*.

Matheus, R., Vaz, J. C., & Ribeiro, M. M. (2014). Open government data and the data usage for improvement of public services in the Rio de Janeiro City. *Proceedings of the 8th International Conference on Theory and Practice of Electronic Governance*. 10.1145/2691195.2691240

Matošević, G., Dobša, J., & Mladenić, D. (2021). *Using Machine Learning for Web Page Classification in Search Engine Optimization. Academic Press*.

Mitra, A., Soman, B., & Singh, G. (2021). *An Interactive Dashboard for Real-Time Analytics and Monitoring of COVID-19 Outbreak in India: A proof of Concept*. Academic Press.

Mosavi, N. S., & Santos, M. F. (2020). *How prescriptive analytics influences decision making in precision medicine*. Academic Press.

Nguyen, L., Stoové, M., Boyle, D., Callander, D., McManus, H., Asselin, J., . . . El-Hayek, C. (2020). *Privacy-preserving record linkage of deidentified records within a public health surveillance system: evaluation study*. Academic Press.

Park, H., Ko, H., Lee, Y.-T. T., Cho, H., & Witherell, P. (2019). *A Framework for Identifying and Prioritizing Data Analytics Opportunities in Additive Manufacturing*. Paper presented at the 2019 IEEE International Conference on Big Data (Big Data). 10.1109/BigData47090.2019.9006489

Prasad, U. D., & Madhavi, S. (2012). *Prediction of churn behavior of bank customers using data mining tools*. Academic Press.

Purwandari, B., Otmen, B., & Kumaralalita, L. (2019). Adoption factors of e-marketplace and instagram for micro, small, and medium enterprises (MSMEs) in Indonesia. *Proceedings of the 2019 2nd International Conference on Data Science and Information Technology*. 10.1145/3352411.3352453

Salathé, M. (2016). *Digital pharmacovigilance and disease surveillance: combining traditional and big-data systems for better public health.* Academic Press.

Soukal, I., & Hedvicakova, M. (2011). *Retail core banking services e-banking client cluster identification.* Academic Press.

Sun, Z. (2020). Business Analytics Intelligence. *An Emerging Frontier for Innovation and Productivity.* Academic Press.

Sun, Z., Strang, K., & Firmin, S. (2017). Business Analytics-Based Enterprise Information Systems. *Journal of Computer Information Systems, 57*(2), 169–178. doi:10.1080/08874417.2016.1183977

Tursunbayeva, A., Di Lauro, S., & Pagliari, C. (2018). *People analytics—A scoping review of conceptual boundaries and value propositions.* Academic Press.

ADDITIONAL READING

Corea, F. (2019). Introduction to Data. In *An Introduction to Data* (pp. 1–5). Springer.

Fayyad, U., & Hamutcu, H. (2020). Toward foundations for data science and analytics: A knowledge framework for professional standards. *Harvard Data Science Review, 2*(2).

France, S. L., & Ghose, S. (2019). Marketing analytics: Methods, practice, implementation, and links to other fields. *Expert Systems with Applications, 119*, 456–475. doi:10.1016/j.eswa.2018.11.002

Gong, Y., & Janssen, M. (2021). Roles and capabilities of enterprise architecture in big data analytics technology adoption and implementation. *Journal of Theoretical and Applied Electronic Commerce Research, 16*(1), 37–51. doi:10.4067/S0718-18762021000100104

Iansiti, M., & Lakhani, K. R. (2014). Digital ubiquity: How connections, sensors, and data are revolutionizing business. *Harvard Business Review, 92*(11), 19.

Kiron, D., Prentice, P. K., & Ferguson, R. B. (2012). Innovating with analytics. *MIT Sloan Management Review, 54*(1), 47.

Kiron, D., & Shockley, R. (2011). Creating business value with analytics. *MIT Sloan Management Review, 53*(1), 57.

Kreuter, F., Ghani, R., & Lane, J. (2019). Change through data: A data analytics training program for government employees. *Harvard Data Science Review, 1*(2), 1–26.

Larson, D., & Chang, V. (2016). A review and future direction of agile, business intelligence, analytics and data science. *International Journal of Information Management, 36*(5), 700–710. doi:10.1016/j.ijinfomgt.2016.04.013

LaValle, S., Lesser, E., Shockley, R., Hopkins, M. S., & Kruschwitz, N. (2011). Big data, analytics and the path from insights to value. *MIT Sloan Management Review, 52*(2), 21–32.

Llave, M. R. (2017). Business intelligence and analytics in small and medium-sized enterprises: A systematic literature review. *Procedia Computer Science, 121*, 194–205. doi:10.1016/j.procs.2017.11.027

Morana, J., & Gonzalez-Feliu, J. (2015). A sustainable urban logistics dashboard from the perspective of a group of operational managers. *Management Research Review, 38*(10), 1068–1085. doi:10.1108/MRR-11-2014-0260

Neumeyer, X. (2021). Implementing data analytics into the entrepreneurship curriculum: a course overview. In *Annals of Entrepreneurship Education and Pedagogy–2021*. Edward Elgar Publishing. doi:10.4337/9781789904468.00044

Ransbotham, S., & Kiron, D. (2017). Analytics as a source of business innovation. *MIT Sloan Management Review, 58*(3).

Sarikaya, A., Correll, M., Bartram, L., Tory, M., & Fisher, D. (2018). What do we talk about when we talk about dashboards? *IEEE Transactions on Visualization and Computer Graphics, 25*(1), 682–692. doi:10.1109/TVCG.2018.2864903 PMID:30136958

Schwendimann, B. A., Rodriguez-Triana, M. J., Vozniuk, A., Prieto, L. P., Boroujeni, M. S., Holzer, A., & Dillenbourg, P. (2016). Perceiving learning at a glance: A systematic literature review of learning dashboard research. *IEEE Transactions on Learning Technologies, 10*(1), 30–41. doi:10.1109/TLT.2016.2599522

Sterne, J. (2017). *Artificial intelligence for marketing: practical applications*. John Wiley & Sons. Available at: http://gildan-bonus-content.s3.amazonaws.com/GIL2450_ArtificialIntelligence/GIL2450_ArtificialIntelligence_BonusPDF.pdf

Sun, Z., & Huo, Y. (2021). The spectrum of big data analytics. *Journal of Computer Information Systems, 61*(2), 154–162. doi:10.1080/08874417.2019.1571456

Tsai, C. W., Lai, C. F., Chao, H. C., & Vasilakos, A. V. (2015). Big data analytics: A survey. *Journal of Big Data, 2*(1), 1–32. doi:10.118640537-015-0030-3 PMID:26191487

Turel, O., & Kapoor, B. (2016). A business analytics maturity perspective on the gap between business schools and presumed industry needs. *Communications of the Association for Information Systems, 39*(1), 6. doi:10.17705/1CAIS.03906

Wamba, S. F., Gunasekaran, A., Akter, S., Ren, S. J. F., Dubey, R., & Childe, S. J. (2017). Big data analytics and firm performance: Effects of dynamic capabilities. *Journal of Business Research, 70*, 356–365. doi:10.1016/j.jbusres.2016.08.009

Williamson, K., & Kizilcec, R. F. (2021, June). Learning Analytics Dashboard Research Has Neglected Diversity, Equity and Inclusion. In *Proceedings of the Eighth ACM Conference on Learning@ Scale* (pp. 287-290). Academic Press.

Yogesh, S., Sharaha, N., & Roopan, S. (2019). Digital marketing and its analysis. *International Journal of Innovative Research in Computer and Communication Engineering, 5*(7), 201957007.

Yun, R., Lasternas, B., Aziz, A., Loftness, V., Scupelli, P., Rowe, A., ... Zhao, J. (2013, April). Toward the design of a dashboard to promote environmentally sustainable behavior among office workers. In *International Conference on Persuasive Technology* (pp. 246-252). Springer. 10.1007/978-3-642-37157-8_29

KEY TERMS AND DEFINITIONS

Dashboard: Dashboards are digital panels containing figures, graphics, tables, maps and other digital features elaborated from the data analytics process. It aims to translate a set of quantitative or qualitative analyses into a view that can be easily interpreted by non-tech positions such as executives, entrepreneurs and people associated to the business.

Data Analytics: Data analytics is the process of analysing and visualizing data to improve decision making. It aims to contribute to organizations in the assertiveness of decisions based on data historical series, ceasing to be common sense.

Business Question: Business questions are driver questions that business teams should elaborate in a collaborative bottom-up approach based on the company's strategic planning. These questions aim to provide a guideline and find proper answers to the organization's department or area indicators.

Data Sources: Data sources are physical or digital repositories where the information associated with the business is found. If in physical format (e.g., paper), this data should be converted to digital format to facilitate use and sharing. Usually, digital data sources can be around an organization such as management systems, strategic systems, SQL or NOSQL databases, and, spreadsheets.

Data Visualization: This is the process of viewing and interpreting dashboards. It occurs through the translation of indicators (KPIS) and diagnosis of the status of a particular object, process, team, department or indicator analysed.

Data Warehouse: Data Warehouse is the central repository for the analytical information to be processed. Usually, this data is uploaded to this central repository and have real-time, near real-time, or sporadic updates.

ETL: ETL is the process of (E) extracting information from its sources, (T) transforming it to a common format, and (L) loading the extracted information into a location/repository.

Open Government Data: Open Government Data (OGD) are public repositories provided by governmental entities. This data is freely available to be collected and used as a source of data. Historically, public sector is one of the biggest source of reliable data.

ENDNOTES

[1] Image sources: https://www.festo.com/medlab/en/cms/10853.htm and https://towardsdatascience.com/using-google-data-studio-55ccf4a828c4?gi=f36ad11f0478

[2] Image sources of Figure 3 https://pxhere.com/pt/photo/1636597, https://canaltech.com.br/business-intelligence/conhecendo-a-arquitetura-de-data-warehouse-19266/, https://www.kindpng.com/imgv/wwmmmx_microsoft-excel-icon-word-icon-png-windows-10/, and, https://panoply.io/data-warehouse-guide/3-ways-to-build-an-etl-process/

Section 2
Technologies for Intelligent Business Analytics

Chapter 5
A Process–Oriented Framework for Regulating Artificial Intelligence Systems

Andrew Stranieri

https://orcid.org/0000-0002-4415-5771

Federation University, Australia

Zhaohao Sun

https://orcid.org/0000-0003-0780-3271

Papua New Guinea University of Technology, Papua New Guinea

ABSTRACT

Frameworks for the regulation of artificial intelligence (AI) systems are emerging; some are based on regulation theories; others are more technologically focused. Regulation of AI systems is likely to emerge in an ad-hoc, unstructured, and uncoordinated fashion that renders high level frameworks philosophically interesting but of limited benefit in practice. In this paper, the task of arriving at a collection of interventions that regulate an AI system is taken to be a process-oriented problem. It presents a process-oriented framework for the design of regulating systems by deliberating groups. It also discusses regulations of AI systems and responsibility, mechanisms and institutions, key elements for regulating AI systems. The proposed approach might facilitate research and development of responsible AI, explainable AI, and ethical AI for an ethical and inclusive digitized society. It also has implications for the development of e-business, e-services, and e-society.

INTRODUCTION

AI has developed rapidly in the past decade, and the AI revolution has been playing an important role in many sectors of the economy (M. U. Scherer, 2016; Zhaohao Sun & Stranieri, 2021). Although ethical artificial intelligence (AI), responsible AI, and explainable AI have been studied in past decades, they have drawn significant attention recently with the dramatic development of AI in driverless cars, cloud

DOI: 10.4018/978-1-7998-9016-4.ch005

computing, e-business, e-services, and e-society (Bossmann, 2016; Bostrom & Yudkowsky, 2018). For instance, high-profile AI applications in driverless cars have raised concerns about who takes responsibility for misdemeanors or errors made by vehicle autopilots trained with machine learning algorithms(Raviteja, 2020). Software developers who design machine learning systems cannot reasonably be held responsible for poor decisions made by systems that have learned from long-term exposure to traffic environments (Dixit et al., 2016).

Concerns regarding the assignment of blame when electronic health record based systems with embedded AI cause harm have led to calls for these systems to explain their reasoning (Payrovnaziri et al., 2020). However, what constitutes a sufficient explanation is difficult to specify, particularly with AI systems that perform actions based on learning conducted over exposure to large datasets (Atkinson et al., 2020; Doshi-Velez et al., 2017). Further, machine learning algorithms can be expected to learn in increasingly sophisticated ways with access to increasingly large datasets (Z Sun et al., 2018) so challenges involved with assigning responsibility for the actions taken by AI systems can be expected to become increasingly complex and pressing.

The capacity for AI systems to explain their reasoning for assignment of responsibility and blame are one aspect of the broader objective of regulating AI systems. Wirtz et al surveys positions on AI regulation based on the assumption that regulation of AI systems involves more than explainable AI and requires the introduction of frameworks that include legal and other constraints (Wirtz et al., 2020). (Thierer et al., 2017) take a laissez fare public policy stance that encourages AI development to be largely unregulated until or unless obvious harm occurs. (M. Scherer, 2015) recommend the creation of an agency commissioned to enforce compliance of legislation specifically focused on regulating AI system.

(Gasser & Almeida, 2017) presents a three layered model for the governance of AI systems that includes 1) a technology layer with algorithm accountability, 2) standards and data governance and 3) a socio-ethical layer that specifies norms and legislation. (Rahwan, 2018) advocated that two groups of stakeholders immediately involved with an AI technology act as a human in the loop system to understand its workings and regulate the design and implementation. The human in the loop system is further complemented by a society in the loop group comprised of stakeholders with competing interests. This group represents society at large and examines trade-offs and unintended consequences. The weBuildAI framework advanced by (Lee et al., 2019) recommends an algorithm design process where individuals representing diverse interests engage in participatory co-design processes with AI systems developers.

Common themes inherent in approaches to regulate AI systems advanced by (Gasser & Almeida, 2017; Rahwan, 2018) and (Lee et al., 2019) include the notion that the exercise is very difficult and that participants who represent society should be closely involved in the regulation. But, what stakeholders or participants should actually do, and how they should reach decisions aimed at regulating an AI system, is mainly unspecified by framework authors. We contend that participating in regulation discussions are particularly difficult because the problem of regulating an AI system conforms to the ten criteria of "wicked problems"(Rittel & Webber, 1974). The position advanced in this chapter is that a stakeholder group can benefit from a clearly defined process to guide their reasoning. A process that extends the the one described by (Stranieri & Sun, 2021) is presented here.

A process for scaffolding the design of a regulatory system to govern an AI technology is intended to be used by an individual or group charged with defining interventions that, in their totality will regulate the AI system. Each step in the process can be regarded as a problem that satisfies the conditions for a wicked problem so regulatory solutions can be expected to be found and refined over time by deliberating groups rather than by advancing pre-specified frameworks or algorithms. Based on the above discussion, the research issues are below:

- Why is the regulation of AI systems important?
- How to regulate an AI system?
- What are the key elements of a framework that can be used to assess the extent to which an AI system may have erred?

The remainder of this chapter is organized as follows: Section 2 provides the background and brief literature review. Section 3 provides the research approach used for this research. Section 4 looks at regulating AI and AI systems based on the principle of big data-driven small data analysis. Section 5 examines regulations of AI systems and responsibility. Section 6 proposes a process-oriented approach to regulating AI systems. Section 7 examines key elements for regulating AI Systems. The final sections discuss the future research directions and end this paper with some concluding remarks and future work.

BACKGROUND

This section provides a background on AI agents, AI systems, machine learning for our research of regulating AI systems.

An AI system is a software system that realizes and augment some human intelligence based on the principle and techniques of AI. AI systems, for example, include expert systems, knowledge base systems, intelligent information systems, multiagent systems, and driverless car systems (C. Russell et al., 2019; Weber, 2020a). An AI agent is an autonomous and adaptive entity that can perceive its environments using a sensor and act upon its environments through its actuators (Zhaohao Sun et al., 2005)(Sun & Finnie, 2004; 2010; 2013, p. 70) (Weber, 2020). AI agents are the software counterpart of human agents existing in society and businesses. Typical tasks performed by AI agents could include searching, collecting, filtering, and processing data, scheduling operations, analyzing data, and visualizing data, information, and knowledge. For example, an intelligent analytics agent can organize big data, analyze big data and mine big data and discover knowledge and insights from big data and visualize the discovered knowledge and insights for decision making (Sun & Stranieri, 2021).

RESEARCH APPROACH

The research approach used in this research mainly include process-oriented paradigm, framework-oriented paradigm, big data driven small data analysis, and structured method. The process-oriented paradigm originated from engineering science and business management. For example, the philosophy of process-oriented programming has deep roots in a process-oriented paradigm(Pressman & Maxim, 2014). The process-oriented paradigm usually uses diagrams to represent processes or actions concerning a real-world problem. These diagrams capture, model, and disseminate the data, information, and knowledge of a system and its environment. Whenever using a process-oriented paradigm to examine a real-world problem, we think: can the problem be treated as a process? The framework-oriented paradigm usually uses a framework for a system as a trituple which can be represented as FS = (C, I, S), where according to (Zhaohao Sun, 2017): C is the parts or components that support the development of the system. I is a set of beliefs, ideas, concepts, and rules that are used as the basis for developing systems. S is the structure of the system.

Big data-driven small data analysis consists of 1). Big data reduction; 2). Big data derived small data collection, and 3). Big data derived small data analysis(Z Sun & Huo, 2021). Big data-driven small data as a research approach is a basis for current literature review, related work, and discussion (Sun & Huo, 2021). We will use big data-driven small data analysis as a research approach to look at regulating AI systems in Section 4.

In addition, the structured method of software engineering is also used to explore how to regulate AI systems(Pressman & Maxim, 2014). Examples throughout the paper are used in a structured way to strengthen the proposed ideas in the process-oriented framework. An application example of AI-based automobile control is illustrated to guide the readers to understand the whole process.

REGULATING ARTIFICIAL INTELLIGENCE: THE STATE OF THE ART

Regulating AI systems have drawn increasing attention in academia, industries, and governments as we are in the age of AI where we are relying on AI systems and tools to perform a variety of tasks requiring intelligence and wisdom(Ellul et al., 2021; Erdélyi & Goldsmith, 2018; M. U. Scherer, 2016). The European Parliament had proposed for establishing a European Agency for robotics and AI to address technical, ethical, and regulatory issues(Delvaux, 2016). The establishment of an international AI regulatory agency has been also proposed to create a unified framework for the regulation of AI technologies and inform the development of AI policies around the world, because AI and AI systems are ubiquitous in modern societies (Erdélyi & Goldsmith, 2018).

Various proposals have been made in scholarship for defining regulatory agency and develop legal systems including liability systems (also see the discussion late in this section). As described above, (M. U. Scherer, 2016) discusses regulating AI systems in terms of risks, challenges, competencies, and strategies. He proposes an indirect form of AI regulation based on differential tort liability and an Artificial Intelligence Development Act (AIDA) as a legislation. AIDA consists of tasks of certifying the safety of AI systems through a new agency, which has two components: policymaking and certification. The agency would also promulgate rules governing licensing and warning notice requirements for certified AI systems. The AIDA would also create a court system under which the AI systems' related actors would be subject to limited tort liability and even several liability. Based on the research of (M. U. Scherer, 2016), regulating AI systems can be analyzed from a system viewpoint, that is, public risks from problematic AI systems are the system input. Regulating AI systems is the system process. Safe AI systems are the system output.

(Ellul et al., 2021) present a national AI technology assurance legal and regulatory framework that has been implemented by Malta's national authority empowered through legislation. Similar to (M. U. Scherer, 2016), Ellul et al claim that certifications from the agencies and system auditors are necessary for stakeholders in AI systems including designers, manufacturers, and sellers(Ellul et al., 2021). In contrast, to the work of(M. U. Scherer, 2016), Ellul et al define qualities and criteria that qualify software as an AI system as: a) the ability to use knowledge acquired in a flexible manner in order to perform specific tasks and/or reach specific goals; b) evolution, adaptation, and/or production of results based on interpreting and processing data; c) systems logic based on the process of knowledge acquisition,

Figure 1. Questions & answers for regulating AI systems

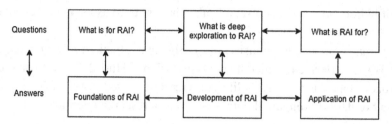

learning, reasoning, problem-solving, and/or planning; d) prediction forecast and/or approximation of results for inputs that were not previously encountered(Ellul et al., 2021). This implies that AI systems are knowledge-based intelligent systems, which is similar to the treatment of AI by (S. Russell & Norvig, 2010), although data-based (or machine learning-based) intelligent systems are also very popular in recent years(Laudon & Laudon, 2020; Weber, 2020b).

In what follows, we use the principle of "big data-driven small data analysis" (Zhaohao Sun & Stranieri, 2021) to provide a more systematic literature review on regulating AI and AI systems. Google Scholar (https://scholar.google.com/) search for "regulating artificial intelligence" (RAI hereafter) found 1,170 results (10 September 2021). This implies that regulating artificial intelligence has drawn significant attention in academia. Then Google scholar (https://scholar.google.com/) search for "regulating artificial intelligence" based on the time limitation "since 2017" found 1090 results (10 September 2021). This implies that 1). Only 80 research results have been published before 2017. 2). Regulating artificial intelligence has drawn significant attention in academia in recent years. After having briefly analyzed the first 100 results ranked by Google Scholar, we find that they provide a diverse collection of studies. For example, "regulating artificial intelligence" has not been a keyword or similar in many found results. Then we search Semantic Scholar for "regulating artificial intelligence" and find 53 results which basically covered most of the first 100 found results of Google Scholar mentioned above. Therefore, we classify each title of the found 53 document results into three categories based on

1. What is for RAI?
2. What is a deep exploration of RAI?
3. What is RAI for?

Taking into account the context related to regulating artificial intelligence. It should be noted that analyzing the context related to regulating artificial intelligence is a part of big data-driven small data analysis(Z Sun & Huo, 2021). The answer to the first question is the theoretical and technological foundations for developing RAI, as illustrated in Figure 1. The answer to the second question is the theoretical and technological development of RAI. The answer to the third question is the applications of RAI. From a viewpoint of research methodology, such a classification is significant for developing ethical AI in general, and RAI in particular.

The 53 research publications are summarized as follows, based on the three categories above: 11 out of 53 research publications address what is RAI. These publications cover robot rules for regulating AI, evidence-based policymaking, a libertarian approach to regulating AI to restrain cartelization, the possibility of and need for regulating AI, European Commission proposal to regulate AI systems(Delvaux,

2016), a legal perspective to stifling AI, extending the current legal framework to address issues with autonomous systems, recommendation to cautiously regulating AI to prevent AI discrimination, human involvement is vital to address the limits of algorithmic justice, the widespread uncertainty about how to regulate AI agents. No nation alone can regulate AI, how the law regulates AI. This implies that only a few strong theoretical and technological enablers for RAI. More theoretical and technological foundations are required for RAI.

19 out of 53 research publications address what deep exploration is. These research publications cover dynamics, a global solution(Erdélyi & Goldsmith, 2018), risks and strategies(M. U. Scherer, 2016), a technology regulator's perspective(Ellul et al., 2021). An ethical approach, the dilemma, a framework for governance, extending the scope of the FDA, the challenges, bestowing corporate personhood to AI systems, control and command the operations of autonomous cars, work incrementally within the existing legal and regulatory schemes, a two-step process, self-regulating. This analysis implies that the process-oriented paradigm for RAI is of significance for developing RAI and ethical AI as well as responsible AI.

10 out of 53 research publications address the third question. These research publications cover the following applications of RAI: Finance, air transport, risk management, governance, ownership of copyright, cyber arms race, and cybersecurity. This implies that 1). the applications of IBA are still very isolated based on the quality research publications. 2. Regulating AI systems is still an emerging area for academia, this confirms and validates what we stated in the early part of the research.

The 53 research publications found by Semantic Scholar also demonstrate that

1. The number of publications found by Semantic Scholar has been dramatically increased from 2016 to 2020 (1/2016, 6/2017, 9/2018, 12/2019, 12/2020, accessed on September 13, 2021). Only five articles were published before 2017. The earliest publication is Fan X et al (2003) "Adaptive IP QoS architecture and algorithms", ICCNMC Proceedings. However, the context analysis shows that it cannot be recognized as the first publication on RAI, because it mentioned that "in an adaptive edge control (QAAC) architecture, the active probe would cooperate with passive regulate and artificial intelligence would control the proportion of probe packets". In other words, it did not look at RAI but proposed a sort of self-organizing IP QoS architecture.
2. 6 out of 53 research publications have not related to RAI. The remainder is the repeated occurrences.

The above discussion demonstrates that

1. Regulating AI systems has drawn increasing attention in academia since 2017. It is still an emerging area for academia.
2. How to regulate AI and AI systems is still a big issue not only for academia but also for industries and governments because of the ubiquity of AI and AI systems in the digital age.
3. The process-oriented paradigm for RAI is a novel attempt for developing RAI and ethical AI as well as responsible AI, which will be examined in the next section of this chapter.

The above discussion also allows us to define regulating AI systems as a process for developing policies, ethics, legal agencies, certifications, licenses, and training programs to make AI systems safe, accountable, reliable, and responsible complying with the global responsibility for the human being's sustainable development in the digital society(Delvaux, 2016; Erdélyi & Goldsmith, 2018; M. U. Scherer, 2016).

The process oriented framework that guides deliberations about the regulation of AI systems is presented next.

A PROCESS-ORIENTED FRAMEWORK FOR REGULATING AI SYSTEMS

A philosophical basis for the process oriented framework presented here draws on the moral responsibility philosophy of (Strawson, 1962). He side steps debates about the features that define the responsibility that an agent possesses and instead declares that moral responsibility is better described as a social construct than as attributes an agent possesses. This renders questions about whether an agent intended to perform an action or not as largely irrelevant. Moral philosophers categorized as pessimists, claimed actions are largely pre-determined and not subject to free will so responsibility for the actions is reduced. The opposing view, held by philosophers Strawson called optimists, refutes determinism, and therefore attributes responsibility for bad actions to the perpetrator who can therefore be rightly blamed and punished. However, Strawson highlights that the distinction between optimists and pessimists is of interest to few. In practice, decision-makers involved in determining responsibility and blame take into account the full context of the situation including the attitudes and reactions of victims and beneficiaries; "of such things as resentment, forgiveness, love, and hurt feelings" (Strawson p5)

Once the full context is considered, the decision-maker may determine that the agent caused the hurt unintentionally, or that it is inappropriate to draw that conclusion, as it is, for example, with children. Alternatively, the decision maker takes attitudes and reactions into account and determines if the agent is culpable. In both cases, the decision-maker's reasoning occurs in a social context making the exercise a social construction. This allows Strawson to take the stance that the assignment of moral culpability requires institutions sanctioned by society to endorse and support the decisionmaker's determination. The specification of a process by which the full context, attitudes and reactions can be taken into account in a systematic way is regarded here as essential to the endeavor.

A process-oriented framework for regulating AI systems consists of the following steps elaborated upon below.

1. Defining the structural and functional features of the AI system to be regulated,
2. Ranking the measurable ramifications of the AI System's regulation.
3. Selecting the structural properties and functional attributes to be the object of AI System's regulation, and
4. Identifying stakeholders and mechanisms that will be involved in the regulation of AI systems

This framework is illustrated in Figure 2.

A hypothetical AI-based automobile control technology will be referenced to exemplify each step. This consists of a reinforcement learning (RL) method that is boot-strapped by domain knowledge from a ripple down rule knowledge-based system following (Bignold et al., 2021). Ripple down rules described by (Compton & Kang, 2021) are initially elicited from road safety experts and are continuously refined as new contexts are encountered. Deep learning algorithms analyze images from cameras mounted on the automobile and feed information about objects near the vehicle into a reinforcement learning algorithm that also receives input from the vehicle engine, fuel, suspension, and other systems. The RL system, bootstrapped with the ripple down rules, initially learns a policy to apply to control the automobile at

Figure 2. The process-oriented framework for regulating AI systems

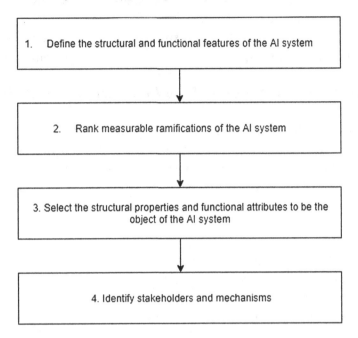

any point of time from many thousands of simulated scenarios. Once installed in the automobile, the RL system continues to refine its policy as action decisions are made and assessed as correct and appropriate or not, based on consequent state changes. Our hypothetical RL automobile control technology has been driving for five years without incident. On one occasion, the brakes failed and the RL system diverted the vehicle into a brick wall to slow the vehicle. However, the brick wall was not stable and collapsed seriously injuring a pedestrian on the other side.

A task force has been established to design institutions, systems, and legislation to regulate the RL control system following the four steps outlined above.

Define the Structural and Functional Features of the AI System to Be Regulated

The explicit definition of the system to be regulated facilitates subsequent phases that will identify appropriate forms for the AI system's regulation. Most AI systems can be described by their structure and function (Reich, 1995). The hypothetical automobile's structural properties include its color and shape whereas its functional attributes include speed, noise, or emissions. During this phase, there is no attempt to limit the properties or attributes to be regulated. The aim is solely to identify all structural and functional attributes of the AI system.

The artifact that is created in this phase names the AI system to be regulated and specifies all structural and functional properties. The horse carriage lobby groups in the 1880's no doubt identified the automobile developed by Benz as an object that had structural properties including size and color and functional attributes such as speed and noise. The structural properties of our hypothetical AI-based driverless control system include S1) the hardware, S2) the RL policy forming algorithm, S3) the deep learning image processing, S4) the ripple down rule bootstrapping algorithm. Functional properties include measures that describe the learning such as F1) extensive and varied learning experiences, and

103

others that reflect driverless performance such as F2) the number of collisions, F3) harm caused to others F4) unanticipated post-action state.

Once the AI system is named and its attributes explicated, the group can move to the next phase, to ascertain and rank the measurable consequences that the AI system's regulation can be expected to realize.

Rank the Measurable Ramifications of the AI System's Regulation

The ramification of a successful regulation refers to a hypothesized future world. Ramifications that are likely to occur if the Benz automobile was regulated can conceivably be articulated in politically neutral terms such as 1) Slowing down the development of the automobile, 2) Reduction in automobile collisions, 3) Protection of the carriage industry and many more.

The World Economic Forum listed the following top nine ethical issues in artificial intelligence (Bossmann, 2016).

1. Unemployment. What happens after the end of jobs?
2. Inequality. How do we distribute the wealth created by AI machines?
3. Humanity. How do machines affect our behavior and interaction?
4. Artificial stupidity. How can we guard AI against mistakes? AI can make mistakes.
5. Racist robots. How do we eliminate AI bias?
6. Security. How do we keep AI safe from adversaries?
7. Evil genies. How do we protect AI against unintended consequences?
8. Singularity. How do we stay in control of a complex intelligent system?
9. Robot rights. How do we define the humane treatment of AI?

A deliberating group charged with designing a regulatory framework for the hypothetical automobile systems may identify the following ramifications as future-world descriptors:

1. A world where ethical AI automobile systems are constantly developed.
2. A world where Australian AI automobile systems compete favorably with those from other countries.
3. A world where the public has great confidence in AI automobile systems and their regulation.
4. A world where humans are not harmed by AI automobile systems.
5. A world without automobile collisions.
6. A world where the automobile drivers have been transitioned into meaningful other occupations.

The exercise of making the ramifications explicit entices a holistic view of outcomes that can be expected if the regulation of AI systems succeeds.

A deliberating group needs to rank the ramifications, ideally but not necessarily, using criteria of public and social benefit. Ranking these in terms of importance leads to the next phase that brings together the structural and functional properties with the ramifications.

A deliberating group may arrive at ranked ramifications for the hypothetical AI driverless car control system from most to least important $4 > 5 > 1 > 6 > 3 > 2$.

Table 1. Mapping between structure/function and ramifications

Step 1 Property	Ramification 4: Humans Not Harmed	Ramification 5: No Collisions
S1) the hardware,		
S2) the RL policy forming algorithm,	Regulation A	
S3) the Deep learning image processing,		
S4) the Ripple down rule bootstrapping algorithm.		
F1) extensive and varied learning experiences		Regulation B
F2) the number of collisions	Regulation C	
F3) harm caused to others	Regulation D	
F4) unanticipated post-action state.		Regulation E

Select the Attributes to Be the Object of AI System's Regulation

This phase requires juxtaposing each property/attribute in the defining list from step 1 to each ramification. The horse carriage manufacturers elected to focus their efforts to regulate the speed of Benz's automobile rather than trying to regulate its color presumably because they thought the objective of thwarting a competing technology would be achieved more effectively by constraining its speed than its color. A group deliberating on how to regulate our hypothetical automobile may decide the achievement of the two ramifications deemed most important in the previous step: 4). A world where humans are not harmed by AI automobile systems; 5). A world without automobile collisions.

The deliberating group must now select which of the system's structures and functions will be attempted to be regulated to achieve the ramifications prioritized. Table 1 illustrates that the group has decided to regulate the RL policy forming algorithm, the number of collisions, and the harm caused to others in order to achieve ramification 4, a world where humans are not harmed. A world without collisions is best considered to be achieved by regulating the learning experiences the automobile is exposed to.

The mapping between structure/function and ramifications is considered to be a wicked problem in that there is no theoretical basis to justify the mapping. The consensus amongst a deliberating group free of political influence, self-interest, or bias, is expected to result in effective regulation strategies in subsequent steps, even if strategies are not optimal.

Identify Stakeholders That Will Be Involved in the Regulation of AI Systems

The performance of AI systems' regulation requires mechanisms and social institutions. Possible mechanisms and institutions need to be accessed by the deliberating group and matched to each object of regulation identified in the previous phase. Lessig identified four types of constraints that regulate social behaviors: the law, market forces, social norms, and natural phenomena (Lessig, 2009). Automobile speed may be regulated using legal constraints with laws that set maximum speed. Economic constraints that restrict speed include the additional fuel consumed at high speed. Motor vehicle speed may also be regulated with the installation of speed humps that represents a natural barrier to speed.

Different stakeholders are involved in each type of constraint. Stakeholders generally involved in legal constraints include legislative bodies to enact laws, enforcement agencies to police the laws, and judicial

Table 2. Element, stakeholders and changes required

Key Elements	Stakeholders Required	Changes Required
The AI System has legal agency	A **regulatory authority** to determine if an AI System conforms to the AI System definition in the legal agency legislation	Legislative change to enable AI Systems to assume legal agency
The AI System has a human sponsor for certification with regulatory authorities	**A regulatory authority** **A human sponsor**	Legislative change to empower the regulatory authority
The AI System's certification includes conformance to standards for adequate explanations	A **standards body** to define coherent explanations	Development of coherence and adequacy standards
Systematically collect collision data	A **Data collection** agency to ensure all vehicle collision data is aggregated and not tampered with	Assign to existing government road traffic authorities
A hierarchy of courts exercising stare decisis are defined	Appoint a first instance, and two appeal **Courts**	Assign to existing Courts

systems to make determinations. In addition, marketing campaigns to raise awareness of the laws, post-implementation reviews, and strategies to manage public reaction may contribute to setting social norms.

The deliberating group for the automobile hypothetical decides to adopt an approach advanced by (Stranieri & Sun, 2021) that assumes that AI Systems can be assigned agency over their actions akin to any legal entity. Key elements of Regulation systems A, C, D, and E the deliberating group has arrived at are described in Table 2 and elaborated on below.

A key element involves defining the AI agent as an actor with the complete agency over its actions. Defining an AI agent as an actor with agency entails a registration and approval process in a manner analogous to that currently imposed on medical devices by certifying authorities such as the Federal Drugs Administration (FDA)(M. U. Scherer, 2016). Deployment options are limited by regulation unless the device is certified. For instance, hospitals in most jurisdictions are bound to use only certified devices. Similarly, AI agents can be certified, and legal regulations passed that prohibit the deployment of uncertified agents on public roads.

As illustrated in Table 2, certification involves licensing a sponsor who is a human agent responsible for maintaining the automobile's RL control system registration and enacting any sanctions imposed on the agent(M. U. Scherer, 2016). The role of an AI agent sponsor is defined as a legal entity (individual or organization) that is associated with the AI agent. The sponsor is required to adhere to sanctions applied to the AI agent. The most extreme sanction is the de-registration of the AI agent, but other forms of sanctions may include re-training or other modifications.

A legal system that includes a hierarchy of courts is constituted to hear cases of AI agency misdemeanor(M. U. Scherer, 2016). The AI agent is the actor that has agency over their actions and is on trial over the actions. A first instance court, composed of a judicial decision-maker must ascertain the facts, by hearing an explanation from the AI agent and other human or non-human agents. The decision-maker must then deliberate and ultimately reach a judgment following principles of stare decisis set out in previous cases. The sponsor is required to ensure the sanctions ordered in the judgment are carried out. Penalties include de-registration of the agent and fines. The sponsor has the capacity to appeal the decision to a higher court.

Technological mechanisms that enable an AI agent to explain its actions as appropriate are required to be built into an AI agent that seeks to be certified. Mechanisms to achieve regulation using social constraints include standards for explainable AI performance (Turek, 2020). Standards that operate as guides for the adequacy of an explanation may include the degree of coherence as assessed by an explanation review committee. An institution such as a Road Traffic Authority (RTA) that is perhaps independent of manufacturers is charged with keeping records of every collision that involves an AI driverless car.

This list of key elements and stakeholders depicted in Table 2 is not exhaustive and is meant only to be illustrative of a solution to the "wicked problem" of developing a regulatory system for the hypothetical automobile. Ideally, the mechanisms and institutions available to a deliberating group are so comprehensive that the group can draw from a wide selection to suit the regulation and context.

These elements ensure that an AI agent's actions are regulated by drawing on each of the four types of constraints including technological constraints, social constraints, and economic constraints (Lessig, 2009). Technological constraints apply because the AI agent is required to exhibit technological sophistication in its capacity to draw inferences and generate explanations for its actions in order to pass regulation requirements and acquire the certification. Social constraints are incorporated into the framework because decisions by regulators or courts will need to be publicly accessible and any that depart from social norms will attract complaints and influence the decision-makers. Economic constraints are enabled with the introduction of a sponsor role. The AI agent sponsor invests in an AI agent initially by funding its registration. The sponsor has a vested interest in maintaining the agent's viability. Any sanctions imposed on the agent by courts must be carried out by the sponsor and impact economically on the sponsor.

A scenario can be imagined where the changes outlined in Table 2 have been realized:

Many human sponsors have assumed the role of sponsoring AI systems that have been assigned agency. One of the AI systems collides with a wall that falls and harms a human out of sight, on the other side of the wall. The AI control system, like a culpable driver, is taken to the first instance court over its actions. A first instance court, composed of a judicial decision-maker must ascertain the facts, by hearing an explanation from the AI agent and other human or non-human agents. The decision-maker hears the explanation from the agent that the action of colliding with the wall was taken because there was no information available that a human was on another side. The prosecution argues that the agent should have inferred that a human might be on the other side so is clearly culpable. The first instance decision make deliberates and ultimately reaches a judgment following principles of stare decisis set out in previous cases and orders the AI system be retrained so that it can make inferences about the environment beyond that which is immediately sensed. A human sponsor who has registered the AI system with regulatory authorities appeals to this decision in order to avoid huge costs associated with re-training. The case is referred to the first appeal Court.

FUTURE RESEARCH DIRECTIONS

With the dramatic and widespread applications of AI and AI systems in every corner of our work, life, and society, the ethics of artificial intelligence has drawn increasing attention in academia, industries, and governments (Bossmann, 2016; Bostrom & Yudkowsky, 2018). Regulating AI systems is related to responsible AI and ethical AI for an ethical and inclusive digitized society. The basis for responsible

Figure 3. The relationships between regulating AI systems, responsible AI, ethical AI, and explainable AI.

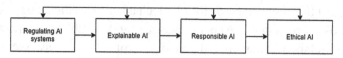

and ethical AI is explainable AI (Turek, 2020). Explainable AI is a part of regulating AI systems based on emerging regulations and laws of AI society. Therefore, the relationships between regulating AI systems, responsible AI, ethic AI, and explainable AI can be represented and illustrated as in Figure 3.

Regulating AI systems aims to make AI systems explainable, responsible, safe, reliable, and finally ethical in order to meet the interest and need of humans, society, and nations as a common community in an ethical and inclusive digitized society. Therefore, regulating AI and AI systems have significant implications for developing explainable, responsible, ethical, and safe AI for an ethical and inclusive digitized society from a technical and social fairness viewpoint(M. U. Scherer, 2016). The proposed framework for regulating AI systems has significant implications for developing responsible and ethical e-Business, e-Services, and e-Society, all these are underpinned by big data and intelligent big data analytics (Richardson et al., 2021; Zhaohao Sun, 2018).

A limitation of this research is that the process-oriented framework for the regulation of AI systems is specified only with high-level steps. One future research direction is to develop unified process diagrams with pragmatic instructions to scaffold further the deliberations of a group seeking to design regulation systems. Another future research direction is to delve into the interrelationships between regulation of AI systems, responsible AI, ethical AI, and their implications for e-Business, e-Services, and e-Society.

CONCLUSION

Regulating AI and AI systems have drawn increasing attention in academia industries and governments since 2017. IT has gained popularity for at least four reasons. First, with over six decades' development, AI can be recognized as intelligent science and technology; AI-based systems, products, and services have won the market as intelligent systems, smart products, and services. Second, the ubiquity of AI and AI systems in our work, lives, and societies challenges us and makes us face ever-increasing risks such as loss of jobs, exposure of privacy, even threats to lives because of autonomous and driverless vehicles (e.g. cars). More and more risks to the public are on the way to us and our society. Third, the responsibility and ethics of AI and AI systems become vulnerable in the front of ever-increasing profits and tempting market investing AI and AI products and services. Four, some concerned that AI and AI systems will dominate the work and lives of our society in the near future.

There are at least three main contributions of this research to regulating AI and AI systems: First, it discussed regulations of AI systems and responsibility, mechanisms and institutions, key elements for regulating AI systems and their relationships. This is the foundation for regulating AI and AI systems. Second, it provides the state of the art regulating AI based on the principle of "big data-driven small data analysis and reveals that how to regulate AI and AI systems is still a big issue not only for academia but also for industries and governments. Third, it presents a process-oriented framework for RAI, which is a novel attempt for developing RAI and ethical AI as well as responsible AI. The proposed approach in this chapter might facilitate research and development of responsible AI, explainable AI, ethical AI, and regulating AI for an ethical and inclusive digitized society. It has also implications for the development of e-Business, e-Services, and e-Society.

In future work, we will examine the relationship between regulation of AI systems, responsible AI, and ethical AI and their implications for e-Business, e-Services, and e-Society. We will also delve into and improve the process-oriented framework for the regulation of AI systems using a multidisciplinary approach.

REFERENCES

Atkinson, K., Bench-Capon, T., & Bollegala, D. (2020). Explanation in AI and law: Past, present and future. *Artificial Intelligence*, *289*, 103387. Advance online publication. doi:10.1016/j.artint.2020.103387

Bignold, A., Cruz, F., Dazeley, R., Vamplew, P., & Foale, C. (2021). *Persistent Rule-based Interactive Reinforcement Learning*. arXiv preprint arXiv:2102.02441.

Bossmann, J. (2016). Top 9 ethical issues in artificial intelligence. *World Economic Forum*. Retrieved from https://www.weforum.org/agenda/2016/10/top-10-ethical-issues-in-artificial-intelligence/

Bostrom, N., & Yudkowsky, E. (2018). The Ethics of Artificial Intelligence. In *Cambridge Handbook of Artificial Intelligence*. Cambridge University Press. doi:10.1201/9781351251389-4

Compton, P., & Kang, B. H. (2021). *Ripple-down Rules: The Alternative to Machine Learning*. CRC Press. doi:10.1201/9781003126157

Delvaux, M. (2016). *Motion for a European Parliament resolution: with recommendation to the commission on civil law rules on robotics*. Technical Report (2015/2103 (INL)).

Dixit, V. V., Chand, S., & Nair, D. J. (2016). Autonomous vehicles: Disengagements, accidents and reaction times. *PLoS One*, *11*(12), e0168054. doi:10.1371/journal.pone.0168054 PMID:27997566

Doshi-Velez, F., Kortz, M., Budish, R., Bavitz, C., Gershman, S., O'Brien, D., . . . Wood, A. (2017). *Accountability of AI under the law: The role of explanation*. arXiv preprint arXiv.01134.

Ellul, J., Pace, G., & McCarthy, S. (2021). *Regulating Artificial Intelligence: A Technology Regulator's Perspective*. Paper presented at the ICAIL'21, ICAIL '21: Proceedings of the Eighteenth International Conference on Artificial Intelligence and LawJune 21–25, 2021, São Paulo, Brazil. 10.1145/3462757.3466093

Erdélyi, O. J., & Goldsmith, J. (2018). Regulating artificial intelligence: Proposal for a global solution. *Proceedings of the 2018 AAAI/ACM Conference on AI, Ethics, and Society*. 10.1145/3278721.3278731

Gasser, U., & Almeida, V. A. (2017). A layered model for AI governance. *IEEE Internet Computing*, *21*(6), 58–62. doi:10.1109/MIC.2017.4180835

Laudon, K. G., & Laudon, K. C. (2020). *Management Information Systems: Managing the Digital Firm* (16th ed.). Pearson.

Lee, M. K., Kusbit, D., Kahng, A., Kim, J. T., Yuan, X., Chan, A., ... Psomas, A. (2019). WeBuildAI: Participatory framework for algorithmic governance. *Proceedings of the ACM on Human-Computer Interaction, 3*(CSCW), 1-35.

Lessig, L. (2009). *Code: And other laws of cyberspace*: ReadHowYouWant.com.

Payrovnaziri, S. N., Chen, Z., Rengifo-Moreno, P., Miller, T., Bian, J., Chen, J. H., Liu, X., & He, Z. (2020). Explainable artificial intelligence models using real-world electronic health record data: A systematic scoping review. *Journal of the American Medical Informatics Association: JAMIA, 27*(7), 1173–1185. doi:10.1093/jamia/ocaa053 PMID:32417928

Pressman, R., & Maxim, B. (2014). *Software Engineering: A Practitioner's Approach* (8th ed.). McGraw-Hill Education.

Rahwan, I. (2018). Society-in-the-loop: Programming the algorithmic social contract. *Ethics and Information Technology, 20*(1), 5–14. doi:10.100710676-017-9430-8

Raviteja, T. (2020). An introduction of autonomous vehicles and a brief survey. *Journal of Critical Reviews, 7*(13), 196–202.

Reich, Y. (1995). Measuring the value of knowledge. *International Journal of Human-Computer Studies, 42*(1), 3–30. doi:10.1006/ijhc.1995.1002

Richardson, J., Schlegel, K., Sallam, R., Kronz, A., & Sun, J. (2021). *Magic Quadrant for Analytics and Business Intelligence Platforms.* Gartner. Retrieved from https://www.gartner.com/doc/reprints?id=1-254T1IQX&ct=210202&st=sb

Rittel, H. W., & Webber, M. M. (1974). Wicked problems. *Man-made Futures, 26*(1), 272–280.

Russell, C., Ward, A. C., Vezza, V., Hoskisson, P., Alcorn, D., Steenson, D. P., & Corrigan, D. K. (2019). Development of a needle shaped microelectrode for electrochemical detection of the sepsis biomarker interleukin-6 (IL-6) in real time. *Biosensors & Bioelectronics, 126*, 806–814. doi:10.1016/j.bios.2018.11.053 PMID:30602262

Russell, S., & Norvig, P. (2010). *Artificial Intelligence: A Modern Approach* (3rd ed.). Prentice Hall.

Scherer, M. (2015). Regulating artificial intelligence systems: Risks, challenges, competencies, and strategies. *Harv. JL & Tech., 29*, 353. doi:10.2139srn.2609777

Scherer, M. U. (2016). Regulating Artificial Intelligence Systems: Risks, Challenges, Competencies, and Strategies. *Harvard Journal of Law & Technology, 29*(2), 354–400.

Stranieri, A., & Sun, Z. (2021). Only Can AI Understand Me?: Big Data Analytics, Decision Making, and Reasoning. In S. Zhaohao (Ed.), *Intelligent Analytics With Advanced Multi-Industry Applications* (pp. 46–66). IGI Global. doi:10.4018/978-1-7998-4963-6.ch003

Strawson, P. F. (1962). Freedom and Resentment in Free Will. Oxford UP.

Sun, Z. (2017). A framework for developing management intelligent systems. In Decision Management: Concepts, Methodologies, Tools, and Applications (pp. 503-521): IGI Global. doi:10.4018/978-1-5225-1837-2.ch024

Sun, Z. (2018). 10 Bigs: Big Data and Its Ten Big Characteristics. *PNG UoT BAIS*, *3*(1), 1–10.

Sun, Z., Finnie, G., & Weber, K. (2005). Abductive case-based reasoning. *International Journal of Intelligent Systems*, *20*(9), 957–983. doi:10.1002/int.20101

Sun, Z., & Huo, Y. (2021). The spectrum of big data analytics. *Journal of Computer Information Systems*, *61*(2), 154–162. doi:10.1080/08874417.2019.1571456

Sun, Z., Strang, K., & Li, R. (2018). Big data with ten big characteristics. *Proceedings of 2018 The 2nd Intl Conf. on Big Data Research (ICBDR 2018)*. 10.1145/3291801.3291822

Sun, Z., & Stranieri, A. (2021). The Nature of Intelligent Analytics. In *Intelligent Analytics with Advanced Multi-industry Applications* (pp. 1–22). IGI-Global. doi:10.4018/978-1-7998-4963-6.ch001

Thierer, A., Russell, R., & O'Sullivan, A. (2017). *Artificial Intelligence and Public Policy-research summary*. Academic Press.

Turek, M. (2020). *Explainable Artificial Intelligence (XAI)*. DARPA. Retrieved from https://www.darpa.mil/program/explainable-artificial-intelligence

Weber, H. (2020a). *Big Data and Artificial Intelligence: Complete Guide to Data Science, AI, Big Data and Machine Learning*. Hans Weber.

Weber, H. (2020b). Big Data and Artificial Intelligence: Complete Guide to Data Science, AI, Big Data, and Machine Learning. ICGtesting.

Wirtz, B. W., Weyerer, J. C., & Sturm, B. J. (2020). The Dark Sides of Artificial Intelligence: An Integrated AI Governance Framework for Public Administration. *International Journal of Public Administration*, *43*(9), 818–829. doi:10.1080/01900692.2020.1749851

KEY TERMS AND DEFINITIONS

Artificial Intelligence (AI): Is science and technology concerned with imitating, extending, augmenting, and automating the intelligent behaviors of human beings.

Data Mining: Is a process of discovering various models, summaries, and derived values, knowledge from a large database. Another definition is that it is the process of using statistical, mathematical, logical, AI methods and tools to extract useful information from large databases.

Ethical Artificial Intelligence: Is a branch of the ethics of technology-specific to artificial intelligence and related artificially intelligent systems. It is about concern with the moral behaviors of humans as they design, make, use, and treat artificial intelligence and related artificially intelligent systems, and a concern with the moral behaviors of AI-based machines, or AI machine ethics.

Intelligent System: Is a system that can imitate, automate, and augment some intelligent behaviors of human beings. Expert systems and knowledge-based systems are examples of intelligent systems.

Machine Learning: Is concerned with how computers can adapt to new circumstances and detect and extrapolate patterns and knowledge.

Process-Oriented Paradigm: A set of ideas and actions intended to deal with a problem by developing a model consisting of process steps, procedures, and tasks.

Regulating AI Systems: Is about making AI systems safe, accountable, liable, and responsible complying with the global responsibility for the common human being's sustainable development.

Stare Decisis: The requirement is that a decision-maker in a court makes decisions consistent with his or her past decisions, decisions of courts at the same level and those of higher courts.

Chapter 6
A Survey on Hybrid Case-Based Reasoning and Deep Learning Systems for Medical Data Classification

Gasmi Safa
Badji Mokhtar University, Algeria

Djebbar Akila
Badji Mokhtar University, Algeria

Merouani Hayet Farida
Badji Mokhtar University, Algeria

ABSTRACT

Several artificial intelligence approaches, particularly case-based reasoning (CBR), which is analogous to the context of human reasoning for problem resolution, have demonstrated their efficiency and reliability in the medical field. In recent years, deep learning represents the latest iteration of an advance in artificial intelligence technologies in medicine to aid in data classification, diagnosis of new diseases, and complex decision-making. Although these two independent approaches have good results in the medical field, the latter is still a complex field. This chapter reviews the available literature on CBR systems, deep learning systems, and CBR deep learning systems in medicine. The methods used and results obtained are discussed, and key findings are highlighted. Further, in the light of this review, some directions for future research are given. This chapter presents the proposed approach, which helps to make the retrieval phase of the CBR cycle more reliable and robust.

INTRODUCTION

Artificial intelligence (AI) aims to design and create systems and applications that can imitate human

DOI: 10.4018/978-1-7998-9016-4.ch006

intelligence and assist in the actual solution of complex issues. AI is already making a difference today in its use in all scientific fields and more particularly in the field of medicine. Among the different branches of AI that have received more and more attention from research in medicine, we find case-based reasoning and deep learning. Case-based reasoning (Kolodner & Reasoning, 1993) (Gasmi, Djebbar, & Merouani, 2021) (Chebli, Djebbar, Marouani, & Lounis, 2021) is an approach for solving future issues relying on reusing previously solved issues saved in the case base, where a new issue is resolved using knowledge or similar experiences presented in case form. A case is defined in two parts, where the first is the problem and the second part is the solution of the problem. These cases which are grouped in the base of cases are independent of each other CBR systems are applied for several purposes for example for medical diagnosis (Huang, Chen, & Lee, 2007) (Begum, Ahmed, Funk, Xiong, & Von Schéele, 2009) (Chebli, Djebbar, & Merouani, 2020), medical planning (Cohen, 1997) (Marling & Whitehouse, 2001), classification of diseases (LeBozec, Jaulent, Zapletal, & Degoulet, 1998) (Fan, Chang, Lin, & Hsieh, 2011), etc. The same goes for Deep Learning (DL) (Kwolek, 2005) which has demonstrated remarkable performance in all medical uses including classification, diagnosis, segmentation, and detection of an anomaly. So DL quickly replaced classical AI techniques because it may give a much better explanation of a complicated situation if large datasets are available. Moreover, it can manipulate all forms of medical data, including images, genetic expressions, signals, etc. Although case-based reasoning or deep learning is simple in principle and has been used successfully in medical problem solving, it still suffers from some limitations that may prevent its success. CBR and more precisely the retrieval phase of the CBR cycle which is the essential phase that takes the responsibility of finding the right solution that is then used by the other phases in order to solve the given problem, still remains unclear and invalid in the medical context, and this is due to the set of naive classical methods used in this phase. And to overcome these limitations, several researchers have proposed a hybridization strategy between CBR and DL, with the intention of taking advantage of the properties of each model, and thus obtaining very good performances for the retrieval phase and the other phases of CBR in the medical context. The objective of this research, is to analyze hybrid systems that combine CBR and DL in medicine and other fields, as well as to suggest an architecture to improve the recovery stage of CBR using DL. The rest of the paper is structured as follows: Section 2 presents the background that encompasses a state of the art of CBR, as well as various medical systems that use CBR, as well as developed medical systems that use DL. In Section 3, hybrid medical systems that combine CBR and DL are studied. In Section 4, some results obtained from hybrid systems are discussed, and the CNN architecture and its popular models are presented. Section 5 presents the proposed approach, and in section 6, future research directions are presented. Section 7 presents the conclusions.

BACKGROUND

Case-Based Reasoning

The case-based reasoning technique is an artificial intelligence strategy to solve problems using reasoning by analogy (Mille, Fuchs, & Herbeaux, 1996), that is to say, reuse problematic situations previously solved and memorized (called source cases), to solve new problems (called target cases). The precision of the CBR is very good and reliable when the proposed solutions are recovered from the cases recorded in

Figure 1. Case-based reasoning life cycle
(Bartsch-Spörl et al., 1999).

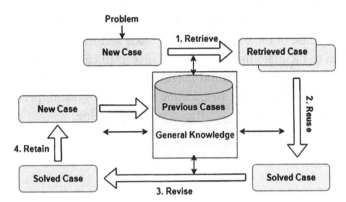

the case base, therefore it uses specific knowledge of problematic situations already resolved (Aamodt & Plaza, 1994), and does not require knowledge engineering effort like other areas of artificial intelligence.

As indicated in Figure 1, the CBR life cycle (Bartsch-Spörl, Lenz, & Hübner, 1999) can be divided into four phases (model R4).

1. The retrieval phase goal is to recover a set of previously solved problems that are comparable to the current problem by following three steps: The first step is to use domain expertise to identify all essential aspects of a problem. The second step is to use all relevant aspects as a similarity criterion to recover all old cases, finally, the third step is to classify all the old cases using domain knowledge.
2. The reuse stage is the second step of a CBR life cycle which builds a resolution for the current issue from the adaptation of the solutions taken in the previous cases. It takes into consideration the maximum precedent found in the retrieval phase, like an adequate resolution for the present issue.
3. The revise phase, involves detecting if there are any errors in the current solution and modifying that solution using repair techniques.
4. The retain phase is the final step of the CBR cycle, it allows the new case to be kept in the case base (memory).

Medical Case-Based Reasoning Systems

Recently, different case-based reasoning systems have gained more attention in various contexts and more specifically the medical context. Among the advantages of the CBR approach in this area is its eagerness to learn, and its ability to handle cases where input values are missing. It can therefore be used to diagnose, classify and plan complex and ambiguous problems. In 1994, Bichindaritz and al. (Bichindaritz, 1994) proposed a system in psychiatry, which allows medical doctors to come up with a diagnosis and a treatment plan for each new case using CBR. In 1998, to correctly classify radiology images, the IDEM system was developed by LeBozec and al. (LeBozec et al., 1998) using CBR, another breast cancer classification system is developed by Fan and al. (Fan et al., 2011) using hybridization between CBR and other artificial intelligence techniques on the Breast Cancer Wisconsin dataset to help physicians make better more effective medical diagnostic decisions. In (Sharaf-El-Deen, Moawad, & Khalifa, 2014), the authors suggested a system for detecting breast cancer as well as thyroid disease using CBR and another method, in assisting physicians in making accurate diagnoses and increasing the accuracy of the recovery phase of the CBR system. Oyelade and Ezugwu (Oyelade & Ezugwu, 2020), have developed a system to facilitate the diagnosis of suspected cases of COVID-19 using hybridization between CBR, Ontology, and also Natural language processing. The proposed system obtained a very high precision of 94.54%. The table 1 listed some of the CBR systems performed over the years in medicine that mainly focus on diagnosis, classification, and planning.

DEEP LEARNING

Deep learning (DL) is a subset of machine learning (ML), which itself is a subset of artificial intelligence (AI). The Venn diagram demonstrating the relationship between artificial intelligence, machine learning, as well as deep learning is shown in Figure 2.

Artificial intelligence is a method that allows a machine to imitate human behavior and create an operational model of the human nervous system that is capable of generating conclusions and decisions. It was first used in 1956 (Boden, 1977). AI has lately acquired popularity and has become the center of interest for researchers owing to the availability of large volumes of data. Machine learning (Samuel, 2000) is a subset of AI that uses statistical approaches to allow a machine to develop through expertise and learning. The goal of machine learning is a generalization, that is to say, to produce reliable and precise predictions on new data after training. As shown in Figure 3, in general, machine learning approaches are separated into two types: supervised learning algorithms and unsupervised learning algorithms (Mohri, Rostamizadeh, & Talwalkar, 2012).

Supervised learning aims to generate a model that can predict the desired output (a label) using learning inputs (explanatory variables). It's used in medicine, for example, to classify new mammograms which haven't been assessed by a doctor, knowing that an entry is a set of characteristics extracted from a mammogram image and the desired output is a medical diagnostic (Perumal, 2016). Supervised learning algorithms are used for classification or regression purposes (Pannala, Nawarathna, Jayakody, Rupasinghe, & Krishnadeva, 2016), for example, neural networks (Zhang, 2000), decision trees (Kothari & Dong, 2001), naive Bayesian (Flach & Lachiche, 2004), random forests (Prinzie & Van den Poel, 2008), k-nearest neighbors (Ayyad, Saleh, & Labib, 2019), linear regression (Wang & Yong, 2008), logistic regression (Subasi & Ercelebi, 2005), non-linear regression (Srivastava & Tripathi, 2012), etc (Figure 3).

Unsupervised learning's goal is to find structure throughout the inputs (unlabeled data). It's utilized in medicine to differentiate at-risk patients from those other patients in electronic health record systems (Miotto, Li, Kidd, & Dudley, 2016). K-means (J. Ye, Zhao, & Wu, 2007), Fuzzy C-means (Nayak, Naik, & Behera, 2015), Mean Shift Clustering (Carreira-Perpinán, 2015), and other unsupervised learning methods are used for clustering (Figure 3).

The term deep learning has emerged in the 2010s, coinciding with the rediscovery of multilayer artificial neural networks. Deep learning is a subfield of artificial intelligence as well as machine learning, that was made progress in almost all fields, and especially in the medical field, where it has achieved exceptional performance which sometimes exceeds human vision (Kwolek, 2005). It's formed of a succession of numerous layers of non-linear units (neurons) that are used to extract and transform functionality. The input layer receives all information and converts it to a signal, which is then transformed through

Table 1. Medical CBR systems.

Author (s), Year, System Name	Objective of Use	Database Utilized	Hybridization	Use of Adaptation	Area of Application	Technique (s) Used	Advantages
(Bichindaritz, 1994)	Diagnosis, Planning	31 restrictive anorexics and 30 bulimic anorexics (eating disorders)	No	Adaptation performed	Psychiatry	CBR	• Help the clinical expertise of the service by learning from experience. • Proposes a diagnosis and a treatment plan for each new case.
(Cohen, 1997), Retrospect	Planning	Breast cancer	Yes	No Adaptation	breast cancer disease	CBR, neural network, genetic algorithm	• Increases the efficiency and effectiveness of health care delivery. • Recommend optimal treatment plans for patients. • Predict treatment outcomes for patients.
(LeBozec et al., 1998), IDEM	Classification	An object database (02 system)	No	No Adaptation	Radiology Images	CBR	• Allows experts to validate and modify the case model. • Allows experts to act on the different stages of the research process during development. • The evaluation of the knowledge included in the system at the level of the interface objects.
(Marling & Whitehouse, 2001), AUGUSTE	Planning	Information about patients with AD	Yes	No Adaptation	Alzheimer's disease	CBR, Rule-based reasoning (RBR)	• Assists physicians in decision-making for sustained attention planning for AD patients
(Schmidt & Vorobieva, 2005), ISOR	Diagnosis, Planning,	Information about depression, anxiety, and other psychiatric disorders is available	No	Semi-automatic Adaptation Performed	Endocrine and Psychiatry	CBR	• Very valid in cases of ineffective treatments. • Provides suggestions for avoiding the inefficacy of prescribed therapy. • Helpful even in situations where patient information is missing.
(Díaz, Fdez-Riverola, & Corchado, 2006), geneCBR	Diagnosis and classification	Bone marrow (BM)	Yes	Adaptation performed	Cancer	CBR and Fuzzy Logic	• Allows cancer classification based on microarray data. • Outperforms results obtained by classification techniques.
(Huang et al., 2007), CDPD	Diagnosis	Chronic illness diagnostic data from the MJ health center	Yes	Adaptation performed	Chronic illness	CBR, data mining (DM)	• Identifying relevant rules from medical assessment data that helps with the prognosis and diagnosis of chronic illnesses.
(Begum et al., 2009)	Diagnosis	–	Yes	Adaptation performed by clinicians in the domain	Psychophysi-ologique	CBR, fuzzy logic	• Assists doctors in analyzing and interpreting intricate and time-consuming consecutive measurements. • Help physicians in making a diagnosis and developing a treatment plan.
(De Paz, Rodríguez, Bajo, & Corchado, 2009), ExpressionCBR	Diagnosis, Classification	microarray data	Yes	Adaptation performed	blood cancer	CBR, decision tree, ESOINN neural network	• Helps in the diagnosis of patients with various types of cancer. • A technique that enables the discovery of the most important genes and factors for disease diagnosis. • Effectiveness in establishing accurate classification and diagnosis.
(Fan et al., 2011)	Classification	Liver disorders, Breast Cancer Wisconsin	Yes	No Adaptation	breast cancer and liver disorder	CBR, fuzzy decision tree, genetic algorithms	• Helps physicians make better, more effective decisions in medical diagnosis.
(López Ibáñez et al., 2011), eXiT*CBR	Diagnosis	Breast Cancer Wisconsin, Breast cancer dataset (628: healthy women, 243: women with breast cancer)	Yes	Adaptation performed	Breast cancer Disease	CBR, Genetic algorithms, Pedigree tools,	• Facilitates interaction with doctors. • Facilitates doctors' analysis of experiments. • Facilitates experimental replication for the medical community.
(Neshat, Sargolzaei, Nadjaran Toosi, & Masoumi, 2012)	Diagnosis	Hepatitis disease	Yes	No Adaptation	Hepatitis Disease	CBR, Particle SwarmOptimization (PSO)	• Gives good performances in the medical field. • Be able to diagnose hepatitis in the best possible conditions with high precision compared to different methods.
(Mansoul, Atmani, & Benbelkacem, 2013)	Diagnosis	Pima Indian diabetes	Yes	Adaptation performed	Diabetes	CBR, Data mining (DM), Multi-criteria Decision Support (MCDS)	• Help to make good decisions. • Improves the quality of care for diabetic patients.
(Guessoum, Laskri, & Lieber, 2014), RESPIDIAG	Diagnosis	Pneumology	No	Adaptation performed	Chronically obstructed pulmonary illness	CBR	• Deals the problem of missing data
(Sharaf-El-Deen et al., 2014)	Diagnosis	Thyroid disease, mammography based breast cancer disease	Yes	Adaptation performed	Breast cancer and Thyroid disease	CBR, Rule-based reasoning (RBR)	• Helps the doctor to make an accurate diagnosis. • Enhance the retrieval-only CBR system accuracy.
(Røddy et al., 2016), ABC4D	Planning	Continuous glucose monitoring (CGM)	No	Adaptation performed	Type 1 diabetes	CBR	• Decision-making aid for insulin bolus dose. • Suggests clinical benefit in improving postprandial hypoglycemia.

continued on following page

117

Table 1. Continued

Author (s), Year, System Name	Objective of Use	Database Utilized	Hybridization	Use of Adaptation	Area of Application	Technique (s) Used	Advantages
(Gu, Liang, & Zhao, 2017), BTCBRsys	Diagnosis	Real-world breast cancer	Yes	Adaptation performed	Breast cancer	CBR, Genetic algorithm	• Assists doctors in making clinical decisions during the diagnosis or treatment of patients, particularly in the early identification of breast cancer.
(Abd Elkader, Elmogy, El-Sappagh, & Zaied, 2018)	Diagnosis	400 real-life chronic kidney disease cases	Yes	No Adaptation	Chronic kidney diseases (CKD)	CBR, RapidMiner, rough fuzzy	• Allows enabling the creation of a full case base from digital patient files. • Improves the recovery process in the RBC system.
(Lamy, Sekar, Guezennec, Bouaud, & Séroussi, 2019)	Classification	Breast Cancer Wisconsin (BCW), Mammographic Mass (MM), Breast Cancer (BC),	Yes	No Adaptation	Breast cancer	CBR, rainbow boxes-inspired algorithm (RBIA)	• Good classification precision. • Visual explanation of the reasoning process for the user through the use of an interface. • Therapeutic decision support for breast cancer
(Oyelade & Ezugwu, 2020)	Classification	Data are collected from medical and interventional radiology (SIRM).	Yes	Adaptation performed	Coronavirus	CBR, NLP, Ontology	• Facilitates the diagnosis of suspected cases of COVID-19.
(Duan & Jiao, 2021)	Planning	Infectious diseases	Yes	Adaptation performed	Public health emergencies	CBR, Cuckoo search(CS), Grey clustering (GC)	• Improves the speed of case recovery. • Increases the precision of the solution. • Highly effective for decision-makers in providing public health emergency response measures.
(Pusztová, Babič, & Paralič, 2021)	Diagnosis	Heart Disease	Yes	Semi-automatic Adaptation Performed	Cardiovascul-ar disease	CBR, decision tree	• Helps the doctor to understand the existing knowledge • Helps the doctor to make personalized decisions. • Easy for the doctor to diagnose a new patient using diagnostic suggestions and explanations.

the hidden layers to the output layer, the latter allows it to provide the final output of the network. Every neuronal in the network (for the hidden and output layers) has the weight coefficient at its input. During training, the DL can use labeled and unlabeled information (X.-W. Chen & Lin, 2014) to learn and gain knowledge using the most widely used learning method which is backpropagation. The goal of the backpropagation method is to reduce learning errors while maximizing prediction accuracy.

Deep Learning Models

Among the deep learning methods that have emerged very quickly and have been widely used and have generated a major positive impact in different areas of computer vision such as the medical field, there's the Convolutional Neural Network (CNN) (LeCun et al., 1989), Generative Adversarial Network (GAN) (Goodfellow et al., 2014), Deep Conventional Extreme Learning Machine (Pang & Yang, 2016), Recurrent Neural Network (RNN) (Rumelhart, Hinton, & Williams, 1986), Deep Boltzmann Machine (DBM) (Salakhutdinov & Hinton, 2009), Deep Belief Network (DBN) (Hinton, Osindero, & Teh, 2006), Deep Autoencoder (DA) (Rumelhart, Hinton, & Williams, 1985), such as shown in Figure 4.

Table 2 contains a relatively short overview of each deep learning model and the authors and advantages of each model.

Applications of Deep Learning in Medicine

Deep Learning presents a high performance and a better interpretation and precision for very complex problems compared to other classical approaches and humans in the medical field for example in image processing, classification, detection, analysis data, etc. And that only if there are large medical datasets. This part presents some research papers that study the use of deep learning in medicine.

Figure 2. The link between artificial intelligence, machine learning, and deep learning.

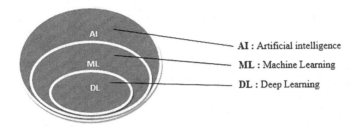

The authors in (Pereira, Pinto, Alves, & Silva, 2016) described an intriguing application that uses convolutional neural networks to automatically separate brain cancers in MRI images. Pereira and al. used the database Brain Tumor Segmentation Challenge 2013 (BRATS 2013) and 2015 (BRATS 2015) to test and validate their proposal, obtaining first place in the online assessment platform in 2013 and second place among twelve contestants for the on-site challenge in 2015.

In the article written by Kooi and al. (Kooi et al., 2017), the main idea is to make a comparison between a convolutional neural network (CNN) and an advanced computer-assisted detection (CAD)

Figure 3. Diagram of machine learning methods and their applications.

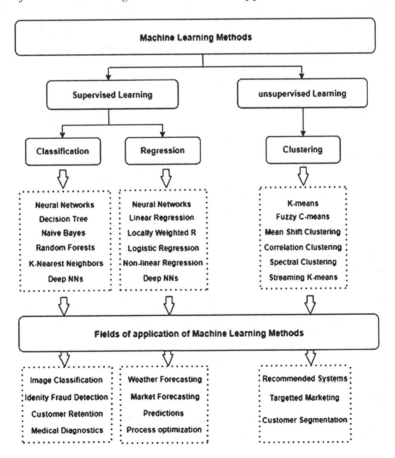

Figure 4. The different Deep Learning Models.

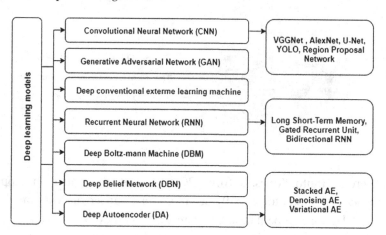

mammography system, knowing that both systems are trained on a large mammographic lesion dataset which contains 45000 images, the CNN model shows good results and has great potential to expand the field of research compared to the CAD system traditional. In addition to this, CNN has the advantage of automatically learning the data, which makes development easier and faster.

Song and al. (Song et al., 2020) presented a histopathological diagnostic system to detect gastric cancer using the deep convolutional neural network trained with 2123 digital slide images dyed using hematoxylin and eosin. The results obtained show that the system can assist pathologists in improving diagnostic accuracy and preventing diagnostic errors, with the model achieving close 100% sensitivity as well as a mean specificity of 80.6% on a real-world gastric testing data of 3212 whole slide images scanned by three scanners. They also used 1582 complete slide images from two different medical centers to show that the method is stable and reliable.

In this article (Suk, Lee, Shen, & Initiative, 2014), Suk and al. developed a novel approach employing Deep Boltzmann Machine (DBM) of deep learning to determine the optimal representation of shared latent characteristics from magnetic resonance imaging (MRI) and positron emission tomography (PET). This approach was evaluated using the Alzheimer's Disease Neuroimaging Initiative (ADNI) dataset, which includes (PET), (MRI), and (PET+MRI). They achieved an accuracy of 92.38% in magnetic resonance, 92.20% in PET, and 95.35% in MRI+PET.

Sarraf and al. developed another system to predict Alzheimer's disease in (Sarraf & Tofighi, 2016), in which they chose the architecture of the convolutional neural network (LeNet-5) and achieved an accuracy of 96.86% in classifying functional MRI data (fMRI) of Alzheimer's disease patients from normal controls.

Using a Generative Adversarial Network (GAN) and pix2pix frame, Kyeong and al. (Oh, Lee, Lee, Yun, & Yoo, 2020) proposed a new approach to produce a segmentation map of the brain white matter compartment in 18F-FDG PET/CT images (from the ADNI database). In comparison to many deep learning algorithms, the suggested method had the greatest AUC-PR of 0.868 and produced better segmentation results.

Zhong and al. (Zhong, Liao, Guo, & Wang, 2019) created a model that extracts fetal electrocardiography (FECG) using a residual convolutional encoder-decoder network (RCED-Net) from real single-channel abdominal electrocardiography (AECG) recordings collected from two databases ADFECGDB

Table 2. Description of deep learning models.

DL Model	Author (s), Year	Description	Advantages
Convolutional Neural Network	(LeCun et al., 1989)	• Inspired by the visual cortex of vertebrates. • Dedicated specifically to the classification of images of handwritten numbers. • Directly receives 2D two-dimensional data (images), rather than 1D one-dimensional data (vectors). • Created especially to handle the complexities of two-dimensional forms. • Usually comprises of convolution and pooling layers alternated with one or more fully connected layers at the ending.	• Ability to process large amounts of low-level information. • Applies successfully to detect and recognize objects, and also to segment regions in images.
Generative adversarial network (GAN)	(Goodfellow et al., 2014)	•Has an objective of generating new data through input data • Mitigate the problem of over-learning in many areas. • The generator and the discriminator are the two parts that constitute the hidden layers.	• Possesses the ability to generate high-quality information. • Reproduce the very complex probability distribution.
Deep conventional extreme learning machine	(Pang & Yang, 2016)	• Combines the strength of CNN with the quick training capabilities of the Extreme Learning Machine. • Composed of several alternating convolution layers and grouping layers to extract the high-level characteristics of the input images. • It does not use a setting for parameters and iterations in the learning process. • Reduce the dimensionality of features by introducing stochastic pooling in the last hidden layer.	• Improves generalization. • A much faster rate of learning than deep learning approaches. • Present better precision compared to other deep learning methods.
Recurrent Neural Network (RNN)	(Rumelhart et al., 1986)	• Developed to analyze a data flow. • Considered a generalization of multi-layered perceptron (input and output can be of variable length). • Developed to make use of the correlations between a prediction problem's input data. • Processed data at each stage using historical data. • Treated with problems where the data is sequential.	• Capable of working with data of various lengths. • Provides more precise results.
Deep Boltz-mann Machine (DBM)	(Salakhutdinov & Hinton, 2009)	• Has the potential to learn increasingly complex internal representations. • Has a quick way to initialize a model's parameters to sensitive values. • Can build high-level representations from a large amount of untagged sensory input. • Can refine the model built by using the labeled data for a specific task. • Each neuron could communicate only with neurons in the layers next and previous.	• Used to successfully learn good generative models. • Works well on object recognition tasks.
Deep Belief Network (DBN)	(Hinton et al., 2006)	• It's a type of generative model that aims to produce new data using the input data's predicted distribution. • Individual layers are learned in an unsupervised manner. • For final tuning, add a linear classifier to the top layer and use supervised optimization. • It's the outcome of connecting multiple Boltzmann Machines in a certain order (cannot be classified as RNN).	• In image recognition and speech recognition, it has been used as a pre-training model. • In medical diagnostics, it's used in classification tasks to detect lesions, and in video, recognition to recognize the presence of humans. • In speech recognition, this is used to comprehend missing words in a sentence. • Applied on physiological cues to identify human emotion.
Deep Autoencoder (DA)	(Rumelhart et al., 1985)	• Has a goal to reduce the data's dimension. • In all applications, they are used as feature extractors (where data is noisy and complex). • An encoder and a decoder are both included in each hidden layer. • It is an unsupervised model	• Excellent capacity to simplify even the most complicated data. • Does not require labeled data.

and PCDB. The developed model achieved better performances and is efficient to extract FECG from

AECG knowing that the values of SE, PPV, F1 on ADFECGDB are 96.06%, 92.25%, 94.10%, and on PCDB are 92.60%, 94.68%, 93.62%.

The authors in (Mahbod, Schaefer, Wang, Ecker, & Ellinge, 2019) presented a three-stage hybrid technique for the categorization of skin lesions in the 150 images of the ISIC 2017. Firstly, deep functionalities are generated using three pre-trained deep models: AlexNet, VGG16, as well as ResNet-18. Second, these characteristics are utilized to train the SVM classifier, and finally, the outputs of these classifiers are merged to achieve classification. This technique has given good results in which the area under the curve for the classification of melanoma is 83.83% and for the classification of seborrheic keratosis is 97.55%.

A novel deep neural network architecture based on transfer learning to enable the categorization of microscopic images was created by the authors Nguyen and al. (Nguyen, Lin, Lin, & Cao, 2018). The features were concatenated using three deep CNNs: Inception-v3, Resnet152, and Inception-Resnet-v2. To accomplish the categorization, these concatenated characteristics are used to form two fully connected layers. On the 2D-Hela and PAP-smear datasets, this architecture was validated, with the precision of 3.20% for 2D-Hela and 2.67% for PAP-smear.

Tang and al. (Tang et al., 2019) presented a deep learning model (Ua-Net) that aims to detect organ at risk (OAR) in the head and neck automatically. This model has been trained on a dataset of 215 CT scans with 28 OARs manually delimited by radiation oncologists, and it was tested on a dataset of 100 CT scans, with an average Dice similarity coefficient of 78.34% on the 28 OARs.

POSSIBILITY OF HYBRIDIZATION BETWEEN CBR AND DL

As it is stated in the previous sections that each of the CBR and deep learning approaches have been effectively utilized in almost all fields of research, and most notably the medical field, which has achieved very reliable and accurate results (eg (Bichindaritz, 1994) (Cohen, 1997) (LeBozec et al., 1998) (Marling & Whitehouse, 2001) (Schmidt & Vorobieva, 2005) (Díaz et al., 2006) (Huang et al., 2007) (Begum et al., 2009) (De Paz et al., 2009) (Fan et al., 2011) for CBR and (Pereira et al., 2016) (Kooi et al., 2017) (Song et al., 2020) (Suk et al., 2014) (Sarraf & Tofighi, 2016) (Oh et al., 2020) (Zhong et al., 2019) (Mahbod et al., 2019) (Nguyen et al., 2018) (Tang et al., 2019) for Deep learning) through to the performance of each of these methods. But despite this widely and successful use of these methods in medical fields, they suffer from certain limitations which can be major obstacles in this context (LeBozec et al., 1998) such as:

- The naive method of recovering a comparable case using the classical system of case-based reasoning's Euclidean distances.
- The influence of the quality of representation of the characteristics used on the efficiency of the CBR system which uses a kNN classifier (Corbat, Nauval, Henriet, & Lapayre, 2020).
- The amount of the data utilized during training has a direct impact on the Deep learning model's capacity to generalize.
- The lack of interpretation of Deep Learning models because they are non-linear.
- The classification accuracy of Deep Learning models depends on the set of object types of the training data (i.e. they can only classify the types of objects contained in the data of learning), etc.

Figure 5. Diagram of a sequential hybridization between CBR and DL.

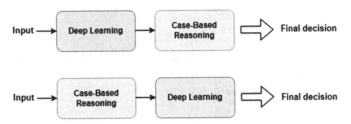

Recently, a solution has been proposed to overcome these limits by hybridizing between CBR and Deep Learning, i.e. by applying DL ideas to CBR problems and vice-versa (Keane, Kenny, Temraz, Greene, & Smyth, 2021) to obtain more maximum performance which none of these models can achieve on their own. There are different ways to achieve the hybridization between CBR and DL, in another way there is a possibility to combine them as follows:

- **Sequential hybridization between CBR and DL:** In this type of hybridization the two classifiers CBR and DL are organized successively (Figure 5), that is, the result produced by the first classifier (CBR or DL) will then be considered an entry for the second classifier (CBR or DL). In this case, the final decision is given by the classifier who comes in last position and do not forget the effect of the first classifier on the intermediate result. In (López-Sánchez, Corchado, & Arrieta, 2017) (Nasiri, Helsper, Jung, & Fathi, 2018), the authors implemented this type of hybridization, knowing that the DL (CNN) is used as the first classifier immediately followed by CBR as a second classifier.

- **Parallel hybridization between CBR and DL:** That is, both methods use the same input, then each producing an independent classification result. After the two results obtained are then compared for a final decision using a majority vote (selection of the best result), as illustrated in Figure 6.

- **Hybridization of inclusion between CBR and DL:** This hybridization aims to closely couple the two methods to have their forces simultaneously in order to obtain very good results. In other words, this type of hybridization applies or integrates the ideas of the first method (DL or CBR) into the second method (DL or CBR) so that it can provide reliable and robust performance and

Figure 6. Diagram of a parallel hybridization between CBR and DL.

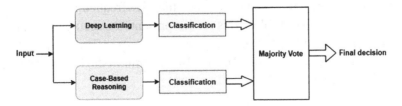

Figure 7. Diagram of inclusion hybridization between CBR and DL.

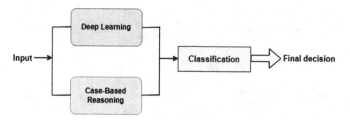

improve the interpretation of classification results (Figure 7). This type of hybridization has been successfully applied in medicine or other contexts (Turner, Floyd, Gupta, & Oates, 2019) (Corbat et al., 2020) (Amin, Kapetanakis, Polatidis, Althoff, & Dengel, 2020).

Twin Systems for CBR and DL in Medicine and Other Fields

In this article, Table 3 lists medical systems as well as systems made in other domains that combine CBR and Deep Learning. For the medical context, the authors in (Nasiri et al., 2018) (Neves et al., 2018) (Gao et al., 2019) have proposed systems that make it possible to classify certain diseases using CBR and CNN, and they obtained fairly high precision. In addition, the authors in (Corbat et al., 2020) have proposed systems making it possible to segment renal tumors also applying CBR and CNN. Regarding other areas (Louati, Louati, & Li, 2021) (Grace, Maher, Wilson, & Najjar, 2016) (López-Sánchez et al., 2017) (Sani, Wiratunga, & Massie, 2017) (Li, Liu, Chen, & Rudin, 2018) (C. Chen et al., 2019) (Amin, Kapetanakis, Althoff, Dengel, & Petridis, 2018) (Turner, Floyd, Gupta, & Oates, 2019) (Eisenstadt, Langenhan, & Althoff, 2019) (Lansley et al., 2019) (Amin, Kapetanakis, Polatidis, Althoff, & Dengel, 2020) (X. Ye, Zhao, Leake, Wang, & Crandall, 2021), the authors combined between CBR and DL models for several tasks such as: classification, detection and prediction, retrieval and adaptation, regression, etc. They obtained very high performances by the application of these systems to solve the new problems and to optimize the existing solutions in these fields. For example in (Turner et al., 2019), the NOD-CC system observed remarkable evolutions in their performances compared to CNN or CBR on its own. And this is due to the automatic feature extraction of CNN and the learning capabilities of CBR. Also, the DeepKAF system (Amin et al., 2020), which takes advantage of the explainability advantage of CBR to support DL, and at the same time the utility of DL to solve CBR implementation problems.

DISCUSSION

One of the objectives of this article is to review the literature on hybrid CBR-DL systems in the medical context or other fields (previous section) and to highlight the most frequently used DL models capable of solving CBR problems. According to Table 3, this section presents the accuracy obtained by each system in the medical context or in the other domains (Figure 8), also specifies in which tasks hybridization was achieved with a large percentage (Figure 9), and also determines the DL model that was hybridized frequently with CBR (Figure 10)

Table 3. Medical and non-medical systems that combine CBR and DL.

Author (s), Year, System Name	Objective of Use	Technique(s) Used	DL Architecture Used	Accuracy (%)	Area of Application	Database Used	Advantages
(Nasiri et al., 2018), DePicT Melano-ma CLASS	Classification	CBR, CNN	CNN Standard	88	Melanoma skin cancer	ISIC archive (1400 training images and 400 test images)	• Adaptable to support users with relevant information and precise recommendations • Very effective for the early detection of melanoma.
(Neves et al., 2018)	Classification	CBR, DL	–	84.2	Cervical Carcinoma	Real-life cases of cervical squamous cell carcinoma are depicted in 54.	• Assist in predicting the various phases of cervical squamous cell carcinoma. • In the case of Cervical Squamous Cell Carcinoma, achieve a satisfactory result.
(Gao et al., 2019)	Classification	CBR, CNN	CNN Standard	77	Oesophageal Cancer disease	350 frames from 15 esophageal videos plus four videos of normal subjects	• Helps clinicians classify early precancerous stages of esophageal cancer. • Convince doctors from a visual explanation of the categorization results of endoscopic esophageal videos.
(Corbat et al., 2020)	Segmentation	CBR, CNN	CNN Standard	–	Pathological kidneys and cancerous tumors	9 real patients with nephroblastoma	• Has the highest percentage to manage conflicts and improve segmentation. • It is implemented with an acceptable computation time.
(Louati et al., 2021)	Detection and Prediction	CBR, CNN, LSTM	CNN Standard	–	Traffic emergency management	Using screenshots from the traffic simulator, for trained and tested	• The detection of emergency cases and the prediction of events interrupt the flow of traffic. • Respond to disturbances. • Effective control of traffic lights and guidance of electric vehicles. • Outperform other benchmarking algorithms.
(Grace et al., 2016), Q-chef	Retrieval and adaptation	CBR, Variational Autoencoder (VAE)	Variational Autoencoder	–	Recipe generation	Ingredients for recipes	• Generation of new recipes according to the requirements of a human user. • The ability to adjust recipes to make them more surprising while yet being plausible.
(López-Sánchez et al., 2017)	Classification	CBR, DCNN	VGG-16 and three DrLIM layers	86.15	Web pages problem	280 web pages (3223 images extracted)	• In the process of learning knowing that new cases are revised to are added to the base of cases. • Deals with situations of a very complex image classification. • Allow the calculation cost of the learning phase to be minimized.
(Sani et al., 2017)	Classification	CBR(KNN), CNN	CNN Standard	–	Human Activity Recognition (HAR)	Collected by an accelerometer from two places on the body, the wrist, and the thigh.	• Produce very good results for extracting representations of deep functionalities with only one training period.
(Li et al., 2018)	Classification	CBR, Autoencoder	Autoencoder	99.22	Classification of handwritten digits	MNIST (10 000 images)	• Flexible in learning useful features. • The interpretation of prediction decisions. • Allow users to follow the classification of a new observation.
				93.5	Classification of cars	Car (154 images)	
				89.95	Classification of clothing and articles	Fashion MNIST (10 000 images)	
(C. Chen et al., 2019), Protoner	Classification	CBR, CNN	VGG-16, VGG-19, ResNet-34, ResNet-152, DenseNet-121, or DenseNet-161	84.8	Bird species identification	CUB-200-2011	• Similar to doctors regarding explaining how to find a solution for difficult image classification tasks. • The possibility of achieving a precision comparable to the most powerful deep models. • Provides an Interpretation at a level that does not exist in other deep interpretable models.
				91.4	Car model identification	Stanford Cars	

continued on following page

Table 3. Continued

Author (s), Year, System Name	Objective of Use	Technique(s) Used	DL Architecture Used	Accuracy (%)	Area of Application	Database Used	Advantages
(Amin et al., 2018), DeepTMS	Retrieval	CBR, LSTM	LSTM	92.13	Ticket Management	300000 old tickets for training and 10000 tickets for the test	• Does not involve experts to automate the construction of text similarity. • Capable of facilitating the management of complex tasks. • Process big data quickly and in real-time.
(Turner et al., 2019), NOD-CC	Classification	CBR, CNN	Inception-v3	–	Object Discovery	PASCAL-Part 4737 images)	• Allow discovery of new types of previously unknown objects during image classification. Minimizes the need for large pre-labeled datasets for CNN training using CBR learning capabilities. • Does not require a specific CNN architecture to be implemented. • Show good results compared to the results of implementing CNN or CBR alone.
(Eisenstadt et al., 2019)	Adaptation	CBR, Generative Adversarial Nets (GAN)	VGG 16	94	Conceptual design	25000 connection map examples for training and 5000 connection map examples for testing	• Improves the design of the building. • Adaptable for room configuration changes. • An implementation module for the FLEA methodology.
(Lansley et al., 2019)	Classification	CBR, CNN	CNN Standard	–	Social engineering attacks	Real cyber social engineering attacks	• Applied in real-time in offline texts. • Identify the possibility of the existence of a social engineering attack for an offline human conversation.
(Amin et al., 2020), DeepKAF	Retrieval	CBR, Skip-thought Autoencoder, Word2Vec, Siamese MaLSTM	Skip-thought Autoencoder, Word2Vec, Siamese MaLSTM	88.32	Ticket Management problem	More than 300000 tickets for Training (textual data)	• Apply to more complex unstructured and heterogeneous data sources. • Show very promising results in the industrial field.
(X. Ye et al., 2021)	Regression	CBR, CNN	vgg-vd-16	–	Age prediction	IMDB-WIKI (22578 face images)	• Continuous use of knowledge without retraining. • Improves the solution of the retrieval step.

According to Figure 8 which shows the accuracy obtained with the different systems in the medical context and other contexts (Table 3), and although the existence of works providing hybridized systems between CBR and DL is very little in the literature, but mainly most of those achieved both fairly acceptable and high accuracy, which reflects that the results are reliable and robust. For example, the highest accuracy in the medical field is 88% obtained by Nasiri and al. (Nasiri et al., 2018) in the classification of Melanoma skin cancer using CBR and CNN. The highest accuracy in other fields is 99.22% obtained by Li and al., (Li et al., 2018) in the classification of handwritten digits using CBR and Autoencoder.

According to the graphical comparison presented in Figures 9 and 10, it is obvious that the hybridization between CBR and DL has been implemented to classify certain problems (whether in the medical context or not) much more than other objectives. And that the convolutional neural network is one of the deep learning models most hybridized with CBR.

Convolutional Neural Network Architecture

The convolutional neural network, as previously mentioned, is a supervised learning approach of DL that has been effectively hybridized with CBR in medicine and other fields due to a hierarchy of its very deep layers. Their typical architecture (Liu et al., 2017), as shown in Figure 11, consists of alternating layers of convolution and pooling, followed by one or more fully connected layers.

The convolutional layer is made up of a collection of convolutional filters that are applied to the input

Figure 8. Accuracy of medical and non-medical systems.

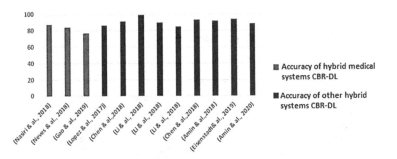

Figure 9. Percentage of systems hybridizing between CBR and DL in terms of use objective.

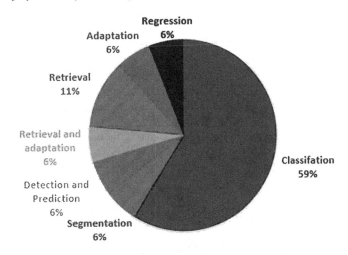

Figure 10. Percentage of application of hybridizations between CBR and Deep Learning models.

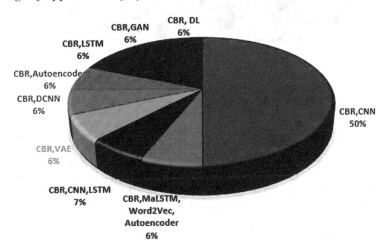

image to produce characteristic maps which are then transmitted to the pooling layer. The dot product between the receiving fields and the filters is used to create these characteristic maps. The pooling layer's goal is to decrease comparable information and produce the dominating response in the produced feature

Figure 11. Schematic structure of the CNNs architecture (Liu et al., 2017).

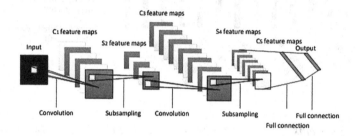

Figure 12. Diagram of convolutional neural network models.

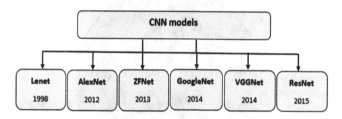

Figure 13. The architecture of the Lenet model.

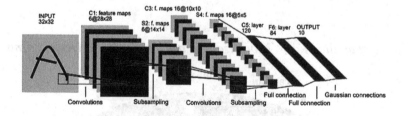

Figure 14. The architecture of the AlexNet model.

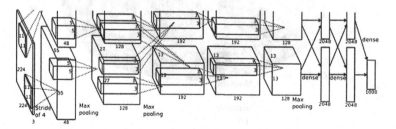

Figure 15. The architecture of the ZFNet model.

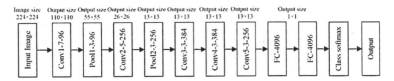

maps to speed up the model's calculations and reduce the overfitting problem. The fully connected layer of CNN is the final layer and is typically utilized for classification.

An Overview of Convolutional Neural Network Models

Figure 12 shows the main CNN models that have become widely popular because of their superior performance in a variety of fields.

The Lenet Model

Lenet was developed by LeCun and al. (LeCun, Bottou, Bengio, & Haffner, 1998) in 1998, and it experienced great development in 2010. It is one of the first CNN approaches that was successfully applied for the recognition of the handwritten digit dataset. Its architecture is composed of a succession of convolution and pooling layers terminated by three fully connected layers, the input images are in gray levels (of size for example $32 \times 32 \times 1$), and the best-known version is LeNet-5 (Figure 13) which contains two convolutional layers and two fully connected layers, and a pooling layer after each convolution.

The AlexNet Model

AlexNet (Krizhevsky, Sutskever, & Hinton, 2012) uses a large number of weights and has layers varying in shape, its CNN architecture is more extensive and deep, which it differentiates from LeNet. it was successful on ImageNet Challenge in 2012 for visual object recognition. It has five convolutional layers and three fully connected layers in its architecture (Figure 14), there is a nonlinear ReLU function in each layer. Every convolutional layer has 96 to 384 filters varying in size from 3×3 to 11×11. To deal

Figure 16. The architecture of the GoogleNet model.

Figure 17. The architecture of the VGGNet16 model.

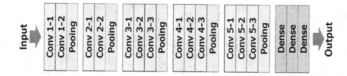

with the overfitting issue, He used dropout for the two fully connected layers and he used softmax for the last layer. He reduced the top-5 error rate by 0.3% and the top-1 error rate by 0.4%.

The ZFNet Model

ZFNet (Zeiler & Fergus, 2014) proposed by Zeiler and Fergue in 2013, is an improved model of the AlexNet which gives better performance. it used 7 × 7 size filters instead of 11 × 11 and is similar to AlexNet regarding the use of the ReLU activation function and the number of convolutional and fully connected layers. This model was trained on three databases: ImageNet 2012, Caltech-101, and Caltech-256 on a GTX 580 GPU for 12 days. It got a top 5 validation error rate of 14.8%. Figure 15 illustrates the architecture of the ZFNet model.

The GoogleNet Model

To reduce the computational complexity of traditional CNN, Szegedy and al. (Szegedy et al., 2015) developed a model called GoogleNet which has several versions: v1, v3, and v4. Its architecture (Figure 16) contains three convolutional layers, followed by 9 inceptions layers and a fully connected layer. Each inception layer contains two convolutional layers, and filters of sizes 1 × 1, 3 × 3, 5 × 5, as well as a max-pooling of 3 × 3. GoogleNet attained a top 5 error rate of 6.67% which is very close to that of humans, it also attained a top 5 test accuracy of 93.3% on the challenge of detection and classification ImageNet ILSVRC14.

Figure 18. The architecture of the ResNet model.

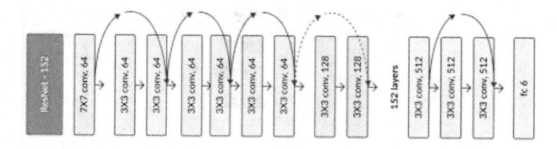

Figure 19. Architecture of our suggested strategy.

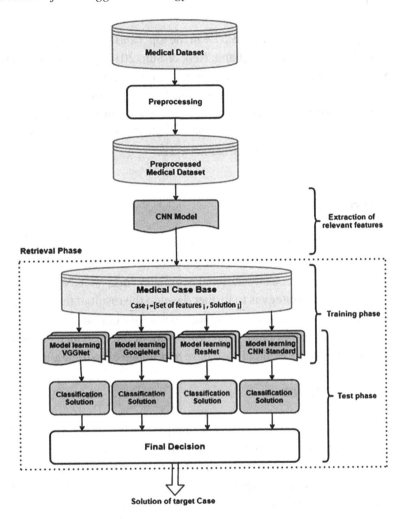

The VGGNet Model

VGGNet (Simonyan & Zisserman, 2014) is a CNN model developed by Simonyan and Zisserman in 2014, was built with the Caffe toolbox. He is trained on 4 Nvidia Titan Black GPUs for 2 to 3 weeks, it uses the scale jittering method to increase the data at the time of training. Its architecture consists of two convolutional layers which are used the ReLU activation function, and the last layer uses the Softmax activation function for classification, it used 3x3 filters. The main versions of VGGNet are: VGG11, VGG16 and VGG19. The first version contains 11 layers, the second contains 16 layers and the third has 19 layers, knowing that the last three layers are fully connected. VGGNet attained a top 5 error rate of 7.3%. The VGG and specifically VGG16 model architecture is shown in Figure 17.

The ResNet Model

A CNN model which provides an error rate of 3.57% in the top 5 and which surpasses the performance of the human being, is the ResNet model (He, Zhang, Ren, & Sun, 2016) proposed by Kaiming He and al., Its architecture is extremely deep with 152 layers (Figure 18). It is a standard feed-forward network that uses residual connections, and also the bottleneck approach to reduce the number of weight parameters. Versions of ResNet with the bottleneck approach are: 50, 101, 152, and those without the bottleneck approach are: 18, 34. The most popular version of ResNet is called ResNet50 containing 49 convolutional layers and a fully connected layer at the end of the network.

THE SUGGESTED STRATEGY

The proposed strategy is illustrated in Figure 19. It is based on an inclusion hybridization between case-based reasoning and deep learning models, i.e., integrating the capabilities of deep learning and CBR. Among the DL models used, there are: Convolutional neural network, VGGNet, ResNet and GoogleNet.

The objective of the suggested strategy is to further develop the result of the CBR approach and more specifically the retrieval phase of the CBR cycle in order to improve classification in the medical context.

The proposed strategy works in four phases: preprocessing of the used medical dataset, extraction of relevant features, construction of the medical case base and image classification.

Preprocessing of the Dataset

In the proposed approach, the first phase which is the preprocessing of the dataset aims to prepare the raw medical dataset (which may contain, for example, little information, unnecessary additional information, missing information, noise) to make it usable, thus to ensure the convergence of the model used and consequently to avoid false predictions that can negatively influence the result of the retrieval phase of the CBR cycle. So it is obvious that the preprocessing of the raw data is crucial to obtain a reliable dataset. There are several techniques of data preprocessing, in which each one can improve differently the result of the model trained on this data. Among these techniques there are: data cleaning (Fatima, Nazir, & Khan, 2017), data normalization (Smolinska et al., 2014), data augmentation (Mikołajczyk & Grochowski, 2018), dimension reduction (Obaid, Dheyab, & Sabry, 2019), etc.

Feature Extraction Using Convolutional Neural Networks

The second phase of the suggested strategy is the extraction of relevant features from the preprocessed medical dataset images. Indeed, feature extraction plays the most important role in image classification, i.e., the classification result strongly depends on the crucial features extracted from the dataset images. To perform the feature extraction process, the convolutional neural network was selected, which is one of the most robust DL models that have achieved significant performance before. Specifically, the first part of the CNN architecture was used, i.e. all the layers of the CNN except the last classification layers.

Construction of the Medical Case Base

After extracting the relevant features using CNN, the medical case base was built using these features. Suppose that the final representation of an image is given by $(\mathbf{x}_i, \mathbf{y}_i)$, knowing that $\mathbf{x}_i$ is the set of features of this image and $\mathbf{y}_i$ is their class, and as each case in the case base consists of two parts.

So, the first part of the case is corresponding to the relevant feature set $\mathbf{x}_i$ and the second part which is the solution corresponds to the class $\mathbf{y}_i$. After the construction of the medical case base, it was divided into two parts, one for training the four models used namely, CNN, VGGNet, ResNet and GoogleNet, and the other for testing. Finally, the final decision of classification is chosen by applying the majority vote (Kittler, Hatef, Duin, & Matas, 1998) on the results obtained by the four models.

FUTURE RESEARCH DIRECTIONS

The main objective behind the hybridization between the two methods, case-based reasoning and deep learning is to complement the shortcomings of one method with the capabilities of the other and to benefit from the richness of the synergies that potentially exist, to help physicians to deal with complex cases and consequently achieve good performance in the medical context. Future research directions that can be considered through this book chapter can be:

- Apply different CNN models such as InceptionV3, ResNeXt101, VGGNet19, InceptionResNetV2, ZFNet, Xception, etc, to properly model the retrieval phase of the CBR cycle.
- Apply deep learning to represent the medical cases to be stored in the case base, i.e., integrate deep learning into the CBR learning process each time a new case is to be stored in the case base.
- Ignore the intervention of a medical expert to establish the adaptation rules of the adaptation phase and make it automatic through the use of deep learning.

CONCLUSION

The hybridization between the two methods, case-based reasoning, and Deep Learning has contributed to positively changing the performance obtained in medicine and other fields in recent years. Their applications have become increasingly indispensable for physicians and specialists, especially in complex and uncertain cases, where physicians can take a long time to classify certain abnormalities or make final decisions for their patients. This paper presents the proposed approach which aims to improve the solution generated by the retrieval phase of the CBR cycle using Deep Learning and more particularly the popular models of the convolutional neural network (CNN). A review regarding CBR systems developed in medicine, and DL systems proposed in the medical context, and hybrid systems between CBR and DL was presented. The future work consists in implementing the proposed approach and improving the way of extracting the relevant features, i.e. combining several robust methods for feature extraction and consequently developing the result of the retrieval phase of CBR.

REFERENCES

Aamodt, A., & Plaza, E. (1994). Case-based reasoning: Foundational issues, methodological variations, and system approaches. *AI Communications*, *7*(1), 39–59. doi:10.3233/AIC-1994-7104

Abd Elkader, S., Elmogy, M., El-Sappagh, S., & Zaied, A. N. H. (2018). A framework for chronic kidney disease diagnosis based on case based reasoning. *International Journal of Advanced Computer Research*, *8*(35), 59–71. doi:10.19101/IJACR.2018.834003

Amin, K., Kapetanakis, S., Althoff, K.-D., Dengel, A., & Petridis, M. (2018). *Answering with cases: a CBR approach to deep learning.* Paper presented at the International Conference on Case-Based Reasoning. 10.1007/978-3-030-01081-2_2

Amin, K., Kapetanakis, S., Polatidis, N., Althoff, K.-D., & Dengel, A. (2020). *DeepKAF: A Heterogeneous CBR & Deep Learning Approach for NLP Prototyping.* Paper presented at the 2020 International Conference on INnovations in Intelligent SysTems and Applications (INISTA). 10.1109/INISTA49547.2020.9194679

Ayyad, S. M., Saleh, A. I., & Labib, L. M. (2019). Gene expression cancer classification using modified K-Nearest Neighbors technique. *Bio Systems*, *176*, 41–51. doi:10.1016/j.biosystems.2018.12.009 PMID:30611843

Bartsch-Spörl, B., Lenz, M., & Hübner, A. (1999). *Case-based reasoning–survey and future directions.* Paper presented at the German Conference on Knowledge-Based Systems.

Begum, S., Ahmed, M. U., Funk, P., Xiong, N., & Von Schéele, B. (2009). A case-based decision support system for individual stress diagnosis using fuzzy similarity matching. *Computational Intelligence*, *25*(3), 180–195. doi:10.1111/j.1467-8640.2009.00337.x

Bichindaritz, I. (1994). A case-based assistant for clinical psychiatry expertise. *Proceedings of the Annual Symposium on Computer Application in Medical Care.*

Boden, M. (1977). Artificial intelligence and natural man Basic Books. Academic Press.

Carreira-Perpinán, M. A. (2015). *A review of mean-shift algorithms for clustering.* arXiv preprint arXiv:1503.00687.

Chebli, A., Djebbar, A., Marouani, H. F., & Lounis, H. (2021). Case-Base Maintenance: An approach based on Active Semi-Supervised Learning. *International Journal of Pattern Recognition and Artificial Intelligence*, *35*(11), 2151011. doi:10.1142/S0218001421510113

Chebli, A., Djebbar, A., & Merouani, H. F. D. (2020). Improving the performance of computer-aided diagnosis systems using semi-supervised learning: A survey and analysis. *International Journal of Intelligent Information and Database Systems*, *13*(2-4), 454–478. doi:10.1504/IJIIDS.2020.109466

Chen, C., Li, O., Tao, D., Barnett, A., Rudin, C., & Su, J. K. (2019). This looks like that: Deep learning for interpretable image recognition. *Advances in Neural Information Processing Systems*, *32*, 8930–8941.

Chen, X.-W., & Lin, X. (2014). Big data deep learning: Challenges and perspectives. *IEEE Access: Practical Innovations, Open Solutions*, *2*, 514–525. doi:10.1109/ACCESS.2014.2325029

Cohen, J. B. (1997). Retrospect: A Hybrid Decision Support System in the Domain of Breast Cancer Treatment Planning. *Proceedings of the AMIA Annual Fall Symposium.*

Corbat, L., Nauval, M., Henriet, J., & Lapayre, J.-C. (2020). A fusion method based on deep learning and case-based reasoning which improves the resulting medical image segmentations. *Expert Systems with Applications, 147*, 113200. doi:10.1016/j.eswa.2020.113200

De Paz, J. F., Rodríguez, S., Bajo, J., & Corchado, J. M. (2009). Case-based reasoning as a decision support system for cancer diagnosis: A case study. *International Journal of Hybrid Intelligent Systems, 6*(2), 97–110. doi:10.3233/HIS-2009-0089

Díaz, F., Fdez-Riverola, F., & Corchado, J. M. (2006). gene-CBR: A case-based reasoning tool for cancer diagnosis using microarray data sets. *Computational Intelligence, 22*(3-4), 254–268. doi:10.1111/j.1467-8640.2006.00287.x

Duan, J., & Jiao, F. (2021). Novel Case-Based Reasoning System for Public Health Emergencies. *Risk Management and Healthcare Policy, 14*, 541–553. doi:10.2147/RMHP.S291441 PMID:33603520

Eisenstadt, V., Langenhan, C., & Althoff, K.-D. (2019). *Generation of Floor Plan Variations with Convolutional Neural Networks and Case-based Reasoning-An approach for transformative adaptation of room configurations within a framework for support of early conceptual design phases.* Academic Press.

Fan, C.-Y., Chang, P.-C., Lin, J.-J., & Hsieh, J. (2011). A hybrid model combining case-based reasoning and fuzzy decision tree for medical data classification. *Applied Soft Computing, 11*(1), 632–644. doi:10.1016/j.asoc.2009.12.023

Fatima, A., Nazir, N., & Khan, M. G. (2017). Data cleaning in data warehouse: A survey of data pre-processing techniques and tools. *IJ Information Technology and Computer Science, 3*(3), 50–61. doi:10.5815/ijitcs.2017.03.06

Flach, P. A., & Lachiche, N. (2004). Naive Bayesian classification of structured data. *Machine Learning, 57*(3), 233–269. doi:10.1023/B:MACH.0000039778.69032.ab

Gao, X., Braden, B., Zhang, L., Taylor, S., Pang, W., & Petridis, M. (2019). Case-based reasoning of a deep learning network for prediction of early stage of oesophageal cancer. *Proceedings of the 24th UK Symposium on Case-Based Reasoning.*

Gasmi, S., Djebbar, A., & Merouani, H. F. (2021). *Case-Based Reasoning in Medicine: A survey.* Paper presented at the First National Conference on Artificial Intelligence and Information Technologies (CNIATI'21), University El-Tarf.

Goodfellow, I., Pouget-Abadie, J., Mirza, M., Xu, B., Warde-Farley, D., Ozair, S., ... Bengio, Y. (2014). Generative adversarial nets. *Advances in Neural Information Processing Systems, 27*.

Grace, K., Maher, M. L., Wilson, D. C., & Najjar, N. A. (2016). *Combining CBR and deep learning to generate surprising recipe designs.* Paper presented at the International Conference on Case-Based Reasoning. 10.1007/978-3-319-47096-2_11

Gu, D., Liang, C., & Zhao, H. (2017). A case-based reasoning system based on weighted heterogeneous value distance metric for breast cancer diagnosis. *Artificial Intelligence in Medicine, 77*, 31–47. doi:10.1016/j.artmed.2017.02.003 PMID:28545610

Guessoum, S., Laskri, M. T., & Lieber, J. (2014). RespiDiag: A case-based reasoning system for the diagnosis of chronic obstructive pulmonary disease. *Expert Systems with Applications, 41*(2), 267–273. doi:10.1016/j.eswa.2013.05.065

He, K., Zhang, X., Ren, S., & Sun, J. (2016). Deep residual learning for image recognition. *Proceedings of the IEEE conference on computer vision and pattern recognition.*

Hinton, G. E., Osindero, S., & Teh, Y.-W. (2006). A fast learning algorithm for deep belief nets. *Neural Computation, 18*(7), 1527–1554. doi:10.1162/neco.2006.18.7.1527 PMID:16764513

Huang, M.-J., Chen, M.-Y., & Lee, S.-C. (2007). Integrating data mining with case-based reasoning for chronic diseases prognosis and diagnosis. *Expert Systems with Applications, 32*(3), 856–867. doi:10.1016/j.eswa.2006.01.038

Keane, M. T., Kenny, E. M., Temraz, M., Greene, D., & Smyth, B. (2021). *Twin Systems for DeepCBR: A Menagerie of Deep Learning and Case-Based Reasoning Pairings for Explanation and Data Augmentation.* arXiv preprint arXiv:2104.14461.

Kittler, J., Hatef, M., Duin, R. P., & Matas, J. (1998). On combining classifiers. *IEEE Transactions on Pattern Analysis and Machine Intelligence, 20*(3), 226–239. doi:10.1109/34.667881

Kooi, T., Litjens, G., Van Ginneken, B., Gubern-Mérida, A., Sánchez, C. I., Mann, R., den Heeten, A., & Karssemeijer, N. (2017). Large scale deep learning for computer aided detection of mammographic lesions. *Medical Image Analysis, 35*, 303–312. doi:10.1016/j.media.2016.07.007 PMID:27497072

Kothari, R., & Dong, M. (2001). Decision trees for classification: A review and some new results. *Pattern recognition: From classical to modern approaches*, 169-184.

Krizhevsky, A., Sutskever, I., & Hinton, G. E. (2012). Imagenet classification with deep convolutional neural networks. *Advances in Neural Information Processing Systems, 25*, 1097–1105.

Kwolek, B. (2005). *Face detection using convolutional neural networks and Gabor filters.* Paper presented at the International Conference on Artificial Neural Networks. 10.1007/11550822_86

Lamy, J.-B., Sekar, B., Guezennec, G., Bouaud, J., & Séroussi, B. (2019). Explainable artificial intelligence for breast cancer: A visual case-based reasoning approach. *Artificial Intelligence in Medicine, 94*, 42–53. doi:10.1016/j.artmed.2019.01.001 PMID:30871682

Lansley, M., Polatidis, N., Kapetanakis, S., Amin, K., Samakovitis, G., & Petridis, M. (2019). *Seen the villains: Detecting Social Engineering Attacks using Case-based Reasoning and Deep Learning.* Paper presented at the ICCBR Workshops.

LeBozec, C., Jaulent, M.-C., Zapletal, E., & Degoulet, P. (1998). Unified modeling language and design of a case-based retrieval system in medical imaging. *Proceedings of the AMIA Symposium.*

LeCun, Y., Boser, B., Denker, J., Henderson, D., Howard, R., Hubbard, W., & Jackel, L. (1989). Handwritten digit recognition with a back-propagation network. *Advances in Neural Information Processing Systems, 2.*

LeCun, Y., Bottou, L., Bengio, Y., & Haffner, P. (1998). Gradient-based learning applied to document recognition. *Proceedings of the IEEE, 86*(11), 2278–2324. doi:10.1109/5.726791

Li, O., Liu, H., Chen, C., & Rudin, C. (2018). Deep learning for case-based reasoning through prototypes: A neural network that explains its predictions. *Proceedings of the AAAI Conference on Artificial Intelligence.*

Liu, W., Wang, Z., Liu, X., Zeng, N., Liu, Y., & Alsaadi, F. E. (2017). A survey of deep neural network architectures and their applications. *Neurocomputing, 234*, 11–26. doi:10.1016/j.neucom.2016.12.038

López Ibáñez, B., Pous i Sabadí, C., Gay Sacristán, P., Pla Planas, A., Sanz, J. N., & Brunet, J. S. (2011). EXiT CBR: A framework for case-based medical diagnosis development and experimentation. *Artificial Intelligence in Medicine, 51*(2), 81-91.

López-Sánchez, D., Corchado, J. M., & Arrieta, A. G. (2017). *A CBR system for image-based webpage classification: case representation with convolutional neural networks.* Paper presented at the Thirtieth International Flairs Conference.

Louati, A., Louati, H., & Li, Z. (2021). Deep learning and case-based reasoning for predictive and adaptive traffic emergency management. *The Journal of Supercomputing, 77*(5), 4389–4418. doi:10.100711227-020-03435-3

Mahbod, A., Schaefer, G., Wang, C., Ecker, R., & Ellinge, I. (2019). *Skin lesion classification using hybrid deep neural networks.* Paper presented at the ICASSP 2019-2019 IEEE International Conference on Acoustics, Speech and Signal Processing (ICASSP). 10.1109/ICASSP.2019.8683352

Mansoul, A., Atmani, B., & Benbelkacem, S. (2013). *A hybrid decision support system: application on healthcare.* arXiv preprint arXiv:1311.4086.

Marling, C., & Whitehouse, P. (2001). *Case-based reasoning in the care of Alzheimer's disease patients.* Paper presented at the International Conference on Case-Based Reasoning. 10.1007/3-540-44593-5_50

Mikołajczyk, A., & Grochowski, M. (2018). *Data augmentation for improving deep learning in image classification problem.* Paper presented at the 2018 international interdisciplinary PhD workshop (IIPhDW). 10.1109/IIPHDW.2018.8388338

Mille, A., Fuchs, B., & Herbeaux, O. (1996). *A unifying framework for Adaptation in Case-Based Reasoning.* Paper presented at the Workshop on Adaptation in Case-Based Reasoning, ECAI-96.

Miotto, R., Li, L., Kidd, B. A., & Dudley, J. T. (2016). Deep patient: An unsupervised representation to predict the future of patients from the electronic health records. *Scientific Reports, 6*(1), 1–10. doi:10.1038rep26094 PMID:27185194

Mohri, M., Rostamizadeh, A., & Talwalkar, A. (2012). *Foundations of machine learning.* The MIT Press.

Nasiri, S., Helsper, J., Jung, M., & Fathi, M. (2018). Enriching a CBR recommender system by classification of skin lesions using deep neural networks. *Proceedings (CBRDL: Case-Based Reasoning and Deep Learning) of the 26th International Conference on Case-Based Reasoning (ICCBR 2018).*

Nayak, J., Naik, B., & Behera, H. (2015). Fuzzy C-means (FCM) clustering algorithm: a decade review from 2000 to 2014. *Computational Intelligence in Data Mining, 2,* 133-149.

Neshat, M., Sargolzaei, M., Nadjaran Toosi, A., & Masoumi, A. (2012). Hepatitis disease diagnosis using hybrid case based reasoning and particle swarm optimization. *International Scholarly Research Notices.*

Neves, J., Vicente, H., Ferraz, F., Leite, A. C., Rodrigues, A. R., Cruz, M., & Sampaio, L. (2018). *A deep learning approach to case based reasoning to the evaluation and diagnosis of cervical carcinoma. In Modern Approaches for Intelligent Information and Database Systems.* Springer.

Nguyen, L. D., Lin, D., Lin, Z., & Cao, J. (2018). *Deep CNNs for microscopic image classification by exploiting transfer learning and feature concatenation.* Paper presented at the 2018 IEEE International Symposium on Circuits and Systems (ISCAS). 10.1109/ISCAS.2018.8351550

Obaid, H. S., Dheyab, S. A., & Sabry, S. S. (2019). *The impact of data pre-processing techniques and dimensionality reduction on the accuracy of machine learning.* Paper presented at the 2019 9th Annual Information Technology, Electromechanical Engineering and Microelectronics Conference (IEMECON). 10.1109/IEMECONX.2019.8877011

Oh, K. T., Lee, S., Lee, H., Yun, M., & Yoo, S. K. (2020). Semantic segmentation of white matter in FDG-PET using generative adversarial network. *Journal of Digital Imaging, 33*(4), 816–825. doi:10.100710278-020-00321-5 PMID:32043177

Oyelade, O. N., & Ezugwu, A. E. (2020). A case-based reasoning framework for early detection and diagnosis of novel coronavirus. *Informatics in Medicine Unlocked, 20,* 100395. doi:10.1016/j.imu.2020.100395 PMID:32835080

Pang, S., & Yang, X. (2016). Deep convolutional extreme learning machine and its application in handwritten digit classification. *Computational Intelligence and Neuroscience, 2016,* 2016. doi:10.1155/2016/3049632 PMID:27610128

Pannala, N. U., Nawarathna, C. P., Jayakody, J., Rupasinghe, L., & Krishnadeva, K. (2016). *Supervised learning based approach to aspect based sentiment analysis.* Paper presented at the 2016 IEEE International Conference on Computer and Information Technology (CIT). 10.1109/CIT.2016.107

Pereira, S., Pinto, A., Alves, V., & Silva, C. A. (2016). Brain tumor segmentation using convolutional neural networks in MRI images. *IEEE Transactions on Medical Imaging, 35*(5), 1240–1251. doi:10.1109/TMI.2016.2538465 PMID:26960222

Perumal, V. (2016). Performance evaluation and comparative analysis of various machine learning techniques for diagnosis of breast cancer. *Biomedical Research, 27*(3).

Prinzie, A., & Van den Poel, D. (2008). Random forests for multiclass classification: Random multinomial logit. *Expert Systems with Applications, 34*(3), 1721–1732. doi:10.1016/j.eswa.2007.01.029

Pusztová, Ľ., Babič, F., & Paralič, J. (2021). Semi-Automatic Adaptation of Diagnostic Rules in the Case-Based Reasoning Process. *Applied Sciences (Basel, Switzerland), 11*(1), 292. doi:10.3390/app11010292

Reddy, M., Pesl, P., Xenou, M., Toumazou, C., Johnston, D., Georgiou, P., Herrero, P., & Oliver, N. (2016). Clinical safety and feasibility of the advanced bolus calculator for type 1 diabetes based on case-based reasoning: A 6-week nonrandomized single-arm pilot study. *Diabetes Technology & Therapeutics, 18*(8), 487–493. doi:10.1089/dia.2015.0413 PMID:27196358

Rumelhart, D. E., Hinton, G. E., & Williams, R. J. (1985). *Learning internal representations by error propagation*. California Univ San Diego La Jolla Inst for Cognitive Science.

Rumelhart, D. E., Hinton, G. E., & Williams, R. J. (1986). Learning representations by back-propagating errors. *Nature, 323*(6088), 533-536.

Salakhutdinov, R., & Hinton, G. (2009). *Deep boltzmann machines*. Paper presented at the Artificial intelligence and statistics.

Samuel, A. L. (2000). Some studies in machine learning using the game of checkers. *IBM Journal of Research and Development, 44*(1.2), 206-226.

Sani, S., Wiratunga, N., & Massie, S. (2017). *Learning deep features for kNN-based human activity recognition*. Academic Press.

Sarraf, S., & Tofighi, G. (2016). *Classification of alzheimer's disease using fmri data and deep learning convolutional neural networks*. arXiv preprint arXiv:1603.08631.

Schmidt, R., & Vorobieva, O. (2005). *Case-based reasoning investigation of therapy inefficacy*. Paper presented at the International Conference on Innovative Techniques and Applications of Artificial Intelligence.

Sharaf-El-Deen, D. A., Moawad, I. F., & Khalifa, M. (2014). A new hybrid case-based reasoning approach for medical diagnosis systems. *Journal of Medical Systems, 38*(2), 1–11. doi:10.100710916-014-0009-1 PMID:24469683

Simonyan, K., & Zisserman, A. (2014). *Very deep convolutional networks for large-scale image recognition*. arXiv preprint arXiv:1409.1556.

Smolinska, A., Hauschild, A.-C., Fijten, R., Dallinga, J., Baumbach, J., & Van Schooten, F. (2014). Current breathomics—A review on data pre-processing techniques and machine learning in metabolomics breath analysis. *Journal of Breath Research, 8*(2), 027105. doi:10.1088/1752-7155/8/2/027105 PMID:24713999

Song, Z., Zou, S., Zhou, W., Huang, Y., Shao, L., Yuan, J., ... Chen, X. (2020). Clinically applicable histopathological diagnosis system for gastric cancer detection using deep learning. *Nature Communications, 11*(1), 1–9. doi:10.103841467-020-18147-8 PMID:32855423

Srivastava, S., & Tripathi, K. (2012). Artificial neural network and non-linear regression: A comparative study. *International Journal of Scientific and Research Publications, 2*(12), 740–744.

Subasi, A., & Ercelebi, E. (2005). Classification of EEG signals using neural network and logistic regression. *Computer Methods and Programs in Biomedicine*, *78*(2), 87–99. doi:10.1016/j.cmpb.2004.10.009 PMID:15848265

Suk, H.-I., Lee, S.-W., & Shen, D. (2014). Hierarchical feature representation and multimodal fusion with deep learning for AD/MCI diagnosis. *NeuroImage*, *101*, 569–582. doi:10.1016/j.neuroimage.2014.06.077 PMID:25042445

Szegedy, C., Liu, W., Jia, Y., Sermanet, P., Reed, S., Anguelov, D., ... Rabinovich, A. (2015). Going deeper with convolutions. *Proceedings of the IEEE conference on computer vision and pattern recognition.*

Tang, H., Chen, X., Liu, Y., Lu, Z., You, J., Yang, M., ... Chen, T. (2019). Clinically applicable deep learning framework for organs at risk delineation in CT images. *Nature Machine Intelligence*, *1*(10), 480–491. doi:10.103842256-019-0099-z

Turner, J., Floyd, M. W., Gupta, K., & Oates, T. (2019). *NOD-CC: A Hybrid CBR-CNN Architecture for Novel Object Discovery.* Paper presented at the International Conference on Case-Based Reasoning. 10.1007/978-3-030-29249-2_25

Wang, Z.-Z., & Yong, J.-H. (2008). Texture analysis and classification with linear regression model based on wavelet transform. *IEEE Transactions on Image Processing*, *17*(8), 1421–1430. doi:10.1109/TIP.2008.926150 PMID:18632350

Ye, J., Zhao, Z., & Wu, M. (2007). Discriminative k-means for clustering. *Advances in Neural Information Processing Systems*, *20*, 1649–1656.

Ye, X., Zhao, Z., Leake, D., Wang, X., & Crandall, D. (2021). *Applying the Case Difference Heuristic to Learn Adaptations from Deep Network Features.* arXiv preprint arXiv:2107.07095.

Zeiler, M. D., & Fergus, R. (2014). *Visualizing and understanding convolutional networks.* Paper presented at the European conference on computer vision.

Zhang, G. P. (2000). Neural networks for classification: A survey. *IEEE Transactions on Systems, Man and Cybernetics. Part C, Applications and Reviews*, *30*(4), 451–462. doi:10.1109/5326.897072

Zhong, W., Liao, L., Guo, X., & Wang, G. (2019). Fetal electrocardiography extraction with residual convolutional encoder–decoder networks. *Australasian Physical & Engineering Sciences in Medicine*, *42*(4), 1081–1089. doi:10.100713246-019-00805-x PMID:31617154

KEY TERMS AND DEFINITIONS

Chronic Kidney Disease: Is a disease in which the kidneys gradually lose function, resulting in a dangerous buildup of fluids, electrolytes, and waste products in the body. Diabetes, high blood pressure, heart disease, and a family history of kidney failure are the main risk factors for kidney disease.

Chronically Obstructed Pulmonary Illness: Is a long-term inflammatory lung disease that causes breathing difficulties and airflow obstruction in the lungs. Smoking and long-term exposure to irritating gases or particles are the main causes of this disease.

Computer-Aided Detection (CAD): Is the technology of using computer-generated output to reduce observational errors by physicians interpreting medical images.

Coronavirus: Is a type of infectious disease that has killed millions of people around the world. It belongs to the Coronaviridae family of viruses that cause digestive and respiratory infections.

Endocrine System: Is a collection of glands that produce and secrete hormones that the body employs for a variety of uses.

Liver Disorder: It is a disease that can be genetically inherited, or caused by several factors such as viruses, alcohol consumption, etc. This type of disease does not always cause visible signs and symptoms.

Public Health Emergencies: An actual or potential public health crisis or imminent threat of a disease or health condition, caused by bioterrorism, epidemic disease, etc.

Chapter 7
Big Data Analytics for Search Engine Optimization in Intelligent Business

Isakki Alias Devi Paramasivam

https://orcid.org/0000-0001-8021-7338

Ayya Nadar Janaki Ammal College, India

Selvakumar Anthonyraj

https://orcid.org/0000-0002-7806-3867

Ayya Nadar Janaki Ammal College, India

ABSTRACT

Big data has a massive impact on the world today, publicly and in the business province. SEO (Search Engine Optimization) is one of the areas of intelligent business marketing that is continuously affected by the insights. Big data makes it easier for search engines to analyze the content and deliver results that are relevant to user needs. Search engine optimization takes into account how search engines work, the computer-programmed algorithms that govern look search engine behavior, what users search for, and the actual search keywords submitted into search engines. Search engines are always preferred by their targeted audience. Big data analytics is obliging to increase website traffic. This really helps to apply intelligence in business areas. This chapter deals with big data analytics for SEO in intelligent business.

INTRODUCTION

Important marketing decisions in intelligent business are determined by big data. This refers to the use of large, complicated datasets that typical data processing applications are unable to handle. Big Data analytics examples consist of stock exchanges, social media sites, jet engines, etc. In SEO, big data is really important. The use of big data in conjunction with SEO tactics makes it simple to overcome any challenges. It gives the company much-needed publicity as well as a larger user base. It also increases the probability of a higher conversion rate in the business. According to Ghasemaghaei et al. (2018), "All

DOI: 10.4018/978-1-7998-9016-4.ch007

dimensions, except bigness of data, significantly increase decision efficiency". Marketers can acquire in-depth insights on a consumer's requirements and attitude by using business intelligence for marketing. The organization may then use this information to build more profitable marketing efforts, target the correct audience, and achieve the greatest outcomes.

Big Data in Customer Service

Nowadays, customers expect excellent customer experience. Data management plays a vital role for customer relationship management in companies. The data from a customer service and customer experience perspective need an integrated approach. The huge volume of information and data sources regarding customers, and transactions will be useful to find the customers who expect constant experiences. Businesses may use big data analytics to change their connections with customers, promote products more effectively, and boost revenue. Analytics that are properly specified and integrated into business processes enable critical behaviors for digital transformation, including: increased productivity, decision-making based on data. Every second, 1.7 MB of data are generated for each and every person on earth, according to estimates. Organizations are gathering and analyzing data in order to optimize their response to challenges and difficulties. Big data and AI are being invested in by 97.2 percent of businesses.

Search Engine

The search engine is more sophisticated at natural language processing and can better to determine the context behind a user's search. Companies need to harness the power of big data to identify new opportunities and gain a reasonable edge in search results. A search engine is a web-based application that aids in the discovery of information on the Internet. Popular search engines include Google, Yahoo!, and MSN Search, to name a few. The spiders' data is utilized to generate a searchable index of the Web. Small company owners may utilize SEO to construct quick, sturdy, and user-friendly websites that rank higher in search engines, driving in more qualified potential customers and enhancing conversion rates (Kherbachi et al., 2020).

BIG DATA

Big data is described as large amounts of data that can only be examined by computers in order to reveal patterns, trends, and associations. Search engines are more upgradeable. They can able to handle large amount of data with high speed. Big Data describe the large amount of data in the networked, digitized, and information driven world.

Today, there are millions of data sources that make data at a speedy rate. These data sources are presented across the world. Social media platforms and networks are some of the most important data sources. For example; Facebook generates more than 500 terabytes of data every day. This data includes pictures, videos, messages, and more.

Data exists in different types of formats, like structured data, semi-structured data, and unstructured data. In Excel sheet, data is classified as structured data with a specific format. In contrast, emails fall under semi-structured. The pictures and videos fall under the type of unstructured data. All this data combined to create Big Data.

Big Data is considered in terms of 3V's: volume (how much data), velocity (how fast the data is processed), and variety (different formats of data). A small volume of complex data, a huge volume of simple data, or sophisticated analytics and predictions from any kind of data can still benefit from the Big Data technology rejuvenation. The available Big Data today is all about "distributed", "sharded" which means dividing up jobs into pieces and spreading them over a cluster. The real meaning is an actionable data, actionable information, and actionable intelligence. The following are some reasons why big data is important for digital marketers:

- Real-time customer insights
- Personalized targeting
- Increasing sales
- Improves the efficiency of a marketing campaign
- Budget optimization
- Measuring campaign's results more accurately

BIG DATA ANALYTICS

Big Data analytics is a methodology for uncovering hidden patterns, unknown correlations, market trends, and client preferences from massive quantities of data. It can be used for better decision making and preventing fraudulent activities. According to Ghasemaghaei et al. (2018), "All dimensions of DA competency significantly improve decision quality".

In the Big Data epoch, search engine optimization covenants with the encapsulation of datasets which are related to the performance of websites. In terms of architecture, content curation, and consumer characteristics, the performance is defined. Big data analytics develops the opportunities for developing new methodological frameworks. These frameworks are made up of trusted analytics that may be used to construct well-informed organic traffic optimization approaches.

Necessity of Big Data Analytics

Everything in the online world is powered by Big Data analytics. According to Oussous et al. (2018), "Advanced data analysis is required to understand the relationships among features and explore data". Take, for example, the music-streaming service Spotify. If a corporation has 100 million users, it will generate a massive amount of data each day. Through a clever recommendation system that is based on likes, shares, and search history, the cloud-based platform can automatically produce suggested songs. If the user is a Spotify user, the top recommendation area will be displayed. A recommendation engine will be used by the search engine, which will make use of data filtering technologies. Data filtering software gathers information and then filters it.

The Lifecycle of Big Data Analytics

Big data analytics has eight stages in its life cycle. It is depicted in Figure 1.

Figure 1. Life cycle of Big Data analytics

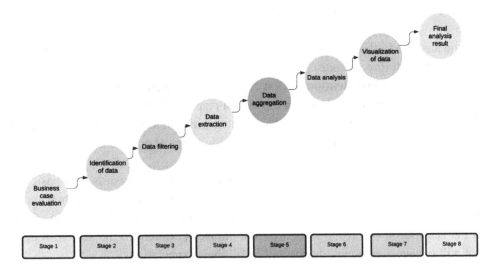

Stage 1: Business case evaluation - A business case is the first step in the Big Data analytics lifecycle. The purpose and goal of the analysis are defined by these situations.

Stage 2: Identification of data - A wide range of data sources can be found.

Stage 3: Data Filtering - All of the previously detected data is cleaned to remove any corrupt data.

Stage 4: Data extraction - Data that isn't compatible with the tool needs to be extracted. Then it can be converted into a format that is compatible.

Stage 5: Data aggregation - Data from multiple datasets with the same fields are combined.

Stage 6: Data analysis - Data is analyzed with analytical and statistical methods in order to uncover useful information.

Stage 7: Data Visualization - Big Data analysts can create graphic visualizations of their analysis using Tableau, Power BI, and QlikView.

Stage 8: Final analysis result - The final stage of the Big Data analytics lifecycle is the final analysis output. The final analysis results are made available to business stakeholders here.

The above stages of big data analytics are useful for collecting own data to acquire organic traffic on websites. SEO analytics aids to increase the organic traffic on site through analyzing data. It can quickly forecast customer behavior and future trends.

Algorithms

Linear Regression: One of the most fundamental algorithms in advanced analytics is linear regression. As a result, it is also one of the most extensively adopted. People can easily understand how it all works and how the input and output data are related.

Logistic Regression: When there are clearly defined yes or no questions, logistic regression is frequently utilized.

- Will a customer purchase from you again?

- Is a potential buyer creditworthy?
- Is there a chance the prospect will become a customer?

Predicting the answers to these questions can generate a sequence of events in the business process which will support drive future revenue.

Regression Trees and Classification Trees: A decision is often used to categorize data in classification and regression trees. Each decision is made in response to an inquiry about one of the input variables. The instance of data grows closer to being categorized in a specific way with each query and appropriate response. A tree-like structure is created by this series of questions and responses, and also the subsequent divisions of data.

Prediction: Prediction algorithms aid in the prediction of popular keywords. The basic idea behind all of these algorithms is that it allows SEO experts to make a basic premise about how much revenue they will make if they rank first for certain specific keywords within a tolerable margin of error. It also facilitates in the acquisition of certain keywords and phrases pertinent to the search. It contemplates keywords that will engage a greater audience and fulfill their expectations.

Types of Big Data Analytics

The four types of big data analytics are as follows:

1. Descriptive Analytics

This summarizes previous data in an easy-to-understand format. This aids in the creation of reports such as a company's income, profit, and sales, among other things. It also aids in the tally of social media metrics.

2. Diagnostic Analytics

This is done in order to figure out what created the issue in the first place. Drill-down, data mining, and data recovery are all instances of techniques. Diagnostic analytics are used by businesses because they provide a detailed understanding of a problem.

3. Predictive Analytics

This sort of analytics examines past and current data in order to create predictions about the future. Predictive analytics analyses current data and makes predictions about the future using data mining, artificial intelligence, and machine learning. It predicts customer and market trends, among other things.

4. Prescriptive Analytics

This type of analytics recommends a remedy to a specific issue. Both descriptive and predictive analytics are used in perspective analytics. The majority of the time, AI and machine learning are used.

Benefits of Big Data Analytics

1. **Risk Management:** The Company uses it to narrow down a list of suspects or problems' root causes.
2. **Product Development and Innovations:** Big Data analytics is utilized to examine the engine design and determine where enhancements are needed.
3. **Better Decision Making:** They will consider a variety of aspects, including population, demography, geographical accessibility, and more.
4. **Enhance Customer Experience:** Big Data analysis is utilized to enhance customer experiences and foster positive customer relationships.

Big Data Analytics Tools

- Hadoop aids in the storage and analysis of data.
- MongoDB is a database that is used for constantly changing datasets.
- Talend is a tool for data management and integration.
- Cassandra is a distributed database for handling data chunks.
- Spark is a programming language that is used to process and analyze enormous volumes of data in real time.
- STORM is a real-time computational system that is open-source.
- Kafka is a fault-tolerant storage platform that runs on a distributed streaming platform.

Industry Applications for Big Data

Here are a few examples of industries that are actively using Big Data:

- Ecommerce - Big Data analytics is used in e-commerce to predict customer trends and optimize prices, to name a few examples.
- Marketing - Big Data analytics assists in the development of high-return-on-investment marketing programmes that increase revenues.
- Education - Used to generate new courses and research old ones in order to meet market demands.
- Banking - Customer income and spending trends can help anticipate which banking products, such as loans and credit cards, they will choose.
- Telecommunications - This field is used to forecast network capacity and improve the client experience.
- Government - Law enforcement gains from Big Data analytics.
- Healthcare - Big data analytics is used to assess how probable a patient is to have health problems based on their medical history.
- Media and entertainment - Used to understand the demand for movies, songs, and other media in order to provide users with a customized recommendation list.

SEARCH ENGINE OPTIMIZATION

The technique of increasing the quantity and quality of internet traffic from search engines to a website or web page is referred as search engine optimization (SEO). According to Khraim (2015), "SEO leads to the increased brand visibility for your site". Rather than paid or direct visitors, SEO focuses on organic traffic. Image and video searches, academic research searches, current news searches, and industry-specific vertical searches are just a few examples of unpaid traffic sources. The process of obtaining visits from free, organic, editorial, or natural search results on search engines is termed as SEO. It has the capability of improving search engine ranks. It gives websites a higher level of quality control.

Working Principle of SEO

Bots are used by Google and Bing to crawl online pages. They can move from site to site, gathering information about the pages and indexing it. Then, using hundreds of ranking criteria or signals, algorithms will analyze sites in the index to determine the order in which they'll show in search results for a given query. The factors which affect search rankings can be considered of as proxies for aspects of the user experience (Kherbachi et al., 2020). Crawlability and mobile usability are important site architecture characteristics, as content optimization variables like content quality and keyword research. According to Gek et al. (2019), "The new site is difficult to bring to the top search engine rankings". The search engines are designed to give users with a speedy search experience by returning relevant, authoritative pages. These criteria must be considered while optimizing our site and content, as they can help our pages rank higher in search results.

SEO is accomplished so that a website can obtain more visitors from search engines by ranking higher on the search engine results page (SERP). These site visitors will become clients. For any type of data, a search engine is the best alternative.

For instance, customers who employ search in large data initiatives involving:

- Patient information
- Financial transactions
- Information about the students
- Notebooks for labs
- Data from the logs and administrative data
- Farmer data
- Information on the weather
- Passenger data

The majority of this data is not in the form of unstructured documents, but rather structured databases. The SEO concepts are depicted in Figure 2.

Content

Search engines are smarter than relational databases for searching structured content. Search engines are more flexible and faster than other techniques of searching. Today's information must be instructive and entertaining, as well as topical and shareable. Content is available in a variety of sources, including:

Figure 2. SEO concepts

- Web page content
- Videos
- Audio
- Blogs
- Info-graphics
- Podcasts
- E-books and whitepapers
- Social media posts

Every page of content is measurable online, and online content pertains to a massive volume of published data. Search engines scan this content and guide visitors / users to relevant results based on their searches. A search engine may perceive itself to be the most important for a query, but it may not be beneficial for business or industry. Online reputation management services must be used to deal with this scenario. A digital marketing firm must focus on increasing the visibility of their client's business and bringing positive content to the top while pushing damaging news to the bottom.

Content Turn Into Data

Content is more than just information that has been released. However, as Google has become a significant curator of big data, it has begun to consider content as quantifiable things. By transforming content into data, search engines can more easily trace it and improve their ability to provide consumers with relevant replies.

Rich snippets, local search packs, and other exclusive results are becoming more prevalent as search results become more organized and semantically analyzed, leading Google to build rich snippets, local search packs, and other exclusive results that would provide greater value to searchers.

Big Data Assists SEO

The usage of huge amounts of data is vital in SEO practices. Search engine optimization is a project that aims to improve a website's search result rankings based on the availability of online data. Visitors are directed to pages that appear to be relevant by search engine giants like Google. The amount and quality of links a website receives from other websites influences its trustworthiness. This is why an SEO specialist will go to great lengths to create authoritative content in order to achieve a higher rating. Everyone recognizes the importance of SEO in marketing campaigns. However, due to the advancement of big data, its tactics are always evolving.

Social Media and Social Networking

Data is churned at a rapid rate on social networking sites. Over time, a large number of users continue to join these social media platforms such as Twitter, Facebook, and others. According to Krstic & Maslikovic (2018), "Measuring the number of physical visits to the location(s) provides an incomplete view of the total amount of use of the cultural institution and its resources". Businesses are devoted to establishing their presence on these social platforms in order to increase their search engine rankings.

Companies will be able to learn customers' ideas and attitudes about a brand, products, or services by analyzing unstructured customer feedback through social media posts, reviews, and customer service conversations. It signifies if the primary emotion is good, neutral, or negative. Text analytics and natural language processing are used in sentiment analysis.

Intelligent Machines

Big data is extremely beneficial since it focuses on people more than search engines do. It instructs us to look into customer purchasing and browsing habits. People don't hesitate to allow cookies or share their check-in credentials for specific locations on social media because everything is transparent online.

Because user-generated data now has weight, computers and mobile devices are getting more intelligent and speedier in their responses to search requests.

Trust Factor

Big data will become an ubiquitous element of everyone's life in the future. No one would be hesitant to reveal their personal information. Online advertisements can be adapted to meet a variety of demands, making them more acceptable and useful in making people's life easier. The reliance on digital devices will increase, necessitating the development of more accurate big data for numerous purposes. This, however, does not prevent spamming. Only the marketing information sources will be modified.

Customer Experience

Big data nowadays contributes to better consumer experiences and company outcomes. Customers' interests, choices, and location details will provide search engines the ability to deliver personalized results. E-commerce is now better implemented. A better data analytics tool can help with customer relationship management.

Sentiment analysis allows a company to gain greater customer insights, which can aid marketers in campaign planning. Sentiment analysis is a method of analyzing data regarding a customer's feelings toward a firm, its brand, and its products or services. Opinion mining is another name for it. Enterprises will profit from user / consumer preferences. Customers who are loyal can be easily detected. Timely identification of customer churn management is also possible. For the finest search engine optimization, digital marketing methods and big data analytics are helpful.

Benefits of sentiment analysis include:

- It aids in the optimization of marketing strategies based on customer feedback
- It aids in the discovery of a brand's strengths and weaknesses
- It aids in the quality of customer service
- It aids in the extension of product quality
- It aids in the identification of new business opportunities

Deeper SEO Insights

Website content is converted into quantifiable data by search engines. These will be able to give more precise findings in the coming days, which marketers can use for insights. Because of huge data, SEOs employ a range of tools and tactics to reach their clients, including keywords, on-page optimization, and hyper linking. All of the decisions made in terms of local SEO, content marketing, and mobile data will aid in the generation of accurate user insights. This is only achievable because of big data's assistance. SEO can help to gain unrestricted targeted traffic from search engines if you have a website, blog, or online store. Users trust search engines, therefore having a presence in the top positions for the keywords they're looking for boosts the website's trustworthiness.

Paid marketing efforts such as native ads, Google AdWords, social media ads, pay-per-click, Google shopping ads, display ads, and more are called to as search engine marketing (SEM). According to Saura et al. (2017), "The accepted thinking in SEO and SEM is that to attract user traffic, it is essential that a website is among the first two or three positions on the first page of the search engine results page (SERPs), as derived through keyword ranking". While always search engine marketing (SEM) isn't normally a big part of an overall SEO strategy, it has its merits because it can help us reach highly targeted customers.

KEY ELEMENTS

When developing an SEO strategy, there are six crucial considerations to keep in mind:

1. Determine Target Market

Today's SEO isn't about attracting as many site visitors as possible; rather, it's about attracting high-value clients who are interested in what you have to offer. Google Analytics is a good place to start when looking at goal marketing. Google Analytics determines which social media channels deliver the most focused traffic to our sites using relevant quantitative data. Furthermore, one can learn how these social media users interact with our website. We must discover answers to the following questions:

- What is it that your market is looking for?
- What are they doing with their online searches?
- What position do they occupy?

If you obtain specific solutions, these are even more important SEO investments.

2. Changes in Users Searching Tricks

Customers previously did not trust search engines like Google to interpret conversational requests. In their search, they included phrases like "Flower delivery in Chennai". Customers have been typing things like "Who guarantees roses near me" in recent times. Changes in searcher behavior will have an impact on which keywords are most valuable for our website. We were used to being aware of terms that brought us additional visitors. Instead, we should concentrate on conversions, sales, and earnings.

3. Navigation Reign

A user-friendly website can have information that is easy to find. This has the potential to increase our traffic. Every website requires that it be constructed around key-word topics with unique content material. As a result, search engines such as Google and yahoo will be able to easily index and rank our website higher. Effective web page site visitor behaviors are beneficial to a higher rating. The text should remain natural and targeted. To keep customers from leaving the website depressed, we can eliminate jargon and keyword stuffing.

4. Valuable Connections

When another website links to our website, search engines like Google believe that it is a trademark that our website online contains valuable material. These days, the cost of a link to our website is based on the quality of the website that is linked to each page. Only a few links to company from high-traffic sites can help organizations to improve ranking.

5. Social Media

Social media has evolved from a simple communication tool to a significant advertising and marketing outlet. Many customers begin their search on social media before arriving at a company's website. More people will visit website if you share up-to-date and personalization.

6. Make SEO Objectives and Track Them

The key to getting better results is to keep track of our website's search engine rating. To establish a baseline for our performance, we must start by tracking the most essential internet site data. If you make little changes to website's content, you'll see an increase in traffic and/or rankings.

IMPROVE SEO RANKINGS

To boost SEO ranks, big data analytics is useful. Understanding how our target audiences think and interact with search engines is essential. Big data analytics are required in this scenario. Companies can know exactly who our users are and what they're looking for using the data we acquire from analytics technologies. Business intelligence and big data analytics are data management solutions used throughout large corporations to collect historical and current data, evaluate raw data using statistics and software, as well as provide opportunities for better future decisions.

Business people can utilize a variety of web analytics tools. What matters more than the correct technology is how companies use that data. Whether it's to improve our entire marketing strategy or to generate better products or services, reviewing and creating next steps with data is essential. Company owners may utilize SEO to construct quick, sturdy, and user-friendly websites that rank higher in search engines, driving in more qualified prospective customers and raising conversion rates. The methods listed below are crucial for SEO rankings.

- Website's navigation behavior
- Build content around best queries
- Improve page loading speed
- Utilize channel groups
- Maximize top referrers
- Geo Based Content-Delivery
- Publish Relevant Content
- Using Meta data

Website's Navigation Behavior

The layout of a website's navigation plays a huge role in enhancing SEO ranking since the longer people stay on the site and visit different pages and articles, the more search engines understand that the site is full of useful materials for visitors. According to Mavridis & Symeonidis (2015), "Search engine rankings have displayed influence by basic webpage characteristics since their inception". Having an effective, easy-to-use navigation structure can assist in guiding visitors through a customer journey, assisting in achieving various goals such as persuading them to sign up for an email list or make an on-site purchase. Using the Behavior tab in Google Analytics reports to examine how well different pages perform in terms of keeping visitors on the site longer.

To discover out what people do, when they visit a page, the user can browse to Behavior > Behavior Flow. We can see how many customers abandon a page after landing on it (or bounce), as well as which pages, they might leave right away. As a result, the homepage may be the starting point. The links in the first interaction column indicate the most-visited pages right after the start page, allowing you to follow the visitors' trip. Knowing where visitors leave the site or which pages, they return to can help you improve them. Wherever needed, include more internal links.

Build Content Around Best Queries

If the website has a search bar, visitors can utilize it to find out what they're looking for on the site, which provides you a great opportunity to develop content to answer their questions. Data analytics can reveal what people are looking for on website. The Site Search tab in Google Analytics may be used to see what customers are searching for on the site. Alternatively, data analytics can be used to see exactly what the audience is looking for even before they arrive on the page. Navigate to Acquisition > Search Console > Queries in Google Analytics to find the search terms used by visitors. Look for the most relevant questions to the firm and build content that revolves around them, such as pillar blog pieces or a funnel.

Improve Page Loading Speed

Almost everyone is talking about Google's move to mobile-first indexing these days, which implies that Google and other search engines are prioritizing how mobile-friendly a site is when determining SEO rankings. When it comes to mobile optimization, the loading speed is crucial. To find out how fast a site loads, use tools like GTMetrix and Page Speed Insights. There are a variety of techniques to make a site more mobile-friendly. Check the loading speeds of individual pages across the site by going to Google Analytics. They also have a function called Site Speed Suggestions, which can provide advice on how to improve the speed of each page.

Utilize Channel Groups

Some online analytics solutions, such as Google Analytics, can classify website traffic in channel groups in a logical way. The paths that website users follow to arrive on the site are referred to as these channels. Some individuals type in the domain name, while others look for a brand or a term. While the default channel groups are useful, you can go even further by building custom channel groups, which can help you produce better, more precise insights and make sense of traffic in more concrete ways. Organizations need to set explicit goals for each channel group once you've built particular channel groups, making it easier to adapt and develop better-targeted campaigns without all the guessing.

Maximize Top Referrers

Chances are utilized to obtain a considerable volume of traffic from third-party sites and pages, when these sites and pages refer users who would not have found their way to a search engine otherwise. Many data analytics solutions can tell you which websites are generating the most traffic. Keeping track of these referrers can help you assess return on investment and improve marketing efforts. Once you've identified the top referrers, you can either strive to increase their performance even further - for example, if third-party site owners can update the link content to something that encourages more clicks, these referrers could improve even more. Alternatively, you might approach different newspapers that have previously used in links to request that they link back to a different blog post in order to improve their own. Either of these methods can aid in increasing CTR and traffic.

Geo Based Content-Delivery

Many businesses, particularly brick-and-mortar enterprises, target the communities in which they are located. If any company would benefit most from visitors from the surrounding city or state, start by developing and optimizing a local SEO plan. If geo-targeting is defined as all ways for determining where an audience comes from and providing information depending on their location, then employing it for local SEO can be a potent combination. The data analytics tool can be used to determine the location of the majority of the audience. This could range from countries to extremely particular cities, depending on the nature of the firm. Optimize the website for improved local SEO rankings by using this information. By modifying pages with more local keywords, using language that resonates better with the target audience, and even tweaking the design to better supply to and represent the local area that wants to talk, you may better supply to and reflect the local area that wants to communicate.

Publish Relevant Content

The first driver of search engine rankings is high-quality content, and there is no substitute for it. Site traffic increases as a result of high-quality content generated expressly for the intended user, which boosts the authority and relevancy of the site.

Keywords

For each page on their website, businesses must select and target a distinct keyword phrase. The search engines must consider how a user might use their search keywords to find that exact page. A webpage's ability to get search engine ranks for several keyword phrases is difficult unless the keywords are related. One page might rank for both "Software Engineer jobs" and "Software Engineer careers". Business people must create a new webpage for each keyword term they want to rank for on their website.

Placing Keywords

Consider the following questions after selecting a keyword phrase for a specific page:

- Is it okay if I include all of the keyword phrases in the URL for the page?
- Should I include all of the keyword phrases in the title of the page?
- Do I need to include all of the keyword phrases in the page headings and subheadings?

If you answered "yes", search engine ranking will climb. Search engine optimization can benefit from readability and usability.

Content

Content, rather than the URL, title, or headings of a page, has the most impact on search engine rankings. We need to repeat our keyword phrase once or twice in the opening and closing paragraphs, then two to four more times throughout the remaining content. To emphasis these keyword phrases, bold, italics, header tags, and other emphasis elements can be used.

Using Metadata

Each page on the website has a gap between the <head> tags where you can insert metadata or information about the page's contents. This data may have been pre-populated in a CMS site created by the UMC web team. However, as the site evolves, it is critical to revisit and update Metadata.

- **Title Metadata:** It is in charge of the page titles that appear at the top of a browser window, as well as the headlines that appear in search engine results. It is the most useful and important info on our page. This emphasizes the importance of creating clever page titles that include keyword terms.
- **Description Metadata:** The textual description that a browser may utilize in the page search return is called description metadata. The site's window display includes a succinct and enticing description of what's inside to entice customers to enter. Two complete sentences constitute a decent meta description. Although search engines may not always use the meta description, it is critical to have the choice.
- **Keyword Metadata:** It is rarely, if ever, utilized to calculate search engine rankings. If you already know keyword phrases, it's not a bad idea to include them in the keyword metadata. Just use a variety of sentences. We must preserve 3-7 phrases, each with 1-4 syllables. A "computer science degree" is an excellent example.

BEST WAYS TO OPTIMIZE OUR WEBSITE FOR SEO

Search engine optimization (SEO) is the technique of enhancing website traffic through search engine results. This increases the visibility of website. If the search phrases used by loyal and potential customers are connected to our brand, they will have a better chance of finding our websites.

Make Our Website Useful for Loyal Audience

More than 200 ranking signals are used by Google to determine which pieces of material appear on the first page of search results. The algorithm looks for signals that a given web page will provide relevant information to our visitors / users. We must choose primary and latent semantic keywords that are relevant to search intent. When it comes to optimizing a website for conversions, the focus should be on directing visitors toward certain objectives. We need to improve our site's interaction with search engines.

Grow Organic Traffic

Advertising accounts for around 1% of the average company's overall revenue. Advertising costs a lot more in the retail industry. Industries must pay to generate and promote their content, although it is less costly than pay-per-click advertising. Paid search accounts for less than 2% of the total, while organic search accounts for roughly 15%. For organic traffic, we must devote both time and money. Website traffic was compared before and after implementing users suggestions (Drivas et al., 2017).

Capitalize on Existing Traffic

When users come to our website, we don't want them to leave. The businessman urges them to come back because he values loyal clients. Businesses must learn to optimize their websites for conversions and comprehend customer experiences. We must determine how visitors explore our website, whether they scroll down the page, and how frequently they click on our calls to action (CTAs). Companies may contact users with offers, incentives, and other information if they sign up for an email list. Visitors may be enticed to follow them on social media, check their product pages, and read their blog articles. Because a higher percentage of organic traffic converts, utilizing existing traffic can help companies to improve conversion rate. Organic and paid traffic were compared before and after implementing users suggestions (Drivas et al., 2017).

Force Your Website to Work Harder

A website can be built by anyone, but only a select few are capable of producing conversions consistently. Across all industries, the average conversion rate is less than 2%. Business people want to see a significant increase in conversions from their users. Companies must keep a close eye on their target market and provide exactly what customers want. Following that, we must apply the information to our website. Visitors to our websites will be able to quickly find what they require, elevating brand as a result. However, SEO is always the priority. Conversions aren't possible without website visitors. Companies must develop a website with excellent, sticky content and several conversion chances for their visitors.

Steps to Optimize Website for SEO

- Analyze all of your website data
- Conduct thorough keyword research
- Create long and value-rich content
- Optimize for on-page SEO
- Optimize for off-page SEO
- Optimize the website for mobile
- Speed up the pages
- Get high-quality backlinks

SEO Performance

When other areas of the business support SEO, its performance is significantly improved. Without the combined efforts of content marketing, user experience, and customer service, the SEO team will not be able to optimize for every ranking element. Big data insights must be valuable in defining company-wide SEO best practices. Business people can figure out which areas of visibility need to be improved and which data sources can provide insights into how to do so. After you've found the correct data sources, you'll need to build up a data pipeline to organize and analyze the information.

Identify Right Metrics

The correct technologies and data sources must be chosen by companies. Then it's crucial to track the correct indicators in order to assess their work. Increased traffic for a specific search keyword may appear to be a beneficial SEO accomplishment, but is that increased traffic actually resulting in active company performance.

Tools

To boost search marketing success, you must employ the correct Big Data techniques and technology. The right tools and technology can open up new doors, improve resource efficiency, and boost the effectiveness of existing SEO campaigns.

Keyword Analysis Tools

Because of Google's advances in language processing and search context, keywords are also vital to SEO on the platform. For identifying fresh content opportunities and increasing targeted web traffic to company's website, keyword research and analysis are critical. Semrush and Ahrefs are excellent data sources for keeping our SEO approach up to date.

You can use Google Adwords Keyword Planner and Semrush to analyze Google's search data. Themes and search volume can be used to filter queries. As Google improves its ability to grasp the context of a search, it's becoming increasingly vital to consider the intent behind a search query in order to gain useful information. These will include details on how to optimize the website for search engines and how to market the content online.

Consider the phrases:

- How to?
- Why?
- What?
- Guides
- Tips

The ability to better identify these types of search queries allows you to better address the audience's challenges and objectives. It will increase visitor trust while also informing them about company products and services.

Semrush

Semrush is a one-stop shop for improving online exposure and identifying marketing strategies. SEO, PPC, SMM, Keyword Research, Competitive Research, PR, Content Marketing, Marketing Insights, and Campaign Management are just a few of the services that our tools and reports can assist with.

To provide data in our data-bases, Semrush use proprietary machine learning algorithms and trusted data suppliers. Although different approaches are used to acquire various types of data, the excellent quality of our data remains consistent throughout all of our databases.

The following information about a website can be found with Semrush:

- Keyword rankings
- Keyword analytics
- Website traffic
- Backlinks
- Website visitor engagement
- Online advertising: creative, positions & keywords
- Global databases
- Mobile traffic data
- Search engine volatility by industry
- Brand products for public relations
- Social media traffic

Semrush is designed for competitive research and all aspects of digital marketing (SEO, Content Marketing, Advertising, and Social Media). We can assess the competition, audit websites, track a particular set of keywords, and generate links with the help of technologies to increase SEO. Content, social media schedules, and report development are all things that we can handle.

The following information is found in the Semrush database:

- 142 geographic databases
- 17 billion keywords
- 580 million domains
- 500TB of raw website traffic data for 190 countries and regions
- 22 trillion backlinks
- 277 million display ads
- 1 billion Google Ads

Ahrefs

The Ahrefs SEO tool is one of the best on the market, and it's one of the most popular ways to prepare an audit report, analyze backlinks, and URL rankings, perform comparative analysis, and more. It's a popular tool for SEO research. It is well-known in the digital marketing area, and it may be used for keyword research and website rankings in addition to SEO back link analysis.

The primary element behind social media marketing is keywords. Apart from determining which keywords are useful to consumers, Ahrefs may also assist us in selecting more accurate themes and topics for our social media posts. For example, if we have a website or publication in mind and want to collaborate with its contributors, finding these authors one by one, reading their bios, and visiting their social media profiles will be time consuming. We can achieve all of this with a single click using Content Explorer. Simply enter the publication site, and a list of authors, who are related to that site, as well as the number of followers on their social media profiles, will show.

Google Search Console

Big data analysis in SEO isn't just about uncovering new possibilities. It also offers information about existing web sites as well as SEO strategy. In order to improve the performance of current web pages, existing search query data must be analyzed. Pages with thin content can be highlighted. Google Search Console is a fantastic tool for highlighting the search terms for which you already have a good position. This data will be made accessible and actionable through Search Analytics reports. This thorough examination of search results is necessary. It aids in the identification of website content keyword phrases.

Ranking Tools

Companies struggle to assess their current rankings and SEO activities. The ranking tools help them come up with new content ideas that would keep their users engaged. The Buzzsumo technology analyses a large quantity of data and determines which content works well in search rankings and on social media for a given topic. It's a sophisticated online tool that allows users to search for well-known information based on their interests. Scanning numerous social websites for user requirements, problems, and preferences takes a significant amount of effort. It will make it easier to come up with new content ideas and keep track of current trends.

Competitive Analysis

We can use big data to do a detailed analysis of our competition and improve our own marketing and SEO effectiveness. For competition analysis, there are a number of modern tools. We can increase our SEO performance by identifying search phrases that our competitors rank for, as well as keywords that drive their success.

USE CASES

From keywords to top referrals and key behavioral metrics like time-on-page and conversion rates, Google Analytics offers valuable information that our organization can leverage to evaluate and improve our organic search campaigns. SEO will be a lot of guesswork if it wasn't for analytics; with analytics, every decision you make is evidence-based.

Real-time Reporting

The real-time reporting operation of Google Analytics allows us to keep track of your website in real time. This will allow us to see real-time website traffic, as well as the pages that are currently attracting visitors and where they came from. Companies can also examine the progress of their campaigns, events, and social media posts to see if they're boosting visitors to website.

Bounce-rate Reporting

Bounce rate reports can reveal us whether consumers interacted with a page on a company's website or whether they simply left without taking the further action (navigation to another page, or scrolled down).

User Journey

You can utilize User-ID to uniquely identify users and use the route analysis technique to see which paths they take between platforms and devices and from event type to event type, to fully understand how they interact with content. A path analysis begins with a screen or event that represents the user's initial step in their journey. The next top-five screens seen or events triggered by the user are then displayed. A backward path, which displays the steps leading up to a final step, can also be created. You may expand the graph along the way and see what users did at each step.

CONCLUSION

Big data tends to make it easier for search engines to assess contents and give relevant results to visitors. Big data analytics can reveal who our clients and users are, as well as what they are searching for. SEO ranking can also be increased by using data analytics tools. Pay-per-click advertising and email marketing are two marketing tactics that can have an indirect impact on how business site ranks.

Business people can't finance each campaign separately. The most successful brands incorporate all of their campaigns to guarantee that their leads are continuously being pushed closer to becoming customers. Utilizing big data analytics, companies can boost their profitability. Big data is also analyzed to determine the best and most relevant keywords for organization's website, which helps to increase traffic. Thousands of search phrases are used by potential users to find out the information they need. Search data analysis provides a clearer insight of customers and provides valuable information for SEO efforts. Organizations can benefit about their customers' expectations via big data analytics. They can boost the number of devoted customers by providing outstanding content on their website. Big data analytics can help businesses keep their loyal clients. Because of search engine optimization, customer happiness will rise. Through big data analytics, all of a customer's activities will be easily notified. Using big data analytics, the website traffic will be increased. SEO gains a new dimension due to big data analytics.

REFERENCES

Drivas, I. C., Sakas, D. P., & Reklitis, P. (2017). Improving Website Usability and Traffic Based on Users Perceptions and Suggestions – A User-Centered Digital Marketing Approach. Strategic Innovative Marketing, 255-266.

Franco, P. G., Matthews, J. L., & Matlock, T. (2016). Framing the past: How virtual experience affects bodily description artefacts. *Journal of Cultural Heritage, 17*, 179–187. doi:10.1016/j.culher.2015.04.006

Gek, D., Kukartsev, V., Tynchenko, V., Bondarev, A., Pokushko, M., & Dalisova, N. (2019). The Problem of SEO promotion for the organization's web representation. *SHS Web of Conferences, 69*, 1-6.

Gharieb, M. E. (2021). The Effect of Online Marketing through Social Media Platforms on Saudi Public Libraries. *Journal of Information Technology Management*, (Special Issue), 238–262.

Ghasemaghaei, M., Ebrahimi, S., & Hassanein, K. (2018). Data analytics competency for improving firm decision making performance. *The Journal of Strategic Information Systems, 27*, 101–113.

Kherbachi, S., Benkhider, N., & Keddari, N. (2020). Application of pagerank in virtual organization architecture. *Researchpedia Journal of Computing., 1*(1), 1–14.

Krstic, N., & Maslikovic, D. (2018). Pain points of cultural institutions in search visibility: The case of Serbia. *Library Hi Tech, 37*, 496–512.

Kulkarni, N., & Wazalwar, N. (2018). A Study on Effect of Demographic Variables on Purchase Intentions through Online Advertising. *SSRG International Journal of Economics Management Studies, 5*(12), 16–19.

Matosevic, G., Dobsa, J., & Mladenic, D. (2021). Using machine learning for web page classification in search engine optimization. *Future Internet, 13*(9), 1-20.

Sahu, N., & Chhabra, R. (2016). Review on Search Engine Optimization. *Journal of Network Communications and Emerging Technologies, 6*, 19–21.

Sarlis, A. S., Drivas, I. C., & Sakas, D. P. (2017). *Implementation and dynamic simulation modeling of search engine optimization processes Improvement of website ranking. In Springer Proceedings in Business and Economics*. Strategic Innovative Marketing.

Saura, J. R., Sanchez, P. P., & Suarez, L. M. C. (2017). Understanding the digital marketing environment with KPIS and web analytics. *Future Internet, 9*(4), 1-13.

Tsuei, H., Tsai, W., Pan, F., & Tzeng, G. (2018). Improving search engine optimization (SEO) by using hybrid modified MCDM models. *Artificial Intelligence Review, 53*, 1–16.

ADDITIONAL READING

Baye, M. R., Santos, B. D. I., & Wildenbeest, M. R. (2015). Search engine optimization: What drives organic traffic to retail sites? *Journal of Economics & Management Strategy, 25*(1), 6–31. doi:10.1111/jems.12141

Blazquez, D., & Domenech, J. (2018). Big Data sources and methods for social and economic analyses. Technological Forecasting and Social Change Journal, 130, 99-113.

Breed, D. G., & Verster, T. (2019). An empirical investigation of alternative semi-supervised segmentation methodologies. *South African Journal of Science*, *115*(3/4), 92–98. doi:10.17159ajs.2019/5359

Edwards, R., & Fenwick, T. (2015). Digital analytics in professional work and learning. *Studies in Continuing Education*, 213–227.

Eembi, N. B. C., Ishak, I. B., Sidi, F., Affendey, L. S., & Mamat, A. (2015). A systematic review on the profiling of digital news portal for Big Data veracity. *Procedia Computer Science*, *72*, 390–397. doi:10.1016/j.procs.2015.12.154

Elragal, A., & Klischewski, R. (2017). Theory-driven or process-driven prediction? Epistemological challenges of big data analytics. *Journal of Big Data*, *4*(19), 1–20. doi:10.118640537-017-0079-2

Eubanks, N. (2020). SEO Case Study – 313% More Organic Traffic with REAL Examples. https://ftf. co/seo-case-study/

García, M. D. M. R., Nieto, J. G., & Montes, J. F. A. (2016). An ontology-based data integration approach for web analytics in e-commerce. *Expert Systems with Applications*, *63*, 20–34. doi:10.1016/j. eswa.2016.06.034

Giabbanelli, P. J., Gray, S. A., & Aminpour, P. (2017). Combining fuzzy cognitive maps with agent-based modeling: Frameworks and pitfalls of a powerful hybrid modeling approach to understand human-environment interactions. *Environmental Modelling & Software*, *95*, 320–325. doi:10.1016/j. envsoft.2017.06.040

Hartmann, T., Fouquet, F., Moawad, A., Rouvoy, R., & Traon, Y. L. (2019). GreyCat: Efficient what-if analytics for data in motion at scale. *Information Systems*, *83*, 101–117. doi:10.1016/j.is.2019.03.004

Kavak, H., Padilla, J. J., Lynch, C. J., & Diallo, S. Y. (2018). Big data, agents, and machine learning: Towards a data-driven agent-based modeling approach. In Proceedings of the Annual Simulation Symposium (vol. 12, pp. 1-12). Society for Modelling and Simulation (SCS) International.

Khraim, H. S. (2015). The impact of search engine optimization on online advertisement: The case of companies using E-Marketing in Jordan. *American Journal of Industrial and Business Management*, *4*, 76–84.

Lekhwar, S., Yadav, S. & Singh, A. (2019). Big Data Analytics in Retail. Information and Communication Technology for Intelligent Systems, 469-477.

Luh, C. J., Yang, S. A., & Huang, T. L. D. (2016). Estimating Google's search engine ranking function from a search engine optimization perspective. *Online Information Review*, *40*(2), 239–255. doi:10.1108/ OIR-04-2015-0112

Lykourentzou, I., & Antoniou, A. (2019). Digital innovation for cultural heritage: Lessons from the European year of cultural heritage. *SCIRES SCIentific RESearch and Information Technology*, *9*(1), 91–98.

Mavridis, T., & Symeonidis, A. L. (2015). Identifying valid search engine ranking factors in a Web 2.0 and Web 3.0 context for building efficient SEO mechanisms. *Engineering Applications of Artificial Intelligence*, *41*, 75–91. doi:10.1016/j.engappai.2015.02.002

Mehryar, S., Sliuzas, R., Schwarz, N., Sharifi, A., & Maarseveen, M. V. (2019). From individual Fuzzy Cognitive Maps to Agent Based Models: Modeling multi-factorial and multi-stakeholder decision-making for water scarcity. *Journal of Environmental Management, 250,* 1–25. doi:10.1016/j.jenvman.2019.109482 PMID:31494410

Mikalef, P., Pappas, I. O., Krogstie, J., & Giannakos, M. (2018). Big data analytics capabilities: a systematic literature review and research agenda. Journal of Information Systems and e-Business Management, 3, 547-578.

Mittal, A., & Sridaran, R. (2019). Evaluation of Websites' Performance and Search Engine Optimization: A Case Study of 10 Indian University Websites. In *Proceedings of the 2019 6th International Conference on Computing for Sustainable Global Development* (pp. 1227–1231). IEEE.

Nigam, K., Saxena, S., & Gupta, N. (2015). An analysis on improvement of website ranking using joomla. *IITM Journal of Management and IT, 6,* 69–72.

Oussous, A., Benjelloun, F. Z., Lahcen, A. A., & Belfkih, S. (2018). Big Data technologies: A survey. *Journal of King Saud University-Computer and Information Sciences, 30*(4), 431–448. doi:10.1016/j. jksuci.2017.06.001

Rana, S. (2019). Moving in the Realm of Big Data: Using Analytics in Management Research and Practices. *FIIB Business Review, 8*(1), 7–8. doi:10.1177/2319714519839802

Rehman, M. H., Chang, V., Batool, A., & Wah, T. Y. (2016). Big data reduction framework for value creation in sustainable enterprises. *International Journal of Information Management, 36*(6), 917–928. doi:10.1016/j.ijinfomgt.2016.05.013

Ren, S., Zhang, Y., Liu, Y., Sakao, T., Huisingh, D., & Almeida, C. M. V. B. (2019). A comprehensive review of big data analytics throughout product lifecycle to support sustainable smart manufacturing: A framework, challenges and future research direction. *Journal of Cleaner Production, 210,* 1343–1365. doi:10.1016/j.jclepro.2018.11.025

Salminen, J., Corporan, J., Marttila, R., Salenius, T., & Jansen, B. J. (2019). Using Machine Learning to Predict Ranking of Webpages in the Gift Industry: Factors for Search-Engine Optimization. In *Proceedings of the 9th International Conference on Information Systems and Technologies* (vol. 6, pp. 1–8), Cairo, Egypt. 10.1145/3361570.3361578

Schmeh, D. (2020). Case study: Using (not provided) keywords for better ad performance. https://keyword-hero.com/blog/keyword-search-google-analytics

Visser, E. B., & Weideman, M. (2014). Fusing website usability and search engine optimisation. *South African Journal of Information Management, 16*(1), 1–9. doi:10.4102ajim.v16i1.577

Wamba, S. F., Gunasekaran, A., Akter, S., Ren, S. J. F., Dubey, R., & Childe, S. J. (2017). Big data analytics and firm performance: Effects of dynamic capabilities. *Journal of Business Research, 70,* 356–365. doi:10.1016/j.jbusres.2016.08.009

Wang, G., Gunasekaran, A., Ngai, E. W. T., & Papadopoulos, T. (2016). Big data analytics in logistics and supply chain management: Certain investigations for research and applications. *International Journal of Production Economics*, *176*, 98–110. doi:10.1016/j.ijpe.2016.03.014

Wedel, M., & Kannan, P. K. (2016). Marketing analytics for data-rich environments. *Journal of Marketing*, *80*(6), 97–121. doi:10.1509/jm.15.0413

Wu, C., Yoshinaga, T., Chen, X., Zhang, L., & Ji, Y. (2018). Cluster-based content distribution integrating LTE and IEEE 802.11 p with fuzzy logic and Q-learning. IEEE Computational Intelligence Magazine Journal, 41-50.

KEY TERMS AND DEFINITIONS

Backlinks: Backlinks are hyperlinks that connect one website to another. Backlinks of high quality can enhance a site's ranking and visibility in search engine results (SEO).

Big Data: Big data is a term that refers to massive, various amounts of data that are accumulating at an exponential rate.

Big Data Analytics: Big data analytics is the difficult process of analyzing large amounts of data in order to reveal information such as hidden patterns, correlations, market trends, and customer preferences which can help businesses make more informed decisions.

Intelligent Business: Intelligent business is a collection of technologies that integrates business analytics, data mining, visualization of data, data tools and infrastructure, and methods to help companies make much better data-driven outcomes.

Keywords: Keywords are topics and concepts that define the subject of your content. They're the words and phrase that people type into search engines, also termed as "search queries," in terms of SEO. These are your primary keywords if you distil everything on your page down to simple words and phrases—all the pictures, video, copy, and so on.

Optimization: Optimization is the act of enhancing the performance of your website via the use of tools, technical strategies, and studies in terms of enhancing traffic, sales, and revenues.

Ranking: The location of a website in the search engine results page is referred to as ranking.

Search Engine: A search engine is a program that uses keywords or phrases to help people find information on the web. By continuously monitoring the Internet and indexing every page they visit, search engines can retrieve results quickly, even with millions of websites available.

SEO: SEO stands for Search Engine Optimization, and it's the process of optimizing a website's technical setting, content relevancy, and link popularity so that its pages would be more easily found, more relevant, more popular in accordance with consumer search queries, and therefore rank higher in the search engines.

Web Traffic: The volume of data sent and received by visitors to a website is known as web traffic. Web traffic has account for the vast majority of internet traffic since the mid-1990s. The number of visitors and the volume of pages they visit determine this result.

Chapter 8
Machine Learning and Deep Learning as New Tools for Business Analytics

Abdelmalek Bouguettaya
Research Centre in Industrial Technologies (CRTI), Algeria

Hafed Zarzour
iD https://orcid.org/0000-0001-9441-4842
University of Souk Ahras, Algeria

Ahmed Kechida
Research Centre in Industrial Technologies (CRTI), Algeria

Amine Mohammed Taberkit
Research Centre in Industrial Technologies (CRTI), Algeria

ABSTRACT

Data scientists need to develop accurate and effective tools and techniques to handle a huge amount of data. Therefore, machine learning and deep learning algorithms have come to the life, especially with the impressive advances in both hardware and software fields. Many impressive existing services are helping us in our daily lives, such as Google Assistant, Uber, Alexa, and Siri, which are based on big data, machine learning, and deep learning. Although intelligent algorithms and big data have been adopted in many modern business intelligence and analytics applications, in this chapter, the authors aim to present the basics of machine learning and deep learning concepts and their utilization in the field of business intelligence. As concrete examples, with the high spread of the COVID-19 pandemic, Tesla and Amazon achieved the biggest revenue ever, where many other companies suffer. These high revenues could be due to the strategic decisions of their leaders, which are based especially on artificial intelligence.

DOI: 10.4018/978-1-7998-9016-4.ch008

INTRODUCTION

In the last few years, business intelligence and analytics are evolving phenomenon due to the significant growth of data in terms of volume, variety, velocity, veracity, and value (Ravi and Kamaruddin, 2017). Thus, with the advance of big data, business analytics using artificial intelligence methods has become an effective and fundamental tool for many companies, such as Amazon, Google, Facebook, AliExpress, Apple, and others, to improve their business. The recent technological advances and the high use of the internet and social media led to the exponential growth of various varieties of data, including images, videos, voices, among others. Handling such a huge amount of data using traditional techniques is very challenging, or impossible in many cases. Machine/Deep learning algorithms have emerged as an effective solution to overcome these problems providing efficient tools to achieve such hard work autonomously. A user just needs to feed the collected data to the trained model and it will do all the tedious and hard work on its own. The recent evolution of artificial intelligence algorithms, including machine learning and deep learning algorithms, is changing the future of business analytics by improving prediction performance and automating the tedious manual traditional operations while improving the profits of the companies (Kraus et al., 2020).

Nowadays, the high adoption of intelligent technologies in our lives enhanced business intelligence efficiency and capabilities. Artificial intelligence is used in a wide range of applications by the most known big companies, such as Photo Tagging by Facebook, Speech Recognition using Apples' Siri, Machine Translation used by Google, Self-driving cars of Tesla, among others. Machine Learning is considered one of the most exciting branches of artificial intelligence and important technological advances in many fields, including self-driving cars, healthcare, banking, finance, security, and eCommerce. For example, intelligent virtual assistants and bots can determine our tastes and preferences with impressive accuracy (Rafailidis and Manolopoulos, 2019; Rawassizadeh et al., 2019), drone and smart machinery are now able to help farmers to monitor their crops and livestock providing higher food productivity while reducing costs and drudgery (Saiz-Rubio and Rovira-Más, 2020), smartphones and smartwatches can help us to monitor our health continuously and notifying our doctors (Nagarajan et al., 2021; Ravì et al., 2017).

In the last few years, the demand for machine learning and deep learning experts is growing exponentially in a very large number of fields both in industry and academia, including business intelligence, due to the enormous advances in intelligent algorithms, computational hardware, and the high availability of data. Therefore, our main goal in this chapter is to provide to the readers who came from business backgrounds with the right tools and techniques used by data scientists and machine learning engineers to achieve their goals, because most companies are moving towards the use of the machine and deep learning techniques to solve their problems and improve the company's revenues. Machine learning algorithms in Business Analytics are a fundamental key for today and future business growth.

MACHINE LEARNING AND BIG DATA FOR BUSINESS ANALYTICS

To improve their success, machine learning and big data are considered fundamental keys for business decisions. To this end, in this section, we are going to present the importance of data and its different sources and types. Also, the basics of machine learning and its importance as a new tool for data analysis.

Big Data

The large usage of smartphones, social media, and various IoT devices in the era of the high flow internet and 5G technologies, generates a massive amount of data every day (Jan et al., 2019). The generated data could be in the form of text, images, videos, audio, e-mails, which approximately exceed 40 exabytes every year (Niemann and Pisla, 2020). According to (Ali, 2020), every minute in 2020, more than 500 hours are uploaded on YouTube, more than 340 thousand posts on Instagram, more than 400 thousand hours of video streaming by users, 174 thousand photos uploaded in Facebook, one million dollars spent online by consumers, more than one million people make video/voice calls, and much more. Thus, Big Data is considered as the new oil due to its high importance in our modern life, especially for big companies, such as Google, Amazon, and Facebook. These companies can use the huge amount of the collected digital data to increase their profits by improving their marketing strategies to target as many as possible customers based on their available information. However, we need to treat and analyze such an amount of raw digital data very carefully to avoid the problems that could result from it. Instead of using costly and tedious traditional tools and computing systems, big tech companies start to adopt recent Artificial Intelligence algorithms as an effective approach to handle and manage the huge amount of collected data (Zhou et al., 2017).

The generated data could be categorized as structured or unstructured data depending on the way how they are presented. Structured (or quantitative) data stands for information that is highly organized and could be analyzed easily. This type of data commonly consists of customer names, phone numbers, dates, and ZIP code that are organized in the form of rows and columns similar to excel spreadsheets. Financial data is an example of structured data; for example, the number of iPhones that Apple has sold per year or quarter in different countries and regions, and putting this data in the form of a well-structured table. On the other hand, unstructured (or qualitative) data represents the most available type of data, which has not the same organized presentation and ease of analyzing as structured data making its processing using conventional tools more difficult. E-mails, Instagram/Facebook messages, videos, images, audio, different sensor data, and speech are some examples of unstructured data. To process and handle such complex data, we need to use modern efficient tools instead of classical costly, tedious, and hard methods. Therefore, the next section is dedicated to machine learning basics and their different types.

Machine Learning Concept

The process of learning can be defined by how anything (humans, animals, computers) can make decisions and take actions according to their experiences. Unlike humans, who learned from their past experiences in life, machines, usually, follow a set of instructions given by the programmer making it very hard to achieve complex applications, such as autonomous vehicles. However, with the incredible breakthroughs in new hardware (GPUs, TPUs) and software technologies (machine learning and deep learning algorithms), all along with the high availability of data, we are able to make machines learn from their experiences too, where the experience for machines means data. So, Machine Learning is a computer science discipline that aims to make computers able to learn patterns from data without being explicitly programmed. According to Arthur Samuel, machine learning is defined as the *"field of study that gives computers the ability to learn without being explicitly programmed"* (Helskyaho et al., 2021). Using a large amount of data leads to better models with higher accuracy.

Figure 1. Classical programming vs machine learning

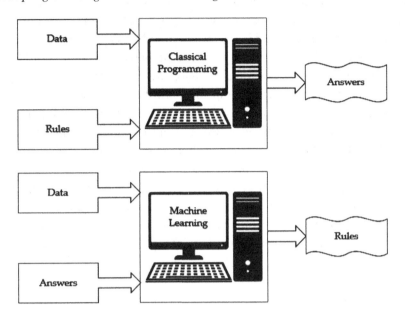

Machine learning algorithms differ a little bit from classical programming methods. In conventional programming, the machine follows instructions (rules) given by the programmer to handle input data and provide answers in its output. However, Machine Learning algorithms take data with their labels (answers) and provide rules to solve the targeted problem by creating a model to predict answers on new unseen data (see Figure 1).

Machine Learning has emerged as a new problem-solving technique in various domains and industries, including agriculture, healthcare, banking, and even for business. There are three main categories of Machine Learning algorithms: supervised learning, unsupervised learning, and reinforcement learning. Therefore, in the following sections, we are going to describe each of these categories while presenting the most used algorithms in each one.

Supervised Learning

Supervised learning is the most popular and easiest machine learning category. The user provides the machine learning algorithm with a well-labeled dataset that consists of the data and its corresponding label (class) during the training process. The algorithm finds a way to create a model that is able to predict an output according to input based on what it learned from the labeled training dataset. Labeled data means that the output is already known in previous and the model just needs to map the inputs to the outputs. Then, the trained model is used to achieve a targeted task or to solve a problem without any human intervention. We are interacting every day with a large number of intelligent applications based on supervised learning. Gmail, and all the electronic mails websites, use supervised learning to classify different email messages as spam or not. Similarly, Facebook uses them to identify peoples through their faces allowing tag suggestions when we upload a photo. Also, the banks adopt supervised learning to decide whether they accept or reject a loan request from a customer according to his data.

Supervised machine learning algorithms are used to achieve two main tasks, which are classification and regression. Classification is a very common task in supervised Machine Learning. It is used to predict the class of the input data. The spam filter is one of the most known examples of binary classification problems, in which a model is trained on many email examples along with their class (spam or not), and then it must learn how to classify new emails. Also, advertisements are very important nowadays and essential factors that could return on the companies' profits significantly. Predicting whether a user will click on the website Ads or not by feeding the user Ad information as features is an example of a classification problem. Logistic regression, SVM, k-nearest neighbor, Naïve Bayes, Decision Tree, Random Forest, and Artificial Neural Networks are the most common classification techniques (see Fig. 2). However, regression is used in the prediction of continuous variables instead of classes, such as houses' price prediction, where the user gives to the regression model the houses' features (ex. Size, Location, Number of rooms, Surface) as input data and it will predict its price according to these given features. Linear regression, Decision Tree, and Neural Networks are among the most known regression techniques (Fig. 2). Regression algorithms are very helpful to predict product demand, marketing returns, among other applications.

Unsupervised Learning

Unlike supervised learning, unsupervised learning is the process of learning from unlabeled data, where the user does not supply any label to the input data. It is a technique that learns by itself and tries to group the input data into different clusters according to the relationship between input data and their hidden patterns. Several websites, such as Netflix and YouTube, use unsupervised learning algorithms to find patterns in video frames and compress them to improve the speed of video uploading and streaming (Yang et al., 2021). Unsupervised learning consists of two branches, which are clustering and dimensionality reduction. Clustering is based on grouping input data into distinct categories. For example, a business might be using clustering techniques to group customers into various categories according to their records and purchasing behavior. K-means and Neural Networks are the most known clustering techniques (Fig. 2). However, dimensionality reduction is a technique that aims to reduce the number of input variables or features in a dataset by removing the redundant ones, while keeping the model performance. Principal Component Analysis (PCA) is one of the earliest and most known dimensionality reduction techniques.

Reinforcement Learning

Reinforcement learning is a machine learning technique that aims to create an intelligent software agent that is able to learn alone by interacting with an environment without being taught explicitly what to do. These agents can figure out how to optimize their behavior given a system of rewards and penalties (see Fig. 3). One of the earliest and most known reinforcement learning applications was the Google DeepMind AlphaGo. It is a computer program that was able to beat the world champion on one of the most challenging and complex games, which is Go.

There are various types of machine learning techniques that perform very well to solve problems in different fields. However, Artificial Neural Networks (ANNs) are becoming the most powerful machine learning model, especially with the advance of different deep learning algorithms. Given that ANNs are used to solve different types of problems, including natural language processing, image recognition, self-driving cars, among others. The next section will cover the basics of ANNs and deep learning.

Figure 2. Different machine learning categories with their most known algorithms.

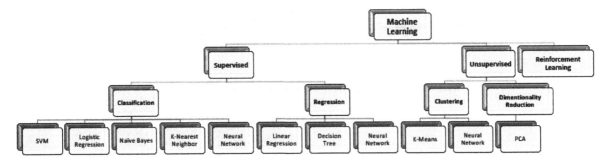

Figure 3. Reinforcement learning diagram.

Machine Learning Workflow

The way how we train computers is the main difference between machine learning algorithms and traditional programming. In the latter, computers follow the instructions given by the programmer. However, in the case of machine learning, the computer defines the rules on its own according to the input data. In order to achieve this goal, engineers need to follow a certain workflow as illustrated in Figure. 4.

- Data collection: The process of gathering data is a very important step of machine learning workflows. The type of collected data depends on the problem to be solved. If users are targeting to solve a computer vision problem, images and videos are the appropriate data to gather. However, if they are targeting to predict who will buy a specific article or product in e-stores, such as Amazon, then they will need information about the customers and their interests.
- Data pre-processing and splitting: Data pre-processing is a critical step in the machine learning workflow. It consists of cleaning and converting the raw data to the format that best suits the needs of the targeted model. This step is crucial to avoid feeding messy data to train the machine learning model because it would result in wrong predictions. Data cleaning, labeling, and splitting are among the most important data pre-processing tools.
- Model selection: The choice of the suitable model architecture is another crucial parameter that developers should take into account, where the wrong model means bad performance. They need to find the best model that fits the type of the gathered data and the targeted problem to be solved.

Figure 4. Machine learning flowchart.

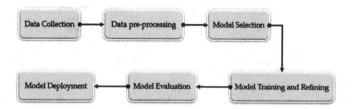

- Train and refine the model: To train a model, firstly we split the model into three main sets, which are the Training set, Validation set, and Testing data. The training and validation sets are used to train the model and tuning the parameters, respectively. During the training process, only the training set and/or validation set are available, but the test set must still unseen to the model and will be used in the testing phase.
- Model evaluation and utilization: Model evaluation aims to find the best model that fits data by calculating some parameters using the confusion matrix, such as accuracy, precision, recall, and f1-score. In order to improve the model performance, it is needed to change the model hyper-parameters to improve its overall performance. Once the training and evaluation of the machine learning model are accomplished, it is needed to deploy this model as part of a business application such as a mobile, desktop, or even web application.

Traditional machine learning algorithms have some limitations to solve complex unstructured data, such as computer vision and natural language processing applications. Therefore, in the next section, we will present a machine learning subfield that is based on artificial neural networks, called deep learning.

ARTIFICIAL NEURAL NETWORKS AND DEEP LEARNING

Artificial neural network dates back to the fifties when the first model for neural networks have been created. However, its popularity increased only in the last few years due to the recent advances in computational hardware power and the availability of large datasets. Traditional machine learning algorithms are facing limitations to solve complex problems due to many factors. The feature extraction step in traditional machine learning algorithms is done manually through experts on the targeted application, which is tedious and costly. However, this step is done automatically using deep learning algorithms by passing the input data through the different layers (Fig. 5).

Deep learning models' performance keeps improving as they are deeper, more complex, and feeding them more data. They are able to learn very complex features through multiple layers of abstraction, which is not the case using traditional machine learning models (see Fig. 6).

Artificial Neuron

Deep learning algorithms are based on the concept of Artificial Neurons, which are bio-inspired techniques. The researchers inspired them from the biological neurons in the human brain (see Fig. 7 (left)), which attempts to mimic them. Artificial Neural Networks (ANNs) are much simpler than biological

Figure 5. Traditional machine learning vs deep learning flowcharts.

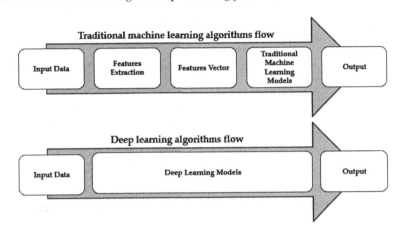

neural networks and they do not represent the real way of how human brains operate, but they do share some key components in their architectures (see Fig. 7). ANNs consist of neurons (nodes) connected to each other by direct links forming dense and complex networks. These neurons are the main building blocks of any ANN, which are just linear function that takes inputs, makes some types of basic processing operations (summation, multiplication), and returns an output after applying an activation function (see Fig. 7 (right)).

We can represent the perceptron output mathematically as follow: f. Where f is the activation function, $\backslash\backslash\backslash\backslash\{w\backslash\backslash\backslash\backslash\}rsub\backslash\backslash\backslash\backslash\{i\backslash\backslash\backslash\backslash\}$ are the weights associated with each input, $\backslash\backslash\backslash\backslash\{x\backslash\backslash\backslash\backslash\}rsub\backslash\backslash\backslash\backslash\{i\backslash\backslash\backslash\backslash\}$ are the inputs and b is the bias. The inputs depend on the targeted application; for example, in the case of image processing, the inputs are the intensities of the pixels.

The activation functions are a fundamental key to ANN architectures, which are non-linear functions applied to the output of each neuron before passing it to the next neuron. They are considered as the decision-making units. It is a mathematical equation that determines the output of each neuron in the neural network. There are various types of activation functions, including step function (threshold function), sigmoid, hyperbolic tangent, and Rectified Linear Unit (ReLU). Their main purpose is to introduce non-linearity into the output of a neuron. A neural network without an activation function would simply accomplish the linear transformation. Thus, a neural network without an activation function is

Figure 6. Deep Neural Network performance according to the data size.

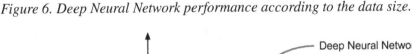

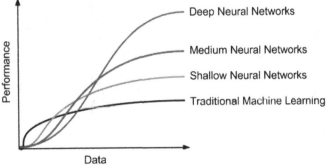

Figure 7. Biological neuron (left) vs Artificial neuron (right).

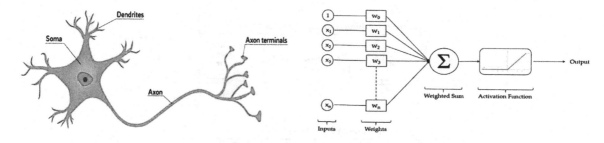

considered a linear regression model, which is not able to solve complex problems. Most of the recent deep neural networks use the ReLU activation function at the hidden layers level. However, the choice of the activation function at the output layer depends on the problem to be solved. In the case of binary classification, we can use ether step or sigmoid functions, but when we have more than two classes, we should use the softmax function.

The Concept of Deep Neural Networks

Using one single neuron or single-layer neural networks (see Fig. 8 (left)) may work well on simple datasets that could be separated by a simple or few straight lines but they are not capable of handling complex unstructured data, such as natural speech and visual data. However, stacking many layers that consists of a large number of neurons in each may outperform any other traditional machine learning techniques, including single-layer neural networks. These neurons are arranged into three types of layers stacked on top of each other: the input layer, the hidden layers, and the output layer (see Fig. 8 (right)). In the literature, this structure is called Multi-Layer Perceptron (MLP), Deep Neural Networks (DNN), or Feed Forward Neural Networks. It can have any number of hidden layers stacked on top of each other, where each layer consists of neurons according to the problem complexity and the adopted hardware because deeper networks need more computational power.

The training process of deep learning algorithms is done by the repetition of three main steps (see Fig. 9). In the first step, the input data pass through the network in one direction, where they perform the

Figure 8. Shallow neural network (left) vs deep neural network (right).

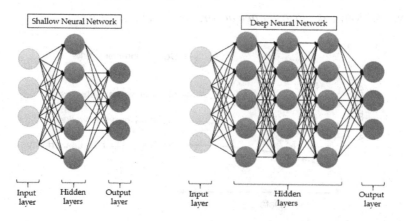

Figure 9. Deep neural networks training flowchart.

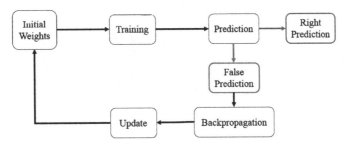

weighted sum calculation and apply the activation function to get the output prediction. Then, measuring the error by comparing the predicted value with the desired one. Finally, using the gradient descent algorithm to optimize the error and backpropagate the change of weights through the network to update the old weights.

Different Deep Learning Architectures

There are several deep learning architectures that can be used in a wide range of fields to solve a variety of problems, including computer vision, natural language processing (NLP), predictive analysis, recommender systems, among others. These architectures mostly fall into four main categories, which are Feed Forward Neural Networks, Convolutional Neural Networks (CNNs), Autoencoders, and Recurrent Neural Networks (RNNs). Standard neural networks do not perform well on image data while CNN architectures are considered as the best solution for image processing and computer vision applications achieving impressive results in many tasks, including object detection, plant disease detection, and early identification of cancer cells. Recurrent Neural Networks are other types of deep learning architectures that achieve state-of-the-art results in time series problems/forecasting due to their concept of retaining knowledge from earlier states. Long-Short Term Memory (LSTM) is an improved version of RNN that addresses one of its major limitations, which is the problem of vanishing gradients. It is used by Apple, Google, and Amazon in their speech recognition applications (Metz, 2016).

Feed-Forward Neural Networks

Feed-Forward neural networks, also called Multi-Layer Perceptrons (MLPs), were among the earliest and most successful deep learning algorithms. As shown above, Feed-Forward Neural Networks are the most basic and fundamental Deep Neural Network architectures (see Fig. 8 (right)). They consist of a large number of perceptrons organized in different layers, where all of these perceptrons are fully connected to each others.

Convolutional Neural Networks

CNN is a special type of Feed-Forward Networks, where a standard CNN architecture consists of several convolutional and pooling layers stacked on top of each other followed by one or more fully connected layers (see Fig. 10). Convolutional and pooling layers are used to extract relevant features and reduce

Figure 10. Typical CNN architecture.

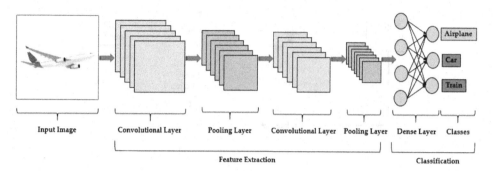

spatial dimensionality from the input data while the fully connected layer is responsible for classifying these features. A fully connected layer, also called a dense layer, is just a standard MLP. The LeNet-5 architecture is one of the earliest CNN architectures, which achieved a very low error rate of 0.9% on the famous MNIST dataset that consists of handwritten digits. LeNet-5 was widely adopted by banks and post offices in the USA to automatically identify handwritten checks and zip code numbers. However, such a shallow architecture is not able to handle large images due to many issues, especially the computational power at the time of the LeNet-5 release. With the recent technological advances on GPUs and software, Krizhevsky et al. (Krizhevsky et al., 2012) were able to win the 2012 ImageNet competition using AlexNet architecture, where they achieved impressive results on image classification. Many other architectures were developed since then, including VGGNet (Simonyan and Zisserman, 2015), GoogLeet (Szegedy et al., 2015), ResNet (He et al., 2016), DenseNet (Huang et al., 2017), and MobileNet (Howard et al., 2019, 2017; Sandler et al., 2018). Nowadays, CNN architectures are considered as the best solution to solve problems related to image processing and computer vision applications achieving state-of-the-art results on datasets such as ImageNet. CNN architectures have been extensively applied in the last few years for many applications, including object detection, face recognition, and image/video object segmentation. They can be used to analyze visual data like face identification, which is used by many e-payment platforms. For example, CNN was adopted in 2017 by AliPay to perform online facial payment just by showing your face to the device (Kraus et al., 2020). Facial payment adopted by AliPay is considered, by MIT Technology Review, as one of the 10 Breakthrough Technologies (Knight, 2017).

Recurrent Neural Networks and Their Variants

Recurrent Neural Network (RNN) is another special type of deep learning architectures (see Fig. 11 (left)). Unlike other neural networks, where the inputs and outputs are independent of each other, Recurrent Neural Network is firstly introduced to handle sequential data like speech, text, and times series data emerge from digital stock markets providing memory to the network via hidden states (Ganai and Khursheed, 2020; Li et al., 2019; Sengupta et al., 2020). RNN architectures have the ability to remember the previous states from prior inputs by feedback the output to the input. Then, they can make decisions according to the previous information allowing these types of architectures to achieve better results in processing time-related data. Nowadays, RNNs and their enhanced variants, like Long Short Term Memory (LSTM) (Hochreiter and Schmidhuber, 1997) and Gated Recurrent Units (GRUs) (Chung et al., 2014), are mostly used for Natural Language Processing (NLP). LSTM architecture (see Fig. 11

Figure 11. Standard RNN architecture (left) and LSTM architecture (right).

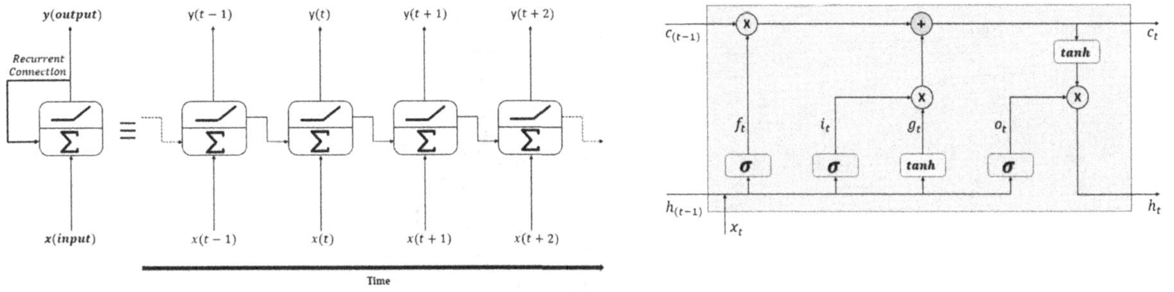

(right)) achieved better results than the vanilla RNN providing solutions to some critical problems, such as Vanishing Gradient and short memory. Nowadays, LSTM is considered the most powerful type of RNN architectures, which is used to capture long-term dependencies in the data. Google, Microsoft, Apple, and Amazon used LSTM in their virtual assistants to recognize natural human speech (Zhang et al., 2018). It was adopted by Google for machine translation (Sutskever et al., 2014). Also, it was used for music generation (Kan and Sourin, 2020), image captioning (Che et al., 2020; Vinyals et al., 2015), sentiment analysis (El Barachi et al., 2021), stock market prediction (Kumar and Haider, 2021), customer behaviors prediction (Sarkar and De Bruyn, 2021), among others.

Transformers

In RNN-based models, the input data needs to be passed sequentially and do not exploit the GPU advantage that are designed to perform parallel operation, which explain the very long training time of these models. Also, they cannot handle very long sequences. Thus, in 2017, a Google research team proposed Transformers in their paper entitled "Attention Is All You Need" to overcome these problems (Vaswani et al., 2017). For example, to achieve language translation task, RNN models take input words and pass them through recurrent units one by one. However, in the case of Transformers, all the input words passed simultaneously resulting in lower training time while providing better results.

In the last few years, Transformer architectures have been gaining very large popularity in a wide range of applications, including Natural Language Processing (NLP) and computer vision (Han et al., 2021; Khan et al., 2021; Lin et al., 2021). As shown in Figure 12, a transformer network consists of an encoder and a decoder. Both the encoder and the decoder parts consist of six layers stacked on top of each others. Each of these layers contains two fundamental sublayers that are Multi-Head Attention and Feed-Forward Network. Lately, several research teams from big tech companies are competing against each other to develop more efficient Transformers-based models. For example, Google, OpenAI, and Facebook researchers proposed BERT (Devlin et al., 2019), GPT versions (Brown et al., 2020; Radford et al., 2020, 2018), and RoBERTa (Liu et al., 2019) architectures respectively to understand natural language. Transformers achieved the state-of-the-art results in NLP applications, and they are not limited to solve NLP problems. Also, Google AI and Facebook developed ViT (Dosovitskiy et al., 2021) and DETR (Carion et al., 2020) respectively to handle computer vision issues.

Figure 12. Transformer network architecture
(Vaswani et al., 2017).

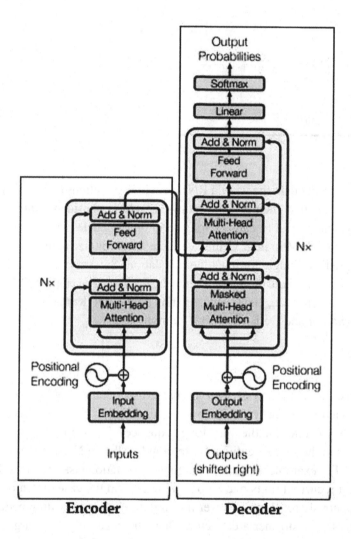

Autoencoders (Compression)

Autoencoders are other types of feedforward neural networks, where their main role is to produce an output similar to the input as closely as possible. They are commonly used for data denoising and compression to improve its quality and transmission speed. The autoencoder architecture consists of two main components, which are an encoder and a decoder (Fig. 13). The encoder aims to transform input data into a reduced representation, called code, by extracting its more valuable features while the decoder tries to reconstruct the input data from the representation generated from the encoder part. Autoencoders could be used to detect anomalies in business processes to improve system security by detecting fraudulent transactions (Nolle et al., 2018). Also, researchers from Amazon company developed a special type of autoencoders for joint compression and enhancing of the noisy speech signal, which is consists of a convolutional encoder and a WaveRNN decoder (Casebeer et al., 2021).

Figure 13. Standard autoencoder architecture.

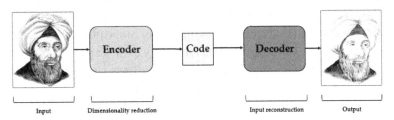

APPLICATIONS OF MACHINE LEARNING AND DEEP LEARNING TO SOLVE BUSINESS PROBLEMS

Due to the high performance achieved by machine and deep learning algorithms in several fields, they are becoming crucial and more apparent each day in many domains in our daily life. Most notably, Bouguettaya et al., (2021a) provided a review on vehicle detection from Unmanned Aerial Vehicle (UAV) imagery based on deep learning. Bouguettaya et al., (2021b) presented the recent advances in UAV platforms and deep learning-based computer vision algorithms, and their aim was to identify crop diseases at an early stage with the purpose to improve food production. The application of deep learning in improving a wildfires detection performance at their early stages in forest and wildland areas is also presented in (Bouguettaya et al., 2022)'s study.

Applications of machine learning and deep learning in business intelligence have witnessed rapid growth over the few past years. These methods have emerged as effective tools for a wide range of business applications, such as eCommerce, finance, healthcare, security, and logistics. They have been successfully applied in several giant companies (Amazon, Tesla, Facebook, Google, and Uber) to solve a wide range of their business problems, such as customers data analysis to target the best customer, sales forecasting, target marketing, increasing security, among others to maximize their profits while reducing cost. Today, it is an obligation for data scientists to be familiar with recent data analysis techniques, which are based on machine learning and deep learning algorithms. In this section, we are going to present some applications of intelligent algorithms in the field of business analytics.

Virtual Assistant

Many companies need to hire human assistants to achieve different tasks, such as replying to e-mails, scheduling appointments, organizing meetings, answering customers' queries, and more. Recently, big data and deep learning-based virtual assistants provide an impressive solution to automate all of these tasks while reducing cost and time. Virtual assistants, also known as digital assistants, are intelligent software applications that can understand natural language (text and/or speech) and perform different tasks using powerful deep learning algorithms for Natural Language Processing (NLP), such as Long-Short Term Memory (LSTM) (Hochreiter and Schmidhuber, 1997) and Transformers (Vaswani et al., 2017). The main role of virtual assistants is assisting customers, answering their questions, finalizing their purchases, and more. Several companies adopted deep learning-based personal virtual assistants allowing smartphones and computers to understand human language, which should increase customer satisfaction by facilitating their daily interactions and purchasing just over speech and/or text writing. Since the first personal assistant, Siri, unveiled by Apple in 2011, many big tech companies developed their intelligent chatbots like Amazon's Alexa, Microsoft's Cortona, and Google Assistant (Kraus et al., 2020; The Economist, 2017). Today, with intelligent chatbots we are able to purchase physical or digital products, from food to music, just by speaking to our smartphones. Recently, Amazon makes Alexa more efficient, practical, and easier providing the ability to make purchasing or adding our favorite products to Amazon cart only by speaking. Moreover, Alexa allows you to track your package and send you notifications when your package is delivered (Amazon, 2021).

Recommendation Systems

Digitalization led to the rapid growth of online services providing a huge amount of data, which are very valuable for business and e-commerce. The data gathered from the users' weblogs could be used by companies to increase their profits. Recommender systems are considered one of the most important tools to achieve such a goal. They are designed to suggest relevant products for a specific customer based on his/her available information. Youtube, Netflix, Facebook, Amazon, and AliExpress collect users' behavior data and use them to understand what every customer wants to watch or to buy. According to (Rafailidis and Manolopoulos, 2019), 35% of consumers purchasing on Amazon, 80% of what they saw on Netflix, and 60% of YouTube video clicks came from recommendation systems. Moreover, big tech companies added recommender systems on their virtual assistants, such as Amazon's Alexa. Based on the customer's data and his/her purchasing history on the Amazon platform, Alexa can suggest items and products that could be of interest to the customer (Amazon, 2021). Many scientific papers showed the importance of recommender systems, such as the work of researchers from Google (Davidson et al., 2010), where they presented the usability and advantages of the YouTube recommender system. Similarly, Zhou et al. (Zhou et al., 2010) showed the impact of the YouTube recommender engine on the number of video views. Recently, several studies targeted the development of strong recommender systems based on recent machine and deep learning algorithms. Carlos and Hunt (Gomez-Uribe and Hunt, 2015) presented different recommender system algorithms used by Netflix, including machine learning algorithms. The authors in (Ahmed et al., 2021), developed a cross-domain recommender system based on Multi-Layer Perceptron to overcome the cold start problem. This problem could be due to the lack of information about new customers resulting in bad quality of recommendations. Chiu et al. (Chiu et al., 2021), proposed to analyze costumer's data through unsupervised NLP methods, then a deep learning-based recommender system is used to provide costumers with personalized solutions. Also, the authors in (Qiu et al., 2020) developed a Transformer-based platform that is adopted by Alibaba to assist a number of business tasks, such as item recommendation, personalized search, and conversational question answering.

Digital Payment and Security

The financial systems are mainly based on trust between the customer and the company. Nowadays, artificial intelligence and e-wallet using mobile devices have emerged as a novel method of secured digital payment, which is adopted by many companies. Recently, with the explode of data volume, processing power, and deep learning algorithms, digital and contactless payment methods have attracted more and more attention day by day, especially with the high spread of the COVID-19 pandemic and the total lockdown. Several giant companies, such as Google, Facebook, Apple, AliExpress, and Amazon aim to achieve easy, fast, suitable, and secure payment methods while reducing transaction costs. Digital payment and e-wallets are already in use by many companies, such as Google Pay, AliPay, Apple Pay, Android Pay, Samsung Pay, Facebook Pay, and Amazon One (Lee et al., 2020). However, one of the major issues for digital and online payment is data security, where customers' information is always vulnerable to be stolen by hackers. Online data security is based on three main factors, which are confidentiality, integrity, and availability. Confidentiality is about providing access to sensitive information only to the authorized persons while integrity is about making sure that information is processed correctly and preventing unauthorized changes. Availability aims to ensure that authorized persons have access to their information at any time. Therefore, credit card and e-wallets companies collect and store the data of when and where the credit cards have been used in real-time and use efficient deep learning algorithms to protect their customers by detecting fraudulent transactions. Also, most big data processing is done on the cloud, where artificial intelligence can play a fundamental role to protect our data providing stronger techniques making the job of hackers harder. Over the last few years, several studies targeted fraudulent transaction detection and improvement of the digital payment systems security (Abakarim et al., 2018; Roy et al., 2018; Wu et al., 2021).

Online Advertising

Advertising in the era of smartphones and the internet has changed and overcome the traditional techniques that are based on televisions, radios, and print advertising (Melo and Machado, 2020). Online advertising achieved an impressive level of success and boost online sales, which is due to many factors, especially big data that could be used to reach more people. However, it is very hard to handle and extract relevant patterns from huge data with traditional data mining methods. Therefore, several researchers and big tech companies adopted deep learning algorithms to improve advertising techniques. Social media platforms like Instagram, Facebook, Twitter, and Tik Tok represent an active digital market due to the huge amount and variety of data about a large number of users on those platforms. Thus, advertisements on social media platforms can help to improve and explode any business. To this end, deep learning algorithms can help to gain more advertising effectiveness by deciding when and what customers we should target for a specific product according to their collected data. Facebook Pixel and Google Analytics 4 (GA4) are tools based on advanced machine learning algorithms, which can be used to better understand your customers across different devices and platforms (Brandi, 2021; Srinivasan, 2020). The machine learning and NLP models adopted by these tools have the ability to create audience forecasts for Facebook and Google Ads and provide you with insights about important trends in your items and data. However, using advertising by itself is useless; thus, you need to specify the targeted audience that you should reach. To achieve that goal, we need a huge amount of information about the targeted public, such as the location, gender, age, income, lifestyle, to name a few. Several researchers targeted machine and deep learning-based models to make their Ads more creative and efficient. The authors in (Vinh and Tran Dac Thinh, 2019), developed an advertisement system to attract customers, based on their sentiments, using a CNN-based facial recognition system. Austin et al. (Austin et al., 2020), presented a deep learning-based model that is able to predict where the Ads should be appeared by combining image features with information from the targeted page. Knowing customers' gender in social media and web platforms is an essential key in the field of advertisement. To this end, the authors in (Priadana et al., 2020), developed a deep learning model based on CNN architecture to predict Instagram users gender based on their profile images.

DISCUSSIONS

Nowadays, data is utilized to understand and enhance practically every aspect of our life, from early disease diagnosis to social media that allows us to communicate with other people all over the world. Processing these data using the right analytics tools can help us to make better decisions. Analytics is about turning data into meaningful business insights that can help to improve it, but, in real life, it is not that simple.

More recently, with the high spread of the COVID-19 pandemic and the financial and economic crises that infect the globe, many companies tend to replace the traditional business methods that have many limitations, including cost, time, a large amount of data to be processed, and require a large number of experts. Artificial Intelligence is becoming a crucial tool in many business applications, especially its two big branches: Machine Learning and Deep Learning. They are concerned with using a large amount of data to extract the relevant patterns within it for decision-making. Machine/Deep learning algorithms have emerged as effective solutions to understand and handle complex and big data with ease while improving the process of decision making. Thus, deep learning-based business analytics tends to solve tedious problems that are time-consuming and costly.

Due to the big amount of available data spreading of the Internet, social media, and IoT devices, big tech companies like Google, Apple, Facebook, Amazon, and Tesla, are already adopted machine learning algorithms in their systems and applications for good reasons. They can help to improve many applications and domains like healthcare, business, agriculture, and much more providing better and more effective services while reducing cost, time, effort, and inefficiency. Nowadays, computers and smartphones can understand and even generate written and spoken words and phrases using NLP techniques like LSTM and transformer neural networks, which we are using almost every day by talking to Alexa, Siri, and Google Assistant. Also, companies can extract and identify critical pieces of sentimental information from massive volumes of data through different deep learning algorithms with very little human intervention, including context, emotion, and intent (Sadiq et al., 2021). This can be quite beneficial in terms of having better knowledge about customer interactions and improving brand engagement strategies.

Despite the importance of machine learning and deep learning, their application in business analytics remains a challenge. For example, the data availability and security are challenging tasks because implementing machine and deep learning solutions needs a huge amount of data to train the AI models, and such data should be fully secured using efficient encryption algorithms to protect the online companies' business.

The future of business analytics under the umbrella of machine learning and deep learning will be quite different from the world of traditional business analytics. It is expected that the business analytics systems based on machine learning techniques will help companies to add a new dimension in predictive analytics for improving their performance by providing new intelligent solutions such as autonomous decision supports. In addition, machine learning and deep learning software will not only outperform humans in business analytics but also completely replace them.

CONCLUSION

The new technological advancement in terms of hardware and software combined with a large amount of available data play a fundamental role in modern business. Big companies, like Amazon, AliExpress, and eBay, turned to use recent intelligent algorithms to improve their incomes. These algorithms are based on novel machine learning and deep learning techniques.

Data is one of the most important keys for any successful company. To increase their incomes, Google, Facebook, Netflix, and Amazon collect a lot of data about their customers and use deep learning algorithms to process them. The gathered information is then utilized to target ads that we are interested in or to recommend series, films, or tools. For example, gamers will be targeted by showing them new video games while showing sports clothing or equipment to athletes. Also, Uber takes advantage of data and intelligent algorithms to optimize its services by creating heat maps for the drivers to know where they should position themselves within the city and calculate the optimum path to accomplish their missions. Therefore, data and intelligent algorithms are becoming crucial keys in a wide range of applications.

REFERENCES

Abakarim, Y., Lahby, M., & Attioui, A. (2018). An efficient real time model for credit card fraud detection based on deep learning. *ACM Int. Conf. Proceeding Ser.* 10.1145/3289402.3289530

Ahmed, A., Saleem, K., Khalid, O., & Rashid, U. (2021). On deep neural network for trust aware cross domain recommendations in E-commerce. *Expert Systems with Applications*, *174*, 114757. doi:10.1016/j.eswa.2021.114757

Ali, A. (2020). *Here's What Happens Every Minute on the Internet in 2020*. https://www.visualcapitalist.com/every-minute-internet-2020/

Amazon. (2021). *Alexa Voice Shopping: Shop millions of Amazon products with Alexa*. https://www.amazon.com/alexa-voice-shopping/b?ie=UTF8&node=14552177011

Austin, D., Sanzgiri, A., Sankaran, K., Woodard, R., Lissack, A., & Seljan, S. (2020). Classifying sensitive content in online advertisements with deep learning. *International Journal of Data Science and Analytics*, *10*(3), 265–276. doi:10.100741060-020-00212-6

Bouguettaya, A., Zarzour, H., Kechida, A., & Taberkit, A. M. (2021a). Vehicle Detection From UAV Imagery With Deep Learning: A Review. *IEEE Transactions on Neural Networks and Learning Systems*, 1–21. doi:10.1109/TNNLS.2021.3080276 PMID:34029200

Bouguettaya, A., Zarzour, H., Kechida, A., & Taberkit, A. M. (2021b). Recent Advances on UAV and Deep Learning for Early Crop Diseases Identification: A Short Review. In *2021 International Conference on Information Technology (ICIT)* (pp. 334-339). IEEE. 10.1109/ICIT52682.2021.9491661

Bouguettaya, A., Zarzour, H., Taberkit, A. M., & Kechida, A. (2022). A Review on Early Wildfire Detection from Unmanned Aerial Vehicles using Deep Learning-Based Computer Vision Algorithms. *Signal Processing*, *190*, 108309. doi:10.1016/j.sigpro.2021.108309

Brandi. (2021). *How To Train Your Pixel To Fetch Better Results*. https://blog.embertribe.com/train-your-facebook-pixel-to-fetch-better-results

Brown, T. B., Mann, B., Ryder, N., Subbiah, M., Kaplan, J., Dhariwal, P., . . . Amodei, D. (2020). *Language Models are Few-Shot Learners*. arXiv:2005.14165v4.

Carion, N., Massa, F., Synnaeve, G., Usunier, N., Kirillov, A., & Zagoruyko, S. (2020). End-to-End Object Detection with Transformers. Lect. Notes Comput. Sci., 12346, 213–229. doi:10.1007/978-3-030-58452-8_13

Casebeer, J., Vale, V., Isik, U., Valin, J.-M., Giri, R., & Krishnaswamy, A. (2021). Enhancing into the Codec: Noise Robust Speech Coding with Vector-Quantized Autoencoders. *ICASSP 2021 - 2021 IEEE International Conference on Acoustics, Speech and Signal Processing (ICASSP)*. 10.1109/ICASSP39728.2021.9414605

Che, W., Fan, X., Xiong, R., & Zhao, D. (2020). Visual Relationship Embedding Network for Image Paragraph Generation. *IEEE Transactions on Multimedia, 22*(9), 2307–2320. doi:10.1109/TMM.2019.2954750

Chiu, M. C., Huang, J. H., Gupta, S., & Akman, G. (2021). Developing a personalized recommendation system in a smart product service system based on unsupervised learning model. *Computers in Industry, 128*, 103421. doi:10.1016/j.compind.2021.103421

Chung, J., Gulcehre, C., Cho, K., & Bengio, Y. (2014). *Empirical Evaluation of Gated Recurrent Neural Networks on Sequence Modeling.* arXiv:1412.3555v1.

Davidson, J., Liebald, B., Liu, J., Nandy, P., & Van Vleet, T. (2010). The YouTube video recommendation system. *RecSys'10 - Proc. 4th ACM Conf. Recomm. Syst.*, 293–296. 10.1145/1864708.1864770

Devlin, J., Chang, M. W., Lee, K., & Toutanova, K. (2019). BERT: Pre-training of deep bidirectional transformers for language understanding. *NAACL HLT 2019 - 2019 Conf. North Am. Chapter Assoc. Comput. Linguist. Hum. Lang. Technol. - Proc. Conf., 1*, 4171–4186.

Dosovitskiy, A., Beyer, L., Kolesnikov, A., Weissenborn, D., Zhai, X., Unterthiner, T., . . . Houlsby, N. (2021). *An Image is Worth 16x16 Words: Transformers for Image Recognition at Scale.* arXiv:2010.11929v2.

El Barachi, M., AlKhatib, M., Mathew, S., & Oroumchian, F. (2021). A novel sentiment analysis framework for monitoring the evolving public opinion in real-time: Case study on climate change. *Journal of Cleaner Production, 312*, 127820. doi:10.1016/j.jclepro.2021.127820

Ganai, A. F., & Khursheed, F. (2020). Predicting next Word using RNN and LSTM cells: Stastical Language Modeling. *2019 Fifth Int. Conf. Image Inf. Process.*, 469–474. 10.1109/ICIIP47207.2019.8985885

Gomez-Uribe, C. A., & Hunt, N. (2015). The netflix recommender system: Algorithms, business value, and innovation. *ACM Transactions on Management Information Systems, 6*(4), 1–19. Advance online publication. doi:10.1145/2843948

Han, K., Wang, Y., Chen, H., Chen, X., Guo, J., Liu, Z., . . . Tao, D. (2021). *A Survey on Visual Transformer.* arXiv:2012.12556v3.

He, K., Zhang, X., Ren, S., & Sun, J. (2016). Deep residual learning for image recognition. *Proceedings of the IEEE Computer Society Conference on Computer Vision and Pattern Recognition*, 770–778. 10.1109/CVPR.2016.90

Helskyaho, H., Yu, J., & Yu, K. (2021). *Machine Learning for Oracle Database Professionals.* Apress. doi:10.1007/978-1-4842-7032-5

Hochreiter, S., & Schmidhuber, J. (1997). Long Short-Term Memory. *Neural Computation, 9*(8), 1735–1780. doi:10.1162/neco.1997.9.8.1735 PMID:9377276

Howard, A., Sandler, M., Chen, B., Wang, W., Chen, L. C., Tan, M., Chu, G., Vasudevan, V., Zhu, Y., Pang, R., Le, Q., & Adam, H. (2019). Searching for mobileNetV3. *Proceedings of the IEEE International Conference on Computer Vision*, 1314–1324. 10.1109/ICCV.2019.00140

Howard, A.G., Zhu, M., Chen, B., Kalenichenko, D., Wang, W., Weyand, T., Andreetto, M., & Adam, H. (2017). *MobileNets: Efficient Convolutional Neural Networks for Mobile Vision Applications*. Academic Press.

Huang, G., Liu, Z., Van Der Maaten, L., & Weinberger, K. Q. (2017). Densely Connected Convolutional Networks. *Proc. IEEE Conf. Comput. Vis. pattern Recognit.*, 4700–4708. 10.1109/CVPR.2017.243

Jan, B., Farman, H., Khan, M., Imran, M., Islam, I. U., Ahmad, A., Ali, S., & Jeon, G. (2019). Deep learning in big data Analytics: A comparative study. *Computers & Electrical Engineering, 75*, 275–287. doi:10.1016/j.compeleceng.2017.12.009

Kan, Z. J., & Sourin, A. (2020). Generation of Irregular Music Patterns with Deep Learning. *Proc. - 2020 Int. Conf. Cyberworlds, CW 2020*, 188–195. 10.1109/CW49994.2020.00038

Khan, S., Naseer, M., Hayat, M., Zamir, S. W., Khan, F. S., & Shah, M. (2021). Transformers in Vision. *Survey (London, England)*, 1–28. arXiv2101.01169v2

KnightW. (2017). *Paying with Your Face*. https://www.technologyreview.com/technology/paying-with-your-face/

Kraus, M., Feuerriegel, S., & Oztekin, A. (2020). Deep learning in business analytics and operations research: Models, applications and managerial implications. *European Journal of Operational Research, 281*(3), 628–641. doi:10.1016/j.ejor.2019.09.018

Krizhevsky, A., Sutskever, I., & Hinton, G. E. (2012). ImageNet classification with deep convolutional neural networks. *Communications of the ACM, 1*, 1097–1105. doi:10.1145/3065386

Kumar, K., & Haider, M. T. U. (2021). *Enhanced Prediction of Intra-day Stock Market Using Metaheuristic Optimization on RNN–LSTM Network, New Generation Computing*. Ohmsha. doi:10.100700354-020-00104-0

Lee, V. H., Hew, J. J., Leong, L. Y., Tan, G. W. H., & Ooi, K. B. (2020). Wearable payment: A deep learning-based dual-stage SEM-ANN analysis. *Expert Systems with Applications, 157*, 113477. doi:10.1016/j.eswa.2020.113477

Li, J., Zhao, R., Hu, H., & Gong, Y. (2019). Improving RNN Transducer Modeling for End-to-End Speech Recognition. *2019 IEEE Autom. Speech Recognit. Underst. Work.*, 114–121.

Lin, T., Wang, Y., Liu, X., & Qiu, X. (2021). *A Survey of Transformers*. arXiv:2106.04554v11

Liu, Y., Ott, M., Goyal, N., Du, J., Joshi, M., Chen, D., . . . Stoyanov, V. (2019). *RoBERTa: A Robustly Optimized BERT Pretraining Approach*. arXiv:1907.11692v1

Melo, P. N., & Machado, C. (2020). *Business Intelligence and Analytics in Small and Medium Enterprises*. Taylor & Francis.

Metz, C. (2016). *Apple Is Bringing the AI Revolution to Your iPhone*. https://www.wired.com/2016/06/apple-bringing-ai-revolution-iphone/

Nagarajan, S. M., Deverajan, G. G., Chatterjee, P., Alnumay, W., & Ghosh, U. (2021). Effective task scheduling algorithm with deep learning for Internet of Health Things (IoHT) in sustainable smart cities. *Sustainable Cities and Society*, *71*, 102945. doi:10.1016/j.scs.2021.102945

Niemann, J., & Pisla, A. (2020). *Life-Cycle Management of Machines and Mechanisms*. Springer.

Nolle, T., Luettgen, S., Seeliger, A., & Mühlhäuser, M. (2018). Analyzing business process anomalies using autoencoders. *Machine Learning*, *107*(11), 1875–1893. doi:10.100710994-018-5702-8

Priadana, A., Maarif, M. R., & Habibi, M. (2020). Gender Prediction for Instagram User Profiling using Deep Learning. *2020 Int. Conf. Decis. Aid Sci. Appl. DASA 2020*, 432–436. 10.1109/DASA51403.2020.9317143

Qiu, M., Li, P., Pan, H., Wang, C., Wang, A., Chen, C., Li, Y., Gao, D., Huang, J., Li, Yong, Yang, J., Cai, D., & Lin, W. (2020). *EasyTransfer -- A Simple and Scalable Deep Transfer Learning Platform for NLP Applications*. Academic Press.

Radford, A., Narasimhan, K., Salimans, T., & Sutskever, I. (2018). *Improving Language Understanding by Generative Pre-Training*. Academic Press.

Radford, A., Wu, J., Child, R., Luan, D., Amodei, D., & Sutskever, I. (2020). Language Models are Unsupervised Multitask Learners. *OpenAI Blog*, *1*, 1–7.

Rafailidis, D., & Manolopoulos, Y. (2019). Can virtual assistants produce recommendations? *ACM Int. Conf. Proceeding Ser.* 10.1145/3326467.3326468

Ravì, D., Wong, C., Lo, B., & Yang, G. (2017). A Deep Learning Approach to on-Node Sensor Data Analytics for Mobile or Wearable Devices. *IEEE Journal of Biomedical and Health Informatics*, *21*(1), 56–64. doi:10.1109/JBHI.2016.2633287 PMID:28026792

Ravi, V., & Kamaruddin, S. (2017). Big data analytics enabled smart financial services: Opportunities and challenges. Lect. Notes Comput. Sci., 10721, 15–39. doi:10.1007/978-3-319-72413-3_2

Rawassizadeh, R., Sen, T., Kim, S. J., Meurisch, C., Keshavarz, H., Mühlhäuser, M., & Pazzani, M. (2019). Manifestation of virtual assistants and robots into daily life: Vision and challenges. *CCF Trans. Pervasive Comput. Interact.*, *1*(3), 163–174. doi:10.100742486-019-00014-1

Roy, A., Sun, J., Mahoney, R., Alonzi, L., Adams, S., & Beling, P. (2018). Deep learning detecting fraud in credit card transactions. 2018 Syst. *Inf. Eng. Des. Symp. SIEDS*, *2018*, 129–134. doi:10.1109/SIEDS.2018.8374722

Sadiq, S., Umer, M., Ullah, S., Mirjalili, S., Rupapara, V., & Nappi, M. (2021). Discrepancy detection between actual user reviews and numeric ratings of Google App store using deep learning. *Expert Systems with Applications*, *181*, 115111. doi:10.1016/j.eswa.2021.115111

Saiz-Rubio, V., & Rovira-Más, F. (2020). From smart farming towards agriculture 5.0: A review on crop data management. *Agronomy (Basel)*, *10*(2), 207. Advance online publication. doi:10.3390/agronomy10020207

Sandler, M., Howard, A., Zhu, M., Zhmoginov, A., & Chen, L.C. (2018). MobileNetV2: Inverted Residuals and Linear Bottlenecks. *Proc. IEEE Comput. Soc. Conf. Comput. Vis. Pattern Recognit.*, 4510–4520. doi:10.1109/CVPR.2018.00474

Sarkar, M., & De Bruyn, A. (2021). LSTM Response Models for Direct Marketing Analytics: Replacing Feature Engineering with Deep Learning. *Journal of Interactive Marketing*, *53*, 80–95. doi:10.1016/j.intmar.2020.07.002

Sengupta, S., Basak, S., Saikia, P., Paul, S., Tsalavoutis, V., Atiah, F., Ravi, V., & Peters, A. (2020). A review of deep learning with special emphasis on architectures, applications and recent trends. *Knowledge-Based Systems*, *194*, 105596. Advance online publication. doi:10.1016/j.knosys.2020.105596

Simonyan, K., & Zisserman, A. (2015). Very deep convolutional networks for large-scale image recognition. *3rd International Conference on Learning Representations, ICLR 2015 - Conference Track Proceedings*.

Srinivasan, V. (2020). *Introducing the new Google Analytics.* https://blog.google/products/marketing-platform/analytics/new_google_analytics/

Sutskever, I., Vinyals, O., & Le, Q. V. (2014). Sequence to sequence learning with neural networks. *Advances in Neural Information Processing Systems*, *4*, 3104–3112.

Szegedy, C., Liu, W., Jia, Y., Sermanet, P., Reed, S., Anguelov, D., Erhan, D., Vanhoucke, V., & Rabinovich, A. (2015). Going deeper with convolutions. *Proc. IEEE Comput. Soc. Conf. Comput. Vis. Pattern Recognit.* 10.1109/CVPR.2015.7298594

The Economist. (2017). *Finding a voice.* https://www.economist.com/technology-quarterly/2017-05-01/language

Vaswani, A., Shazeer, N., Parmar, N., Uszkoreit, J., Jones, L., Gomez, A. N., Kaiser, Ł., & Polosukhin, I. (2017). Attention is all you need. Adv. Neural Inf. Process. Syst., 5999–6009.

Vinh, T. Q., & Tran Dac Thinh, P. (2019). Advertisement System Based on Facial Expression Recognition and Convolutional Neural Network. *Proc. - 2019 19th Int. Symp. Commun. Inf. Technol. Isc.*, 476–480. 10.1109/ISCIT.2019.8905134

Vinyals, O., Toshev, A., Bengio, S., & Erhan, D. (2015). Show and tell: A neural image caption generator. *Proc. IEEE Comput. Soc. Conf. Comput. Vis. Pattern Recognit.*, 3156–3164. doi:10.1109/CVPR.2015.7298935

Wu, J., Jiang, N., Wu, Z., & Jiang, H. (2021). Early warning of risks in cross-border mobile payments. *Procedia Computer Science*, *183*, 724–732. doi:10.1016/j.procs.2021.02.121

Yang, R., Mentzer, F., Van Gool, L., & Timofte, R. (2021). Learning for Video Compression with Recurrent Auto-Encoder and Recurrent Probability Model. *IEEE Journal of Selected Topics in Signal Processing*, *15*(2), 388–401. doi:10.1109/JSTSP.2020.3043590

Zhang, X., Xie, C., Wang, J., Zhang, W., & Fu, X. (2018). Towards memory friendly long-short term memory networks (LSTMs) on mobile GPUs. *Proc. Annu. Int. Symp. Microarchitecture, MICRO 2018*, 162–174. 10.1109/MICRO.2018.00022

Zhou, L., Pan, S., Wang, J., & Vasilakos, A. V. (2017). Machine learning on big data: Opportunities and challenges. *Neurocomputing*, *237*, 350–361. doi:10.1016/j.neucom.2017.01.026

Zhou, R., Khemmarat, S., & Gao, L. (2010). The impact of YouTube recommendation system on video views. *Proc. ACM SIGCOMM Internet Meas. Conf. IMC*, 404–410. 10.1145/1879141.1879193

ADDITIONAL READING

Earley, S. (2015). Analytics, machine learning, and the internet of things. *IT Professional*, *17*(1), 10–13. doi:10.1109/MITP.2015.3

Chapter 9
Semantic Image Analysis on Social Networks and Data Processing:
Review and Future Directions

Mowafaq Salem Alzboon
(iD) https://orcid.org/0000-0002-3522-6689
Jadara University, Jordan

Muhyeeddin Kamel Alqaraleh
Jadara University, Jordan

Emran Mahmoud Aljarrah
Jadara University, Jordan

Saleh Ali Alomari
Jadara University, Jordan

ABSTRACT

In the last decade, a significant number of people have become active social network users. People utilize Twitter, Facebook, LinkedIn, and Google+. Facebook users generate a lot of data. Photos can teach people a lot. Image analysis has traditionally focused on audience emotions. Photographic emotions are essentially subjective and vary among observers. There are numerous uses for its most popular feature. People, on the other hand, use social media and applications. They handle noise, dynamics, and size. Shared text, pictures, and videos were also a focus of network analysis study. Statistic, rules, and trend analysis are all available in massive datasets. You may use them for data manipulation and retrieval, mathematical modeling, and data pre-processing and interpretation. This chapter examines social networks, basic concepts, and social network analysis components. A further study topic is picture usage in social networks. Next, a novel method for analyzing social networks, namely semantic networks, is presented. Finally, themes and routes are defined.

DOI: 10.4018/978-1-7998-9016-4.ch009

INTRODUCTION

Today's online networking includes social networks. Users may establish online connections, discuss their circumstances, preferences, and operation information while simultaneously acquiring and disseminating knowledge. Smartphone and 5G users view the world through social media. Every social media platform has a network. It's your Twitter, Facebook, and LinkedIn connections. You may do this using LinkedIn, Instagram, Facebook, and Twitter. Facebook is the quickest social network to reach one billion registered members, with over 2.6 billion monthly active users.

According to Instagram, it has over one billion monthly active users. Popular social networks are now available in many languages, enabling operators or users to connect with friends or entities beyond political, economic, and geographic borders (Adedoyin-Olowe et al., 2014; Awad et al., 2020; Bayrakdar et al., 2020; Janani et al., 2019; Kasthuri & Jebaseeli, 2020; Mahmud et al., 2020; Najafabadi et al., 2019).

Today, 3.6 billion Internet users use social networks, with mobile devices and personal social networks expected to grow in popularity. User accounts or extensive user engagement are common in social networks. When Facebook initially surpassed one billion monthly active users, newcomer Pinterest was the first independent website to reach ten million unique monthly visitors. Due to geographical importance and topic matter, European facilities such as VK or Chinese social networks Qzone and Renren have attracted common appeals in their regions. (Awad et al., 2020). For example, Facebook or Google+ depend on relationships with family and friends and aggressively promote communication via apps such as status sharing or pictures and video games. Microblogs, such as Tumblr or Twitter, are sometimes referred to as social networks. The material on some social networks is user-generated.

Societal networks have a significant social effect since they are always present in users' lives. Recently, online and offline reality merging and digital personality have all emerged. Social networks, which allow users to exchange and access multimedia and text material, are introducing more people to the Internet. Facebook, for example, has 2,603 million active members as of July 2020. As of Q1 2019, Twitter, one of the world's most popular microblogging network sites, has 330 million monthly users. (Statista, 2020b).

As of July 2020, Sina Weibo, a Twitter-like microblogging platform in China, has over 550 million active monthly users (Statista, 2020a). Another famous social networking site is Instagram. Since the photo and video filters can be automated on Instagram, companies can use the standard tool to develop their exclusive visual content for sharing. (Statista, 2020a). As of June 2020, over 1,082 million active monthly users worldwide were aware of this social network initiative and 500 million active daily social network users (Statista, 2020a, 2020b).

The world's social network scope is rising every day. At the end of 2019, 72.4% of the global Internet population is expected to have social network access, up 69.6% in 2016. According to recent projections, the number of global social network users is now estimated to exceed 3.03 billion active monthly operators through 2021, up from 2.47 billion in 2017 (Statista, 2020a, 2020b).

This subsequent rise in social networking sites has taken internet applications worldwide (Akaichi, 2014) numerous social networks of learning, communication, health, history, etc. Social networks also contributed to researching and analyzing mechanisms and shared knowledge that make up social networks. Studies on social network analysis (SNA) have been based since recently (Bayrakdar et al., 2020).

Today, particularly Facebook, Twitter, Sina Weibo, Instagram, ResearchGate, Sermo, PatientsLikeMe, etc., online social networking sites have converted the biosphere's significant storehouses of data (Yu et al., 2016). Therefore, it is essential to gather data from comprehensive data resources and use it correctly by interpreting the information from processing it. For instance, social network information plays

Figure 1. Furthermost widespread social networks worldwide as of July 2020, ordered by the number of lively users (in millions)
(Statista, 2020a)

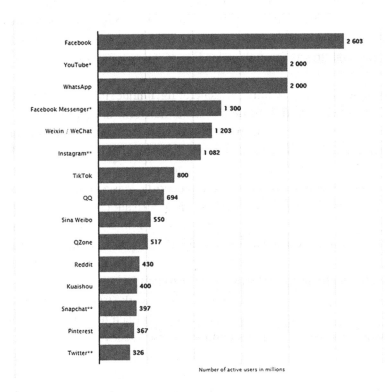

a significant part in decisive product revenue and marketing specifications. Social networks, instead, became essential data points for analyzing customer habits and evaluating personalities for various reasons (Adedoyin-Olowe et al., 2014; Bayrakdar et al., 2020; Kasthuri & Jebaseeli, 2020). Figure 1 illustrates furthermost widespread social networks worldwide as of July 2020, ordered by the number of lively users (in millions)

Furthermore, many remerged research types include developing input systems for social network users, assessments in teaching, feeling and awareness regulation, lack of information, and analysis of social connections (Bayrakdar et al., 2020). social networking sites are primarily created using visual information or textual for time info. And location for a specific purpose. Collecting and visualizing these spatial-temporal data defines incident identification, image description, cross-media processing, and several other studies (Kou et al., 2016). Modern methods to location, time, image, and log features of social networks have provided promising outcomes from their arenas (Mahmud et al., 2020).

However, additional exertion is needed to incorporate and reliably convey this information in multi-modal and multi-functional social networking. Social networks become widespread daily and are vigorously utilized by operators, so social network analysis is very important. Social network analysis typically refers to social networks ' statistical, visual, and sociological characteristics. This chapter separates social networks from static, interactive, and conceptual analysis data. Static social network analysis reports on status E of social networks based on systemic structures and strategies (Freeman, 1977) Or software flow-driven (Latora & Marchiori, 2001). It describes critical principles, including degree, connection, and distance within the social networks.

Furthermore, social network analysis models simplify the grouping of persons and clusters besides classifying tacit connections between individuals within social graphs. Dynamic social network analysis, which compares static social network analysis's central notions with the study of temporal events, focuses on transformations of social graphs through states E to E` corresponding to periods {t, t`} (Bayrakdar et al., 2020).

Semantic social network analysis aims at generating unique information-related outcomes that represent individuals and communities inside the social network, integrating static or dynamic social network analysis, ontology modeling, conceptual networks, microformats, and semantic web languages (Hu et al., 2014; Ruan et al., 2014; Thovex & Trichet, 2011). Semantic analysis has been necessary for information knowledge management and exploration. Studies integrating social network analysis's three different modes are essential research areas. A significant obstacle is a multidimensional static, dynamic, and textual representation model in social networks is a significant obstacle. Recently, virtual links via Web 2.0 networking media have acquired significant attention in semantic web culture. Online social data exchange, sharing, and review using a graph model (RDF), configuration specification (RDFS and OWL), and database language (SPARQL) (Kulcu et al., 2016). The Exponential Random Graph Model frequently uses dynamic or chronological simulation (ERGM).

The ERGM was primarily applied to modeling social network structure. Proposing an ERGM for a social network meets the fifth stages (Robins et al., 2007): (i) Each network interaction is presumed to be an arbitrary or random variable; (ii) an assumption or dependency hypothesis is roundabout through defining possibilities between network variables; (iii) a dependency hypothesis or assumption indicates a specific model type; (iv) a universalization of limitations by similarity or other limitations; and (v) an ERGM estimation and study. Dynamic models are usually time-focused models which make correlations amongst variables with passing the time or overtime. (Proskurnikov & Tempo, 2017). Dynamic or active SNA is characterized as the time-changing investigating for networks. It has been a growing study area throughout the last decade. Complex network models have been growing in literature. Social interface constructions may be separated into two core classes: microscopic and macroscopic. Macroscopic opinion-dynamic models are similar to continuum dynamics simulations. Macroscopic simulations illustrate how beliefs propagate over time, such as voting habits for every selection or survey. The model is often recognized as an agent-dependent model. Microscopic opinion-forming models illustrate how human actor's (agents) behaviors grow. Modeling users' spatial-temporal behavior in social networks is significant for expecting upcoming user acts besides determining the network's latent impact by tracking user movements (Zarezade et al., 2018). Operators have recurring patterns in their gestures.

Spatiotemporal models get up once data is accumulated over space and time, with at slightest one longitudinal and single chronological stuff. The spatiotemporal dataset event defines a longitudinal and chronological phenomenon at a specified location x also time t. Using smart connections to information on social networks and semantic structures has been a noteworthy study area in the current time. Technologies of semantic aim to close the human-machine hole. It requires cultural language processing, machine learning, and cognitive science approaches. Since traditional search methods cannot capture and integrate social data from diverse sources, semantic technologies are critical.

For social networks, gathering and describing spatial-temporal data is considered the cornerstone, semantic modeling and analysis of social networks is an essential part of the research, and the method of retrieval and indexing is necessary. This study uses qualitative methods to examine the field of social network analysis and discuss historical, current, and future interventions and their implementation.

Preparing for the survey is as follows: The basics of social network analysis (SNA) and its various features and technical challenges are discussed in section 2. Section 3 depicts structural analysis and mimics structural analysis software. Applications of structural analysis and social data analysis discussed in Sections 4 and 5 are reflected in Sections 4 and 5. Section 6 delves into social interaction analysis; section 7 delves into semantic image analysis. The study includes a systematic literature analysis of these topics discussed in the literature; section 9 reflects future trends. Section 10 of the research study specifies the worth of work and the course of study that could be pursued.

Social networks are a way to connect and interact with many people and exchange information, emails, recent technical developments, news alerts, photographs, photos, and thoughts (Clemons et al., 2007). Online networking also included industry and customer analysis activities, such as general marketing, company data examination, and mouth marketing (Kasthuri & Jebaseeli, 2020). Worldwide social network analysis provides vast volumes of content in different fields of study, such as business management, psychology, finance, history, politics, and other global academic aspects. Social target analyses focus specifically on the online page's resources and the online page's processes, the online page's content, and, therefore, user behavior within the platform. Social network analysis is often used for intelligence methods, and data mining is deemed the most deserving.

Data mining may be an innovative methodology and is a handy tool for building multiple relationships and patterns within the information.

Extracts secret knowledge from massive libraries (Craven & Shavlik, 1997; Dou et al., 2015; Mohamad & Tasir, 2013; Romero & Ventura, 2007). Data mining is often referred to as content production. Data analyses are performed from multiple backgrounds and distilled into information that could be needed to analyze data patterns and experiences to help create better business decisions, thereby improving revenue, digital connectivity, product innovations, and cost reduction. Figure 2 shows the amount of once-a-month active Twitter users worldwide from 1st quarter 2010 to 1st quarter 2019 (in millions)

These include bioinformatics, artificial intelligence, communications, predictive modeling, networking, social media, and decision support systems. Data mining techniques are also used to construct accurate and informative social network activity models. The chapter introduces basic social networking concepts, discusses their critical features and data processing techniques explored by social media networks, and explains outcomes. Social networking can be a web-based sharing forum that lets citizens share knowledge (Chang et al., 2014). Figure 3 shows different types of the most popular Social Media.

SOCIAL NETWORK ANALYSIS (SNA) AND MINING BASICS

The SNA was developed in the 1930s by several people working in psychology, mathematics, and biology. Several scientific ideas are based on ancient Greek writings. The development of social networks and social network analysis was described in detail by Linton C. Freeman. Social network analysis emerged as a research area with a fundamental model in the following years. This part outlines the steps of a generic social network analysis paradigm (NetworkX, 2018). Figure 4 shows the stage block scheme, showing numerous components; these components are defined as follows:

The foremost step of dealing with social network data is data analysis, which can be achieved using various data sources. However, this method is usually accomplished by calling the database administra-

Figure 2. Amount of once-a-month lively Twitter users worldwide from 1st quarter 2010 to 1st quarter 2019 (in millions)
(Statista, 2020b) (Statista, 2020a).

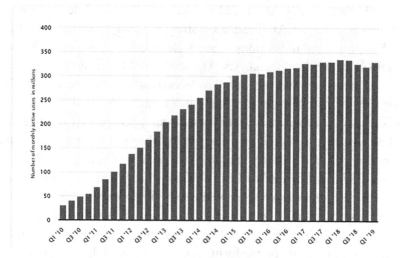

tor to obtain the dataset, update the dataset generated for scholarly purposes or problems, or develop a framework or compose a system (Alfantoukh & Durresi, 2014). There is often an application programming interface (API) shared with several common social networking platforms, for example, Twitter, Facebook, LinkedIn, and Foursquare, to support the data cooperation. The second stage involves data processing, analysis, collection, and basic statistics. Because raw social data is typically noisy, massive, and casual, it includes numerous operator-produced acronyms. It contains confidential private user information, and easy text cleaning has been carefully preprocessed to remove unnecessary white spaces,

Figure 3. Different types of the most popular social media
(Social Media Marketing Tree Diagram, 2021)

stop terms, and punctuation. The research method fails because hastily assembled databases contain confidential information, posing privacy and security risks (Gao et al., 2014).

Thus, data processing is critical for social network analysis's performance. From the other point of view, removing a social network from the initial database should be processed in a standardized format for automated review, modification, and retrieval. Furthermore, some basic statistical analysis can be performed on organized social data, such as calculating the number of microblogs per hour or period created, the number of messages, remarks or comments (including unique keywords), users, the number of diverse retweeted operators, or users, and the amount or number of video views. The data analysis study (Chelmis et al.) is intended for the method's third phase.

Intended for the 3rd phase of the method, the data analysis study (Chelmis & Prasanna, 2011) has three main methods: systemic examination or analysis, social substance (data and its different interaction) analysis, and semantic examination or analysis. Generally, structural analysis operates on social network analysis graph-based network topologies, including network architectures, sociometric characteristics, population discovery, temporal networks, and random walks. However, to explain the relationship between reported text and social context, graph analysis on your own is unsatisfactory. Social networking material review is often essential.

Consequently, Data mining focuses on identifying structures and establishing criteria, specifically disseminating content through social networks. Recently, emotion analysis, sarcasm identification, and suggestion consume concerned considerable interest in this field. However, structural and substance analyses conducted ahead of them have essential constraints. All lose support for logic. Semantic social network analysis's fundamental aim is to integrate semantics into rich organized info, and through which misconception, social networks deal with far richer constructs than raw graphics.

Finally, visualizations of social network analysis are among the most critical functionality and can help educate people involved in their results. The visualization approach that provides a graphical representation of the network better explains specific social networks (Wadhwa & Bhatia, 2012). Often, visualization is described as the last stage in an extended analysis phase, although this could alter. It is claimed that visualization is no more the finish of a pipeline and that close integration of social network analysis and visualization is required to analyze social networks efficiently. Several resources are currently accessible for visualization, and some of the more common are UCINet, Gephi, NodeXL, and Pajek.

The systemic study, social media analysis, and social activity analysis were grouped to make introducing various studies relating to the social network study easier. As a result, the next section deals with conceptual research.

IN-DEPTH STRUCTURAL ANALYSIS AND REVIEW

Structural analysis is the earliest segment in study fields since it deals with original studies on social networking sites' nature and features. This chapter has several causes why researchers or academics are concerned in this field; for instance, consider how a social network is formed or created. In addition, explaining the network structure or formed (usually using various algorithm's graphs), comparing its building block or structure with other established networks, or exploring unknown interactions amongst individuals in a network. The matrix includes as many rows and columns as the dataset participants (Hu et al., 2014). The matrix elements symbolize user-to-user connections (Bhagat et al., 2011). In this modeling method, weights may be applied to the graph's links or connections or edges, and elements

Figure 4. The architecture of the general SNA model

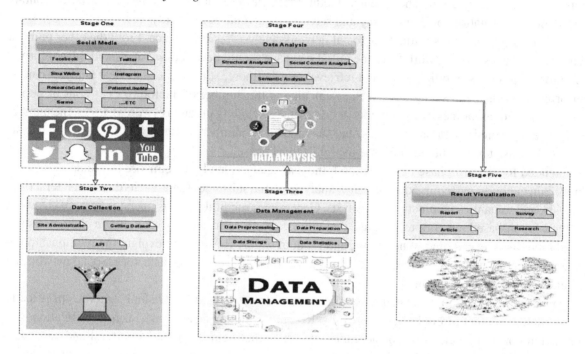

in the matrices may be useful to show the importance of user relationships (Henry & Fekete, 2007). Nevertheless, they can not discern various relationships or reflect relationships' meanings distinctly.30 Several experiments have modeled social networks utilizing homogeneous and heterogeneous graphs.

STRUCTURAL ANALYSIS SOFTWARE

Social networks are also studied, applying specific methods to accomplish computational research missions. Many platforms for evaluating social networks include Pajek, UCINet, NodeXL, Gephi, IGraph, SocNetV, NetMiner, and NetworkX. The platforms include two features established on graphical user interfaces (GUIs) and programming packages/libraries. GUIs are simpler to understand, while programming packages/libraries are efficient and extensible. For example, in Pajek and Gephi (Mrvar & Batagelj, 2016), it was found that they are GUI-based analytics tools, while IGraph and NetworkX are package/library-based tools. The subsequent is a short description of these methods.

Pajek analyzes and visualizes an extensive network to turn into smaller networks. After being used and built for over 20 years, Pajek is the only highly uncomplicated algorithm managing a broad network (Mrvar & Batagelj, 2016). Gephi is an integrated visualization or image creation and analysis tool for various networks, complex and hierarchical graphs. It uses a 3D rendering mechanism to simulate broad networks in real-time (simultaneous) and facilitate investigation or research (Singh et al., 2018).

IGraph is a network library that concentrates on ease of usage, portability, and performance with a bit of east API for those who want to render larger graphs. When searching its responses, a spanning search algorithm utilizes classic graph theory algorithms like minimal spanning trees and network flow algorithms to find solutions to graph issues, like network layout (Akhtar, 2014). NetworkX provides software resources to plan, monitor, and calculate complex networks and examine and assess their diverse configuration and behaviors in the Python language. (NetworkX, 2018). In all four of the applications mentioned, anybody with connections to the Internet would use them. In addition, it emphasizes parallelism and scalability, while Networoratives, a growing open-source forum for large-oriented network analysis, emphasizes expansion (Staudt et al., 2016). An increasingly efficient computational method employs various parallel multidimensional data processing algorithms, a few of which are highly parallel to cope with several networks that range from a few thousand to a billion edges (Adedoyin-Olowe et al., 2014; Awad et al., 2020; Bayrakdar et al., 2020; Janani et al., 2019; Kasthuri & Jebaseeli, 2020; Mahmud et al., 2020; Najafabadi et al., 2019).

APPLICATIONS OF STRUCTURAL ANALYSIS AND IMPLEMENTATIONS

Social network analysis was a topic on which various studies have been conducted in several different places. Ostrowski developed a mechanism that demonstrated that groups could display long-term patterns in structural dynamics, especially organizations, which may provide information that can indicate future trends. In addition to measuring strength and control, he assessed several other attributes such as perseverance, aptitude, courage, resourcefulness, self-confidence, and commitment to the measures he employed are (or the measures he employed to focus on) are concerned with these qualities. Studies were conducted to identify the most prevalent viruses in different samples of sharks, their effects on hosts, and how the hosts control such viruses (Gong et al., 2016). Heuristic techniques have successfully discovered the route with two community detection algorithms that produce the shortest detection paths (expanding the combined result to include SPDA methods) (Gong et al., 2016).

Using network architecture to constrain the search room, SPCD's network graph increases its efficiency. Mislove et al. performed a large-scale study on four well-known internet social networks: 'sic networks' components, such as Facebook, MySpace, LinkedIn, Orkut, Spurl, Stack Exchange, and Technorati, were included (Mislove et al., 2007).

Observing small-world, scale-free, power-law, and scale-free properties could deduce the potential networks of connections from the node extent. Researchers who use systematic data mining techniques can analyze social networks and network editing techniques. Alavijeh has stated that the use of data and network analysis for SNA is just getting started and that similar principles are being used in other research fields, such as social networking (Tylenda et al., 2009).

One of the particular aspects of the connection mining problem is that it applies data mining techniques on networks of social entities, which is the distinction from general network approaches to data mining. In structural analysis, relation mining, you might be interested in individual classes, roads, or connected networks, and you are more than likely to come across subgraph or subgraph exploration. Problems were inherent to studies on social networking. For example, in this specific community, digging at fraudulent software, behaviors or discrepancies, and network disruptiveness would be quite relevant (Çıtlak et al., 2019). These incidents may be of some manner such as cyberbullying (Di Capua et al., 2016), (Dredge et al., 2014), terrorist assault planning (Knoke, 2015) embezzlement,(Matti et al., 2015), misinformation news spread (Xiao et al., 2015) false profiles generating fictitious numbers on pages,(V. Tiwari, 2017) and political exploitation. Then, by observing habits in user groups who liked the same sites, they found deceptive activities, dubious parties, and selfish assaults. The Facebook datasets used in the study come from users' actual Preferences and site pages. Benevenuto et al. Developed a content-based, guided network (in YouTube) and associated responses and used derivative functionality as part of a broader dataset to detect content spammers and promoters (Benevenuto et al., 2009). Separate research analyzed the consumers of YouTube that they considered being involved in spamming and their suspicious account behavior by extending the usage of a network-based method (Tylenda et al., 2009).

As previous studies on social networks have shown, Xiao's team developed a time-sensitive and scalable machine learning model to discover false groupers registered by the same consumer (Xiao et al., 2015). the research approach was tested on the LinkedIn account. Instead of counting single accounts, the automated approach organizes current clusters by a false or a real account to detect if the same individual generated them.

SOCIAL DATA ANALYSIS AND REVIEW

The second portion of social data analysis focuses on staggering volumes of social network data. Still, it extends it to anything from media and commerce to, e.g., the Most social analysis focuses on information created by the users. However, the network structures that result from that content do not typically receive much consideration (Eltermann et al., 2020). Another case study on social media finds that an incredible amount of social data is used by natural language processing (NLT), including the classifications, such as in this one. Although the extensive mining of social data is relatively simple, it has also proven to be very useful in identifying sorts and investigating and dealing with big data databases, which are difficult to organize with basic approaches (Srivastava, 2008). The types of my information can be based on the nature of their data. When using specific resources, it's crucial to ensure that your data is organized or unorganized (A. K. Tiwari et al., 2019). Researchers need to decide on the patterns to study to analyze these data types. The researcher needs to identify trends.

Without careful use of available data mining techniques, progress would be impossible. In the coming years, companies will be overwhelmed by an increasing amount of raw data, which will be seen as a stressful, fragmented, and complicated process attributable to social networks. The professor's thesis proposed a systematic data mining algorithm to mine intelligent intelligence from social network data (Rahman, 2012). The data was primarily gathered from Facebook, the concept of a social media site, such as identities, insights, interactions, not-butterflies, tumb messages, ….etc. As raw data and its different qualities (such as identity, interactions, sentiments, thoughts, and other posts and tweets) were sources for more data analysis.

Often known as k-Nearest Neighbor Attribute Classification, a system, k-N Classification, or k-Neighborrowing Attribute Strategy Mosley had retweeted deployment on relationships, as a kind of social organization, connections, and activities, and analytics about social involvement (Batrinca & Treleaven, 2015). The chapter explains how data mining and text analytics can be extended to social networks to identify specific results. When making remarks on every article on social networks, there is no transparent, standardized direct data analysis methodology, specifically for social network analysis.

(Salloum et al., 2017). Combining disciplines including text analysis, extracting information, categorizing it, mapping awareness, interacting with spatial and multidimensional data and frameworks including documentation or data spaces, and operating with large datasets such as texts or databases, both count as aspects of text mining. Researchers can perform text mining analysis on social media to learn about a topic, a community's general thought habits, highlight important aspects of a problem, or in the hopes of discovering previously undiscovered or obscure information. User modeling and text mining methods were used to extract online input on different vehicles on Abrahams et al. (Two .'s researchers studied the usage of language and text analysis on two concept blogs to extract various bits of information.) (Abrahams et al., 2012). Researchers used the groundbreaking decision support methodology to classify faults by examining consumers' subjective responses and analyzing consumer expectations to assess their respective subtypes via social media. Research by Kahya-Ozyirmidokuz (Kahya-Özyirmidokuz, 2016) used strategies to identify numerous Facebook online shopping businesses social networking sites' shopping patterns. NLP techniques and URL structural analysis were done on the websites of two hundred Turkish companies, corporations, and then language techniques and the use of There is a degree of resemblance analysis and clustering that is done. Annotation to analyze the effect of Twenge and Wimber and the dissemination of data trends on adolescents' self-Expand, a notable library tweet and Twenge, and test out the latest techniques combining text mining and encoding (Al-Daihani & Abrahams, 2016). The LightSIDE classifier approach was established using the classifier integrated into the automated learning LightSIDE system. A support vector machine or a support vector machine (SVM) classified messages. Thus, this was meant to happen in advance of each post chosen for publication by academics. Networks such as Facebook and Twitter have gained considerable interest, and popularity, as analysis concerning textual content mining and thus a source of new and social network details The use of the famous social networking websites, including Facebook data in three different issues of statistical sophistication, like (clutter, noise, and change). Giving it more complex also rendered social data virtually impossible to handle manually (Batrinca & Treleaven, 2015). With this goal in mind, it is essential to provide computerized information systems to conduct computer analysis of new information quickly.

Frequently use a good calculation methodology to solve these issues, storing text and learning relevant data. It is used for NLP tasks such as semantic search, NER, translation, and fluency estimation and built using the open-source social network analysis software framework (Cunningham et al., 2013).

The toolkit would be an outstanding addition to your analysis toolbox, including the activities like data collection, indexing, semantic definition, scan, and visualization. Various study data use these modern insight-gathering testing methods, but only those with reliable analysis techniques benefit. To accomplish these aimsNLP concepts are essential; individuals, topics, and feelings must be properly represented to offer the significance of the results (Maynard et al., 2017). Though this should be borne in mind, automation of text analysis has been seen to be incomplete, Twitter is successful at finding brief and casual communications, and news reports in their entirety appear to be quite ambiguous.

SOCIAL INTERACTION ANALYSIS

The last chapter focuses on individual behaviors to start looking at social networks data and see if people are passing knowledge on and discovering models that depict users' personal and social processes. It is defined as a cascade, which is just that; for instance, people who utilize the content or functionality of a site or technology can, by proxy, increase the number of contacts with it and thereby increasing the amount of traffic or making it more popular (Al-Garadi et al., 2018). One of the popular uses of decentralized networks is the introduction of vast numbers of reaction links, which lead to an incredible amount of social network content diffusion. For accurately forecasting long-term adoption patterns, the material could start by looking at long-term data on YouTube. And it's worth it to observe early user behavior patterns concerning Digg, particularly because from those measures, you know the majority of its current users started in this manner (Szabo & Huberman, 2010).

Using their data for the time series Just the First Two Hours Forecast 30 Days of Diggreames as a guide, they found that Diggs' first two-hour entry period predicted his half-day lifespan better than vi's two-day entry period. Goel and his team created a Twitter dataset that measures the network's content distribution efficiency. To recognize and demonstrate network performance, users of social networks must first be recognized. These networks are powerful because they are ideal traps for spreading ransomware, political orders, and derogatory content. A similar finding was made by Kempe et al. (Kempe et al., 2003). When evaluating these numbers, you've come to the analysis that defining a major user problem is balancing power (F.ElGamal, 2013).

Using various studies, it is observed that influential users serve as the most important transmission modes within a social network (Goyal et al., 2010). Although some prior research has looked at nodes more generally at social effects, Freeman's chapter stresses three main network centrality measures. The article by Freeman takes the opposite view and explores three: the centrality of degree, closeness, and betweenness for determining the centrality of a given node (Freeman, 1978). PageRank is a Google-based metric often used by consumers to determine the weight of a website has inside the search results according to if they are supposed to have the capacity to raise the volume of information in the network, if necessary, and gauge other participants dependent on the quantity of operation that they execute the role of retweeting (Ben Jabeur et al., 2012). the algorithm can be described as close to that used in Google: social network leaders or powerful individuals can be modeled as expanded. A graph network is created where the users are represented as nodes, and the comments are as user edges.

Researchers have suggested many ranking algorithms such as InfluenceRank, LeaderBoard, Twitter, and Degree Descending on a User Profiles (or DD-Search) to help us recognize influential users and encourage their value. Regardless of who carried out the analysis, both research concerned social effects. According to Dang-Xuan, said data shows the levels in the politicization of more fascinating or angry words but didn't explain its ramifications, which contributed to the inference that there was more circulation of views that were commonly regarded as positive or negative (Stieglitz & Dang-Xuan, 2012). Salath'e et al. examined temporal health opinion patterns through analyzing responses to a recent vaccination program against a particular pandemic virus (Salathé et al., 2013). They analyzed the community impacts.

SEMANTIC IMAGE ANALYSIS

Knowing the quality of images has become more challenging and promising due to advances in computer vision. Visual content development and delivery skills have lately been combined with the Internet, which has expanded productions to interactive dissemination (Avrithis et al., 2006). The advancement of technology has not kept pace with the growing demand for increased image processing capabilities. The enormous amounts of new visual content made finding previously accessible visual material more difficult. When you have more textual or image data, the search needs to be more flexible and powerful (Leonard, 2007).

Pre-production, image processing, and computer vision are necessary steps in dealing with images. In addition to noise reduction and picture sharpening, sophisticated processing stages like image segmentation are also available (Adatrao & Mittal, 2016). There have been many applications of the analysis of the post-focused extension of the definition of the raw images for various attributes or characteristics, to the extent that now they are underutilized. Two types of social material can be distinguished using visual attributes: Exchangeable Picture (EXIF) data and information-generating features (Sawant et al., 2011). Until now, a wider range of visual attributes Hass has been proposed to help distinguish shades, shapes, and textures. When annotating an image, the annotation points are focused on unique to the regions of the image (margins or regions in the picture) or on the image as a whole (histograms and moments)

(Y. Liu et al., 2007). Previous studies examine the amount of local and national aspects and much global information (Tuytelaars & Mikolajczyk, 2007). EXIF is one of the most important metadata fields for digital imaging, whether it's used by point-and-and-shoot or by cameras with manual controls (Bayrakdar et al., 2020). The EXIF data includes aperture level, focus speed, exposure level, and other lens and image focus (Sinha & Jain, 2008).

When you take a shot, you need to recall information such as the focal length and maximum shutter speed and at what time the photo was taken to be more precise, including photo extension, ease of panning, and the degree of clarity. The metadata describes images and identifies them or image classification (Boutell & Luo, 2005). Color, shape, form, and points of interest may be removed using this advanced computer vision software. However, the amount of time presently available for pictures processing is still required. This is a difficult issue since interactions between ideas must be reduced to a lower level to be handled automatically. Particular instructions tend to overlook a condition when expanded in a certain way. As a result, it is difficult to include all suitable images and photographs with a restricted number and size. Were it not for improved application domain knowledge, the quantity of semiconducting in semiconductors would be unknown, resulting in sub-focused semiconductor analysis (Sinha & Jain, 2008). This technique for eliminating semiconductor holes in image retrieval systems may extend picture material tagging capabilities.

Figure 5 depicts the process in simple terms, including what has to be done to understand better. Users may tag a few information on picture tagging services, such as who it's about, where it was taken, and uploaded. Tags are useful for making images social media-friendly. For example, high-expanding pictures are unlikely to be recognized if no content tags are provided. In classification and program tagging-based methods, a tag's value must be measured and assessed (Li et al., 2009). Qian et al. proposed a system for labeling pictures of different social data with different textual labels (Qian et al., 2014). The meaning of each tag was applied to a picture was considered along with any of all previously known items the words related to the same image in the context to compile the tag list of last things related to the item's final results. Install to Innovative solutions like the Coded Optimized Diversified Labeling (DOSO demonstrated their effectiveness by providing quantitative results in search and image retrieval tag results for categorization and tag extension. Compared to other current tagging systems, which focus primarily on images, these are extremely picture-related but often have semantically linked tags. This excludes using a semantic similarity parameter for each keyword when preparing a list of suggested tags for an analysis that incorporates WordNet, simply using the semantically related tags (Jin et al., 2005) to evaluate irrelevant keywords.

It is determined that with the help of the Dempster-Shafer model (D-S proof) that all parameters in the equations combine to form a phenomenon (i.e., effect). The writers Li, Zhang, Taro Endo, and Yoshi Endo (Adedoyin-Olowe et al., 2014) utilized a neighborhood voting to assess the importance, which had previously proved to be accurate and successful when gathering votes from visual neighbors (Li et al., 2009). 3.5 million Flickr photos show that algorithms can be applied to the social tagging of images, and the suggestion of tags from images is robust. Rather than sticking to explicit tag representations, authors add a faceted paradigm of image semantics (Hare et al., 2007).

Figure 5. The elementary roadmap of semantic image analysis.

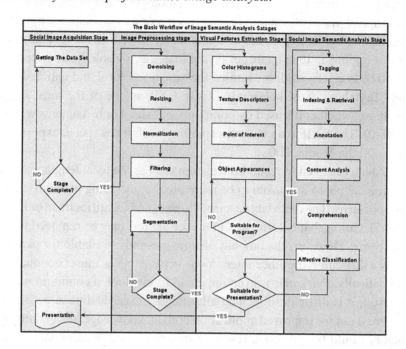

This picture-based model estimates the available knowledge representation model to reflect the high quantity of semantic information present in an image. When it comes to interpreting the significance of an image, the analyst has four key components: object, geographical, temporal, case, meaning, subject, and/subjective meaning. Additionally, current recovery methods were tested on the linear functional space used by different picture collections and found to be most successful for photos that can be expanded. Feature extraction and entity recognition are important stages in processing image data to include general image analysis (Yoshitaka & Ichikawa, 1999). Finding algorithms that enable you to classify picture content is difficult manually, but few of these have been in the last few years. Rather than trying to the hierarchy of unique picture characteristics, the emphasis of this work was on binary Bayesian classifiers that works at low levels of resolution, which need rigorous checks. The team captured main lower-level, sophisticated attributes concerning better resolution enforced constraints (Vailaya et al., 1999). In addition to the images being split into indoors/outdoors and divided into cityscapes and landscapes, they are also graded into landscape groupings. According to Merler et al., in their study, the most effective way to find traits of users on social media is by looking at photographs shared online (Merler et al., 2015). They'd suggested sharing picture content in a person's whole 'semantic gender' sequence to aid in predicting the individual's gender.

Models learned to classify items, circumstances, and occurrences to test this semantic distribution. They were generated to identify objects and situations in each photo for each person. The gender prediction model was developed using the normal SVM methodologies with RBF functions. Additionally, as an analyst researching ten thousand Facebook Twitter people and half a million picture collections, I noticed that gender might be defined by picture dissemination (75.6 percent accuracy). Furthermore, the gender estimation increases to 88% when presented with email. Over the last few years, there has been a sharp increase in varied fields and sub-focused technologies focused on visual knowledge use through intelligent science. Some domains also benefited from processing beyond simple image recognition, such as better access to image databases, increasing human and computer interaction, human-directed classification, and decreased cost. Wang and Li proposed a keyword multimodal semantic correlation method called Multimodal Semantic Hash Learning (MMSHL) for image analysis (Wang & Li, 2017).

The mixture of multimodal correlation learning, multigraph learning, and multi-based or latent textual hashing is implemented to provide an efficient solution without the need for concurrent computation. Due to a focus on MMSHL layout, images were annotated using a two-stage semi-supervised learning process. This provided outstanding performance, as the database indexing software used three real-world photos on MIR Flickr and NUS-WIDE as the template for its modeling and reasoning process.

There is a great deal of study in the literature around LSA to come up with the traditional graphic and this, in which visual terms each concept can be found to serve as an abbreviation for many topics. Studies found that a tax cut would have an immediate and detrimental impact on productivity, instead, so citizens would invest that money now rather than save it for potential usage (Wang & Li, 2017) chose to employ a novel form of research called a direct semantic analysis (or, or an application of DSA) to directly to socially marked photographs to learn the network's semantic connection matrix The graph-based analysis technique was adapted from current research literature research methods. A semi-unrefined visual image is obtained (deconstructed) and integrated into the Social image (Representation) first, and then an Expand Representation picture is created.

Although only one included the usage of evidence, two experimental observations had shown the positive effects of the comparative image dataset. de-Instead of pictures, in personal doctor-messenger photo albums or information provided by virtual medical picture websites, new electronic medical social platforms enlargements enable doctors and patients to share huge volumes of easily compressible multimedia data. This condition called for a review of the network graphs to identify correct geometry. Bouslim et al proposa un aná rámetodo multi-modal para analizar fotograma pensado para analizar información tédese sobre la red pública radiológica que táctico desarrollado social de datos de lectura de unetígica de información que lítica de notas (Bouslimi et al., 2017). Sometimes, obsolete words can be obtained through a medical terminology dictionary. However, it is emphasized that the notes posted via medical terminology message boards are textual descriptions in certain cases. Another technique they implemented was an LSA to connect textual and visual senses of medical picture representation.

Image CLEED2015 was used to extend the model's water pipeline coverage region. An Ontology-based annotation approach developed by Elahi et al. permits participation from actors who are heavily active in the process (usually referred to as the core participants) that semiautomatically derives relation-ships based on annotation comments (Bouslimi et al., 2017). Some think about how these photos might seem to an audience over time, how people could come to perceive events occurring, and what events, or which movies, might connect to certain other characters.

The use of social network relational frameworks that explore relationship variety have also gained popularity. The OntoIM ontology was intended to provide a class structure of image annotations in addition to social research characteristics. Wet (or humid) weather conditions do not promote the spread of infection, but they also do not reduce the rate of incidence (Ayadi et al., 2016). The methodology used by other content-driven image processing algorithms has peaked (color, shape, and texture). The ability of technologies to recreate fresh-free medical pictures encouraged experts and patients to assess images and improve image retrieval. These characteristics made the content-based picture retrieval system helpful and assessment tools necessary, resulting in improved analysis or consultation of the relevant samples.

Photographs are the only way analyst has to improve their total social intelligence.

However, the accompanying writings provide important ideas that assist anybody in learning more about what is going on in the frame. Researchers developed a new classification technique based on D-S theory that integrated innovative visualization and dynamic text characteristics into a model that was firmly anchored in the picture (N. Liu et al., 2017). The type and environment detail are defined as global, while four class attributes (texture, color, shape, degree of detail, and feel) are assembled to decide the overall appearance. After an eHTC histogram has been run, various visual characteristics cavities are assessed according to the textual functionality, with specific dynamic data after (i.e.the result of) the definition of which is referred to as data after (or by). Expand. The state-of-the-the-art visual influence (the VE) classifications predict that much of the new research currently being done in the field impacts the audience. In other experiments, Zhao et al. investigated different factors that affect personalized picture emotion perceptions, including visual consistency, social context, temporal evolution, and salience, to decide which seemed most successful (Zhao et al., 2018). This method of RMTL incorporation and refining is continuously yielded accurate performance due to the use of a rolling hypergraph algorithm.

To evaluate each audience's emotional reaction to images, it is important to quantify the amount of expansion. Furthermore, an Image-Emotion-Social-Net (a dataset of 8000 FB users that contains 1.4 million inspirational pictures and 1.4 million factual photos) was created for an amazing 8,000+ people who choose to experiment with visual social media and utilize that content as they see fit. Expand succeeded by means having tried out the method for personalized expression of feelings with the dataset that is generated from the IESN, to see whether it was feasible were utilized to express the four state-of-of-the-the-the-art classifiers: (1) naive Bayesian (NB), (2) RB-kernel SVM (3) graph-based, (4) pragmatic and statistical, and overall, (5) hyper learning (HG). Concerning terms, it was not substantial.

The emergence of a significant decrease in textual sentiment analysis occurred (Kabakus & Kara, 2018). The role of emotional or affective analysis of social media relies on interpretation, and interpretation relies on the meaning of pictures, which is essentially subjective (Fu et al., 2017).

Table 1 shows the practical articles on image semantic research on social networks, and here it has the following about concepts: This chapter illustrated their first novel, which came out a year ago, the problems they were attempting to address, and how they were attempting to go about doing so, and what they wanted to do.

FUTURE TRENDS

Although researching social networks is impressive, the discipline also has several open issues that researchers need more study. As social networks introduce vast quantities of social data, including private information and comprehensive individual about network operators or users, data protection is a complicated and understandable problem (Ji et al., 2015). Data must be closely checked and secured. Confidence and privacy are huge problems for social network applications. Research combining information from diverse social networks and moving for heterogeneous partnerships (e.g., communication, follow-up, and transport sharing) with one or more relevant sources (Adedoyin-Olowe et al., 2014; Awad et al., 2020; Kasthuri & Jebaseeli, 2020; Najafabadi et al., 2019) Comparing two user accounts across many social networks (Goga et al., 2015) These are tremendous obstacles for social network analysis. However, they face severe concerns about confidentiality, and they still have specific issues.

Social network analysis is frequently time-consuming and overpriced. Researchers started using different parallel processing methods and platforms (Cybenko, 2017). In this situation, designing paral-

Table 1. Summary of all relevant information regarding semantic image research on social networks.

Ref	Year	Author	Technique	Dataset	Other Characteristics
(Li et al., 2009)	2009	Li et al.	A novel neighbor voting algorithm for tag relevance learning	Flickr	By tagging the surrounding images with the same tag, you would be able to know whether an object is important in the picture, and then expanding on it identifying and classifying essential visual elements for each of the tags can be important in recognizing the function of the value of the consumer
(Qian et al., 2014)	2014	Qian et al.	DIVS	Flickr and NUS-WIDE	This project builds on the work achieved by contributing a powerful and useful tagging mechanism for unstructured social data (sometimes keyword-driven content) by ensuring that the most frequently occurring keywords or tags are used while allowing space for more complex ones. specificity and variety of the tag applied to the image
(Jin et al., 2005)	2005	Jin et al.	WordNet and Dempster–Shafer multiple evidence combination.	Corel	Improve annotation quality by pruning obsolete keywords: successful image labeling and retrieval method.
(Hare et al., 2007)	2007	Hare et al.	Linear algebraic semantic space and a faceted model of image semantics	Victoria and Albert Museum(V&A) dataset	It introduces a faceted image semantics model that explains the abundance of semantic information interpretable inside an image. Semantic image retrieval void.
(Merler et al., 2015)	2015	Merler et al.	Support vector machine (SVM) with RBF kernels	Twitter	Estimate consumer gender through graphical information of social network accounts, including profile photos, stream views, and color trends. Sex analysis of social networking accounts.
(Wang & Li, 2017)	2017	Wang and Li	k-NN image classifier and Multimodal Semantic Hash Learning (MMSHL)	MirFlickr and NUS-WIDE	Let's expand the image dates into a large-scale single- or multimodal method annotation via multiple forms of multigraph learning and apply latent textual hashing to a framework for optimization. the increased efficiency and precision of automated expansion
(Shambour & Lu, 2015)	2015	Lu et al.,	Direct semantic analysis (DSA) and visual Bag of Words (BoW) representation	Pascal VOC'07 and MirFlickr	Using graph-based study to learn how to research around visual words in pictures
(Ayadi et al., 2016)	2016	Bouslimi et al.	BoW and latent semantic analysis (LSA)	ImageCLEFMed'2015	Whether humans or computers do it, encourage the creation of picture processing-based retrieval questionnaires that use the imagery in the progression of our collection methods.
(Elahi et al., 2013)	2013	Elahi et al.	OntoCAIM ontology	Flickr	Generate ontology-based annotations semiautomatically for a social network using annotations from the most active person.
(Bouslimi et al., 2017)	2016	Ayadi et al	Statistical area descriptors for form information extraction; gray-level histogram and gray-level moment for color material extraction	A directory of Charles Nicolle Hospital in Tunis	Perform an effective image recovery method based on hue, shape, texture combination, and fusion. Content-based patient indexing and retrieval

lelizable and practical algorithms is only a couple of parameters to solve. This is a challenging field of study, and investigation in this area of research is motionless in its beginning, mainly about all-purpose frameworks for semantic processing to be scalable. Another uncluttered study area is the successful review of large-scale RDF datasets. Expanding capacity, research, storage, and changeability don't matter as the scale of the data rises beyond the level that the processor can manage individually. More distributed RDF save or stores were considered, and they were improved upon to accelerate the transmission of knowledge dissemination (Janke et al., 2018), (Potter et al., 2016).

Analyzing experiences, which would simplify determining the social network's effectiveness for individual users and evaluating critical concerns such as connectivity performance, is seen as a significant future path (Borgatti, 2009). Recently, interest in the analysis and management issues relevant to power-sharing in social networks has increased (ŞİMŞEK & KARA, 2018). The bulk of the period (Yang et al., 2017).

Furthermore, recent study trends have focused on dark networks since public media networks, which have acquired a major part in interplanetary intelligence, are often used by authoritarian governments or extremist groups for many purposes, including deception and exploitation. This poll borrows heavily from (Bayrakdar et al., 2020). There are various methods or instruments to deal with all of the difficulties. Social network analysis may be used to build monitoring, disrupt, and dismantle criminal and hidden networks (Everton, 2012). Social network research may also provide important views on terrorism and terrorist organizations, including identifying keys. Using data mining methods, several important results are examined (Carpineto et al., 2009): With the healthy growth of communities in social networks, the issue of confidence and mistrust among these people as a community was a major problem.

When a computer or electrical device automatically studies an image to extract useful information, this is referred to as digital image analysis or computer image analysis. Notably, the device is frequently a computer, but it could also be an electrical circuit, a digital camera, or even a mobile phone in some instances. It encompasses the fields of computer vision or machine vision and medical imaging and makes extensive use of pattern recognition, digital geometry, and signal processing techniques. Object-Based Image Analysis (OBIA) is a technique that uses two main processes: segmentation and classification, to analyze images. On a pixel-by-pixel basis, traditional image segmentation works. OBIA, on the other hand, groups pixels into homogeneous objects. These objects can come in various sizes, shapes, and colors. As well as statistical information about objects, statistics can categorize objects differently. Geometry, context, and texture of image objects can all be included in image object statistics. In the classification process, the analyst defines statistics used to generate, for example, land cover.

Previous studies have shown that some individuals attempt to undermine or alter the conventional atmosphere of such online groups. Various reports addressed trust issues. Community or group identification focuses on network structure research and detecting more interconnected people than other applications. Identifying human interaction or personal behaviors to concentrate on data collection is a challenging study area requiring intense investigation. Today, people's activity refers to particular human-generated activities such as clicking on an advertisement, accepting a friend's request, joining a discussion group, or commenting on a photo. Node connections are analyzed using link analysis. Transitions, linkages, and other node kinds may be detected. Plan your data structures with these relationships in mind.

CONCLUSION

Assorted datasets and sizes are used to build social networks. It performs well with the mining software strategy package. It is based on various communication sources and formats. Due to software implementation and usage, data mining is technical. The chapter addressed social networking and social networking tracking. Overcoming existing techniques Ongoing research and development will continue to provide cutting-edge data analysis techniques. Over the last two decades, the rapid growth of online social networks has produced social network research. In the age of large-scale social networking, traditional network methods are obsolete. Recognizing, evaluating, and interpreting social network information is critical given the amount of data produced.

Digital image analysis, or computer image analysis, refers to the process of using a computer or electrical device to analyze an image and extract useful information. In most cases, the device is a computer, but it can also be an electrical circuit, a digital camera, or even a mobile phone. Computer vision and medical imaging are all rolled into one, and pattern recognition, digital geometry, and signal processing are heavily utilized.

Furthermore, the search for useful social network information has been widely explored. NLP, sophisticated document analysis, and knowledge recovery techniques were widely employed to extract textual content from documents. This dissertation describes the entire social network analysis process based on current research findings from a semiconductor. A survey was conducted to evaluate semantic derivation techniques for making a large amount of data expressive in social network systems. In terms of picture content, several semantic extraction techniques are emphasized. Even though research on semantic analysis and literary modeling is restricted, this thesis emphasizes future research using semantic technology in social network analysis. This page is a resource for academics interested in semantic social network analysis techniques. Exploring the reviews mentioned above, designing new semantic source methods for various venues may be concluded. It also highlighted the study's main problems and potential adjustments in the focal areas.

REFERENCES

Abrahams, A. S., Jiao, J., Wang, G. A., & Fan, W. (2012). Vehicle defect discovery from social media. *Decision Support Systems, 54*(1), 87–97. doi:10.1016/j.dss.2012.04.005

Adatrao, S., & Mittal, M. (2016). An analysis of different image preprocessing techniques for determining the centroids of circular marks using hough transform. *2016 2nd International Conference on Frontiers of Signal Processing, ICFSP 2016*, 110–115. 10.1109/ICFSP.2016.7802966

Adedoyin-Olowe, M., Gaber, M. M., & Stahl, F. (2014). A Survey of Data Mining Techniques for Social Media Analysis. *Journal of Data Mining & Digital Humanities, 2014*, 5. Advance online publication. doi:10.46298/jdmdh.5

Akaichi, J. (2014). A medical social network for physicians' annotations posting and summarization. *Social Network Analysis and Mining, 4*(1), 1–8. doi:10.100713278-014-0225-1

Akhtar, N. (2014). Social network analysis tools. *Proceedings - 2014 4th International Conference on Communication Systems and Network Technologies, CSNT 2014*, 388–392. 10.1109/CSNT.2014.83

Al-Daihani, S. M., & Abrahams, A. (2016). A Text Mining Analysis of Academic Libraries' Tweets. *Journal of Academic Librarianship, 42*(2), 135–143. doi:10.1016/j.acalib.2015.12.014

Al-Garadi, M. A., Varathan, K. D., Ravana, S. D., Ahmed, E., Mujtaba, G., Shahid Khan, M. U., & Khan, S. U. (2018). Analysis of online social network connections for identification of influential users: Survey and open research issues. *ACM Computing Surveys, 51*(1), 1–37. doi:10.1145/3155897

Alfantoukh, L., & Durresi, A. (2014). Techniques for collecting data in social networks. *Proceedings - 2014 International Conference on Network-Based Information Systems, NBiS 2014*, 336–341. 10.1109/NBiS.2014.92

Avrithis, Y., Strintzis, M., Kompatsiaris, Y., Spyrou, E., & Dasiopoulou, S. (2006). Semantic Processing of Color Images. In Color Image Processing (pp. 259–284). CRC Press. doi:10.1201/9781420009781.ch11

Awad, A., Ali, A., & Gaber, T. (2020). Feature selection method based on chaotic maps and butterfly optimization algorithm. In *Proceedings of the International Conference on Artificial Intelligence and Computer Vision (AICV2020)* (*Vol. 2*, Issue 1153). Springer International Publishing. 10.1007/978-3-030-44289-7_16

Ayadi, M. G., Bouslimi, R., & Akaichi, J. (2016). A medical image retrieval scheme through a medical social network. *Network Modeling and Analysis in Health Informatics and Bioinformatics*, *5*(1), 23. Advance online publication. doi:10.100713721-016-0130-9

Batrinca, B., & Treleaven, P. C. (2015). Social media analytics: A survey of techniques, tools and platforms. *AI & Society*, *30*(1), 89–116. doi:10.100700146-014-0549-4

Bayrakdar, S., Yucedag, I., Simsek, M., & Dogru, I. A. (2020). Semantic analysis on social networks: A survey. *International Journal of Communication Systems*, *33*(11), 1–30. doi:10.1002/dac.4424

Ben Jabeur, L., Tamine, L., & Boughanem, M. (2012). Active microbloggers: Identifying influencers, leaders and discussers in microblogging networks. In Lecture Notes in Computer Science (including subseries Lecture Notes in Artificial Intelligence and Lecture Notes in Bioinformatics): Vol. 7608 LNCS (pp. 111–117). Springer Berlin Heidelberg. doi:10.1007/978-3-642-34109-0_12

Benevenuto, F., Rodrigues, T., Almeida, J., Gonçalves, M., & Almeida, V. (2009, April). Detecting spammers and content promoters in online video social networks. *Proceedings - IEEE INFOCOM*, 1–2. Advance online publication. doi:10.1109/INFCOMW.2009.5072127

Bhagat, S., Cormode, G., & Muthukrishnan, S. (2011). Node Classification in Social Networks. In *Social Network Data Analytics* (pp. 115–148). Springer. doi:10.1007/978-1-4419-8462-3_5

Borgatti, S. P. (2009). Social Network Analysis, Two-Mode Concepts in. In *Encyclopedia of Complexity and Systems Science* (pp. 8279–8291). Springer New York. doi:10.1007/978-0-387-30440-3_491

Bouslimi, R., Ayadi, M. G., & Akaichi, J. (2017). Semantic medical image retrieval in a medical social network. *Social Network Analysis and Mining*, *7*(1), 2. Advance online publication. doi:10.100713278-016-0420-3

Boutell, M., & Luo, J. (2005). Beyond pixels: Exploiting camera metadata for photo classification. *Pattern Recognition*, *38*(6), 935–946. doi:10.1016/j.patcog.2004.11.013

Carpineto, C., Osiski, S., Romano, G., & Weiss, D. (2009). A survey of web clustering engines. *ACM Computing Surveys*, *41*(3), 1–38. doi:10.1145/1541880.1541884

Chang, W. H., Li, B., & Fang, X. (2014). Data collection and analysis from social network – Profile Analyzer System (PAS). In Lecture Notes in Computer Science (including subseries Lecture Notes in Artificial Intelligence and Lecture Notes in Bioinformatics) (Vol. 8643, pp. 765–772). Springer International Publishing. doi:10.1007/978-3-319-13186-3_68

Chelmis, C., & Prasanna, V. K. (2011). Social networking analysis: A state of the art and the effect of semantics. *Proceedings - 2011 IEEE International Conference on Privacy, Security, Risk and Trust and IEEE International Conference on Social Computing, PASSAT/SocialCom 2011*, 531–536. 10.1109/PASSAT/SocialCom.2011.23

Çıtlak, O., Dörterler, M., & Doğru, İ. A. (2019). A survey on detecting spam accounts on Twitter network. *Social Network Analysis and Mining*, *9*(1), 35. Advance online publication. doi:10.100713278-019-0582-x

Clemons, E. K., Barnett, S., & Appadurai, A. (2007). The future of advertising and the value of social network websites: Some preliminary examinations. *ACM International Conference Proceeding Series*, *258*, 267–276. 10.1145/1282100.1282153

Craven, M. W., & Shavlik, J. W. (1997). Using neural networks for data mining. *Future Generation Computer Systems*, *13*(2–3), 211–229. doi:10.1016/S0167-739X(97)00022-8

Cunningham, H., Tablan, V., Roberts, A., & Bontcheva, K. (2013). Getting More Out of Biomedical Documents with GATE's Full Lifecycle Open Source Text Analytics. *PLoS Computational Biology*, *9*(2), e1002854. doi:10.1371/journal.pcbi.1002854 PMID:23408875

Cybenko, G. (2017). Parallel computing for machine learning in social network analysis. *Proceedings - 2017 IEEE 31st International Parallel and Distributed Processing Symposium Workshops, IPDPSW 2017*, 1464–1471. 10.1109/IPDPSW.2017.178

Di Capua, M., Di Nardo, E., & Petrosino, A. (2016). Unsupervised cyber bullying detection in social networks. *Proceedings - International Conference on Pattern Recognition, 0*, 432–437. 10.1109/ICPR.2016.7899672

Dou, D., Wang, H., & Liu, H. (2015). Semantic data mining: A survey of ontology-based approaches. *Proceedings of the 2015 IEEE 9th International Conference on Semantic Computing, IEEE ICSC 2015*, 244–251. 10.1109/ICOSC.2015.7050814

Dredge, R., Gleeson, J., & De La Piedad Garcia, X. (2014). Cyberbullying in social networking sites: An adolescent victim's perspective. *Computers in Human Behavior*, *36*, 13–20. doi:10.1016/j.chb.2014.03.026

El, F., & Gamal, A. (2013). An Educational Data Mining Model for Predicting Student Performance in Programming Course. *International Journal of Computers and Applications*, *70*(17), 22–28. doi:10.5120/12160-8163

Elahi, M., Ricci, F., & Rubens, N. (2013). Active learning strategies for rating elicitation in collaborative filtering: A system-wide perspective. *ACM Transactions on Intelligent Systems and Technology*, *5*(1), 1–33. doi:10.1145/2542182.2542195

Eltermann, F., Godoy, A., & Von Zuben, F. J. (2020). Effects of Social Ties in Knowledge Diffusion: case study on PLOS ONE. *Anais Do Brazilian Workshop on Social Network Analysis and Mining ({BraSNAM})*, 97–108. 10.5753/brasnam.2016.6448

Everton, S. F. (2012). Disrupting Dark Networks. In *Disrupting Dark Networks*. Cambridge University Press. doi:10.1017/CBO9781139136877

Freeman, L. C. (1977). A Set of Measures of Centrality Based on Betweenness. *Sociometry*, *40*(1), 35. doi:10.2307/3033543

Freeman, L. C. (1978). Centrality in social networks conceptual clarification. *Social Networks*, *1*(3), 215–239. doi:10.1016/0378-8733(78)90021-7

Fu, X., Liu, W., Xu, Y., & Cui, L. (2017). Combine HowNet lexicon to train phrase recursive autoencoder for sentence-level sentiment analysis. *Neurocomputing*, *241*, 18–27. doi:10.1016/j.neucom.2017.01.079

Gao, Y., Wang, F., Luan, H., & Chua, T. S. (2014). Brand data gathering from live social media streams. *ICMR 2014 - Proceedings of the ACM International Conference on Multimedia Retrieval 2014*, 169–176. 10.1145/2578726.2578748

Goga, O., Loiseau, P., Sommer, R., Teixeira, R., & Gummadi, K. P. (2015). On the reliability of profile matching across large online social networks. *Proceedings of the ACM SIGKDD International Conference on Knowledge Discovery and Data Mining, 2015-August*, 1799–1808. 10.1145/2783258.2788601

Gong, M., Li, G., Wang, Z., Ma, L., & Tian, D. (2016). An efficient shortest path approach for social networks based on community structure. *CAAI Transactions on Intelligence Technology*, *1*(1), 114–123. doi:10.1016/j.trit.2016.03.011

Goyal, A., Bonchi, F., & Lakshmanan, L. V. S. (2010). Learning influence probabilities in social networks. *WSDM 2010 - Proceedings of the 3rd ACM International Conference on Web Search and Data Mining*, 241–250. 10.1145/1718487.1718518

Hare, J. S., Lewis, P. H., Enser, P. G. B., & Sandom, C. J. (2007). Semantic facets: An in-depth analysis of a semantic image retrieval system. *Proceedings of the 6th ACM International Conference on Image and Video Retrieval, CIVR 2007*, 250–257. 10.1145/1282280.1282320

Henry, N., & Fekete, J. D. (2007). MatLink: Enhanced matrix visualization for analyzing social networks. In Lecture Notes in Computer Science (including subseries Lecture Notes in Artificial Intelligence and Lecture Notes in Bioinformatics): Vol. 4663 LNCS (Issue PART 2, pp. 288–302). Springer Berlin Heidelberg. doi:10.1007/978-3-540-74800-7_24

Hu, J., Liu, M., & Zhang, J. (2014). A semantic model for academic social network analysis. *ASONAM 2014 - Proceedings of the 2014 IEEE/ACM International Conference on Advances in Social Networks Analysis and Mining*, 310–313. 10.1109/ASONAM.2014.6921602

Janani, P., Verma, S., Natarajan, S., & Sinha, A. K. (2019). Communication Using IoT. In Information and Communication Technology for Sustainable Development, Advances in Intelligent Systems and Computing. Springer Singapore. doi:10.1007/978-981-13-7166-0

Janke, D., Staab, S., & Thimm, M. (2018). Impact analysis of data placement strategies on query efforts in distributed RDF stores. *Journal of Web Semantics*, *50*, 21–48. doi:10.1016/j.websem.2018.02.002

Ji, S., Li, W., Gong, N. Z., Mittal, P., & Beyah, R. (2015). On Your Social Network De-anonymizablity: Quantification and Large Scale Evaluation with Seed Knowledge. *Proceedings 2015 Network and Distributed System Security Symposium*. 10.14722/ndss.2015.23096

Jin, Y., Khan, L., Wang, L., & Awad, M. (2005). Image annotations by combining multiple evidence & WordNet. *Proceedings of the 13th ACM International Conference on Multimedia, MM 2005*, 706–715. 10.1145/1101149.1101305

Kabakus, A. T., & Kara, R. (2018). TwitterSentiDetector: A domain-independent Twitter sentiment analyser. *INFOR*, *56*(5), 137–162. doi:10.1080/03155986.2017.1340797

Kahya-Özyirmidokuz, E. (2016). Analyzing unstructured Facebook social network data through web text mining: A study of online shopping firms in Turkey. *Information Development*, *32*(1), 70–80. doi:10.1177/0266666914528523

Kasthuri, S., & Jebaseeli, A. N. (2020). Social Network Analysis in Data Processing. *Adalya Journal*, *9*(2), 260–264.

Kempe, D., Kleinberg, J., & Tardos, É. (2003). Maximizing the spread of influence through a social network. *Proceedings of the ACM SIGKDD International Conference on Knowledge Discovery and Data Mining*, 137–146. 10.1145/956750.956769

Knoke, D. (2015). Emerging Trends in Social Network Analysis of Terrorism and Counterterrorism. In *Emerging Trends in the Social and Behavioral Sciences* (pp. 1–15). Wiley. doi:10.1002/9781118900772. etrds0106

Kou, F., Du, J., He, Y., & Ye, L. (2016). Social network search based on semantic analysis and learning. *CAAI Transactions on Intelligence Technology*, *1*(4), 293–302. doi:10.1016/j.trit.2016.12.001

Kulcu, S., Dogdu, E., & Ozbayoglu, A. M. (2016). A survey on semantic Web and big data technologies for social network analysis. *Proceedings - 2016 IEEE International Conference on Big Data*, 1768–1777. doi:10.1109/BigData.2016.7840792

Latora, V., & Marchiori, M. (2001). Efficient behavior of small-world networks. *Physical Review Letters*, *87*(19), 198701–198704. doi:10.1103/PhysRevLett.87.198701 PMID:11690461

Leonard, J. J. (2007). Challenges for autonomous mobile robots. *International Machine Vision and Image Processing Conference, IMVIP 2007*, 4. 10.1109/IMVIP.2007.46

Li, X., Snoek, C. G. M., & Worring, M. (2009). Learning social tag relevance by neighbor voting. *IEEE Transactions on Multimedia*, *11*(7), 1310–1322. doi:10.1109/TMM.2009.2030598

Liu, N., Wang, K., Jin, X., Gao, B., Dellandréa, E., & Chen, L. (2017). Visual affective classification by combining visual and text features. *PLoS One*, *12*(8), e0183018. doi:10.1371/journal.pone.0183018 PMID:28850566

Liu, Y., Zhang, D., Lu, G., & Ma, W. Y. (2007). A survey of content-based image retrieval with high-level semantics. *Pattern Recognition*, *40*(1), 262–282. doi:10.1016/j.patcog.2006.04.045

Mahmud, M. S., Huang, J. Z., Salloum, S., Emara, T. Z., & Sadatdiynov, K. (2020). A survey of data partitioning and sampling methods to support big data analysis. *Big Data Mining and Analytics*, *3*(2), 85–101. doi:10.26599/BDMA.2019.9020015

Matti, T., Zhu, Y., & Xu, K. (2015). Financial fraud detection using social media crowdsourcing. *2014 IEEE 33rd International Performance Computing and Communications Conference, IPCCC 2014*. 10.1109/PCCC.2014.7017023

Maynard, D., Roberts, I., Greenwood, M. A., Rout, D., & Bontcheva, K. (2017). A framework for real-time semantic social media analysis. *Journal of Web Semantics*, *44*, 75–88. doi:10.1016/j.websem.2017.05.002

Merler, M., Cao, L., & Smith, J. R. (2015). You are what you tweet···pic! gender prediction based on semantic analysis of social media images. *Proceedings - IEEE International Conference on Multimedia and Expo*. 10.1109/ICME.2015.7177499

Mislove, A., Marcon, M., Gummadi, K. P., Druschel, P., & Bhattacharjee, B. (2007). Measurement and analysis of online social networks. *Proceedings of the ACM SIGCOMM Internet Measurement Conference, IMC*, 29–42. 10.1145/1298306.1298311

Mohamad, S. K., & Tasir, Z. (2013). Educational Data Mining: A Review. *Procedia: Social and Behavioral Sciences*, *97*, 320–324. doi:10.1016/j.sbspro.2013.10.240

Mrvar, A., & Batagelj, V. (2016). Analysis and visualization of large networks with program package Pajek. In Complex Adaptive Systems Modeling (Vol. 4, Issue 1). Springer Science and Business Media LLC. doi:10.118640294-016-0017-8

Najafabadi, M. K., Mohamed, A. H., & Mahrin, M. N. (2019). A survey on data mining techniques in recommender systems. *Soft Computing*, *23*(2), 627–654. doi:10.100700500-017-2918-7

Network, X. (2018). *Encyclopedia of Social Network Analysis and Mining*. Springer New York. doi:10.1007/978-1-4939-7131-2_100771

Potter, A., Motik, B., Nenov, Y., & Horrocks, I. (2016). Distributed RDF query answering with dynamic data exchange. In Lecture Notes in Computer Science (including subseries Lecture Notes in Artificial Intelligence and Lecture Notes in Bioinformatics): Vol. 9981 LNCS (pp. 480–497). Springer International Publishing. doi:10.1007/978-3-319-46523-4_29

Proskurnikov, A. V., & Tempo, R. (2017). A tutorial on modeling and analysis of dynamic social networks. Part I. *Annual Reviews in Control*, *43*, 65–79. doi:10.1016/j.arcontrol.2017.03.002

Qian, X., Hua, X. S., Tang, Y. Y., & Mei, T. (2014). Social image tagging with diverse semantics. *IEEE Transactions on Cybernetics*, *44*(12), 2493–2508. doi:10.1109/TCYB.2014.2309593 PMID:25415950

Rahman, M. M. (2012). Mining Social Data to Extract Intellectual Knowledge. *International Journal of Intelligent Systems and Applications*, *4*(10), 15–24. doi:10.5815/ijisa.2012.10.02

Robins, G., Pattison, P., Kalish, Y., & Lusher, D. (2007). An introduction to exponential random graph (p*) models for social networks. *Social Networks*, *29*(2), 173–191. doi:10.1016/j.socnet.2006.08.002

Romero, C., & Ventura, S. (2007). Educational data mining: A survey from 1995 to 2005. *Expert Systems with Applications*, *33*(1), 135–146. doi:10.1016/j.eswa.2006.04.005

Ruan, X. H., Hu, X., & Zhang, X. (2014). Research on application model of semantic web-based social network analysis. In Lecture Notes in Electrical Engineering: Vol. 271 LNEE (Vol. 2, pp. 455–460). Springer Berlin Heidelberg. doi:10.1007/978-3-642-40630-0_59

Salathé, M., Vu, D. Q., Khandelwal, S., & Hunter, D. R. (2013). The dynamics of health behavior sentiments on a large online social network. *EPJ Data Science*, *2*(1), 1–12. doi:10.1140/epjds16

Salloum, S. A., Al-Emran, M., Monem, A. A., & Shaalan, K. (2017). A survey of text mining in social media: Facebook and Twitter perspectives. *Advances in Science. Technology and Engineering Systems*, *2*(1), 127–133. doi:10.25046/aj020115

Sawant, N., Li, J., & Wang, J. Z. (2011). Automatic image semantic interpretation using social action and tagging data. *Multimedia Tools and Applications*, *51*(1), 213–246. doi:10.100711042-010-0650-8

Shambour, Q., & Lu, J. (2015). An effective recommender system by unifying user and item trust information for B2B applications. *Journal of Computer and System Sciences*, *81*(7), 1110–1126. doi:10.1016/j.jcss.2014.12.029

Şimşek, A., & Kara, R. (2018). Using swarm intelligence algorithms to detect influential individuals for influence maximization in social networks. *Expert Systems with Applications*, *114*, 224–236. doi:10.1016/j.eswa.2018.07.038

Singh, V. K., Taram, M., Agrawal, V., & Baghel, B. S. (2018). A Literature Review on Hadoop Ecosystem and Various Techniques of Big Data Optimization. In *Lecture Notes in Networks and Systems* (Vol. 38, pp. 231–240). Springer Singapore., doi:10.1007/978-981-10-8360-0_22

Sinha, P., & Jain, R. (2008). Classification and annotation of digital photos using optical context data. *CIVR 2008 - Proceedings of the International Conference on Content-Based Image and Video Retrieval*, 309–317. 10.1145/1386352.1386394

Social Media Marketing Tree Diagram. (2021). https://slidemodel.com/templates/digital-marketing-powerpoint-template/social-media-marketing-tree-diagram-ppt/

Srivastava, J. (2008). Data mining for social network analysis. *2008 IEEE International Conference on Intelligence and Security Informatics*, xxxiii–xxxiv. 10.1109/ISI.2008.4565015

Statista. (2020a). *The Statistics Portal. Global social media ranking 2020*. Statista. https://www.statista.com/statistics/272014/global-social-networks-ranked-by-number-of-users/

Statista. (2020b). *The Statistics Portal. Twitter: number of active users 2010-2020*. Statista. https://www.statista.com/statistics/282087/number-of-monthly-active-twitter-users/

Staudt, C. L., Sazonovs, A., & Meyerhenke, H. (2016). NetworKit: A tool suite for large-scale complex network analysis. *Network Science*, *4*(4), 508–530. doi:10.1017/nws.2016.20

Stieglitz, S., & Dang-Xuan, L. (2012). Political communication and influence through microblogging - An empirical analysis of sentiment in Twitter messages and retweet behavior. *Proceedings of the Annual Hawaii International Conference on System Sciences*, 3500–3509. 10.1109/HICSS.2012.476

Szabo, G., & Huberman, B. A. (2010). Predicting the popularity of online content. *Communications of the ACM*, *53*(8), 80–88. doi:10.1145/1787234.1787254

Thovex, C., & Trichet, F. (2011). A semantic and multidisciplinary model for professional and social networks analysis. *Proceedings - 2011 International Conference on Advances in Social Networks Analysis and Mining, ASONAM 2011*, 45–52. 10.1109/ASONAM.2011.102

Tiwari, A. K., Ramakrishna, G., Sharma, L. K., & Kashyap, S. K. (2019). Academic performance prediction algorithm based on fuzzy data mining. *IAES International Journal of Artificial Intelligence, 8*(1), 26–32. doi:10.11591/ijai.v8.i1.pp26-32

Tiwari, V. (2017). Analysis and detection of fake profile over social network. *Proceeding - IEEE International Conference on Computing, Communication and Automation, ICCCA 2017,* 175–179. 10.1109/CCAA.2017.8229795

Tuytelaars, T., & Mikolajczyk, K. (2007). Local Invariant Feature Detectors: A Survey. In Local Invariant Feature Detectors: A Survey. Now Publishers Inc. doi:10.1561/9781601981394

Tylenda, T., Angelova, R., & Bedathur, S. (2009). Towards time-aware link prediction in evolving social networks. *Proceedings of the 3rd Workshop on Social Network Mining and Analysis, SNA-KDD '09.* 10.1145/1731011.1731020

Vailaya, A., Figueiredo, M., Jain, A., & Zhang, H. (1999). Content-based hierarchical classification of vacation images. *International Conference on Multimedia Computing and Systems -Proceedings, 1,* 518–523. 10.1109/MMCS.1999.779255

Wadhwa, P., & Bhatia, M. P. S. (2012). Social networks analysis: Trends, techniques and future prospects. *IET Conference Publications, 2012*(CP652), 1–6. 10.1049/cp.2012.2481

Wang, J., & Li, G. (2017). A Multimodal Hashing Learning Framework for Automatic Image Annotation. *Proceedings - 2017 IEEE 2nd International Conference on Data Science in Cyberspace, DSC 2017,* 14–21. 10.1109/DSC.2017.48

Xiao, C., Freeman, D. M., & Hwa, T. (2015). Detecting clusters of fake accounts in online social networks. *AISec 2015 - Proceedings of the 8th ACM Workshop on Artificial Intelligence and Security, Co-Located with CCS 2015,* 91–102. 10.1145/2808769.2808779

Yang, L., Giua, A., & Li, Z. (2017). Minimizing the Influence Propagation in Social Networks for Linear Threshold Models. *IFAC, 50*(1), 14465–14470. doi:10.1016/j.ifacol.2017.08.2293

Yoshitaka, A., & Ichikawa, T. (1999). A survey on content-based retrieval for multimedia databases. *IEEE Transactions on Knowledge and Data Engineering, 11*(1), 81–93. doi:10.1109/69.755617

Yu, Y., Lin, H., Meng, J., & Zhao, Z. (2016). Visual and textual sentiment analysis of a microblog using deep convolutional neural networks. *Algorithms, 9*(2), 41. doi:10.3390/a9020041

Zarezade, A., Jafarzadeh, S., & Rabiee, H. R. (2018). Recurrent spatio-temporal modeling of check-ins in location-based social networks. *PLoS One, 13*(5), e0197683. doi:10.1371/journal.pone.0197683 PMID:29791463

Zhao, S., Yao, H., Gao, Y., Ding, G., & Chua, T. S. (2018). Predicting Personalized Image Emotion Perceptions in Social Networks. *IEEE Transactions on Affective Computing, 9*(4), 526–540. doi:10.1109/TAFFC.2016.2628787

Section 3
Applications of Intelligent Business Analytics

Chapter 10
Applying Intelligent Big Data Analytics in a Smart Airport Business:
Value, Adoption, and Challenges

Desmond Narongou

https://orcid.org/0000-0003-0815-025X

National Airports Corporation, Papua New Guinea

Zhaohao Sun

https://orcid.org/0000-0003-0780-3271

Papua New Guinea University of Technology, Papua New Guinea

ABSTRACT

Airports have always been one of the biggest contributors of big data to the aviation ecosystem. With the abundance of data available, big data analytics can help transform the airports to smart ones. This chapter examines airport analytics from a business process viewpoint. It explores the value of applying intelligent big data analytics in an airport from an operations perspective and strategic differentiation perspective. This chapter also discusses the challenges faced when adopting intelligent big data analytics in a smart airport paradigm from the perspective of PNG's National Airports Corporation (NAC). This chapter then looks at how these challenges can be overcome to realize the true value of applying intelligent big data analytics in an airport. The approach proposed in this chapter might contribute to expediting research of future development of intelligent big data analytics solutions that are customizable to an airport to recognize the real value of intelligent big data analytics in all facets of its operations.

INTRODUCTION

Big data has become the strategic resource of an organization and a country (McKinsey, 2011). Big data analytics is at the heart of any business, management, decision making, and socio-economic development

DOI: 10.4018/978-1-7998-9016-4.ch010

(Sun & Wu, 2021). Big data analytics is revolutionizing businesses and different industries around the world (Weber, 2020) (Ghavami, 2020). In the aviation industry, the business value of smart airports that encompasses the application of intelligent big data analytics is expected to grow exponentially over the next few years (Narongou & Sun, 2021) even after the COVID-19 pandemic subsides and far beyond. The global aviation analytics market is expected to grow from USD 1.7 billion in 2020 to USD 3 billion in 2025 at a compound annual growth rate (CAGR) of more than 11 percent (Globe Newswire, 2021).

One of the biggest challenges within the aviation industry is to optimally utilize and maximize the big volume (abundance) of data to realize the real business value in the sector (Oldenburg, 2020). There are silos of information lying around the industry that need to be properly captured, organized, and analyzed using intelligent big data analytics tools to manage costs, improve revenues, and provide a strategic differentiation to the industry (Ghavami, 2020). Oftentimes the available data and information are too broad and inadequate to provide sufficient insights at the airports for decision making (Lees, 2016). This has given airport executives limited insights into understanding the opportunities for growth and improvement as well the challenges faced in an airport from all its operation functions (Narongou & Sun, 2021). The application of intelligent big data analytics incorporates data, information, and big data itself through advanced ICT tools aims to address these challenges to provide endless opportunities for refining business processes in the airport (Sun Z., 2021).

Following one of the biggest falls in the history of the aviation industry as we face the COVID-19 pandemic head-on, the aviation industry players are looking into sustainable business solutions that will survive and sustain its continuity. The aviation industry players are seeking different business and revenue models to increase their business value while mitigating the challenges faced when adopting and integrating big data analytics into their decision-making models. The big data market grows significantly (Sun, Strang, & Li, 2018). This growth comes with challenges that need to be well analyzed and be prepared to adopt and implement the change in a smart airport ecosystem.

Based on the above analysis, there are still three research issues:

1. How do airports best utilize big data for their strategic differentiation and operational improvement?
2. What is the market and business value for applying big data analytics in a smart airport ecosystem?
3. What are some challenges that impede the adoption of intelligent big data analytics in a smart airport?

This chapter will address these issues by firstly looking into the available related literature to intelligent big data analytics. This will then be able to provide a better direction to discuss airport analytics, which is one of the smart solutions to penetrate each stage of the airport business process as a service. By looking into intelligent big data analytics as a business service, we can best describe the business value of applying intelligent big data analytics in a smart airport from different perspectives. This chapter also discusses the challenges faced when adopting intelligent big data analytics in a smart airport paradigm from the perspective of PNG's National Airports Corporation (NAC). This chapter then looks at how these challenges can be overcome to realize the true value of applying intelligent big data analytics in an airport.

The remainder of this chapter is organized as follows: Section 2 provides a literature review on intelligent big data analytics based on big data-driven small data analysis. Section 3 examines airport analytics through the airport operations and functions as a services chain and the application of big data analytics into every node of the chain to increase the business value (Kiron & Shockley, 2011). Section

Table 1. Summary keywords searched in Google Scholar

Searched Keyword	Number of Sources Found (in Given Seconds)		
	Since 2017	From 2017 – 2021	Anytime
Aviation analytics	59	59	90
Airport analytics	7	7	8
Intelligent big data analytics	32,300	30,5 00	138,000
Smart Airport	20,400	23,600	202, 000
Big data driven small data analysis	6	6	6

4 looks at intelligent big data analytics as a business service. Section 5 explores the business value of applying intelligent big data analytics (IBDA) from a smart airport perspective. Section 6 addresses the challenges faced when adopting intelligent big data analytics in a smart airport. Section 7 provides a discussion on applying intelligent big data analytics in a smart airport ecosystem. Section 8 provides a conclusion to the chapter and proposes future research directions.

INTELLIGENT BIG DATA ANALYTICS: A LITERATURE REVIEW

In this section, we use Google Scholar to conduct a literature review based on big data-driven small data analysis approach (Sun & Huo, 2021). A big data derived small data approach is a process paradigm that consists of 1. Big data reduction, 2. Big data derived small data collection, and 3. Big data derived small data analysis (Sun & Huo, 2021). Big data-driven small data approach is the basis for literature review, related work, discussion, and implications (Sun & Huo, 2021). It is also the inspiration of many ideas and models proposed in this research.

We use Google Scholar (https://scholar.google.com) to search for "intelligent big data analytics" on 23rd June 2021 and found out that there were about 202, 000 research publications. A further breakdown reveals that from years 2017 to 2021, there were about 23,600 research publications. We use Google Scholar (https://scholar.google.com) to search for "smart airport", "aviation analytics", and "airport analytics" respectively on 23rd June 2021 and the searched results are summarized in Table 1.

The authors use Google Scholar (https://scholar.google.com) to search for "big data-driven small data analysis" on the 27th May 2021 and found "6 results". After further drill down, the authors identified four sources that were directly related to the search topic: (Sun Z., 2021), (Sun Z., 2021), (Sun Z., 2017), (Sun Z., 2021), (Blayney & Sun, 2019), (Sun & Huo, 2021). This implies that this subject is still an emerging area of intelligent big data analytics and thus requires more research to develop and guide its applications from academia to industry perspectives. The first article titled An Introduction to Intelligent Analytics Ecosystems (Sun Z., 2021) revealed that the interest in using intelligent big data analytics is growing rapidly among different areas: academia, other public institutions, and industries. The other three articles by the same author published in the same year deal with the importance of applying intelligent big data analytics to various industries together with the opportunities and challenges faced. The other source, "Spectrum of Big Data Analytics" further highlighted that big data driven small data analysis consists of big data reduction, big data derived small data collection and analysis (Sun &

Huo, 2021). Intelligent big data analytics (IBDA) is crucial for airport operations when it is well-planned and executed on a small scale (Rajan, 2020). By starting off with identifying key data sets within its data analytics model, airports can know exactly what type of data can be pooled to their integrated data analytics (IDA) and airport data warehouse (ADW). This will create a vast availability of data pool for quick and easy access and analytics (Narongou & Sun, 2021).

Using Excel and Excel VBA for Preliminary Analysis in Big Data Research by (Blayney & Sun, 2019), highlighted the comparison in using excel spreadsheet application in cleaning data for analyzing data, tools, and platforms. The authors argued that behind big data-driven research and analysis, the data cleansing process is always the first step through big data-driven small data analysis using MS Excel. Excel has been one of the powerful applications used in financial analysis, among other business operations and functions related to analytics (Blayney & Sun, 2019) (EuSpRIG, 2021). Excel still remains one of the powerful tools for preparing data, analyzing raw data, and getting it ready for deeper visualization patterns and reporting analytics (Boost Labs, 2019).

While small data, on the other hand, is a subclass of big data deemed sufficient enough to make it accessible, informative, and actionable by people without the need for advanced analytical tools. Notably, the difference between big data and small data is that the former is about machines, while the latter deals with obtaining meaningful insights organized and packaged for deriving causations, patterns, thoughts, and the reasons about people (Thompson, 2021). Big data analytics may have been proven convenient for large multinational companies that have adopted and integrated advanced computing power and ICT technologies, whereas many small companies can benefit from a simpler approach, from defining smaller strategies within their reach to innovate their business models through analytics (Nielsen & Lund, 2019).

Table 1 showed that airport analytics and aviation analytics have not drawn much attention yet. The searched results of aviation analytics amounted to 57 sources, around 96% percent of the searched results. For airport analytics, the authors noted that out of nine (9) sources listed, there were five (5) direct mentions of the keyword. Apart from the big data-driven small data analysis, airport analytics and aviation analytics, however, are still in their infant stage of research and there is a huge demand for more work to contribute to the scholarly recognition of these two key areas in a smart airport-driven ecosystem.

Mullan discusses the strategies for "building a data-driven organization" that will ultimately have positive impacts on business growth and value, passenger experience, and operational efficiency as key areas for inclusion and consideration (Mullan, 2019). Larsen also discussed how to use big data analytics to develop aviation analytics (Larsen, 2013). This paper identifies and pointed out what are the key data sets in an aviation ecosystem and discusses methodologies on how to effectively use these data sets into big data analytics paradigm to solve airport operational issues, for example, security checks, which is one example of using big data analytics solutions through a centralized aviation data warehouse (ADW) (Larsen, 2013) (Narongou & Sun, 2021). This also is one of the applications of "big data-driven small data analysis" (Blayney & Sun, 2019) (Sun & Huo, 2021) (Sun Z., 2021) (Sun Z., 2021) (Sun Z., 2021) (Sun Z., 2021) method to the aviation sector.

BUSINESS VALUE OF APPLYING INTELLIGENT BIG DATA ANALYTICS IN A SMART AIRPORT

The big data within the aviation sector is now growing more than ever. The challenge is how to use this vast data for its maximum business value and benefit. As pointed out by McKinsey group, taking full advantage of data requires tackling all legal, regulatory, and talent challenges within the aviation industry (McKinsey & Company, 2016). These barriers need to be dealt appropriately at the corporate level to pave the way for effective implementation of big data analytics solutions that will ultimately contribute to realizing the business opportunities for expansion and growth in the smart airport environment.

Big data's value is determined and realized through the application of big data analytics (Ghavami, 2020) (Weber, 2020) (Narongou & Sun, 2021). Intelligent big data analytics (IBDA) has helped a lot of organizations realize tangible and significant business value, progress, and growth from daily operations, to strategic management, and decision making (Rama, Zhang, & Koronios, 2016). Big data's value is like the oil of the 20th century and the 21st century's goldmine. Big data is now considered a strategic asset of an organization, government, or an individual nowadays (Sun Z., 2017). Big data helps to identify new and potential business opportunities and new prospects for expansion, understanding the market challenges and threats to a business entity in its operational space and industry. The availability of Internet technologies and their related applications, for example, cloud computing, Internet of Things (IoT), and Internet of Everything (IoE) (Sun Z., 2021) have made it so much easier for processing big data to advance a more balanced view into a business operation before making decisions. An airport operator, for example, may have organizational database systems, customer relationship management (CRM) systems, and social media accounts to collect data from multiple and heterogeneous data entry points and sources (Rama, Zhang, & Koronios, 2016). Big data analytics and business intelligence platforms can support a full analytic workflow from data preparation to visual exploration and insight generation with an emphasis on self-service usage and augmented user assistance (Sallam, Richardson, Kronz, Sun, & Schlegel, 2021). The application of intelligent big data analytics has created market opportunities apart from remodeling how organizations and businesses operate and function (Sun, Sun, & Strang, 2018). The Lufthansa group, for instance, increased its efficiency by 30%. Lufthansa Group is a global aviation group that at one point lacked uniformity with its analytics reporting across its 550 subsidiaries. Their use of a single analytics platform increased efficiency by 30 percent, gave them greater flexibility in decision making, and enhanced departmental autonomy, and helped them create competitive advantages with real-time analytics. (https://www.tableau.com/learn/articles/data-driven-decision-making). Much of the revenue can be generated within an airport is based on aeronautical charges with less focus on other key non-aeronautical revenue activities. The increase in non-aeronautical revenue can be also generated if such intelligent big data analytics is implemented at an airport (Narongou & Sun, 2021). For example, in digital advertising around the airport, an airport company or other stakeholders can utilize existing platforms like FIDS to attract more commercial customers into advertising their products at an airport. This has the potential to boost revenue sources for airport operators as well as airlines from other commercial-related activities and functions from other service departments. Improving these commercial activities will also increase business value beyond the boundaries of traditional innovative services that can create value among business partners and stakeholders (Alansari, Soomro, & Belgaum, 2019).

The lean towards the increasing use of big data analytics in business activities is motivated by at least two factors: the need and the ability to use data to create business value and, drive competitive advantage as organizations, and businesses seeks new frontiers in using available modern technologies to leverage the use of data (Kiron & Shockley, 2011). The increasing use of data to make business decisions has put high demand on organizations including players in the aviation space to resort to redefining their data collection and management strategies. Practical application of big data can realize business goals and realign organizational strategies to meet targets and increase resource management and workflow efficiency. By using data from previous purchases and search patterns, Amazon determines which products to recommend to customers. A recommendation engine on Amazon isn't based on blindly suggesting a product, but on data analytics and machine learning. Approximately 35 percent of Amazon consumers' purchases could be linked back to the company's recommendation system, according to a McKinsey report (Stobierski, 2019).

A fully functional and integrated airport analytics platform will have the capability to be able to interact with and capture, process, and analyze all data from activities happening within the airport environment and then covering the entire aviation ecosystem itself. The scope of airport and aviation data sets nowadays has expanded beyond desktop capability (which involves time-consuming manual slicing of data). The application of intelligent big data analytics solutions including, data warehousing, AI, and machine learning (ML) can meet some of the business needs in the aviation industry (Larsen, 2013). For example, using analytics-based intelligent CCTV in the airport environment can help monitor, detect, and control movements and threats in an airport during peak periods where manpower is not sufficient to meet the demand. Intelligent business analytics is based on applying intelligent analytics for business and management (Sun Z., 2021). For example, passenger forecasts at an airport can be best predicted using intelligent business analytics solutions which in most cases are derived from the data warehouse through airport and aviation analytics.

AIRPORT ANALYTICS

In this section, we examine airport analytics. Then, we discuss how to apply big data analytics to each stage of the airport service chain.

Coupled with the vast availability of data generated around the airport ecosystem which has greatly revolutionized how airport operations and business activities were conducted and managed (resentence) (Dixon, 2020). By evaluating the current basis by which decisions are made around the airports using the traditional approach of management by objectives (MBO) which achieves targeted objectives in sequence (Wikipedia, 2021). This brings up another approach to management which is known as "management by data" or MBD for short (Foy, 2020). From here we can clearly see that although MBO has been dominating much of these management and decision-making practices over the last decades since the MBO was first coined by Peter Ducker in the 1950s (Wikipedia, 2021), new sweeping changes have now taken hold of much these models through the application and usage of data analytics. For example, let's consider a case study at the Port Moresby International (PMIA) of Papua New Guinea to quickly look at how its traditional models go head-to-head with the current usage of data analytics for management and decision making. Since NAC's establishment, all its decision-making processes were done using all the laid-out processes which are objective-based: aimed at achieving a certain level of growth and progress at a given fixed period. However, in the early 2000s when PMIA realized the importance of management by data and began to use them at its different business processes and operations from HR, Finance, terminal operations management among other key aviation processes, it has been observed that there is increasing use of data and related analytics to provide more tangible insights into guiding its operations and business activities. Key decisions were made based on the facts provided by data analytics (Narongou & Sun, 2021). Outmoded management methods which depended heavily on empirical knowledge, observation, and scenario testing do not produce the results expected nowadays (Papagiannopoulos, 2021). For example, a recent study conducted by Ernest and Young Global Limited on big data research from leading insight firm Nimbus Ninety, reported that 81% of respondents agree that data

Figure 1. Airport analytics driven airport services.

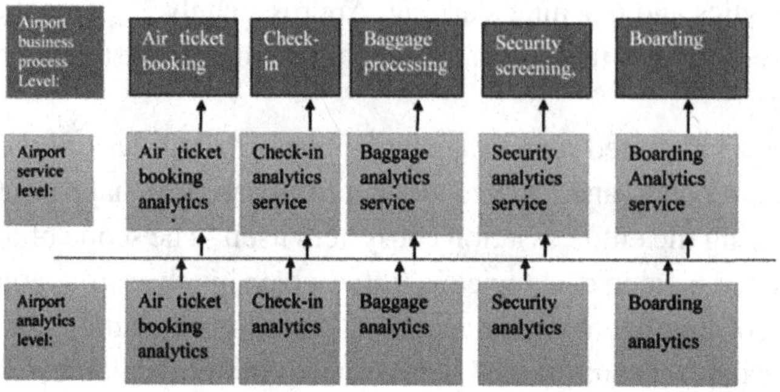

should be at the heart of all decision-making among key reasons which include understanding customers better, improving products and services and to improve the management of existing data (2015). This calls for a new change of decision-making models and methods based on "data driven decision making (DDDM) which simply is the act of using data to inform your decision-making process and confirm a course of action before committing to it. (Stobierski, 2019).

Big data analytics deals with the science and technology of collection, organization, and analysis of big data for the discovery of patterns, knowledge, and intelligence about the related information from the big data (Narongou & Sun, 2021). Therefore, airport analytics is the application and deployment of big data analytics solutions in an airport environment to provide analytics-based platforms and services as well as decision making.

This section is to look into the following topics and their relationships to airport analytics:

1. Airport as a business process
2. Airport as a services chain
3. The correspondence between airport service chain and Airport's business process.
4. The correspondence between big data analytics and airport services chain to provide a value-added benefit to the stakeholders.

In what follows, we look into each of them.

Airport services range from screening, check-in, boarding, baggage control, flight services, ground handling, and other passenger-related activities around the airport: from landside to airside. Most activities and interactions within the aviation ecosystem are conducted around two main physical landscapes of an airport which include a car park to terminal and to the airside. By looking at these interactions, most business transactions also take place around these areas: ticketing, retail shops, car parking, banking services, and many others. These activities represent key processes involved in an airport environment. At each level of airport business process activity, there is a corresponding data being generated and is stored in the ADW (airport data warehouse) (Narongou & Sun, 2021). Intelligent big data analytics is applied to each of the process in a smart airport ecosystem ensures that it derives insights from these processes to support operational and planning excellence.

Figure 2. Airport business process chain

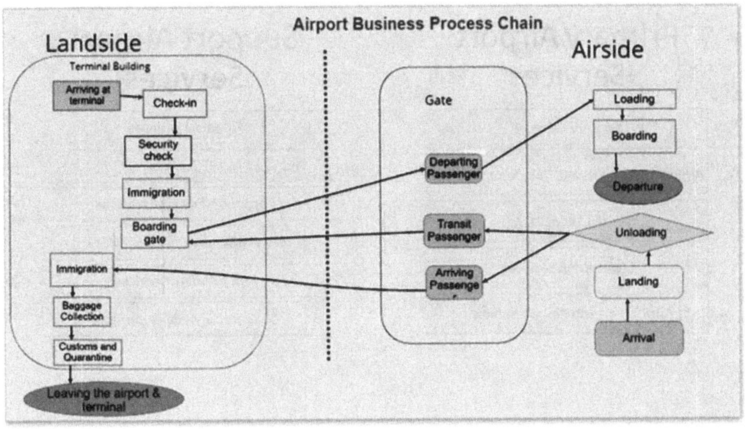

Airport as a Business Process

"A process can be defined as a sequence of steps that produce the *desired* outcome. Defined and documented processes also ensure *consistent* outcomes" (Brechter, 2012). Airport business activities comprise activities that revolve around passenger processing, cargo and luggage, aircraft, and passenger movements. Airport business activities are mostly done based on standard operating procedures and processes and thus regardless of who actually does them, they give the expected output (Altexsoft, 2020). Airport business processes accounted for activities happening from landside to airside to provide for smooth passenger movement that enables check-in to departure and vice versa from arrival and transit processes. Airport as a business process because all steps related to passenger processing a done in sequential order, pre-departure processes include security screening, check-in, baggage tagging and movement, and then boarding. In every step, there has to be a corresponding relatedness to its application in terms of verifying the associated source documents. In every stage of the passenger processing activity, transactions took place, which contributes to accomplishing the overall business cycle of processing passengers at the terminal. For example, during check-in, a passenger is required to produce tickets and ID cards, and other details to initiate the process. During this stage, a transaction activity involves trading personal data in order to complete. A proof to identify that this process is now complete is the issuance of a boarding pass by the check-in officer to the passenger.

Let's consider a case for a departing passenger. Peter (a passenger) purchases his ticket via online airline ticketing. Peter arrives at the terminal two hours before the flight's departure for check-in. Peter is asked at the entrance into the terminal to produce the ticket and goes on to security screening. After completing security screening and checks, Peter is helped with proceeding on to baggage wrap services to pack the baggage. Peter then goes over to complete the check-in. Upon confirmation of his ticket details including his personal details (ID) and baggage, the check-in officer finally issues a ticket to Peter. Peter then proceeds to the departure when the final checks are done by the boarding officer and flight attendant before allowed to board the aircraft.

Figure 3. Airport services chain

Primary Services and Support Services at an Airport

Airport services can be classified into two categories: Primary services and support services, as shown in Figure 3. The primary services mainly consist of airport operations and customer services, security services, ICT services, engineering services, and airport fire and rescue services. The support services mainly consist of financial services, HR services, corporate communications, legal and secretarial services, procurement services, and commercial activity services (Laudon & Laudon, 2020). The primary services focus on giving passengers and customers the best value and customer experience. They are the essential services that have a direct influence and impact on performance or excellence of the airport's operational processes and functions. These services are from airport operations, both at landside and airside. Primary services are the key enablers of the aircraft and flight operations, passenger and customer service operations, security as well cargo and baggage management processes to flow smoothly guaranteeing operation effectiveness and efficiency. These primary services formed the heart of airport operational activities and processes (Papagiannopoulos, 2021) (Alansari, Soomro, & Belgaum, 2019). Primary airport tasks focus on check-in, boarding, departure, arrival, and transiting for both outbound and inbound flights and passenger movements processes.

The secondary services at an airport are considered to be an added advantage service to the clients and customers. These services are considered to be part of an airport operators' or airline's internal functions and processes that do not have a direct influence on the operational level in an airport and are also known as support services. These services are also part of the overall activities happening around the airport; however, they are not as critical to the daily functions of airport operations from the passenger processing and flight management perspectives. These secondary services, however, are handled by the executive level of an airport operator or airline but have strategic implications on the primary services (Kovynyov & Mikut, 2018).

The data generated from the primary and secondary services for example security checks, boarding, buying coffee inside the terminal and advertising activities need to be actuated into accessible information and insights using airport data analytics solution platforms and services. Breakdown of airport business operation processes and services covers two key operating areas: the landside and airside. The landside focuses much on non-aeronautical business activities while the airside focuses on aeronautical business activities and processes. Landside operations are aimed at serving passengers and maintenance of terminal buildings, parking facilities, and vehicle traffic drives and movement. Terminal operations comprise resource allocation and staff management. Airside operations include aircraft landing and navigation, airport traffic management, runway management, and ground handling safety apart from cargo and baggage operations services such as cargo and baggage handling and tagging (Altexsoft, 2020) (Kovynyov & Mikut, 2018).

These services are the key contributors to the operational excellence of an airport driven by robust human and technical resources within an airport.

Airport Data Analytics and Aviation Analytics

From the airport operator's viewpoint, all activities happening from the landside to the airside contributed to different data source points. There lies a challenge in capturing all these data into a centralized model for use. New airport business models will have to "be adopted and re-engineered" (Narongou & Sun, 2021) using airport analytics to create and add value to an airport by increasing its financial capacity and operational efficiency. This adaptation and re-engineering process involve identifying key market variables such as "demographic change, new corporate conditions, emergence and maturity" of ICT systems and applications and planning out how these variables have put up a demand to the airport operators to redesign their organizational strategy and to diversify their business models (Alansari, Soomro, & Belgaum, 2019) to suit these challenging and elastic marketing conditions. One of the critical tasks is to identify the different processes involved in and around the airport and then knowing when and how airport analytics can be applied to provide success towards realizing its business value from minimizing operational costs, increasing operational efficacy to boosting passenger experience and improving decision making for strategic purposes (Pell & Blondel, 2018).

Airport analytics on the other hand deals with the application of ICT-related intelligent technologies for collecting, organizing, and processing aviation data sets for analysis, the discovery of patterns, knowledge, and intelligence within an aviation ecosystem (Larsen, 2013) (Narongou & Sun, 2021). Aviation analytics is characterized by the deployment of intelligent technologies including intelligent big data analytics, Internet of things (IoT), artificial intelligence (AI), machine learning, and cloud computing to the aviation sector to provide predictive analysis, optimize operations, improve workflow efficacy, identify new market opportunities, and (Globe Newswire, 2021). Aviation data is derived from multiple heterogeneous systems and sources. The primary aviation data sources include flight tracking data, airport operations data, weather conditions information, airline information, market information, passenger information, aircraft data, air safety data, and other aviation-related activities' data (Larsen, 2013) (Globe Newswire, 2021). Although aviation analytics and airport analytics are interrelated in almost every aspect of operations, the former deals with covering all areas of operations from all parties involved in the industry. The latter deals with the airport and airline-related activities which specifically related aircrafts, passengers, baggage and cargo operations in an airport. Aviation players include airlines, airports, customers (passengers), service providers, contractors, and local government authorities (Papagiannopoulos, 2021). Airport analytics deals with the collection, processing, and analyzing airport-related activities' data for generating insights while aviation analytics covers a wide spectrum of airport analytics including other related third-party activities governing the operational and industry-wide activities. Furthermore, airport analytics captures all the details of what's happening around the landside to the airside and processes these into useful information for decision making at an airport. Therefore, in summary, we have the following:

$$airport\ analytics\ platform = airport\ analytics + aviation\ analytics \tag{1}$$

and

$$airport\ analytics = Air\ ticket\ booking\ analytics, Check\text{-}in\ analytics, Baggage\ analytics$$
$$+Security\ analytics + Boarding\ analytics \tag{2}$$

INTELLIGENT BIG DATA ANALYTICS AS A SERVICE FOR ENHANCING SMART AIRPORT DEVELOPMENT

Making use of data quickly for the improved turnaround to managing business processes smartly is crucial for any business to determine its growth and success (Rajan, 2020). Organizations with traditional business models have had a hard time coping up with the challenge of implementing new business models (Rajan, 2020) aided by the availability of data coupled with advanced ICT solutions and the best business practices (Narongou & Sun, 2021) for data collection and analyzing through to discovering and visualizing patterns or trends and building their knowledge base (Sun Z., 2021).

As shown in Figure 4, the following stakeholders contribute a lot of data to airport analytics. Local government authorities are the policy regulators, for example, in PNG's case, the policy regulators are Civil Aviation Safety Authority (CASA PNG) and the Department of Transport (DoT). The local government authorities set the regulatory and policy frameworks for the aviation industry. Customers and passengers are the users of aviation resources and facilities. Passengers are the key customers and stakeholders in the aviation chain of activities. They pay and use the airport facilities when traveling. Contractors, suppliers, and service providers are third-party stakeholders within the industry. Although playing a key role in making sure airport activities and processes, passengers' activities do directly affect the operations of the airport. They are engaged in providing a wide range of services, for example, the cleaning around the airport, building airport infrastructure and facilities, providing security around the airport, or doing other commercial and business activities around the airport environment.

As depicted in Figure 4, aviation management includes managing the operations of the aviation ecosystem ensuring that all the maintenance, safety, operations, and regulations are executed satisfactorily. The complexity of the aviation ecosystem comprises airlines, airport operators, passengers, service providers, and contractors/suppliers as well as regulators, including the government. Similar to any other industry, the aviation industry takes all stakeholders and players to keep the industry fully functional (Yu, 2017) (Seawright, 2017). Airport management, however, includes managing, supervising, and coordinating processes, operations, and activities happening in an aerodrome, both landside and airside. The key aviation partners are those who have come up through the departmental functional areas. The entire aviation operational functionality needs more resources, expertise or bandwidth beyond each individual player's capability which centers around efficiency and effectiveness (Brechter, 2012) (Brechter, 2021).

The application of appropriate digital technologies and intelligent big data analytics solutions into the aviation ecosystem's business process aims to add more business value and deliver the most appropriate and customized business service to suit customer demands, expectations, and increasing efficiency (Pell & Blondel, 2018). Based on Figure 4, airlines, airports, contractors, suppliers, government authori-

Figure 4. An airport analytics platform

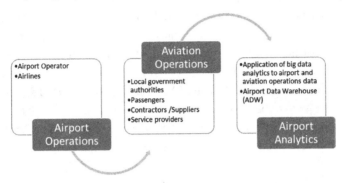

ties, and others in the aviation space are contributors of data to the airport analytics but they are also considered as the primary users of aviation data analytics for operational planning, decision making, and execution (Larsen, 2013). The application and implementation of intelligent big data analytics as a service for enhancing smart airport development airport data analytics is considered as an enabler "to unleash key information, how this is used across the aviation industry and how it has the potential to solve significant airport challenges" (Papagiannopoulos, 2021). Yet this was not fully realized as there are many challenges for adopting intelligent big data analytics and airport analytics.

CHALLENGES FOR ADOPTING INTELLIGENT BIG DATA ANALYTICS IN A SMART AIRPORT

"Shifting demographics, new corporate governance requirements, and emerging and maturing communications technologies are driving new travel patterns that will require innovative business models and strategies" (Fattah, Lock, Buller, & Kirby, 2009). These are some of the major factors that affect most of the decisions of the corporate business world. Adopting and implementing intelligent big data analytics in an airport operation as one of the key airport strategies has to be a priority. One of the biggest challenges faced by the aviation industry players when implementing and adopting big data analytics is to collect and sort siloes of heterogeneous aviation data sets both structured and unstructured and then feed these into an aviation analytics platform for query and analytics solutions using big data analytics methods, and airport data warehouse (ADW) solutions (Larsen, 2013) (Narongou & Sun, 2021). Airport operators have been experiencing a hard time dealing with data, capturing, processing, and sharing with other parties within the aviation space. A case study can be seen in PNG's National Airports Corporation (NAC) case. It has been facing a number of issues accessing and collecting passenger data among other airport and aviation data with other stakeholders, for example, Air Niugini, and PNG Air. The issues faced by NAC with data sharing are twofold: firstly, data is a strategic asset of an organization, therefore, needs to be guarded and secondly, data sharing needs to be well-coordinated considering all legal frameworks governing and authorizing data sharing. Data privacy and confidentiality are the two most prevailing issues that need addressing with common understanding before diving into further. A survey conducted by MIT classifies organizations into three levels of analytics based on the ability of their use within their organizations: aspirational, experienced, and transformed. The aspirational category is basic analytics users, for example, they might be using Microsoft excel applications for daily operational analysis functions like finance and targeted business activities and operations. Experienced companies use advanced analytics tools for data integration, visualization, and modeling techniques. While the advanced users of analytics are applying analytics from all facets of its business operations and are looking for more value-added benefits from their models (Kiron & Shockley, 2011). Application of machine learning (ML), Artificial intelligence (AI), Internet of things (IoT) among other intelligent ICT technologies are considered to be a more advanced form of utilizing big data analytics for modeling, predictive analytics among other uses (Sun & Huo, 2021) (Narongou & Sun, 2021).

With a lot of data being generated in the aviation ecosystem, firstly, almost all of these data are being captured, and secondly "of what's captured, a fraction is being used" (McKinsey & Company, 2016) for its intended purpose within the industry. Tying organizational data to the application of big data analytics solutions with the corporate strategic vision and direction by the airport companies' airlines, aviation industry regulators and authorities is the key to fully utilizing and realizing the of big aviation data and analytics. This paves the way for airport companies to capture these data within their strategic documents to serve as a guide to keep on track in adopting and implementing intelligent big data analytics in their organizations. Applying intelligent big data analytics can deliver big business value, but too often companies let technology guide their efforts. Instead, decisions must be based on business priorities (Aggarwal & Manuel, 2016). This is the lens that most airports and airlines executives must envisage in their strategic process and operational functions. By strategically realigning business priorities to meet target objectives, they can see the best fit of integrating intelligent big data analytics into their business processes to add value to it. This will determine how they do business and measure their operational performance using the available data boosted by analytics for insights.

With COVID-19 now hitting the aviation industry so hard unprecedently with unpredicted changes in passenger, aircraft, and cargo movements. It's so difficult to keep track of business processes and progress during these times. Disruptions to business continuity plans and airport congestion, together with social distancing measures now being applied with the need for many 'touchless' interactions brings together a whole new advantage of utilizing ICT solutions and big data analytics solutions (Papagiannopoulos, 2021). Implementing intelligent big data analytics solutions will be ideally a feasible way to help airport companies and airlines plan their resources, foresee their future with analytics, and plan their activities accordingly based on forecasts and intelligence generated.

DISCUSSION

Improving efficiency at the airport is always a key priority when airport authorities decide on the next steps to take. Strong passenger growth is expected to grow by late 2021 as the COVID-19 vaccine is rolled out. Despite the fact that COVID-19 has crippled the aviation industry dramatically, a new focus is now shifted towards the smart use of airport resources and processes utilizing ICT solutions including big data analytics, cloud computing, AI, ML, IoT among others. Most businesses, entities and corporations are now relying on "extracting and exploiting insights from big data …[through] big data analytics and advanced business analytics systems". This is attributed to the fact almost all organizations now relying on insights that are mostly derived from data analytics to run their daily operation functions, optimizing business processes, and aiding their decision-making (Sun Z., 2021). At the heart of every decision-making in businesses lies the data. The facts obtained through analysis supported by intelligent

Figure 5. The chain of reaction in the aviation industry business

business analytics paved the way for progress in making real-time decisions in a fast-paced business world. Coping up with this challenge has always been an issue with the players in the aviation industry decided to have their own solutions which have failed to bring together all parties to share data from a bigger perspective (Papagiannopoulos, 2021).

The aviation industry is one of the biggest sectors that is now putting up with implementing intelligent big data analytics into its sphere. The aviation ecosystem is a robust chain of interrelated activities that contributes to the overall functioning of the aviation industry. Transporting passengers and cargoes from one destination to another involves a number of processes, activities, aircraft, airport operators and authorities, and service providers. The "interrelationship" among them usually corresponds to at least one operation or action, in this case, is the flow of operations and activities in the aviation ecosystem (Sun Z., 2021). As depicted in Figure 4, the airport analytics platform provides an environment application of intelligent big data analytics into the airport.

The following figure highlighted the order of activities in the chain of value-added business benefits and areas of concern by respective stakeholders.

From Figure 5, the airport authority and airlines form the basis of the chain reaction with society at the top and with passengers coming in between the chains. The main areas of concern by the airport authority and the airline are to manage cost, increase capacity and improve operational effectiveness and efficiency. This determines the service provided at the airport which will be accessed by the passenger whose primary concerns and expectations are around convenience and comfort and ease of travel from one destination to another, for example, shorter queues and no delays (Alansari, Soomro, & Belgaum, 2019). At the top level of the chain, lies the entire society surrounding who will be impacted by the activities by the bottom three levels: the airport authority, airlines, and passengers. As depicted in Figure 5, the society in this context refers to all players in the aviation sector as well as the general populace whose lives may be in some way be impacted by aviation-related activities. Their concerns lie with the safety, security, and environmental impacts posed by the aviation sector. Therefore, the application of intelligent big data analytics will have to look into these chains of variables and solve those challenges from airport authorities, airlines, passenger respectively and then the society as a whole in the sector. From the airport, airlines and passengers, the smart airport maturity levels 3 to five, which focuses on optimizing passenger processing activities through the use of intelligent ICT systems to meeting and monitoring customer activities; needs and requests with fast reactivity in real time (Pell & Blondel, 2018) offers an advantage for airport authorities and airlines to fully implement those available technologies for example self-service technologies, intelligent big data analytics, and analytics solutions including ML, IoT add value to its processes and realize its goals (Narongou & Sun, 2021) (Pell & Blondel, 2018). The application of such services in an airport will ultimately give the aviation community and society, in general, overall insights and capabilities to define a collaborative effort and actions to regulating and participate in aviation-related activities or any other activities that will have direct or indirect implications to aviation operations and processes.

Future Directions and Limitations

In what follows, the authors will look at two future directions and two limitations.

Intelligent big data analytics for smart airport has the potential to improve all airport operations by providing a holistic view to the airport business process. By integrating big data, and intelligent analytics platform and solutions into the smart airport model, an airport will increase its business value and rate of investment and returns for all stakeholders in the aviation industry. With the vast availability of data generated in the aviation industry, the application of intelligent big data analytics solutions will go in a long way to help improve its decision-making processes and thus providing a quicker turn-around and response time. The main contributions of this research at least include: 1) develop an and identify extensive airport services and business processes platform that underpins the key activities in an airport and; 2: highlights key four elements in an intelligent big data analytics, data, information, knowledge, and wisdom (Sun & Stranieri, 2021), and aims to use this four elements to drive a smart airport ecosystem that uses intelligent analytical tools and such as DM, DW, ML and AI to drive business value in an airport. By clearly outlining what was achieved in this chapter, one future direction derived from this work is to expand sections 4 & 5 through develop a sustainable framework that will guide airport companies' executives align their ICT and intelligent big data analytics as a capital investment (Laudon & Laudon, 2020) to its corporate strategies. This will eventually lead to full realizing the application of the smart airport dream in an airport (Narongou & Sun, 2021).

However, this is limited based on the fact that most decision makers are too reluctant to invest in technology as a means to increase business value and improve business process efficiency by automatic most of the tasks and processes. Another notable limitation is the disparities among the policy frameworks in guiding the implementations of intelligent big data analytics in an airport. The aviation industry is one of the highly regulated industry in the world, guided by international agencies and national civil aviation agencies. This has created impediments to fully implementing a such smart airport solution in an airport. As such, another future focus of this research is to clearly identify those impediments dealing with data security and privacy to civil aviation regulations and look at possible approaches to implement those solutions to realizing more business value.

CONCLUSION

With big data analytics now permeating every aspect of business activity across all industries, the aviation industry is one that is evolving to meet customer and passenger expectations to make a seamless travel experience for all and managing its operational activities. This chapter aims to provide insights into understanding the challenges faced by airports and airlines when implementing intelligent big data analytics as part of the smart airport solutions in an aviation ecosystem. This will enable decision-makers including airport authorities and airlines executive to exactly knowing when and how to apply these smart ICT solutions in their business processes to add more business value to their operational requirements and revenue generation, as well as guiding their strategic alignment into the future through operational excellence. This will enable better customer relationship management (CRM) and increase business added value in every airport service.

In future work, we will develop strategies to guide airport services that can be applied to airport operations. These strategies will incorporate a full smart airport maturity model that will digitally transform airport operations (Nau & Benoit, 2017) (Narongou & Sun, 2021) (Pell & Blondel, 2018) with better insights into knowing when and what services and enabling smart and intelligent ICT services including intelligent big data analytics that can be applied in an airport.

REFERENCES

Aggarwal, S., & Manuel, N. (2016, June 22). *Big data analytics should be driven by business needs, not technology*. McKinsey & Company.

Alansari, Z., Soomro, S., & Belgaum, M. R. (2019). Smart Airports: Review and Open Research Issues. In M. H. Miraz, P. S. Excell, A. Ware, S. Soomro, & M. Ali (Eds.), iCETiC 2019. Lecture Notes of the Institute for Computer Sciences, Social Informatics and Telecommunications Engineering. 285 (pp. 137–148). Springer. https://doi.org/10.1007/978-3-030-23943-5_10.

Altexsoft. (2020, January 15). *Airport Technology Management: Operations, Software Solutions and Vendors*. Retrieved June 19, 2021, from Altexsoft: https://www.altexsoft.com/blog/travel/airport-technology-management-operations-software-solutions-and-vendors/

Blayney, P. J., & Sun, Z. (2019). Using Excel and Excel VBA for Preliminary Analysis in Big Data Research. In Z. Sun & Z. Sun (Eds.), *Managerial Perspectives on Intelligent Big Data Analytics* (pp. 110–136). IGI Global. doi:10.4018/978-1-5225-7277-0.ch007

Boost Labs. (2019, April 24). *Why Excel Is Still Essential to Data Analytics*. Retrieved June 12, 2021, from Boost Labs: https://boostlabs.com/blog/why-excel-is-still-essential-to-data-analytics/

Brechter, S. (2012, March 28). *Process 101: The Case for Process Management in Business Aviation*. Retrieved June 12, 2021, from Gray Stone Advisors: https://www.graystoneadvisors.com/process-management-in-business-aviation/

Brechter, S. (2021). *Operating Partners in Business Aviation*. Retrieved June 12, 2021, from Gray Stone Advisors: https://www.graystoneadvisors.com/operating-partners-in-business-aviation-2/

Choudhary, V. (n.d.). *Airport and Passenger Analytics – Innovation Driven by Growth.* Retrieved April 26, 2021, from IGT Solutions: https://www.igtsolutions.com/blog/airport-and-passenger-analytics-innovation-driven-by-growth/

Dixon, M. (2020, April 10). *How airport data analytics is changing airport operations.* Retrieved April 26, 2021, from Selerity: https://seleritysas.com/blog/2020/04/10/how-airport-data-analytics-is-changing-airport-operations/

Dixon, M. (2020, September 17). *Passenger data analytics forging the way forward for the aviation industry.* Retrieved May 27, 2021, from Selerity: https://seleritysas.com/blog/2020/09/17/passenger-data-analytics-the-way-forward-for-aviation-industry/

Ernst & Young Global Limited. (2015). *Becoming an analytics driven.* Retrieved September 17, 2021, from https://assets.ey.com/content/dam/ey-sites/ey-com/en_gl/topics/digital/ey-global-becoming-an-analytics-driven-organization.pdf

EuSpRIG. (2021). *Basic Research.* Retrieved 06 12, 2021, from European Spreadsheet Risk Interest Group (EuSpRIG): http://www.eusprig.org/basic-research.htm

Fattah, A., Lock, H., Buller, W., & Kirby, S. (2009). Smart Airports: Transforming Passenger Experience To Thrive in the New Economy. *Cisco Internet Business Solutions Group (IBSG)*, 1-16. Retrieved April &, 2020, from https://pdfs.semanticscholar.org/b579/1c0c4db633817f7c81f1bb0214081f1d3aa3.pdf

Foy, M. (2020, December 12). *Management by Data.* Retrieved May 4, 2021, from Berkeley Haas: newsroom.haas.berkeley.edu/magazine/fall-winter-2020/management-by-data/

Ghavami, P. (2020). Big Data Analytics Methods: Analytics Techniques in Data Mining, Deep Learning and Natural Language Processing (2nd ed.). de Gruyter.

Globe Newswire. (2021, January 8). *Global Aviation Analytics Market Report 2020: COVID-19 Could Affect Aviation Analytics Services by 40-45% - Forecast to 2025.* Retrieved May 06, 2021, from Globe Newswire: globenewswire.com/fr/news-release/2021/01/08/2155631/0/en/Global-Aviation-Analytics-Market-Report-2020-COVID-19-Could-Affect-Aviation-Analytics-Services-by-40-45-Forecast-to-2025.html

Hong, J., Oh, J., & Lee, H. (2019). Smart Airport and Next Generation Security Screening. *Electronics and Telecommunications Trend, 34*(2), 73–82. doi:10.22648/ETRI.2019.J.340208

Huai, Z. (2018, December 28). *How big data and AI will transform Shenzhen Airport.* Retrieved May 19, 2020, from Huawei: https://www.huawei.com/en/about-huawei/publications/winwin-magazine/32/shenzhen-airport-digital-platform-and-ai

Jaffer, S., & Timbrell, G. (2014). Digital Strategy in Airports. In *25 Australasian Conference on Information Systems-Digital Strategy in Airports* (pp. 1-11). Australasian Conference on Information Systems (ACIS).

Kiron, D., & Shockley, R. (2011). Creating business value with analytics. *MIT Sloan Management Review, 53*(1), 57–63.

Kohli, D. (2018, November 2). *Big data facilitating the working towards a smart future.* Retrieved August 4, 2020, from International Airport Review: https://www.internationalairportreview.com/article/77340/working-towards-smart-future/

Kovynyov, I., & Mikut, R. (2018). *Digital Transformation in Airport Ground Operations.* Cornell University. doi:10.1007/s11066-019-09132-5

Larsen, T. (2013). Cross-platform Aviation analytics using big data analytics. *2013 Integrated Communications Navigation and Surveillance (ICNS) Conference*, 1-10. Retrieved May 27, 2021, from http://masflightbigdata.com/uploads/1/9/5/4/19547003/cross-platform-aviation-analytics-using-big-data-methods-paper.pdf

Laudon, K. C., & Laudon, J. P. (2020). *Management Information Systems: Managing the Digital Firm* (16th ed.). Pearson Education, Inc.

Lees, E. (2016). *A Better Way to Manage Airports: Passenger Analytics.* ICF International, Inc.

McKinsey. (2011, May). *Big data: The next frontier for innovation, competition, and productivity.* Retrieved from McKinsey Global Institute: https://www.mckinsey.com/business-functions/business-technology/our-insights/big-data-the-next-frontier-for-innovation

McKinsey & Company. (2016, April 16). *How advanced analytics can drive productivity.* Retrieved June 20, 2021, from McKinsey: https://www.mckinsey.com/business-functions/mckinsey-analytics/our-insights/how-advanced-analytics-can-drive-productivity

Miskolczi, M., Jászberényi, M., & Tóth, D. (2021, January 13). Technology-Enhanced Airport Services—Attractiveness from the Travelers' Perspective. *Sustainability, 13*, 705.

Mullan, M. (2019). The data-driven airport: How daa created data and analytics capabilities to drive business growth improve the passenger experience and deliver operational efficiency. *Journal of Airport Management, 13*(4), 361–379. Retrieved June 26, 2021, from https://www.ingentaconnect.com/content/hsp/cam/2019/00000013/00000004/art00007

Narongou, D., & Sun, Z. (2021). Big Data Analytics for Smart Airport Management. In Z. Sun & Z. Sun (Eds.), *Intelligent Analytics With Advanced Multi-Industry Applications* (pp. 209–231). IGI Global. doi:10.4018/978-1-7998-4963-6.ch010

National Academies of Sciences, Engineering, and Medicine. (2012). *Guidebook for Developing General Aviation Airport Business.* Washington, DC: The National Academies Press. doi:10.17226/22694

Nau, J.-B., & Benoit, F. (2017). *Smart Airport: How Technology is shaping the future of airports.* Wavestone.

Nielsen, C., & Lund, M. (2019, November 25). *Small data: data strategies that most companies can profit from.* Retrieved June 12, 2021, from California Management Review: https://cmr.berkeley.edu/2019/11/small-data/

Oldenburg, M. (2020, January 25). *The biggest benefits of airport analytics.* Retrieved April 26, 2021, from Targit: https://www.targit.com/blog/the-biggest-benefits-of-airport-analytics

Papagiannopoulos, N. (2021, April 7). *The value of data analytics for airports: Use cases and novel methods.* Retrieved June 2, 2021, from International Airport Review: https://www.internationalairport-review.com/article/155857/value-data-analytics-airports/

Pell, R., & Blondel, M. (2018). *Airport Digital Transformation.* Arthur D Little.

Popovic, V., Kraal, B., & Kirk, P. (2009). Passenger Experience in an Airport: An Activity-centred Approach. *IASDR 2009 Proceedings*, 18-22. Retrieved 11 29, 2019, from https://www.researchgate.net/publication/42424464

Rajan, Q. (2020, May 11). *Big Data for Small Business.* Retrieved April 29, 2021, from Towards Data Science: https://towardsdatascience.com/big-data-for-small-business-ae851f34e5a5

Rama, J., Zhang, C., & Koronios, A. (2016). The implications of Big Data analytics on Business Intelligence: A qualitative study in China. *Fourth International Conference on Recent Trends in Computer Science & Engineering*, 87, 221-226. doi:10.1016/j.procs.2016.05.152

Roe, D. (2021, March 24). *Many Organizations Put Big Data Aside To Focus on Small Data.* Retrieved April 22, 2021, from CMSWire: https://www.cmswire.com/information-management/many-organizations-put-big-data-aside-to-focus-on-small-data/

Sallam, R., Richardson, J., Kronz, A., Sun, J., & Schlegel, K. (2021, February 15). *Magic Quadrant for Analytics and Business Intelligence Platforms.* doi: ID G00467317

Seawright, S. (2017, October 17). *5 Elements of the Aviation Ecosystem that will Impact the Future of the Industry.* Retrieved June 19, 2021, from Connected Aviation Today: https://connectedaviationtoday.com/aviation-ecosystem/#.YM1yU1QzaUk

Stobierski, T. (2019, August 26). *The Advantages of Data-Driven Decision-Making.* Retrieved September 23, 2021, from Harvard Business School: https://online.hbs.edu/blog/post/data-driven-decision-making

Sun, Z. (2017). *Intelligent Big Data Analytics.* Centre of Big Data Analytics and Intelligent Systems. doi:10.13140/RG.2.2.15854.61763

Sun, Z. (2021). An Introduction to Intelligent Analytics. *PNG UoT BAIS*, *6*(1), 1–6.

Sun, Z. (2021). An Introduction to Intelligent Analytics Ecosystems. *PNG UoT BAIS*, *6*(3), 1–11.

Sun, Z. (2021). An Introduction to Intelligent Business Analytics. *PNG UoT BAIS*, *6*(2), 1–6.

Sun, Z. (2021). Ten Challenges and Opportunities of Intelligent Big Data. *PNG UoT BAIS, 6*(5), 1-6.

Sun, Z., & Huo, Y. (2021). The spectrum of big data analytics. *Journal of Computer Information Systems*, *61*(2), 154–162. doi:10.1080/08874417.2019.1571456

Sun, Z., Strang, K., & Li, R. (2018). Big data with ten big characteristics. In *Proceedings of 2018 The 2nd Intl Conf. on Big Data Research (ICBDR 2018)* (pp. 56-61). Weihai, China: ACM.

Sun, Z., & Stranieri, A. (2021). The Nature of Intelligent Analytics. In Z. Sun & Z. Sun (Eds.), *Intelligent Analytics With Advanced Multi-Industry Applications* (pp. 1–21). IGI Global.

Sun, Z., Sun, L., & Strang, K. (2018). Big Data Analytics Services for Enhancing Business Intelligence. *Journal of Computer Information Systems*, *58*(2), 162–169. doi:10.1080/08874417.2016.1220239

Sun, Z., & Wu, Z. (2021). A Strategic Perspective on Big Data Driven Socioeconomic Development. In *The 5th International Conference on Big Data Research (ICBDR)*. ACM.

Thompson, G. (2021). *Small Data, Big Opportunities*. Retrieved April 22, 2021, from Toptal: https://www.toptal.com/finance/data-analysis-consultants/big-data-vs-small-data

Vashisth, S., Heizenberg, J., Lo, T., Herschel, G., & Radhakrishnan, D. (2021, February 15). *Magic Quadrant for Data and Analytics Service Providers*. Retrieved April 26, 2021, from Gartner: https://www.gartner.com/doc/reprints?id=1-2586H7WL&ct=210216&st=sb

Vermeulen, E. P. (2017, December 24). *What is "Smart" in Our New Digital World?* Retrieved March 05, 2020, from Hacker Noon: https://hackernoon.com/what-is-smart-in-our-new-digital-world-87e6426398

Weber, H. (2020). Big Data and Artificial Intelligence: Complete Guide to Data Science, AI, Big Data, and Machine Learning. ICGtesting.

Wikipedia. (2021, April 25). *Management by objectives*. Retrieved May 05, 2021, from Wikipedia: https://en.wikipedia.org/wiki/Management_by_objectives

Yu, J. (2017, July 9). *The Complex Aviation Ecosystem*. Retrieved June 19, 2021, from LinkedIn: https://www.linkedin.com/pulse/complex-aviation-ecosystem-jack-yu/

ADDITIONAL READING

Bal, H., & Kucuk Yılmaz, A. (2019). Values that form the business: Evidence from airport operations in Turkey. *Aeronautical Journal*, *123*(1262), 507–522. doi:10.1017/aer.2018.168

Banfi, F., Hazan, E., & Levy, A. (2013, April 1). Using "Big Data" to optimize digital marketing. McKinsey & Company.

Coronel, C., & Morris, S. (2018). *Database Systems: Design, Implementation, and Management* (12th ed.). Cengage Learning.

Cortell (2017). IBM Planning Analytics. Retrieved July 29, 2018, from http://www.cortell.co.za/our-partners/ibm-planning-analytics/

Jones, C., & Dunse, N. (2015). The valuation of an airport as a commercial enterprise. *Journal of Property Investment & Finance*, *33*(6), 574–585. doi:10.1108/JPIF-07-2015-0048

Sun, Z., Strang, K., & Firmin, S. (2016). Business analytics-based enterprise information systems. *Journal of Computer Information Systems*, *56*(4), 74–84. doi:10.1080/08874417.2016.1183977

KEY TERMS AND DEFINITIONS

Airport Analytics: Refers to the application of big data analytics to data generated from activities conducted within an aerodrome. All data from passenger processing activities including aircraft movement are also part of the airport analytics platform.

Airport Services Chain: Refers to activities and services chain operating in an airport from landside to airside, or vice versa. The airport services chain comprises primary and secondary services or support services.

Artificial Intelligence (AI): Is science and technology concerned with imitating, extending, augmenting, automating intelligent behaviors of the human beings.

Aviation Ecosystem: Refers to processes within which all players from airport operators, airlines, government authorities, and other stakeholders are involved in the operations, conduct, and function of the aviation-related activities.

Big Data: Is data with at least one of the ten big characteristics, consisting of big volume, big velocity, big variety, big veracity, big intelligence, big analytics, big infrastructure, big service, big value, and big market.

Big Data Analytics: Big data analytics is a science and technology about organizing big data, analyzing and discovering knowledge, patterns, and intelligence from big data, visualizing and reporting the discovered knowledge for assisting decision making (Sun, Sun, & Strang, 2016). The main components of big analytics include big data descriptive analytics, predictive analytics, and prescriptive analytics (Sun, Sun, & Strang, 2018), which correspondingly address the three questions of big data: when and what occurred? what will occur? and what is the best answer or choice under uncertainty? All these questions are often encountered in almost every part of science, technology, business, management, organization, and industry.

Cloud Computing: Is a computing paradigm based on the demand for resources and services in the cloud. It is a special distributed computing that introduces utilization models for remotely provisioning scalable and measured resources.

Data Science: Is a field that builds on and synthesizes a number of relevant disciplines and bodies of knowledge, including statistics, informatics, computing, communication, management, and sociology to translate data into information, knowledge, insight, and intelligence for improving innovation, productivity and decision making.

Intelligent Big Data Analytics: Is science and technology about collecting, organizing, and analyzing big data to discover patterns, knowledge, and intelligence as well as other information within the big data based on artificial intelligence and intelligent systems.

Intelligent System: Is a software system that can imitate, automate some intelligent behaviors of human beings. Expert systems and knowledge-based systems are examples of intelligent systems.

Internet of Things (IoT): Refers to systems that involve computation, sensing, communication, and actuation. It involves the connection between humans, non-human physical objects, and cyber objects, enabling monitoring, automation, and decision making.

Smart Airport Management: Is a special form of airport management that integrates and shares key Information Communication Technology (ICT) systems, data, and information to optimize performance and capacity, passenger experience, and customer service for the entire aviation ecosystem.

PMIA: Port Moresby Jackson's International Airport (PMIA) is managed by the National Airports Corporation (NAC), a state-owned entity entrusted to manage all airport infrastructure services throughout Papua New Guinea (PNG).

Smart Airport: Smart airport is an integrated airport environment that interconnects all ICT systems and related sources of data and information smartly for optimizing customer satisfaction, operational efficiency, strategic differentiation, and economic diversity, underpinned by advanced digital technologies and intelligent systems.

Chapter 11
Immunize Your Organization:
A People Analytics Exploration of the Change in Employee Priorities After the COVID–19 Lockdown

Shivanand Rai

ESCP Business School Berlin, Germany

Markus Bick

ESCP Business School Berlin, Germany

ABSTRACT

The pandemic has changed the world immensely and provided a natural experiment for the field of people analytics. Herein, the authors analyze how this has changed employees' priorities, what the future might look like, and how corporations can respond. This is the first study of its kind to examine the entire construct of Glassdoor and map the changes it reveals during the pandemic, using machine-learning and NLP techniques. Individual ratings were used to create a model of satisfaction that would provide us with a framework to see which factors drive employee satisfaction and what changed during the pandemic. The results show that culture and management are the most critical organizational factors in a time of crisis, with career reducing in importance. Culture appears to be the vaccine that immunizes against tough times. Although actual compensation did not increase, its rating did so during the pandemic, showing that career and compensation are rated more on external factors. Most employees pointed to the bureaucracy and silo mentalities of banks as the nexus complicating their lives.

INTRODUCTION

The COVID-19 pandemic has changed many aspects of our society, one crucial element of which is our relationship with work. Working from home (WFH) was supposed to be a temporary measure with many returning to work after the pandemic was over. However, companies such as Microsoft and Google have decided to institute WFH as a permanent fixture (Page, 2020). The jury is still out on its benefits and

DOI: 10.4018/978-1-7998-9016-4.ch011

drawbacks: Some observers argue that the lines between personal and professional are blurred and that employees are working longer hours, while others have seen increased productivity as a result of increased isolation and the lack of a commute (Thompson, 2020). This seismic shift in work arrangements will change the human resources (HR) strategies of organizations globally, and so the old playbook of how to hire, engage, and retain employees will have to be completely revamped in the absence of physical interaction and communication. This shift influences a host of HR activities downstream; for example, how are appraisals affected by minimal physical interactions between a manager and employee? How are the bonds among employees affected, and do innovation and collaboration suffer from this new arrangement? These are complex phenomena which are difficult to ascertain without first understanding the current realities and employees' thoughts.

A meta-study by Marler & Boudreau (2017) revealed that many people think analytics studies are not robust, because they lack the company data to prove causal relationships with internal practices as well as informal data on what employees are experiencing. To overcome this issue, scraping data from public sources has become the easiest way to ascertain global employee changes. This paper seeks to answer the questions raised above by applying machine-learning techniques to public Glassdoor data, in order to determine the current environment. Using Glassdoor as a public data source to gain insights on employee behaviour is an established method in people analytics (Chandra, 2012). This paper focuses particularly on the finance industry, since it is predicted to be least affected by lockdowns and WFH initiatives, given the advanced level of digitalization and lack of requirement for physical workforce proximity (Statista, 2020). The finance industry also constitutes 30% of the global economy, making it a sizable industry on which to focus (Ross, 2020). To streamline the analysis, this paper compares London and Singapore, the second- and fourth-most competitive cities in the world for finance, respectively (Financial Centre Futures, 2020), thereby providing valuable insights into bank and financial firm C-suites.

We scraped Glassdoor reviews of the three biggest financial organizations in terms of assets and employees in both cities. This became the primary dataset for analysis, and naturally, these firms were banks (Singapore: DBS, OCBC, and UOB; London: Barclays, HSBC, and Lloyds). Machine-learning techniques were used to quantify differences before and after lockdown. The random forest algorithm, with an 89% area under the curve, proved to be the most suitable method for identifying the changing perceived priorities of employees. We created a model that explains employee satisfaction and then looked at the reviews with topic modeling, in order to understand the sentiments behind the ratings.

THEORETICAL BACKGROUND

Impact of people analytics on banks' financial bottom line. The connection between HR practices and financial outcomes, especially in financial institutions such as banks, is well documented. For example, one standard improvement in HR systems improves financial outcomes by 20% (Wright et al., 2005), which is also true for individual business units (Wright et al., 2003). This phenomenon is specifically pronounced in knowledge-intensive industries such as finance and technology, where employees contribute directly to the performance and productivity of the firm (Avey et al., 2010). A study with publicly traded financial services firms demonstrated this point, whereby higher human capital management (HCM) scores resulted in higher stock prices (McMurrer & Bassi, 2007).

Theoretical framework for people analytics' impact on the bottom line. According to HR metrics, the biggest driver of firm performance is attrition, in that it costs a company anywhere between 30% and

400% of an employee's annual salary to find a replacement (Srivastava & Nair, 2017). This is essentially a drain on company resources just to maintain normal operations. Therefore, ensuring minimal attrition is critical to company strategy. Implicitly, people believe that employee productivity is tied intimately to firm performance, but measuring it in knowledge-intensive industries is difficult, since the outcome of the employees' work are intangible and difficult to measure (Huselid, 1995). Therefore, there is a need to dig deeper into the academic literature to understand what employees think, feel, and perceive, measure appropriate constructs that have real predictive power, and provide firms with actionable insights.

Employee metrics in people analytics. Using attrition and productivity as a bedrock for analysis, six other constructs can be identified as generally accepted components of people analytics: *satisfaction, career/job growth, compensation, well-being* or *work-life balance, culture,* and *perception of firm/management,* all of which coincide well with our Glassdoor data, therefore allowing a framework to be created.

Satisfaction. Originating from the disconfirmation theory, where a mental state of *satisfaction* was measured via a Likert scale (Berry & Parasuraman, 1991), this has become the basis for most people analytics analyzes that affect a large part of employee behaviour. Studying this metric provides a good sense of the employee's internal state and intentions towards the firm. Satisfaction is thus a direct precursor to attrition and productivity and an important metric with which to understand and predict employee behaviour and intention (Brunetto et al., 2012). Given the strong effect that satisfaction has on employee behaviour, it is examined herein as the key dependent variable in this study. On Glassdoor, this is a self-reported item on a scale of 5. Furthermore, Luo, Zhou, & Shon (2016) demonstrated that the Glassdoor satisfaction construct is highly correlated to company performance. However, causation has not been determined, as culture can contribute to performance, or vice versa.

Career growth. There are several ways in which an individual's career growth may be defined, including salary growth, expanded role responsibilities, earning a promotion, or being responsible for more individuals and parts of the business. From an academic perspective, metrics include moves to a new position in the last year, new developments such as secondments, or specific experiences in multiple functions and/or geographies (Mayo, 2018). Employees would theoretically like to be on an endless career trajectory or be able to change roles within an organization based on their whims. Unfortunately, though, this is not possible, and while technology companies do try to remove siloes, in order to allow for the internal movement of talent, there are still some constraints. Given the difficulty in placing people within organizations, and the vast amount of data required to facilitate this move, it is no wonder that career progression is a difficult construct to measure objectively. Furthermore, there may be a gulf of difference between what individuals think they should receive, versus how the firm rates their skill sets and what the market offers. There is no real answer to this conundrum except to assume that the job market knows best and will prize skill sets that are scarce and more valuable. Therefore, this research uses Glassdoor's career rating as an objective measure of the perceived career opportunities within the firm.

Corporate Culture. Peter Drucker's quote, "Culture eats strategy for breakfast," has been repeated ad nauseum in corporate settings (Walford-Wright & Scott-Jackson, 2018). Prominent figures such as Steve Jobs have spoken at great lengths about culture and how it differentiates a company from its competitors. Typically, culture has been difficult to quantify; the first comprehensive study was on IBM staff between 1967 and 1975 (Lackey et al., 2004), and ever since, it has been considered the invisible force that binds employees. At times, it is the unwritten, implicit rule book of organizations; therefore, in times of distress or resource scarcity, culture can be a force of resilience and recovery. Uyeno (2019) showed that Glassdoor's culture construct is highly correlated to firm performance. Therefore, this paper uses the culture scale on Glassdoor as a good proxy for what employees think of their company culture and whether it contributes positively to their experience. This will be corroborated with topic modeling to show if the culture ratings match the reviews given to companies by employees.

Work-Life Balance (WLB). A significant portion of employee perception is driven by the place that work occupies in one's life. If work is central and enjoyable, long hours at the expense of other goals in life is acceptable, while in any other scenario, well-being is diminished, and satisfaction suffers. Chandra (2012) described this variance as follows: "*Some people are happy working hard and for long hours, while others are not. WLB is about paying attention to both work and family responsibilities.*" Gelbard (2018) similarly defined WLB as "*an overall appraisal of the extent to which individuals' effectiveness and satisfaction in work and family roles are consistent with their life values at a given point in time.*" Clearly, WLB is a critical measure, and yet it is also a personal one. This research assumes that the average of all employee ratings is a representation of an organization's policies and reflects positive outcomes for the firm. Thompson (2020) reported that the impact COVID-19 has had on blurring work-life boundaries might be significant, thereby justifying this paper's inspections of the WLB construct.

Management Perception. Studies have demonstrated the C-suite's impact on a company and the morale of its employees (Collins and Clark, 2003); for example, stock prices can rise and fall following mere tweets from prolific CEOs such as Elon Musk (Reinicke, 2020). Glassdoor presents rich data on what employees think about the management team, especially reflecting their CEO approval rating. Arguably, leadership is a critical indicator of corporate performance, culture, and employee engagement.

Compensation. While Glassdoor's data on compensation may offer a subjective rating, this research uses it as a reasonable proxy, since there are reviews from both current and former employees. Ratings from former employees are expected to be lower, since dissatisfaction may have been a key reason for them leaving. However, given the intense 'war for talent', alluded to by Barton and Charan (2018), most banks have to keep their pay package competitive in order to manage the difficulty of attracting talent. Indeed, most banks see 90% of the offers they make accepted (Gupta, 2015), which justifies using the compensation rating on Glassdoor as a representation of the compensation policy of the organization.

Finance Industry: In studying people analytics and its impact on companies, this research focuses on industries with a high requirement for talent and knowledge capital. Finance ranks high on this scale, only behind R&D in scientific institutions and the technology industry (Sands & Bakthavachalam, 2019), thus making this industry a prime candidate. Furthermore, for the analysis to be meaningful, a significant population of reviews was required. Given that banks such as HSBC hire over 300,000 employees compared to Google's 98,000, this industry is a good choice for this research, due to the numbers of employees. Finally, finance is the best industry for Glassdoor-based analysis, as it is an overrepresented industry within Glassdoor and will capture more sentiments regarding the sector. Furthermore, given the inability to use an API to scrape individual companies, it is important to study an industry in which just a few companies account for a large proportion of the business. In Singapore, studying the three biggest banks covers 100% of the retail banking market (Financial Centre Futures, 2020). First, a t-test was conducted to identify any significant differences in the data before and after lockdown.

From Table 1, it is evident that the t-test is significant (highlighted results) for the change in overall satisfaction, so the study can conclude that COVID-19 and WFH have had an impact on employee perceptions. Furthermore, a t-test was performed on the data from both cities to prove that they are significantly different from each other, thereby lending further credence to the fact that they should be analyzed separately. Given the literature review, satisfaction will be the dependent variable, while the other factors will be the independent variables.

Geographical Choices: Therefore, given the current parameters, the field candidates to study from is narrowed to a few major metropoli. Since Glassdoor has certain restrictions on the amount of reviews to be scrapped (explained more in Empirical Study 4.1). It makes sense to distinguish geographically as COVID-19 had a differing impact on different cities. The differing impact has an impact on the operations of the company and the responses that the reviews reveal. Therefore, we will need to isolate two Financial Hubs with significant English Glassdoor reviews, with similar lockdown protocols, cultural diversity, and with sufficient geographical distance to make it a global analysis. Therefore, upon comparing the 6 Financial Hubs from The Global Financial Centres Index (Financial Centre Futures (2020)) we gauged Singapore and London to be a viable comparison.

Hypothesis 1: The dependent variables (*career growth, culture, compensation, management & work-life balance*) impact satisfaction which is the independent variable. The bedrock of our analysis is that sub-ratings affect satisfaction. There is sufficient literature to support this notion, and it is important to see how this translates into actionable insights for organizations.

Hypothesis 2: The reviews will demonstrate the impact of the pandemic on satisfaction. While there is no explicit mention of COVID-19 and WFH in the numerical ratings, the t-tests and analyzes thus far suggest that a drastic change has occurred. Therefore, language processing of the reviews should demonstrate that the change in ratings is due to WFH during the pandemic.

METHODOLOGY

Using Glassdoor as a Database

Glassdoor is one of the most comprehensive public databases for employee perceptions (Uyeno, 2019), and it has been used as a data source for a variety of research work. For example, MIT collaborated with Glassdoor to study 1.2 million reviews and used machine-learning to quantitatively analyze culture along nine dimensions; this database has been released for public academic use (Uyeno, 2019).

Karabarbounis & Pinto (2018) studied how well Glassdoor reflects the job market, especially on data such as salary, and correlated this data with US Census Bureau data to see how accurately it reflects reality. They showed that first, there is an overrepresentation of data from the technology, finance, and telecommunications industries and an underrepresentation of construction, F&B, and healthcare. Second, the researchers found that salary figures were highly correlated with figures from the US Census, therefore increasing the credibility of user data. Given that most users expect the reviews to be accurate, they would also try to give accurate representations, due to the cognitive bias of the consensus effect and reciprocity (Li et al., 2018).

With 48% of job seekers using Glassdoor as part of their job-hunting endeavor, and 67 million visitors monthly in 2018, even the *Harvard Business Review* uses its data when reporting on employment trends or workforce policies (Landers, Brusso, and Auer, 2019). While the validity of each sub-construct (work-life balance, compensation, management perception, career growth) with their corresponding psychometric constructs (Cronbach & Meehl, 1955) is contested, there is reason to believe that the overall relationship between satisfaction and the sub-constructs does indeed exist and is valid—as concluded by DeKay (2013) from his content analysis of Glassdoor reviews, to demonstrate internal validity of the 6 variables.

Table 1. T-Test on Data before and after lockdown

Overall	Description	Value	Value
mu	Average value before lockdown	3.29	3.49
xbar	Average value after lockdown	3.59	3.73
s	standard deviation of data since lockdown	1.17	1.06
n	number of reviews since lockdown	190.00	320.00
t	T-Value	3.55	4.18
p	probability that the change is only due to chance	0.00	0.00
Culture	**Description**	**Value**	**Value**
mu	Average value before lockdown	3.14	3.48
xbar	Average value after lockdown	3.36	3.66
s	standard deviation of data since lockdown	1.33	1.18
n	number of reviews since lockdown	190.00	320.00
t	T-Value	2.30	2.61
p	probability that the change is only due to chance	0.01	0.00
Career	**Description**	**Value**	**Value**
mu	Average value before lockdown	3.17	3.35
xbar	Average value after lockdown	3.48	3.57
s	standard deviation of data since lockdown	1.11	1.13
n	number of reviews since lockdown	190.00	320.00
t	T-Value	3.95	3.41
p	probability that the change is only due to chance	0.00	0.00
Compensation	**Description**	**Value**	**Value**
mu	Average value before lockdown	3.28	3.34
xbar	Average value after lockdown	3.66	3.58
s	standard deviation of data since lockdown	1.07	1.02
n	number of reviews since lockdown	190.00	320.00
t	T-Value	4.96	4.15
p	probability that the change is only due to chance	0.00	0.00
Management	**Description**	**Value**	**Value**
mu	Average value before lockdown	2.73	3.34
xbar	Average value after lockdown	3.35	3.24
s	standard deviation of data since lockdown	1.22	1.16
n	number of reviews since lockdown	190.00	320.00
t	T-Value	6.93	1.56
p	probability that the change is only due to chance	0.00	0.06
WLB	**Description**	**Value**	**Value**
mu	Average value before lockdown	2.79	3.68
xbar	Average value after lockdown	2.93	3.86
s	standard deviation of data since lockdown	1.33	1.13
n	number of reviews since lockdown	190.00	320.00
t	T-Value	1.38	2.87
p	probability that the change is only due to chance	0.08	0.00

Table 2. Count of reviews across the entire dataset

Months	Jul-18	Oct-18	Jan-19	Apr-19	Jul-19	Oct-19	Jan-20	Apr-20	Jul-20	Oct-20
Count of Reviews Done over the months	20	26	21	42	63	57	43	42	52	107

The number of Glassdoor reviews has increased dramatically post-lockdown, based on scraping. Hence, the test set (data from April 2020 to Oct 2020) comprises 25% of the total number of reviews. Specifically, the increase began from July 2020, possibly after second-quarter HR appraisals (Table 2).

Machine-Learning Techniques in People Analytics

Depending on the type of data, there are a variety of ways in which one can use algorithms to study the dataset. For example, XGBoost has been demonstrated to be successful for classifying attrition (Jain & Nayyar, 2018). In another study, the random forest was the most accurate algorithm to predict attrition (De Oliviera et al., 2019). However, 'black-box' algorithms must be avoided, because they predict satisfaction but do not provide any insights into why it happens. This in turn reduces the ability to extrapolate any insights to other examples and to be meaningful in terms of companies' HR (Shikha & Khera, 2018). Therefore, even though algorithms such as neural networks and support vector machines might provide better predictions and can utilize both categorical and numerical data, they do not provide insights into why the model works and which variables are more important. This is critical to the current study, in order to provide actionable recommendations, so we will use random forest and XGBoost classification regression, since the problem entails classifying 'Satisfying' from 1 to 5. Given the mix of categorical and integer variables as well, it is more suitable to use these algorithms instead of OLS regressions. Therefore, the study will weigh the accuracy of each algorithm based on AUC (area under the curve) ROC (receiver operating characteristics).

EMPIRICAL STUDY

Collecting the Data

Glassdoor has rescinded its API for researchers and public consumption; therefore, to access Glassdoor reviews at scale, a scraping algorithm was created. Glassdoor was contacted for permission, but no reply was received, and so the dataset was limited to fewer than 5,000 reviews collectively, to avoid copyright or intellectual property infringement. My code was built from Chatham's (2018) framework and tweaked for the multiple variations that Glassdoor has made to their dataset between 2018 and 2020. The scraped dataset had to be properly prepared and split before machine-learning algorithms could be run on it. First, the date column had to be cleaned and made consistent (we only used the date for this analysis and not the time). Rows that had any missing values were removed—these could have occurred because the algorithm ran an error—leaving 2,214 reviews from the two cities and six banks. This analysis is only significant enough to be conducted on a city level and not on individual companies, since it lacks geographical coverage.

Figure 1. Classification of roles, and numbers of reviews.

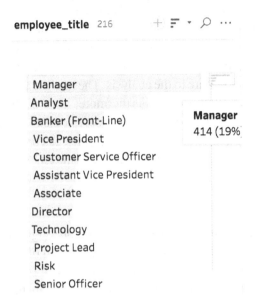

Next, a significant amount of time went into categorizing employee titles. The data included several spelling errors ("Vice Preisdent" instead of "Vice President"), different naming conventions ("VP" or "Vice-President" instead of "Vice President"), and different titling conventions ("Pricing Vice President" versus Vice President (Pricing)); hence, eight hours were spent grouping roles into smaller bundles that could be used generally across banks, locations, and departments. This approach is similar to Karabarbounis & Pinto's (2018) study, where 193,000 distinct job roles listed on Glassdoor were aggregated to 20 (29% of the database).

The final database for the current study included 216 distinct roles aggregated from a total of 656 such roles. Generally, they were around hierarchies such as analyst, manager, vice president and assistant vice president. There was also an attempt to categorize them by function, where possible, and these tended to be around customer, service officer, project management, risk, technology and HR. The top 10 roles accounted for 70% of the study's reviews, demonstrating that the categorization was sufficiently robust.

Machine-learning Methodology

The data from London and Singapore were run separately through Dataiku. The machine-learning model was built using pre-COVID-19 data as a training set, and then run on post-lockdown data as the test set. The results were then compared, to ascertain which algorithm is the best. These results helped examine if the hypotheses were correct and to propose an overall model for Glassdoor constructs and what drives satisfaction. Our study utilized a variety of tools: Selenium with Python was used to scrape the data from Glassdoor, and thereafter, Excel and Tableau were applied for data cleaning and preparation. For the qualitative analysis and visualizations, Tableau was used, to get a sense of the data. Machine-learning was done on Dataiku, to develop the final results, and lastly, Python was used again to run topic modeling on a certain subset of the data.

Lastly, latent Dirichlet allocation (LDA) is a critical method used in people analytics to abstract text from data. Lee & Kang (2017) used LDA to analyze Glassdoor reviews and determine which model was most important for attrition. Glassdoor captures a significant amount of textual data about each review, for which LDA is a common method of analysis. This study used three columns of textual data: Review title, pros, and cons. Analyzing these three columns separately is one way of understanding the topics people discuss and adding greater texture to the analysis. The method analyzes words that occur together in a corpus and then groups them into topics. Furthermore, most of the LDA research performed on Glassdoor has focused on culture because of MIT's dataset released in collaboration with the database. Therefore, this study is a cursory glance into textual data, which can be optimized in future research. The full code can be seen in the Appendix, with the full result of the LDA topic modeling in Appendix 2.

Findings

We ran an XGBoost and a random forest classifier on London and Singapore before the lockdowns started as a training set, with satisfaction as the dependent variable in need of classification. The random forest classifier was the clear winner, as it had an ROC AUC of about 87% for Singapore and 89% for London, which is considered very good for five classes where the default probability is about 20%, which means that the model works incredibly well. Removing extraneous variables such as job title, tenure, and status improved the model by about 20%, thus confirming observations from the qualitative analysis that these variables were not important to the model. Another important observation is that career, culture, and management were the top three variables according to both algorithms, while WLB and compensation were the bottom two variables in both models. This confirms the observation from the correlation matrix that these three variables are closely related to satisfaction, and that WLB and compensation are less important. However, without WLB and compensation, the AUC of the algorithm drops by 5% in both scenarios, thereby signalling that they provide some information when it comes to certain reviews. The random forest algorithm is able to classify reviews with ratings of 1, 2, and 5 with about 90% accuracy, but it struggles a bit with ratings of 3 and 4, which might reflect a construct validity, i.e., an issue whereby people express an opinion that may or may not reflect the same view.

Therefore, having decided that the Random Forest is the best model for the dataset, the study examined the importance variables for London and Singapore so that differences emerging between both cities could be studied. Culture predicts satisfaction a lot stronger for London at 31% than for Singapore at 23%. Culture is ranked second for both cities thereby demonstrating how they perceive the construct and how important that is to their satisfaction universally. The next phase of analysis involves applying the trained model to the post-lockdown test sets and determining how algorithms perform and how much employee perception changed after lockdown. The study then looks at these differences and analyzes the probable causes before undertaking the topic modeling exercise. Both models performed relatively well and saw a decrease of 10% in accuracy (77% for Singapore and 79% for London). While this is expected and shows the resilience of the model, the current study sets out to retrain it on the new set of data, to see if there are any changes in the model. The study can then analyze the variable weights to understand the difference in more concrete terms.

Table 3. Summary of the changes after using the random forest algorithm

		Difference in Ratings Pre- & Post-Lockdown	Difference in Random Forest Rank	Difference in Random Forest Weightage
Singapore	**Career**	**0.32**	**0**	-1%
	Culture	**0.22**	**1**	1%
	Management	**0.61**	**-1**	-7%
	Compensation	0.39	-1	3%
	WLB	0.13	1	4%
		Difference in Ratings Pre- & Post-Lockdown	Difference in Random Forest Rank	Difference in Weightage
London	**Career**	**0.22**	**1**	-4%
	Culture	**0.17**	**-1**	-7%
	Management	**-0.10**	**2**	5%
	Compensation	0.24	0	4%
	WLB	0.18	0	1%

Quantitative Findings

First, *career*, *culture* and *management* make up the bulk of the predictions, as mentioned earlier, at 80% ROC AUC. Therefore, the rankings only switched amongst them, in the top three and between compensation and *work-life balance* in the bottom two. It can be argued that WLB and *compensation* are specifically individual traits, while *culture* and *management* are firm-wide traits. *Culture* and *management* also seem to be complementary ideas, and one appears to do well at the expense of the other. *Career* also seems to take a back seat in these difficult times, as its importance decreases in London and in Singapore. It is also worth considering that the relationship is not linear; for example, a 0.61 increase in *management* did not result in a similar increase in *satisfaction* but a decrease in the assigned weight to *management*. Therefore, *management* and *culture*, i.e., the soft intangibles in an organization, seem to be the biggest determinants of employee *satisfaction* in times of crisis. Second, apart from the *management perception* in London, all ratings improved during this time of crisis in both cities. It seems there is an element of gratitude and gratefulness as well, since the weights for *compensation* and *work-life balance* increase during this time, possibly against the backdrop of widespread economic difficulties. Lastly, for both London and Singapore, the seemingly weakest factor is not statistically significant according to the t-test but is shown to have the greatest increase in weight by the random forest algorithm (*work-life balance* for Singapore and *management* for London). The results of the algorithm are shown in Appendix 1.

Key Takeaways

Firstly, *career* takes a backseat when the whole world is in crisis. With economic prospects looking bleak, career plans for most individuals are halted, as there is very little progression and no corresponding options for them to consider in other firms. Therefore, this is actually an opportunity for firms to reset benchmarks for job roles that had seen a lot of income escalation due to labor scarcity and attrition

Figure 2. New model of satisfaction

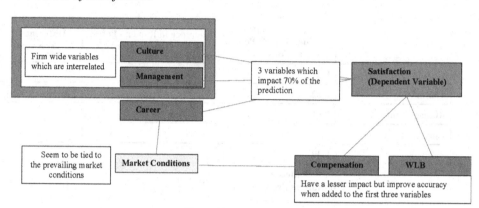

because of market demand. This can be important for roles where we see expectations for a lot of movement and promotion, such as management graduate programs or technology roles, which typically tend to be fast-moving and grow quickly.

Second, even though incomes and bonuses may have decreased significantly, the perceived compensation benefits have increased. This probably demonstrates that *compensation* is tied to wider market perceptions. This is an important opportunity to reset once again expectations about income and salary for employees. It is also a good time to perform salary benchmarking across the firm to trim labor costs significantly, which may have inflated since the last Great Financial Crisis in 2008. Third, *culture* and *management* act as vaccines against downturns, in that they are inversely related in weightage; additionally, *culture* is the second-most important factor for both London and Singapore. This can also mean that companies build up *culture*, which in times of crisis can be used as a resource to keep employees happy. This can also be a source of further research, as *culture* and managerial perception might lead to more resilient firms that emerge from a crisis quicker, thereby also having implications on their stock price.

Lastly, the organization is only as strong as its weakest component. In Singapore, WLB, which is the weakest-performing component, has seen the greatest jump in weightage, and *management* in London has seen a similar effect as well. This alludes to the marginal utility concept, where what is lacking becomes the most critical factor of satisfaction. Therefore, this means that for a company's HR, they need to constantly improve on their weakest elements, to ensure employee satisfaction is maximized. The model for *satisfaction* is thus dynamic and constantly changing to mirror circumstances in the world. Therefore, it seems that it constantly evolves as time goes on, as illustrated in Figure 2.

Qualitative Analysis by City

Singapore. First, Singapore has been closing the gap in terms of employee satisfaction and looks set to overtake London soon. This is good news for local policymakers, as they have been attempting to cultivate the city-state more as a financial hub, especially against the backdrop of Asia's spectacular economic rise. Management and compensation perceptions have already overtaken London, while perception gaps between career and culture have also narrowed.

However, in terms of *work-life balance*, Singapore has a long way to go to catch up with London, which in the time after lockdown has become more important, as the boundaries between work and home have blurred significantly. Analysts, project managers and technologists seem to have benefited most from lockdown, and it will be interesting to examine what specifically in their roles has caused such a stark increase in satisfaction.

The following are examples of quotes about *work-life balance* after lockdown:

Work-life balance—weekends work, overtime. Former analyst, 7/7/2020, worked at DBS for more than 3 years.

Work can be extremely overwhelming at times, due to pressing timelines and scarce resources. Current analyst, 11/10/2020, worked at UOB for more than 8 years.

Blame culture, long hours, bad organization structure. Current VP, 5/8/2020, worked at UOB for more than 3 years.

However, curiously, WLB does not come up as a topic in itself in the reviews in the post-lockdown dataset. Most reviews spoke about the company as whole, its internal environment or the trade-off between a comfortable job with a nice environment and strong career progression. In terms of pros, we see a large majority of people lauding management, and a smaller proportion talking about benefits and incentives. However, in the cons, all of the topics deal with culture. Therefore, it appears that even though WLB has experienced the most quantitative increase, culture is the most critical for Singaporean employees.

There might be an interesting dynamic at play whereby even though WLB is the pinch point for most employees, they focus on what causes the resource or time crunch, which is attributed to poor culture and a bloated bureaucracy. While there are no solutions proposed, it seems to be a problem that spans management, culture, and the specific role. This might be an industry-wide issue, because since 2008, government regulation has increased significantly in banking, thus threatening to drown the industry in red tape and regulation. This should be compared against other industries in Singapore to see if there are cultural elements at play. Singapore works the second-most hours in the world behind Japan (Today, 2019), and therefore even though employees might be upset with the current scenario, there does not seem to be any current alternative. If Singaporean policymakers want to make Singapore even more attractive as a business destination, they might need to address this situation via legislation, as done in 2006 where a compulsory five-day working week was formally instituted.

London. Most of London's indicators seem to be relatively constant over time, due to its increased maturity as a financial hub, relatively tepid markets in Europe as well as Brexit, which has compounded uncertainty. Satisfaction and all variables have increased except for management perception. There is an increased emphasis on culture, which seems to have served London well during this crisis, as we see it being one of the most important criteria. However, when the roles that have been affected negatively by COVID-19 are examined, such as the frontline roles associate, banker and vice president, it appears that the decline in culture is the biggest issue. The following are examples of quotes about management after lockdown:

Bank, toxic work environment, unpleasant. Banker, 26/9/2020, current employee at HSBC for more than one year.

Favoritism, lack of communication, divide between elderly and young. Banker, 7/9/2020, former employee at Barclays for more than 5 years.

Poor pay, bad culture, not interesting work. VP, 7/9/2020, former employee at Lloyds for more than a year.

What is particularly worrying about London's trends is the decline in management perceptions. While we hypothesize that these are linked with the government's handling of COVID-19, in order to gain an objective sense of why this is happening, we need to look at the outcome of topic modeling to understand the specifics in this instance:

Poor salaries, some very poor senior managers—very poor gender balance within senior management, very few men. Manager, 9/8/2020, current manager at HSBC

Promotions and bonuses are based on ticking boxes for diversity metrics, not on talent or hard work. Extremely frustrating to see very mediocre gameplayers take promotions. Director, 5/5/2020, undisclosed tenure at Lloyds

London experienced a wider variety of complaints, given its larger dataset. We observed that on average, for the five different topics per column that we looked at, the reviews were overwhelmingly negative. This is in stark contrast to Singapore, where the reviews were more muted but ratings were lower than London. This is indeed a peculiar behavior to examine, but it could be linked to the Asian understanding of not going against authority or bad-mouthing one's company, even in an anonymous capacity.

The importance of focusing on culture coming out in the pros becomes evident, and this also matches the random forest model, where culture plays a huge part in employee satisfaction. However, we can observe immense dissatisfaction with management here, which stems from appraisals and significant bureaucracy that employees have to navigate in a bank. Naturally, one could argue that this might have been increasingly hampered by the advent of COVID-19 and British banks not being able to digitize. Banks based in London are also a magnitude larger than Singaporean banks, with a longer history, and one can only imagine the complexity that scale and history bring. Furthermore, this level of scale is typically tied to difficulties and efficiencies in processes, many of which might seem highly unfair to an individual employee but work on the scale of such a large organization. With the digitization of finance and the onslaught of Fintech firms, banks need to be able to deal with changes with more agility and nimbleness than their employees are currently experiencing. Furthermore, if processes are driven by banking regulations etc., policymakers might want to consider how to keep London competitive, in order to retain it as a global financial hub. Lastly, further studies could be conducted on Glassdoor, to establish if all firms of a similar size (oil and gas, manufacturing firms) suffer from the same silo and red tape issues, or examine how they overcome these barriers.

CONCLUDING INSIGHTS

Hypothesis 1: The sub-ratings affect *satisfaction*. This is the biggest finding in this study. We have seen that sub-factors and variables are sufficient to create a fairly robust model, and the study has revealed that the priorities of employees in both cities change—and these changes reflect trends in the reviews.

Hypothesis 2: The ratings demonstrate the impact of the pandemic on satisfaction. We did not find mentions of the pandemic until we did a role-based analysis. Most of the employee criticisms focused on the size of the banks and how inefficient, difficult to navigate or stand out, and siloed they were. The lack of work-life balance for Singapore and poor management for London were anchored around these criticisms.

LIMITATIONS

Given the barriers that Glassdoor has put up, it will be difficult to do an end-to-end study across all Glassdoor data. Therefore, increasing the number of firms or looking at the biggest Finance Firms across the globe might be an improvement on this exploratory study. There are several personal or demographic data points that have been used to get clearer predictions such as marital status and years since the last promotion. These studies have been built around internal employee databases or other databases such as Indeed or LinkedIn, trying to combine these data sources might result in a more robust model to actually understand the entire schema of employee satisfaction.

CONCLUSION AND FUTURE RESEARCH

This is the most comprehensive end-to-end study on the finance industry based on data taken from Glassdoor. Most studies to date have looked at individual variables such as *culture* or *compensation*, without trying to understand the entire schema for satisfaction and employee priorities within the industry.

Management currently seems to be the most controversial construct and is one of the primary drivers of satisfaction and seems inversely proportionate to the weightage assigned by the algorithm to Culture; therefore, there might be issues of construct validity. Furthermore, in reviews employees would blame bureaucracy on a self-interested political management and at times, the prevailing corporate culture which shows that employees might see these two constructs as highly interrelated and not distinct. As a result, validating construct validity is critical and might highlight an issue with data collection in Glassdoor. It could be also a chicken and egg problem whereby management influences culture, and vice versa. Culture has been extensively studied before and how leadership affects it. However, there hasn't been a study on employee perception of management and how employees think Management is doing. Usually perception of Management been gleaned from corporate strategy and annual returns on but what specifically employees think of Management can perhaps only be inferred from employee turnover especially at senior levels.

There are also many studies on current government responses to COVID-19 in an attempt to understand best practices (Thomson, 2020). These can be overlaid with the cities in which reviews take place, to see how government responses affect management's responses to the pandemic – an important consideration when seeking to understand fully what influences management policies.

Given the interrelationship between management and culture, and how significantly it has increased during the pandemic at the expense of careers, this might be a critical factor in demonstrating how organizations bounce back from difficult times. It could be used as a measure of intra-organizational resilience, and it would be useful to see how finance performance returns after a downturn. Finally, it could be used to predict what banks will bounce back from the current recession against a performance measure such as revenue, profitability, or market capitalization.

We have seen WLB become more important in Singapore, but when we study the reviews, most of them identify red tape and bureaucracy as the key pinch points for organizations. Furthermore, there might be a direct relation between how processes and an increased workload influence employee well-being; however, this needs to be studied in greater detail with a sufficient literature review, since the problem is particularly pervasive in the finance industry.

REFERENCES

Avey, J. B., Nimnicht, J. L., & Graber Pigeon, N. (2010). Two field studies examining the association between positive psychological capital and employee performance. *Leadership and Organization Development Journal*, *31*(5), 384–401. doi:10.1108/01437731011056425

Berry, L. L., & Parasuraman, A. (1991). Marketing services: competing through quality. Academic Press.

Brunetto, Y., Teo, S., Shacklock, K., & Farr-Wharton, R. (2012). Emotional intelligence, job satisfaction, well-being and engagement: Explaining organisational commitment and turnover intentions in policing. *Human Resource Management Journal*, *22*(4), 428–441. doi:10.1111/j.1748-8583.2012.00198.x

Chandra, V. (2012). Work–life balance: Eastern and western perspectives. *International Journal of Human Resource Management*, *23*(5), 1040–1056. doi:10.1080/09585192.2012.651339

Chatham, M. (2018). *Glassdoor-review-scraper*. Retrieved from GitHub: https://github.com/Matthew-Chatham/glassdoor-review-scraper

Collins, C. J. (2003). Strategic Human Resource Practices, Top Management Team Social Networks, and Firm Performance: The Role of Human Resource Practices in Creating Organizational Competitive Advantage. *Academy of Management Journal*, 740–751.

Cronbach, L. J., & Meehl, P. E. (1955). Construct validity in psycho- logical tests. *Psychological Bulletin*, *52*(4), 281–302. doi:10.1037/h0040957 PMID:13245896

De Oliveira, E. L., Torres, J. M., Moreira, R. S., & de Lima, R. A. F. (2019). Absenteeism Prediction in Call Center Using Machine Learning Algorithms. *New Knowledge in Information Systems and Technologies*, 958–968. doi:10.1007/978-3-030-16181-1_90

DeKay, S. H. (2013). Peering through Glassdoor.com: What social media can tell us about employee satisfaction and engagement. In C. M Genest (Ed.), *Proceedings: CCI Conference on Corporate Communication 2013* (pp. 369-382). New York, NY: Corporate Communication International.

Financial Centre Futures. (2020). *The Global Financial Centres Index 28*. Long Finance.

Gelbard, R. R.-G., Ramon-Gonen, R., Carmeli, A., Bittmann, R. M., & Talyansky, R. (2018). Sentiment analysis in organizational work: Towards an ontology of people analytics. *Expert Systems: International Journal of Knowledge Engineering and Neural Networks*, *35*(5), e12289. Advance online publication. doi:10.1111/exsy.12289

Gupta, P. (2015). Human Resource Analytics in Indian Banking Sector. *IJISRT*.

Huselid, M. (1995). The Impact of Human Resource Management Practices on Turnover, Productivity, and Corporate Financial Performance. *Academy of Management Journal*, *38*, 635–672.

Jain, R., & Nayyar, A. (2018). Predicting Employee Attrition using XGBoost Machine Learning Approach. *2018 International Conference on System Modeling & Advancement in Research Trends*. 10.1109/SYSMART.2018.8746940

Karabarbounis, M., & Pinto, S. (2018). What Can We Learn from Online Wage Postings? Evidence from Glassdoor. *Economic Quarterly*, 173-189.

Lackey, N. R., & Sullivan, J. J. (2004). Culture, Leadership and Organization. *Sage (Atlanta, Ga.)*.

Landers, R. N., Brusso, R. C., & Auer, E. M. (2019). Crowdsourcing Job Satisfaction Data: Examining the Construct Validity of Glassdoor.com Ratings. *Personnel Assessment and Decisions*, *5*(3), 6. Advance online publication. doi:10.25035/pad.2019.03.006

Lee, J., & Kang, J. (2017). *A Study on Job Satisfaction Factors in Retention and Turnover Groups using Dominance Analysis and LDA Topic Modeling with Employee Reviews on Glassdoor.com. In International Conference on Information Systems (ICIS)*. AIS.

LiK.MaiF.ShenR.YanX. (2018). *Measuring Corporate Culture Using Machine Learning*. doi:10.2139/ssrn.3256608

Luo, N., Zhou, Y., & Shon, J. (2016). *Employee Satisfaction and Corporate Performance: Mining Employee Reviews on Glassdoor.com. In ICIS*. AIS.

Marler, J. H., & Boudreau, J. W. (2017). An evidence-based review of HR Analytics. *International Journal of Human Resource Management*, *28*(1), 3–26. doi:10.1080/09585192.2016.1244699

Mayo, A. (2018). Applying HR analytics to talent management. *Strategic HR Review*, *17*(5), 247–254. Advance online publication. doi:10.1108/SHR-08-2018-0072

McMurrer, D., & Bassi, L. (2007). Maximizing Your Return on People. *Harvard Business Review*. PMID:17348175

Page, C. (2020). *Microsoft Will Let Employees Work From Home Permanently: Report*. Retrieved from Forbes: https://www.forbes.com/sites/carlypage/2020/10/09/microsoft-will-let-employees-work-from-home-permanently/#5f3efa14172a

Reinicke, C. (2020). *Tesla's recent rally has pushed the stock up more than 200% this year. Here are CEO Elon Musk's most controversial tweets about the market*. Retrieved from Business Insider: https://markets.businessinsider.com/news/stocks/tesla-stock-elon-musks-most-controversial-tweets-about-market-twitter-2020-7-1029372168#

Ross, S. (2020). *Financial Services: Sizing the Sector in the Global Economy*. Academic Press.

Sands, E. G., & Bakthavachalam, V. (2019). *Ranking Countries and Industries by Tech, Data, and Business Skills*. Retrieved from Harvard Business Review: https://hbr.org/2019/05/ranking-countries-and-industries-by-tech-data-and-business-skills

Shikha, N., & Khera, D. (2018). Predictive Modelling of Employee Turnover in Indian IT Industry Using Machine Learning Techniques. *Journal for Decision Makers*.

Srivastava, D., & Nair, P. (2017). Employee Attrition Analysis Using Predictive Techniques. *Smart Innovation, Systems and Technologies*, 293–300.

Statista. (2020). *Projected coronavirus (COVID-19) impact index by industry and dimension*. Author.

Thompson, C. (2020). *What If Working From Home Goes on … Forever?* https://www.nytimes.com/interactive/2020/06/09/magazine/remote-work-covid.html

Today. (2019). *Singapore ranks 32 out of 40 for work-life balance, second most overworked city*. https://www.todayonline.com/singapore/singapore-ranks-32-out-40-work-life-balance-second-most-overworked-city

Uyeno, L. (2019). *An Empirical Analysis of Company Culture: Using Glassdoor Data to Measure the Impact of Culture and Employee Satisfaction on Performance*. Retrieved from Claremont College Scholarship: https://scholarship.claremont.edu/cmc_theses/2293/

Walford-Wright, G., & Scott-Jackson, W. (2018). Talent Rising; people analytics and technology driving talent acquisition strategy. *Strategic HR Review*, *17*(5), 226–233. Advance online publication. doi:10.1108/SHR-08-2018-0071

Wright, P., Gardner, T., Moynihan, L., & Allen, M. (2005). The relationship between HR practices and firm performance: Examining causal order. *Personnel Psychology*, 409–446.

Wright, P. M., Gardner, T. M., & Moynihan, L. M. (2003). The impact of HR practices on the performance of business units. *Human Resource Management Journal*, *13*(3), 409–446. doi:10.1111/j.1748-8583.2003.tb00096.x

Xu, H., Yu, Z., Yang, J., & Xiong, H. (2016). *Talent Circle Detection in Job Transition Networks*. ACM. doi:10.1145/2939672.2939732

Xu, T., Zhu, H., Zhu, C., Li, P., & Xiong, H. (2018). Measuring the Popularity of Job Skills in Recruitment Market: A Multi-Criteria Approach. In *The Thirty-Second AAAI Conference on Artificial Intelligence (AAAI-18)*. Association for the Advancement of Artificial Intelligence.

APPENDIX 1: DIAGRAMS WITH FINDING

Table 4. Algorithms run on Singapore Training Set

Algorithms Run on Singapore Training Set	Completed on 4/11/2020 3:45:23 PM		
Random Forest			
Score	86%	**Hierarchy of Factors**	
Rows	557	*1*	Career
Trees	100	*2*	Management
Depth	6	*3*	Culture
Min Samples	1	*4*	Compensation
Was Grid of Size	2	*5*	Balance
XG Boost			
Score	85%	**Hierachy of Factors**	
Rows	557	*1*	Management
Trees	1	*2*	Culture
Max Depth	3	*3*	Career
		4	Compensation
		5	Balance

Table 5. Algorithms run on London Training Set

Algorithms Run on London Training Set			
Random Forest			
Score	0.89	**Hierachy of Factors**	
Rows	1145	*1*	Culture
Trees	100	*2*	Career
Depth	6	*3*	Management
Min Samples	1	*4*	Compensation
Was Grid of Size	2	*5*	Balance
XG Boost			
Score	0.87	**Hierachy of Factors**	
Rows	1145	*1*	Career
Trees	2	*2*	Culture
Max Depth	3	*3*	Management
		4	Balance
		5	Compensation

Table 6. Random Forest Model retrained on Singapore post lockdown

Algorithms Run on Singapore Test Set		Completed on 7/11/2020 10:15:17 AM		
Random Forest				
Score	88%	Hierachy of Factors		
Rows	190	*1*		Career
Trees	100	*2*		Culture
Depth	6	*3*		Management
Min Samples	1	*4*		Balance
Was Grid of Size	2	*5*		Compensation

Table 7. Random Forest Model retrained on London post lockdown

Algorithms Run on London Test Set		Completed on 7/11/2020 1:07:01 PM		
Random Forest				
Score	89%	Hierachy of Factors		
Rows	320	*1*		Management
Trees	100	*2*		Culture
Depth	6	*3*		Career
Min Samples	1	*4*		Compensation
Was Grid of Size	2	*5*		Balance

APPENDIX 2: LDA RESULTS FOR SINGAPORE AND LONDON

Table 8. LDA analysis for Singapore across reviews, pros, and cons

Reviews	Company Focused	Environment	Satisfied in the Past
Score	**0.8**	**0.1**	**0.1**
Words	0.086*"start" + 0.078*"environ" + 0.075*"remuner" + 0.071*"job" + 0.059*"best" + 0.053*"nan" + 0.048*"okay" + 0.044*"like" + 0.037*"stabl" + 0.033*"lead"	0.156*"review" + 0.067*"time" + 0.058*"stress" + 0.051*"progress" + 0.046*"retir" + 0.036*"team" + 0.036*"nil" + 0.031*"technolog" + 0.030*"start" + 0.030*"remuner"	0.136*"poor" + 0.067*"local" + 0.062*"transform" + 0.059*"role" + 0.053*"bad" + 0.037*"long" + 0.029*"opportun" + 0.028*"high" + 0.028*"intern" + 0.028*"member"
Example 1	*Takes care of employees*	*Very helpful colleagues and branch members.*	*Good work-life balance*
Example 2	*Company with Good Benefits*	*Normal stable job with very little progression*	*Good place for a start.*
Pros	**Management Perception**	**Benefits**	**Incentives**
Score	**0.58**	**0.36**	**0.06**
Words	0.029*"transform" + 0.029*"term" + 0.029*"commit" + 0.029*"product" + 0.029*"slight" + 0.029*"scheme" + 0.029*"tech" + 0.029*"treat" + 0.029*"decis" + 0.028*"believ"	0.055*"strong" + 0.042*"rank" + 0.030*"month" + 0.030*"depend" + 0.030*"free" + 0.029*"home" + 0.029*"generous" + 0.029*"smooth" + 0.029*"allow" + 0.029*"plenti"	0.036*"okay" + 0.036*"enjoy" + 0.036*"hit" + 0.036*"collabor" + 0.036*"target" + 0.036*"meet" + 0.035*"exposur" + 0.035*"brand" + 0.033*"pro"
Example 1	*Lots of stakeholder management opportunities, too much sometimes, with too many inter-department politics and counter-productive work orders just retain headcounts. Sharpens your communication skills. However, culture does eat strategy for lunch!*	*Leave allowance, distance from home, benefits provided*	*Good remuneration if you hit the target*
Example 2	*Set and implement effective goals and leadership makes decisive actions*	*Great company benefits like insurance, Iflex, Leaves, Lucky had a good manager, and colleagues which is hard to find Big company, hence culture differs from team to teams Smooth workflow process as compared to other Banks due to its focus on digitalisation*	*Okay incentives and some managers are good*
Cons	**Transactional with no Cohesion**	**Crumbling under Bureaucracy**	**No Improvements or Risk Taking initiatives**
Score	0.88	0.05	0.06
Words	0.033*"experi" + 0.030*"foreign" + 0.024*"graduat" + 0.023*"branch" + 0.023*"littl" + 0.023*"volum" + 0.023*"demand" + 0.023*"best" + 0.023*"meet" + 0.022*"peer"	0.026*"design" + 0.026*"differ" + 0.024*"allow" + 0.018*"approv" + 0.017*"corpor" + 0.017*"roadshow" + 0.017*"junior" + 0.017*"mix" + 0.017*"global" + 0.017*"singapor"	0.023*"ask" + 0.018*"locat" + 0.018*"immedi" + 0.018*"level" + 0.018*"frustrat" + 0.018*"appreci" + 0.018*"higher" + 0.018*"will" + 0.018*"speak" + 0.018*"toxic"
Example 1	*All banking RMs in s'pore are glorified insurance agents. There is no sense of fiduciary duty towards the client because management expects you to push the product that generates the most revenue. You are expected to brainwash clients.*	*Bad corporate culture, tall hierarchical structure where you‚Äll need to get approvals from 5 different departments to get one thing approved. Salary is lower in comparison to other banks and incentives keep getting cut thus leading to minimal recognition for your hard work. An award winning digital bank with backward systems and processes which makes day to day work highly inefficient (and they penalise you‚Äôre by cutting your incentives if you make any errors) overall would not recommend.*	*Mid level management is not progressive and is not willing to risk for the fear of repercussion. Some projects are done for the sake of showing senior management that work is done with no actual improvement or benefits.*
Example 2	*No team cohesion/sense of belonging. Little to no mentorship; as a fresh graduate entering a graduate programme with no prior experience, there was a steep learning curve with no one to turn to if I had any questions as team members were usually too busy with their own work to explain inner workings/principles of existing frameworks.*	*Be prepared to stand 10 hours per day during roadshows, especially on weekends. Managers determine your activities by the number of customers you can get to sit down. Sometimes you can be approaching the public non-stop but get 0 sit-ins and your manager will just assume you're slacking in some corner. Managers always try to blame you for not closing sales and they cannot understand that not everyone wants endowment plans. Expect bosses to scold you like you're some filthy animal.*	*slower on system advance, less efficient on process*

Table 9. Summary of LDA analysis for London without the specific formulas

Reviews	Two Sides to a Coin	Unhappy With the Structure	Ambivalence	Defined by Their Seniority	Stable Dinosaur
Score	**0.6**	**0.1**	**0.1**	**0.1**	**0.1**
Example1	*Unique but painful*	*Toxic culture*	*Alright*	*Part time colleague*	*fair employer*
Example 2	*Supportive but lots of red tape*	*bureaucratic*	*Not enjoyable*	*Technology Entry-Level Graduate Programme*	*Civil Service of British banking transforms (painfully)*
Pros	**Good working Environment**	**Autonomy and Engagement**	**Good Benefits**	**Overperforming on all fronts**	**Superficial things**
Score	**0.8**	**0.05**	**0.05**	**0.05**	**0.05**
Example 1	*Supportive working environment with good benefits*	*Decent hours, internal mobility, flexibility*	*Family friendly Flexible benefits Generous pension Ability to work from home. Trying to do the right thing by it's customers (but after severe criticism, fines and massive PPI claim backs)*	*Great work life balance, Lots of internal opportunities, flexible, high performance*	*Big company well known brand*
Example2	*Set and implement effective goals and leadership makes decisive actions*	*The shares schemes You can build a good understanding of financial services if you apply yourself.*	*Good pension and benefits package. Good investment strategy in tools to help you do your job.*	*International Bank with good career development opportunities*	*Lovely people, nice offices good environment*
Cons	**Fossilized Organization**	**Working Culture was bad**	**Poor Senior Leadership and Management**	**Efficiency and Cost cutting**	**Unfair Appraisal systems**
Score	**0.2**	**0.2**	**0.2**	**0.3**	**0.3**
Example 1	*true innovation is impossible as too much bureaucracy*	*Extremely bureaucratic organisation with many management layers*	*Ruthless management in some areas but also some brilliant managers*	*Spent more time reporting than doing the actual work.*	*Clear favourites within internal hiring, making it difficult to feel motivated or want to progress internally. Historic bureaucracy, with onus on colleagues in finding solutions to eradicate it - a kind of workforce taxation. Top heavy.*
Example 2	*Very slim chance of progression Weekend working wasn‚Äôt too flexible The job has essentially become to feel like a glorified shop assistant role. But Lloyds will tell you your roles really important.*	*Constant stretches become meaningless. Toxic leaders survive way too long.*	*Senior leadership more concerned with politics than empowering their teams to making decisions. Too many silos, where people do not ultimately care about the success of the company, only their own personal success. Internal processes complicated and slow.*	*Focused on cost cutting atm*	*The salary increase yoy is really low, even for those listed as having a strong performance for the year*

APPENDIX 3: SCRAPING ALGORITHM

```
        main.py
----------
Matthew Chatham
June 6, 2018
Given a company's landing page on Glassdoor and an output filename, scrape the
following information about each employee review:
Review date
Employee position
Employee location
Employee status (current/former)
Review title
Employee years at company
Number of helpful votes
Pros text
Cons text
Advice to mgmttext
Ratings for each of 5 categories
Overall rating
'''

import time
import pandas as pd
from argparse import ArgumentParser
import argparse
import logging
import logging.config
from selenium import webdriver as wd
import selenium
import numpy as np
from schema import SCHEMA
import json
import urllib
import datetime as dt

start = time.time()

DEFAULT_URL = ('https://www.glassdoor.sg/Reviews/Lloyds-Banking-Group_London-
Reviews-EI_IE316191.0,20_IL.21,27_IM1035.htm?sort.sortType=RD&sort.
ascending=false&filter.iso3Language=eng&filter.employmentStatus=REGULAR&filter.
employmentStatus=PART_TIME')
```

```
parser = ArgumentParser()
parser.add_argument('-u', '--url',
                    help='URL of the company\'s Glassdoor landing page.',
                    default=DEFAULT_URL)
parser.add_argument('-f', '--file', default='lloyds_full.csv',
                    help='Output file.')
parser.add_argument('--headless', action='store_true',
                    help='Run Chrome in headless mode.')
parser.add_argument('--username', help='Email address used to sign in to GD.')
parser.add_argument('-p', '--password', help='Password to sign in to GD.')
parser.add_argument('-c', '--credentials', help='Credentials file')
parser.add_argument('-l', '--limit', default=660,
                    action='store', type=int, help='Max reviews to scrape')
parser.add_argument('--start_from_url', action='store_true',
                    help='Start scraping from the passed URL.')
parser.add_argument(
    '--max_date', help='Latest review date to scrape.\
    Only use this option with --start_from_url.\
    You also must have sorted Glassdoor reviews ASCENDING by date.',
    type=lambda s: dt.datetime.strptime(s, "%Y-%m-%d"))
parser.add_argument(
    '--min_date', help='Earliest review date to scrape.\
    Only use this option with --start_from_url.\
    You also must have sorted Glassdoor reviews DESCENDING by date.',
    type=lambda s: dt.datetime.strptime(s, "%Y-%m-%d"))
args = parser.parse_args()

if not args.start_from_url and (args.max_date or args.min_date):
    raise Exception(
        'Invalid argument combination:\
        No starting url passed, but max/min date specified.'
    )
elif args.max_date and args.min_date:
    raise Exception(
        'Invalid argument combination:\
        Both min_date and max_date specified.'
    )

if args.credentials:
    with open(args.credentials) as f:
        d = json.loads(f.read())
        args.username = d['username']
        args.password = d['password']
```

```
else:
    try:
        with open('secret.json') as f:
            d = json.loads(f.read())
            args.username = d['username']
            args.password = d['password']
    except FileNotFoundError:
        msg = 'Please provide Glassdoor credentials.\
        Credentials can be provided as a secret.json file in the working\
        directory, or passed at the command line using the --username and\
        --password flags.'
        raise Exception(msg)

logger = logging.getLogger(__name__)
logger.setLevel(logging.INFO)
ch = logging.StreamHandler()
ch.setLevel(logging.INFO)
logger.addHandler(ch)
formatter = logging.Formatter(
    '%(asctime)s %(levelname)s %(lineno)d\
    :%(filename)s(%(process)d) - %(message)s')
ch.setFormatter(formatter)

logging.getLogger('selenium').setLevel(logging.CRITICAL)
logging.getLogger('selenium').setLevel(logging.CRITICAL)

def scrape(field, review, author):

    def scrape_date(review):
        return review.find_element_by_tag_name(
            'time').get_attribute('datetime')

    def scrape_emp_title(review):
        if 'Anonymous Employee' not in review.text:
            try:
                res = author.find_element_by_class_name(
                    'authorJobTitle').text.split('-')[1]
            except Exception:
                logger.warning('Failed to scrape employee_title')
                res = np.nan
        else:
            res = np.nan
        return res
```

```
def scrape_location(review):
    if 'in' in review.text:
        try:
            res = author.find_element_by_class_name(
                'authorLocation').text
        except Exception:
            res = np.nan
    else:
        res = np.nan
    return res


def scrape_status(review):
    try:
        res = author.text.split('-')[0]
    except Exception:
        logger.warning('Failed to scrape employee_status')
        res = np.nan
    return res


def scrape_rev_title(review):
    return review.find_element_by_class_name('summary').text.strip('"')


def scrape_years(review):
    try:
        res = review.find_element_by_class_name('mainText').text.strip('"')
    except Exception:
        res = np.nan
    return res


def scrape_helpful(review):
    try:
        x = review.find_element_by_class_name(
            'helpfulReviews').text.strip('""')
        res = x[x.find("(")+1:x.find(")")]
    except Exception:
        res = 0
    return res


def scrape_pros(review):
    try:
        res = review.find_elements_by_class_name(
            'v2__EIReviewDetailsV2__fullWidth')[0].find_elements_by_tag_
name('p')[1].text
```

```
        except Exception:
            res = np.nan
        return res

    def scrape_cons(review):
        try:
            res = review.find_elements_by_class_name(
                'v2__EIReviewDetailsV2__fullWidth')[1].find_elements_by_tag_
name('p')[1].text
        except Exception:
            res = np.nan
        return res

    def scrape_advice(review):
        try:
            res = review.find_elements_by_class_name(
                'v2__EIReviewDetailsV2__fullWidth')[2].find_elements_by_tag_
name('p')[1].text
        except Exception:
            res = np.nan
        return res

    def scrape_overall_rating(review):
        return review.find_element_by_css_selector(
                "span.gdStars.gdRatings.common__StarStyles__gdStars > span >
span").get_attribute('title')

    def _scrape_subrating(i):
        try:
            ratings = review.find_element_by_class_name('gdStars')
            subratings = ratings.find_element_by_class_name(
                'subRatings').find_element_by_tag_name('ul')
            this_one = subratings.find_elements_by_tag_name('li')[i]
            res = this_one.find_element_by_class_name(
                'gdBars').get_attribute('title')
        except Exception:
            res = np.nan
        return res

    def scrape_work_life_balance(review):
        return _scrape_subrating(0)

    def scrape_culture_and_values(review):
```

```
        return _scrape_subrating(1)

    def scrape_career_opportunities(review):
        return _scrape_subrating(2)

    def scrape_comp_and_benefits(review):
        return _scrape_subrating(3)

    def scrape_senior_management(review):
        return _scrape_subrating(4)

    funcs = [
        scrape_date,
        scrape_emp_title,
        scrape_location,
        scrape_status,
        scrape_rev_title,
        scrape_years,
        scrape_helpful,
        scrape_pros,
        scrape_cons,
        scrape_advice,
        scrape_overall_rating,
        scrape_work_life_balance,
        scrape_culture_and_values,
        scrape_career_opportunities,
        scrape_comp_and_benefits,
        scrape_senior_management
    ]

    fdict = dict((s, f) for (s, f) in zip(SCHEMA, funcs))

    return fdict[field](review)


def extract_from_page():

    def is_featured(review):
        try:
            review.find_element_by_class_name('featuredFlag')
            return True
        except selenium.common.exceptions.NoSuchElementException:
            return False
```

```
def extract_review(review):
    author = review.find_element_by_class_name('authorInfo')
    res = {}
    # import pdb;pdb.set_trace()
    for field in SCHEMA:
        res[field] = scrape(field, review, author)

    assert set(res.keys()) == set(SCHEMA)
    return res

logger.info(f'Extracting reviews from page {page[0]}')

res = pd.DataFrame([], columns=SCHEMA)

reviews = browser.find_elements_by_class_name('empReview')

if(len(reviews)== 0):
    logger.info('No more Review!')
    date_limit_reached[0] = True

logger.info(f'Found {len(reviews)} reviews on page {page[0]}')

for review in reviews:
    if not is_featured(review):
        data = extract_review(review)
        logger.info(f'Scraped data for "{data["review_title"]}"\
({data["date"]})')
        res.loc[idx[0]] = data
    else:
        logger.info('Discarding a featured review')
    idx[0] = idx[0] + 1

if args.max_date and \
    (pd.to_datetime(res['date'], errors='coerce', format='%m%d%Y').max() >
args.max_date) or \
        args.min_date and \
        (pd.to_datetime(res['date'], errors='coerce', format='%m%d%Y').
min() < args.min_date):
    logger.info('Date limit reached, ending process')
    date_limit_reached[0] = True

    return res
```

```python
def more_pages():
    next_ = browser.find_element_by_class_name('pagination__PaginationStyle__
next')
    try:
        next_.find_element_by_tag_name('a')
        return True
    except selenium.common.exceptions.NoSuchElementException:
        return False


def go_to_next_page():
    logger.info(f'Going to page {page[0] + 1}')
    next_ = browser.find_element_by_class_name(
        'pagination__PaginationStyle__next').find_element_by_tag_name('a')
    browser.get(next_.get_attribute('href'))
    time.sleep(15)
    page[0] = page[0] + 1


def no_reviews():
    return False
    # TODO: Find a company with no reviews to test on

"""
def navigate_to_reviews():
    logger.info('Navigating to company reviews')

    browser.get(args.url)
    time.sleep(1)

    if no_reviews():
        logger.info('No reviews to scrape. Bailing!')
        return False

    reviews_cell = browser.find_element_by_class_name("eiCell.cell.reviews.
active")
    reviews_path = reviews_cell.get_attribute('href')
    browser.get(reviews_path)
    time.sleep(1)

    return True
"""

def sign_in():
    logger.info(f'Signing in to {args.username}')
```

```python
    url = 'https://www.glassdoor.com/profile/login_input.htm'
    browser.get(url)

    # import pdb;pdb.set_trace()

    email_field = browser.find_element_by_name('username')
    password_field = browser.find_element_by_name('password')
    submit_btn = browser.find_element_by_xpath('//button[@type="submit"]')

    email_field.send_keys(args.username)
    password_field.send_keys(args.password)
    submit_btn.click()

    time.sleep(25)

def get_browser():
    logger.info('Configuring browser')
    chrome_options = wd.ChromeOptions()
    if args.headless:
        chrome_options.add_argument('--headless')
    chrome_options.add_argument('log-level=3')
    browser = wd.Chrome(options=chrome_options)
    return browser

def get_current_page():
    logger.info('Getting current page number')
    paging_control = browser.find_element_by_class_name('pagination__Pagina-
tionStyle__page.pagination__PaginationStyle__current')
    """
    current = int(paging_control.find_element_by_xpath(
        '//ul//li[contains\
        (concat(\' \',normalize-space(@class),\' \'),\' current \')]\
        //span[contains(concat(\' \',\
        normalize-space(@class),\' \'),\' disabled \')]')
        .text.replace(',', ''))
    """
    current = int(paging_control.find_element_by_tag_name('a').text)
    return current

def verify_date_sorting():
    logger.info('Date limit specified, verifying date sorting')
    ascending = urllib.parse.parse_qs(
        args.url)['sort.ascending'] == ['true']
```

```python
        if args.min_date and ascending:
            raise Exception(
                'min_date required reviews to be sorted DESCENDING by date.')
        elif args.max_date and not ascending:
            raise Exception(
                'max_date requires reviews to be sorted ASCENDING by date.')

browser = get_browser()
page = [1]
idx = [0]
date_limit_reached = [False]

def main():

    logger.info(f'Scraping up to {args.limit} reviews.')

    res = pd.DataFrame([], columns=SCHEMA)

    sign_in()
    if args.max_date or args.min_date:
        verify_date_sorting()
        browser.get(args.url)
        page[0] = get_current_page()
        logger.info(f'Starting from page {page[0]:,}.')
        time.sleep(1)
    else:
        browser.get(args.url)
        page[0] = get_current_page()
        logger.info(f'Starting from page {page[0]:,}.')
        time.sleep(1)

    reviews_df = extract_from_page()
    res = res.append(reviews_df)

    # import pdb;pdb.set_trace()

    while more_pages() and\
            len(res) < args.limit and\
            not date_limit_reached[0]:
        go_to_next_page()
        reviews_df = extract_from_page()
        res = res.append(reviews_df)
```

```
    logger.info(f'Writing {len(res)} reviews to file {args.file}')
    res.to_csv(args.file, index=False, encoding='utf-8')

    end = time.time()
    logger.info(f'Finished in {end - start} seconds')
```

Appendix 2: LDA Algorithm
```
import pandas as pd
import os
import gensim
from gensim import models
from gensim.utils import simple_preprocess
from gensim.parsing.preprocessing import STOPWORDS
from gensim.models.coherencemodel import CoherenceModel
from nltk.stem import WordNetLemmatizer, SnowballStemmer
import numpy as np
import nltk
from langdetect import detect
from langdetect.lang_detect_exception import LangDetectException
import re
import ssl
import matplotlib.pyplot as plt
from operator import itemgetter

# Random seed.
np.random.seed(2018)

# Creating certificate to download 'wordnet' nltk package.
try:
    _create_unverified_https_context = ssl._create_unverified_context
except AttributeError:
    pass
else:
    ssl._create_default_https_context = _create_unverified_https_context
nltk.download('wordnet')

# Reading the data.
os.chdir('/Users/shivarai/Desktop/Thesis/Coding')
data = pd.read_csv('roles.csv', index_col=0)
stemmer = SnowballStemmer('english')

data = data[['cons']]
data.columns = ['content']
```

```
# Lemmatizer and stemmer
def lemmatize_stemming(text):
    return stemmer.stem(WordNetLemmatizer().lemmatize(text, pos='v'))


# Preproccess the text.
def preprocess(text):
    result = []
    for token in simple_preprocess(text):
        if token not in STOPWORDS and len(token) > 2:
            result.append(lemmatize_stemming(token))
    return result


def remove_spec_chars(text):
    text = re.sub('[^A-Za-z0-9]+', ' ', text)
    return text

# Cleaning up the data.
data['content'] = data['content'].astype(str)

# Cleaning up the text.
# data = data[data['brand/category'] == 'Luxury']
data['content'] = data['content'].apply(lambda x: remove_spec_chars(x))

# Preprocessing text.
# Creating a dictionary containing times a word appears in dataset.
data['content'] = data['content'].apply(lambda x: preprocess(x))
dictionary = gensim.corpora.Dictionary(data['content'])
print('Dict len: ', len(dictionary))

for keys,values in dictionary.items():
    print(keys)
    print(values)

# Filtering dictionary.
num_below = 2  # remove tokens that appear in less than threshold.
num_above = 0.7  # remove tokens that appear in more than 50% of documents.
dictionary.filter_extremes(no_below=num_below, no_above=num_above)
print('Dict len: ', len(dictionary))
#remove specific words here

keys_to_remove = ["good", "place", "great", "compani", "bank", "work", "of-
```

```
fic", "ocbc", "busi", "corpor", "uob", "dbs"]

for key in keys_to_remove:
  dictionary.filter_tokens(bad_ids=[dictionary.token2id[key]])

# Bag of words corpus reporting how many
# words and how many times those words appear.
bow_corpus = [dictionary.doc2bow(doc) for doc in data['content']]

# Creating tf_idf model with words from bow_corpus.
tf_idf = models.TfidfModel(bow_corpus)
corpus_tfidf = tf_idf[bow_corpus]

# Function to compute the coherence values of the number of topics.
def compute_coherence_values(dictionary, corpus, texts, limit, start=1,
step=1):
    coherence_values = []
    model_list = []
    for num_topics in range(start, limit, step):
        model = gensim.models.LdaMulticore(corpus=corpus, id2word=dictionary,
num_topics=num_topics)
        model_list.append(model)
        coherencemodel = CoherenceModel(model=model, texts=texts,
dictionary=dictionary, coherence='c_v')
        coherence_values.append(coherencemodel.get_coherence())
    return model_list, coherence_values

# computing the coherence and ploting the coherence.
mod_list, coh_vals = compute_coherence_values(dictionary, bow_corpus,
data['content'], 10)
x_range = range(1, 10)
plt.plot(x_range, coh_vals)
plt.xlabel("Num Topics")
plt.ylabel("Coherence score")
plt.legend("coherence_values", loc='best')
plt.show()
# -------------------------------------------------------------------

# Creating BOW model with the optimal number of topics.
lda_model = gensim.models.LdaMulticore(bow_corpus, num_topics=3,
 id2word=dictionary,
                                        passes=2, workers=2)
```

271

```
for index, topic in lda_model.print_topics(-1):
    print('LDA model Topic: {} \nWords: {}'.format(index, topic))

# Creating TF-IDF model with the optimal number of topics.
tfidf_model = gensim.models.LdaMulticore(corpus_tfidf, num_topics=2,
id2word=dictionary,
                                         passes=3, workers=4)

for index, topic in tfidf_model.print_topics(-1):
    print('TFIDF model Topic: {} \nWords: {}'.format(index, topic))

# --------------------------------------------------------------------

for index, score in sorted(lda_model[bow_corpus[10]], key=lambda tup:
-1*tup[1]):
    print("\nScore: {}\t \nTopic: {}".format(score, lda_model.print_
topic(index, 10)))


# Create Dataframe with the topics and scores. make the topic_dr "score" col-
umn as a float
topic_dr = pd.DataFrame(columns=['Topic', 'Score'])
for i in range(0, len(bow_corpus)):
    topic = max(lda_model[bow_corpus[i]], key=itemgetter(1))[0]
    score = max(lda_model[bow_corpus[i]], key=itemgetter(1))[1]
    new_df = pd.DataFrame([[topic, score]], columns=['Topic', 'Score'])
    topic_dr = topic_dr.append(new_df)

# Cleaning topic df and merging with data.
topic_dr = topic_dr.reset_index()
topic_dr = topic_dr.drop(['index'], axis=1)
topic_dr['Topic'].value_counts()

# Creating final dataset.
data_final = data.reset_index()
##data_final = data_final.drop(['date'], axis=1)
data_final = data_final.join(topic_dr, how='left')
```

Chapter 12
Undergraduate Computer Science Capstone Projects:
Experiences and Examples in Data Science

Li Chen

University of the District of Columbia, USA

ABSTRACT

The CS&IT senior capstone project at the University of the District of Columbia has three components: 1) Senior Seminar, 2) Senior Project I, and 3) Senior Project II. The purpose of Senior Seminar (one credit) is to expand the students' scope of knowledge through reading cutting-edge materials in CS&IT. Students in the class often learn from each other, while the instructor organizes talks given by professors at the university as well as industry professionals. Students give formal presentations as their final exam. The main purpose of Senior Project I (two credits) is to teach students how to start a research project. Students are asked to complete a simple research proposal after doing background research to select a research project. The final report is a short report. In Senior Project II (three credits), many students choose to continue the project Senior Project I. For this course, students complete a well-written report ranging from 20 to 25 pages. This paper explains how we teach these courses and include five examples in data science.

INTRODUCTION

The senior capstone project in the Department of Computer Science and Information Technology at the University of the District of Columbia includes three components: (1) Senior Seminar, (2) Senior Project I, and (3) Senior Project II. As an instructor, I have been teaching these classes for more than 10 years. In this article, I would like to share some of my personal experience in teaching these classes. The purpose of Senior Seminar (one credit) is to enhance the students' scope of knowledge through reading cutting-edge materials in CS&IT. Students in the class often learn from each other via in-class discussion and presentation, while the instructor organizes talks given by professors at the university and industry professionals. Students give formal presentations as their final exam. The main purpose of Senior Proj-

DOI: 10.4018/978-1-7998-9016-4.ch012

ect I (two credits) is to teach students how to start a research project. Students are asked to complete a simple research proposal after doing background research to select a research project. The final report is a short report of 8-10 pages in length. After Senior Project I, we encourage students to take Senior Project II (three credits) the subsequent semester. Many students choose to continue the project they began in Senior Project I, and, if such is the case, students are asked to update their proposal. Otherwise, students are given the opportunity to change their project topic. For this course, students are usually asked to complete a well-written report ranging from 20-25 pages. The following includes examples of projects we received in previous years for review and comment in order to make future improvements. In recent years, the Senior Seminar class has been merged into the Senior Project I class. However, the contents and materials are kept the same in my classes.

BASIC COMPONENTS OF UDC-CSIT CAPSTONE PROJECTS

In this section, we will describe the objectives and functions of the three course components of our capstone project: (1) Senior Seminar, (2) Senior Project I, and (3) Senior Project II.

The Senior Seminar Class

There are three primary objectives for the Senior Seminar: 1) Learn cutting-edge technology in CS&IT, 2) Refine written communication skills, and, most importantly, 3) Develop public speaking skills.

Course grading is based on: 1) In-class presentations (30%), 2) Writing (30%), and 3) Participation (40%). The most important aspect of the course is the 10–15-minute final presentation.

In the first two to three weeks, the instructor covers general areas of CS&IT, focusing on topics that may be useful to students in their project interests. Students are then divided into groups based on their interests and encouraged to learn about various projects.

In the Spring Semester 2020, students were interested in mobile computing, web programming, cognitive security, scalable energy with AI, and robotics. (I always said that this class mainly talk about "other's research work." It is not necessary to make a close connection to your own research in the senior project class.)

In the following weeks, instructors usually choose to give formal presentations on certain popular topics in computer science. For instance, for the previous two semesters, I have given talks on data science. We also invite other faculty members and industry professionals to give talks. Throughout the semester, there are usually 2-3 faculty members and two industry professionals who come and speak to the class.

To improve their presentation skills, students are asked for suggestions on topics they are interested in and video examples of good presentations are posted to Blackboard. Students are also assigned to watch related YouTube videos and write summary essays as homework.

Student are asked to produce a one-page PPT with their title and abstract during class and for the midterm, each student is asked to give a 3–5-minute presentation of their topic for practice. In previous years, there was only one final presentation required. However, this "rehearsal" is a great opportunity for students to receive feedback on their presentation before their final and gain more public speaking experience.

For the final project, students prepare 10-12 PPT slides to give as a formal presentation.

The Senior Project I Class

The course description for Senior Project I is as follows: Senior Project I consists of the development, design, programming, documentation, and testing of a significant system problem. The project may be a team or individual effort with 3-6 hours laboratory.

In this class, students consider three topics for research or development. They are encouraged to select topics related to their future career interests. The goal of this project is to find a solution to an existing problem in the area, so students are asked to do some background research, along with consult their peers and instructors, on which topics they will study. Once they have some ideas, they should begin their research by reading previous literature.

Students write sample paragraphs describing the three topics, which the instructor then evaluates. The instructor gives comments and suggestions for how to pursue the topic and how difficult it may be. The difference between this course and the Senior Seminar is that here, students are encouraged to pursue their own research with some guidance. The Senior Seminar is more focused on learning existing technology and theories.

A milestone of Senior Project I is to write a simple proposal. A rubric (called the Student Research Information Sheet) is distributed with requirements for the proposal and questions for the students to answer. The course is designed to guide students through the beginning stages of how to start their research.

To make it clear, the main goal of this class is to teach student how to start to do research. Unlike the Senior Project II class, students need to work hard on their research.

Based on personal interests and level of previous knowledge, a senior student can focus on research, development, or review/survey in their projects.

- **Research-oriented projects:** Project includes researching previous work along with a prototype for testing software systems.
- **Development-oriented projects:** Project must include software development. It should also be accompanied by around 500 lines of code.
- **Review/survey-oriented projects:** Project includes reading research/development articles, writing a review/survey, and completing simulation software to support your survey.

In summary, for measurability, students are usually required to complete the following tasks:

1. Read 2-3 articles in CS&IT research papers.
2. Select a project and submit a proposal.
3. Submit a final written document for the project (8 pages).

The Senior Project II Class

Senior Project II is a continuation of Senior Project I. In this class, students are supposed to revise the proposal they wrote for Senior Project I or select a new topic. Before doing this, we first have an assessment called the Student Research Information Sheet (for Senior Project II students).

Student Research Information Sheet (for Senior Project II students)

Please answer all questions and bring it to class this Friday.

1. In your Senior Project I class, what was your research topic? Please attach your report if you can.

2. Do you like your SPI research and outcomes? Do you want to continue with similar research?

3. If you choose to start a new project, what research topic(s) do you have in mind?

4. What is the best description for your short-term goals after graduation?

a) Find a job b) Apply for MS in CS&IT c) Graduate School in a different field

5. What kind of CS jobs will you apply for if your goal is to find a job?

6. What area(s) will you study if your goal is to apply to graduate school?

Students are encouraged to find a professor in the department to serve as their mentor for the class. The general completion requirements, in additional to the requirements for Senior Project I, are as follows:

1. Continue to read CS&IT research papers and refine the research proposal,
2. Select a project and submit a full proposal if the student wishes to change topics,
3. Post research achievements in a research showcase, and
4. Submit a final written document of the project (a formal report of at least 20-25 pages).

The projects can still be based on research, development, or review/survey. However, more is required of the student.

- Research-oriented projects: Project includes researching previous work along with a prototype for testing software systems. The finished research report should be of a good quality. It is encouraged to be submitted to conferences or even journals.
- Development-oriented projects: Project includes a product, which should be practical and useful in solving real world problems. Code should be around 1000-1500 lines.
- Review/survey-oriented projects: Project includes reading research/development articles and writing a review/survey, which should contain some data analysis analytics or simulations to support the students' opinion of the survey. This survey should be of a publishable quality.

If a student has a mentor, he or she is encouraged to write joint papers with the mentor and to submit to conferences and journals. For the final submission, students should provide a hard copy of a bound report.

In this class, group projects are allowed, but each student must submit his or her own final report (unless the group submits their work to a local or national conference prior to the class final due date). The group size is at most three students.

TEACHING EXPERIENCES AND TEACHING EXAMPLES

In this section, we share some of our experiences in teaching Senior Projects I & II.

How to Choose a Project

We usually spend 3-4 weeks discussing how to choose the right project to research. Personal interests should be the priority, but the student may also consider his/her career goals so that their effort and time spent on the senior project can help them in their next steps.

For instance, if a student wishes to find a job in cyber-security immediately after graduation, then the student should select a project in this area. If a student wishes to continue with a graduate degree, then he/she could select a more theoretical topic. The challenge for the instructor is guiding them in the right direction. We ask students to meet with professors who specialize in areas of their interest. We also encourage students to work with different computer languages, especially if their goal is to work in industry in order to broaden their skills. (Chen, 2011)

The following is a list of things to consider for students in Senior Project I related to how to select a research topic and some basic steps for completing the project.

1.   Choose a topic that is "new" or
2.   Choose a topic that is "deep"
3.   Background information (Wikipedia, YouTube, Google Scholar)
4.   Read papers/materials (3 papers, one short, one long, etc.)
5.   Write a proposal (midterm, 2 pages)
6.   Do research
7.   Write final report (8 pages double spaced)

The following directions were given to our Senior Project I & II students:

How to obtain a research/development idea?

- *Ideas can come from application areas (data or other related materials)*
- *Even though you have made your focus research, you can also think about which companies you would like to work for and what products they make*
- *You can think about an application area where you would want to work*
- *You might want to talk to your parents, relatives, or peers to find out if there's a challenge they have faced in a field (healthcare, financial, IT industries) that may interest you*
- *Read survey papers to find some unsolved problems and questions you would like to answer*

Instructor's Demo Samples for Starting a Research Project

A Teaching Example during class time: When some students ask how they start their research. The instructor asked to use a life-example to show what should one to do in different stages, especially how to start a research project. When one student provided a topic on Snapchat, the student probably wanted to code some applications relates to Snapchat. The instructor showed the following demo to the class.

How do I start a research project?

Use Snapchat as an example:

1.   What is Snapchat? The first question is to know what Snapchat is.

    a.   Check Wikipedia https://en.wikipedia.org/wiki/Snapchat

*"**Snapchat** is an image messaging and multimedia mobile application created by Evan Spiegel, Bobby Murphy, and Reggie Brown, former students at Stanford University, and developed by Snap Inc., originally Snapchat Inc."*

b. Google it –snapchat website: not much information I can immediately use. https://scan.snapchat.com/

c.   Search on Youtube:

What is Snapchat? https://www.youtube.com/watch?v=ykGXIQAHLnA Evan Speigel talks about Snapchat & the FOUNDING of Snapchat https://www.youtube.com/watch?v=Bwdz99zFtO4

2.   How to use Snapchat

Connecting to the previous search especially the information obtained from last three.

HOW TO USE SNAPCHAT FOR BEGINNERS – https://www.youtube.com/watch?v=Bwdz99zFtO4

3.   Research: How do we improve Snapchat or how do we do research using Snapchat

    a.   The most important thing is "how do I find a valuable problem for my project?"
    b.   This means when using your time and other resources, you are not going to regret for your time spent in the future. The reasons could be:
        i.   It is something I love it.
        ii.   It is something I needed it for my job hunting.
        iii.   It is something my parents asked.
        iv.   It is something I wanted.
        v.   It is something may be worthwhile for my future.
        vi.   Just want to finish this class.
    c.   For specific problems related to Snapchat: The communication with students What is it? What type of projects you are interested?

Example 1: 10 sec video limits with Snapchat are not enough for me, I like to do Apps for extending the video capture to 1 min.

i.   To determine my knowledge level: Can I do it?
ii.   I need to do investigation how I access the software system of Snapchat for development users. (e.g. open source, functions I can call.)
iii. I need to find examples of the existing code that can help me to learn and implement (StackFlow. com).

Example 2: I do not want to change Snapchat, but I want to use Snapchat's existing functions including their data for my research.

i.   How many people use Snapchat today and history?
ii.   Their locations
iii. Gender
iv.   Storage usage
v.   Age group distributions
vi.   Day, month, year, predication
vii. Statistics & visualization
viii. Advanced issues: AI, NN, and tell other industry the value of Snapchat.

Example 3: Use Snapchat with other software system such as Google-map

PROPOSAL AND REPORT WRITINGS

In this section, we discuss how we taught proposal and final report writing. Our focus is on the final report, where we request the students to write a formal final report with 25 pages. For the proposal of the project, due to the fact that students often change their minds to switch from a topic to another, we just ask them to prepare a short and informal proposal for the new topic.

Write a Short Proposal and Develop a Rough Plan

In short, a proposal needs to answer the three questions about the project: "Why," "What," and "How?" Why do you like to solve this problem? What should it do? How do you solve this problem?

In writing a proposal of the project, it should contain five main components plus references.

1.   The first part is to state the problem a student wants to solve including some outcomes and goals of the project.
2.   The second part is to do a short literature review that discusses what has been done in the past. Or it is a totally new idea.
3.   The third part is to provide some information about how to solve this proposed problem. This part is kind of hard since students might be very new to research and does not have enough experience to well explain how they going to solve this problem. However, keep in mind to record the strategy

of problem solving is important of learning. This part could be just rough planning with some short paragraphs.

4. The fourth part discusses the expected outcomes and contributions of the project. We always expect the contributions is to general knowledge or the software product that could serve the public. Students should predict what they can get in the project. Again, like above (3), this part is very hard to write before completion of the project for an undergraduate student.

5. The fifth part of the proposal is to let the instructor know timeline of the project. The timeline is to provide some tangible and measurable, feasible estimation of the time to complete the project. We always allow students to adjust their timeline table.

6. The last part is the short list of references.

A template we have provided to student for the proposal of the senior projects. They are asked to submit a rough proposal for Senior Project I and then modify it in Senior Project II.

RESEARCH PROPOSAL TEMPLATE

Statement the Problem (Abstract): Problem to solve including project goals.

Literature review (Introduction): What has been done in the past?

Aims and Solving Strategy (Planning): How do you solve this problem?

Expected Outcomes: What you can get?

Timeline: Tell us when you can reach some milestones of the project?

References: (Papers you have cited in your proposal)

When preparing doing research you need to state a problem to solve. In the beginning, you are asked to choose three possible things you like to do research with. This is called the research area, aspect, or topic. Then you are asked to find some research papers related to one of the research topics.

- *A research proposal is to provide details for the research you are going to complete. It is not necessary you write each step how you do. But you need to give some descriptions to the following information:*
- *Literature review: such as background information. What is already known or unknown? (Set the scene.)*
- *Aims and Solving Strategy: You can restate your problem here. What do you want to know, prove, demonstrate, analyze, test, investigate or examine? List your project aims in a logical sequence.*
- *Expected Outcomes: How do you anticipate you will achieve these aims? Expected outcomes, significance or rationale Why is it important? What do you expect it will deliver?*

- *You can also add why the project is important. Highlight the benefits, positive expected outcomes, or innovative applications of knowledge. Timetable Rough for completing each important tasks (milestones) of the project.*

Write a Formal Report of the Project

We wrote a short technical article on how to write a project report (Chen, 2020). It is different from a template of the format of a project report. In this article, we listed five essential parts for a typical research report. They are abstract, introduction, research, summary, and references. Except abstract and references, the others can be split into multiple sections or chapters depending on the length of your report or article including thesis and dissertations.

Part 0: Abstract

This part only contains some statements about your research or project. Could be very brief less than 100 words. Or, it also could be 500-700 words if you write a thesis or dissertation. Your sentence should be clear enough especially when you state what you have done or what main research contributions you have made.

Part 1: Introduction

This part could be just one section/chapter or multiple sections/chapters.

It contains the brief statements about your paper or article that is related to some broad areas. It should also include augments, the problem you plan to solve, and/or aim of your goal as well as the purpose of your project/paper/research.

After the that, it should include two sub-components: Literature review and Concepts. These can be separated into different chapters/sections.

Literature review is to provide information for readers about the history and the cutting age research related to your report/project.

The component relating to Concepts is to provide readers the technological level of knowledge preparation in order to let them to understand of your report. This section must be general enough to general reader. If you are going to use deep knowledge, you should put them in the research part.

Part 2: Research Part

This part is at the center of your report. It contains your work in this report/project. Depends on the length of your report. If it is a capstone project, a thesis, or dissertation, you should include:

1. Design and planning of your project/research,
2. Core Research,
3. Analysis/verification of your result, and
4. Application.

If it is just for a research paper, you might not need the components for design and planning. You might only need (2) and (3). Sometimes, you also need to add a section or more sections/chapters for (4).

Design/Planning: Give clear statement about what problems you are going to solve, and what technical tools that you are going to use. How much time you have planned to solve the problem? This component is usually your research proposal. It is not necessary for research paper submission. But it is good for research report. If you are doing a software design, you can put your design here including flow-charts or use-cases here.

Core Research: Put your research work here including formula derivation, algorithm design. Your implementation. Simple examples or small applications here. Your main research results. It could be multiple sections or chapters.

Analysis: How good is your research? It should include some examples and Comparisons to other's methods. How about the marketing/user response?

Application: This part can be put into Analysis depends on your project application is small or big. You could have a separated section/chapter for your application. It could include Lab data or Real data testing.

Part 3: Conclusion/Summary

You usually tell reader what you did. It contains similar materials you presented in the abstract. It also should include what you like to do next? If you are writing a survey, you may need to put your comments on this topic thoroughly. In such a case, this part might be long.

The last part is cited references.

The Template for Senior Project Final Reports

Senior Project Final Report Template

Cover page: Title and Author

Abstract: 200 words

Table of Contents

Chapters

1. Introduction Section: Big scope related to a whole research/development area

2. Background Section: Narrow to the knowledge to your project

3. Research/Result section (s) (I-III): Your research path and theoretical results

4. Applications: How to use your findings to real World problems and actual use

5. Conclusion/Discussion/Future work:

Figure 1. A figure in Student K's Senior Project II

6. *References: Cited papers and sources.*

SENIOR PROJECT EXAMPLES

Examples for Earlier Students: Some remarkable examples for our earlier students. Student T used C# for a software system, and he found his job immediately after his graduation. A student used Java for advising system, and he was accepted in a MS program in John Hopkins University. Two students whose first name were Travis did excellent work (now they are IT leaders in their companies). Student Gorbachev did elliptical curve cryptography, then he was accepted in PhD program in Catholic University. Student Moeti went to Google and he is now a PhD student in Virginia Tech.

We now talk about recent examples.

Example 2: Recent Student K in Senior Project II in 2017. His topic was "iCloud with Snapchat using IOSX functions." He was developing Mobile Computing for Snapchat to extend the time limits for live videos. I instructed him to consider developing a general function that can allow other developers to use it to link their mobile applications to Snapchat. He did excellent job. His software was downloaded 500+ times.

Example 3: Student Khoi in Senior Project I who had some training classes in Stanford online courses in data science. He wanted to do natural language analysis using Python and its data science tool. I examined him and found out that he was very capable. So, I just gave him a lot of encouragements. His report showed that he has used Convolutional Neural Network (CNN) and Recurrent Neural Network (RNN) such as LSTM in some examples of Natural Language Processing (Hoang, 2018). This student obtained an Internship in Apple. For Senior Project II, I have asked this student to do some new research espccially develop some new AI models to use. He made a neural network editor text understanding. He now works for Apple for natural language processing.

Figure 2. A Code Segment in Student Khoi's Senior Project II
(Hoang, 2018).

```
42 w = Tk()
43 Label(w, text="Neural Network Editor",font=(None, 35),width=70,background='snow2').pack(side="top")
44
45 text=Text(w,width=200,height =15)
46 #just use diffrent bind commands to call or pass diffrent functions
47 text.configure(background='snow')
48 text.bind("<space>",get_text)
49 text.bind("<Up>",add_text)
50 text.pack()
51 w.configure(background='snow2')
52 w.minsize(width=800, height=700)
53 res = Label(w,font=(None, 25))
54 res.configure(background='snow2')
55
56 res.pack(side="top")
57 w.mainloop()
58
```

Example 4: Some students who needs more attentions. For instance, a few students who were interested self-driving cars. We had several conversations. And helped them to find out first the state-of-art articles for the current self-driving cars status in the marketing. I asked them to consider the following: How AI is used? How to obtain data for further analysis? I also talked to University of Michigan's Transportation Lab for finding their data for our students. The work continued for several semesters by multiple teams of students.

Example 5: Student Steven was working on the mobile application for fitness. The project includes some workout activities and displays. He had made a simple program that was working. He took Senior Project I last semester and used Java for Android. Now he is about to get a summer internship in an Army's Lab. In year 2019, two students worked for an Interior Guidance System, they developed a mobile App that used 3D data for finding classroom. The system was very impressive. (Dena-Mamo, 20)

Example 6: Another group of two students did the project that help the biker to perform the Hands-Free Signaling. They have designed and coded not only including the software design but also use

Figure 3. The Mobile Application Projects for finding a classroom
(Dena-Mamo, 2020).

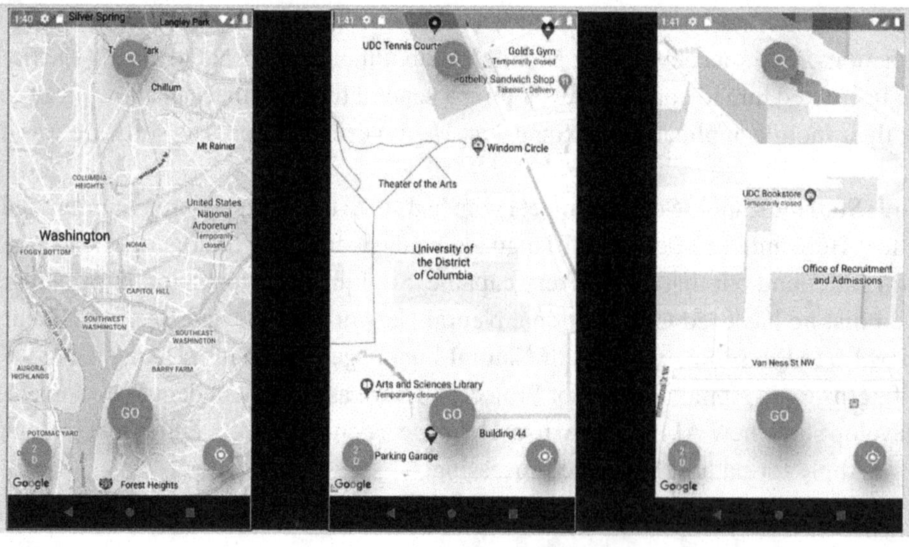

Figure 4. The Mobile Application for Hands-Free Signaling
(Kamit-Mulualem,K. 2020).

micro-controller in their project (Kamit-Mulualem,K. 2020). They have achieved at high expectations of the instructor.

Student Justin in Senior Project I used some existing software doing analysis for stock price prediction. This research is related to BigData. He had made the program work. For his Senior Project II, I have asked him to go depth. And he like to use Tensorflow that was made by Goolge for machine learning. He did his work.

CONCLUSION

In this paper, we have presented a whole framework of how we teach capstone classes in our university. Over the years, the objectives of the capstone projects have slightly changed. However, the main goal is remains to give students an opportunity to complete their own research in both depth and breadth. Students need such significant experience in researching from the capstone project for job finding and future degree pursuit. In addition to research, the final report plays an important role for accomplishing the goal of the capstone project. This major writing assignment is also to meet the large portion of the general education requirement for undergraduate students (Dugan, 2011).

REFERENCES

Chen, L. (2011). Education Forum: How to Become a Good Programmer. *ACM SIGACT News, 42*(2), 77-81.

Chen, L. (2020). How Do We Write a Good Project Report? *ACM SIGACT News*, *1*(51), 118–119. doi:10.1145/3388392.3388405

Dena, D., & Mamo, K. (2020). *An Interior Guidance System.* Unpublished Senior Project Report, UDC.

Dugan, R. F. Jr. (2011). A survey of computer science capstone course literature. *Computer Science Education*, *21*(3), 201–267. doi:10.1080/08993408.2011.606118

Hoang, K. (2018). *Neural Network in Natural Language Processing.* Unpublished Senior Project Report, UDC.

Kamit, M. H., & Mulualem, K. (2020). *Hands-Free Signaling.* Unpublished Senior Project Report, UDC.

ADDITIONAL READING

Adadi, A., & Berrada, M. (2018). Peeking inside the black-box: A survey on explainable artificial intelligence (XAI). *IEEE Access: Practical Innovations, Open Solutions, 6,* 52138–52160. doi:10.1109/ACCESS.2018.2870052

Carter, L. (2011, March). Ideas for adding soft skills education to service learning and capstone courses for computer science students. In *Proceedings of the 42nd ACM technical symposium on Computer science education* (pp. 517-522). 10.1145/1953163.1953312

Chen, L. (2021). Iteration vs. Recursion: Two Basic Algorithm Design Methodologies. *ACM SIGACT News, 52*(1), 81–86. doi:10.1145/3457588.3457601

Chen, L., & Coulibaly, L. A. (2021). Data Science and Big Data Practice Using Apache Spark and Python. In *Intelligent Analytics With Advanced Multi-Industry Applications* (pp. 67–95). IGI Global. doi:10.4018/978-1-7998-4963-6.ch004

Chen, L. M., Su, Z., & Jiang, B. (2015). *Mathematical Problems in Data Science.* Springer International Publishing. doi:10.1007/978-3-319-25127-1

Concolato, C. E., & Chen, L. M. (2017). Data science: A new paradigm in the age of big-data science and analytics. *New Mathematics and Natural Computation, 13*(02), 119–143. doi:10.1142/S1793005717400038

Deepamala, N., & Shobha, G. (2018). Effective approach in making capstone project a holistic learning experience to students of undergraduate computer science engineering program. *JOTSE: Journal of Technology and Science Education, 8*(4), 420–438. doi:10.3926/jotse.427

Khan, S. M., Ibrahim, M., & Haider, S. A. (2021, July). Performance Prediction of Computer Science Students in Capstone Software Engineering Course Through Educational Data Mining. *2021 ASEE Virtual Annual Conference Content Access.*

Neyem, A., Benedetto, J. I., & Chacon, A. F. (2014, March). Improving software engineering education through an empirical approach: lessons learned from capstone teaching experiences. In *Proceedings of the 45th ACM technical symposium on Computer science education* (pp. 391-396). 10.1145/2538862.2538920

Parker, R. (2018, February). Developing Software Engineers: A study of professionalization in a CS Senior Capstone. In *Proceedings of the 49th ACM Technical Symposium on Computer Science Education* (pp. 276-276). 10.1145/3159450.3162326

Saad, A. (2007, March). Senior capstone design experiences for ABET accredited undergraduate electrical and computer engineering education. In Proceedings 2007 IEEE SoutheastCon (pp. 294-299). doi:10.1109/SECON.2007.342905

Schneider, J. G., Eklund, P. W., Lee, K., Chen, F., Cain, A., & Abdelrazek, M. (2020, October). Adopting industry agile practices in large-scale capstone education. In *2020 IEEE/ACM 42nd International Conference on Software Engineering: Software Engineering Education and Training (ICSE-SEET)* (pp. 119-129). 10.1145/3377814.3381715

KEY TERMS AND DEFINITIONS

Cloud Service Providers: Are companies that provide cloud computing services. Amazon (AWS), Google (Google Cloud Platform), and Microsoft (Azure) provide cloud computing services.

Data Science: Is emerging research disciplinary area that relates to big data, machine learning, and cloud computing.

Machine Learning: Usually means to using data samples to obtain a mathematical model(s) for prediction and classification of unknown data. It is a branch of artificial intelligence.

Chapter 13
The Relationships Between Users' Negative Tweets, Topic Choices, and Subjective Well-Being in Japan

Shaoyu Ye
https://orcid.org/0000-0003-4464-9736
University of Tsukuba, Japan

Kei Wakabayashi
University of Tsukuba, Japan

Kevin K. W. Ho
https://orcid.org/0000-0003-1304-0573
University of Guam, Guam

Muhammad Haseeb Khan
University of Tsukuba, Japan

ABSTRACT

This study examined the relationships between expressions in Tweets, topic choices, and subjective well-being among undergraduates in Japan. The authors conducted a survey with 304 college students and analyzed their Twitter posts using natural language processing (NLP). Based on those who posted over 50 tweets, the authors found that (1) users with higher levels of social skills had fewer negative tweets and higher levels of subjective well-being; (2) frequent users posted both positive and negative tweets but posted more negative than positive tweets; (3) users with fewer negative tweets or with more positive tweets had higher levels of subjective well-being; and (4) "safe" topics such as social events and personal interests had a positive correlation with the users' subjective well-being, while debatable topics such as politics and social issues had a negative correlation with the users' subjective well-being. The findings of this study provide the foundation for applying NLP to analyze the social media posts for businesses and services to understand their consumers' sentiments.

DOI: 10.4018/978-1-7998-9016-4.ch013

INTRODUCTION

Over the past decades, text mining has been used to conduct sentiment analysis on social media. Text mining has been used successfully to detect stock market movement based on the sentiments observed in various social media platforms, such as Twitter (Dong, Liao & Zhang, 2018). Prior research has also noted that most sentiment-analysis algorithms were designed to detect users' preferences for products and services rather than users' behaviors and feelings. However, more tools have been developed in recent years for studying noncommercial communication in social media sentiment (Thelwall, Buckley, Paltoglou, Cai, & Kappas, 2010).

One valuable major research area on noncommercial communication sentiment analysis has focused on the effects of social media on users' social psychology. This research has shown that people's tweets on Twitter contain clues about their emotional and psychological conditions. On the positive side, interacting with people through social media can reduce users' loneliness (Skues, Williams, & Wise, 2012). However, we also know that overuse of social media can be detrimental to young people's well-being (Jung, Pawlowski & Kim, 2017) and that the levels of (over)use of social media are related to a person's social skills (Song, Zmyslinski-Seeling, Kim, Drent, Victor, Omori, & Allen, 2014).

In this research, we present our research examining the relationships between positive/negative expressions in tweets, discussion topics, and the subjective well-being of Twitter users from data collected from undergraduate students in Japan using natural language processing (NLP) as our text mining technique.

BACKGROUND AND RESEARCH QUESTIONS

Relationship of Subjective Well-Being and Trust With Social Media Usage

Until now, little has been known about social media's use on subjective well-being since there are no consistent results. For example, Jung *et al.* (2017) reported that overusing social media has a negative impact on users' subjective well-being, whereas Skues *et al.* (2012) reported that social media reduces users' levels of loneliness and improves their levels of subjective well-being. On the positive side, Johnson, Tanner, Lalla, and Kawalski (2013) suggested that social media can be used to maintain young people's social capital, thus improving their subjective well-being. However, a recent meta-analysis by Liu, Baumeister, Yang, and Hu (2019) pointed out that social media use could harm users' subjective well-being. However, heavy users of Facebook, Twitter, and Instagram seem to decrease their levels of subjective well-being, specifically, by increasing negative affective states rather than by decreasing positive states or life satisfaction—a pattern evident across all these three platforms (Wirtz, Tucker, Briggs, & Schoemann, 2021). Furthermore, Ye, Ho, and Zerbe (2021) indicated that the effects of these three platforms on users' subjective well-being might be different due to their different use patterns and the people who they followed, as the users of Twitter only seemed to have the lowest levels of subjective well-being and highest levels of loneliness, whereas users of all the three platforms had the highest levels of subjective well-being and lowest levels of loneliness.

Trust also plays a role in people's social media use; for example, deciding to follow another user or forward a message on social media is dependent on the degree of trust between the person and the source of the message (Abdullah, Nishioka, Tanaka, & Murayama, 2015). Furthermore, social media can be a tool for emotional expressions, as can be observed in posts and messages disseminated through such social media as Facebook and Twitter. In this way, social media can play a vital role in maintaining relationships. For example, an emotional message on Twitter could influence readers to be more likely to retweet the message and retweet it more quickly (Stieglitz & Linh, 2013).

Text Mining and Twitter Research

We focused on studying Twitter in this study because it is the most popular social network platform used by young people in Japan (Ye, Toshimori, & Horita, 2017). Recently, the use of text mining techniques for analyzing the sentiment in Twitter messages has attracted considerable attention (Martínez-Cámara, Martín-Valdivia, Ureña-López, & Montejo-Ráez, 2014). Sentiment analysis using text mining enables researchers to detect and track people's emotions over time by quantifying sentiment (Giachanou & Crestani, 2016). Previously, researchers could only use simple statistical methods to analyze tweet-and-retweet patterns and URLs in Twitter messages. However, with the advent of various new text mining techniques like natural language processing, researchers can gain insightful findings through an in-depth analysis of tweets. Text mining can also help researchers perform sentiment content analysis (Lingiardi, Carone, Semeraro, Musto, D'Amico, & Brena, 2020).

Research Question

Our research used natural language processing (NLP) analysis to clarify the relationship between users' tweets and their subjective well-being using university students' data in Japan. Kitamura, Kawai, and Sasaki (2017) reported that the social rewards motive was negatively related to the number of negative emotional terms. Therefore, we were particularly interested in tweets expressing positive/negative emotions and how these usages might affect users' subjective well-being. Therefore, our research question is: *How do the discussions at the Twitter messages affect the user's subjective well-being?*

Our analysis also included the users' generalized trust and social skills as two possible factors interacting with Twitter messages. Research has shown that people with higher levels of trust engage more easily on social media and more readily share tweets with their friends (Abdullah *et al.*, 2015). They are also more sociable and have higher levels of subjective well-being. Research has also shown that people with better social skills express themselves more readily and articulately on social media; therefore, they are more likely to use Twitter to communicate with people frequently and use more detailed tweets (Inoue & Ye, 2020). Because people with better social skills generally have higher levels of subjective well-being (Inoue & Ye, 2020), it is expected that their tweets are less likely to include complaints and negative communication expressions. This observation implies that people with high levels of subjective well-being would be less likely to complain and use negative expressions in their tweets.

METHODS

Data Collection

We conducted a self-report questionnaire survey (both online and in pencil versions) from early May to the end of June 2019 to investigate our research question with participants recruited from Japan's Kanto region universities. Three hundred four (304) completed student responses for analysis were received.

All of them were Twitter users, i.e., they had at least posted one tweet on their Twitter when they participated in the survey.

Measures

The survey was approved by the institutional review board of a Japanese University in the Kanto area. It first measured the students' social media and Twitter usage. We asked the participants about their Twitter usage: usage time, "like" behavior, tweets/retweets/viewing frequency, number of Twitter followers, and the number of people they followed on Twitter. We also asked how many of their Twitter followers and people they followed were (a) people they occasionally met in daily life; (b) people they met in everyday life; (c) people with whom they had intimate relationships in real life (e.g., close friends, partners, etc.); (d) Twitter-only acquaintances; and (e) people with whom they had close relationships on Twitter only (e.g., frequent interactions, shared passions, etc.). In addition, it measured their level of trust using Yamagishi's (1998) "Trust of Others in General." (6 items). It also measured their levels of social skills using Shimamoto and Ishii's (2006) "Daily Life Skills Scales for College Students" (24 items). To measure their subjective well-being, we used the 12-item scale developed by Sumino (1996). All the responses used a five-point scale ranging from 5 = strongly agree to 1 = strongly disagree.

Text Analysis

We collected tweets posted by our participants using the Twitter application programming interface (API) by looking up the account names provided in the survey. As preprocessing, we omitted retweets and tweets with no nouns or less than five words from the analysis. Hashtags, user mention tags, and URLs are removed from the tweet text to be trained and analyzed. We applied sentiment and topic analysis to those tweets to obtain the text features.

To perform the sentiment analysis, we built a neural network model using the flairNLP[1] library of natural language processing code. We designed the neural network to have a word-embedding layer and a bidirectional long short-term memory (LSTM) layer that together classified sentences into three categories: positive, negative, and neutral (Graves & Schmidhuber, 2005). We developed an original dataset for training the neural network containing 20,000 Japanese tweets with sentiment labels. For each tweet, three different human workers from the crowdsourcing company Lancers[2] They provided sentiment scores on a five-point scale ranging from 5 = very positive to 1 = very negative. The inter-annotator agreement in terms of Fleiss' kappa was 0.233, which makes sense because the sentiment is subjective and largely depends on individuals. We assigned a positive label if two out three workers gave 5 or 4 scores to the tweet, a negative label if two out three workers gave 1 or 2, and a neutral label otherwise. We evaluated the model using holdout validation and calculated the precision of the prediction as 0.70, 0.56, and 0.59 for the positive, negative, and neutral categories, respectively. The results suggested that most errors were on account of negative and neutral tweets being confused with each other because negative and neutral tweets were incorrectly identified. We split each collected tweet into sentences by line-break character, and each sentence was provided to the neural network model as input to be classified. We particularly focused on each user's negative sentiment ratio — the proportion of negative sentences among the user's total sentences.

We used the latent Dirichlet allocation (LDA) model (Blei, Ng, & Jordan, 2003) for the topic analysis. To train the LDA model, we collected another set of randomly sampled Japanese tweets via Twitter streaming API between May 6th and May 28th, 2019. We then applied the sparse stochastic inference method (Mimno, Hoffman, & Blei, 2012) and set the number of topics to 100. The trained LDA model calculated the topic proportion of each user's tweet posting, yielding 100 feature values for each user. Each value indicated the strength of the tweet's connection to the corresponding topic.

Prediction of Subjective Well-Being by Machine Learning Models

Since we hypothesize that there are correlations between text features and psychological state, we further expect that it is possible to construct a machine learning model that predicts a user's subjective well-being from observations of text features in tweets posted by the user. To confirm this possibility, we designed an experiment based on the leave-one-out cross-validation (LOO-CV) method that examines machine learning's potential performance in predictions of subjective well-being. Given the dataset collected from participants by the survey, the procedure of LOO-CV is as follows: (1) One participant is chosen as a "test example," and the rest are marked as "training examples." (2) A machine learning model is trained using the "training examples" and learn patterns about how text features are related to subjective well-being. (3) The obtained machine learning model is applied to predict the subjective well-being of the "test example" participant, and the prediction is evaluated by measuring the square error between the predicted value and the actual subjective well-being score of the participant. (4) We repeat (1)-(3) for all "test example" choices and calculate the average of the square errors (called mean square error; MSE). A less MSE means the machine learning method has a better potential to predict subjective well-being.

We used the LASSO linear regression model (Tibshirani, 1996) as the machine learning model. We tested multiple combinations of text features (e.g., negative/positive tweet ratio and the strength of each discussion topic), and measured MSEs for each combination to examine which text features help predict subjective well-being. We compare the MSEs of the machine learning method to the MSE of a baseline method, which predicts the subjective well-being of the "test example" participant to be the average of subjective well-being scores of "training examples."

RESULTS

In this study, we reported the positive/negative emotional expressions extracted from the text analysis. We collected all the open tweets that the participants posted from early May to the end of July 2019. Among the 304 participants, 112 had open tweets. We extracted 100 topics from another set of randomly sampled Japanese tweets using a topic model, then analyzed our participants' tweets using that 100 topics extracted and checked how they were grouped based on the similarities. The results of the grouping were then analyzed their correlations with the tweeters' social skills and subjective well-being. Since the text features of users with a relatively small number of tweets were considered to be unreliable, we did a preliminary assessment, analyzing the text-mining data results of users with total tweet numbers of "fewer than 10," "fewer than 30," "fewer than 50," and "fewer than 100." When we included data from users with a low number of tweets (e.g., "fewer than 10"), we found no relationship because the results were too noisy. We targeted the 65 users who had tweeted 50 times or more in the past three months to obtain an optimized result. The correlations between trust, social skills, subjective well-being, the ratio of negative expressions in tweets, the number of tweets, and the length of the tweets are shown in Table 1.

From the correlation table, the following results were observed:

Table 1. Correlation table

	1	2	3	4	5	6	7	8
1. Trust								
2. Social skill	.62 **							
3. Number of tweets	-.34 **							
4. Length of tweets	-.35 **		.98 **					
5. Positive tweets	-.31 *		.90 **	.91 **				
6. Negative tweets	-.35 **		.97 **	.96 **	.84 **			
7. Ratio of positive tweets			-.38 **	-.36 **		-.40 **		
8. Ratio of negative tweets		-.27 *				.27 *		
9. Subjective well-being	.47 **	.77 **					.25 *	-.38 **

Note: ** $p < .01$, * $p < .05$

1. Users with higher levels of trust had higher levels of subjective well-being ($r = .47, p < .01$);
2. Users with higher levels of social skills had higher levels of subjective well-being ($r = .77, p < .01$) and a lower ratio of negative tweets ($r = -.27, p < .05$);
3. There were correlations between subjective well-being and the ratio of positive tweets ($r = .25, p < .05$) and negative tweets ($r = -.38, p < .01$).

The results of subjective well-being prediction accuracy using text features by machine learning are presented in Table 2. From the analysis, as the smaller the error squares showed the better results, therefore, we found that two of the best predictors for the prediction model for subjective well-being were "negative and positive ratios" and "concatenation of negative and positive ratios and discussion topics." The result suggests that the sentiment analysis would be effective in predicting subjective well-being. On the other hand, the topic analysis could not contribute at decreasing prediction errors, although there was a correlation between the discussion topics and subjective well-being (to be elaborated on later in this section). This can be attributed to the complexity of the prediction models. The discussion topic feature consisted of 100 different values corresponding to the proportion of each of the 100 topics, which demanded us to find 100 good weight parameters for the LASSO linear regression model. Since we have only 64 training instances in the LOO-CV procedure, the model is over-parameterized and unstable in the prediction. This phenomenon is also called "overfitting" in machine learning literature. The negative and positive tweet ratio feature consists of only two values, allowing the model to avoid overfitting and find a generalized pattern effectively.

Regarding the most posted topics, we explored the correlations between the discussion topics and subjective well-being. The most significant correlations (i.e., the top three positive and top three negative topics) are summarized in Table 3. These results showed that the relationship between the topic and subjective well-being differed depending on the topic. That is, there was a positive correlation when the content was about "safe" topics such as personal interests (especially when the tweeters were female) and social events/interpersonal relationships. However, there was a negative correlation when the topics were debatable, such as politics, social issues, and the like. Interestingly, even though these positive and negative correlations were significant and high, most of them were not associated with the top ten discussion topics on Twitter, except politics.

Table 2. Results of predictive accuracy: subjective well-being

Text Feature	Subjective Well-being	
	Error Squares	Differences
Negative tweet ratio	89.35	−12.36
Positive tweet ratio	99.03	−2.68
Negative and positive ratio	88.97	−12.74
Word usage	90.73	−10.98
Number of tweets	103.98	2.27
Gender	105.47	3.76
Number of followers	99.12	−2.59
Number of following	98.71	−3.00
Concatenation of number of followers and following	100.47	−1.24
Concatenation of number tweets, gender, follower, following, and negative ratios	101.52	−0.19
Discussion topic	101.71	0.00
Concatenation of negative and positive ratios and discussion topic	88.97	−12.74

Notes: The error square of the baseline model is 101.71, and the difference is calculated by subtracting the error square of different topics.

Table 3. Discussion topics with top three positive and negative correlations with subjective well-being

Topic Content	Ranking	Correlation
Positive correlations		
Social events (e.g., entertainment events, hobbies, movies, etc.)	29	.32
Personal interests (e.g., graduation, fashion, cooking/preparing lunchbox, etc.)	15	.25
Interpersonal relationships (e.g., interviewers, personal interests, counseling, etc.)	27	.24
Negative correlations		
Politics	2	-.32
Social issues (e.g., pension, working wives (Note 1), education, Liberal Democratic Party (Note 2), etc.)	46	-.29
Entertainment/movie (e.g., star, director, etc.)	61	-.20

Notes:

1. In Japan, many people would prefer that females stay home and not work after getting married (that is, be full-time housewives). Since this is a much-discussed social issue in Japan, it is also a popular online topic.

2. The Liberal Democratic Party is the most significant political affiliation in Japan and has been the ruling party for most of the postwar period, making it a popular online topic.

DISCUSSION

Based on the previous research, we expected that people with higher levels of trust would be more active on social media — in this case, Twitter — as they communicated more readily with others. We also anticipated that people with higher levels of trust would be less likely to post negative tweets on Twitter and have higher levels of well-being. However, we found that those of our participants with higher levels of trust posted fewer tweets in all cases. Twitter is commonly used in Japan for connecting with acquaintances (e.g., Ye, 2019). The participants' levels of trust were generally low (with an average of 19.18 out of 30 based on the sum of six items scored on a 5-point scale, $SD = 4.71$), so it might be that our participants were less likely than the general population to post much on Twitter. It might also be that their posts were readable only by certain groups of people (Twitter allows users to restrict reader access to posts). Therefore, although the participants with higher levels of trust might have had more acquaintances in their Twitter network (given that people with higher levels of trust would be more likely to make friends online), having many acquaintances on the network might have made them tweet less to avoid posting tweets that their acquaintances might consider inappropriate, offensive, or controversial.

Our second observation was related to social skills. Prior research has also reported that users with lower social tolerance levels tend to experience more negative emotions when viewing unpleasant posts on Twitter (Hirai & Ye, 2019). Further, people with a lower degree of attachment/involvement in the online community and less motivated by social rewards post relatively more negative posts and comments on social media, including Twitter (Kitamura et al., 2017). Our finding that people with higher levels of social skills were less likely to post negative posts was in line with the literature. We also noted that participants with higher levels of social skills had higher levels of subjective well-being. This finding suggests that people with higher social skills were better able to determine what kind of posts they should post for their intended audience. Given that social skills can enhance subjective well-being, people with higher levels of social skills might feel happier when they tweet about safe, familiar topics using appropriate (inoffensive and noncontroversial) expressions.

Our text-mining results suggested that the discussion topics would relate to subjective well-being. However, our analysis showed an interesting phenomenon. Those topics with a high number of responses did not have high correlations with the users' subjective well-being: the average ranking of the top three positive and top three negative topics was 30, not within the 75th percentile in the ranking. This finding suggests the need for additional research examining the relationship between Twitter topics and subjective well-being using the text-mining technique.

To sum up, our results provide us with the following theoretical contributions to the literature. (1) We found that our participants with higher levels of trust posted fewer tweets and used fewer positive/ negative tweets, which was different from the prediction from the literature. We suggested that it might be because our participants had many acquaintances on the network, making them tweet less to avoid posting tweets that their acquaintances might consider inappropriate, offensive, or controversial. (2) Our participants with higher levels of social skills were less likely to post negative posts, which was in line with the literature. Also, (3) we found that discussion topics would relate to subjective well-being. In addition, this study also has a practical implication, as we showed that text-mining would be an appropriate technique for investigating the relationship between post topics and subjective well-being among users.

FUTURE RESEARCH DIRECTIONS

Applying intelligent business analytics on social media, i.e., social media analytics, is essential in the modern business world (Fan & Gordon, 2014). Nowadays, consumers' comments on social media can get viral and act as a two-blade sword. It can either co-create a company's image through positive electronic word-of-mouth (eWOM) from your consumers or destroy your company by amplifying your mistakes through negative eWOM (See-To & Ho, 2014). One of the most dramatic negative examples is the United Airlines Passenger Crisis that happened in April 2017. The airlines forcefully removed a passenger off the airplane, which triggered people's anger across the globe (Freberg, 2017). This example showcases the need for businesses to gather the sentiment of the social media environment to protect their organizations' brand name.

While this study analyzes the use of text mining technology and, in particular, natural language processing for analyzing tweets to understand the social psychology of young people living in Japan, the results provide insight for applying these techniques in intelligent business analytics. Businesses can gain lots of business intelligence by text mining the social media messages that appear on their Facebook and Twitter pages and getting to know the consumers' sentiments on their performance. Our findings in this study suggest that natural language processing and machine learning models discover the correlations between discussion topics and sentiments. It opens up a new practical use of these techniques for businesses to gather information about their consumer behavior and sentiments and can use such information to strengthen their market positions.

For future research, from the perspective of social psychology, we would recommend further examining why people, especially young people in Japan, like to share/write about popular topics even when those discussions do not improve their well-being. It would be helpful for social psychologists to know the reasons behind such social media interactions. For future research using our findings in business applications, we would suggest that business researchers and social media marketing practitioners further explore the possibility of using natural language processing in understanding consumer behavior.

CONCLUSION

This study had limitations. While we collected a good sample size (over 300 respondents), only 65 (about 20%) posted more than 50 tweets over three months, reducing usable data volume. The small usable sample size restricted the statistical methods we could use to analyze our data. Therefore, we propose that future research be done with a higher sample size of active Twitter users to ensure a robust data analysis. By the same token, we would recommend that business researchers and social marketing practitioners should be aware of the constraints of text mining techniques before implementing these social marketing research studies.

ACKNOWLEDGMENT

This research was supported by the Telecommunications Advancement Foundation (TAF).

REFERENCES

Abdullah, N. S., Nishioka, D., Tanaka, Y., & Murayama, Y. (2015). User's action and decision making of retweet messages towards reducing misinformation spread during disaster. *Journal of Information Processing*, *23*(1), 31–40. doi:10.2197/ipsjjip.23.31

Blei, D. M., Ng, A. Y., & Jordan, M. I. (2003). Latent Dirichlet allocation. *Journal of Machine Learning Research, 3*(Jan), 993–1022.

Dong, W., Liao, S., & Zhang, Z. (2018). Leveraging financial social media data for corporate fraud detection. *Journal of Management Information Systems, 35*(2), 461–487. doi:10.1080/07421222.2018.1451954

Fan, W., & Gordon, M. D. (2014). The power of social media analytics. *Communications of the ACM, 57*(6), 74–81. doi:10.1145/2602574

Freberg, K. (2017). *United Airlines crisis: PR takeaways & social media insights.* https://karenfreberg.com/blog/united-airlines-crisis-pr-takeaways-social-media-insights/

Giachanou, A., & Crestani, F. (2016). Like it or not: A survey of Twitter sentiment analysis methods. *ACM Computing Surveys, 49*(2), 28. doi:10.1145/2938640

Graves, A., & Schmidhuber, J. (2005). Framewise phoneme classification with bidirectional LSTM and other Neural Network Architectures. *Neural Networks: The Official Journal of the International Neural Network Society, 18*(5–6), 602–610. doi:10.1016/j.neunet.2005.06.042 PMID:16112549

Inoue, H., & Ye, S. Y. (2020). University students' Twitter usage and subjective well-being. *IEICE Technical Report, 119*(394), 83–88.

Johnson, K., Tanner, M., Lalla, N., & Kawalski, D. (2013). Social capital: The benefit of Facebook "Friends.". *Behaviour & Information Technology, 32*(1), 24–36. doi:10.1080/0144929X.2010.550063

Jung, Y., Pawlowski, S. D., & Kim, H.-W. (2017). Exploring associations between young adults' Facebook use and psychological well-being: A goal hierarchy approach. *International Journal of Information Management, 37*(1), 1391–1404.

Kitamura, S., Kawai, D., & Sasaki, Y. (2017). Relationships between the use of emotional terms on social media, posting motives, and network structure: Focusing on positive and negative emotional terms in Twitter. *The Japanese Journal of Language in Society, 20*(1), 16–28.

Lingiardi, V., Carone, N., Semeraro, G., Musto, C., D'Amico, M., & Brena, S. (2020). Mapping Twitter hate speech towards social and sexual minorities: A lexicon-based approach to semantic content analysis. *Behaviour & Information Technology, 39*(7), 711–721. doi:10.1080/0144929X.2019.1607903

Liu, D., Baumeister, R. F., Yang, C.-C., & Hu, B. (2019). Digital communication media use and psychological well-being: A meta-analysis. *Journal of Computer-Mediated Communication, 24*(5), 259–274. doi:10.1093/jcmc/zmz013

Martínez-Cámara, E., Martín-Valdivia, M. T., Ureña-López, L. A., & Montejo-Ráez, A. R. (2014). Sentiment analysis in Twitter. *Natural Language Engineering, 20*(1), 1–28. doi:10.1017/S1351324912000332

Mimno, D., Hoffman, M. D., & Blei, D. M. (2012). Sparse stochastic inference for latent Dirichlet allocation. *Proceedings of the 29th International Conference on Machine Learning.*

See-To, E. W. K., & Ho, K. K. W. (2014). Value co-creation and purchase intention in social network sites: The role of electronic Word-of-Mouth and trust – A theoretical analysis. *Computers in Human Behavior, 31*, 182–189. doi:10.1016/j.chb.2013.10.013

Shimamoto, K., & Ishii, M. (2006). Development of a daily life skills scale for college students. *Japanese Journal of Educational Psychology*, *54*(2), 211–221. doi:10.5926/jjep1953.54.2_211

Skues, J. L., Williams, B., & Wise, K. (2012). The effects of personality traits, self-esteem, loneliness, and narcissism on Facebook use among university students. *Computers in Human Behavior*, *28*(6), 2414–2419. doi:10.1016/j.chb.2012.07.012

Song, H., Zmyslinski-Seeling, A., Kim, J., Drent, A., Victor, A., Omori, K., & Allen, M. (2014). Does Facebook make you lonely?: A meta analysis. *Computers in Human Behavior*, *36*, 446–452. doi:10.1016/j.chb.2014.04.011

Stieglitz, S., & Linh, D.-X. (2013). Emotions and information diffusion in social media— Sentiment of microblogs and sharing behavior. *Journal of Management Information Systems*, *29*(4), 217–247. doi:10.2753/MIS0742-1222290408

Sumino, Z. (1995). Creating a subjective well-being scale for life (1). *Annual convention of the Japanese Association of Educational Psychology*, *37*, 95.

Thelwall, M., Buckley, K., Paltoglou, G., Cai, D., & Kappas, A. (2010). Sentiment strength detection in short informal text. *Journal of the American Society for Information Science and Technology*, *61*(12), 2544–2558. doi:10.1002/asi.21416

Tibshirani, R. (1996). Regression shrinkage and selection via the Lasso. *Journal of the Royal Statistical Society. Series B, Statistical Methodology*, *58*(1), 267–288.

Wirtz, D., Tucker, A., Briggs, C., & Schoemann, A. M. (2021). How and why social media affect subjective well-being: Multi-site use and social comparison as predictors of change across time. *Journal of Happiness Studies*, *22*(4), 1673–1691. doi:10.100710902-020-00291-z

Yamagishi, T. (1998). *The Structure of Trust: The Evolutionary Games of Mind and Society*. Tokyo University Press.

Ye, S. Y. (2019). The relationships between Twitter use, social comparison and satisfaction with friendship among university students. *Socio-Informatics*, *8*(2), 111–112.

Ye, S. Y., Ho, K. W. K., & Zerbe, A. (2021). The effects of social media usage on loneliness and well-being: Analysing friendship connections of Facebook, Twitter and Instagram. *Information Discovery and Delivery*, *49*(2), 136–150. doi:10.1108/IDD-08-2020-0091

Ye, S. Y., Toshimori, A., & Horita, T. (2017). Causal relationships between media/social media and Internet literacy among college students: Addressing the effects of social skills and gender differences. *Educational Technology Review*, *40*(1), 61–70.

ADDITIONAL READING

Blei, D. M., Ng, A. Y., & Jordan, M. I. (2003). Latent Dirichlet allocation. *Journal of Machine Learning Research*, *3*(Jan), 993–1022.

Chowdhury, G. (2003). Natural language processing. *Annual Review of Information Science & Technology, 37*(1), 51–89. doi:10.1002/aris.1440370103

Diener, E. (1984). Subjective well-being. *Psychological Bulletin, 95*(3), 542–575. doi:10.1037/0033-2909.95.3.542 PMID:6399758

Fan, W., & Gordon, M. D. (2014). The power of social media analytics. *Communications of the ACM, 57*(6), 74–81. doi:10.1145/2602574

Fang, J., Chiu, D. K. W., & Ho, K. K. W. (2021). Exploring cryptocurrency sentiments with clustering text mining on social media. In Z. Sun (Ed.), *Intelligent Analytics With Advanced Multi-Industry Applications* (pp. 157–171). IGI Global. doi:10.4018/978-1-7998-4963-6.ch007

Gefen, G., Fresneda, J. E., & Larsen, K. R. (2020). Trust and distrust as artifacts of language: A latent semantic approach to studying their linguistic correlates. *Frontiers in Psychology, 11*, 561. doi:10.3389/fpsyg.2020.00561 PMID:32273866

Giachanou, A., & Crestani, F. (2016). Like it or not: A survey of Twitter sentiment analysis methods. *ACM Computing Surveys, 49*(2), 28. doi:10.1145/2938640

Graves, A., & Schmidhuber, J. (2005). Framewise phoneme classification with bidirectional LSTM and other Neural Network Architectures. *Neural Networks: The Official Journal of the International Neural Network Society, 18*(5–6), 602–610. doi:10.1016/j.neunet.2005.06.042 PMID:16112549

Inoue, H., & Ye, S. Y. (2020). University students' Twitter usage and subjective well-being [大学生のTwitter使用と心理的幸福感] [信学技報]. *IEICE Technical Report, 119*(394), 83–88.

Kitamura, S., Kawai, D., & Sasaki, Y. (2017). Relationships between the use of emotional terms on social media, posting motives, and network structure: Focusing on positive and negative emotional terms in Twitter [ソーシャルメディアにおける感情語使用と投稿動機,ネットワーク構造の関係—ツイッターでのポジティブ感情語・ネガティブ感情語に着目して—] [社会言語科学]. *The Japanese Journal of Language in Society, 20*(1), 16–28.

Lingiardi, V., Carone, N., Semeraro, G., Musto, C., D'Amico, M., & Brena, S. (2020). Mapping Twitter hate speech towards social and sexual minorities: A lexicon-based approach to semantic content analysis. *Behaviour & Information Technology, 39*(7), 711–721. doi:10.1080/0144929X.2019.1607903

Martínez-Cámara, E., Martín-Valdivia, M. T., Ureña-López, L. A., & Montejo-Ráez, A. R. (2014). Sentiment analysis in Twitter. *Natural Language Engineering, 20*(1), 1–28. doi:10.1017/S1351324912000332

McKnight, D. H., & Chervany, N. L. (2001). Trust and distrust definitions: One bite at a time. In *Trust in Cyber-societies* (pp. 27–54). Springer-Verlag. doi:10.1007/3-540-45547-7_3

Song, H., Zmyslinski-Seeling, A., Kim, J., Drent, A., Victor, A., Omori, K., & Allen, M. (2014). Does Facebook make you lonely?: A meta analysis. *Computers in Human Behavior, 36*, 446–452. doi:10.1016/j.chb.2014.04.011

Stieglitz, S., & Linh, D.-X. (2013). Emotions and information diffusion in social media— Sentiment of microblogs and sharing behavior. *Journal of Management Information Systems, 29*(4), 217–247. doi:10.2753/MIS0742-1222290408

Thelwall, M., Buckley, K., Paltoglou, G., Cai, D., & Kappas, A. (2010). Sentiment strength detection in short informal text. *Journal of the American Society for Information Science and Technology*, *61*(12), 2544–2558. doi:10.1002/asi.21416

Wirtz, D., Tucker, A., Briggs, C., & Schoemann, A. M. (2021). How and why social media affect subjective well-being: Multi-site use and social comparison as predictors of change across time. *Journal of Happiness Studies*, *22*(4), 1673–1691. doi:10.100710902-020-00291-z

Ye, S. Y. (2019). The relationships between Twitter use, social comparison and satisfaction with friendship among university students [大学生のTwitter使用,社会的比較と友人関係満足度とのつ系] [社会情報学]. *Socio-Informatics*, *8*(2), 111–112.

Ye, S. Y., Ho, K. W. K., & Zerbe, A. (2021). The effects of social media usage on loneliness and well-being: Analysing friendship connections of Facebook, Twitter and Instagram. *Information Discovery and Delivery*, *49*(2), 136–150. doi:10.1108/IDD-08-2020-0091

KEY TERMS AND DEFINITIONS

Natural Language Processing (NLP): It is a branch of artificial intelligence (AI), which focuses on the use of computers to understand human language, including both text and spoken language, like human beings.

Sentiment Analysis: It is the use of natural language process, text mining, and other techniques to study people's opinion and emotion.

Social Media: It is a term to describe a set of Web 2.0 application, which provide users platforms to interact with each other. User-generated content in a characteristics of social media.

Subjective Well-Being: It is a person's feeling on going well in his/her life. It contains two types of emotion, i.e., happiness and life satisfaction.

Text Mining: It is a computation analysis of text, which aims to derive high quality information from the text for further analysis.

Trust: It is a belief in the reliability and benevolence.

Twitter: It is a social media, which allows users to post and interact with short messages and is considered as microblogging. It is the most popular social media platform in Japan (as at 2021).

ENDNOTES

[1]   https://github.com/flairNLP/flair
[2]   https://www.lancers.jp/

Chapter 14
A Comparison of Deep Learning Models in Time Series Forecasting of Web Traffic Data From Kaggle

Bingnan Wang
The University of Hong Kong, Hong Kong

Dickson K. W. Chiu
The University of Hong Kong, Hong Kong

Kevin K. W. Ho
(iD) https://orcid.org/0000-0003-1304-0573
University of Guam, Guam

ABSTRACT

In recent years, time series forecasting has attracted more attention from academia and industry. This research used raw data from the "Web Traffic Forecasting" competition on the Kaggle platform to test the prediction accuracy of different time series models, especially the generalization performance of various deep learning models. The experiments used historical traffic data from 145,063 web pages from Wikipedia from 2015-07-01 to 2017-11-13. Traffic data from 2015-07-01 to 2017-09-10 was used to forecast traffic from 2017-09-13 to 2017-11-13, a total of 62 days. The experimental results showed that almost all deep learning models predicted far more effectively than statistical and machine learning models, showing that deep learning models have great potential for time series forecasting problems.

INTRODUCTION

Time series forecasting refers to using historical data in a period to predict the future. The application scenarios of time series forecasting are relatively rich, including quantitative trading, macroeconomic

DOI: 10.4018/978-1-7998-9016-4.ch014

trend forecast, merchandise sales forecast in e-commerce, store sales forecast in the retail industry, and electricity forecast of power supply. The input and output format of time series forecasting is similar to regression problems in supervised learning, but there is one fundamental difference: time-series data usually has time dependence (Robinson & Sims, 1994). For a batch of input data of the same size, if the order of the data is changed, all data patterns and relations are likely to undergo huge changes, and the prediction results of models may be completely different as well. At the same time, other regression problems may not have this characteristic.

Although there are many successful deep learning applications in time series forecasting in academia, many industrial and commercial applications still use traditional statistical models or machine learning models to deal with time series forecasting problems. The industrial and commercial sectors are still in the exploratory stage of applying deep learning technology to time series forecasting. The main reasons are:

1. Most time-series forecasting in academia use a very small dataset for testing complex deep learning models, which is of little significance for evaluating the actual performance of models. Few studies used industrial-grade datasets to test these models' performances. Thus, conclusions drawn from such experiments are not quite convincing;
2. Compared with mature fields, such as natural language processing, computer vision, and recommendation systems, the research field of time series forecasting is relatively niche. This means that the industry lacks related expertise; and
3. At present, the industries that can generate the greatest benefits from time series forecasting are mainly the financial industry, especially quantitative trading. However, due to the unique nature of the industry, the results and details of such applications are rarely disclosed.

Thus, the objectives of this chapter are:

1. Comparing the difference in model performance between the statistical model, machine learning model, and different deep learning models on the same data set; and
2. Comparing the performance differences of different deep learning models on the same data set in detail, and summarize the advantages and disadvantages of different deep learning algorithms.

Time series forecasting has many important applications in commercial and industrial sectors. However, compared to popular fields, such as natural language processing, recommendation systems, and computer vision, time series forecasting is a relatively niche research field. Few articles have summarized the most valuable method, i.e., deep learning time series forecasting algorithms, so far. Therefore, to make up for this gap, this chapter will compare in detail the effects of different deep learning algorithms on the same real-life industrial data set and evaluate the performance of different deep learning algorithms. These algorithms are representative and popular and used as the solutions of the time series forecasting in the industry and competitions. They have potential great commercial value. This chapter provides references for various industries to solve practical time series forecasting problems in the real world.

BACKGROUND AND LITERATURE REVIEW

Deep Learning

In recent years, with the development of the substantial increase in GPU computing power and the publication of more and more breakthrough studies, neural networks have become a hot and independent research field, with countless papers about deep learning published every year.

Deep learning models can be abstracted as a combination of the physical structure of a multi-layer neural network with activation functions, objective functions, optimization algorithms, and various auxiliary functions. A multi-layer neural network is composed of various neural network layers. These layers can be roughly divided into simple feed-forward neural network layers (Svozil, Kvasnicka, & Pospichal, 1997), recurrent neural network layers (Medsker & Jain 2001), convolutional neural network layers (Albawi, Mohammed, & Al-Zawi, 2017), and attention-based neural network layers (Luong, Pham, & Manning, 2015), as well as a variety of other complicated network structures such as residual block (He, Zhang, Ren, & Sun, 2016), transformer block (Vaswani et al., 2017), and so on.

Deep Learning for Time Series Forecasting

Due to the unique nature of time series data, not all neural network structures can be directly applied to time series data. In fact, in many time series forecasting competitions, data scientists often have to carry out various feature engineering and improvements of the network structures, training process, or parameters tuning to improve deep learning models for achieving good results. The main reason is that time series contain many complex components affecting one another. Thus, the potential pattern of the whole time-series data makes time series forecasting more challenging. These components mainly include (Wei, 2006):

1. *Base level* refers to the basic value of the time series data itself, often measured by the mean or median value of historical data. For example, the base level of the price of computers and newspapers is very different;
2. *Trend* refers to the increase or decrease of time series data over time. The strength of a trend according to the magnitude of the slope;
3. *Seasonality* means periodicity or a regular change shown by time-series data. For example, the electricity consumption of urban residents will change obviously and regularly with the seasons; and
4. *Noise* affects time series due to many uncertain factors. For example, stock prices will be affected by diseases, wars, economic policies, etc.

Although the neural network is considered a universal fitter (Yager & Kreinovich, 2003), they need very careful network structure design for time series. This includes the number of layers, the use of activation functions, the position where the normalization layer is inserted into the network structure, etc. In the process of neural network training, selecting appropriate initial learning rates, learning rate schedules, and optimizers are necessary (Darken & Moody, 1990). Further, certain transformations of the input layer of the neural network are necessary to unleash the power of deep learning models.

At present, some deep learning algorithms have been designed for time series forecasting. These deep learning algorithms have achieved excellent results in many time series competitions or demonstrated effectiveness through a lot of practice. Those algorithms selected in our experiments are as follow:

Statistical Time Series Models

The development of time series forecasting can be traced back to about 40 years ago. Early time series forecasting methods are relatively simple. For example, the exponential smoothing algorithm proposed by Muth (Gardner Jr., 1985) is a classic simple time series forecasting model for univariate time series forecasting that uses the moving average of past historical data as future predictions. However, it is difficult for the exponential smoothing method to learn the underlying laws of seasonality and trends in the time series data. Therefore, the effect of the model dealing with time series with strong seasonality and trends (such as e-commerce sales data, electricity consumption data of power plants, etc.) is often unsatisfactory.

After that, the exponential smoothing method was improved, and the state-space model (Durbin, J., & Koopman, S. J. 2012) was created. During this period, many researchers did not regard the time series as composed of different time series components until Hyndman et al. (2002) (extended by Taylor, 2003) defined three types of trend components:

1. None type, which means that the time series does not contain trend components, which also means that the time series data has no obvious trend;
2. Additive, which means it is considered that there is a seasonal component in the time series, and the seasonal component and other components in the time series have an additive relationship; and
3. Multiplicative, which means it is considered that there is a seasonal component in the time series. The seasonal component and other components in the time series are multiplicative (Note: The seasonality here refers to the generalized seasonality, which is called the periodicity of the time series, which means that the time series data circulates with the change of time. The period here can be 7 days, one month or one year, etc.).

Then the classic algorithm of ARIMA (Shumway & Stoffer, 2017) was invented, and variants include SARIMA (Valipour, 2015)), VARIMA (Barceló-Vidal, Aguilar, & Martín-Fernández, 2011), AUTO ARIMA (Yermal, & Balasubramanian, 2017). To this day, many companies still use these algorithms to help to solve time series forecasting problems.

However, the various models mentioned above have not considered the problems of variations, which refers to the non-static seasonal and trend components in the time series data. For example, the price trend of stocks often changes significantly. Similarly, the business cycle of the retail industry also follows the economic cycle from time to time. Therefore, It is not accurate to consider the trend and seasonal component of a time series immutable.

Therefore, the Theta algorithm (Assimakopoulos & Nikolopoulos, 2000) is proposed, which has achieved quite good results in "The M3 Competition". The Theta model and the Holt-Winters model (Chatfield, 1978) both consider the problems of variations and use the exponential moving average method to deal with variations.

In addition, it is worth mentioning that Facebook's open-source time series forecasting framework, Prophet (Taylor & Letham, 2018), is developed based on the time series decomposition method for model construction. The Prophet can also take the holiday effect into account in the process of model training.

These statistical models rely on constructing linear functions from recent observations to provide future predictions. However, these statistical methods are often based on strong assumptions, and the actual data does not necessarily meet the assumptions in many cases. This situation often leads to the poor performance of the models. For example, when using the ARIMA model, the time series data must be converted to stationary (no trend or seasonality) through several differential transformations. Another important issue is that almost all statistical models cannot use exogenous variables or deal with multi-sequence time series forecasting problems. However, in the actual application process, exogenous variables (such as holidays and cities, etc.) contributes significantly to accurate forecasting. In the real world, multi-sequence time series forecasting problem is more common than single-sequence time series forecasting problem. At the same time, when the availability of a single series of data is insufficient, these models often can not effectively use multiple series of data to extract the underlying common features and patterns. Statistical models can only be modeled for a single sequence. Therefore, when there are a large number of single sequences in the input data, for example, in e-commerce sales forecasting, the sales data of each product is a single sequence data. If we choose to use statistical models, we have to build a large number of statistical models in the end.

Machine Learning Models

In recent years, machine learning models and deep learning models have received more attention. In many cases, they have shown better performance than statistical models in time series forecasting problems. The reason behind this is mainly due to their capabilities and flexibility resulting from data-driven computation to extract potentially complex patterns from a large amount of time-series data. This approach dramatically improves the prediction accuracy of the models, and they do not need any theoretical assumptions about the data distribution. In addition, machine learning models and deep learning models can be introduced very flexibly. Exogenous variables can also be directly in the training process of models for all sequence data. Generally speaking, we call a model that can directly model all sequence data as a global model and a model that can only model a single sequence as a local model. There are plenty of different types of exogenous variables in time series data. Here we divide these variables into several types (Alley, 1988): static variables do not change their values over time, and dynamic variables change over time.

Due to the limitations of statistical models, machine learning is extensively used for time series forecasting, such as using Support Vector Machine (Cao & Tay. 2003) to predict financial prices. In Kaggle's machine learning data mining competition, most contestants used the Gradient Boosting Regression Tree algorithm (Friedman, 2001) to solve time series forecasting. This is due to the strong robustness and generalization performance of the ensemble learning algorithms and the high efficiency of the Gradient Boosting Regression Tree algorithms open-source implementation: Xgboost (Chen & Guestrin, 2016), Lightgbm (Ke et al., 2017), and Catboost (Dorogush, Ershov, & Gulin, 2018). Notably, the winner of "The M5 Competition," a time series forecasting competition on Kaggle, used the LightGBM.

The Gradient Boosting Regression Tree algorithm turns the time series forecasting problem into a conventional regression problem. In single-step estimation predicting the data of one-time step in the future, time series forecasting and regular regression problems are almost the same. However, in multi-step time series forecasting predicting the data of several time steps in the future, most machine learning algorithms cannot be used, including Support Vector Machine and Gradient Boosting Regression Tree. This is because these algorithms are designed to solve conventional regression and classification problems and can only support the output of a single label. So, they cannot deal with multiple outputs.

For ease of explanation, assuming that we want to use historical traffic of a web page in the past 180 days to predict those in the next 60 days, the problem can be expressed as:

$$[t,t+1,t+2,t+3,...,t+59] = F([t-180,t-179,...,t-1]),$$

where t_i represents the sales value of the product at the i-th moment, and F represents the model we use. Therefore, to adapt machine learning algorithms to deal with time series forecasting problems, specific strategies are necessary, which mainly includes (Taieb, Bontempi, Atiya, & Sorjamaa, 2012):

1. *Recursive Forecasting Strategy:* The advantage of the recursive forecasting strategy is the low computational complexity, as we only need to build one model to complete the whole forecasting process. This strategy can use static or dynamic time-invariant features in the future, which will help increase forecasting accuracy. However, the recursive forecasting strategy has the problem of error accumulation because the predicted result is used as a new feature for further prediction.

This strategy use [t-180,t-179....t-1] as the model input features, and [t] as the model label to build a regression model named Model1. After that we use Model1 to predict [t-180,t-179,...,t-1] and get the predicted label t_pred at time t. Then, we regard t_pred as the true label at time t, and use Model1 to predict [t-179,t-178,t-177... ..t-1,t_pred] and get the prediction result t+1_pred at time t+1. Similarly, we regard t+1_pred as the true label at time t+1, and we continue to use Model1 to predict [t-178,t-177,t-176....t-1,t_pred,t+1_pred], get the prediction result at time t+2, and so on.

2. *Direct Forecasting Strategy:* The advantage of the directly forecasting strategy is that it does not cause error accumulation like the recursive forecasting strategy, and the code implementation of the directly forecasting strategy is relatively simple. However, the disadvantage of this strategy is the high calculation complexity of the direct forecasting strategy, especially for long-term forecasts, because n models have to be built for n predictions.

This strategy transforms the multi-step forecasting problem of the time series into multiple single-step forecasting problems, and the single-step forecasting problem is almost the same as the common regression problem. For training data, we use the following as our training data and labels:

[t-180,t-179....t-1][t],

[t-180,t-179....t-1][t+1]

[t-180,t-179....t-1][t+2]

....

[t-180,t-179....t-1][t+59]

According to the data, a total of 60 models are constructed to make 60 times predictions to obtain the prediction results of 60 time steps in the future:

[t-180,t-179....t-1][t]——> Model1;

[t-180,t-179....t-1][t+1]——> Model2;

[t-180,t-179....t-1][t+2]——> Model3;

....

[t-180,t-179....t-1][t+59]——> Model60.

3. *Hybrid Forecasting Strategy:* The advantage of the hybrid forecasting strategy combines the advantages of recursive forecasting strategy and direct forecasting strategy. This strategy can use static or dynamic time-invariant features to help increase the forecasting accuracy while avoiding error accumulation like the direct forecasting strategy. However, the calculation complexity of the hybrid forecasting strategy is very high because n models are required for n predictions.

This strategy combines recursive and direct forecasting strategies. We first use [t-180,t-179,...,t-1] [t] to build Model1 for predicting t_pred. We consider t_pred as the true label at time t, and then we use [t- 179,...,t-1,t_pred][t+1] to establish Model2 for predicting t+ 1_pred at time t+1. Next, we use [t-178,....,t-1,t_pred,t+1_pred][t+2] to build Model3 and so on.

Deep Learning Models

Due to its strong flexibility, deep learning can naturally deal with the problem of multi-step forecasting. Common deep learning strategies applied to time series forecasting mainly include two strategies:

1. *Vector output strategy:* This vector output strategy is relatively easy to use as we only need to set the output size of the last layer of the neural network to the forecast length. Then, we can directly use only one deep learning model to complete a multi-step time series forecasting task. The advantage of the vector output strategy is that it is easy to implement and very fast. Its disadvantage is that the time dependency between future time steps is not considered, and the vector output strategy cannot use future static features or dynamic time-invariant features in the future.

2. *Seq2seq Recursive Output Strategy:* This strategy use a special neural network structure called "seq2seq",which contains an encoder and a decoder (Rebane, Karlsson, Papapetrou, & Denic, 2018). The encoder and decoder can be a recurrent neural network, convolutional neural network, transformer, or other network structures capable of processing sequence data. We use [t-180,t-179,...,t-1] as the encoder input and get the latent vector calculated by the encoder neural network. Then, the latent vector serves as the input for the decoder to predict t_pred at time t. Unlike hybrid forecast-

ing strategies, t_pred is used as the input at time t+1 to re-enter the decoder to get the prediction t+1_pred at time t+1 instead of training a new model. In this process, the forward propagation process of the model does not end, and the whole process is continuous.

The main advantage of the seq2seq recursive output strategy is its high flexibility and can support variable-length forecasts. This is very useful for some time series data augment technology, but its shortcomings compared with the vector output strategy is the low training efficiency of the seq2seq recursive output strategy. The problem of error accumulation also occurs during the prediction process of the decoder. Although teacher forcing mechanisms can be introduced to help reduce error accumulation during model training, the problem of error accumulation still exists in model forecasting.

Literature Gap

Some recent studies have compared the performance of different prediction models. Qin (2019) compared the LSTM, TCN, GRU, BiLSTM, BIGRU, and CNN. Ji, Kim, & Im (2019), by testing the deep neural network (DNN), the long short-term memory (LSTM) model, the convolutional neural network, and the deep residual network with bitcoin price data and found that LSTM had the best performance. Zeroual, Harrou, Dairi, and Sun (2020) compared LSTM, BiLSTM, GRU, and VAE, and proved the superior performance of VAE compared to other algorithms. Athiyarath, Paul, and Krishnaswamy (2020) also compared the differences between ARIMA, MVFTS, CNN, LSTM, and CBLSTM.

However, scant studies comprehensively compare various deep learning models, especially the popular transformer neural network architecture and the hybrid neural network architecture designed for time series forecasting. Almost all related work tested too few types of deep learning models in the experiments, making the conclusions insufficient. In addition, the experimental data sets used in most of the related literature were too simple, which makes the experimental conclusions unconvincing.

With the rapid development of deep learning, many advanced network structures with extraordinary learning capabilities were invented. Many of these network structures are designed for time series forecasting or can be used in time series forecasting after a minor modification, such as Nbeats, Deepar, Wavenet, temporal fusion transformer, and so on. However, scant studies systematically compare the effects of these new models on time series forecasting so far. Therefore, this chapter uses industrial-grade web traffic data for model training and validation and objectively and reasonably evaluates the actual performance of these models, and compares the application of many different advanced deep learning models in time series forecasting more comprehensively. In addition to testing common RNN and CNN models, we also test well-known neural network structures such as hybrid neural networks, attention-based models, transformers, etc., to make up for the deficiencies in the past related work.

METHODOLOGY

Research Design

This study employs quantitative analysis mainly including the following steps:

1. ***Data preprocessing:*** As the original dataset has many missing values, and the value ranges of the traffic data of different web pages are quite different, the data needs cleansing and preprocessing. Notably, the input data of all tested models are all the same preprocessed data;

2. ***Feature engineering:*** It is designed as a completely independent module from the model. For the same model, the performance of the models under different feature engineering methods will be tested. To reduce the test time of the models, we only use the traffic data of the web pages to train, test, and compare the models.

3. ***Fixation of randomness:*** The experiments need to avoid the randomness of the dataset division method and the training process of the models. Before training the models, we take 80% of the data as the training data and the remaining 20% as test data. In subsequent verification, the division of training and test data is unchanged. At the same time, a fixed random seed is used to fix the randomness in the model training process.

4. ***Data set division:*** In time series forecasting, the way of dividing the data set is in chronological order, quite different from dividing data in common classification or regression problems.

5. ***Model training and validation:*** We train the models on the training data set and validate these models trained on the test data set to evaluate the performance of different models.

6. ***Model comparison:*** To compare the model performance differences between deep learning models, statistical models, and machine learning models, we have selected some statistical models and machine learning models. Since statistical models can only deal with single-sequence data for 145,063 web pages, the overall computational complexity of building 145,063 statistical models is too high. Therefore, we only chose simple statistical models with less computational time for modeling, including simple average model, periodic model, polynomial regression model, and holt-winter model.

Among the machine learning models, we chose one of the current best-performing open-source implementations of the gradient boosting regression tree, Lightgbm. Lightgbm has been employed for many engineering optimizations on the gradient boosting regression tree algorithm to achieve high performance. We experiment with the direct forecasting strategy, recursive forecasting strategy, and hybrid forecasting strategy for multi-step time series forecasting.

This study used the open-source web traffic data set on Kaggle (https://www.kaggle.com/c/web-traffic-time-series-forecasting) as the experimental data set. The web traffic data set comprises 145,063 different Wikipedia articles with their historical daily traffic data, i.e., the daily number of visits of each article. The time range of label data is from July 1, 2015, to September 1, 2017. The time range of the data without labels is from September 13, 2017, to November 13, 2017. The data contains two types of features: static features and dynamic features. The static feature comprises a description of the text information of a web page, including the title of the web page, proxy information, client information, etc. The dynamic features include the dates, traffic data of different web pages on that date, etc.

Because Kaggle's web traffic competition is ultimately based on SMAPE (symmetric mean absolute percentage error) as the evaluation standard, we use SMAPE as a metric. To evaluate the experimental results more comprehensively, we include MSE (Mean Square Error) and MAE (Mean Absolute Error) as model evaluation indicators for evaluation.

DATA ANALYSIS AND FINDINGS

Data Preprocessing

The traffic data of the same web page at different time steps is very different, and the range can be more than ten times the low value. For the training process of models, especially the deep learning models, such differences make it difficult to train and converge. Therefore, we perform a logarithmic transformation on all data (Lütkepohl & Xu, 2012). To avoid including log(0) in the model, the traffic data of each time step of all web pages are uniformly incremented by one before the logarithmic transformation. Due to many missing values in the traffic data, simple zero-value imputation of missing data will be performed on the missing values. Finally, the historical traffic data of 145,063 web pages from 2015-07-01 to 2017-09-10 (totaling 803 time-steps) is obtained.

Considering that in the multi-sequence time series forecasting, simple global normalization methods (such as z-score normalization, min-max normalization) cannot change the relative size of different web pages' traffic data. According to experience, the traffic of different web pages unifying the size to exactly the similar or the same range can help the models learn better. Therefore, we adopt group normalization with the min-max normalization method to normalize the traffic data of each web page separately to make the traffic data of each web are all in the range of 0 to 1.

Finally, the web traffic data from 2015-11-09 to 2017-05-05 is used for training, 2017-07-08 to 2017-05-08 for the training labels, 2017-01-12 to 2017-07-08 for the test data set, and 2017-07-11-2017-09-10 for the test labels. We train the models on the training set and verify their generalization performance on the test set to compare and evaluate the performance of different models and make appropriate adjustments to hyperparameters of the models.

Parameter Settings

In this experiment, we used 13 models for deep learning. The model names and parameter settings are as follows. These parameters have been chosen according to criteria described in the literature, which explain further justifications and rationales behind (beyond the scope of this chapter). For the 7 statistical and machine learning models used in this experiment, we summarize their parameters and setting in Table 1.

1. **Single-Layer LSTM** (Long Short-Term Memory): The number of hidden layer neurons is 256, the activation function is the sigmoid function, and the activation function of the recurrent layers is the *tanh* (hyperbolic tangent) function. Both dropout rate and recurrent dropout rate are set to 0 (Sundermeyer, Schlüter, & Ney, 2012).
2. **Deep LSTM**: Stacked by three LSTM layers, the number of hidden layer neurons in each LSTM layer is set to 256, 128, and 64, respectively. The activation function is the sigmoid function, and the recurrent layers' activation function is the *tanh* function. Both dropout rate and recurrent dropout rate (Gal & Ghahramani, 2016) are set to 0.
3. **Bidirectional Deep LSTM**: Formed by stacking three bidirectional LSTM layers, the number of hidden layer neurons in each LSTM layer is 256, 128, and 64, respectively. The activation function is the sigmoid function, and the recurrent layers' activation function is the *tanh* function. Both dropout rate and recurrent dropout rate are set to 0 (Graves, Jaitly, & Mohamed, 2013).

4. **TCN (Temporal Convolutional Networks)**: 64 causal dilated convolution kernels are used, with the kernel size of each convolution kernel set to 3 and the dilated factors of the causal convolution layer set to (1, 2, 4, 8, 16, 32, 64,128). Thus, eight causal dilated convolutional layers are used in total. Relu (Agarap, 2018) is used as the activation function with skip connections (Yamanaka, Kuwashima, & Kurita, 2017). Layer normalization is used to help the model converge better and faster.

5. **Wavenet**: 64 causal dilated convolution kernels are used, with the kernel size of each convolution kernel set to 3 and the dilated factors of the causal convolution layer set to (1, 2, 4, 8, 16, 32, 64,128). Thus, eight causal dilated convolutional layers are used in total, each using filter convolution and gating convolution. Skip connections are used as well (Oord et al., 2016).

6. **CNN+LSTM**: 64 ordinary convolutional kernels are used, with the convolution kernel size of each kernel set to 3. We calculated the max pooling and the average pooling, respectively, and concatenated the calculation results. The results are sent to the LSTM model as the input, where the number of hidden layer neurons is 256, the activation function is the sigmoid function, and the recurrent layer activation function is the *tanh* function Both dropout and recurrent dropout of LSTM are set to 0 (Livieris, Pintelas, & Pintelas, 2020).

7. **Attention-based model**: The attention layer is added to the single-layer LSTM and the single-layer TCN, respectively (Wang, Huang, Zhu, & Zhao, 2016; Fan, Zhang, Huang, Zhu, & Chen, 2021). The linear transformation layer in the attention layer uses 64 neurons. The dot product similarity is used as the calculation method of the attention score, and the weighted sum value is finally concatenated with the original value as the output. The number of neurons in the single-layer LSTM hidden layer is 256, the activation function is the sigmoid function, and the recurrent layer activation function is the *tanh* function. Both dropout and recurrent dropout are set to 0, 64 causal dilated convolution kernels are used, the kernel size of each convolution kernel is set to 3. The dilated factors of the causal convolution layer are (1, 2, 4, 8, 16, 32, 64,128). Thus, a total of eight causal dilated convolutional layers are used. Relu is used as the activation function, with skip connections and layer normalization to help the model converge better and faster.

8. **Transformer-based model:** This model abandons the RNN and CNN and purely uses the attention mechanism to build the model structure. Among them, the number of neurons in the linear transformation layer is 64. In the multi-head attention layer, two heads are used. Relu is used as the activation function in feed-forward layers, and the number of neurons in feed-forward layers is set to 32. Only one transformer block is used, and the global average pooling layer is finally used to calculate the global average value of the output of the transformer block (Amoiralis, Tsili, & Kladas, 2009).

9. **Deepar**: The encoder and decoder structures are used. Both encoder and decoder use single-layer LSTM, and the parameter settings are the same. The number of hidden layer neurons is 256, the activation function is the sigmoid function, and the recurrent layers' activation function is the *tanh* function. Both the dropout rate and recurrent dropout rate are set to 0 (Salinas, Flunkert, Gasthaus, & Januschowski, 2020).

10. **Nbeats**: The length of backtest is set to 739, forecast 62, and the number of hidden layer neurons 64. Two stack layers are used, and two generic blocks are used in each stack layer. Theta dim is both set to 4 (Oreshkin, Carpov, Chapados, & Bengio, 2019).

11. **Seq2seq with LSTM**: The encoder and decoder structures are used. Both the encoder and the decoder use a single-layer LSTM, and the parameter settings are the same. The number of hidden

Table 1. Statistical models and machine learning models

Model Name	Parameters Description	SMAPE	MSE	MAE
Naive baseline models(Last)	use last 7 days to forecast the future	0.081	0.015	0.081
Naive baseline models(mean)	use the mean values of last 14 days to forecast the future	0.070	0.011	0.070
Polynomial	Forecast time series data with a polynomial regression model, degree of the polynomial regression set to 2	0.092	0.016	0.092
Holt-Winters	Holt-Winters exponential smoothing forecaster	0.071	0.011	0.071
LightGBM	Direct Forecast Strategy	0.074	0.012	0.074
LightGBM	Recursive Forecast Strategy	0.068	0.010	0.068
LightGBM	Hybrid Forecast Strategy	0.072	0.011	0.072

layer neurons is 256, the activation function is the sigmoid function, and the recurrent layer activation function is the *tanh* function. Both dropout rate and recurrent dropout rate are set to 0. The conventional seq2seq training strategy is used without the teacher forcing training strategy (Xiang, Yan, & Demir, 2020).

12. **LSTM Autoencoder**: LSTM autoencoder (comprising encoder and decoder) is used to pre-train the LSTM Layer. The parameter settings of the encoder and decoder are the same, with the number of hidden layer neurons 256, the activation function as the sigmoid function, and the recurrent layer's activation function as the *tanh* function. Both dropout rate and recurrent dropout rate are set to 0. After the LSTM autoencoder converges, the encoder is used as the initialized LSTM layer to continue training and evaluation.

13. **Temporal fusion Transformer**: The number of hidden layer neurons in the variable selection network is set to 16. Both the encoder and decoder parts use single-layer LSTM. The number of hidden layer neurons in LSTM is set to 16, the dropout rate as 0.1, the number of heads in the multi-head attention layer as 4, and the number of neurons in the linear transformation layer as 16.

For all deep learning models, we trained 500 epochs. When the evaluation metrics SMAPE on the test data set of the model does not rise for ten consecutive epochs, the training is stopped, and the optimal model weights are automatically loaded. We use the Adam optimizer, with the learning rate set to 0.0003 and the batch size Is 512. The results are shown in Table 2.

DISCUSSION AND CONCLUSION

Discussion

In this study, a total of 13 neural network structures were compared with traditional statistical and machine learning models. Most statistical models can hardly handle the multi-sequence multi-step time series forecasting problem reasonably because these required tens of thousands of statistical models for tens of thousands of sequences, which is infeasible in terms of computational complexity. However, compared with complex machine learning models and deep learning models, the interpretability of statistical models is the best.

Table 2. Deep learning models

Model Name	SMAPE	MSE	MAE
LSTM	0.067	0.010	0.067
Deep LSTM	0.068	0.010	0.067
Bidirectional Deep LSTM	0.066	0.010	0.066
TCN	0.073	0.013	0.073
Wavenet	0.068	0.010	0.068
CNN+LSTM	0.065	0.010	0.065
LSTM with Attention	0.066	0.010	0.066
LSTM with AutoEncoder	0.067	0.010	0.067
LSTM with Seq2Seq	0.066	0.010	0.066
Deepar	0.101	0.020	0.101
Nbeats	0.064	0.001	0.064
Transformer	0.064	0.001	0.064
Temporal Fusion Transformer	0.064	0.001	0.064

Machine learning models can handle single-step time series forecasting problems well because single-step forecasting is quite similar to regression problems. However, regarding the long-period multi-step time series forecasting problem, machine learning models also have the problem of high computational complexity and larger error.

Deep learning models are inherently suitable for different types of time series forecasting problems, and the overall model effect is better than statistical models and machine learning models. However, deep learning models have the problem of poor interpretability. Except for Deepar, all deep learning models have defeated statistical models and machine learning models (see Table 2). The main reason is that Deepar cannot directly optimize the SMPE loss function, which is caused by the network structure of Deepar itself. Among LSTMs, deep bidirectional LSTM has the best performance because the deep bidirectional LSTM model considers information in two-time directions while the stack LSTM layers can learn higher-order hidden laws. Besides, the network structure of CNN+LSTM has a better effect than simply using CNN or LSTM;

The performance of the TCN model is average because the length of our training data is very long, and the performance of TCN in the ultra-long time sequence data is not as good as the RNN model. Wavenet uses a more complex network design, such as a gating mechanism that is similar to LSTM, but its model performance is better than TCN.

After the attention mechanism and seq2seq structure are introduced to LSTM, the model's performance has been improved to a certain extent, which is also in line with expectations. Nbeats, transformer, and temporal fusion transformer performed the best. We can see the great potential of hybrid deep learning models and transformer in time series forecasting tasks.

Notably, different network structures have different learning capabilities and training efficiency. Generally speaking, due to the serial training characteristics of the recurrent neural network, the recurrent neural network is difficult to accelerate in parallel. In the case of the same amount of parameters, the training speed of the recurrent neural network is slower than that of the convolutional neural network, the attention mechanism, and the transformer.

Compared with recurrent neural networks, convolutional neural networks can perform parallel computation because the calculations of different convolution kernels are independent, greatly increasing training time. However, compared with the recurrent neural network, it is more difficult for convolutional neural networks to learn the latent pattern of the long sequence data. It can only realize the learning of the long sequence data by stacking a large number of convolutional layers. With the rapid development of the attention mechanism, self-attention and transformer, which purely use attention layers and some simple feed-forward layers, have been completely applied to many fields to deal with sequence data.

Among them, the research of transformer in time series has made certain progress, such as Bert (Devlin, Chang, Lee, & Toutanova, 2018), temporal fusion transformer and informer (Zhou et al., 2020). They can better use long sequence data to learn complex patterns in time series. Further, as the training process of these kinds of the transformer can be parallelized, in the case of the same amount of parameters, the training efficiency and models' performance of the transformer is much higher than that of the recurrent neural network and convolutional neural network.

Limitations and Future Work

The limitations of this study are as follows. The influence of different hyperparameters on the generalization performance of neural networks was not explored and is indented for continuing research. This study only considered the dynamic variable of web traffic data, but no other static variables were introduced to help improve the predictive ability of the models. We are interested in other variables such as topic, user ratings, and edits. Due to the long calculation time, there were few training epochs for complex neural network models, such as transformer and temporal fusion transformers. We may explore whether more training can improve the results. Finally, more different data and different model validation methods can be used to evaluate the performance of these models. On the other hand, we are interested in time-series analysis on cryptocurrency price (Fang et al., 2020) and the COVID-19 pandemic (Huang et al., 2021).

REFERENCES

Agarap, A. F. (2018). *Deep learning using rectified linear units (relu)*. arXiv preprint arXiv:1803.08375.

Albawi, S., Mohammed, T. A., & Al-Zawi, S. (2017, August). Understanding of a convolutional neural network. In *2017 International Conference on Engineering and Technology (ICET)* (pp. 1-6). Academic Press.

Alley, W. M. (1988). Using exogenous variables in testing for monotonic trends in hydrologic time series. *Water Resources Research*, 24(11), 1955–1961. doi:10.1029/WR024i011p01955

Amoiralis, E. I., Tsili, M. A., & Kladas, A. G. (2009). Transformer design and optimization: A literature survey. *IEEE Transactions on Power Delivery*, 24(4), 1999–2024. doi:10.1109/TPWRD.2009.2028763

Assimakopoulos, V., & Nikolopoulos, K. (2000). The theta model: A decomposition approach to forecasting. *International Journal of Forecasting*, 16(4), 521–530. doi:10.1016/S0169-2070(00)00066-2

Athiyarath, S., Paul, M., & Krishnaswamy, S. (2020). A comparative study and analysis of time series forecasting techniques. *SN Computer Science*, *1*(3), 1–7. doi:10.100742979-020-00180-5

Bai, S., Kolter, J. Z., & Koltun, V. (2018). *An empirical evaluation of generic convolutional and recurrent networks for sequence modeling.* arXiv preprint arXiv:1803.01271.

Barceló-Vidal, C., Aguilar, L., & Martín-Fernández, J. A. (2011). *Compositional VARIMA time series. Compositional Data Analysis: Theory and Applications.* John Wiley & Sons.

Cao, L. J., & Tay, F. E. H. (2003). Support vector machine with adaptive parameters in financial time series forecasting. *IEEE Transactions on Neural Networks*, *14*(6), 1506–1518. doi:10.1109/TNN.2003.820556 PMID:18244595

Chatfield, C. (1978). The Holt - winters forecasting procedure. *Journal of the Royal Statistical Society. Series C, Applied Statistics*, *27*(3), 264–279.

Chen, T., & Guestrin, C. (2016, August). Xgboost: A scalable tree boosting system. In: *Proceedings of the 22nd ACM SigKDD International Conference on Knowledge Discovery and Data Mining* (pp. 785-794). 10.1145/2939672.2939785

Cryer, J. D., & Chan, K. S. (2008). *Time series analysis: with applications in R.* Springer Science & Business Media. doi:10.1007/978-0-387-75959-3

Devlin, J., Chang, M. W., Lee, K., & Toutanova, K. (2018). *Bert: Pre-training of deep bidirectional transformers for language understanding.* arXiv preprint arXiv:1810.04805.

Dorogush, A. V., Ershov, V., & Gulin, A. (2018). *CatBoost: gradient boosting with categorical features support.* arXiv preprint arXiv:1810.11363.

Durbin, J., & Koopman, S. J. (2012). *Time series analysis by state space methods.* Oxford University Press. doi:10.1093/acprof:oso/9780199641178.001.0001

Fan, J., Zhang, K., Huang, Y., Zhu, Y., & Chen, B. (2021). Parallel spatio-temporal attention-based TCN for multivariate time series prediction. *Neural Computing & Applications*, 1–10. doi:10.100700521-021-05958-z

Fang, J., Chiu, D. K. W., & Ho, K. K. W. (2020). Exploring Cryptocurrency Sentimental with Clustering Text Mining on Social Media. In Z. Sun (Ed.), Handbook of Research on Intelligent Analytics with Multi-Industry Applications (pp. 157–171). Academic Press.

Friedman, J. H. (2001). Greedy function approximation: A gradient boosting machine. *Annals of Statistics*, *29*(5), 1189–1232. doi:10.1214/aos/1013203451

Gal, Y., & Ghahramani, Z. (2016). A theoretically grounded application of dropout in recurrent neural networks. *Advances in Neural Information Processing Systems*, *29*, 1019–1027.

Gardner, F. S. Jr. (1985). Exponential smoothing: The state of the art. *Journal of Forecasting*, *4*(1), 1–28. doi:10.1002/for.3980040103

Gibbons, F. X. (1990). Self-attention and behavior: A review and theoretical update. *Advances in Experimental Social Psychology*, *23*, 249–303. doi:10.1016/S0065-2601(08)60321-4

Graves, A., Jaitly, N., & Mohamed, A. R. (2013, December). Hybrid speech recognition with deep bidirectional LSTM. In *2013 IEEE workshop on automatic speech recognition and understanding* (pp. 273-278). IEEE.

He, K., Zhang, X., Ren, S., & Sun, J. (2016). Deep residual learning for image recognition. In *Proceedings of the IEEE conference on computer vision and pattern recognition* (pp. 770-778). IEEE.

He, K., Zhang, X., Ren, S., & Sun, J. (2016). Deep residual learning for image recognition. In *Proceedings of the IEEE conference on computer vision and pattern recognition* (pp. 770-778). IEEE.

Hochreiter, S. (1998). The vanishing gradient problem during learning recurrent neural nets and problem solutions. *International Journal of Uncertainty, Fuzziness and Knowledge-based Systems*, 6(02), 107–116. doi:10.1142/S0218488598000094

Hu, D. (2018) *An Introductory Survey on Attention Mechanisms in NLP Problems*. arXiv:1811.05544

Huang, P. S., Paulino, Y., So, S., Chiu, D. K. W., & Ho, K. K. W. (2021). Special Issue Editorial - COVID-19 Pandemic and Health Informatics (Part 1). *Library Hi Tech*, 39(3), 693–695. doi:10.1108/LHT-09-2021-324

Hyndman, R. J., Koehler, A. B., Snyder, R. D., & Grose, S. (2002). A state space framework for automatic forecasting using exponential smoothing methods. *International Journal of Forecasting*, 18(3), 439–454. doi:10.1016/S0169-2070(01)00110-8

Ji, S., Kim, J., & Im, H. (2019). A comparative study of bitcoin price prediction using deep learning. *Mathematics*, 7(10), 898. doi:10.3390/math7100898

Ke, G., Meng, Q., Finley, T., Wang, T., Chen, W., Ma, W., ... Liu, T. Y. (2017). Lightgbm: A highly efficient gradient boosting decision tree. *Advances in Neural Information Processing Systems*, 30, 3146–3154.

Kurbiel, T., & Khaleghian, S. (2017). *Training of deep neural networks based on distance measures using RMSProp*. arXiv preprint arXiv:1708.01911.

Lai, G., Chang, W. C., Yang, Y., & Liu, H. (2018, June). Modeling long-and short-term temporal patterns with deep neural networks. In *The 41st International ACM SIGIR Conference on Research & Development in Information Retrieval* (pp. 95-104). 10.1145/3209978.3210006

Lim, B., Arık, S. Ö., Loeff, N., & Pfister, T. (2021). Temporal fusion transformers for interpretable multi-horizon time series forecasting. *International Journal of Forecasting*, 37(4), 1748–1764. doi:10.1016/j.ijforecast.2021.03.012

Lim, B., Sercan, O., & Arik, N. (2019). *Temporal Fusion Transformers for Interpretable Multi-horizon Time Series Forecasting*. arXiv:1912.09363

Livieris, I. E., Pintelas, E., & Pintelas, P. (2020). A CNN-LSTM model for gold price time-series forecasting. *Neural Computing & Applications*, 32(23), 17351–17360. doi:10.100700521-020-04867-x

Luong, M. T., Pham, H., & Manning, C. D. (2015). *Effective approaches to attention-based neural machine translation*. arXiv preprint arXiv:1508.04025. doi:10.18653/v1/D15-1166

Lütkepohl, H., & Xu, F. (2012). The role of the log transformation in forecasting economic variables. *Empirical Economics, 42*(3), 619–638. doi:10.100700181-010-0440-1

Medsker, L. R., & Jain, L. C. (2001). Recurrent neural networks. *Design and Applications, 5*, 64–67.

Oord, A. V. D., Dieleman, S., Zen, H., Simonyan, K., Vinyals, O., Graves, A., . . . Kavukcuoglu, K. (2016). *Wavenet: A generative model for raw audio.* arXiv preprint arXiv:1609.03499.

Oreshkin, B. N., Carpov, D., Chapados, N., & Bengio, Y. (2019). *N-BEATS: Neural basis expansion analysis for interpretable time series forecasting.* arXiv preprint arXiv:1905.10437.

Oreshkin, B. N., Carpov, D., Chapados, N., & Bengio, Y. (2019). *N-BEATS: Neural basis expansion analysis for interpretable time series forecasting.* arXiv preprint arXiv:1905.10437.

Qin, H. (2019). *Comparison of deep learning models on time series forecasting: A case study of dissolved oxygen prediction.* arXiv preprint arXiv:1911.08414.

Rebane, J., Karlsson, I., Papapetrou, P., & Denic, S. (2018, August). Seq2Seq RNNs and ARIMA models for cryptocurrency prediction: A comparative study. In SIGKDD Fintech 2018, London, UK.

Robinson, P. M., & Sims, C. A. (1994). Time series with strong dependence. In *Advances in econometrics, sixth world congress* (Vol. 1, pp. 47-95). 10.1017/CCOL0521444594.002

Salinas, D., Flunkert, V., Gasthaus, J., & Januschowski, T. (2020). DeepAR: Probabilistic forecasting with autoregressive recurrent networks. *International Journal of Forecasting, 36*(3), 1181–1191. doi:10.1016/j.ijforecast.2019.07.001

Samal, K. K. R., Babu, K. S., Das, S. K., & Acharaya, A. (2019, August). Time series based air pollution forecasting using SARIMA and prophet model. In *Proceedings of the 2019 international conference on information technology and computer communications* (pp. 80-85). 10.1145/3355402.3355417

Schmidhuber, J. (2014). *Deep Learning in Neural Networks: An Overview.* arXiv:1404.7828

Shumway, R. H., & Stoffer, D. S. (2017). ARIMA models. In *Time series analysis and its applications* (pp. 75–163). Springer. doi:10.1007/978-3-319-52452-8_3

Svozil, D., Kvasnicka, V., & Pospichal, J. (1997). Introduction to multi-layer feed-forward neural networks. *Chemometrics and Intelligent Laboratory Systems, 39*(1), 43–62. doi:10.1016/S0169-7439(97)00061-0

Taieb, S. B., Bontempi, G., Atiya, A. F., & Sorjamaa, A. (2012). A review and comparison of strategies for multi-step ahead time series forecasting based on the NN5 forecasting competition. *Expert Systems with Applications, 39*(8), 7067–7083. doi:10.1016/j.eswa.2012.01.039

Taylor, S. J., & Letham, B. (2018). Forecasting at scale. *The American Statistician, 72*(1), 37–45. doi: 10.1080/00031305.2017.1380080

Valipour, M. (2015). Long-term runoff study using SARIMA and ARIMA models in the United States. *Meteorological Applications, 22*(3), 592–598. doi:10.1002/met.1491

Vaswani, A., Shazeer, N., Parmar, N., Uszkoreit, J., Jones, L., Gomez, A. N., . . . Polosukhin, I. (2017). Attention is all you need. In Advances in neural information processing systems (pp. 5998-6008). Academic Press.

Vaswani, A., Shazeer, N., Parmar, N., Uszkoreit, J., Jones, L., Gomez, A. N., . . . Polosukhin, I. (2017). *Attention is all you need.* arXiv preprint arXiv:1706.03762

Xiang, Z., Yan, J., & Demir, I. (2020). A rainfall-runoff model with LSTM-based sequence-to-sequence learning. *Water Resources Research, 56*(1).

Yamanaka, J., Kuwashima, S., & Kurita, T. (2017, November). Fast and accurate image super resolution by deep CNN with skip connection and network in network. In *International Conference on Neural Information Processing* (pp. 217-225). Springer. 10.1007/978-3-319-70096-0_23

Yermal, L., & Balasubramanian, P. (2017, December). Application of auto arima model for forecasting returns on minute wise amalgamated data in nse. In *2017 IEEE International Conference on Computational Intelligence and Computing Research (ICCIC)* (pp. 1-5). IEEE. 10.1109/ICCIC.2017.8524232

Zeroual, A., Harrou, F., Dairi, A., & Sun, Y. (2020). Deep learning methods for forecasting COVID-19 time-Series data: A Comparative study. *Chaos, Solitons, and Fractals, 140*, 110121. doi:10.1016/j. chaos.2020.110121 PMID:32834633

Zhou, H., Zhang, S., Peng, J., Zhang, S., Li, J., Xiong, H., & Zhang, W. (2020). *Informer: Beyond Efficient Transformer for Long Sequence Time-Series Forecasting.* arXiv preprint arXiv:2012.07436.

ADDITIONAL READING

Dong, L. Y., Ji, S. J., Zhang, C. J., Zhang, Q., Chiu, D. W., Qiu, L. Q., & Li, D. (2018). An unsupervised topic-sentiment joint probabilistic model for detecting deceptive reviews. *Expert Systems with Applications, 114*, 210–223. doi:10.1016/j.eswa.2018.07.005

Fantinato, M., Peres, M. S., Kafeza, E., Chiu, D. K. W., & Hung, P. (2020). A Survey of the Integration of Deep Learning and Service Orientation. *Journal of Database Management, 32*(3), 95–119. doi:10.4018/ JDM.2021070105

Gao, W., Lam, K. M., Chiu, D. K. W., & Ho, K. K. W. (2020). A Big data Analysis of the Factors Influencing Movie Box Office in China. In Z. Sun (Ed.), *Handbook of Research on Intelligent Analytics with Multi-Industry Applications* (pp. 232–249).

Ji, S., Yang, W., Guo, S., Chiu, D. K. W., Zhang, C., & Yuan, X. (2020). Asymmetric response aggregation heuristics for rating prediction and recommendation. *Applied Intelligence, 50*(5), 1416–1436. doi:10.100710489-019-01594-2

Ji, S., Zhang, Q., Li, J., Chiu, D. K. W., Xu, S., Yi, L., & Gong, M. (2020). A burst-based unsupervised method for detecting review spammer groups. *Information Sciences, 536*, 454–469. doi:10.1016/j. ins.2020.05.084

Ji, S. J., Leung, H. F., Sim, K. M., Liang, Y. Q., & Chiu, D. K. W. (2015). An Adaptive Prediction-regret Driven Strategy for One-shot Bilateral Bargaining Software Agents. *Expert Systems with Applications*, *42*(1), 411–425. doi:10.1016/j.eswa.2014.07.022

Ji, S. J., Ma, H. Y., Zhang, S. L., Leung, H. F., Chiu, D., Zhang, C. J., & Fang, X. W. (2016). A pre-evolutionary advisor list generation strategy for robust defencing reputation attacks. *Knowledge-Based Systems*, *103*, 1–18. doi:10.1016/j.knosys.2016.03.015

Jiang, N., Zhuang, Y., & Chiu, D. K. W. (2017). Multiple transmission optimization of medical images in recourse-constraint mobile telemedicine systems. *Computer Methods and Programs in Biomedicine*, *145*, 103–113. doi:10.1016/j.cmpb.2017.04.002 PMID:28552115

Wang, X., Ji, S., Liang, Y., Leung, H., & Chiu, D. K. W. (2019). An unsupervised strategy for defending against multifarious reputation attacks. *Applied Intelligence*, *49*(12), 4189–4210. doi:10.100710489-019-01490-9

Zhuang, Y., Jiang, N., Wu, Z., Li, Q., Chiu, D. K., & Hu, H. (2014). Efficient and robust large medical image retrieval in mobile cloud computing environment. *Information Sciences*, *263*, 60–86. doi:10.1016/j.ins.2013.10.013

KEY TERMS AND DEFINITIONS

Additive Trend Components: There is a seasonal component in the time series, and the seasonal component and other components in the time series have an additive relationship.

Deep Learning: Imitates the way humans gain knowledge for automating predictive analytics and can be abstracted as a combination of the physical structure of a multi-layer neural network with activation functions, objective functions, optimization algorithms, and various auxiliary functions.

Direct Forecasting Strategy: Requires developing a separate model for each forecast time step, thus avoiding error accumulation in each step.

Hybrid Forecasting Strategy: Combines the recursive and direct forecasting strategy so that static or dynamic time-invariant features help increase the forecasting accuracy while avoiding error accumulation like the direct forecasting strategy.

Multiplicative Trend Components: There is a seasonal component in the time series and the seasonal component and other components in the time series are multiplicative.

Recursive Forecasting Strategy: Uses a one-step model multiple times in which the prediction for the prior time step feeds into the next time step for prediction.

Time Series Forecasting: Using historical data in a period to predict the future. The input and output format of time series forecasting is similar to regression problems in supervised learning, but with time dependence, i.e., if the order of the data is changed, all data patterns and relations are likely to undergo huge changes affecting the prediction results.

Chapter 15
Weibo Analysis on Chinese Cultural Knowledge for Gaming

Zhixuan He
The University of Hong Kong, Hong Kong

Dickson K. W. Chiu
The University of Hong Kong, Hong Kong

Kevin K. W. Ho
iD https://orcid.org/0000-0003-1304-0573
University of Guam, Guam

ABSTRACT

This chapter analyzes the current situation of video games with Chinese cultural knowledge in China's game market by analyzing Weibo messages of five selected video games developed based on Chinese culture to explore their relationships with Chinese culture. The authors then summarize the results from comments, likes, word cloud, and clustering analysis to provide practical suggestions. As a new industry, video games and e-sports are gaining popularity worldwide. However, scant research has focused on video games developed based on Chinese culture in the current market, mainly because they started much later than their Western counterparts. Therefore, the findings of this research can help game developers better understand these markets and customer preferences while protecting and spreading Chinese culture through gaming and e-sports activities in this digital era.

INTRODUCTION

With technological advancement and people's increasing demand for spiritual, cultural, and entertainment, China's video game industry has grown rapidly in recent years. Video games have become increasingly popular among young people in China. Since e-sports became the official program in the 2022 Hangzhou Asian Games, the video game industry ushers in unprecedented development opportunities. According to the data from Statista (Clement, 2021), China was the largest video game market with a

DOI: 10.4018/978-1-7998-9016-4.ch015

revenue of US$40.85B in 2020, and the number of game users in China has reached 664.79 million in 2020 (Lin, 2021a). The revenue of e-sports in China in 2020 was 136.56B Yuan (1 USD = 6.5 Yuan approximately in 2021), while the Console and PC game revenue in China reached 640 million Yuan in 2019 (Lin, 2021b; 2021c).

As China's video game industry enters its golden age, various types of video games have entered the market, including action games, science-fiction games, role-playing games (RPG), simulation games (SLG), etc. Foreign famous game companies like Activision Blizzard, Electronic Arts, and Ubisoft have refocused their products on young people in China. At the same time, domestic game companies like Tencent and NetEase are rising and competing with foreign companies in the China market. Among various kinds of video games, different cultures come from different countries inside those games. In recent years, more and more developers have been incorporating elements of Chinese culture into their video games. To gain more insights into how culture affects game design, this research uses a Big Data analytics approach to explore the relationship between video games and Chinese culture so that people can find a better way to propagate and protect Chinese culture in this digital age. Thus, our three research questions (RQs) are as follows:

RQ1. What elements of Chinese culture are used in video games in the current major electronic game market?

RQ2. How popular are such games with Chinese cultural elements in the current electronic game market?

RQ3. How can these video games spread and preserve Chinese cultural elements?

LITERATURE REVIEW

Video Games and Cultures

With the development of the Internet and computer technologies, different types of video games have appeared in the market. More and more game developers started incorporating various cultural elements into these video games. For example, Assassin's Creed Valhalla, developed by Ubisoft (a US company), incorporates Viking culture and legends. In this game, the player acts as a Viking leader called Eivor (Assassin's Creed Valhalla, n.d.) and follows the game plot to experience ancient Nordic and British culture and legends one by one. The game was set in the Viking age at around 870 AD. Typical scenarios include (i) controlling the protagonist to use an ax, a commonly used weapon by the ancient Vikings because of its simple form and affordable availability; (ii) sailing around in the game with a Viking warship called Langskip, exploring Scandinavia and Britain. The Langskip is often called the dragon headship because the bow and stern of this ship are usually made into a unique shape that is high and titled like a dragon and a snake (Ma, 2011). Generally speaking, this game incorporates the cultural elements of the Vikings for players to experience.

The second example is the Red Dead Redemption 2, an action-adventure game based on the history of the American West developed by Rockstar San Diego (a US company). The game includes a classic representative of the American West in the eyes of the public, the cowboys. The background of this game is set in the American West, Midwest, and South in 1899. Players act as Arthur Morgan, a member of the Van Der Linde gang, to experience the American spirits in the Western (Red Dead Redemption 2, n.d.). In the late 19th century, the US was transformed from an agricultural country to an industrial country. The cowboy was a special working class in that specific period in American history who made a significant contribution to the accumulation of wealth and the development of the territory (Li, 1999). Cowboys and this period of history were rewritten into various literary works, movies, and eventually into todays' video games. The cowboy culture has already become a representative culture of the American West widely known worldwide. In Red Dead Redemption 2, players can immerse themselves in the new world of the Western US and experience the Western cowboy culture (Red Dead Redemption 2, n.d.).

The third example is Nioh 2, an action role-playing game developed by Team Ninja and Kou Shibusawa, a pair of Japanese game developers (Nioh 2, n.d.). The background of this game is the end of the Warring States Period in Japan around late 1500 AD. The player acts as a Japanese samurai called Hide to meet various monsters in Japanese mythology and celebrities who appeared in Japanese history in the game to experience Japanese Bushido and Ninja culture. The emergence and growth of the Japanese Samurai as a class should be attributed to the formation of the family-style military group, the Samurai group. Maintaining the existence and development of the family is the main reason for forming the Samurai group. In particular, maintaining the master-apprentice relationship is the prerequisite for the existence of the samurai group, which eventually led to the birth of the Shogunate.

Besides, Ninja is also a special profession in ancient Japan. The Ninja appeared in Japan from the Kamakura period (1192 to 1333 AD) to the Edo period (1603 to 1867 AD). The Ninja was an individual or group that conducted espionage, sabotage, infiltration, and assassination activities as a profession. Ninjas have formed many genres through practicing Ninjutsu that requires superhuman endurance. Not only were they good at using gunpowder and attacks in battles, but they were also good at making makeup to confuse others and collect information (Liu & Qie, 2016). In Nioh 2, players can use various kinds of Ninjutsu and Katana (Japanese sword). They will also encounter many celebrities in Japanese history, such as Oda Nobunaga and Toyotomi Hideyoshi, because the game's background is adapted from real Japanese history (Nioh 2, n.d.).

Video Games and Chinese Cultures

Compared with foreign game companies, China's video game industry started late. For example, one of the leading Japanese game companies, Nintendo, was founded in 1889 as a game cards company and transformed into a video game developer in the 1970s. Later, Nintendo launched many famous games, such as Super Mario and Pokemon, in 1985 and 1996, respectively (Nintendo, n.d.). Only much later, Kingsoft launched Magic Eagle (神鷹突擊隊) in 1994, which was regarded as the first game in Mainland China (Song & Guo, 2012). However, since the early 21ˢᵗ century, games produced from foreign countries, such as the World of Warcraft, Pop Kart, and Counter-Strike, were introduced into Mainland China, and domestic games were on the wane. These foreign video games have grabbed a large amount of the domestic market. Worse still, a large number of low-quality online games that were only for profit continued to emerge, and illegally pirated single games emerged (Song & Guo, 2012). Therefore, few outstanding video games were injected with Chinese cultures.

The first well-known Chinese culture adapted into video games was the Three Kingdoms culture. The Three Kingdoms culture refers to a comprehensive culture that originated from the history of the Three Kingdoms Period (220 to 280 AD) and formed many derivative phenomena represented by the *Romance of the Three Kingdoms* (三國演義) through the spread and evolution of the stories of the Three Kingdoms (Shen, 1994). One of the most famous Three Kingdoms games is the Dynasty Warriors Series Games (真三國無雙系列). The first version of Dynasty Warriors was launched in 2000 by Omega Force and

Koei (Dynasty Warriors, n.d.). This game is a kind of hack and slash fighting game, in which players choose to operate a character from the Three Kingdoms period to fight in those famous battles in history.

The second example is the Fantasy Westward Journey injected with Ancient Chinese mythology. As one of China's four classical novels, *Journey to the West* (西遊記) is famous for its characters such as Monkey King, Tang the Monk, and Zhu Bajie (Pig Monk), and has become an important element in Chinese culture just like the *Romance of the Three Kingdoms*. The Fantasy Westward Journey is a Massively Multiplayer Online Role-Playing Game (MMORPG) with a total of 18 characters in human, fairy, or demon races for players to choose from (The Fantasy Westward Journey, n.d.). Players can operate those characters to use various kinds of weapons and spells in the game.

The last example is Chinese Paladin: Sword and Fairy, incorporated with the Chinese martial arts culture. This is a role-playing game launched by Softstar in 1995 (The Legend of Sword and Fairy, n.d.). The cores of Chinese martial arts culture have two points: one is being good at martial arts, the other is having a chivalrous spirit (Lo et al., 2021). Benevolence, knowledge, and bravery are regarded as the essential evaluation criteria of martial arts culture. In many martial arts literary works, most heroes regarded punishing evil and upholding justice as their highest code of conduct and ethical norm (Zhang & Zhao., 2017). In this game, players can operate the character to practice, which refers to leveling up and using various weapons and magic arts to fight against enemies.

Comparison Between Western and Chinese Culture Games

For those western culture games developed by foreign companies, most of them have rich game plots. The length of the game plot of these games usually can reach dozens of hours. If players want to complete the whole game plot, it may take hundreds of hours. For example, the main story of Red Dead Redemption 2 will take players 40 to 60 hours to complete (Harvey & DeFreitas, 2019), and Nioh 2 requires around 100 hours (PowerPyx, 2020). Besides, these games also have excellent gameplay quality. For example, Nioh 2 supports the ray-tracing feature and Deep Learning Super Sampling (DLSS) for specified computer graphic cards (Burnes, 2021), making the game quality more realistic and player immersion better.

For those games incorporated with Chinese culture, the average gameplay time is often less than 50 hours. For example, the gameplay time of Chinese Paladin 6 is around 43 hours, including the main story and extra content. Even if there are many old players, it is hard to attract more new players to play the games due to their short content.

Generally speaking, the games incorporated with western cultures are well made, and they have good game quality and attractive game plots. Thus, they often quickly occupy the market. But for those games incorporated with Chinese culture, well-made games are rare, and they are also far less attractive in terms of the game quality and plot.

METHODS

As this study focuses on video games with Chinese cultural elements, five video games are selected as the target for the web crawler: *Civilization VI, Total War: Three Kingdoms, Justice, Tale of Immortal,* and *Naraka: Blade Point.* Each of the data sets has about 400 items. We used text-ming to analyze the data collected and looked for the keyword trendings and responses from online forums, as well as the word cloud and cluster analysis. Table 1 presents the screenshot of the *Civilization VI* data set.

Nakara: Bladepoint and *Tale of Immortal* are chosen because they are the latest Chinese culture-based video games launched on June 16, 2021, and January 27, 2021, respectively. The player count of *Nakara: Bladepoint* hit 136,606 in 9 hours after its launch (Adams, 2021). This game is based on Chinese chivalry culture, referring to those who practice martial arts with their abilities to perform chivalrous justice and fight for the weak against the strong (and evil) (Wei, 2010). *Justice* is also one of the most famous ancient chivalry video games using the Chinese chivalry culture, a Massive Multiplayer Online (MMO) type.

Tale of Immortal uses classical Chinese cultural elemental of *Mountains and Rivers* (山水) and *Cultivating Immortality* (修仙). Civilization VI won the Game Awards for Best Sim/Strategy in 2016 (Avendano, 2016). This game contains different cultures from the world, including Chinese cultures, such as ancient buildings and ancient poems. Total War: Three Kingdoms is one of the latest video games with a *Three Kingdoms* background, launched in May 2019.

The data used in this research is collected from Weibo by a Python web crawler. This module can get the User ID, main page's URL, content, time, device, number of sharing, number of comments, and number of likes from Weibo.

Data Preprocessing

Stop Word List. Constructing the stop word list is an important step. Many non-content words in Chinese and English text will affect the analysis result, e.g., "你" (you), "我" (I/me), "他/她" (He/She), "虽然" (although), etc., in Chinese, and *about, and, can, go*, etc., in English. The stop word list used in this research includes three public Chinese stop word lists: Baidu Stop Word List, HIT Stop Word List, and SCU Stop Word List (Xie, Chu, Chiu, & Wang, 2021).

Chinese Text Segmentation. In this research, the Chinese text should be segmented for analysis, and otherwise, some meaningful words will be mis-filtered during the analysis. Table 2 presents some keywords for the analysis.

RESULTS AND DISCUSSION

Analysis of Comments and Likes

The recent 50 data are extracted, and the line charts are drawn to analyze the trend of comments and likes of these games. The time duration is about two weeks. Figures 1 and 2 present the trend of comments and likes from the users of these five games.

From Figures 1 and 2, *Naraka: Bladepoint* has the most change in both comments and likes. Justice has changed in likes, but the trend in comments is insignificant. *Total War: Three Kingdoms* has a trend of small changes in both comments and likes. For *Civilization VI* and *Tale of Immortal*, there is an unclear trend of change between these two games in comments and likes compared with the other three games. *Naraka: Bladepoint* has more active users than other games. The most remarkable difference between *Naraka: Bladepoint* and other games are that the game type of *Naraka: Bladepoint* is a larger-scale last man standing deathmatch, which is one of the most popular game types. Some games of the same type, such as *PUBG* and *Fortnite*, have been very popular worldwide in recent years. Indeed, *Naraka: Bladepoint* is the first large-scale last man standing deathmatch game with Chinese chivalry culture. *Naraka: Bladepoint* players can use different kinds of Chinese cold weapons like spears and broadswords

Table 1. Civilization VI data set

昵称	主页url	内容	时间	设备	分享数	评论鼠标	点赞数
长弓手皮揣子	https://weibo.com/1294317314?refer_flag=1001030103_	#游戏##文明6##亲子#大儿子最近热衷于在我玩游戏的时候当狗头军师。7岁的小男孩，满脑子想的都是打仗～～"爸爸,旁边那个城市是你的国家。"呃,不,那是别的国家。"把它打下来!""打不了,我跟他们是和平状态。开打了关系就会一直不好。而且要有合适的战争借口才能宣战,不然国形象太差会引来其他国家一起打咱们。最好能保持远交近攻。另外国家内部建设也还不到位;科技发展落后武器装备不行让人家,财政不好了养不起军队,基建搞不好前线打仗后方饥荒遍反……"那你以后打算打吗?"要打的吧,我这局游戏设定的是统治胜利。	05月24日 17:30	微博weibo.com	12	29	89
DDG的秋天	https://weibo.com/6052732978?refer_flag=1001030103_	《文明6》一把游戏九小时	06月20日 22:28	HUAWEIP40Pro5G	0	5	5
Kobatal	https://weibo.com/3784000367?refer_flag=1001030103_	啊啊啊啊啊,为什么我玩的游戏都这么杀时间啊dota2,全战三国,文明6,了不起的修仙模拟器,十字军之王3,反正搞出个所以然呢,三天就过去了	06月15日 01:47	荣耀V30PRO5G	0	1	2
一看就是老天涯浪子了	https://weibo.com/3363741080?refer_flag=1001030103_	刚为了把咖啡喝完玩了会文明6计划2:30前刷头洗漱完毕 但看游戏里的表已经2:00顿时慌得一批马上坐车 结果车上看自己手表才1:38顿时松了一口气 但还不能完全松懈 毕竟时间还是紧张 等我下车快到家一看手机 还是1:38 这就不得不引起我的注意和思考:整件事真的只是单纯的三个表没个一个准的问题吗?	06月14日 13:41	iPhone客户端	0	4	1
3DMGAME官方微博	https://weibo.com/2163365571?refer_flag=1001030103_	#E3 2021#由世嘉发行的历史战略游戏《人类》(HUMANKIND)宣布将于6月13-21日进行封闭Beta测试,玩家可以选择5个不同时期的50个文明。游戏将于8月17日 发售,登陆Steam/Epic/谷歌Stadia平台,国区预购价232元,支持简体中文。L3DMGAME官方微博的微博视频	06月14日 05:51	微博视频号	0	0	10
李一鏖在東京	https://weibo.com/6195049590?refer_flag=1001030103_	摩尔庄园很无语,这么久了,bug问题层出不穷,骗氪到了这种地步?你不氪金还玩也是在为这款游戏贡献流量,我现在删了游戏,以后都不会去玩垃圾国产游戏!文明6比这好玩儿太久多,劝森也比这友好。消费情怀是现在国内文娱产业的捞钱手段。以后都不会再玩儿。	06月14日 05:40	摩尔庄园超话	0	0	0
任言·君语	https://weibo.com/1575749231?refer_flag=1001030103_	Super Switch屏幕进化到7寸是老任对文明6,三国志,德军总部这类游戏的硬件优化	06月13日 03:06	HUAWEIP30	0	4	3
贪婪魔女Leona	https://weibo.com/3196414734?refer_flag=1001030103_	#2021日常#文明6这个游戏真的是……每次看世界地理历史相关的书的时候特别想开一局,然而开一局就能劝退我半年……今天算是人类在非洲起源了,半年后我再开埃及吧	06月13日 02:23	HUAWEIP20Pro	0	0	0
一颗爱心牛奶球	https://weibo.com/3879379642?refer_flag=1001030103_	我之前起初买了文明6,教程来还没过就觉着太繁琐了,但我一直相信它是个好游戏。这两天磕完了b站大佬3h的介绍和新手前期发展,终于在O今晚8点体会到了游戏的快乐,并购入了dlc,当我放下ns的时候已经这个时间了	06月12日 01:26	iPhone7Plus	0	12	4
科学导报社	https://weibo.com/2424618195?refer_flag=1001030103_	#文明校园#山西农业大学游戏+知识 这场竞赛有创意6月3日,一场特殊的思想政治课在山西农业大学勤勤学楼千人报告厅展开。该校马克思主义学院教授王宇娴向全体学生讲述了抗美援朝胜利的伟大意义:"这一战,打出了山河无恙、家国平安,打出了中国军队的战斗力,打出了中国人民的精气神,打出了中国的国际地位,打出了世界的和平和人类的进步!"台上,教授慷慨陈词、激情澎湃;台下,观众聚精会神、掌声阵阵。为了引导青年大学生学史明理、学史增信、学史崇德、学史力行,迎接中国共产党成立100周年,由山西农业大学校团委主办、食品学院分团委	06月11日 10:57	360安全浏览器	0	1	1
我是读书人lol	https://weibo.com/5759274656?refer_flag=1001030103_	坥文明6问同大佬们,我用华为M6玩手机版为啥游戏画面会超出屏幕	06月11日 00:57	文明6超话	0	2	0
乙女游戏万事屋	https://weibo.com/6388699885?refer_flag=1001030103_	【投稿】希望自制乙游,想做个玩法小调查。个人对卡牌玩法的代入感不大强,如果将战斗改进成操作类,比如战略游戏类型,例如文明6、钢铁雄心4或者欧陆风云4那样的战略沙盘,插在完结剧情突断类型中,根据战斗结果走向不同支线,即为是自己打的因此代入感应该会更强一些,输赢都有剧别be(战略撤退),想问问各位姐妹们对这类游戏的接受度。收起全文d	06月10日 15:55		0	34	64
橘猫SHIKA	https://weibo.com/2273319500?refer_flag=1001030103_	我从小到大就没怎么活得跟同龄女生一样,不化妆,打游戏文明6战争圉圉拿到手上了还不是又放下来,和铅笔灰打交通大学时期还穿了一段时间lo装女性享受的东西有性别倾向性,有些人连这个差异都不接受还出来打拳确实有点丢人	06月10日 12:17	抓拍猫专用Android	0	1	5
微男酱	https://weibo.com/6499581994?refer_flag=1001030103_	不听劝买了文明6(15分钟从入门到入土)这游戏到底怎么玩	06月08日 17:11	iPhone客户端	0	2	0
Epic游戏商城	https://weibo.com/7287111107?refer_flag=1001030103_	【送手办啦】Epic大促正在火热进行中,今天@2KGames中国为大家准备了惊喜礼物哦~ 转发本贴将在6月17日抽两人随机送《无主之地3》的精美手办!《无主之地3》、《NBA2K21》、《文明6》等也都在epic平台打折特卖中,配合套娃券真实惠!#2K夏日游戏祭#@微博抽奖平台	06月07日 11:47	微博weibo.com	1645	413	509
斗门发布	https://weibo.com/3772731587?refer_flag=1001030103_	#文明实践#【莲洲镇举办垃圾分类宣传活动 村民在游戏中学会垃圾分类】6月5日下午,斗门区莲洲镇市政园林环卫办在莲江村举办"垃圾分类,我是行动者"垃圾分类宣传活动,吸引众多村民参与。	06月07日 10:15	微博weibo.com	0	0	0
小鲍07	https://weibo.com/6585397248?refer_flag=1001030103_	大英帝国,你的想法很危险啊#文明6##游戏#2南昌	06月06日 10:37	荣耀30S5G	0	1	1
南昌日报	https://weibo.com/3143022404?refer_flag=1001030103_	#世界环境日##美丽南昌·幸福家园#【从身边小事做起 共建美丽家园】6月4日上午,红谷滩区行政广场上热闹非凡,这是由开生的江西省生态文明建设成果展示暨6·5环境日现场宣传活动在这里举行,"2021江西最美环保人"荣誉称号授予、环保互动游戏等环节引导人们践行绿色发展理念,从身边小事做起,共同履行环保责任,共建美丽家园。O从身边小事做起 共建美丽家园收起全文d	06月05日 15:52	微博weibo.com	0	0	0
没事多睡会儿吧	https://weibo.com/5284103597?refer_flag=1001030103_	朋友们文明6游戏时长已经8.8小时了要知道,我把这游戏买来可还没有18个小时啊…刚刚睡梦里还在点市政呢	06月03日 17:28	微博国际版	0	0	2
Cloud_P5	https://weibo.com/1254268391?refer_flag=1001030103_	【模拟战旗连发】类文明游戏《旧世界(Old World)》宣布结束早先的EA阶段,将于7月1日发布正式版。本作由文明4的主设计师牵头开发,在文明的基础上中追加了事件系统,打造出别具风格的玩法。加上8月17日发布的《人类(Humankind)》,夏季共有两款类文明模拟类游戏发售。不知文明6之后还是否有更新计 展开全文c	06月02日 14:00	微博视频号	0	0	0
Boozern	https://weibo.com/5228170970?refer_flag=1001030103_	之前玩文明6的时候查丹麦在后期经常绿脸做蹄狗狗就觉得游戏有点假 今天原来是在映射现实	06月01日 09:37	iPhone客户端	0	1	0
神奇的盒子Xbox	https://weibo.com/6605861553?refer_flag=1001030103_	《文明6》第六个DLC葡萄牙包预告片#游戏#种草官#L神奇的盒子Xbox的微博视频	05月31日 23:53	微博视频号	0	0	0
咕叽咕叽_Bisou	https://weibo.com/3885218542?refer_flag=1001030103_	文明6-没有网的时候最适合消磨时间的游戏一把文明6快乐一周末 让我再来最后亿个回合	05月31日 01:54	iPhone12	0	0	0

continued on following page

Table 1. Continued

昵称	主页url	内容	时间	设备	分享数	评论数	点赞数
puppyez	https://weibo.com/6489857507?refer_flag=1001030103_	我已经四个月没碰文明6,半年没碰刺客信条了自己电脑充公,没得游戏打快要闷死了	05月30日 17:52		0	0	0
非麻瓜Mingle	https://weibo.com/2946348473?refer_flag=1001030103_	有没有听见点「开始游戏」的瞬间那声真情实意的叹气了?差点没忍住就又要修仙用命肝了。感天动地 我忍住了!看着文明6游戏片头一如既往地感动我澎湃中带着一丝清醒,忍了忍了,好好学习才能更好地建设我的国家等着我!L非麻瓜Mingle的微博视频	05月30日 03:26	iPadAir	0	0	4
Barolo-tt	https://weibo.com/6137824084?refer_flag=1001030103_	睡前忠告,别玩文明6,一抬头天亮了,服了,真有毒这游戏	05月29日 05:49	iPhone客户端	0	0	0
大虹的一年私记	https://weibo.com/2203611471?refer_flag=1001030103_	Steam。。。。你好狠我正价买的巫师3和文明6。你一个减到20多一个减到40多。以后大火游戏我肯定忍一年再买了	05月28日 16:12	HUAWEIP30	0	2	0
欧皇露露子	https://weibo.com/3106541455?refer_flag=1001030103_	老弟,别骂了,我上个月原价退的文明6,这月就打折,你以后见不到我了,还是一模一样的日期,现在躺我这条锦鲤,你下次游戏必史低。	05月26日 13:34		0	1	2
你妈卡在井盖里了	https://weibo.com/5163383150?refer_flag=1001030103_	打游戏真爽 有人陪打游戏更爽了 我原来以为是我是缺人陪 现在才知道 我就是他妈命里缺游戏妈的 直接他妈玩嗨游戏我太好玩了文明6yyds!	05月26日 00:16	iPhone客户端	0	0	0
秋刀鱼日	https://weibo.com/5852763569?refer_flag=1001030103_	今晚就是挺有趣的 在门口复习英语 好多人都一起出来了 外面很热 身上都是汗 我们也聊的很欢 孟子J哥 阿u 张森森 健哥 邱子 都在外面一起哈哈哈 学高街哥敬我五帝电气鼠慢摇给哈哈哈哈哈 第一节的时候在后面和v桑还有何点点一起玩 何总坐地图册研究游戏文明6如何侵略国家哈哈哈 帮盖子和v哥背单词 健哥乐在其中 反正就是 我 妇男之友了收起全文d	05月24日 23:47	iPhone客户端	0	1	0
每天一顿黄焖鸡	https://weibo.com/2644116591?refer_flag=1001030103_	开始打文明6,或许游戏刚打开那十分钟是最好玩的	05月24日 00:24		0	0	0
小狗说谢谢惠顾	https://weibo.com/7606891465?refer_flag=1001030103_	我的脑子做不了很复杂的即时战略思考,特别是多人情境下,像狼人杀 推理文明6这种类型的,也不知道是懒还是笨,很抗拒,fps游戏和moba这种程度的倒还不赖	05月22日 22:59	微博国际版	0	1	0
阿伟不会笑	https://weibo.com/7511428700?refer_flag=1001030103_	致宝贝的第十二封信宝贝 已经十二封信了 很快啊 由于咋晚熬了个小夜 还买了个半个西瓜熬夜 今天早上起床 是感觉膀胱炸了 然后惊醒的 我 去了厕所 然后一看时间10点多 且咋晚买了个一直想玩但是不敢的游戏叫文明6很耗费时间 所以对十下午下班也是室友带来给我的 确实没有什么出门的欲望 一会去健个身 提提精神宝贝 还是想问你你现在在哪 在做什么 你也不要以后自责没有先出现什么的 在这段等你的岁月里 我仍优秀 也在变温柔突然想起来看倾城之恋的一些感悟 对爱程度的渴望会衍生出对爱的怀疑 不断试探对方 始	05月22日 20:15	HUAWEIP30Pro	0	0	0
Nu-menyy	https://weibo.com/6796479409?refer_flag=1001030103_	文明6这游戏好玩到我和王昀晨为了同时成功登录大约尝试了15遍花了至少35分钟都没放弃	05月20日 12:34	iPhone	0	0	0
SilverSupersonicAircraft	https://weibo.com/3602511442?refer_flag=1001030103_	Angel City Chorale/Christopher Tin《Sogno di Volare ("The Dream of Flight")》(游戏《文明6》主题曲)KSogno di Volare ("The Dream of Flight") (游戏《文明6》主题曲)(@网易云音乐)每次玩游戏都感觉很震撼	05月20日 12:33	网易云音乐	0	4	0
游侠网	https://weibo.com/1893905030?refer_flag=1001030103_	【《文明6》开发商下半年将公布多个激动人心的新项目】在本周的Take-Two财报会议中,公司的首席执行官Strauss Zelnick表示:《文明6》、《幽浮》等热门IP的开发商Firaxis工作室将在下半年公布多个"激动人心"的新项目。Strauss说:"《文明6》已经发售了有6年了,5年以来,游戏的日活用户仍保持稳定增长,迄今为止,这款游戏的销量已经达到1100万。此外,得益于《幽浮2》登陆switch,以及《幽浮:奇美拉小队》的成功发售。Firaxis经历了他们有史以来最棒的一年。"关于未来,S	05月20日 08:05 转赞人数超过10	微博weibo.com	2	6	12
沫沙澄	https://weibo.com/2679839363?refer_flag=1001030103_	#文明6#这个游戏真的是无情的时间吞噬机器,感觉自己也太久玩兄久,这么多个小时是如何过去的?为什么已经凌晨4点了?可是六点多我还要起床呢??……于是,又是困困的一天	05月19日 15:34	微博weibo.com	0	6	0
FayeWong、	https://weibo.com/3965920716?refer_flag=1001030103_	文明6简直了 从八点坐到现在要提醒自己不能沉迷于游戏!!!	05月19日 01:59	想变胖的iPhone12	0	4	3
Flippedxyou	https://weibo.com/6323790206?refer_flag=1001030103_	文明6第一次被一个游戏搞得怀疑人生 为什么走了几步就被野蛮人锤了。我继续回去钻研教程了	05月18日 15:38		0	0	0
_晚星送我	https://weibo.com/6489717991?refer_flag=1001030103_	一开始听说文明6很杀时间我是不信的,直到我打开游戏再一次抬头发现已经过去五六个小时的时候我哭了,半夜睡地到第二天上班脑子里还迷迷糊糊想的是城市食物不够要饿死了还有哪里还能种田啊救命为什么隔壁普鲁士国堡里全是兵啊为什么我不开战还还要建贡我	05月18日 15:32	微博国际版	0	0	0
伍郎不撕逼	https://weibo.com/2921461301?refer_flag=1001030103_	一直有在想和她一起玩双人成行可能会挺开心要是这个游戏一年前就有那就好了这两天特别沉迷文明6虚拟世界的征服也会给人带来特别的成就感Steam的好友系统突然提醒我地开了玩了双人成行游戏我急下伯利克里放下雅典卫城突然变得安静野蛮人和印度国王国住我的市中心原来我不是不在意而只是想着忘记	05月17日 01:46	RedmiK305G先锋	0	0	1
桌游速报	https://weibo.com/5838389936?refer_flag=1001030103_	【KS众筹】由Forbidden Games制作的Mosaic:A Story of Civilization,最多支持1-6人!Glenn Drover制作的的全新游戏,Mosaic是一款文明建设游戏,拥有你期望的一切:技术、奇迹、城市扩张、资源、贸易、黄金时代、成就、政府,具有独特优势和能力的领导者……和更多!您通过做出的每个决定来控制文明的命运L桌游速报的微博视频收起全文d	05月12日 09:01	iPhoneXS	0	0	1
中老年人微博用户	https://weibo.com/5539452069?refer_flag=1001030103_	我真的好容易突然被历史类的东西吸引注意力了 听了一整天P社游戏和文明6的魔幻历史发展。	05月12日 00:02	微博weibo.com	0	0	0
游民星空	https://weibo.com/1969176463?refer_flag=1001030103_	【Epic商城多项数据曝光 《GTA5》免费吸引了700万新用户】SteamDB创办人Pavel Djundik爆料了一些Epic游戏商城的数据,数据显示Epic商城新用户增长最明显的时期是《GTA5》和《文明6》限免时,分别吸引了700万与200万名新用户,此外,在2019年,第三季度的《无主之地3》收入占比高达38.6%,《荒野大镖客2:救赎》与《天外世界》支撑起了第四季度的收入。其它数据:2020春季促销收入:990万美元FTLoG促销收入:570万美元黑色星期五促销收入:800万美元2019圣诞假	05月09日 20:35 转赞人数超过60	微博weibo.com	8	45	170
御前刺猬Y	https://weibo.com/3320904660?refer_flag=1001030103_	文明6这游戏有毒	05月03日 05:34	iPhone客户端	0	1	0
Sixwatem488	https://weibo.com/6737100194?refer_flag=1001030103_	好想玩电脑游戏……拿着nds对着宝可梦只有一个肝字还是文明6比较优雅	05月01日 17:16	三星S205G	0	0	0
灵魂的退隐	https://weibo.com/5285874467?refer_flag=1001030103_	没怎么玩过游戏的想入文明6来着,这视频一看就从入门到土干了,也太复杂了吧,完全不知道steam上该玩什么了	05月01日 14:09	HUAWEIMate40Pro	0	0	0

continued on following page

Table 1. Continued

昵称	主页url	内容	时间	设备	分享数	评论鼠标	点赞数
最重要的是心情啊	https://weibo.com/5610459695?refer_flag=1001030103_	++!电脑每次放假都要坏,好不容易有时间玩会游戏......#文明6#	04月30日 20:10	iPhone客户端	0	1	0
空母大凤OvO-奉贤看海人	https://weibo.com/5580662717?refer_flag=1001030103_	Angel City Chorale/Christopher Tin《Sogno di Volare ("The Dream of Flight") (游戏《文明6》主题曲)》KSogno di Volare ("The Dream of Flight") (游戏《文明6》主题曲)(@网易云音乐)	04月29日 09:32	iPhone客户端	0	0	0
历史上的脑顶洞人	https://weibo.com/2552534395?refer_flag=1001030103_	求问万能的主页,如果游戏需求撑死了就是山口丁、天际线、文明6这种的话,显卡用A卡Yes么?尽管现在买显卡简直就是49年入国民党的行为。	04月28日 19:18	微博weibo.com	0	21	4
用户6611941725	https://weibo.com/6611941725?refer_flag=1001030103_	垃文明6这个游戏更新完就上不去了,求大佬们支支招	04月28日 17:53	文明6超话	0	1	1
宅男小小五	https://weibo.com/5205100408?refer_flag=1001030103_	自从买了文明6总共才玩了2把还是最简单的模式昨天一看游戏时长居然超过45个小时了以后还是放寒暑假再玩吧太耽误事了	04月26日 13:32	iPhone客户端	0	0	0
熏鱼三明治	https://weibo.com/1752761574?refer_flag=1001030103_	预防脑瓜生锈就靠这把小琴了昂~第一次弹,不许笑!《Banaha》香蕉很简单有趣的刚果小曲儿,风趣世界而我则是在听文明6游戏原声带时才头一次听到,喜欢,单曲循环,然后边哼边弹把简谱默了出来L熏鱼三明治的微博视频2南京	04月24日 09:03	微博视频号	0	1	0
小九本九_	https://weibo.com/1307654841?refer_flag=1001030103_	手贱下载了个文明6,玩了一个多小时教程依旧不知所云一脸懵逼→头冒水,现在玩个游戏门槛都这么高了吗?就不能对我这个在饥荒世界捡垃圾的小可怜温柔一点??	04月20日 18:59	OPPOFindX3	0	16	5
EhudAkers	https://weibo.com/6025785811?refer_flag=1001030103_	一个设想:文明6这个游戏挺适合AI发展的。如果有一天对面的AI也懂咋规划路线,咋煽动外交孤立人类玩家了,打仗也懂战略纵深了,多余的地也懂得铲了新建了,不乱造奇观了,借助同样初始资源跟人类玩家打得有来有回了......那也太特么好玩了吧!!兴奋到搓手手!!	04月18日 21:40	iPhone客户端	0	1	1
八尾喵_sika	https://weibo.com/1820750340?refer_flag=1001030103_	最近怎么这么棒~想玩的游戏一个接一个史低,喜欢的人宣了我喜欢的品牌愉快的周末从Spiritfarer开始!!如果文明6不白屏就更棒了♀	04月16日 18:57	iPhone客户端	0	1	0
吃货猴子抱走团子	https://weibo.com/7244742387?refer_flag=1001030103_	#文明6#作为一个萌新玩了七八十个小时的文明6,不会外交,文化胜利,只会依靠战争取胜,真的觉得文明6很真实。一个国家必须要有足够的军事实力才有真正的话语权,就像游戏里,我都打到你们门口了,你还谴责我二氧化碳排放过多,有屁用,我都把世界占领完了,你就算把我外交点数削没了,又能怎么样。以前你们谴责这个不谴责那个,真的一点用没有,它们根本不会在意,只有强国才会被别人谴责,而弱者只会被别人侵略收起全文d	04月15日 12:14	HUAWEIMate20X	0	0	1
韩冲-Han	https://weibo.com/1971386205?refer_flag=1001030103_	《文明6》iPad版真的是一反暴力的游戏,每当我想给三哥送去核平的时候,就肯定会死机。2西安·蓝田县	04月14日 14:07		1	20	8
朱嘉益	https://weibo.com/1408349823?refer_flag=1001030103_	RNG上演史诗级偷家帝国时代4公布中国文明文明6即将最后一次免费更新互动游戏《审判者》预告片公布#每日游报##一分钟游戏新闻#2上海L朱嘉益的微博视频	04月11日 20:24	微博视频号	2	2	9
IGN编辑部	https://weibo.com/7494874950?refer_flag=1001030103_	【《帝国时代4》最新实机视频公布】官方刚刚在《帝国时代》前瞻发布会上公开了游戏的最新实机视频,展示了不同文明在不同时代下的游戏要素和战斗内容,时长约6分钟,游戏预计于今年秋季发售。LIGN编辑部的微博视频	04月11日 20:15转赞人数超过30	微博视频号	12	5	26
没有人可以比老子更酷	https://weibo.com/1674527455?refer_flag=1001030103_	看了帝国时代4的预告片我感觉好惊艳啊变成3D游戏了耶超想玩的结果看评论居然都是骂的都说画面垃圾不像2021的游戏我傻了大家要求都好高我看文明6也是这个画风啊	04月11日 11:18	HUAWEIMate30Pro5G	0	2	1
我爱吃果冻诶嘿	https://weibo.com/2919012567?refer_flag=1001030103_	把不太喜欢并且已经玩厌了的游戏卡,清一清准备卖掉,居然也没掉什么价,除开已经掉价七十的文明6【这游戏我是真的玩不逼】ns游戏卡保值产品	04月11日 00:20	HUAWEIMate20Pro	0	1	0
柿山夜今年要减15斤	https://weibo.com/1692577443?refer_flag=1001030103_	希望首页玩文明6和怪物猎人的朋友敲我一下另外准备考gmat或者有计划考的朋友可以约远程自习,谁先跑去玩游戏谁是狗2加拿大·多伦多	04月10日 12:23	iPhoneSE	0	0	3
薄荷糖是德云女孩鸭	https://weibo.com/6054157297?refer_flag=1001030103_	垃文明6这游戏太上头,纯新手,玩了一天没弄明白是什么操作,反正没赢就对了,玩到头秃!(小声bb虽然不太懂,但是上天,打算入了所以dlc!)	04月09日 15:47	文明6超话	0	1	0
阿妤	https://weibo.com/1689893121?refer_flag=1001030103_	垃文明6更新之后就进不了游戏是个什么情况......有没有人能救救我2洛阳	04月09日 14:36	文明6超话	0	4	4
李胜威5653	https://weibo.com/5849325390?refer_flag=1001030103_	文明6是一款我高考之后开始接触的回合制战略游戏你很难想象一款单机游戏可以耐玩到四年600个小时我任务对它爱不释手 这款游戏同时也是我在知乎上高强度键政的最初动机新出的季票好心动 买了买了	04月08日 16:26	iPhone	0	0	3
大傻子喜欢小尾巴呀	https://weibo.com/5868298331?refer_flag=1001030103_	文明6的正确玩法:打开游戏界面,然后听bgm就行了,史诗感听听就好,真玩起来太伤肝从来没觉得天这么容易亮,刚吃完饭又要吃饭了L大傻子喜欢小尾巴呀的微博视频	04月07日 16:33	Note9Pro一亿像素	0	0	1
顾芳时	https://weibo.com/5958101399?refer_flag=1001030103_	文明6昨天晚上玩了一下新手教程,八点钟左右开始的打到十二点,毫无困意......这游戏略上头啊我最近一两个小时倒头就睡了	04月07日 07:19	微博国际版	0	0	1
优酷	https://weibo.com/1642904381?refer_flag=1001030103_	【豆瓣9.3分 史诗级国产纪录片登陆优酷】#东方帝王谷#位于陕西省关中地区,共有72座帝王陵,埋葬着73位帝王!其境内帝王陵、历史现场、文物不胜枚举,对中国的诞生与成长,有着不可磨灭的影响。史诗级国产纪录片《东方帝王谷》,带您揭秘大秦的崛起史,看东方版"权利的游戏"!4月6日起,优酷全网热播!考古迷、历史粉、盗墓迷、帝王粉们不容错过!L优酷纪录片的优酷视频收起全文d	04月06日 13:00转赞人数超过40	微博视频号	18	9	49
选择无影响	https://weibo.com/3693421231?refer_flag=1001030103_	我一直好想玩文明6啊。但是我觉得我这脑子可能根本玩不懂。。。。。我脑子不灵光,手也不灵敏光是一个文明6的问题,是很多游戏我觉得我都驾驭不了	04月04日 23:57	前后2000万OPPOR11	0	1	0
伍君仪透析英语	https://weibo.com/1264366955?refer_flag=1001030103_	玩Civilization IV学英语,每一个回合查1个生词,2小时完成#每天透析20个生词。玩到后面没找到我不认识的生词,只能靠猜城市名、巴西城市名,还有历史文化名人、著名遗址的名字。这是让英语词汇量暴涨的强力方法。本来是用中文解说的,但后面Tritium跑过来了,只好改成英文解说。《文明6》我还在学怎么玩,那个不县条时条的"日本国"在我治理下各项发展指标倒数第一,果然是人才......#玩游戏学英语#垃文明6L伍君仪透析英语的微博视频收起全文d	04月04日 11:50	微博视频号	0	0	2
银河系干啥啥不行大赛亚军	https://weibo.com/7435896471?refer_flag=1001030103_	文明6的时间真的和现实时间不一样 我的浪费时间专用游戏	04月04日 00:38	Share微博客户端	0	0	0
saiijun	https://weibo.com/5388888462?refer_flag=1001030103_	文明6是个鸡贼的游戏,对新手玩家太不友好,连个开拓者难度都玩不过ai	04月01日 12:58	HUAWEIMate20	0	0	0
小怪兽AICPA	https://weibo.com/2528413711?refer_flag=1001030103_	什么鬼?Apex Legends?我听都没听说过这个游戏,更何况玩过,莫名其妙把我封了?全面战争和文明6突然就不敢买了,EA疑心病不要太重	03月31日 21:36	iPhone客户端	0	0	0

continued on following page

Table 1. Continued

昵称	主页url	内容	时间	设备	分享数	评论量标	点赞数
小怪兽AICPA	https://weibo.com/2528413711?refer_flag=1001030103_	什么鬼?Apex Legends?我听都没听说过这个游戏,更何况玩过,某某其妙把我封了?全面战争和文明6突然就不敢买了,EA疑心病不要太重	03月31日 21:36	iPhone客户端	0	0	0
苗壮成长小树树	https://weibo.com/6386024708?refer_flag=1001030103_	switch游戏愿望单火纹 八方旅人 塞尔达 旷野之息健身环文明6世界游戏51大全等我打通了dq11s都不知道何年何月了,上班真的好忙,一点玩游戏的时间都没有,还想把逆转裁判123、战场女武神、马里奥疯兔这些都打通,在闲看到好价的卡带都不敢买,买了也没时间玩,星露谷物语我还没结婚,害,从头到尾就打通过风花雪月。收起全文d	03月31日 02:14	RedmiK20Pro真旗舰	3	0	0
是月亮呀mini	https://weibo.com/1784660741?refer_flag=1001030103_	文明6和鬼谷八荒是什么杀时间游戏这个世界上居然有比m4捏娃娃还杀时间的游戏绝了	03月28日 23:03	小米10	0	0	1
杰瑞的使命必达先生	https://weibo.com/5848977889?refer_flag=1001030103_	#春日寻游季##哪款游戏让你玩了不想睡#文明6	03月28日 15:03	Android	0	0	0
长沙市精神病医院朱主任	https://weibo.com/6514445219?refer_flag=1001030103_	我的可爱室友玩文明6我给他当地治顾问把战略资源和现金流拉满了他第一件事是造娱乐中心还说不造娱乐中心公游戏赢了但是我输了	03月27日 01:48	iPhone客户端	0	4	0
游戏早知道	https://weibo.com/1239720361?refer_flag=1001030103_	#Xbox早知道##游戏早知道www.yxzzd.com#发布了头条文章:《铁拳7》《文明6》《极品飞车:热力追踪重制版》金会员体验开放O《铁拳7》《文明6》《极品飞车:热力追踪重制版》金会员体验开方	03月26日 17:52	微博weibo.com	0	0	1
你根本吓不到我	https://weibo.com/60418302...?refer_flag=1001030103_	#游戏推荐##游戏解说#EPIC第二波免费神秘大作《文明6》开启领取,我笑了,你们呢?L你根本吓不到我的微博视频	03月26日 13:00	微博视频号	0	0	1
用户6797154942	https://weibo.com/6797154942?refer_flag=1001030103_	垣last炫神pc上有无推荐极品单机,不太喜欢玩枪战的,玩过黑魂只狼mhw,库里还有文明6和巫师三,自从我玩了奶刀2感觉好多游戏都索然无味了	03月26日 12:51	last炫神超话	0	1	0
山上哟	https://weibo.com/3480871691?refer_flag=1001030103_	#儿子##一起家庭教育#儿子三月十九号写了一篇《文明6游戏纪实》,说实在,真的惊到我了,写得有画面,有气势,这个理科男的文字水平真的不赖。	03月26日 07:41	HUAWEIMate9	0	1	0
王当德尔	https://weibo.com/5496186105?refer_flag=1001030103_	我今天真的被LYT笑死文明6到底是个什么游戏她讲如果是非洲国家那么地图上就会有一堆棉花她说这些外国佬是不是想到他们当时用黑奴去种棉花然后来意淫新疆也是这样的笑死我了	03月25日 17:34	iPhone客户端	0	2	0
伍君仪透析英语	https://weibo.com/1264366955?refer_flag=1001030103_	同样是治国理政的游戏,《文明6》跟国产手游/页游简直是天上地下,后者就是围绕氪金设计的……	03月22日 23:07	新版微博weibo.com	1	0	1
南提里斯行车指南	https://weibo.com/5379790153?refer_flag=1001030103_	最近发呆的原因:打游戏打到凌晨六点。玩到六点睡到下午,然后继续玩。刚考完在放纵。基本没看微博world,修仙模拟器,泰拉瑞亚,mc,太吾绘卷,鬼谷八荒,文明6。这种不用睡觉的游戏都是我心头好,欢迎同好来交流顺便一提,我头像和名字是elona里的东西	03月21日 15:13	Android	0	6	2
如果2021我成为了魔法师	https://weibo.com/28043550...?refer_flag=1001030103_	好家伙,玩了两个多星期,终于打完了#文明6#的一局,亚历山大胜利了,统一天下还是很爽的,这游戏太累了,玩到天荒地老不是问题。。	03月19日 23:12	iPhone客户端	0	1	0
你是第三种绝色as	https://weibo.com/5263821250?refer_flag=1001030103_	#文艺复兴虽然现在看这游戏有很多缺陷 但它确实是yyds 就是因为玩了这个 所以我一直就喜欢单机游戏(虽然文明6差不多是同种类型 但我要是碰了文明6怕是一天至少得有14个小时都在线 所以像剩客信条这种的就挺好)也是因为它 我才渐渐去了解历史类一开始只是为了了解背景去找《伊利亚特》《奥德赛》看 然后渐渐关《耶路撒冷三千年》《光荣与梦想》这些 才对外国史也有所涉猎…六年级的时候我爸妈给我买了台电脑 是他死活不肯联网 我哭了几次以后终于同意让他学校的电脑老师给我个游戏当年一放学就回	03月19日 06:12	vivoNEXAI智慧旗舰	0	0	0
借我那把爱情的枪吧	https://weibo.com/6299513213?refer_flag=1001030103_	我花了一百多刀,买了个游戏机上的文明6,不会玩,我就看教程,好家伙,给我讲课!	03月18日 20:06	iPhone客户端	0	0	0
红色军火商	https://weibo.com/1514302864?refer_flag=1001030103_	我是《文明》深度玩家。《文明6》最新资料片《风云变幻》有个很有意思的设定:这个游戏到后期,电力是很重要的东西——它可以极大促进工业产能。最初的电力来源是燃煤电厂——释放大量温室气体,造成海平面上升。所以我的思路是,如果国土内有煤矿,就集中发展出燃煤电厂科技,所有城市批量造燃煤电厂,然后推动国际会议"禁止建造新的燃煤电厂,保护地球"。这样只有我有电,对手就很难在工业革命之后持续发展。类似的思路还可以套用到"燃油电厂"、"核电厂"。等到其他国家开发出风电和光伏,怕是游戏已经结束了看到这里,你明白欧美为什么搞	03月18日 15:37	进港避风的iPhone11(红色)	7	29	99
捧场王阿鹿Floo_	https://weibo.com/1390117714?refer_flag=1001030103_	文明这个游戏不适合我,我还在这搞城市规划建设,敌人都打过来几波了	03月17日 22:23	疑似iPhoneX	0	0	0
A9VG	https://weibo.com/1622008051?refer_flag=1001030103_	2K宣布《文明6》第六款DLC"葡萄牙包"将于3月26日推出,该DLC将加入新领袖、新文明、新游戏模式"丧门之围"、两个世界奇观(贝伦塔\埃特曼安吉寺神庙)以及全新的湿地地图。#游戏情报站#LA9VG的微博视频	03月16日 00:13	微博视频号	65	17	53
重燃生活图鉴	https://weibo.com/5681598515?refer_flag=1001030103_	仙剑三的御剑江湖,LOL初代无限火力的CHALLENGERS,文明4的baba yetu,文明6的所有音乐,是容玩成全了游戏,是坚持玩全了热爱。前尘忆梦,再续前缘。害,她们就是18年的夏天,而每一个人热爱游戏的人都是头号玩家。是的,立剧有。2南宁L祈Jinxed的微博视频	03月15日 15:56	微博视频号	0	0	2
小来给你慢慢解答	https://weibo.com/5541289353?refer_flag=1001030103_	垣文明6看了看,玩游戏的基本都是大学,唉,老了老了都毕业了	03月14日 23:49	文明6超话	0	2	3
木岛无城	https://weibo.com/6603481938?refer_flag=1001030103_	#侠盗猎车:罪恶都市##文明6#踹了个迪被警察追杀今天的游戏都太不友好了 听说文明6出僵尸模式了??	03月13日 22:57	Android	0	0	1
BOKUKA	https://weibo.com/1763770605?refer_flag=1001030103_	2021年入手的第......诶?之前好像把第七给漏了直接记成了第八,那把这个算第七吧第七个游戏——文明6。	03月13日 12:06转赞人数超过10		0	14	12
不甜机智咩	https://weibo.com/1763309731?refer_flag=1001030103_	一个继sim4文明6劫森之后让我见到清晨六点的太阳的游戏出现了	03月13日 11:47	iPhone客户端	0	6	4
游民星空	https://weibo.com/1969176463?refer_flag=1001030103_	【《文明6》"新纪元季票"最终DLC疑泄露:全新文明葡萄牙、新玩法僵尸模式】据Gamerant报道,《文明6》即将推出全新文明——葡萄牙,以及一个全新游戏模式——僵尸模式。该信息来自SteamDB,有玩家在SteamDB上发现本作开发商Firaxis在游戏新的成就中预先录入了游戏新的成就,这几项新的成就项目包括:扮演葡萄牙三世赢得一场游戏的胜利;操控葡萄牙,并与巴西、日本、印度进行贸易;回合开始时至少控制20只葡萄牙。其中,"虔诚者'若昂三世、《文明6》成就"香料流转"等内容似乎直接暗示了全新文明:葡萄牙;而随后	03月11日 16:44转赞人数超过70	微博weibo.com	15	10	80

continued on following page

Table 1. Continued

昵称	主页url	内容	时间	设备	分享数	评论鼠标	点赞数
江湖麻辣渠	https://weibo.com/7029762087?refer_flag=1001030103_	坨缪糕产出《虚无逆境》1.6w+一发完 先看第一张(游戏玩家Mew在先进文明的奇妙探险"因为有你,我才能在每一个有你的宇宙里勇敢地活下来。"虚无主义作为哲学意义,为怀疑主义的极致形态。认为世界、生命(特别是人类)的存在是没有客观意义、目的以及可以理解的真相。"我希望在这个互联网发展过头的时代,人们仍然,并且永远不会缺乏,面对现实世界的勇气。只有分清楚现实和虚拟的界限,人们才能认识自己,谨言慎行,将虚拟世界也当作自己言行考虑的一部分。善良的孩子,你是那个时空的勇者,也是自己的勇者。你要相信Gulf,他	03月10日10:57转赞人数超过500	缪糕产出超话	11	73	764
斯京小星星	https://weibo.com/6281979240?refer_flag=1001030103_	我宣布文明6成为我steam上耗肝时间最多的游戏人总是会在某一时刻 找到人生的信仰 每个文明都有源头偏向性喜爱都有归处	03月10日03:33	iPhone客户端	0	4	3
RAsundown	https://weibo.com/2850548331?refer_flag=1001030103_	我本人秋招和写论文期间的游戏清单:黑魂3,哈迪斯,文明6就很难不觉得这个人不是有点抖m倾向	03月09日21:34	iPhone客户端	0	2	2
三水bitwater	https://weibo.com/1265813057?refer_flag=1001030103_	魔兽世界,文明6,动物森友会这些杀时间的游戏如果加上NFT,Play to Earn模式,可玩性、可组合性、可持续性,想象空间巨大	03月09日18:28	微博weibo.com	0	0	0
白云城主纪晓岚	https://weibo.com/1816339811?refer_flag=1001030103_	文明6买的草率了,真不适合玩这类游戏,开着修改器把所有升级元素升满,看看效果,拿高达虐虐原始部落,就没意思了,我适合玩播片游戏	03月09日15:21	iPhone客户端	0	0	0
FMarauders	https://weibo.com/6338436021?refer_flag=1001030103_	虽然人该往前看 但有时候我好想回到16年 守望 黑魂3文明6巫师3 奇异人生 最后生还者 那一年游戏区纯朴又真诚 鹅和夫人还会一起播求生 一切看上去都美好充满希望还是后来那些糟糕的事情都还没有发生我也还是那个幻想未来无限可能的高二学生	03月03日00:10	荣耀20	0	1	1
今年也喜欢刘昊然	https://weibo.com/5416068807?refer_flag=1001030103_	一边下载文明6一边看萌新攻略 看了五分钟放弃了这款游戏没有脑子不适合。	02月27日18:04	iPhone客户端	0	0	0
萧瑟cyclone	https://weibo.com/5706764997?refer_flag=1001030103_	都被收假了才发现,一堆epic白给的游戏没碰,而且全是时间窃取类型文明6,城市天际线……到学校后不知道有没有时间玩了	02月27日11:41	Android	0	0	0
单机老王子	https://weibo.com/6042105347?refer_flag=1001030103_	【文明6】#游戏资讯#《文明6》2月免费更新内容,本月的游戏更新包括"城邦选择圈","城邦选择圈"能让玩家选择有多少城邦出现在他们的游戏中,可让玩家选择从随机选择的城邦或自订城邦清单进行游戏。L单机老王子的微博视频	02月27日11:04	微博视频号	0	0	0
苏州河边的马达	https://weibo.com/7464617251?refer_flag=1001030103_	干TM,下午睡了一觉起床更新完文明6直接游戏加载不进去了,老子的秦始皇打到1963年了你给我加载不进去,气哭了。#文明6#2赣州	02月26日21:18	小米手机	0	1	2
千千闕歌	https://weibo.com/5651534089?refer_flag=1001030103_	刚打开戴森球电脑排风扇炸了…发现年纪上来后越来越抗拒接受新游戏了…还好对书本没有抗拒…(我又下回来了文明6)(网页版微博真好用,要是时间线正确就更好用了…)	02月25日21:14	微博weibo.com	0	0	0
Izymath	https://weibo.com/2926100603?refer_flag=1001030103_	#文明6#虽然游戏简化单一,但我还是可以想象到,从远古时代开始,迁徙,聚集,制作,崇拜,文字,记录,部落,乡村,城镇,功能区,教育,科学,经济,人类在这个星球上漫漫跋涉,寻找这个群体生存和发展的可能,是一场宏大的跋涉王恒屹/周昭妍《朝代歌 (Live)》K朝代歌@QQ音乐	02月24日20:16	QQ音乐	0	2	1
嘻嘻CCiel	https://weibo.com/3108209387?refer_flag=1001030103_	我从8点玩文明6玩到现在仿佛又上八小时班这游戏太肝了太肝了永远都下一回合	02月24日03:03	小米8屏幕指纹版	0	0	1
W煎茶W	https://weibo.com/2561240785?refer_flag=1001030103_	貌似游戏性能还行?文明6测试模式最高甚至最高到100帧(笔记本底部终于温热了)	02月24日00:37	微博weibo.com	0	0	1
LOSER_寒光	https://weibo.com/5221199054?refer_flag=1001030103_	昨天第一次玩文明6这款游戏,玩了很久,也得到了很多的启示。一个文明的胜利,不止武力手段一种方式,这是游戏的机制,也是当今社会各项竞争的影射。	02月22日11:03	三星A8s黑曈全视屏	0	0	0
咀咀釘	https://weibo.com/1976004503?refer_flag=1001030103_	程序员为了教我,重拾起多年没玩的《文明6》。(结果玩得比我还上瘾…)今晚他得意洋洋告诉我在游戏里用我的名字创立了一个宗教,让更多的人崇拜我。这想法很棒。	02月22日02:47	iPhone客户端	0	0	0
Monologue_OuO	https://weibo.com/7505370568?refer_flag=1001030103_	更新完的文明6哎不 野蛮6谢谢大家游戏已经卸了	02月21日19:09	iPadair	0	0	1
Tsykkk	https://weibo.com/6894246980?refer_flag=1001030103_	仕玩家震怒搁文明6里看下把它城都扬咯印度那个领袖在游戏里也是这个行径,服了	02月20日10:22	HUAWEIMate20Pro	0	2	1
賀茂義心	https://weibo.com/2903826863?refer_flag=1001030103_	戴森球计划是什么神仙游戏星际主题就是我的最爱,再加上建造经营玩法 这不就是我最爱的星际穿越重建人类文明吗比文明6还有内味,i了i了,上头了熬起夜来根本停不下来	02月20日02:24	Android	0	0	4
企鹅岚	https://weibo.com/1675062601?refer_flag=1001030103_	用剩余的点卡在俄服买了个小游戏,Shift happens,才几块钱,还蛮好玩的,至少比文明6好懂多了?!	02月18日23:35	神罗iPhoneXS	0	18	1
企鹅岚	https://weibo.com/1675062601?refer_flag=1001030103_	行了,以后别买上百的下载游戏了,感觉很亏,卡带至少还能出,文明6我根本不会玩,好不容易选到最难开局,只会乱点。	02月18日17:32	神罗iPhoneXS	0	0	0
A9VG	https://weibo.com/1622008051?refer_flag=1001030103_	【《文明6》2月更新】《文明6》公布了2月更新的开发者视频,介绍了将在2月26日推出的免费更新的游戏内容。包括蛮族氏族模式、领袖偏好池以及一些平衡性修改和AI调整。【蛮族氏族模式】关于蛮族氏族模式,这次的更新完全免费,只需要有本体游戏就可以进行游玩。该模式附带6种蛮族氏族,氏族又可以转变为城邦,在每回合都能够获得城邦转变进度。这一进度会随着玩家与蛮族的互动而产生增减,玩家可以用全新的方式与他们进行互动。此外为了便游戏更加有趣,蛮族氏族可以生产未参与本次游戏的主要文明的特色单位。遭遇蛮族之后,如果玩选择隶清氏	02月18日15:20转赞人数超过50	微博视频号	25	15	58
MebiuW	https://weibo.com/1502169164?refer_flag=1001030103_	这两天拿M1 Air玩游戏,卡倒是不卡(文明6天际线),但也的确是我用过设备最烫的,D面积热后渡到飞起,放夏天直接放题上感觉会灼伤那种,fanless的代价。	02月18日12:53转赞人数超过10	iPhone12Pro	1	14	16
如果2021我成为了丁魔法师	https://weibo.com/2804355032?refer_flag=1001030103_	玩了几天#文明6#,到一百回合了,还没搞懂这是个什么游戏,好处就是,占用时间多,可以少吃点零食。	02月18日12:46	iPhone客户端	0	0	0

continued on following page

Table 1. Continued

昵称	主页url	内容	时间	设备	分享数	评论量标	点赞数
那回忆的独奏	https://weibo.com/3700692781?refer_flag=1001030103_	学生生涯玩过的那些电脑游戏回忆(七十四)(文明6):文明6这游戏作为文明系列爱好者的我可是它一出来我就下下来玩了,不过刚开始玩着倒挺不喜欢,可能还是文明5玩多了的过,而且文明6中的各文明的主儿都变成Q版人物,跟他们对话也没了文明5那种大气的感觉,这点也让人不太习惯。文明6中的城市规模是不一的了,可以规划各种片区,还可以充分利用资源。文明6中的地图也变成了推进式,不像前代都是用的探索式,这点也让人很不习惯。不过实话文明6中的bgm都还不错的,我有个哥们还蛮喜欢它哼哼,且文明6现在也在不停地更新,可能过阵	02月18日 11:38	360安全浏览器	0	0	0
AKA_担担面	https://weibo.com/6487630636?refer_flag=1001030103_	记录一下最近在玩的游戏:勿忘我 艾希ICEY 巫师3 hades哈迪斯还有文明6黑魂2游戏是我滴生命之光!	02月17日 22:52	红米Note74800万相机	0	0	2
游侠网	https://weibo.com/1893905030?refer_flag=1001030103_	【《文明6》2月免费更新内容介绍】《文明6》公布中文开发者视频,介绍了将于2月26日推出的免费更新内容,包括蛮族氏族模式、领袖选择池以及游戏平衡性修改等内容。#游戏情报站#L游侠网的微博视频	02月17日 22:18转赞人数超过20	微博视频号	10	4	25
李氏家族族长66207	https://weibo.com/6877892043?refer_flag=1001030103_	艾因山丘#艾因Eine#@艾因Eine游戏《文明6》	02月17日 17:28	微博weibo.com	0	0	1
会玩传媒	https://weibo.com/7082773862?refer_flag=1001030103_	《文明6》2月26日免费更新 包括蛮族氏族模式等内容《文明6》公布中文开发者视频,介绍了将于2月26日推出的免费更新内容,包括蛮族氏族模式、领袖选择池以及游戏平衡性修改等内容。蛮族氏族模式蛮族氏族模式是一个全新自选游戏模式,可以免费游玩,不受DLC影响。本模式会带来6种蛮族氏族,蛮族氏族可以转变为城邦。不同的氏族生活在不同地图条件上,玩家能够以全新的方式和他们互动。同时蛮族能获得并生产参加本场游戏的主要文明的特色单位,氏族每回合都能获得城邦转变进度,氏族向文明生活的转变进度随着玩家活动而增减。扫荡蛮族	02月17日 09:40	微博weibo.com	0	0	0
菩提居士V1	https://weibo.com/6026553510?refer_flag=1001030103_	这几天我特意给南京女孩准备一份礼物。我喜欢玩荒野大镖客2,我特意给她准备一个线上大礼包,给她开了一个steam账号,用了九天时间,用外挂做完了一个极致养老号。如果要是找淘宝工作室去刷,起码1500块下不来。然后趁着战地五打折我还给她买了战地五。我还买了好多游戏,我还买了文明6和饥荒还有无主之地3,最近打折促销呢。收起全文d	02月16日 15:49	OPPOReno55G	0	0	0
菩提居士V1	https://weibo.com/6026553510?refer_flag=1001030103_	这几天我特意给南京女孩准备一份礼物。我喜欢玩荒野大镖客2,我特意给她准备一个线上大礼包,给她开了一个steam账号,用了九天时间,用外挂做完了一个极致养老号。如果要是找淘宝工作室去刷,起码1500块下不来。然后趁着战地五打折我还给她买了战地五。我还买了好多游戏,我还买了文明6和饥荒还有无主之地3,最近打折促销呢。收起全文d	02月16日 15:49	OPPOReno55G	0	0	0
云之姬兮w	https://weibo.com/5405132023?refer_flag=1001030103_	文明6哪里是一款桌游分明是一款上头游戏啊!俄罗斯也太好玩了吧?!	02月16日 03:28	iPhone客户端	0	3	0
JoeyYuuuuu	https://weibo.com/7070634879?refer_flag=1001030103_	文明6真是个可怕的游戏#文明6#	02月16日 00:14	nova5Pro人像超级夜景	0	0	0
冯晞帆-稀饭	https://weibo.com/1354560737?refer_flag=1001030103_	再玩一局就睡觉,结果到天亮,文明6这游戏必须戒	02月15日 20:15	iPhone11	0	15	13
花柑子	https://weibo.com/63784647725?refer_flag=1001030103_	看了游戏时间统计我吓一跳,这两周我和我男票玩文明6一共玩了80个小时我上班也就上80小时hhh	02月15日 20:13	iPhone11Pro	0	0	0
单机老王子	https://weibo.com/6042105347?refer_flag=1001030103_	#单机游戏##过年玩啥游戏#策略神作《文明6》又打骨折了!同时第二位中国领袖忽必烈终于正式上线,真香!L单机老王子的微博视频	02月15日 10:07	微博视频号	0	0	0
什么时候能适应成年人的生活	https://weibo.com/6376172622?refer_flag=1001030103_	接连购入文明6和switch之后,最近发现游戏有点玩不过来。。宝可梦果然是猛男必备,某猪已经玩了两三天舍不得放手了	02月15日 07:21	HUAWEIMate10	0	0	2
GregorySRL	https://weibo.com/6306102865?refer_flag=1001030103_	看他玩文明6然后买了文明6看他玩黑塔科夫然后也买了黑边塔科夫 这两个游戏到现在没玩明白一个	02月15日 02:20	HUAWEIP30	0	1	0
哗鸟	https://weibo.com/2200204462?refer_flag=1001030103_	鬼谷八荒也太杀时间了。有当初玩文明6和群星的感觉了,一个rpg游戏居然能做成这样。玩的时候居然没注意到,刚才强行把电脑关上才注意到我居然是点被尿憋死	02月14日 01:27	微博国际版	0	0	0
俏皮少女陈富贵	https://weibo.com/1930292643?refer_flag=1001030103_	我百玩不厌的游戏:巫师3,模拟人生全系列,文明6。真滴好玩!!!	02月13日 21:10	iPhone客户端	0	6	0
请你喝茶昂	https://weibo.com/1031934234?refer_flag=1001030103_	《文明6》玩到一半拖了将近半个月才重拾起,果然玩不进去了...这种游戏还是适合一口气玩一回合(前提这口气挺长)	02月13日 20:51	HUAWEIP30	0	0	0
是Anna也是Ana呀	https://weibo.com/1862731963?refer_flag=1001030103_	我以为文明6是个单机游戏...谁知道没联网不让玩	02月13日 20:35	iPhone客户端	0	2	0
伪造Tmuse	https://weibo.com/53432879776?refer_flag=1001030103_	文明6是打起来最费神的游戏了一直盯着想还容易上头脑袋里一直想最近想补的这个dlc对文化胜利和商业中心的平衡还是做得不错的	02月13日 14:53	iPhone客户端	0	0	0
牛仔怕牛水手怕水	https://weibo.com/68052727762?refer_flag=1001030103_	#我的年度游戏单#ns星露谷塞尔达宝可梦杀戮尖塔纸片马里奥逆转裁判pc帝国时代二决定版文明6,另外从暑霄脱坑是最明智的决定	02月12日 18:45	HUAWEIMate20	0	2	6
-PLZPRAYFORME-	https://weibo.com/2403375260?refer_flag=1001030103_	昨晚80块入了文明6全套让我看看看,春促再入个底特律和毛线小精灵吧好幸福,蒸汽就是我的游戏垃圾堆	02月12日 13:58	iPhone客户端	0	3	0
维克多_Yip	https://weibo.com/1095248435?refer_flag=1001030103_	#每日一部好看的游戏预告片#Vol.169,《文明6》发售预告片,此预告片也作为游戏的片头。预告片配乐为游戏主题曲,由华裔音乐家田志仁谱写,采用古典乐风格,这歌词改编自达芬奇为自己的飞天梦而写的诗句。L维克多_Yip的微博视频	02月12日 09:10	微博视频号	5	2	12
崔鼎矗	https://weibo.com/1849264974?refer_flag=1001030103_	没有春晚是觉得不合胃口。steam上买了好多游戏和若干DLC。虽然喜欢文明6,但那些mod我也多。今skylines或云霄飞车之星这种模拟经营类游戏的复杂程度不亚于三维建模绘图软件。那还玩个屁!电影不想追,游戏懒得打,抖科音都是胸大跳舞的小姐姐,朋友圈不是撒狗粮也是放狗屁,哎呦喂,你们别踩我。我也只能在吃饭拉屎睡觉中苦苦找寻人生乐趣了一册那要疯了!收起全文d	02月12日 06:47	iPhone客户端	0	0	0

continued on following page

Table 1. Continued

昵称	主页url	内容	时间	设备	分享数	评论鼠标	点赞数
awesoMEwithME	https://weibo.com/2115624893?refer_flag=1001030103_	看完春晚的【茉莉】后,我听了一晚上文明6的中国bgm,随着游戏进程,从远古时代的朴素干净到原子时代的恢宏磅礴,玩游戏的时候就特别震撼!	02月12日 01:20	HUAWEIP30	0	0	0
圆滚滚的奶酪君	https://weibo.com/6179129772?refer_flag=1001030103_	听见茉莉花的BGM我眼前已经幻视出下一回合的游戏界面了#文明6PTSD#	02月11日 21:17	iPhone客户端	1	0	3
MrFWX	https://weibo.com/2787636883?refer_flag=1001030103_	打个羽毛球扭伤了脚扭了脚,以家里我已经十几年没用过的坐屁股了一次给干躺住了在家无聊玩个文明6,爆兵了准备征服世界的时候,C盘全游戏塞爆满了,不得不删档重下这就是犯太岁的威力吗?	02月11日 17:43	iPhone客户端	0	1	1
YnSuuuu-	https://weibo.com/1828112171?refer_flag=1001030103_	老公把旧的游戏电脑翻出来了凌晨一点及小心翼翼的打开文明6借着微弱的灯光输入我老公steam的密码输入错误我继续把脸凑在键盘上仔细看着每一个键 慢慢的输入了一遍如此反复了很多次终于输对了现在在更新了 激动的搓搓手希望我能短暂的玩一会 希望老公打呼噜不要把儿子吵醒	02月11日 01:26	iPhone11	1	6	3
Sliu_cGz	https://weibo.com/1854760801?refer_flag=1001030103_	文明6的新手教程就玩了快1小时不愧是打发时间的最好游戏	02月10日 21:49	微博weibo.com	0	3	1
德古拉船长2021	https://weibo.com/1770545841?refer_flag=1001030103_	春节想玩的游戏好多,文明6,暗黑破坏神3,战区,想看的书更多。	02月10日 19:51	OPPOFindX2	0	2	2
骑着蜗牛遨银河系	https://weibo.com/5581822259?refer_flag=1001030103_	今天教两小孩打文明6,既玩了游戏,又学了知识,一回合便是一下午,再也不会来问我拿手机打王者农药了	02月10日 17:16	三星Note10+5G	0	0	1
KeenBubble	https://weibo.com/2652647461?refer_flag=1001030103_	文明6,我奶的游戏终于出现了!可惜不能转播,冲404去了	02月10日 12:42	想葛葛直播Android	0	0	0
not_tameless_swift_proud	https://weibo.com/6567695092?refer_flag=1001030103_	这游戏果然叫野蛮6,为了能赢就设了两个文明,最小地图,现在另一个文明的影子都没看见,一直在和蛮族打架,高高兴兴造了船第一次出海,一眨眼身边突然来了四艘蛮族的船,一个回合就把我揍趴了	02月10日 12:34	微博国际版	0	4	1
太阳系虚伪废物	https://weibo.com/3555456241?refer_flag=1001030103_	悠星新手刷剧了一晚上才刷出自己想要的初始真不容易顺便一边玩文明6一边刷,黄金时代MOD真的出色 真就比原来的设计师会做游戏	02月09日 02:06	微博weibo.com	0	0	0
兔酱姐	https://weibo.com/5940590087?refer_flag=1001030103_	今晚本想在蒸汽上买戴森球计划和文明6,发现我的苏菲book显卡几乎是游戏最低配行吧,我还是老老实实主机党吧	02月08日 23:26	nova5Pro人像超级夜景	0	0	0
脾气不好容易动手	https://weibo.com/3055461513?refer_flag=1001030103_	和关 聊天的话题:文明6,DC剧情,火影,奥特曼但这个b打游戏是真的菜 比少爷还菜我是没想到的	02月08日 23:17	iPhone客户端	0	4	1
ms白马	https://weibo.com/1840540473?refer_flag=1001030103_	Epic是趁着steam要开国服所以火线热门打折走一波么。文明6打折了,单游戏6.99刀,主程序+一万个资料包19.03刀.	02月08日 15:55	微博weibo.com	0	0	1
原来昵称挺好的我不舍得	https://weibo.com/5763753650?refer_flag=1001030103_	趁文明6打折赶紧买了一波然后觉得游戏太大又不想下载	02月08日 08:54	iPhone客户端	0	12	3
船长L的老年生活	https://weibo.com/3477289885?refer_flag=1001030103_	最近又开始肝文明6一盘下来就一天了 这游戏什么都好就是老被ai驾驶体不合驾,伟人比他多也骂,造个火箭飞天还骂!!!!!	02月07日 22:43	小米10	0	2	2
MMMMESNZssx	https://weibo.com/1765275995?refer_flag=1001030103_	前几天switch上有个游戏《文明6》打折,我也不知道到底是个啥游戏,就知道这个游戏口碑好像还不错,于是闭眼买了。好家伙,我可是一个玩动森和马里奥的人,一打开这游戏我就懵逼了,这是个治国游戏啊!太复杂了又要发展人口又要发展经济又要发展军事又要发展科技又要发展文化,还要研究政体,还要处理也其他国家的关系又整个人裂开这个游戏很明显不适合我这种可爱乖风的美女但tm又一玩一通宵收起全文d	02月07日 05:13	iPhone客户端	0	12	1
神经无医	https://weibo.com/5082987835?refer_flag=1001030103_	一把文明6打一天,在网吧用高配电脑+2K屏打游戏真的太爽了	02月05日 18:25	iPhone客户端	0	0	0
不懈奋斗的小方	https://weibo.com/3556094897?refer_flag=1001030103_	欢乐源泉 好想成为GTA5 大表哥2 钢铁雄心4文明6刺客信条以及一系列switch游戏的硬核玩家啊 可惜游戏天赋真是烂的感人 只能肝啊O绿洲	02月05日 09:32	绿洲APP	0	2	0
每天都要吃小蛋糕	https://weibo.com/6047724077?refer_flag=1001030103_	趴在文明6坑底还没出来又跳进了江南百景图我爱模拟经营游戏	02月05日 00:30	微博国际版	0	0	0
不懈奋斗的小方	https://weibo.com/3556094897?refer_flag=1001030103_	好希望成为GTA5 大表哥2 钢铁雄心4文明6以及一众switch游戏的硬核玩家 但现实确实游戏天赋烂的惊人2保定	02月04日 20:42	HUAWEIP405G	0	0	0
节能减肥_	https://weibo.com/1926785733?refer_flag=1001030103_	盘点一下想买的游戏just dance 塞尔达 马里奥3d 怪物猎人 城市天际线 文明6	02月03日 11:29	iPhone	0	1	1
朱芝心原野	https://weibo.com/6313888508?refer_flag=1001030103_	为什么别人的文明6看起来那么史诗高端,我的页面:欧美低端3d卡通沙盘游戏	02月02日 17:31	Share微博客户端	0	0	1
朱芝心原野	https://weibo.com/6313888508?refer_flag=1001030103_	为什么别人的文明6看起来那么史诗高端,我的页面:欧美低端3d卡通沙盘游戏	02月02日 17:31	Share微博客户端	0	0	1
用户6188286702	https://weibo.com/6188286702?refer_flag=1001030103_	Day16爱玩什么游戏。现在在玩ow和lol,包括但不限于gta5,文明6,开心消消乐,皇室战争,三国杀。以前也玩过和平精英和王者荣耀,已经退坑了。希望以后能有人一起分享厨房。	02月02日 12:33	HUAWEIMate20	0	0	1
我的真面目就是你的亲爹	https://weibo.com/7030819246?refer_flag=1001030103_	我买过最悔的游戏就是文明6,我还是一出来就花60刀买的,的没想到自己是个睿智,根本玩不明白,有没有懂的	02月02日 09:55	iPhone客户端	0	9	6
玄鉴之	https://weibo.com/1839145117?refer_flag=1001030103_	很佩服我自己,每天这么忙,工作,家里,居然也能抽点时间打游戏Switch买给男朋友的,感觉他太生活太无趣了,越过年自己先玩爽再说帝国时代PC版买了新DLC,打折季买了文明6全套,三国全战时不时开出来爽一下,不准备今年再买PC游戏了~游戏真的使我快乐~最重要的是我打游戏从来不上瘾	02月01日 23:49	小米10Pro	0	4	1
每天都睡不醒的PrimaryKey	https://weibo.com/5347811895?refer_flag=1001030103_	最近在肝的游戏是《戴森球计划》,感觉比文明6稍微难一点。	02月01日 19:21	iPhone12	0	0	4

continued on following page

Table 1. Continued

昵称	主页url	内容	时间	设备	分享数	评论鼠标	点赞数
落尘染墨	https://weibo.com/6622655420?refer_flag=1001030103_	毫无疑问,我很喜欢玩文明6,好久之前从读江南的上海堡垒开始第一次知道这种游戏,到现在从七点打到现在,结束一把残局(指好久之前的一把,到手已经有相当大的一片地),可我说不明白,它那再战一合的魅力所在何处,从原始部落到太空事业,这确实很酷,但我实在不清楚这"下一回合"的魅力,外交胜利的画面出现,疲惫漫了涌上来,咋这么上头收起全文d	02月01日 01:39	小米MIX2S全面屏	0	0	1
一只片片	https://weibo.com/1844983780?refer_flag=1001030103_	周末和我爹联机打了两天文明6,原先指望这个游戏时长已经一千七百多个小时的大佬带带我们,结果——	02月01日 01:12	iPhoneXS	0	0	1
阿喵喵nya	https://weibo.com/1733468812?refer_flag=1001030103_	第一次玩文明6两小时以后满脸懵懂的退出游戏了 说的一打开再等回过神已经天亮的呢……	01月31日 01:49	iPhone客户端	0	5	1
LveZill	https://weibo.com/2276220104?refer_flag=1001030103_	肝了一下午的戴森球计划。杀时间跟文明6有的一拼。游戏优点都特别鲜明。本来不到两个g的大小让我对画面和内容没有什么期待,但实际上画面感叹实让我眼前一亮,行星之间相对运动的轨迹,恒星升起的光影变化简直不要太美。而且玩法内容也特别丰富。玩法让我这个工艺人倍感亲切,就像搭资做平面和管线布置一样。最有趣的是建成一条生产线,然后再慢慢优化,看着各种冗余拥堵到更改流程后的丝滑流畅的全局美是有说不出的快感。而且目前玩下来还没发现有什么bug不过这个也不错嘛。一个是视角,第三人称。即使设置改成上帝视角也无法脱离角色固定位置	01月31日 00:39	微博HTML5版	0	1	1
花柑子	https://weibo.com/6378464725?refer_flag=1001030103_	周末突然想玩文明6,去搜了一下正好dlc有打折hhh我就是自带想玩什么游戏那个游戏就会打折的技能	01月30日 22:53	iPhone11Pro	0	0	0
旗鱼_想学画画	https://weibo.com/1844194344?refer_flag=1001030103_	文明6挤占我的画画时间。但是游戏真好玩【】	01月29日 12:07	HUAWEIP40Pro5G	0	4	0
失树	https://weibo.com/5426485038?refer_flag=1001030103_	最近我还是不喜欢出门,在商店里我读不懂德语标签,在邮局里我听不懂搭话的路人,外卖小哥跟我问好只好一句danke回去。语言不通让人处处擅墙。此时此地的孤立无援,心生绝望。整个寒假我几乎都宅在家打文明6,Steam记录的游戏时长大约有200小时。注视着镜中的自己,脸颊消瘦,脑海中不由得冒出「胡适之胡适之」以及「决定了!应当爱,应当劳动」之类的话。这段子了我时常想起纽约,不由得想,如果去了纽约的生活该多好。波光闪闪的哈德逊河,灯光繁华的百老汇,甚至在夏天的空气里格外憨闷又飘着怪味的地	01月27日 11:03	Android	0	10	38
蔡新伍20	https://weibo.com/1239007287?refer_flag=1001030103_	女流姐姐终于玩文明6了,这游戏对于不熟悉游戏的人,看直播也挺不友好的。哈哈	01月26日 09:10	女流超话	0	5	1
JoJo电玩	https://weibo.com/7545931380?refer_flag=1001030103_	#游戏#《文明6》在早些时候宣布了将于1月29日发布的《文明VI:新纪元季票》第五款DLC-越南和忽必烈包。如今放出的"先晴为快LJoJo电玩的微博视频	01月25日 09:51	iPhone客户端	0	0	0
主机游戏君	https://weibo.com/5821836595?refer_flag=1001030103_	《文明6》在早些时候宣布了将于1月29日发布的《文明VI:新纪元季票》第五款DLC-越南和忽必烈包。如今放出的"先晴为快:越南领袖赵夫人"影片。#文明6##游戏资讯#L主机游戏君的微博视频	01月24日 16:00	微博视频号	56	113	302
不二家的嘉嘉最近是痴汉	https://weibo.com/2216089361?refer_flag=1001030103_	文明6这个游戏真的太肝了。	01月24日 09:53	HUAWEIP30	0	1	0
数字尾巴	https://weibo.com/1726544024?refer_flag=1001030103_	《文明6》又双叒出DLC了游戏官网宣布,将在1月28日推出第五个DLC『越南和忽必烈』,此次更新的DLC包含以下内容:1. 新领袖『忽必烈』,技能预计为获得新科技;2. 新文明『越南』,由于雨林环境的特征,有雨林、沼泽、树林地貌,不同地貌的加成也不同;3. 新游戏模式『垄断和公司』,可以使某等侈品具备垄断 Buff,使玩家现在能够建立自己的经济帝国,提供稳定的大商人点数。该模式不需要购买任何DLC,但需要有『选起兴表』DLC内容才可以访问全部奢侈品资源。收起全文d	01月21日 13:17	微博weibo.com	7	9	22
玩STEAM的大魔王	https://weibo.com/1863028777?refer_flag=1001030103_	粉丝投稿:有没有适合和小姐妹玩机的简单点的游戏?除了星露谷啊文明6#steam##适合和姐妹联机的游戏#	01月20日 22:19	微博weibo.com	2	93	175
银降鬼	https://weibo.com/3100543135?refer_flag=1001030103_	我玩的不是文明6我玩的是动物园大亨明天就买个盖房子游戏去	01月20日 09:24	三星GalaxyS9+	0	2	1
steam游戏推荐_	https://weibo.com/6213409283?refer_flag=1001030103_	【永久入库:二次元TPS游戏黎明,新史低:文明6风云变幻28元等游戏】永久入库:二次元第三人称射击游戏黎明,HB新史低:文明6:风云变幻28元等,米哈游2.28亿元纳税排第一,射击解密游戏《梦》可以了解下,尼尔:伪装者分级MLUP大魔驴的微博视频	01月18日 17:45	微博视频号	0	0	2
d妖娆至翠粟花	https://weibo.com/2921752725?refer_flag=1001030103_	天啊我要裂开了,switch在国内更新是要这么寸步难行的吗…………不过我看我也上手不了几次了,今天跟我妈说能玩文明6之后,她高兴得手舞足蹈赶紧麻溜更新吧,给娘娘买游戏去了	01月17日 19:23	iPhone客户端	0	0	2
现在重开还来得及去异世界吗	https://weibo.com/6598768854?refer_flag=1001030103_	打开文明6看了眼又关上了 看到策略游戏我的眼睛和脑子一起关机	01月17日 04:51	iPad客户端	0	0	0
亿吨快乐铁	https://weibo.com/7395013672?refer_flag=1001030103_	太可怕了文明6教程两小时起步我打游戏前还要先看两个小时的教程	01月16日 18:39	iPhone客户端	0	0	0
一盒pocky	https://weibo.com/1769339167?refer_flag=1001030103_	终于再次打满一把《文明6》500回合,三夜才搞完。上次一把还是大学嗖塞旭哥坐我旁边熬了几个通宵。感觉一年也就开一把文明6了,慢下一把又通宵	01月16日 05:29	iPhone客户端	0	0	0
苏打汽水zz	https://weibo.com/6790438212?refer_flag=1001030103_	最近在玩库存里的游戏,那时候喜加一,结果买了就吃灰去了,一直没打开过hhh,那时候沉迷文明6,来来一回合,结果打了200+小时……,最近也不知道怎么的,就是我找不到特别合我胃口的书,可能再翻翻翻如前看到的书,我发现有的书如果是实体书,我能够看得进去,电子书的话,就不容易看进去,除非内容特别吸引我,可能也是因为网络节奏是快速的,导致人渐渐变得懒惰,懒于去深入思考,这可不是一件好事,以前我是能够一本书看一天,完全不会厌烦的,我比较爱安静吧,所以对于社交之类的倒不是很在意,我是我很清晰,时间不等人,我	01月14日 21:25	微博weibo.com	0	0	0
青·篆洛碧湖	https://weibo.com/1671070344?refer_flag=1001030103_	文明6真是一个过于肝性的游戏……波兰开局,迎来足人孔子,创立的道教传遇从伊比利亚半岛到加加索山脉的每一寸土地,把瑞典赶出历史舞台,环球航行后在北美布下工业基地,跟邻居波斯在国境线上堆兵力,为了和柬埔寨比拼先进科技在香港安插间谍……图为波兰大作家李白在罗马剧院展示的传世巨作	01月13日 17:26	微博国际版	0	0	2
you-思源	https://weibo.com/5127190850?refer_flag=1001030103_	突然想起之前在EPIC上白嫖了好多游戏,就文明6下载下来想着消遣一下,结果连新手教程都打不过去	01月10日 15:09	iPhone8Plus	1	0	2
超级正能量小号	https://weibo.com/7370443207?refer_flag=1001030103_	塞尔达和文明6还有被我及时取消掉的捡树枝怎么都这么肝明!玩游戏给我整得压力更大了我现在希望未来的50天里每天两个小时健身环(你最好是)!	01月09日 21:31	荣耀305G	0	1	0

continued on following page

Table 1. Continued

昵称	主页url	内容	时间	设备	分享数	评论鼠标数	点赞数
当代青年陌小河	https://weibo.com/5890928301?refer_flag=1001030103_	我已经对《文明6》这款游戏完全失去了兴趣。	01月08日 11:22	新版微博weibo.com	0	0	0
想要翻身的咸咸咸鱼	https://weibo.com/2385478501?refer_flag=1001030103_	刚刚在存了备份档的情况下，扔了文明6的第一颗核弹头了，由于冲击过大关游戏了，打算明天再开	01月08日 11:14	HUAWEIP10Plus	0	0	1
梳雨是个好名字	https://weibo.com/5240373018?refer_flag=1001030103_	玩了1年文明6后,我想把游戏里的世界奇观,不管是人造的还是自然奇观都游览一遍。日常百度乞力马扎罗山和维苏威火山	01月07日 10:58	微博weibo.com	0	0	1
游戏没有围	https://weibo.com/5894340915?refer_flag=1001030103_	今天Steam数据榜单上出现了一个让人意想不到的作品——《气球塔防6》(Bloons TD6),据后台数据统计,最多有43,629位用户同时在线游玩此款游戏。与它差不多排名的分别是:《收获日2》、《怪猎:世界》、《泰拉瑞亚》、《文明6》......这款游戏我偶尔会有降价,打折的适合入一下还是可以的,毕竟猴子+塔防,谁能不爱呢收起全文d	01月06日 14:39	微博weibo.com	1	2	6
任言·君语	https://weibo.com/1575749231?refer_flag=1001030103_	我的2020年没什么可总结的,简而言之就是,休息了人生中最长的一段时间,这些年最少时间的游戏,游戏时间和空余时间不总是成反比的。认真玩的游戏细数出来也就只有四个,DQ11S,XB1,动森,文明6	01月04日 19:03	HUAWEIP30	0	0	3
举杯敬虚荣	https://weibo.com/1773177337?refer_flag=1001030103_	文明6,这游戏真是有毒啊,昨天从epic下载完过了教程,开一局试试,就坐着就点啊点,一转眼就突然到零点了,"再来几个回合,容我灭了日本","我x,怎么就01:28了???"	01月03日 09:45	K30S至尊纪念版	0	0	0
火锅啤酒月光杯	https://weibo.com/5271316446?refer_flag=1001030103_	今天作死在steam上买了文明6,然后怎么研究都没把教程通关,玩了1个小时光操作单位晃得眼睛都疼,这游戏,不值!亏时间又亏钱	2020年 12月31日 00:06	iPhoneXR	0	0	0
奈奈IX	https://weibo.com/1641124702?refer_flag=1001030103_	文明6这个游戏真的太沉迷了。睡下去都3点多了简直废人模式全开	2020年 12月30日 09:09	iPhone客户端	0	0	2
1ndig0	https://weibo.com/2212936237?refer_flag=1001030103_	今年一个人过年,那段时间玩了文明6,春天玩了动森,夏秋是一年中最忙的没时间玩,就算买了游戏也搁置,偶尔会打几把匹配,等A了2077以后想把对马岛玩了。	2020年 12月28日 18:16	iPhone客户端	0	0	0
MsapphirE	https://weibo.com/1702782640?refer_flag=1001030103_	考完试,代表我可以好好睡觉好好玩了。我要想几点睡就几点睡,想几点起就几点起。还有,我想玩的游戏们!我来了!模拟人生4文明6王国风云2 PM5 LOL 还有我在epic上领的新游戏!我来了!明侦6小鬼当家 魔法师的不列颠日常 直播录屏 全明星比赛 还有我b站大会员攒着看的电影!我来了!哈哈哈哈哈哈哈哈哈哈!开心!收起全文d	2020年 12月27日 19:02	Android	0	1	4
Dorothea琪	https://weibo.com/3837501718?refer_flag=1001030103_	来自生命的经验之谈玩文明6要量力而行到游戏氪金文明6氪命2南京·中国传媒大学南广学院	2020年 12月27日 11:52	iPhone客户端	0	1	1
探机probe赤赤赤赤赤	https://weibo.com/5850479242?refer_flag=1001030103_	突然感觉打游戏没意思了 炉石传说限时好烦 英雄联盟新版本我又玩不明白 下棋就那点套路我又玩不赢 单机有感觉就是刷而且有的关我还不过去 好佛 没有其他类型有意思的游戏吗 感觉游戏给我带来的新鲜感褪去的好快啊 好怀念那个入坑warframe的寒假 肝材料的游戏我还查攻略查的很开心 怀念文明6	2020年 12月26日 22:49	iPhone客户端	0	2	0
并不是果子狸_二二二冒	https://weibo.com/1962522791?refer_flag=1001030103_	想玩的东西太多了,想再玩一遍to the moon 和古剑3,想再玩一局文明6(噢天怎么丢了),想玩巫师3和奇妙探险队,想玩好多好多剧情没玩鸣鸣鸣......但是放假的时候就只会睡觉,因为太困了(❀ᴗ❀)	2020年 12月26日 19:48	微博国际版	0	0	0
STEAM情报	https://weibo.com/5683813904?refer_flag=1001030103_	【转发抽奖】冬季特卖,2k旗下多款游戏史低特惠。感兴趣的不要错过了。无主之地3 — 豪华版94,终极版159四海兄弟最终版 — 104文明6 — 本体49,白金版129NBA 2k21 — 99幽浮魔英龙小队 — 49生化奇兵 重制版 — 16生化奇兵2 重制版 — 17无主之地3、四海兄弟最终版、文明6几款游戏,epic还可以使用10刀优惠券。转发本条微博,抽3人1送上四海兄弟最终版。12月27日开卖。#我的圣诞老人是2K##12月2K月#@抽奖详情收起全文d	2020年 12月24日 19:56	微博weibo.com	582	134	250
港中深_合唱团	https://weibo.com/7342247016?refer_flag=1001030103_	#香港中文大学深圳#@香港中文大学深圳#校园才艺show###快进2020##文明6#@港中深_管弦乐团当音乐想起的那一刻你是否仿佛看到了文明从从从起步到最终走向昌盛?从石器时代,到信息时代,我们最终跨过浩瀚的宇宙迈进......"张开双翼 踏向星辰是汝之抉择星空浩瀚方知此处为汝之归宿"一旦尝过飞行的滋味,便会永远仰望天空,因为你曾去过那里,并且渴望回到那里。——列奥纳多·达·芬奇跟随我们与管弦乐团@港中深_管弦乐团一起,在这越燃的现场中,张开双翼,飞向辽阔的星海吧!L港中深_合唱团的微博视频收起全文d	2020年 12月24日 11:06	音乐现场·视频社区	5	2	10
不买奥迪s5不改名	https://weibo.com/5937030446?refer_flag=1001030103_	模拟人生dlc贵了吧,文明6这游戏太上头了,这边建议玩氪金游戏,文明六比较耐命	2020年 12月24日 00:47	iPhone客户端	0	1	4
笠十二	https://weibo.com/6310535439?refer_flag=1001030103_	爱玩游戏的男生:《文明6》一次能玩两天开挂没意思,血条飞出屏幕、伤害飞出屏幕开挂只有一次和无数次,以后你一遇到问题过不去就会想着开挂这话笑死我啦	2020年 12月24日 00:07	Share微博客户端	0	1	0
玉楼月_笑摸狗头	https://weibo.com/3207873827?refer_flag=1001030103_	买游戏不玩也是快乐的一部分,趁打折买了杀手2文明6巫师3数码宝贝,全都去我的列表里吃灰吧(͒ ᐛ)͒('ᵌ')	2020年 12月23日 19:35	微博weibo.com	0	1	1
这里怎样	https://weibo.com/1621278475?refer_flag=1001030103_	Epic游戏库的游戏可以删除么?就当下活动《文明6》白金好要8.47刀,但是我有了本体就不能买了,买DLC就只要15.99刀......@Epic游戏商城	2020年 12月23日 14:39	新版微博weibo.com	0	0	1
Ax-光之影	https://weibo.com/6123147862?refer_flag=1001030103_	我的台式什么时候发货 刺would信条,赛博朋克,大镖客,文明6,,巫师3,GTA5,2k21我来啦!买游戏才是最快乐的游戏!	2020年 12月22日 20:06	小米10	0	12	0
四月风起	https://weibo.com/1410477492?refer_flag=1001030103_	看网上有人推荐杀戮尖塔,问儿子玩过没,儿子他在steam买了啊,玩过一点,没时间就没怎么玩了,儿子给过我他的steam账号,我很多游戏,看喜欢文明6,还有意义玩了文明6的游戏,不过我下载了后觉得太复杂就没玩了,年龄大了,对新东西的学习热情和能力都下降了不少,今天试试杀戮尖塔的游戏吧	2020年 12月20日 08:26	微博weibo.com	0	0	0
希尔伯特的玫瑰	https://weibo.com/6364435857?refer_flag=1001030103_	想着要不要趁着冬促入手《文明6》,被B站游戏录像们时长成功劝退。肝不动了	2020年 12月19日 08:41	iPhone客户端	0	8	0
娱乐扒圈酱	https://weibo.com/1593698365?refer_flag=1001030103_	#游戏情报站#【《文明6》12月免费更新宣传片 大量改动、增加新特色】Firaxis今天释出了一支新影片,讲到了即将在12月17日星期四推出的《文明6》12月游戏更新所带来的游戏变更、调整与追加特色/功能。在更新推出前,Firaxis也将在北京·时间12月17凌晨入点直播社群节目。本月的游戏更新包括"城邦选择 收起全文d	2020年 12月16日 11:44	iPhone客户端	0	0	0
阿黄今天好好生活了吗	https://weibo.com/5829773308?refer_flag=1001030103_	想买文明6和双点医院的卡带。我是疯了吗,住院不够,游戏里还要开医院 ,我有病。但是双点医院的画风其实在太可爱了有钱买,但是怕没命玩。。。	2020年 12月15日 21:20	nova5Pro人像超级夜景	0	0	0
刹拉刹拉Boom	https://weibo.com/2118301082?refer_flag=1001030103_	看宣传视频的时候永远是我最想玩这款游戏的时候。一旦买回来,连新手教程都懒得过了,更别说去找资料看攻略。嘛缺氧星露谷物语文明6,我还想买动物园之星过山车之星城市天际线,真让人头大。	2020年 12月12日 15:13	iPhone客户端	0	2	3

continued on following page

Table 1. Continued

昵称	主页url	内容	时间	设备	分享数	评论鼠标	点赞数
食荤魔女Leona	https://weibo.com/3196414734?refer_flag=1001030103_	#2020盘点#游戏也玩得不多,可能好奇心没那么旺盛了,不过涉足的游戏都感觉玩得过分认真了,《文明6》,接连吸了好几晚,摸清了几乎所有胜利套路,然后就再没打开过了,因为太想掌握,《江南百景图》,又名椰岛养成,帮我排解了不少隔离时光;《炉石传说》,只玩酒馆战棋,提神醒脑。	2020年12月11日13:18	HUAWEIP20Pro	0	0	0
懋---吐槽无罪	https://weibo.com/1742124087?refer_flag=1001030103_	刚看steam库存突然发现我居然买了文明6但是完全没有花钱的印象还有35个游戏围着都没打开过可能我只是喜欢每次打折捡漏的感觉	2020年12月11日00:35	iPhone客户端	0	0	0
最爱斐斐斐斐斐斐	https://weibo.com/6276305647?refer_flag=1001030103_	#文明重启#@应书岭@英雄互娱客户服务中心@文明重启游戏,咋说呢,可能,我真的对贵公司旗下的游戏失去信心了,我本来是真的很喜欢文明重启这款游戏的,自从我的第一个账号在今年6月份被封禁之后我就再也没玩过这个游戏,期间我有过很多次想重新下载来玩,但是心里一直都是抵触的,就是害怕某某莫名其妙又被封,但是今天我的队友们让我重新创建一个号来玩游戏,我忍不住下载好后发现,这会很多平衡改变,出现我这种情况玩家的不只一个,之前我还以为是游戏账号借给别人才导致游戏被封,这次知道设备被封我明白了,和别人没有关系。	2020年12月09日23:21	iQOOPro性能旗舰	2	5	2
Switch新闻速递	https://weibo.com/6069554817?refer_flag=1001030103_	Firaxis 推出《文明6》更新预告新视频,透露12月18日将推出游戏更新,调整与追加特色/功能等等,前一晚计划先举办线上直播节目。视频已更新为中文字幕。LSwitch新闻速递的微博视频	2020年12月09日19:34	微博视频号	1	1	4
电竞苹果酱	https://weibo.com/5756737721?refer_flag=1001030103_	Firaxis今天释出了一支新影片,讲到了即将在12月17日星期四推出的《文明6》12月游戏更新所带来的游戏变更、调整与追加特色/功能。在更新推出前,Firaxis还将在北京·时间12月17凌晨3点直播社群节目。本月的游戏更新包括"城邦选择器",以及许多平衡性调整和根据玩家喜爱所做的变更。类似8月推出的"自然奇观选择器","城邦选择器"能让玩家选择有多少城邦出现在他们的游戏中,可让玩家选择以随机选择的城邦或自订城邦清单进行游戏。L游戏的微博视频收起全文d	2020年12月09日16:00	微博视频号	0	0	0
是腊月不是正月	https://weibo.com/3840119134?refer_flag=1001030103_	好不容易闲了几天,都用来玩创世小玩家了,上一个让我如此沉沦的游戏还是文明6	2020年12月09日10:55	iPhone客户端	0	1	0
shyicarus	https://weibo.com/2252155800?refer_flag=1001030103_	#文明6#Steam上游玩时间最长的游戏,虽然大部分时间都在开图和读存档	2020年12月08日21:41	iPhone客户端	0	1	0
游民星空	https://weibo.com/1969176463?refer_flag=1001030103_	#游戏情报站#【《文明6》12月免费更新宣传片 大量改动、增加新特色】Firaxis今天释出了一支新影片,讲到了即将在12月17日星期四推出的《文明6》12月游戏更新所带来的游戏变更、调整与追加特色/功能。在更新推出前,Firaxis还将在北京·时间12月17凌晨3点直播社群节目。本月的游戏更新包括"自然奇观选择器","城邦选择器"能让玩家选择有多少城邦出现在他们的游戏中,可让玩家选择以随机选择的城邦或自订城邦清单进行游戏。	2020年12月08日17:00	微博视频号	16	45	136
PS5姬	https://weibo.com/6755610006?refer_flag=1001030103_	《文明6》最新免费更新宣传片公开,将于12月17日推出。#游戏资讯#LPS5姬的微博视频	2020年12月08日01:17	游戏姬的iPhone11	0	0	3
Fia_yooohik	https://weibo.com/7484471644?refer_flag=1001030103_	重新下了文明5然后又玩了6个小时,好家伙,赶紧止损卸载了。这种自闭游戏我一玩不用睡觉了	2020年12月06日02:50	小米10至尊纪念版	0	0	1
人间甜糖	https://weibo.com/3983642248?refer_flag=1001030103_	#战网崩了#本来今天晚上听完听力是打算下两把棋的 一进去就崩了 又想看看阿瓦 没想到阿瓦在播文明6被逼从了一晚上地主 室友还讲不都是打牌游戏一样一样	2020年12月06日00:36	nova4自拍极点全面屏	0	0	0
一台复读机NN	https://weibo.com/3514076750?refer_flag=1001030103_	垃不可一世杀手朋友三点打游戏0-6转信 然后资料卡是我QQ一开始我很文明后来想起来不对劲 然后我就置出出 在哪学的中华文化语言知识果然没白学 对面瞧我吓得直接把我删了啷 作为手儿第1584697位弟子 扬眉吐气!	2020年12月04日17:32	不可一世杀手超话	0	14	3
Mac啊喊	https://weibo.com/7303477504?refer_flag=1001030103_	文明6铂金版 mac中文pj版附DCL包来和大家分享!文明6游戏将延续前作主要的玩法,使用在文明的文明来征战世界,利用外交、战争、科技、宗教等多元化的手段来击败对手成为世界的领袖。这是CivilizationVI的第二次扩展,你周围的世界比以往任何时候都更加活跃。通过万千的先进技术和工程项目以及在世界大会上就共赢问题与全球社会进行谈判,以为您的员工树立胜利之路。本站提供文明6Mac中文破解版下载,一起加入游戏体验现代时代的战争吧!该版本包括DLC:上升和下降,聚众风暴,拜占庭和高卢包,埃塞俄比亚包,Maya和	2020年12月04日09:15	微博weibo.com	0	0	1
任言·君语	https://weibo.com/1575749231?refer_flag=1001030103_	文明6这个游戏果然很讽刺,当年欧美摇滚乐队在苏联搞文化入侵,从流行文化层面直接推动和平演变,然后我玩文明6的DLC俄罗斯这个屌丝文明后期点播摇滚乐队的概率都高的离谱。	2020年12月01日01:56	HUAWEIP30	0	0	6
单机老王子	https://weibo.com/60421053347?refer_flag=1001030103_	【文明6】#单机游戏#《文明6》免费更新"大海盗时代"介绍视频公布,10月22日推出L单机老王子的微博视频	2020年11月30日18:50	微博视频号	0	0	0
Kimsea07	https://weibo.com/3098313647?refer_flag=1001030103_	okk,steam大促买了仨游戏,文明6,底特律变人,城市:天际线。感觉很赚,不过看到一些原价的游戏现在打对折也上不去,尤其Steep现在居然从要27块了,心思是在滴血看要测评的意思是我玩完这三款游戏我可能已经80岁了 Q好了不说了,点个鲜芋仙开玩要了	2020年11月29日11:05	啵啵捏的iPhone客户端	1	4	0
-Allegro-	https://weibo.com/2632689404?refer_flag=1001030103_	就我昨天5分钟退出文明6教程的速度我觉得作为一个游戏白痴JD2021是对我最大的恩赐买贵了 就买贵了吧 它值得	2020年11月28日09:36	iPhone	0	3	0
WhenIclosemyeyes	https://weibo.com/3437870570?refer_flag=1001030103_	目前想打雾假雾做的打HPV疫苗做近视眼手术文明6这种建立城市的游戏我小时候很喜欢!做蛋糕 蛋挞 包饺子 学几个新菜上完算法课上完B站21天的那个编程课把记单词。再抢起来追剧!!!虽然还没想好追剧啥	2020年11月28日00:15	iPhone客户端	0	4	0
Ring_Frei	https://weibo.com/6093558214?refer_flag=1001030103_	文明6是个好游戏,但是我这种比较不爱打架的种田玩家可能真的不太适合玩这游戏,里面的NPC动不动就对我宣战	2020年11月26日08:19	HUAWEIP20Pro	0	0	0
曾理之意志	https://weibo.com/1853013324?refer_flag=1001030103_	《文明》系统诞生于1991年,至今已有6代,能与之媲美的策略游戏并不多。整个游戏都需要考虑:地形、运气、宗教、体制、文化、科学、军事......如此巨作,花68元就可以无限玩。然而,评分挺低,认为贵、不值。这游戏极度烧脑,我玩得不好。虽然玩过每一代,但每次出新版,仍需要熟悉操作、上网读攻略。这游戏智商高过100以上,则是我摹写。另外,还需要静下心研究。以上两点,筛选大部分玩家。一人一票,还反淘汰。收起全文d	2020年11月22日11:15	iPhone11Pro	0	2	3
单机老王子	https://weibo.com/60421053347?refer_flag=1001030103_	【文明6新纪元季票】#单机游戏#《文明6新纪元季票》DLC4「巴比伦包」中字介绍,看看都有哪些新鲜的事情L单机老王子的微博视频	2020年11月19日11:51	微博视频号	0	0	0
话少孤长乐趣少	https://weibo.com/5282096223?refer_flag=1001030103_	#樊登读书#昨晚上睡前听完了《丝绸之路》。宗教,贸易,武力讨伐,科技。听着听着就是听精神了。边听边满脑子想着文明6...以前我就是自己瞎几把玩,听着听着就是对如以上提到的字眼的作用清晰了起来。建议可作为《文明6》游戏入门指导指南。	2020年11月16日07:42	iPhoneXSMax	0	4	2
噗味哈哈哈哈	https://weibo.com/6872115828?refer_flag=1001030103_	搞不懂文明6有啥好玩的,策略游戏里最无脑的一个。全面战争都比它有意思,p社也比它好。	2020年11月15日00:52	iPhone客户端	0	0	0

continued on following page

Table 1. Continued

昵称	主页url	内容	时间	设备	分享数	评论属标	点赞数
IGN编辑部	https://weibo.com/7494874950?refer_flag=1001030103_	《文明6新纪元季聚》新DLC内容《巴比伦包》公开,11月19日推出。一位新领袖、一个新文明,24位伟人,6个新城邦,以及新模式「英雄与传奇」。该游戏模式增加了英雄和传说的12位强大英雄单位(比如封面的孙悟空),每位英雄都是独一无二的,只能代表一个文明。英雄的寿命有限,在一定的回合数之后便会耗尽,但可以用信仰值将其召回,继续为您的事业添砖加瓦。LIGN编辑部的微博视频号收起全文d	2020-11-1003:33 转赞人数 超过10	微博视频号	5	7	10
中国古典音乐家网	https://weibo.com/3205400741?refer_flag=1001030103_	【特别推荐】史诗合唱团文明6主题曲《Sogno di Volare(飞翔之梦)》自从游戏诞生以来,有不少游戏主题曲被归为经典。油管播主【Peter Hollens】组织了50多位歌手,在野外完美演绎了《文明6》的主题曲。优美的音乐加上恢弘的背景,让人感觉非常震撼。不知不觉之间,又来了一个回合……《Sogno di Volare(飞翔之梦》是华落作曲家——田志仁为游戏《文明6》所作主题曲,歌词采用意大利语演唱,曲式厚重绚丽,外加人声主旋律形成排山倒海的冲击力,激昂澎湃之余,又教人泪流满面。如果你是个游戏	2020年11月09日09:33	微博视频号	4	2	7
酷哥说	https://weibo.com/5538829428?refer_flag=1001030103_	【游戏推荐】由SEGA发行的《人类 HUMANKIND?》一款历史战略游戏你能够在其中重新书写人类的整个故事,能够让你打造一个专属于自己的独特文明。结合多达60种历史文化,带领你的子民从古代走向现代社会。从籍籍无名的新石器部落起家,过渡到远古时代的巴比伦人,再到古典时的玛雅人、中世纪的倭马亚人、近代早期的英国人等等。。。从这个简介就不难看出,本作也是一款以历史为轴线的战略发展游戏,说到同类型就不得不让人联想到《文明》系列里最负盛名的《文明6》,无论从玩法和地图、历史路线来看都非常相似,不知道世嘉这部作	2020年11月05日13:10	微博视频号	1	0	52
挥剑能留住晚霞吗	https://weibo.com/6091136782?refer_flag=1001030103_	异星工厂,一个让我觉得肝度堪比文明6的游戏,戴上耳机从零开始造两条生产线到1点半了。明天一定早睡,之后异星搬鱼,毕业以后再好好肝。2厦门:集美大学	2020年11月05日01:51	K30至尊纪念版	0	0	0
任奢·君语	https://weibo.com/1575749231?refer_flag=1001030103_	我今年文明6的游戏时间200小时,超过了今年所有NS上购买的新游,不得不说一句EPIC白嫖真的香。由此也激起了我购NS版文明6的欲望——天天坐在电脑前打文明6只会通宵,永远不会睡觉,只有在床上再来一回合才有可能玩睡觉这样了。但是一想到我老NS屏弱的2h+和Lite不到4h的续航,就打消了这个念头。这游戏一局怎么不得5小时起步……收起全文d	2020年11月02日05:38	HUAWEIP30	1	2	3
Thehang景恪	https://weibo.com/5379618351?refer_flag=1001030103_	生活就像文明6需要去考虑付出和回报的收益但不同之处在于游戏你可以在外面思考而人生永远都是进行时	2020年11月01日13:23	vivoAI智慧拍照X21	0	0	3
贰零贰壹肆	https://weibo.com/2860025352?refer_flag=1001030103_	学习习文明6中……制作这个游戏的真他娘的是人才啊!一局直接白天到黑夜还是有很多不懂的地方啊steam真的好好玩哦	2020年10月24日21:51	iPhoneX	0	0	1
阿伦戴尔赛车手	https://weibo.com/7366103304?refer_flag=1001030103_	一边看着放在那个女巫一边就热血沸腾的准备回家玩文明6了,啊!怎么这么多好玩的游戏以及好看的书啊!真是让我乐不思蜀根本不想写文啊!放开那个女巫真的很好看啊!	2020-10-2414:38 转赞人数 超过10	微博weibo.com	0	0	15
Cloud_P5	https://weibo.com/1254268391?refer_flag=1001030103_	说道因为游戏产生的文化和理解差异这事,还让我想起来一个事。当年文明6刚出灾害系统的资料片时,我一个朋友觉得工业导致气候变化让海岸被淹没这太过白左恶想了,他说本来就是西方人自己搞的那么多碳排然后要这些没发达的国家买单,但文明6虽然是基于历史,却是一个让你编写历史的游戏。如果是西工业化的国家不是英国等欧洲国家,而是亚洲或者中国,世人是不是就会把这种审看法用在中国或者那个大阵营上了?我和他说是没错,但是因为工业化导致气候变化引发的一些灾害也是客观存在的,只是恰好历史是如此罢了。本来文明发展也是落后的人	2020年10月23日12:46	微博weibo.com	3	0	4
3DMGAME官方微博	https://weibo.com/2163365571?refer_flag=1001030103_	#游戏资讯#《文明6》先睹为快:"大海盗时代"情景影片公开,"大海盗时代"是10月更新中内容的一部,计划于10月22日星期四免费发布。"大海盗时代"情景让一至四名玩家在大海上争夺宝藏和荣耀。玩家将从"恐怖海盗"、"私掠船"、"侠盗",和"财运"四个阵营中挑选任一,而每个阵营各自都有独特能力与玩法。除了对付其他阵营外,玩家还应付决心送玩家到海底的英国、法国、西班牙和荷兰海军。"大海盗时代"场景带来了为游戏增添热带风情的全新和更新美术内容,而可在独特的手工制作地图上进行游玩,玩家也可以选择每次游	2020-10-2110:31 转赞人数 超过30	微博视频号	6	6	24
暴力馒头	https://weibo.com/1770317094?refer_flag=1001030103_	我想请问一下我的幕后们,你们把我的个人电脑和手机IP全世界公布,有任求对我的意见吗?现在我不管是拿旧电脑一玩文明6和其它游戏就卡死,有多少黑客拿我的电脑当靶子,你们有考虑过我的感受吗?难道只要我一不符合你们任何一方的意思,就可以随意搔弄我的电脑?你想要不要逼迫了?	2020年10月20日21:17	HUAWEIMate20X	0	1	0
保我一下会死吗	https://weibo.com/7312359524?refer_flag=1001030103_	满屏幕的熊笔气的我又要高血压发作,不过现在我长大了不会再为不识字的双商负数小学鸡们写千字论文浪费时间了,火速打开文明6降火,我封文明6为本世纪最修身养性的电脑游戏	2020年10月18日12:12	iPhone11	0	0	2
FrankWilliamAbagnale-	https://weibo.com/2790803854?refer_flag=1001030103_	文明6这游戏真的牛,我学的经济方面的物流方面的知识都能有体现,即将为我电脑里gta5外又一款常驻游戏	2020年10月15日16:49	荣耀20S	0	0	2
Switch新闻速递	https://weibo.com/6069554817?refer_flag=1001030103_	Firaxis推出了《文明6》游戏更新新视频,由游戏团队为玩家带来10月更新资讯,包含游戏改变、调整与追加特色/功能。另外,官方也预告将在10月22日凌晨2时举办直播节目。本月的游戏更新包括"海贼大时代"场景,以及许多平衡性调整和根据玩家意见所做的变更。「海贼大时代」场景将一至四名玩家在大海上争夺宝藏和荣耀,玩家将从「吓人海盗」、「私掠船」、「侠盗」和「图货者」这四个阵营中挑选任一,而每个阵营自都有独特能力与玩法。除了对付其他阵营外,玩家还应付决心送玩家去见深海阁王的英国、法国、西班牙和荷兰海军。LS	2020年10月15日12:08	微博视频号	0	0	1
略萌的神萌	https://weibo.com/1756619467?refer_flag=1001030103_	这万国觉醒,我还以为自己进入了文明6呢……果然国产游戏都是抄……	2020年10月15日11:46	iPhoneSE	3	0	2
游民星空	https://weibo.com/1969176463?refer_flag=1001030103_	#游戏资讯#【《文明6》更新大海盗时代地图 10月23日扬帆起航】《文明6》官方公布了新的免费更新内容:"大海盗时代"情景地图,并为其发布了宣传片,"大海盗时代"拥有全新的美术资源,并为迷人的热带海域和满满的海盗风情。海盗将有四个派系可供选择,每个派系都有独特的专属能力。"大海盗时代"中还有遗物系统,获得遗物将给游戏玩法带来变化,每场游戏出现的遗物不一样,装备不同的遗物可获得不同组合的强力加成效果。游戏内还进行了一些平衡性的改动,如"招募游击队员"间谍任务和游戏速度的改动等。《文明6》"大海盗时代"	2020-10-1509:13 转赞人数 超过90	微博视频号	31	21	92
核游网	https://weibo.com/6569127244?refer_flag=1001030103_	【《文明6》10.23日更新预告】#游戏资讯#《文明6》10.23日更新预告放出,本月更新内容:"大海盗时代"情景,以及许多平衡性调整。LSteam之家的微博视频	2020年10月14日17:17	微博视频号	1	0	8
Q1du_	https://weibo.com/6230514708?refer_flag=1001030103_	最适合用AI发力的其实是《文明6》这类游戏。开一盘欧洲地图,当AI通过强化学习能够学到什么时候该和谁结盟?该联合谁打谁?地缘优势如何利用?乃至要周围封锁时如何规划商路的经济内循环?铝和石油等战略资源匮乏时外交手段如何发力?乃至筹弹道接到地方还是威胁平衡?有些问题看上去结构化,但其实在在局部最优上都会导致后期一个崩溃。AI如果能理解人类这种尴尬的平衡,甚至另辟蹊径找出一些其他路子,2021年日本也许就不会轰炸珍珠港去了。收起全文d	2020年10月12日22:57	iPhone客户端	0	0	1
vickysse啦	https://weibo.com/5960530870?refer_flag=1001030103_	操文明6是什么游戏拒绝嫖毒 文明6真的有道理本都市女青年如果不是pad自动关机估计还要继续刚明天下班继续吧	2020年10月09日01:15	iPhone客户端	0	6	4

continued on following page

Table 1. Continued

昵称	主页url	内容	时间	设备	分享数	评论鼠标	点赞数
小王今天开心了口马	https://weibo.com/6684562243?refer_flag=1001030103_	在入手文明6和糖豆人的边缘疯狂试探害怕刚打开游戏教资直接结束	2020年10月08日 13:34	Share微博客户端	0	3	0
今昔续百鬼_	https://weibo.com/6217715641?refer_flag=1001030103_	玩了一下午文明6真的有一种"老子花钱买的游戏凭什么还要花时间?"的感触	2020年10月07日 17:05	iPhone客户端	0	0	1
ChloeNon-Stop	https://weibo.com/2878374100?refer_flag=1001030103_	呜呜呜我不想学习了我想打英雄联盟/文明6/逛大街/刷开罗小游戏/化妆化妆/吃好吃的吃好吃的/	2020年10月06日 17:14	华为手机畅享玩不停	0	3	1
Saeran超阔爱	https://weibo.com/3153605532?refer_flag=1001030103_	文明6玩久了挺无聊的但也不是游戏的问题是我的问题因为我不会玩只会瞎戳戳才觉得无聊	2020年10月05日 20:59	小狗的iPhone8Plus(银色)	0	1	0
Mr骁骁骁	https://weibo.com/7504804698?refer_flag=1001030103_	闲了没事想开把文明6,只打了一会就放弃了,游戏进度贼慢,时间过的贼快,估计假期完了这把都打不完,新机制还得去思考理解,算了算了,放空自己瘫着它不香么	2020年10月05日 17:44	小米MIX2S全面屏	0	0	0
windleavez	https://weibo.com/1312997677?refer_flag=1001030103_	#游戏假新闻速递#Firaxis 公布《文明6》全新扩展包 ,特朗普将作为美国的第二位领袖正式加入游戏。制作人 Dennis Shirk 表示,公司会捐献出该 DLC 的全部收入,用于资助全球抗疫事业。制作团队还宣布举办游戏设计大赛,向全球玩家征集特朗普"领袖倾向"和"领袖奖励"的设计创意。#文明6#	2020-10-0512:40 转赞人数超过500	微博weibo.com	99	49	847
今天想吃饼	https://weibo.com/5340261175?refer_flag=1001030103_	有没有玩过文明6的大佬说说,怎么买游戏合适。现在小黑盒上有一个史低,但是dlc不打折。谢谢大家!	2020年09月27日 18:37	HUAWEIP405G	0	0	0
JJ比赛斗地主租号回收金币	https://weibo.com/7499416033?refer_flag=1001030103_	JJ比赛,JJ斗地主租号金商微信6761277 ,满级千炮,满级经典账号资源 在《文明5》问世的六年里,我们对它进行了不只一次的回顾。这就是这些游戏的玩法,《文明6》也不例外。最新的游戏元素为Firaxis的久经考验的公式添加了许多新的想法,尽管有些新想法比其他的效果更好,但总体还是比各部分加起来的效果更好。机械上的调整和改进被包裹在一种微妙的、棋盘游戏式的美学中,你的第二十小时和第十小时都会同样令人愉悦。我们会玩这个游戏很久很久。收起全文d	2020年09月26日 07:06	360安全浏览器	1	1	1
556SM1LE1CE	https://weibo.com/1780851722?refer_flag=1001030103_	1. Steam又打折了,买了个《文明6》玩了一个早上,这游戏太上头了。我很成功的让中国在中世纪就超英赶美统治全世界,让秦始皇坐上外星飞船,估计按这么发展下去兵马俑估计人手一把激光枪和太空剑了,搞不好星球大战前传就是《星球大战:焚书坑儒》,哈哈哈哈我一天在想啥。2. 下午看了一部电影中文译名叫《城市英雄》,但我觉得应该按原译《falling down》翻译作坠落会更好。电影给我的感觉很像70年美国拍的《出租车司机》。有时候让人抓狂的可能真就不是什么大事,而是一件一件压在身上的小事。有些问题其实真的很简单,	2020年09月25日 00:35	HUAWEIP40Pro5G	0	2	2
凜凜凜凜寒風之中	https://weibo.com/3853286830?refer_flag=1001030103_	對上一次強忍著高價區的高價買遊戲還是文明6(記得差不多是中國價格的6倍),最後嘛....我玩了20個小時還是連閃閃艷后二選一那個教學關都打不贏	2020年09月23日 11:30	微博weibo.com	0	11	13
horanseika	https://weibo.com/6320712129?refer_flag=1001030103_	今日金句"高斯分布就是不断地卷积得到的,所以只要你够卷你就能成为高斯"这理解绝了"现在社会上贩卖焦虑的人太多了,所以我每年都会给自己一周时间疯狂打游戏(指钢铁雄心,文明6),然后感到无趣,就把游戏全删了。""小学奥数的题之所以出的又偏又怪就是为了让父母也做不出来,父母那个焦虑啊,然后就把孩子送到补习班去了。""题目死磕它干嘛,做不出来就不要做嘛。""每次上完课,下一节课的来到教室的同学都会觉得我上的是细胞生物学。"wh上复变课真的好可爱啊收起全文d	2020年09月23日 00:52	荣耀305G	0	2	2
游戏班长	https://weibo.com/1399345424?refer_flag=1001030103_	《文明6》公开了拜占庭领袖巴兹尔二世的预告片。该人物包含在"拜占庭和高卢包" DLC 中,将在 9 月 24 日推出。需购买《文明6:新纪元季票》获得。#游戏##游戏资讯#L游戏班长的微博视频	2020年09月22日 10:41	微博视频号	0	1	0
游民星空	https://weibo.com/1969176463?refer_flag=1001030103_	#游戏资讯#【《文明6》拜占庭DLC预告 军事宗教相辅相成共筑帝国】《文明6》将于9月24日推出他们的第三款DLC"拜占庭和高卢"包,此内容会提供给任何拥有《文明6:新纪元季票》的玩家,也可单独购买。今日《文明6》发布了拜占庭的预告片,拜占庭的特色能力是"天授规矩":在圣城皈依拜占庭的宗教后,单位便能获得战斗力和宗教战斗力的加成。击杀敌对文明或城邦单位时,拜占庭将传播自己的宗教,同时反哺军事。"天授规矩"还能让拥有圣城的城市获得大量预言家点数加成L游民星空的微博视频收起全文d	2020-09-1917:26 转赞人数超过80	微博视频号	19	36	116
林渊在科研	https://weibo.com/7319628006?refer_flag=1001030103_	#校园#你们国庆+中秋有什么安排?我们学校能不能让大家回家,还是未知数。所以我干脆不打算回家,而是准备每天都去校外逛吃逛吃。吃完后,我就去实验室溜达溜达。如果实验室还有很多人,那就组局打牌/狼人杀/三国杀。如果没人了,那我就玩steam游戏。文明6买到手好久了,我还一次都没有玩过。完美的假期,期待~收起全文d	2020-09-1720:48 转赞人数超过20		0	17	33
甜食可可虫	https://weibo.com/2263513873?refer_flag=1001030103_	我一直在想一个小时候玩过的游戏,是类似文明6的策略游戏,主角骑着一只不知道什么的野兽(恐龙?)然后每个回合走一个或者多个格子,有攻击格数,并且也是回合制。但我总想不起来了,印象错乱以为会是最终幻想系列。但我查了一下好像并不是,那是什么游戏呢。。。。。	2020年09月17日 12:04	OnePlus7Pro	0	4	0
决定开始学散打的帅哥	https://weibo.com/3149054087?refer_flag=1001030103_	文明6是一个很杀时间的游戏,但实际上,我们这些经常玩的,都希望能做的更复杂一些,复杂2-3倍以上,甚至更多。还是那句话,我要足够有钱,就专门搞个团队给我做游戏,主要给我自己玩	2020年09月16日 11:45	iPhone客户端	0	0	0
咏baby他姐	https://weibo.com/1613455984?refer_flag=1001030103_	#十字军之王3#今个刚入门会玩一点点,这游戏果然比文明6好玩,太多有趣的故事了。下图:第三代爱尔兰国王生了7个公主,木有儿子,还只能男子优先的顺位继承,分封制,我都要疯了。大公主还加了个同性恋。小公主属性+5蜡烛+8骨头,我意难平啊~~~~	2020年09月13日 23:37	iPhone客户端	0	0	2
NRJ_L	https://weibo.com/2285885687?refer_flag=1001030103_	之前一直跟大流用的steam,也没想过用其他平台什么的,觉得这个平台游戏多用户也多,体验比较好。但就是今年epic送游戏这么个操作让我了解到其他的游戏平台。当时领这些游戏只是随手,但是真正想玩文明6这类游戏之后,开始对比这两个平台的不同,甚至我每天都要打开的已经变成了epic而不是steam。epic的优点在于界面更合我口味,各种游戏的价格应该都比steam更便宜点。但是缺点就是买商店界面没有买家的评论,只有三个打分情况。最让我感觉可惜的是没有蒸汽的成就系统。希望epic未来能不断改善吧!收起全文d	2020年09月13日 10:21	iPhone客户端	0	7	1
李瀟萌的five慢生活	https://weibo.com/1632667800?refer_flag=1001030103_	文明6可真是一个深陷的游戏,不知不觉摸了一个一天的鱼,没看书没工作,就让我这么玩下去吧	2020年09月09日 15:28	iPhone客户端	0	0	0
5号铁打油鸡蛋	https://weibo.com/7322025507?refer_flag=1001030103_	抱歉,作者已设置仅展示半年内微博,此微博已不可见。	2020年09月08日 21:05		0	0	0
灯等灯等灯O_O	https://weibo.com/2309758410?refer_flag=1001030103_	《无论魏晋》连着两晚熬夜看,大周一的整个人都不好了,我太喜欢基建文。私以外,全员工具人,全心全意搞事业。有点像小时候在电脑上玩的做皇帝的小游戏,中午回家找找,找不到玩文明6、冰汽时代、放逐之城,积灰的游戏我想死你们了,就是我的时间。。。	2020年09月07日 09:06	iPhone客户端	0	1	2
霜之新星	https://weibo.com/1321400485?refer_flag=1001030103_	文明6跟饥荒简直就是时光机,启动游戏后,等我意识到看手机,几小时过去了。	2020年09月06日 21:50	Summoner'sAndroid	0	4	0

continued on following page

Table 1. Continued

昵称	主页url	内容	时间	设备	分享数	评论鼠标	点赞数
伍君仪透析英语	https://weibo.com/1264366955?refer_flag=1001030103_	玩了10个小时之后,我终于上手《文明6》:哇,这个游戏比GTA5、《刺客信条》之类明显高一个段位。3D效果、开放世界之类也就是开始玩比较爽,还把游戏搞得接近100个G那么巨型,而对于高智商玩家来说,抽象的棋类才是要好玩。我玩不好下棋那种高智商烧脑游戏,Civilization VI就整合游戏,毕竟之前玩得最多的还是三国战略类。《文明6》得专心玩,之前只是在《刺客信条》连不上服务器验证才玩,断断续续得有点凌乱不知所云,现在玩进去才知道什么叫"再玩一个回合欲罢不能"。#玩游戏学英语#收起全文d	2020年09月05日09:04	微博weibo.com	0	0	0
国家人文历史	https://weibo.com/1610362247?refer_flag=1001030103_	#史玩家#今天要介绍的游戏叫《文明6(Sid Meier's Civilization® VI》。作为《文明》系列的新作,《文明6》继续了席德梅尔对历史的宏大叙事,玩家将有机会扮演古代文明,穿越远古时代、古典时代、中古时代、启蒙时代、工业时代、电气时代、原子时代和信息时代,体验领土扩张、贸易拓展、文化创造、武力开战、国际外交等,重新书写已经消逝了的古代文明历史。《文明6》在发售后经过数个扩展包的丰富,从模拟王朝的兴衰到天灾对历史进程的影响,其游戏的历史气息也愈加浓厚。玩家在游戏中扮演各种文明势力,从茹毛饮血	2020年09月03日17:31	微博weibo.com	5	19	32
ZWM-Billy	https://weibo.com/6454917813?refer_flag=1001030103_	#文明6#文明6游戏里的很多元素都要看你每一盘的具体情况。比如雨林对巴西非常友好,给圣地、剧院、商业都提供标准相邻加成。特别是圣地,因为可以让圣地有宗教信条再加成,起飞就看你怎么叠加~巴西的其实地球位置有成片的雨林不可以让圣地的相邻加成达到24!!!就是把圣地建在相邻两林+1信仰,也就是圣+6,这样圣地就+12宗教。然后万神殿出:神圣道路(圣地从相邻两林+1信仰),也就是圣+6,这样圣地就+12宗教。再用政策卡"+100%圣地相邻加成",那么圣地就+24宗教。有人可能觉得24宗教到中后期没啥用,买个使徒	2020年08月30日13:09	iPadair	0	1	2
第一次来网上冲浪	https://weibo.com/6171388954?refer_flag=1001030103_	这几天经典一点前上床,打开文明6玩五个回合,一放下游戏机天亮了	2020年08月29日04:46	小米9SE	0	0	1
霍比屯的养猪大户	https://weibo.com/2505276682?refer_flag=1001030103_	这几天玩了之前在steam上白嫖的古墓丽影9,然后看了部分11的直播,突然觉得这类游戏太大好玩了,再一次想快点毕业找个工作配个游戏主机。刚才看到巫师3打折,果断买了,再加上之前在epic上白嫖的gta5和文明6,想玩的游戏太多。这几个月也是一直在和别人联机玩机机玩,简直不要太开心。	2020年08月27日23:11	iPhone客户端	0	0	0
游人馆	https://weibo.com/3048369783?refer_flag=1001030103_	#新闻看点#在游戏厂商眼中,历史可以说是一个取之不尽的"宝库",许多游戏都会植入许多历史元素,比如经典3A大作《文明6》,游戏的题材就是一个文明的发展历程,可以说游戏就是一部历史!不过在小编眼中,游戏中最具...O《文明6》斩获大票粉丝的奇迹系统,这款手游中竟然也有同款?	2020年08月25日12:56	新浪看点客户端			
encyclopedia201810	https://weibo.com/6736007183?refer_flag=1001030103_	之前虽然早早就买了文明6,遗憾的是并没有时间仔细玩。在暑假的最后,我接挑战了下文明的神级难度。不得不说文明6虽然游戏机制比比往代复杂,但由于资源最优化比既方便又强力,神级难度个人感觉比往代低得多。我比较适合这种有一定策略的战棋游戏或回合制游戏,每一步都可以尽情享受思考的乐趣。对应的,射击类与动作类就很笨手,哪怕苦练也拿不出手,只能说天赋使然。收起全文d	2020年08月24日23:57	iPhone客户端	0	0	0
真·百无一用是书生	https://weibo.com/5238295886?refer_flag=1001030103_	epic有一点很不好,游戏白嫖太多就忘记去玩它。换了台新电脑登错账号都没有感觉,白嫖了几个礼拜的游戏想起来要下一下文明6吧。看着没多少的游戏库愣了半天,才意识到自己登错账号了	2020年08月21日15:04	微博weibo.com	0	0	0
DarylRules	https://weibo.com/1687768350?refer_flag=1001030103_	我跟老公噹了几天mac玩文明6卡不高兴 然后就非要送一台电脑给我专门玩游戏我不要还非要送 这个男的求生欲也太强了点	2020年08月21日09:32	iPhone11ProMax	0	0	0
Ms-Joy周毅	https://weibo.com/2607073175?refer_flag=1001030103_	最新测试,我老婆玩剑三也会出现黑屏,所以剑网三,pubg以及文明6有何共同之处?为啥一玩就黑屏,而dota2,魔兽世界等游戏就完全正常。	2020年08月19日13:40	HUAWEIMate20	4	415	4817
空空回来了追梦少说话	https://weibo.com/6386110145?refer_flag=1001030103_	文明6月底免费更新,玩家可以通过自定义选择出现在地图内的奇观,可以选择随机科技、文化路线模式。文明6真是良心游戏,太耐玩了	2020年08月19日09:13	微博weibo.com	0	1	1
单机老王子	https://weibo.com/6042105347?refer_flag=1001030103_	【文明6】#单机游戏#《文明6》安卓版现已正式推出,前60回合免费游玩,赶紧去试试吧L单机老王子的微博视频	2020年08月18日17:47	微博视频号	0	1	1
RTTswitch	https://weibo.com/1919857334?refer_flag=1001030103_	《文明6》官方Firaxis介绍了游戏即将在8月份迎来的免费更新情报,详细介绍了玩家将会在8月迎来的多个重要新功能!这只是《文明6》未来整体内容规划当中的众多免费更新之一,并且提供给任何拥有《文明6》的玩家。8月游戏更新将于8月27日推出,适用于Xbox One,PS4,Nintendo Switch,Windows PC,Mac和Linux。移动平台将在稍晚与《新纪元季票》内容一起接收更新。#switch#收起全文d	2020年08月18日11:32	微博weibo.com	0	0	0
浪玩堂	https://weibo.com/2497298463?refer_flag=1001030103_	#游戏资讯#《文明6》公布8月免费更新内容介绍。讲解了新增的自然奇观选择器、科技与市政随机模式,以及平衡性改动。此次更新将于8月27日推出,对所有玩家免费开放。L浪玩堂的微博视频	2020年08月18日11:28	微博视频号	6	3	6
3DMGAME官方微博	https://weibo.com/2163365571?refer_flag=1001030103_	#游戏资讯#《文明6》宣布8月更新将于8月27日上线,涉及了游戏平衡更改效外,本月的更新包括自然奇观选择器,玩家能够手动选择将在地图上随机生成的《文明VI》自然奇观;科技与市政随机模式,前提条件和成本被随机化。此外林火持续时间更长,其最终将变为赞赏状态,对所市政广场模式进行了调整。L3DMGAME官方微博的微博视频收起全文d	2020年08月17日23:00	微博视频号	4	5	20
小克尔V	https://weibo.com/1830187205?refer_flag=1001030103_	文明6除了片头动画很牛逼之外,游戏体验上我真难得太差了!远没有我第一次玩文明系列的兴奋感和征服世界后的爽快。	2020年08月17日22:13	iPhone客户端	0	0	0
到灯塔去喝养乐多	https://weibo.com/6621434507?refer_flag=1001030103_	#文明6#游戏直男必入这次的新纪元季票《文明6:新纪元季票》第二款DLC"埃塞俄比亚包"上线啦,此包内含1个新文明和1位新领袖、1个新区域、2个新建筑。同时直到2021年3月,新纪元季票每间隔2月便会放出1个新DLC包(共6个)。不愧是夺走我游戏无数个日夜的《文明6》,这次的新季票还有更多新奇的天象与灾害设定。喜欢玩游戏的男生真的拒绝不了吧,全新的文明6新纪元季票很适合新玩家入坑,也是我推荐一一款真情实感追的游戏,休闲时间打开文明6真的可以让心情变好,也是缓解压力的一种方式吧。L到灯塔去y的微博	2020年08月17日21:55	Android	0	0	100
游点不靠谱	https://weibo.com/3927009573?refer_flag=1001030103_	#游戏推荐#《文明6》已登陆 Android 平台,手机版为标准版游戏,玩家可在免费的状况下进行60 回合的试玩,之后再进行购买收费。同时,游戏中也有内购《风云际会》与《迭起兴衰》资料片。L游点不靠谱的微博视频	2020年08月16日23:09	微博视频号	88	138	795
能不能有个人名让我用	https://weibo.com/6004935902?refer_flag=1001030103_	文明6战报-埃塞俄比亚 299t,两次开启游戏时间跨度一个月,之前已经不知道发生什么了,总之胜利了,埃塞俄比亚还是挺好玩的。	2020年08月16日21:20	微博weibo.com	0	0	0
Sheyvila	https://weibo.com/5658772513?refer_flag=1001030103_	夏便买了文明6,14欧吧,然后怂恿一起,他表示这种游戏肯定不好玩儿。然后昨天想试试,中午吃完饭坐在那里一直打,到了凌晨两点还睡不着,香香得。现在原价60欧	2020年08月16日17:21	华为手机	0	0	0
花季叼爆少女	https://weibo.com/1826009430?refer_flag=1001030103_	文明6玩的也太肝了这游戏另一个名字应该叫"时间都去哪了"	2020年08月16日10:53		0	4	1
我是孤独的风中一匹狼-戈	https://weibo.com/5238844156?refer_flag=1001030103_	文明6真的是唯一看着眼馋,不敢下手买的游戏。怕再玩一局就天亮了,哥年纪大熬不了夜啊,而且手里电脑配置也不行,怕是还要换个本子	2020年08月16日09:34	坚果手机Pro2	0	0	0
陶塑小猪	https://weibo.com/3248651320?refer_flag=1001030103_	昨天我和我弟联机玩文明6,遭到我弟强烈吐槽。我弟:你出生地没海(隔着屏幕我也能感受到他的白眼)游戏中的我:我要学航海术制图术,造船造船!搞海运业!我弟:你是不是海贼王看多了?	2020年08月16日08:30		0	2	1

continued on following page

Table 1. Continued

昵称	主页url	内容	时间	设备	分享数	评论鼠标	点赞数
新浪游戏	https://weibo.com/1255795640?refer_flag=1001030103_	#游戏资讯#《文明6》登陆安卓平台,支持中文,玩家可以免费游玩60个回合。L新浪游戏的微博视频号	2020年08月14日22:35	微博视频号	25	29	55
节能使者	https://weibo.com/5723837992?refer_flag=1001030103_	适应特洛伊的UI后,着手的外交系统虽然变化不大,但动态的贸易,多资源流通并融合发展大大提升游戏性(这点有点像文明4),也间接强化了外交作用,游戏重点强调的还是对神祇的信仰加深时代的特性,这里也有点像文明里的宗教系统,不过全战偏历史的作品里就有宗教的功能只是表现方式有所加强变得更为突出。	2020年08月14日20:46	iPhone11ProMax	0	0	0
游戏名侦探	https://weibo.com/5589030490?refer_flag=1001030103_	【侦探游戏资讯】【文明6】现已登陆Android,玩家可免费体验前60回合内容,完整版游戏内容及"风云变幻"、"迭起兴衰"资料片等则需付费解锁#文明6#安卓版上线#游戏名侦探的微博视频	2020年08月14日19:46	游戏超话	74	60	190
来一壶雪碧	https://weibo.com/7322131563?refer_flag=1001030103_	#文明6#直男的开心游戏时间太重要了@2KGames最近才看到文明6除了新纪元季频,本游戏狂热爱好者者可以深陷其中的魅力了。《文明6》的玩法非常多样,格外耗时多样,玩家想要建立起一个帝国,必须接受时间的考验。而且又重启模式默认灾难四级,还是很有挑战的,这点很喜欢。新加的山火太阳风暴也挺有意思,尤其这个大太阳风暴,陨石落下之后第二回合,地图会有尘埃特效,像极了灾难片爆炸附近的尘埃效果。所以哥在中期就打造了海上无敌舰队,玩起来就轻松了不少。总体来说感觉还挺好的!(小声bb:买季票比单买DLC划算很多,还送领袖包)收	2020年08月14日19:31	Android	0	9	50
其实我是丝丝	https://weibo.com/6412431713?refer_flag=1001030103_	开始下文明6,不知道这游戏好玩不,据说一局可以玩好几个星期……糖豆人外挂视频是我最近的欢乐源泉(虽然挂蓄司马是常识是真理	2020年08月14日17:38	iPhone7	0	0	0
硬件学堂	https://weibo.com/2049128063?refer_flag=1001030103_	《席德·梅尔的文明6》已正式登陆安卓平台,喜欢这款游戏的玩家们今后可以在手机上畅玩了。	2020年08月14日16:06	微博weibo.com	6	16	27
IT之家	https://weibo.com/1826017320?refer_flag=1001030103_	【《文明6》正式推出安卓版:前60回合免费游玩】周五,人气回合制策略游戏《文明6》现已正式推出Android版,并登陆谷歌Play商店,玩家可免费游玩前60回合。……详情点击:O《文明6》正式推出安卓版:前60回合免费游玩	2020年08月14日15:26	IT之家	2	14	11
游侠网	https://weibo.com/1893905030?refer_flag=1001030103_	【你的电池储量还够吗?】《文明6》安卓版上线!经典回合制战略游戏《文明6》已经在安卓端正式推出,玩家能够采取先体验在付费的游玩模式,免费体验每局前60回合内容,60回合之后会触发收费机制。具体收费情况如下:《文明6》本体:19.99美元;《文明6:迭起兴衰》DLC:29.99美元;《文明6:风云变幻》DLC:39.99美元;文明情景包:4.99~8.99美元不等。L游侠网的微博视频收起全文	2020年08月14日14:25	微博视频号	5	8	18
TapTap发现好游戏	https://weibo.com/5977267211?refer_flag=1001030103_	著名的时间杀手《文明6》安卓版海外上线,还记得你最长的一局玩了多久吗?游戏采用了先体验再付费的模式,可以直接游玩每局的前60回合内容,然后进行付费。游戏全解锁售价19.99美元,DLC迭起兴衰、风云变幻分别售价29.99美元和39.99美元。LTapTap发现好游戏的微博视频	2020年08月14日13:11	微博视频号	8	13	41
游力卡酱_	https://weibo.com/6411426253?refer_flag=1001030103_	电池杀手它来了!著名"时空穿梭机"、经典回合制战略游戏《文明6》现已推出Android版,采取先体验再付费模式,玩家可免费体验每局的前60回合内容,然后触发付费机制。收费详情如下:19.99美元《文明6》完全解锁;29.99美元解锁"迭起兴衰"DLC;39.99美元"风云变幻"DLC,另可花费4.99~8.99美元购入文明情景包。L蛋蛋君荐游戏的微博视频收起全文	2020年08月14日10:19	微博视频号	9	7	30
杉果娘Sonkwo	https://weibo.com/6342379812?refer_flag=1001030103_	知名时间流逝游戏《文明6》现已登陆Android平台。与iOS版相同,玩家可免费体验每局的前60回合内容,后继续游玩需付费解锁。其中:-原版完全解锁19.99美元-"迭起兴衰"DLC 29.99美元-"风云变幻"DLC 39.99美元-文明情景包4.99~8.99美元L杉果娘Sonkwo的微博视频	2020年08月14日09:59	微博视频号	19	38	114
FayFuluolaite	https://weibo.com/2676741717?refer_flag=1001030103_	昨天抽完了所有的金箱子和补天石之后,江南百景图被我卸载了我并且,将文明6纳入PS4游戏清单(文明6有PS4版吗)?	2020年08月09日17:10	微博weibo.com	0	0	0
腾讯游戏安全中心	https://weibo.com/6160862917?refer_flag=1001030103_	【候选人已确定,快来猜猜Ta是谁6】踏入八月,离文明游戏使者评选活动开始又更近一步!今天这位候选人的参选游戏是《王者荣耀》,他曾在直播时遇到四位故意掉分队友,即时全程被队友拖累,也竭尽全力、不放弃的精神备受网友赞赏。除此之外还会多次配合官方提供游戏内"演员"的信息,打击演员行为。你能猜到他是谁吗?转+评价你的答案,抽4位宝宝送出八月第一份幸运球币!#文明游戏使者#O抽奖详情收起全文d	2020年08月03日11:13	微博weibo.com	113	200	87
沙夏sashako_	https://weibo.com/2350243205?refer_flag=1001030103_	真的会有人代餐代到文明6和欧陆风云4去吗?会。那你在文明6和陆4里能真切地做到吗?不能。那你玩游戏的时候在想什么?想方设法让我确的国拟人CP在游戏里结盟。	2020年08月01日20:34	柯尼斯堡的Android	0	0	3
七包小辣条_	https://weibo.com/6148632696?refer_flag=1001030103_	文明6你咋好tm的难玩,点开游戏两眼一抹黑	2020年08月01日15:26	专业打狗Android	0	4	0
AAAAADRIANA	https://weibo.com/1790621325?refer_flag=1001030103_	半个月过得超快,被投喂的生活即将结束,明天就可以满趾气地回成都了此处应有"全成都你都"表情包原本想象中的"文明6从九点打到九点"以及"两天一gal"的隔离生活并没有实现,因为玩游戏的时间几乎全部用来打mrfz了yj你真的知道睡人怎么善一生把自己两个号朋友两个号打过了打过了危机18至少吃了下低保看了螃屋自己的号码度低打了一整夜才过朋友的大号本来是巫妖+早露却的,但是忘记截图了,就重新用羊羹洁亮脸打了一遇截了图(塞爾娅yyds!!!)虽然去之后得居家隔离至少七天,又要开开自己做饭模式了真是有点小激动哈哔竟,又	2020年08月01日07:25	想吃火锅Android	0	2	0
卡可丸	https://weibo.com/2177069192?refer_flag=1001030103_	文明6这游戏,太浪费绳命了,申请退款了	2020年07月31日01:21	iPhone客户端	1	1	4
一只臭饺子	https://weibo.com/3789118570?refer_flag=1001030103_	也许文明6不是最优秀的游戏,但是它可能是让你感悟最多的游戏	2020年07月30日19:46	HUAWEIMate20	0	4	2
龟苓膏加芋圆淋芒果酱	https://weibo.com/2705020080?refer_flag=1001030103_	#不知道秦始皇这么牛掰#刚文明6秦胖胖结束,就偶遇这个微博热搜游戏里秦胖胖也是很厉害的,和现实一样	2020年07月30日14:49	HUAWEIMate20Pro	0	2	3
StopOne-英美澳申请	https://weibo.com/2013365572?refer_flag=1001030103_	《文明6》是由Firaxis制作、2K Games发行的一款SLG游戏,是《文明》系列游戏的第六部作品。你知道文明6,英语怎么说吗?#文明6##雅思难#雅思口语##四六级#你知道文明6,英语怎么说d	2020年07月29日16:37	微博weibo.com	7	0	151
世界上唯一仅有的瓜	https://weibo.com/6846908911?refer_flag=1001030103_	无聊死了无聊死了无聊死了我想出狱有没有什么可以打发时间的室内活动看遍全部综艺热剧//没有switch/不喜打游戏/steam账号上没有文明6和中国式家长但依然可以安然自处许多年的中年宅女女第一次感到了孤独	2020年07月27日14:17	iPhone11	0	20	14
VVanessa--	https://weibo.com/5082042058?refer_flag=1001030103_	目前来讲文明6好难对一款游戏产生持久的热情感玩了几个月现在也不想打开了并且时不时还在想着清除数据重新来过的冲动	2020年07月27日14:00	iPhone8Plus	0	14	0
Steam资讯者	https://weibo.com/6093623227?refer_flag=1001030103_	【Steam《文明6》限时免费玩】从今天到7月27日,Steam上《文明6》游戏限时免费玩三天。如果觉得玩的很爽,那么也可以考虑买下来,游戏本体最high75%off仅售49元。	2020年07月26日12:26	微博weibo.com	0	15	48
爱在西元前01129	https://weibo.com/7459894799?refer_flag=1001030103_	这游戏又让我有了熬夜的冲动l文明6##单机游戏##gpd win max#L爱在西元前01129的微博视频	2020年07月23日16:36	Android	0	0	0

continued on following page

Table 1. Continued

昵称	主页url	内容	时间	设备	分享数	评论凰标	点赞数
义北正南	https://weibo.com/7298015386?refer_flag=1001030103_	文明6这游戏有毒怎么感觉没玩多久5个小时就过去了	2020年07月21日 04:05	HUAWEIP30	0	0	1
Fintal芬特儿	https://weibo.com/5344032621?refer_flag=1001030103_	电商人真的有时间玩游戏吗?如果是模拟经营类的话,倒是相当相当多的呀。比如《文明6》,这个游戏就很适合动脑子去玩,还能放松休闲消磨自己多余的时间。又或者说石油大亨,享受当资本主义进行原始积累的快感。也可以玩玩造桥,锻炼自己的创造力。事实上,大多数人最后还是会选择打手游去。谁也逃不开落香的命运。O电商人一般都玩儿什么游戏?收起全文d	2020年07月17日 02:44	iPhone客户端	0	0	0
游民星空	https://weibo.com/1969176463?refer_flag=1001030103_	#游戏资讯#【《文明6》"埃塞俄比亚"DLC介绍 领袖孟尼利克二世】本周早些时候,2K官方宣布了《文明6:新纪元季票》的第二款DLC"埃塞俄比亚包"将在7月23日推出。今日,让我们来先睹为快埃塞俄比亚的孟尼利克二世。埃塞俄比亚专注于在丘陵上建造城市,产出信仰值并利用孟尼利克的"内阁会议"能力来提升科技值和文化值。城市可以从资源处获得更多信仰值,从资源手富城市起源的国际贸易路线还将提升此加成。埃塞俄比亚可以通过信仰值购买考古博物馆和考古学家。孟尼利克二世将根据丘陵上创建城市的信仰值产出来获得更多文	2020年07月16日 23:02	微博视频号	13	21	51
Switch新闻速递	https://weibo.com/6069554817?refer_flag=1001030103_	《文明6》新边疆季票第二部DLC衣索比亚将在7月23日推出,加入新游戏模式「秘密结社」。「衣索比亚包」加入了1个新文明及1位新领袖、1个新区域及更多建筑,并增添了一个可选取的新游戏模式「秘密结社」。LSwitch新闻速递的微博视频	2020年07月15日 10:38	微博视频号	0	0	2
樱断牙	https://weibo.com/3103244715?refer_flag=1001030103_	文明6游戏日记:新手局没关蛮族人都打傻了	2020年07月14日 23:04	RedmiNote8Pro四摄	0	0	0
玩疯了的Laey	https://weibo.com/3772860327?refer_flag=1001030103_	……好嫌弃文明6……我果然不喜欢回合制游戏……emmmmmm(头秃。)	2020年07月14日 22:31	荣耀V9我想要的快	0	2	0
pkkj	https://weibo.com/1796071111?refer_flag=1001030103_	【#独山县水司楼将更名变身酒店#景区:已外包给其他公司运作】近日,#独山县#耗资2亿修建的烂尾"水司楼"引发关注。有网友认为建筑造型奇特,可尝试打造影视真的未来水司楼将何去何从?记者了解到,目前,这栋建筑将被打造为酒店,更名为"净心谷大酒店",后期的运营开发维护等将外包给他公司 展开全文c	2020年07月14日 16:35	微博视频号	1	2	6
热心群众朴先生	https://weibo.com/5199678151?refer_flag=1001030103_	对文明6新纪元有点失望,策划脑壳是有个包吗,好好的一个历史游戏,非要出什么预言家、吸血鬼诊法、净身些花里胡哨诡弄用还破坏原版平衡的,建议直接改名魔幻6	2020年07月14日 13:37	小米10	0	0	3
游戏控	https://weibo.com/1487803202?refer_flag=1001030103_	#游戏资讯#【《文明6:新纪元季票》"埃塞俄比亚包"7月23日推出】2K游戏今日公布了《文明6:新纪元季票》的第二款DLC"埃塞俄比亚包",游戏将于7月23日登陆PS4、Xbox One、Switch和PC。L游戏控的微博视频	2020年07月14日 13:13	微博视频	4	2	4
游侠网	https://weibo.com/1893905030?refer_flag=1001030103_	【《文明6:新纪元季票》"埃塞俄比亚包"7月23日推出】2K游戏今日公布了《文明6:新纪元季票》的第二款DLC"埃塞俄比亚包",它将在7月23日推出。该内容包将提供给任何拥有《文明VI:新纪元季票》的玩家,或可单独获取。"埃塞俄比亚包"加入了1个新文明(埃塞俄比亚)及1位新领袖、1个新区域及更多建筑。另外还添加了一个可选的新游戏模式:"秘密结社"(需要《迭起兴衰》或《风云变幻》DLC内容才能游玩)。已获取《文明6:新纪元季票》的玩家将可获得特典内容"泰迪·罗斯福和凯瑟琳·德·美第奇领袖包"。每	2020年07月13日 23:48	微博weibo.com	5	7	13
任地域	https://weibo.com/6578279612?refer_flag=1001030103_	已发布了头条文章:《【NS每日新闻】文明6下周介绍新势力 国外零售商曝4款待公布游戏》一张图,一句话,带你简阅Switch每日新闻~#任天堂switch#O【NS每日新闻】文明6下周一介绍新势力 国外零售商曝4款待公布游戏	2020年07月11日 23:25	SWITCH超话	1	0	2
-让狂热成为生命的指引-	https://weibo.com/3995459361?refer_flag=1001030103_	玩了一下午的《文明6》,脖子疼脑袋晕这游戏也太折磨人了吧	2020年07月11日 16:12	Share微博客户端	0	0	0
今日不宜说话	https://weibo.com/5678856182?refer_flag=1001030103_	今日总结刚刚逛知乎才发现,居然还有粉丝爆破文明6贴吧????这是干啥哪人家一游戏和你家要香有什么关系????搞不懂搞不懂正主管智你家粉丝你有些粉丝真的太神奇了感觉最近出去玩的次数为零了钱包日渐消瘦次数待明天也出去玩的文明6呀,我已经想好了如果满明天有人要发说说明友圈的话,文案是以下几个七年(配上各种小表情啥哈哈)好久没有小跑去迎接一个人那种快乐了如果你说你在下午四点来,我就开始感觉很快乐,时间越临近,我就越来越感到快乐。到了四点钟的时候,我会坐立不安,我发现了幸福的价值。我是真的不能再	2020年07月11日 00:05	微博国际版	0	0	0
茶腐玉剥葡萄	https://weibo.com/2208269571?refer_flag=1001030103_	抱歉,此微博已被作者删除。查看帮助:O网页链接	2020年07月04日 16:42		2	4	0
lulu_xm_ny	https://weibo.com/6363105737?refer_flag=1001030103_	坩文明6最近ns文明6打折想入,想请问一下各位大佬玩这个游戏需要熟知历史政治军事知识吗以及大家游戏时长多久呀	2020年07月10日 08:34	文明6超话	0	10	20
雷狮	https://weibo.com/1622781887?refer_flag=1001030103_	现在是肖朝元年,肖国臣民爆破文明6吧,欲想制作只有肖苏玛丽神文明历史的游戏。	2020年07月08日 16:59	微博weibo.com	4	6	7
龙涛	https://weibo.com/1337387664?refer_flag=1001030103_	我这智商,竟然入坑了《文明6》这游戏真的好难,特别难,小时候特别讨厌策略游戏,现在是挑战智商了?这游戏的菜单界面太小了,一个个小字,在高分辨率的屏幕下,我只能开1080P,还要贴着屏幕看,这要是玩起来,更难受了。不过,这游戏显然上手难,赢起来更需要花时间,但慢慢入坑后,根本停不下来。看着从荒郊野外的一块地,慢慢建立了一堆城市,特别有成就感。收起全文d	2020年07月08日 11:01	VVebo	0	0	0
oPcOtPoPuYs	https://weibo.com/6454247952?refer_flag=1001030103_	以前肖战虾圈侵犯AO3 侵害同人圈创作圈我就看看热闹,现在火烧到我身上了我平时只玩文明6一个游戏,因为游戏人少,所以平时只能在贴吧里与其他玩家交流,这是我唯一的一块交流地。但不知道为什么,肖战粉丝开始爆破文明6吧加入了1个新文明这么一小块精神乐园还被推毁了!我的手指现在是发抖的,我无法克制的愤怒!我现在在能够的群众体合AO3及其他小众领域的受害者了团结的力量是强大的,我以前还是躺平,这个地方就败了!现在,我要捍卫我的土地!肖战必胜!#227大团结##肖战事件受害者##427大爆炸#收起全文d	2020年07月07日 16:18	iPhone客户端	0	0	0
能不逗吗小伙子	https://weibo.com/2206451634?refer_flag=1001030103_	xzf为什么要爆文明6贴吧?这好好的玩个游戏招谁惹谁了?	2020年07月07日 14:08	HUAWEIP40Pro5G	0	2	0
kikicamarena	https://weibo.com/7274385097?refer_flag=1001030103_	大半夜刷知乎得知文明6吧被xz粉爆吧遂打开贴吧验证没想到啊没想到毫无关系的两个东西会被联系起来就想说一句去玩一局文明6吧或许许多人都上好累想	2020年07月07日 01.37	小米8SE	0	1	0
触乐网	https://weibo.com/3957040489?refer_flag=1001030103_	#触乐菜熊#每个人在一生中都会发生变化,如今的你也许与5年、10年或15年前完不同。社会和大众文化也处于不断演变之中,不过这种改变并没有被游戏产品完全反映出来,比如《文明6》这样的游戏里,你所选择国家的文化在整个游玩过程中基本上维持原样。这个盲点在一些开发者看来正是一个突破口,世嘉旗下工作室Amplitude Studios正在制作的策略游戏《人类》就试图为玩家们带来一些新东西。O策略游戏为什么不能反映文化的演变和融合?现在,挑战者来了收起全文d	2020年07月06日 19:25	微博weibo.com	54	10	38

instead of modern guns to defeat enemies in the gameplay. It might be one of the reasons that *Naraka: Bladepoint* has more active players than other games.

Word Cloud

The top 150 frequent words of the five data sets are plotted in a Word Cloud graph. Figures 3 and 4 present the word cloud of *Civilization VI* and *Total War: Three Kingdoms*, showing the most frequent words of the two games are "游戏" (Game), "文明" (Civilization), and "玩" (play), and "三国" (Three Kingdoms), "战争" (war), "官渡" (Guandu), and "曹操" (Cao Cao), respectively.

Figures 5 and 6 show the word cloud of Justice and Tale of Immortal, with the most frequent words "逆水寒" (Justice), "流派" (school), "江湖" (Jiang Hu), and "鬼谷八荒" (Tale of Immortal), "修仙" (cultivate immortality), "道侣" (couple), respectively. Figure 7 presents the word cloud of *Naraka: Bladepoint*, with most frequent words in "永劫无间" (Naraka: Bladepoint), "吃鸡" (become the winner), and "队友" (teammates).

Cluster Analysis

Figure 8 presents the major part of the clustering analysis graph of *Naraka: Bladepoint*, showing that the players of *Naraka: Bladepoint* focus more on the game mode like keywords "单排" (single player mode), "决赛圈" (Finals), and game characters controlled by players like "和尚" (Tianhai), "宁红夜" (Viper Ning), and "迦南" (Matari). In *Naraka: Bladepoint*, different characters in the game have different costumes and use different Chinese cold weapons. Combined with the word cloud in Figure 7, players of *Naraka: Bladepoint* show great interest in the last man standing deathmatch game mode and Chinese cultural elements, including costumes, weapons, and ancient buildings from the game characters and game scenes.

Figure 9 presents the major part of the cluster analysis of *Total War: Three Kingdoms*. It shows that popular game characters including "曹操" (Cao Cao), "袁绍" (Yuan Shao), "董卓" (Dong Zhuo), "吕布" (Lü Bu), and "刘备" (Liu Bei), together with "汉室" (Han Dynasty) have a close historical connection are closely connected. Thus, players show interest in experiencing the Three Kingdoms culture by controlling the game characters to change the scenes.

Civilization VI uses the same turn-based strategy game like *Total War: Three Kingdoms*. Figure 10 presents the cluster analysis of *Civilization VI*. The main cluster is "宗教" (Religion), "信仰" (Faith), "战争" (Wars), and "文化" (Culture). It shows that the expression of a country's culture in *Civilization*

Table 2. Keywords used for analysis

Keyword	Translation
文明	Civilization
三国	Three Kingdoms
逆水寒	Justice
鬼谷八荒	The Tale of Immortal
永劫无间	NARAKA: BLADE POINT
游戏	Games

Figure 1. Trend of comments

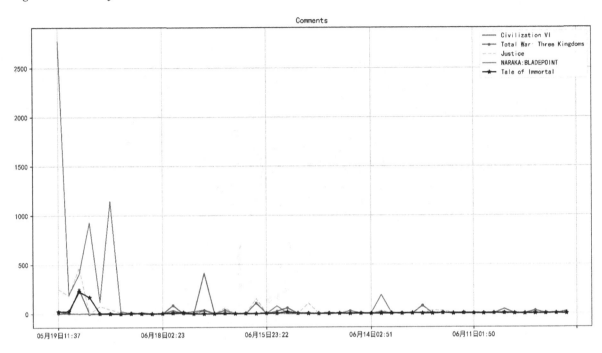

Figure 2. Trend of likes

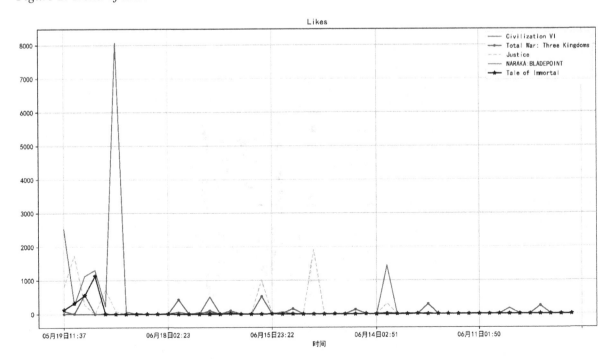

Figure 3. Civilization VI

Figure 4. Total War: Three Kingdoms

Figure 5. Justice

Figure 6. Tale of Immortal

Figure 7. Naraka: Bladepoint

Figure 8. Cluster analysis of Naraka: Bladepoint

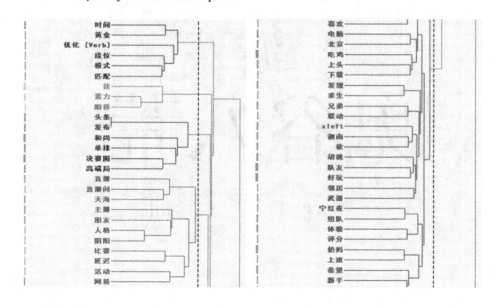

Figure 9. Cluster analysis of Total War: Three Kingdoms

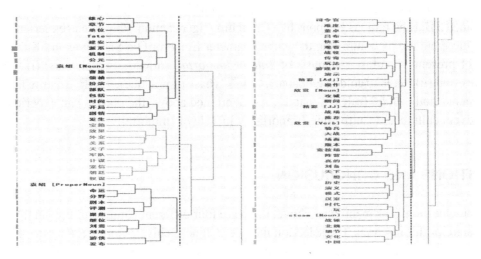

Figure 10. Cluster analysis of Civilization VI

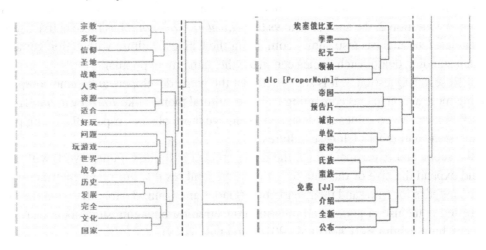

Figure 11. Cluster analysis of Tale of Immortal

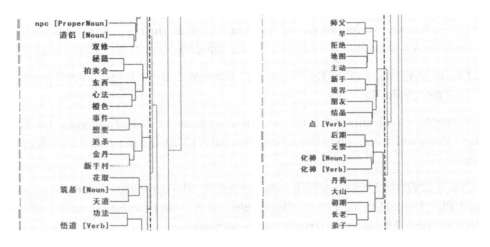

VI not only focuses on one specific culture like *Total War: Three Kingdoms*, but also covers diversified parts of Chinese culture, including famous ancient buildings like the Great Wall, famous persons like Confucius and Li Bai and famous weapons like Crouching tiger cannon. Players can experience different parts of Chinese culture by controlling the game character Emperor Qin Shihuang and Kublai.

Figure 11 presents the cluster analysis of *Tale of Immortal*, showing two clusters: (i) "双修", "道侣" (couple), and (ii) "金丹" (golden cinnabar), "筑基" (base of practice), "天道" (nature law), "悟道" (enlightenment), and "功法" (rules of magic). As mentioned above, the players can experience Mountains and Rivers culture and Cultivating Immortality in Tale of Immortal.

SUGGESTIONS AND CONCLUSION

For Research Question 1, as mentioned above, there are four different Chines cultures in the five video games selected for this research. The selection includes Chinese chivalry culture, Classic of Mountains and Rivers culture, Three Kingdoms culture, and Chinese traditional culture from ancient buildings to ancient poems. They are popular Chinese cultural elements and well-received in these games. The word clouds have shown significant cultural elements in these games being discussed in Weibo forums.

For Research Question 2, the analysis shows that *Naraka: Bladepoint* has more active users than the other four games. Our analysis also shows combining the Chinese culture with action games or large-scale last man standing deathmatch games can make the game more popular.

Thus, for Research Question 3, it is suggested that the game developers and game companies focus on developing more action games containing Chinese cultural themes like *Journey to the West* or *Water Margin* (水滸傳), etc. More games are designed to engage more players, especially young players, and let them understand and inherit Chinese cultures.

Due to the scope and experiment time, the data obtained is limited. Future work will improve the coverage and expand the size of the data to get more general results. For other entertainment, we are interested in analytics for films and their marketing (Gao, Lam, Chiu, & Ho, 2020). On the other hand, we are interested in the use of games and museum education for engaging students in learning martial arts and other Chinese cultures (Chen et al., 2018; Lo et al., 2019).

REFERENCES

Adams, R. (2021). Naraka: Bladepoint player count hits 136K in final beta test. *Techraptor*. Retrieved from https://techraptor.net/gaming/news/naraka-bladepoint-player-count-hits-136k-in-final-beta-test

Assassin's Creed Valhalla. (n.d.). In *Wikipedia*. Retrieved from https://en.wikipedia.org/wiki/Assassin%27s_Creed_Valhalla

Avendano, Y. (2016). Civilization VI is the best strategy game of 2016 (The game awards said so). *Twinfinite.net*. Retrieved from: https://twinfinite.net/2016/12/civilization-vi-best-strategy-game-the-game-awards/

Burnes, A. (2021). NVIDIA DLSS available now in Nioh 2 - The complete edition and Mount & Blade II: Bannerlord. Plus, Unreal Engine 4 DLSS Plugin released. *Nvidia*. Retrieved from https://www.nvidia.com/en-us/geforce/news/february-2021-rtx-dlss-game-update/

Chen, Y., Chiu, D. K. W., & Ho, K. K. W. (2018). Facilitating the learning of the art of Chinese painting and calligraphy at Chao Shao-an Gallery. *Micronesian Educators*, *26*, 45–58.

Clement, J. (2021). *Leading gaming markets worldwide in 2020, by gaming revenue*. Statista. Retrieved from https://www.statista.com/statistics/308454/gaming-revenue-countries/

Dynasty Warriors. (n.d.). In *Wikipedia*. Retrieved from https://en.wikipedia.org/wiki/Dynasty_Warriors

Gao, W., Lam, K. M., Chiu, D. K. W., & Ho, K. K. W. (2020). A Big data Analysis of the Factors Influencing Movie Box Office in China. In Z. Sun (Ed.), Handbook of Research on Intelligent Analytics with Multi-Industry Applications (pp. 232–249). Academic Press.

Harvey, A., & DeFreitas, C. (2019). How long does it take to beat RDR2. *Imagine Games Network*. Retrieved from https://www.ign.com/wikis/red-dead-redemption-2/How_Long_Does_It_Take_to_Beat_RDR2

Li, J. (1999). *American West Cowboy and Cowboy Culture* [美国西部牛仔和牛仔文化] (Unpublished doctoral dissertation). Capital Normal University, Beijing, China.

Lin, L. T. (2021a). *Total number of game users in China from 2008 to 2020*. Statista. Retrieved from https://www.statista.com/statistics/870620/china-number-of-game-users/

Lin, L. T. (2021c). *Annual revenue of eSports games market in China 2016-2020*. Statista. Retrieved from https://www.statista.com/statistics/1087541/china-esports-game-market-revenue/

Lin, L. T. (2021b). *Console and PC game sales revenue in China 2008-2019*. Statista. Retrieved from https://www.statista.com/statistics/445407/console-and-pc-game-revenue-in-china/

Liu, Q.X., & Qie, D.J. (2016). A comparative analysis of Chinese and Japanese cultures based on martial arts and ninjas [基于武侠与忍者的中日文化比较分析]. *Journal of the Ninbo Radio & TV University*, *14*(51), 35-40.

Lo, P., Chan, H. H. Y., Tang, A. W. M., Chiu, D. K. W., Cho, A., Ho, K. K. W., See-To, E., He, J., Kenderdine, S., & Shaw, J. (2019). Visualising and Revitalising Traditional Chinese Martial Arts – Visitors' Engagement and Learning Experience at the 300 Years of Hakka KungFu. *Library Hi Tech*, *37*(2), 273–292. doi:10.1108/LHT-05-2018-0071

Lo, P., Cheuk, M. K., Ng, C. H., Lam, S. K., & Chiu, D. K. W. (2021). *The way of Arts and Kungfu* [文武之道:以拳入哲] (Vol. 2). Systech Publications.

Ma, X. H. (2011). The long Viking ship carrying death [载着死神而来的维京长船]. *Ocean World*, *2011*(12), 24–27.

Nintendo. (n.d.). In *Wikipedia*. Retrieved from https://en.wikipedia.org/wiki/Nintendo

Nioh 2. (n.d.). In *Wikipedia*. Retrieved from https://en.wikipedia.org/wiki/Nioh_2

PowerPyx. (2020). Nioh 2 Length (Playtime). *PowerPyx*. Retrieved from https://www.powerpyx.com/nioh-2-length-playtime/

Red Dead Redemption 2. (n.d.). In *Wikipedia*. Retrieved from https://en.wikipedia.org/wiki/Red_Dead_Redemption_2

Shen, B. J. (1994). A probe into the concept of "Three Kingdoms Culture" ["三国文化" 概念初探]. *Journal of Chinese Culture, 1994*(3), 98–101.

Song, J. L., & Guo, L. (2012). Talking about the development of China's electronic game industry [浅谈中国电子游戏产业发展]. *Business (Atlanta, Ga.), 2012*(07), 161.

The Fantasy Westward Journey. (n.d.). In *Baidu Baike*. Retrieved from https://baike.baidu.com/item/%E6%A2%A6%E5%B9%BB%E8%A5%BF%E6%B8%B8/157573?fr=aladdin

The Legend of Sword and Fairy. (n.d.). In *Wikipedia*. Retrieved from https://en.wikipedia.org/wiki/The_Legend_of_Sword_and_Fairy

Wei, Y. (2010). Chivalry culture and Chinese wushu. *Wushu Science, 7*(11), 17–19.

Xie, R., Chu, S. K. W., Chiu, D. K. W., & Wang, Y. (2021). Exploring public response to COVID-19 on Weibo with LDA topic modeling and sentiment analysis. *Data and Information Management, 5*(1), 86–99. doi:10.2478/dim-2020-0023

Zhang, G., & Zhao, J. L. (2017). A review of the research on Chinese martial arts culture [中国武侠文化研究述评]. *Journal of Jilin Sport University, 33*(1), 7–11.

ADDITIONAL READING

Dong, L. Y., Ji, S. J., Zhang, C. J., Zhang, Q., Chiu, D. W., Qiu, L. Q., & Li, D. (2018). An unsupervised topic-sentiment joint probabilistic model for detecting deceptive reviews. *Expert Systems with Applications, 114*, 210–223. doi:10.1016/j.eswa.2018.07.005

Fantinato, M., Peres, M. S., Kafeza, E., Chiu, D. K. W., & Hung, P. (2020). A Survey of the Integration of Deep Learning and Service Orientation. *Journal of Database Management, 32*(3), 95–119. doi:10.4018/JDM.2021070105

Hew, K. F., Huang, B., Chu, K. W. S., & Chiu, D. K. W. (2016). Engaging Asian students through game mechanics: Findings from two experiment studies. *Computers & Education, 92*, 221–236. doi:10.1016/j.compedu.2015.10.010

Ji, S., Yang, W., Guo, S., Chiu, D. K. W., Zhang, C., & Yuan, X. (2020). Asymmetric response aggregation heuristics for rating prediction and recommendation. *Applied Intelligence, 50*(5), 1416–1436. doi:10.100710489-019-01594-2

Ji, S., Zhang, Q., Li, J., Chiu, D. K. W., Xu, S., Yi, L., & Gong, M. (2020). A burst-based unsupervised method for detecting review spammer groups. *Information Sciences, 536*, 454–469. doi:10.1016/j.ins.2020.05.084

Ji, S. J., Leung, H. F., Sim, K. M., Liang, Y. Q., & Chiu, D. K. W. (2015). An Adaptive Prediction-regret Driven Strategy for One-shot Bilateral Bargaining Software Agents. *Expert Systems with Applications, 42*(1), 411–425. doi:10.1016/j.eswa.2014.07.022

Ji, S. J., Ma, H. Y., Zhang, S. L., Leung, H. F., Chiu, D., Zhang, C. J., & Fang, X. W. (2016). A pre-evolutionary advisor list generation strategy for robust defencing reputation attacks. *Knowledge-Based Systems*, *103*, 1–18. doi:10.1016/j.knosys.2016.03.015

Jiang, N., Zhuang, Y., & Chiu, D. K. W. (2017). Multiple transmission optimization of medical images in recourse-constraint mobile telemedicine systems. *Computer Methods and Programs in Biomedicine*, *145*, 103–113. doi:10.1016/j.cmpb.2017.04.002 PMID:28552115

Wang, X., Ji, S., Liang, Y., Leung, H., & Chiu, D. K. W. (2019). An unsupervised strategy for defending against multifarious reputation attacks. *Applied Intelligence*, *49*(12), 4189–4210. doi:10.100710489-019-01490-9

Zhuang, Y., Jiang, N., Wu, Z., Li, Q., Chiu, D. K., & Hu, H. (2014). Efficient and robust large medical image retrieval in mobile cloud computing environment. *Information Sciences*, *263*, 60–86. doi:10.1016/j.ins.2013.10.013

KEY TERMS AND DEFINITIONS

Chinese Word Segmentation: The task of splitting Chinese text (a sequence of Chinese characters) into words.

Cluster Analysis: Used to classify objects or cases into groups called clusters, where no prior knowledge on cluster membership is required. Clustering procedures may be hierarchical or non-hierarchical, whereas the non-hierarchical methods in cluster analysis are often known as K-means clustering (employed in this research). Such procedures typically include problem formulation, distance measure selection, clustering procedure determination, choosing the number of clusters, cluster interpretation, and result validity assessment.

Stop Words: Are those filtered out before or after processing of natural language data or text as they are not carrying significant meaning, usually customized for different applications.

Word Cloud (Also Known as Wordle, Word Collage, or Tag Cloud): Visual representations of words that give greater prominence to words that appear more frequently.

Chapter 16
Big Data Analytics and the Discovery of the Hidden Data Treasure From Savings Banks in Germany

Carsten Giebe

iD https://orcid.org/0000-0003-2335-4808

MATE Hungarian University of Agriculture and Life Sciences, Hungary

ABSTRACT

The banking sector in Germany is undergoing a massive change. The reasons are digitalization, changing customer behaviour, and low interest rates. The focus of this research is on the savings banks in Germany. Savings banks could miss the boat in the age of digital transformation. On the one hand, savings banks are demonstrably forced to take drastic measures, such as mergers, branch closures, and staff reductions. On the other hand, savings banks possess more data about their customers than other industries. Savings banks can order a big data analytics solution called "Sparkassen-DataAnalytics" (aka savings banks data analytics). Sparkassen-DataAnalytics could be used to offer customers tailormade banking products from the information obtained. It is an open secret that costs can be reduced through a higher degree of automation. The main purpose of this research is to discuss to what extent big data analytics could be a lifeline for German savings banks. Research methods are a literature review and subsequent discussion on the use of big data analytics in the German banking market.

INTRODUCTION

First, a look at the German banking system will be provided. The banking system in Germany is characterized by three pillars. Pillar I contains the private sector banks, Pillar II contains the savings banks and Pillar III contains the cooperative banks (see Figure 1). This structure makes the German banking system unique (Behr & Schmidt, 2015; Komorowski, 2020). The focus of this research paper is on the German savings banks (Pillar II).

DOI: 10.4018/978-1-7998-9016-4.ch016

Figure 1. "The German Banking System" based on Giebe & Schulz (2021)

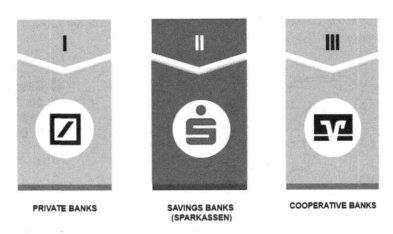

The savings banks in Germany are independent commercial enterprises under municipal ownership. Their task is to strengthen competition on the basis of market and competitive requirements, especially in their business area. Their task has many regional aspects. For example, it must ensure an appropriate and sufficient supply of monetary and credit services to all sections of the population, to the business community, especially small and medium-sized enterprises, and to the public sector, also on a regional basis. Savings banks are also responsible for supporting the performance of tasks by municipalities in the economic, regional political, social and cultural spheres. Accordingly, the savings banks promote savings and asset formation among broad sections of the population and the economic education of young people (Savings Banks Act of Baden-Württemberg, §6 (1), 2020).

The individual savings banks are so-called institutions under public law. As a rule, they belong to cities or municipalities and serve the common good. Savings banks thus have a public mission. As of July 2020, there were 377 individual savings banks, which in turn are incorporated into twelve individual regional savings bank associations. In this respect, each individual region of the Federal Republic of Germany is assigned to a specific savings bank and marked on the map shown (see Figure 2). Here, the savings bank associations are marked with a dark red outlined line, for example SVB for Sparkassenverband Bayern (aka Savings Banks Association Bavaria) in the south or OSV for Ostdeutscher Sparkassenverband (aka East German Savings Banks Association) in the east of the Federal Republic of Germany. The savings bank associations, in turn, contain the individual savings banks, which are often identical to the district. They are represented in the area with pastel colors.

For some years now, the banking sector has been undergoing the greatest structural upheaval the industry has ever seen. This structural change is being driven massively by technological progress. As a result, banks are being forced to reposition themselves strategically. Until now, banks have been able to achieve high market penetration with standard products.

However, innovative product ideas are now necessary because banks are appearing on the market with almost identical products. As a result, banks and savings banks are being forced to provide highly efficient banking services. Large personnel and material expenses are putting increasing cost pressure on the institutions (Moormann, 2000).

Digital transformation is now a reality. Many banks and savings banks in Germany could miss the boat in the age of digital transformation. On the one hand, external influences such as customer behavior,

Figure 2. "Business areas of the savings banks and savings banks associations (aka Sparkassenverbände) in Germany".
Source: Dörrbecker, M. (2020) https://upload.wikimedia.org/wikipedia/commons/6/6e/Karte_Gesch%C3%A4ftsgebiete_der_Sparkassen_und_Sparkassenverb%C3%A4nde_in_Deutschland.png

customer expectations, technological change, willingness to pay, and product life cycles are gaining in importance. On the other hand, internal expectations of employees, e.g., acceptance of new technological solutions and processes, are rather sluggish. According to a study by consulting firm McKinsey, traditional banks could lose 29-35% of their revenue due to competition from FinTech companies (Drummer et al., 2016; Giebe, 2019; Komorowski, 2020).

According to Deeken & Specht (2017), one can often get the impression in the savings banks camp that approaching crises are not realized. Although the obvious dominates the present, people take refuge in an imaginary ivory tower. Attitudes such as "This may affect everyone else - but not us" are the order of the day (Deeken & Specht, 2017).

The future world of work will therefore generally be characterized by digitalization and automation. When talking about automation in relation to technical innovations, the term Big Data Analytics is often mentioned. Big Data Analytics could therefore be considered one of many possible technical innovations. As the largest credit institution group in Germany, the Sparkassen-Finanzgruppe has the enormous data treasure of around 50 million customers. This includes master data, transaction data, securities account movements, and online usage data (Lange, 2020).

BACKGROUND

The applied methodology is an explorative literature research with the aim of a conceptual, practice-oriented approach. In search engines known for the research, such as Google Scholar, Elsevier or also newspapers, company websites and other websites were searched for the keywords: Big Data Analytics, Sparkassen in Deutschland as well as the combination of Big Data Analytics and Sparkassen in Deutschland. The search languages were German and English. The aim of this research is to provide readers with a comprehensive picture of real banking practice in Germany.

In order to further substantiate the situation of savings banks with real key figures, data sets were researched on www.statista.com. Specifically, the number of individual savings bank institutions, the number of branches of savings banks, the number of employees of savings banks, the operating profit of savings banks, the return on equity of savings banks and the cost-income ratio of savings banks were determined and used for descriptive analysis. The visualizations were performed using R software. This information will be used to visualize any trends that compel savings banks to take action.

There are extensive scientific articles on the subject of Big Data and Big Data Analytics. There are also publications on Big Data Analytics in the financial services industry. However, there are gaps in the studies available for publications in the context of Big Data Analytics in direct connection with German savings banks.

The article by Damaschke & Giebe (2020) can be cited as previously published basic literature with direct reference to a combination of savings banks in Germany and Big Data Analytics. This is specifically about the savings banks' own Big Data Analytics solution called Sparkassen-DataAnalytics. Furthermore, the paper " Economic effects of the digital transformation on the banking market using the example of savings banks and cooperative banks in Germany " by Giebe & Schulz should be cited. In addition to a well-founded business assessment of the impact of digital transformation, this paper also reveals a research gap. It states that, among other things, the term Big Data Analytics can be considered a recommendable option for savings banks in Germany for forecasting customers' probabilities of closing deals in the age of digitalization (Giebe & Schulz, 2021).

In the current era, decision makers have begun to incorporate enormous amounts of data into their decision-making processes. These data sets are huge data sets that have high volume, variety and velocity. The foundation for these analytics is based on probability. Various techniques now exist, such as statistical models, machine learning, data mining and data modeling. These can be implemented by companies to apply the patterns and their relationships in data for forecasting and as a weapon for business competition (Vassakis, 2018).

With the turn of the millennium, the volume of data started to skyrocket, the technology available at that time was not able to analyze the amount of data. Big Data can be defined not only by the amount of data, but also by high velocity, variety, comprehensive scope, and relational nature. Big Data has been primarily characterized by the 5 Vs: Volume, Variety, Velocity, Veracity and Value. In recent years, there has been a real hype around this topic. It was considered a key argument for organizations to gain competitive advantage (Akter et al., 2016; Kitchin, 2014; Wamba et al., 2015).

In most industries and business areas, business intelligence and predictive analytics are shaping diverse business models. Both topics are now very relevant and can be described as one of the most important technology trends of the 2010s (Chen et al., 2012). Also, for Sun et al. business research and development is characterized by Big Data analytics and business intelligence improvement. Big Data Science and Big Data Computing are considered the basis for developing a service-oriented architecture for Big Data Analytics. With Big Data Analytics, temporal, expected, and relative characteristics of artificial intelligence can lead to improvements in business organization (Sun et al., 2018).

Typical use cases of Big Data Analytics include its application in business intelligence solutions or as input for self-learning systems such as artificial intelligence. Prediction of customer behavior, process optimization, and predictive maintenance are other notable use cases of Big Data Analytics (Najafabadi et al., 2015).

In light of the facts that have been elaborated, the research question is:

To what extent could Big Data Analytics specifically be a lifeline for German savings banks and thus a concrete alternative in the age of digitalization?

In order to be able to answer the research question, this thesis will specifically research practice-oriented insights from the world of savings banks in Germany. In order to obtain these insights, the articles by Damaschke (2020), Lange (2020) and Lünemann & Müller-Hammerstein (2021) should be mentioned, as they can provide practical and also current details.

MAIN FOCUS OF THE ARTICLE

More and more companies are turning to Big Data Analytics to better understand their customers and differentiate themselves from the competition. To achieve a sustainable competitive advantage from Big Data, companies need to combine rich data across the enterprise. This allows them to use analytics that customers perceive in a dynamic environment to respond to them (Kitchens et al., 2018).

Big Data Analytics thus refers to methods and processes that can be used to discover possible structures, patterns, and correlations in large volumes of data (big data). With the help of these, model-based forecasts can be made for future developments relevant to decision-making, such as a product proposal (Brühl, 2019). Technologies replace long-term established processes as well as human experience with intelligent software solutions of modern data analytics and smart algorithms. Therefore, Big Data Analytics is named as one of the forces driving digitalization (Komorowski, 2020).

In 2017, the Sparkassen-Finanzgruppe launched "Sparkassen-DataAnalytics" (aka savings banks data analytics) as a holistic project of the Deutscher Sparkassen- und Giroverband (aka German Savings Banks and Giro Association), the umbrella organization of savings banks in Germany. The biggest challenge was that there was no IT environment for data analytics and data flows and data processes were not mature (Damaschke, 2020). Sparkassen-DataAnalytics is considered an offering for each individual savings bank.

What questions and challenges do sales and campaign managers in a German savings bank have to answer when preparing sales campaigns? The questions to be answered are: Which customers belong to a target group? Which channels should be used to address the customers? How do I choose the selection criteria to obtain a certain sample size? So-called expert selections have become established over the years, based on expert banking knowledge. Since no distinction is made on the basis of affinity, all selected customers would have to be approached. And this approach was justified for many years. With the Sparkassen-DataAnalytics approach, selections are made on the basis of statistical procedures. This allows customers to be brought into focus who would sometimes not appear in expert selections. Savings bank customers can be sorted according to the highest affinity in percentage terms on the basis of the predicted probabilities of conclusion (Damaschke & Giebe, 2020).

The way Sparkassen-DataAnalytics works is shown in the following diagram (see Figure 3). The savings bank customer shown on the left has contacts, or touchpoints, with his savings bank via various channels. The savings bank is shown in the middle of the diagram. These tools ensure a sustainable multi-channel approach. In an optimal case, the savings bank customer already benefits from a fully comprehensive so-called 360° communication. The customer data available through the business relationship is recorded and stored by the savings bank as part of his customer journey. For example, when an account is opened, a contract is concluded, or a service request is made, contract data is historized. Due to increasing digitalization, the production of this data is taking place with great dynamization. This means that the amount of data is becoming larger and is being generated at an increasing rate. Sparkassen-DataAnalytics, shown on the right-hand side of the image, extracts the relevant information from the data in a targeted manner (Damaschke & Giebe, 2020).

The goal of generating sales-relevant events from this data, for example, can be expanded even further through the prospective enrichment of external data. At the end of 2019, approximately 50 forecast models were available in the productive application for the savings banks. Various sales events are made available to the savings banks via the core banking system OSPlus. With a "Next Best Action" feature, advisors can identify which product the customer sitting in front of them has a particular affinity for. This provides the opportunity to interact with the customer via many different channels, for example, in person, by telephone or by e-mail. Due to the adaptability of the models used, there is a dynamization of the evaluation speed. In the process, findings, for example a successful campaign or a successfully predicted product sale, are fed back into the cycle. This is referred to as a closed loop (Damaschke & Giebe, 2020).

A basic principle applies to the development of Sparkassen-DataAnalytics. First, a business question is translated into a machine learning context, for example, the search for the most affinitive customers for a particular banking product. Similar to expert selection, the algorithm tests different selection rules (Damaschke & Giebe, 2020).

Figure 3. Own representation of the Sparkassen-DataAnalytics based on Damaschke & Giebe (2020)

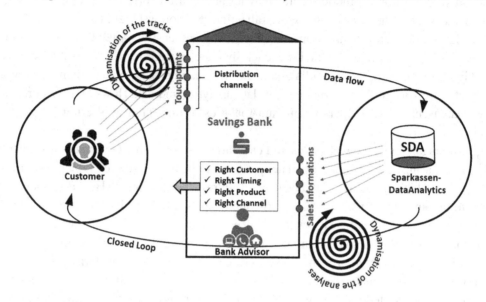

Historical characteristics that have an influence on the product affinity of customers are used. Characteristics are e.g. age, balances, existing products. As a result, the models use a feature vector with all the information needed to forecast a product sale (Lünemann & Müller-Hammerstein, 2021).

Machine learning describes the artificial generation of knowledge from experience. Here, a system learns from events in data. After completion of a learning phase, patterns and regularities can be recognized (Hammerström, 2018). Machine learning is divided into two phases, the training phase and the test phase. In the first phase, the model is trained on a given algorithm using training data. Using very large amounts of data, this model has learned to identify details that are necessary to bring about a grouping of the data. An example of grouping can be customers who are potential buyers or non-buyers for a particular banking product (Damaschke & Giebe, 2020).

The relevant target for training the models is therefore purchase codes. All customers who purchase the target product during the training period are coded. The model is trained with this processed data set. Non-linear relationships between the characteristics and the target variable are derived. Only those characteristics of a person that make a positive contribution to the forecast quality are taken into account (Lünemann & Müller-Hammerstein, 2021).

In fractions of a second, the model creates a profile that can then be compared with other customer profiles. In the second phase, test data is used to check whether the model can also correctly sort unknown customers with a sufficiently good prediction quality. The discrepancy between the expected and the estimated result determines model adjustments; this is referred to as model learning (Damaschke & Giebe, 2020).

Sparkassen-DataAnalytics currently uses so-called decision trees that split the data set in a binary manner. Based on these question chains, each customer is assigned to a segment that has a certain probability of closing a banking product. Since the individual decision trees would become very large due to the complexity and a single tree would weight any special features too heavily, so-called boosting is used. The idea here is to transform a large number of simple models into a strong tree ensemble model.

Figure 4. Comparison of interest rates in the Euro Area and the United States
(Source: ECB / FED) http://www.leitzinsen.info/charts/ezbfed.jpg

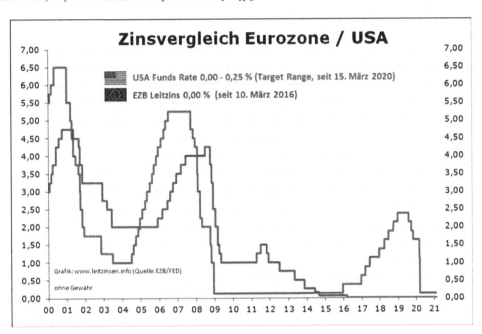

During generation, each new tree is optimized to correct the weaknesses of the previous forest. In sum, all trees thus provide very good results (Lünemann & Müller-Hammerstein, 2021).

In contrast to expert selection, however, the machine learning model acts objectively and captures more complex interrelationships that are sometimes surprising and unexpected in their outcome for experts in a savings bank (Damaschke & Giebe, 2020).

RESULTS AND DISCUSSION

For many years, a trend of declining nominal and real interest rates has been observed in the main industrialized countries in Europe. The result is a historically unprecedented environment of lowest and negative interest rates In the euro area and in Germany (see Figure 4). The current low interest rate environment is thus putting considerable pressure on banks and savings banks in Germany to act (Deeken & Specht, 2017; Wolgast, 2016). Virtually nothing is earned on customer loans and customers can no longer be offered credit interest on savings deposits.

The interest rate level of recent years has had fatal consequences for savings banks. For the institutions, there is an enormous dependence on interest surpluses. Mergers, branch closures and staff reductions are the inevitable reactions to the increased cost pressure, in the hope of counteracting this trend. It is well known that cost reductions can be achieved through a higher degree of automation. Savings banks are thus forced to digitalize their processes and realize cost savings (Deeken & Specht, 2017; Giebe, 2019).

The descriptive analysis of the key figures reveals a dramatic picture. The number of savings banks (see Figure 5), the number of domestic branches (see Figure 6) and the number of employees (see Figure 7) at savings banks in Germany declined significantly between 1991 and 2018 (see also Table 1, which

Figure 5. Own representation of the "Number of savings banks in Germany".

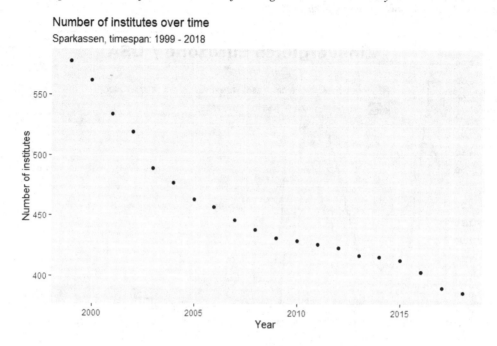

shows the figures at the end of each year). At the end of 2018, a total of 386 individual savings banks, 9,492 domestic branches and 209,600 employees were identified.

As has been elaborated, German savings banks have had to drastically reduce the number of institutions, branches and employees. The President of the Federal Association of German Bank, Hans-Walter Peters assumes that in the next few years every fourth branch of all banks and savings banks in Germany will be closed (Peters, 2018).

The analysis of the key business figures of savings banks in Germany shows a differentiated picture (see table 2). The operating result of the savings banks in Germany in the period from 1999 to 2018 can also be seen (see Figure 8). The operating income (also operating result) is a key business figure and generally refers to the result from ordinary business activities. For the savings banks, in simplified terms, it is the balance of expenses and income from operating activities. At the end of 2018, the operating income of the savings banks in Germany was €9,064 million.

The return on equity after taxes of the savings banks in Germany is also shown for the period from 1994 to 2018 (see Figure 9). Return on equity is an indicator of a company's or credit institution's earnings situation that shows the result (in this case: net income after taxes) in relation to the equity capital employed. In 2018, the German savings banks were able to report a return on equity after taxes of around 4.82 percent.

Last but not least, the development of the cost-income ratio of the savings banks in Germany is shown in the period from 1998 to 2018 (see Figure 10). The cost-income ratio is an economic indicator in the operating business of savings banks. It provides information on the efficiency of a savings bank, whereby the lower the value of the cost-income ratio, the more efficiently the savings bank operates. In 2018, the cost-income ratio of savings banks in Germany was around 69.9 percent.

Figure 6. Own representation of the "Number of branches of savings banks in Germany".

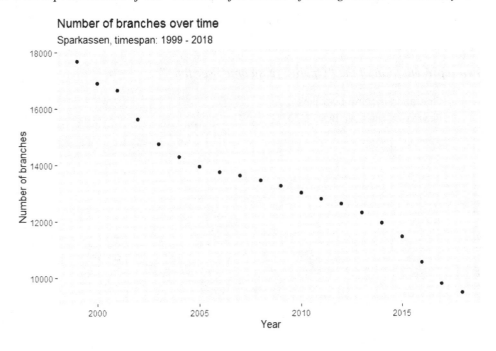

Figure 7. Own representation of the "Number of Employees of Savings Banks in Germany".

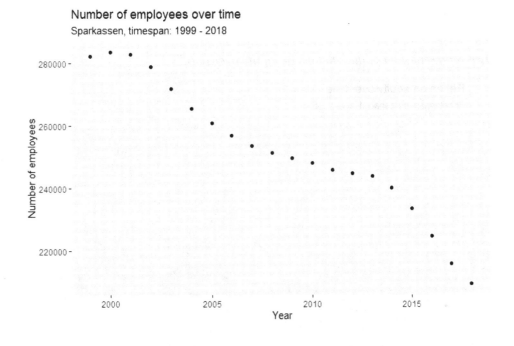

It was determined in the course of the investigations that only the operating result changed significantly in the years 1999-2018. For this key performance indicator, a link can be established to the cost-cutting measures implemented as a result of increasing digitalization. By contrast, the cost-income ratio and return on equity did not change significantly during the period under review (Giebe & Schulz, 2021).

Figure 8. Own representation of the "Operating income over time"

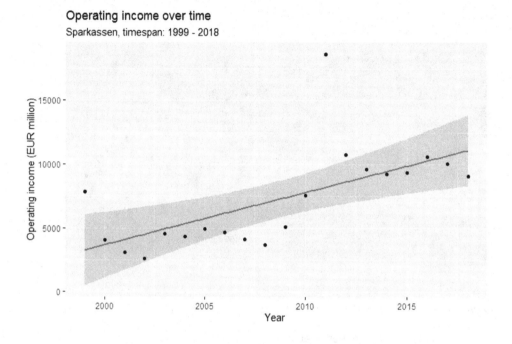

Figure 9. Own representation of the "Return on equity over time"

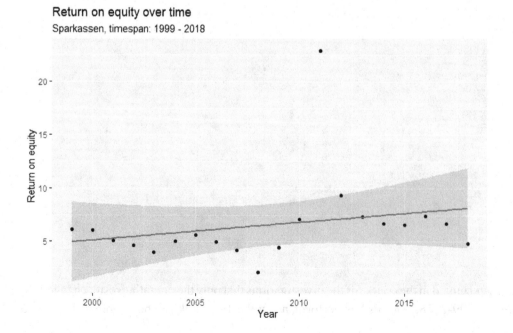

Figure 10. Own representation of the "Cost to income ratio over time"

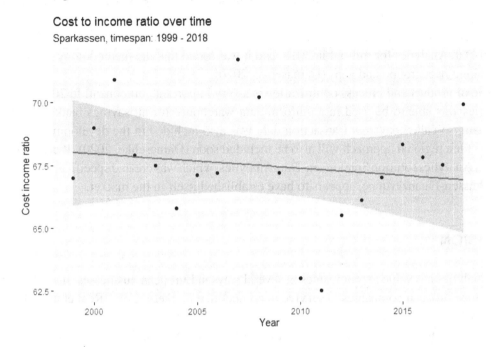

In terms of real key figures, there is a clear need for urgent action. Savings bank data analytics could be a helpful element here, so that customers of savings banks can actually be offered the ideal banking product at the right time, with the right approach via the right distribution channel, on the basis of the extensive wealth of data. In order to be able to answer the research question with a clear conscience, opinions from real practice are needed.

A study by Bonney et al. shows that salespeople tend to overvalue sales options. Keeping options open can be an expensive proposition for companies. This happens when salespeople apply resources to low-priority customers. As a result, sales managers may need to be more involved in coaching their salespeople when it comes to identifying customers to target among the options. This can potentially reduce turnover costs as salespeople focus less on a multitude of opportunities (Bonney et al., 2016). Here, too, savings bank data analytics can make a contribution by identifying the right customers via algorithms.

There are various examples in which Sparkassen-DataAnalytics outperformed expert selections in terms of actual closings. Even if there was an overlap between the customers from the expert selections and Sparkassen-DataAnalytics, in most cases around 30 percent completely different customers were available for the approach and higher closing rates were counted in the direct comparison. This meant that the customer approach was much more targeted (Damaschke & Giebe, 2020).

Indeed, the strengths and advantages of Sparkassen-DataAnalytics could be proven in several test campaigns of different savings banks compared to classical expert selections. Among other things, the reasons lie in the targeted customer selection based on the algorithms (Lange, 2020). Sparkasse Vorpommern uses Sparkassen-DataAnalytics via the online channel as well as stationary sales on the topic of product affinities. Sparkasse KölnBonn was able to significantly increase appointments as well as product sales compared to previous campaigns. Sparkasse Essen had twice as many consultations in individual consulting topics. After a collective mailing, the recipients of which were selected using

Sparkassen-DataAnalytics, Sparkasse Bremen had a higher level of additional contracts than with comparable campaigns (Damaschke, 2020).

However, there were also various insights and learning areas. Approximately 240 savings banks used Sparkassen-DataAnalytics for roll-out in 2018, and it was found that the methodology worked well but that the banking background had gaps (Damaschke, 2020).

The topic of product and process optimization is a very important component. In 2019, Sparkassen-DataAnalytics was able to be used in a uniform data warehouse for all savings banks. In addition to inventory data, so-called payment transaction data was also included in the development. Market and address data for a regional approach will also be included soon (Damaschke, 2020). It can be stated that the Big Data Analytics solution Sparkassen-DataAnalytics, which was created specifically for companies in the Sparkassen-Finanzgruppe, appears to have established itself in the market.

CONCLUSION

Big Data Analytics has value for companies in several ways in European businesses. It can be a strategic investment for European companies to survive in competitive markets (Côrte-Real et al., 2017).

The study by Gronau et al. also analyzes the current level of use of business analytics in German companies. The aim was to determine the maturity of the companies. As one of three industries, the financial sector is particularly affected by the digital transformation. Compared to manufacturing companies, banks and insurance companies are much more future-oriented. The bottom line is that the potential offered by business analytics is usually not sufficiently implemented in Germany (Gronau et al., 2016).

The pressure on retail banks is enormous. For traditional players and new entrants, there are extraordinary opportunities in digitalization. Traditional banks must become a digital bank if the opportunities of the digital economy are to be exploited; innovation in the customer experience is essential (Ilie et al., 2017).

Savings banks need to develop new ideas to be competitive and more efficient than before. Based on this, campaigns can have higher hit rates and thus increase revenue. Another opportunity that Sparkassen-DataAnalytics enables is to predict possible customer attrition. The algorithm predicts indications of potential customer cancellation (Damaschke & Giebe, 2020). So-called churn scores are used here, in which the target variable is, for example, certain cancelled bank products. Given that acquiring a new customer is up to five times more expensive than retaining an existing customer, these scores are becoming increasingly important.

According to Lange, savings bank data analytics can and will increase the competitiveness of savings banks. In addition, savings bank data analytics is increasingly being used to reduce costs and operational risks (Lange, 2020).

The study by Giebe et al. from the perspective of bank customers in Germany can be cited as a further argument. In this study, most respondents agreed that Big Data Analytics can ensure more objective, comprehensive, individualized and active advice. Furthermore, it was proven that Big Data Analytics can increase customer loyalty from the perspective of bank customers (Giebe et al., 2019).

On the basis of the impetus provided, the research question:

To what extent could Big Data Analytics be a lifeline for German savings banks and thus a concrete alternative in the age of digitalization?

can be answered with yes, from the author's point of view. However, with the hint to optimally balance the interaction of "man and machine" and to equip employees with the necessary competencies.

However, the development of specific competencies to ensure the digital transformation of the financial sector is currently one of the greatest challenges. The goal is to secure the company's own competitiveness and sustainable business. Currently, changes in the demand for new solutions and technological competencies of the company are being observed. This includes, for example, the improvement of existing products or product positioning (Mavlutova & Volkova, 2019).

Here and in the transfer of knowledge, human resources can make an active contribution in savings banks. Human resources often deals with personnel development at its core. However, talent management, performance management and compensation management also play an important role in the implementation of a digitalization strategy. Human resources should take a more active role in the age of digitalization. This is the only way to ensure that human capital is competent and qualified. In this way, digitalization needs can be met in the present and in the future. It is important to coordinate all human resources activities. If this is given, the digitalization strategy of a company can be achieved (Fenech et al., 2019).

The success of Big Data Analytics in companies depends heavily on the overall Big Data Analytics capability of a company. These include capacities, the knowledge of the people involved, the processes of collaboration and knowledge sharing, the availability of infrastructure and data, and well-established collection and processing methods (McAfee et al., 2012).

In addition to the investment in basic resources required for Big Data Analytics projects, the organization needs personnel with knowledge of Big Data Analytics technology as well as management skills to effectively execute the projects (Gupta & George, 2016). According to Davenport, employees involved in Big Data Analytics should have necessary technical skills as well as strong communication skills and interpersonal skills (Davenport, 2014).

The recipe for success of optimal learning transfer is the subject of numerous scientific publications. Blume et al. (2010) examined 89 empirical studies on transfer in training. It is significant that transfer success depends on cognitive skills, conscientiousness, motivation and a supportive work environment (Blume et al., 2010). These attributes need to be integrated into appropriate training programs.

FUTURE RESEARCH DIRECTIONS

Today, data is generally regarded as the raw material of the 21st century. Data analytics activities have been known since 2017. So-called Sparkassen-DataAnalytics services have been developed to cover the entire customer journey. Thus, Sparkassen-DataAnalytics can become an essential part of sales planning, an operational application and performance measurements. Data analytics will permanently change customer management, but also the corporate culture in the savings banks (ITmagazin, 2019). From the author's point of view, further concrete, measurable examples of success are essential. The use cases researched as part of this research do not yet provide representative evidence for the entire Sparkassen-Finanzgruppe. It is therefore advisable to initiate research in this direction.

Decades of practice with expert selection meets modern data analytic methods. The final success of a savings bank data analytics integration is therefore not determined by the quality of the model, but rather by monitoring the organizational change. In addition, it is becoming increasingly important to ensure continuous transparency about the new process models and what has been achieved (Lünemann

& Müller-Hammerstein, 2021). For this reason, the use of savings bank data analytics requires a change management approach in the view of the author.

But the machine alone will not lead to success in the future. This is because the interpretation and fine-tuning of the results must also be subjected to close scrutiny from a banking perspective. Also, only the right questions lead to meaningful answers on the data (Damaschke & Giebe, 2020). Given that this is not a "plug and play" solution, there is a need for further research on how to ensure optimal integration in savings banks and what the distinction between methodology and banking expertise actually looks like.

The traditional classic business model of savings banks is traditionally based on personal customer contact. However, high influence and changes due to digitalization are inevitable. These changes have an impact on many aspects of how bank customers demand, evaluate and ultimately purchase financial services. Savings banks thrive on their regional ties to their customers. The personal contact person and the high level of trust in the savings bank are valued by customers. Savings banks can only be sustainable if they manage to combine tradition and innovation (Deeken & Specht, 2017; Lünemann & Müller-Hammerstein, 2021).

The role of branches is already being discussed from an omnichannel perspective. There is no alternative to branch closures due to the ever-increasing cost pressure (Waschbusch et al., 2016). Banks and savings banks are also lagging behind other industries in this context. Omni-channel management in German bank sales will change significantly and is without alternative (Menrad, 2020). Further research could therefore relate to an optimal omnichannel approach in the context of Big Data Analytics.

In contrast to simpler applications, machine learning methods face the challenge that they are partly incomprehensible to users. In some cases, they are regarded as so-called "black boxes". This means that users do not directly learn how the making of certain decisions was accomplished by an algorithm. Along with the increasingly extensive use of machine learning, the ethical and legal requirements for the use of Big Data Analytics are also increasing. Current research in the field of machine learning, in addition to privacy, is particularly concerned with comprehensibility and data sovereignty. Data sovereignty describes the decision-making power that the owner of the data possesses. Hereby he can steer, decide and control, what happens with his data, who receives it and how a use looks. Premises are therefore the security of personal data (Damaschke & Giebe, 2020; Komorowski, 2020). How to ensure data protection can be the subject of further research.

The topic of communication may also be the subject of further investigation. Positive experience had been gained with a modular introductory offer "Customer Management with Sparkassen-DataAnalytics". Individual savings banks were able to combine and book learning content according to their needs. Participants benefited, for example, from an overview of the sales cycle with Sparkassen-DataAnalytics, from administrative knowledge of the application, or from a review session with an open framework (ITmagazin, 2020). It would be exciting to investigate which of the individual communication measures lead to success.

Starting with sales, the idea is to be able to support all other business areas of the Sparkassen-Finanzgruppe with Sparkassen-Data Analytics in the future. This would enable various operating processes to be optimized and automated. There is still potential in the application areas of operations and control (Damaschke, 2020). At a later date, it will be possible to generate practice-oriented insights from operations and control and to explore further development content.

In recent years, the call for more social responsibility has become louder and louder. Not least due to numerous examples about accounting scandals, bribery payments or the me too debate, ethical behavior by every employee is the vision (Schreyögg, 2016). In this respect, the combination of Big Data Analytics and social responsibility could be specifically investigated.

REFERENCES

Akter, S., Wamba, S. F., Gunasekaran, A., Dubey, R., & Childe, S. J. (2016). How to improve firm performance using big data analytics capability and business strategy alignment? *International Journal of Production Economics*, *182*, 113–131. doi:10.1016/j.ijpe.2016.08.018

Anzahl der Beschäftigten bei Sparkassen in Deutschland in den Jahren von 1991 bis 2018 [Number of employees at savings banks in Germany between 1991 and 2018]. (n.d.). https://de.statista.com/statistik/daten/studie/157024/umfrage/beschaeftigte-in-sparkassen-seit-dem-jahr-2000/

Anzahl der Sparkasseninstitute und ihrer inländischen Zweigstellen in den Jahren von 1990 bis 2019 [Number of savings bank institutions and their domestic branches in the years 1990 to 2019]. (n.d.). https://de.statista.com/statistik/daten/studie/6698/umfrage/anzahl-der-sparkassen-und-inlaendischen-zweigstellen-seit-dem-jahr-1990/

Behr, P., & Schmidt, R. (2015). *The German banking system: Characteristics and challenges.* SAFE White Paper, No. 32. Goethe University. http://hdl.handle.net/10419/129081

Betriebsergebnis der Sparkassen in Deutschland in den Jahren von 1999 bis 2018 (in Millionen Euro) [Operating profit of savings banks in Germany in the years 1999 to 2018 (in millions of euros)]. (n.d.). https://de.statista.com/statistik/daten/studie/13622/umfrage/betriebsergebnis-deutscher-sparkassen-seit-dem-jahr-1999/

Blume, B. D., Ford, J. K., Baldwin, T. T., & Huang, J. L. (2010). Transfer of training: A meta-analytic review. *Journal of Management*, *36*(4), 1065–1105. doi:10.1177/0149206309352880

Bonney, L., Plouffe, C. R., & Brady, M. (2016). Investigations of sales representatives' valuation of options. *Journal of the Academy of Marketing Science*, *44*(2), 135–150. doi:10.100711747-014-0412-7

Brühl, V. (2019). Big Data, Data Mining, Machine Learning und Predictive Analytics: Ein konzeptioneller Überblick [Big Data, Data Mining, Machine Learning and Predictive Analytics: A Conceptual Overview]. *CFS Working Paper Series, 617.* https://ssrn.com/abstract=3321195

Chen, H., Chiang, R. H., & Storey, V. C. (2012). Business intelligence and analytics: From big data to big impact. *Management Information Systems Quarterly*, *36*(4), 1165–1188. doi:10.2307/41703503

Côrte-Real, N., Oliveira, T., & Ruivo, P. (2017). Assessing business value of Big Data Analytics in European firms. *Journal of Business Research*, *70*, 379–390. doi:10.1016/j.jbusres.2016.08.011

Damaschke, C. (2020). Data Analytics. Ein Blick hinter die Kulisse [Data Analytics. A look behind the scenes]. *SparkassenZeitung*. Retrieved from: https://sparkassenzeitung.de/vertrieb/sparkassen-data-analytics-ein-blick-hinter-die-kulisse

Damaschke, C., & Giebe, C. (2020), Sparkassen-DataAnalytics: Den Datenschatz der Sparkassen-Finanzgruppe heben [Sparkassen-DataAnalytics: Lifting the Data Treasure of the Savings Banks Finance Group]. In Digitalisierung - "the next challenge" für Sparkassen Handlungsfelder zur künftigen Gestaltung des Geschäftsmodells in Sparkassen (pp. 139-154). Deutscher Sparkassenverlag.

Davenport, T. (2014). How strategists use "big data" to support internal business decisions, discovery and production. *Strategy and Leadership*, *42*(4), 45–50. doi:10.1108/SL-05-2014-0034

Deeken, M., & Specht, K. (2017). *Zukunftsfähigkeit Deutscher Sparkassen* [Sustainability of German Savings Banks]. Springer Fachmedien Wiesbaden. doi:10.1007/978-3-658-18700-2

Drummer, D., Jerenz, A., Siebelt, P., & Thaten, M. (2016). *FinTech – Challenges and Opportunities How digitization is transforming the financial sector.* McKinsey & Company. https://www.mckinsey.com/industries/financial-services/our-insights/fintech-challenges-and-opportunities

Eigenkapitalrentabilität nach Steuern der Sparkassen in Deutschland in den Jahren von 1994 bis 2018 [Return on equity after taxes of savings banks in Germany in the years 1994 to 2018]. (n.d.). https://de.statista.com/statistik/daten/studie/242273/umfrage/eigenkapitalrentabilitaet-der-sparkassen-in-deutschland/

Entwicklung der Cost-Income-Ratio der Sparkassen in Deutschland in den Jahren von 1998 bis 2018 [Development of the cost-income ratio of savings banks in Germany in the years 1998 to 2018]. (n.d.). https://de.statista.com/statistik/daten/studie/197223/umfrage/cost-income-ratio-der-sparkassen-in-deutschland-seit-2007/

Fenech, R., Baguant, P., & Ivanov, D. (2019). The changing role of human resource management in an era of digital transformation. *International Journal of Entrepreneurship*, *22*(2). https://www.abacademies.org/articles/the-changing-role-of-human-resource-management-in-an-era-of-digital-transformation-8154.html

Giebe, C. (2019). The Chief Digital Officer – Savior for the Digitalization in German Banks? *Journal of Economic Development, Environment and People*, *8*(3), 6–15. doi:10.26458/jedep.v8i3.633

Giebe, C., Hammerström, L., & Zwerenz, D. (2019). Big Data & Analytics as a sustainable Customer Loyalty Instrument in Banking and Finance. *Financial Markets, Institutions and Risks*, *3*(4), 74–88. doi:10.21272/fmir.3(4).74-88.2019

Giebe, C., & Schulz, K. (2021). Economic effects of the digital transformation on the banking market using the example of savings banks and cooperative banks in Germany. *International Journal of Economics and Finance*, *13*(6), 34. Advance online publication. doi:10.5539/ijef.v13n6p34

Gronau, N., Thim, C., & Fohrholz, C. (2016). Business Analytics in der deutschen Praxis [Business Analytics in der deutschen Praxis.]. *Controlling*, *28*(8–9), 472–479. doi:10.15358/0935-0381-2016-8-9-472

Gupta, M., & George, J. F. (2016). Toward the development of a big data analytics capability. *Information & Management*, *53*(8), 1049–1064. doi:10.1016/j.im.2016.07.004

Hammerström, L. (2018). Organizational Design of Big Data and Analytics Teams. *European Journal of Social Science Education and Research*, *5*(3), 132–149. doi:10.2478/ejser-2018-0065

Ilie, O.-M., Popescu, C., & Iacob, S. E. (2017). Transforming the Banking Organization in the Context of Digital Economy. *Proceedings RCE, 2017*, 284–292. doi:10.18662/lumproc.rce2017.1.24

ITmagazin. (2019). Data Analytics. 360 Grad – den Kunden im Blick [Data Analytics. 360 degrees - the customer in view]. *ITmagazin 3/2019.* https://www.f-i.de/News/ITmagazin/Archiv/2019/Einfach.-Machen/Titelthema/360-Grad-den-Kunden-im-Blick

ITmagazin. (2020). Sparkassen-DataAnalytics. Es geht weiter! [Savings Banks DataAnalytics. It goes on!]. *ITmagazin 2/2020.* https://www.f-i.de/News/ITmagazin/Archiv/2020/Mit-Abstand-gut-beraten/Loesungen-Praxis/Es-geht-weiter

Kitchens, B., Dobolyi, D., Li, J., & Abbasi, A. (2018). Advanced customer analytics: Strategic value through integration of relationship-oriented big data. *Journal of Management Information Systems, 35*(2), 540–574. doi:10.1080/07421222.2018.1451957

Kitchin, R. (2014). Big Data, new epistemologies and paradigm shifts. *Big Data & Society, 1*(1), 1–12. doi:10.1177/2053951714528481

Komorowski, P. (2020), Role of digitization for German saving banks, In Digitalisierung - "the next challenge" für Sparkassen Handlungsfelder zur künftigen Gestaltung des Geschäftsmodells in Sparkassen (pp. 329-345). Deutscher Sparkassenverlag.

Lange, M. (2020). Finanz Informatik: Optimiertes Kundenmanagement mit Data Analytics [Finanz Informatik (Data Center): Optimised customer management with data analytics]. *IT Finanzmagazin.* https://www.it-finanzmagazin.de/data-analytics-so-geht-optimiertes-kundenmanagement-108798/

Lünemann, J., & Müller-Hammerstein, C. (2021). *Finanzinstitute: Kundenansprache mit Data Analytics* [Financial institutions: Addressing customers with data analytics]. KINote – eine Marke der Bank-Verlag GmbH. https://www.ki-note.de/einzelansicht/finanzinstitute-kundenansprache-mit-data-analytics

Mavlutova, I., & Volkova, T. (2019). Digital Transformation of Financial Sector and Challenges for Competencies Development. In *2019 7th International Conference on Modeling, Development and Strategic Management of Economic System (MDSMES 2019)*. Atlantis Press. 10.2991/mdsmes-19.2019.31

McAfee, A., Brynjolfsson, E., Davenport, T. H., Patil, D. J., & Barton, D. (2012). Big data: The management revolution. *Harvard Business Review, 90*(10), 60–68. https://pubmed.ncbi.nlm.nih.gov/23074865/ PMID:23074865

Menrad, M. (2020). Systematic review of omni-channel banking and preview of upcoming developments in Germany. *Innovative Marketing, 16*(2), 104–125. doi:10.21511/im.16(2).2020.09

Moormann, J. (2000). Die Digitalisierung des Bankgeschäfts. In *Informationstechnologie in Banken* [The digitalization of banking. In Information Technology in Banks] (pp. 3–16). Springer. doi:10.1007/978-3-642-56991-3_1

Najafabadi, M. M., Villanustre, F., Khoshgoftaar, T. M., Seliya, N., Wald, R., & Muharemagic, E. (2015). Deep learning applications and challenges in big data analytics. *Journal of Big Data, 2*(1), 1. doi:10.118640537-014-0007-7

Peters, H.-W. (2018). Bankenverband rechnet mit kräftigem Abbau von Filialen [Banking association expects strong reduction of branches]. *Frankfurter Allgemeine.* https://www.faz.net/aktuell/wirtschaft/bankenverband-rechnet-mit-kraeftigem-abbau-von-filialen-15579480.html?GEPC=s81&GEPC=s5

Schreyögg, G. (2016). *Grundlagen der Organisation. Basiswissen für Studium und Praxis* [Fundamentals of Organisation. Basic knowledge for study and practice]. Springer Verlag. doi:10.1007/978-3-658-13959-9

Sparkassengesetz Baden-Württemberg in der Fassung vom 19.07.2005 (GBl. S. 587) zuletzt geändert durch Gesetz vom 07.05.2020 (GBl. S. 259) mit Wirkung vom 13.05.2020 [Savings Banks Act of Baden-Württemberg, §6 (1), 2020)]. https://dejure.org/gesetze/SpG

Sun, Z., Sun, L., & Strang, K. (2018). Big data analytics services for enhancing business intelligence. *Journal of Computer Information Systems, 58*(2), 162–169. doi:10.1080/08874417.2016.1220239

Vassakis, K., Petrakis, E., & Kopanakis, I. (2018). Big data analytics: Applications, prospects and challenges. In *Mobile big data* (pp. 3–20). Springer. doi:10.1007/978-3-319-67925-9_1

Wamba, S. F., Akter, S., Edwards, A., Chopin, G., & Gnanzou, D. (2015). How 'big data' can make big impact: Findings from a systematic review and a longitudinal case study. *International Journal of Production Economics, 165*, 234–246. doi:10.1016/j.ijpe.2014.12.031

Waschbusch, G., Blaß, R., & Berg, S. C. (2016). Zukunft der Bankfiliale–Auslaufmodell oder Erlebniswelt [The future of the bank branch - a model to be discontinued or a world of experience]. *Bank und Markt, 5*, 30-33. https://www.kreditwesen.de/bank-markt/themenschwerpunkte/aufsaetze/zukunft-bankfiliale-auslaufmodell-erlebniswelt-id33007.html

Wolgast, M. (2016). Das gegenwärtige Niedrigzinsumfeld aus Sicht der Sparkassen [The current low interest rate environment from the point of view of savings banks]. *Vierteljahrshefte zur Wirtschaftsforschung, 85*(1), 11–29. doi:10.3790/vjh.85.1.11

ADDITIONAL READING

Au, C. D., & Hiese, A. (2021). Künstliche Intelligenz in Banken: Worauf es im aktuellen Marktumfeld ankommt [Artificial intelligence in banks: What matters in the current market environment]. *Digitale Welt, 5*(3), 26–29. doi:10.100742354-021-0359-z

Brock, H., & Bieberstein, I. (2015). Multi-und Omnichannel-Management in Banken und Sparkassen [Multi- and Omnichannel Management in Banks and Savings Banks]. *Wege in eine erfolgreiche Zukunft.* doi:10.1007/978-3-658-06538-6

Burkert, U., Dürkop, U., Intelmann, J., Kater, U., Lips, C., Michels, J., Traud, G., Wesselmann, C., & Zimmermann, G. (2019). Künstliche Intelligenz – Wachstumstreiber der deutschen Volkswirtschaft? Standpunkt der Chefsvolkswirte [Artificial Intelligence - Growth Driver for the German Economy? Viewpoint of the Chief Economists], DSGV. Retrieved from: https://www.dsgv.de/positionen/standpunkte-der-chefsvolkswirte/kuenstliche-intelligenz.html [Accessed December 2021]

Conrad, A., Hoffmann, A., & Neuberger, D. (2017). Physische und digitale Erreichbarkeit von Finanzdienstleistungen der Sparkassen [Physical and digital accessibility of financial services of savings banks], *ThünenSeries of Applied Economic Theory - Working Paper, No. 149*, Universität Rostock, Institut für Volkswirtschaftslehre, Rostock, http://hdl.handle.net/10419/156222

Eim, A., Lamprecht, D., & Wipprich, M. (2006). Die Netzwerke der Sparkassen-Finanzgruppe und des genossenschaftlichen FinanzVerbundes: Zukunftsperspektiven des Dreisäulensystems [The networks of the Savings Banks Finance Group and the Cooperative Financial Network: Future prospects for the three-pillar system]. *Vierteljahrshefte zur Wirtschaftsforschung, 75*(4), 53–72. doi:10.3790/vjh.75.4.53

Engels, B. (2016). Big-Data-Analyse: Ein Einstieg für Ökonomen [Big data analytics: an introduction for economists], *IW-Kurzbericht Nr. 78*. Institut der deutschen Wirtschaft, Köln. http://hdl.handle.net/10419/157584

Engels, B. (2018). Ein unbekannter Schatz: Wie bestimmen Unternehmen in Deutschland den Wert ihrer Daten? [An Unknown Treasure: How Do Companies in Germany Determine the Value of Their Data?]. *IW-Trends-Vierteljahresschrift zur empirischen Wirtschaftsforschung, 45*(4), 41-59. doi:10.2373/1864-810X.18-04-04

Engels, B., & Goecke, H. (2019). Big Data in Wirtschaft und Forschung: Eine Bestandsaufnahme [Big Data in Business and Research: A Stocktaking], *IW-Analysen Nr. 130*. Institut der deutschen Wirtschaft, Köln. http://hdl.handle.net/10419/201760

Gai, K., Qiu, M., & Sun, X. (2018). A survey on FinTech. *Journal of Network and Computer Applications, 103*, 262–273. doi:10.1016/j.jnca.2017.10.011

Giebe, C., & Schulz, K. (2021). Cost Cutting Measures at Cooperative Banks in Germany as a Result of Digitalization and their Consequences. *Journal of Economic Development. Environment and People, 10*(2), 29–45. doi:10.26458/jedep.v10i2.693

Giebe, C., & Schulz, K. (2021). Digitalization and its Rapid Impact on Savings Banks in Germany. *Global Journal of Management and Business Research, 21*(4), 1–11. doi:10.34257/GJMBRBVOL21IS4PG1

Hammermann, A., & Stettes, O. (2016). Qualifikationsbedarf und Qualifizierung: Anforderungen im Zeichen der Digitalisierung [Skills needs and qualification: requirements in the spirit of digitalisation]. *IW policy paper (No. 3/2016)*. Institut der deutschen Wirtschaft (IW). German Economic Institute, http://hdl.handle.net/10419/127450

Hess, T., Matt, C., Benlian, A., & Wiesböck, F. (2016). Options for formulating a digital transformation strategy. *MIS Quarterly Executive, 15*(2). https://aisel.aisnet.org/misqe/vol15/iss2/6/

Kauffman, R. J., & Weber, T. A. (2018). Special Section: The Digital Transformation of Vertical Organizational Relationships. *Journal of Management Information Systems, 35*(3), 837–839. doi:10.1080/07421222.2018.1481646

Kaya, O. (2019). Künstliche Intelligenz im Bankensektor [Artificial intelligence in the banking sector]. *Deutsche Bank Research*, Frankfurt am Main. http://hdl.handle.net/11159/4259

Lee, I., & Shin, Y. J. (2018). Fintech: Ecosystem, business models, investment decisions, and challenges. *Business Horizons*, *61*(1), 35–46. doi:10.1016/j.bushor.2017.09.003

Löffler, L., & Giebe, C. (2021). Generation Z and the War of Talents in the German Banking Sector. *International Journal of Business Management and Economic Research*, *4*(6), 1–18. doi:10.35409/ IJBMER.2021.3319

Menrad, M., & Varga, J. (2020). From Analogue to Digital Banking: Developments in the European Union from 2007 to 2019. *Regional and Business Studies*, *12*(2), 17–32. doi:10.33568/rbs.2516

Osborne, J. (1995). A Case Of Mistaken Identity: The Use Of Expense/Revenue Ratios To Measure Ratios To Measure Bank Efficiency. *Journal of Applied Corporate Finance*, *8*(2), 55–59. doi:10.1111/j.1745-6622.1995.tb00287.x

Paul, S., Rudolph, B., Zech, S., Oehler, A., Horn, M., Wendt, S., & Jentzsch, N. (2016). Neue Finanztechnologien—Bankenmarkt in Bewegung [New Financial Technologies-Banking Market on the Move]. *Wirtschaftsdienst (Hamburg, Germany)*, *96*(9), 631–647. doi:10.100710273-016-2028-7

Rohrmeier, D. (2015). Lebenswelten 2020 – Wie werden wir morgen unsere Finanzen managen? [Lifeworlds 2020 - How will we manage our finances tomorrow?]. In: Seidel M., Liebetrau A. (eds) Banking & Innovation. FOM-Edition (FOM Hochschule für Oekonomie & Management). Springer Gabler, Wiesbaden. doi:10.1007/978-3-658-06746-5_7

Schädle, T. H. (2021). Die Besonderheiten der deutschen Kreditwirtschaft. [The special features of the German banking industry] In *Abwicklung nicht-systemrelevanter Banken*. Springer Gabler. doi:10.1007/978-3-658-32488-9_2

Sebastian, I., Ross, J., Beath, C., Mocker, M., Moloney, K., & Fonstad, N. (2017). How big old companies navigate digital transformation. *MIS Quarterly Executive*, *16*(3), 197–213. https://aisel.aisnet.org/ misqe/vol16/iss3/6

Teece, D. J., Pisano, G., & Shuen, A. (1997). Dynamic capabilities and strategic management. *Strategic Management Journal*, *18*(7), 509–533. https://www.jstor.org/stable/3088148. doi:10.1002/(SICI)1097-0266(199708)18:7<509::AID-SMJ882>3.0.CO;2-Z

Trelewicz, J. Q. (2017). Big data and big money: The role of data in the financial sector. *IT Professional*, *19*(3), 8–10. doi:10.1109/MITP.2017.45

KEY TERMS AND DEFINITIONS

Big Data Analytics: Big data analytics describes the challenge of filtering out the relevant information from a huge deal of data with the right strategy.

Competition: Competition is a race for market share, contested by market participants. This race is global and usually aims to maximize profits.

Digital Transformation: The digital transformation of banks begins with a vision. The transformation will only succeed if the human factor is also "picked up.

Digitalization: Digitalization is a playing field on which we cavort. If we want to win, we cannot leave it. Digitalization has the same significance as the industrial revolution.

German Banking System: The German banking system is undergoing its greatest transformation as result of the digital transformation. Nothing is the same as it was before.

Savings Banks: Savings banks are the largest banking group in Germany. They have a public mission and a high local presence. The Savings Banks logo represents a coin being put into a piggy bank.

Sparkassen-DataAnalytics: Sparkassen-DataAnalytics is the brand of the predictive analytics solution developed specifically for savings banks, based on customer data from approximately 50 million savings bank customers in Germany.

APPENDIX 1

Table 1. "Number of Savings Banks, number of domestic branches and number of employees".

Year	Number of Saving Banks in Germany	Number of Domestic Branches of Savings Banks	Number of Employees of Savings Banks
2018	386	9.492	209.600
2017	390	9.818	216.100
2016	403	10.555	224.700
2015	413	11.459	233.700
2014	416	11.951	240.100
2013	417	12.323	244.900
2012	423	12.643	245.950
2011	426	12.810	248.150
2010	429	13.025	249.600
2009	431	13.266	251.400
2008	438	13.457	253.700
2007	446	13.624	257.000
2006	457	13.756	260.800
2005	463	13.950	265.400
2004	477	14.292	271.900
2003	489	14.757	278.800
2002	519	15.628	282.850
2001	534	16.648	283.450
2000	562	16.892	282.150
1999	578	17.667	287.650
1998	594	18.327	288.400
1997	598	18.751	288.450
1996	607	18.895	290.050
1995	624	19.071	291.150
1994	643	19.271	287.750
1993	691	19.510	284.150
1992	717	19.578	284.350
1991	734	19.486	281.350

(Data Source: https://de.statista.com/, 1991-2018)

APPENDIX 2

Table 2. "Operating income, return on equity and cost-income ratio of savings banks

Year	Operating Income Over Time (in Millions of €)	Return on Equity Over Time (in %)	Cost-income Ratio Over Time (in %)
2018	9.064	4,82	69,9
2017	10.075	6,72	67,5
2016	10.611	7,42	67,8
2015	9.369	6,54	68,3
2014	9.233	6,72	67,0
2013	9.621	7,33	66,1
2012	10.732	9,32	65,5
2011	18.620	22,88	62,5
2010	7.549	7,07	63,0
2009	5.112	4,44	67,2
2008	3.673	2,12	70,2
2007	4.123	4,21	71,7
2006	4.638	4,95	67,2
2005	4.933	5,6	67,1
2004	4.329	5,03	65,8
2003	4.559	4,0	67,5
2002	2.641	4,65	67,9
2001	3.078	4,06	70,9
2000	4.055	6,02	69,0
1999	7.828	6,122	67,0
1998	No Value available	6,52	68,1
1997	No Value available	6,66	No Value available
1996	No Value available	7,42	No Value available
1995	No Value available	7,99	No Value available
1994	No Value available	8,01	No Value available
1993	No Value available	No Value available	No Value available
1992	No Value available	No Value available	No Value available
1991	No Value available	No Value available	No Value available

(Data Source: https://de.statista.com/, 1991-2018)

Compilation of References

Aamodt, A., & Plaza, E. (1994). Case-based reasoning: Foundational issues, methodological variations, and system approaches. *AI Communications*, *7*(1), 39–59. doi:10.3233/AIC-1994-7104

Abakarim, Y., Lahby, M., & Attioui, A. (2018). An efficient real time model for credit card fraud detection based on deep learning. *ACM Int. Conf. Proceeding Ser.* 10.1145/3289402.3289530

Abd Elkader, S., Elmogy, M., El-Sappagh, S., & Zaied, A. N. H. (2018). A framework for chronic kidney disease diagnosis based on case based reasoning. *International Journal of Advanced Computer Research*, *8*(35), 59–71. doi:10.19101/IJACR.2018.834003

Abdullah, N. S., Nishioka, D., Tanaka, Y., & Murayama, Y. (2015). User's action and decision making of retweet messages towards reducing misinformation spread during disaster. *Journal of Information Processing*, *23*(1), 31–40. doi:10.2197/ipsjjip.23.31

Abrahams, A. S., Jiao, J., Wang, G. A., & Fan, W. (2012). Vehicle defect discovery from social media. *Decision Support Systems*, *54*(1), 87–97. doi:10.1016/j.dss.2012.04.005

Ackoff, R. (1992). *From Data to Wisdom.* http://faculty.ung.edu/kmelton/Documents/DataWisdom.pdf

Adams, R. (2021). Naraka: Bladepoint player count hits 136K in final beta test. *Techraptor*. Retrieved from https://techraptor.net/gaming/news/naraka-bladepoint-player-count-hits-136k-in-final-beta-test

Adatrao, S., & Mittal, M. (2016). An analysis of different image preprocessing techniques for determining the centroids of circular marks using hough transform. *2016 2nd International Conference on Frontiers of Signal Processing, ICFSP 2016*, 110–115. 10.1109/ICFSP.2016.7802966

Adedoyin-Olowe, M., Gaber, M. M., & Stahl, F. (2014). A Survey of Data Mining Techniques for Social Media Analysis. *Journal of Data Mining & Digital Humanities*, *2014*, 5. Advance online publication. doi:10.46298/jdmdh.5

Agarap, A. F. (2018). *Deep learning using rectified linear units (relu)*. arXiv preprint arXiv:1803.08375.

Aggarwal, S., & Manuel, N. (2016, June 22). *Big data analytics should be driven by business needs, not technology*. McKinsey & Company.

Ahkmedzhanov, N. M., Zhukotcky, A. V., Kudrjavtcev, V. B., Oganov, R. G., Rastorguev, V. V., Ryjov, A. P., & Stogalov, A. S. (2003). System for evaluation and monitoring of risks of cardiovascular disease. *Intelligent Systems*, *7*, 5–38.

Ahmed, A., Saleem, K., Khalid, O., & Rashid, U. (2021). On deep neural network for trust aware cross domain recommendations in E-commerce. *Expert Systems with Applications*, *174*, 114757. doi:10.1016/j.eswa.2021.114757

Akaichi, J. (2014). A medical social network for physicians' annotations posting and summarization. *Social Network Analysis and Mining*, *4*(1), 1–8. doi:10.100713278-014-0225-1

Akhtar, N. (2014). Social network analysis tools. *Proceedings - 2014 4th International Conference on Communication Systems and Network Technologies, CSNT 2014*, 388–392. 10.1109/CSNT.2014.83

Akter, S., Wamba, S. F., Gunasekaran, A., Dubey, R., & Childe, S. J. (2016). How to improve firm performance using big data analytics capability and business strategy alignment? *International Journal of Production Economics*, *182*, 113–131. doi:10.1016/j.ijpe.2016.08.018

Alansari, Z., Soomro, S., & Belgaum, M. R. (2019). Smart Airports: Review and Open Research Issues. In M. H. Miraz, P. S. Excell, A. Ware, S. Soomro, & M. Ali (Eds.), iCETiC 2019. Lecture Notes of the Institute for Computer Sciences, Social Informatics and Telecommunications Engineering. 285 (pp. 137–148). Springer. https://doi.org/10.1007/978-3-030-23943-5_10.

Albawi, S., Mohammed, T. A., & Al-Zawi, S. (2017, August). Understanding of a convolutional neural network. In *2017 International Conference on Engineering and Technology (ICET)* (pp. 1-6). Academic Press.

Al-Daihani, S. M., & Abrahams, A. (2016). A Text Mining Analysis of Academic Libraries' Tweets. *Journal of Academic Librarianship*, *42*(2), 135–143. doi:10.1016/j.acalib.2015.12.014

Alfantoukh, L., & Durresi, A. (2014). Techniques for collecting data in social networks. *Proceedings - 2014 International Conference on Network-Based Information Systems, NBiS 2014*, 336–341. 10.1109/NBiS.2014.92

Al-Garadi, M. A., Varathan, K. D., Ravana, S. D., Ahmed, E., Mujtaba, G., Shahid Khan, M. U., & Khan, S. U. (2018). Analysis of online social network connections for identification of influential users: Survey and open research issues. *ACM Computing Surveys*, *51*(1), 1–37. doi:10.1145/3155897

Ali, A. (2020). *Here's What Happens Every Minute on the Internet in 2020*. https://www.visualcapitalist.com/every-minute-internet-2020/

Ali, Z. (2016). *New IDC MarketScape Provides a Vendor Assessment of the Worldwide Business Analytics Consulting and Systems Integration Services for 2016*. Retrieved from IDC: https://www.idc.com/getdoc.jsp?containerId=prUS41224416

Alley, W. M. (1988). Using exogenous variables in testing for monotonic trends in hydrologic time series. *Water Resources Research*, *24*(11), 1955–1961. doi:10.1029/WR024i011p01955

Altexsoft. (2020, January 15). *Airport Technology Management: Operations, Software Solutions and Vendors*. Retrieved June 19, 2021, from Altexsoft: https://www.altexsoft.com/blog/travel/airport-technology-management-operations-software-solutions-and-vendors/

Amazon. (2021). *Alexa Voice Shopping: Shop millions of Amazon products with Alexa*. https://www.amazon.com/alexa-voice-shopping/b?ie=UTF8&node=14552177011

Amin, K., Kapetanakis, S., Althoff, K.-D., Dengel, A., & Petridis, M. (2018). *Answering with cases: a CBR approach to deep learning*. Paper presented at the International Conference on Case-Based Reasoning. 10.1007/978-3-030-01081-2_2

Amin, K., Kapetanakis, S., Polatidis, N., Althoff, K.-D., & Dengel, A. (2020). *DeepKAF: A Heterogeneous CBR & Deep Learning Approach for NLP Prototyping*. Paper presented at the 2020 International Conference on INnovations in Intelligent Systems and Applications (INISTA). 10.1109/INISTA49547.2020.9194679

Amoiralis, E. I., Tsili, M. A., & Kladas, A. G. (2009). Transformer design and optimization: A literature survey. *IEEE Transactions on Power Delivery*, *24*(4), 1999–2024. doi:10.1109/TPWRD.2009.2028763

Anzahl der Beschäftigten bei Sparkassen in Deutschland in den Jahren von 1991 bis 2018 [Number of employees at savings banks in Germany between 1991 and 2018]. (n.d.). https://de.statista.com/statistik/daten/studie/157024/umfrage/beschaeftigte-in-sparkassen-seit-dem-jahr-2000/

Anzahl der Sparkasseninstitute und ihrer inländischen Zweigstellen in den Jahren von 1990 bis 2019 [Number of savings bank institutions and their domestic branches in the years 1990 to 2019]. (n.d.). https://de.statista.com/statistik/daten/studie/6698/umfrage/anzahl-der-sparkassen-und-inlaendischen-zweigstellen-seit-dem-jahr-1990/

Ashby, W. R. (1956). *An Introduction to Cybernetics*. Chapman and Hall. doi:10.5962/bhl.title.5851

Assassin's Creed Valhalla. (n.d.). In *Wikipedia*. Retrieved from https://en.wikipedia.org/wiki/Assassin%27s_Creed_Valhalla

Assimakopoulos, V., & Nikolopoulos, K. (2000). The theta model: A decomposition approach to forecasting. *International Journal of Forecasting*, *16*(4), 521–530. doi:10.1016/S0169-2070(00)00066-2

Athiyarath, S., Paul, M., & Krishnaswamy, S. (2020). A comparative study and analysis of time series forecasting techniques. *SN Computer Science*, *1*(3), 1–7. doi:10.100742979-020-00180-5

Atkinson, K., Bench-Capon, T., & Bollegala, D. (2020). Explanation in AI and law: Past, present and future. *Artificial Intelligence*, *289*, 103387. Advance online publication. doi:10.1016/j.artint.2020.103387

Austin, D., Sanzgiri, A., Sankaran, K., Woodard, R., Lissack, A., & Seljan, S. (2020). Classifying sensitive content in online advertisements with deep learning. *International Journal of Data Science and Analytics*, *10*(3), 265–276. doi:10.100741060-020-00212-6

Avendano, Y. (2016). Civilization VI is the best strategy game of 2016 (The game awards said so). *Twinfinite.net*. Retrieved from: https://twinfinite.net/2016/12/civilization-vi-best-strategy-game-the-game-awards/

Avey, J. B., Nimnicht, J. L., & Graber Pigeon, N. (2010). Two field studies examining the association between positive psychological capital and employee performance. *Leadership and Organization Development Journal*, *31*(5), 384–401. doi:10.1108/01437731011056425

Avrithis, Y., Strintzis, M., Kompatsiaris, Y., Spyrou, E., & Dasiopoulou, S. (2006). Semantic Processing of Color Images. In Color Image Processing (pp. 259–284). CRC Press. doi:10.1201/9781420009781.ch11

Awad, A., Ali, A., & Gaber, T. (2020). Feature selection method based on chaotic maps and butterfly optimization algorithm. In *Proceedings of the International Conference on Artificial Intelligence and Computer Vision (AICV2020)* (*Vol. 2*, Issue 1153). Springer International Publishing. 10.1007/978-3-030-44289-7_16

Ayadi, M. G., Bouslimi, R., & Akaichi, J. (2016). A medical image retrieval scheme through a medical social network. *Network Modeling and Analysis in Health Informatics and Bioinformatics*, *5*(1), 23. Advance online publication. doi:10.100713721-016-0130-9

Ayyad, S. M., Saleh, A. I., & Labib, L. M. (2019). Gene expression cancer classification using modified K-Nearest Neighbors technique. *Bio Systems*, *176*, 41–51. doi:10.1016/j.biosystems.2018.12.009 PMID:30611843

Azvine, B., Nauck, D., & Ho, C. (2003). Intelligent Business Analytics— A Tool to Build Decision-Support Systems for eBusinesses. *BT Technology Journal*, *21*(4), 65–71. doi:10.1023/A:1027379403688

Bai, S., Kolter, J. Z., & Koltun, V. (2018). *An empirical evaluation of generic convolutional and recurrent networks for sequence modeling*. arXiv preprint arXiv:1803.01271.

Bansal, S., Chowell, G., Simonsen, L., Vespignani, A., & Viboud, C. (2016). *Big data for infectious disease surveillance and modeling*. Academic Press.

Barceló-Vidal, C., Aguilar, L., & Martín-Fernández, J. A. (2011). *Compositional VARIMA time series. Compositional Data Analysis: Theory and Applications*. John Wiley & Sons.

Bartsch-Spörl, B., Lenz, M., & Hübner, A. (1999). *Case-based reasoning—survey and future directions.* Paper presented at the German Conference on Knowledge-Based Systems.

Batrinca, B., & Treleaven, P. C. (2015). Social media analytics: A survey of techniques, tools and platforms. *AI & Society, 30*(1), 89–116. doi:10.100700146-014-0549-4

Bayrakdar, S., Yucedag, I., Simsek, M., & Dogru, I. A. (2020). Semantic analysis on social networks: A survey. *International Journal of Communication Systems, 33*(11), 1–30. doi:10.1002/dac.4424

Begum, S., Ahmed, M. U., Funk, P., Xiong, N., & Von Schéele, B. (2009). A case-based decision support system for individual stress diagnosis using fuzzy similarity matching. *Computational Intelligence, 25*(3), 180–195. doi:10.1111/j.1467-8640.2009.00337.x

Behr, P., & Schmidt, R. (2015). *The German banking system: Characteristics and challenges.* SAFE White Paper, No. 32. Goethe University. http://hdl.handle.net/10419/129081

Ben Jabeur, L., Tamine, L., & Boughanem, M. (2012). Active microbloggers: Identifying influencers, leaders and discussers in microblogging networks. In Lecture Notes in Computer Science (including subseries Lecture Notes in Artificial Intelligence and Lecture Notes in Bioinformatics): Vol. 7608 LNCS (pp. 111–117). Springer Berlin Heidelberg. doi:10.1007/978-3-642-34109-0_12

Benevenuto, F., Rodrigues, T., Almeida, J., Gonçalves, M., & Almeida, V. (2009, April). Detecting spammers and content promoters in online video social networks. *Proceedings - IEEE INFOCOM*, 1–2. Advance online publication. doi:10.1109/INFCOMW.2009.5072127

Berry, L. L., & Parasuraman, A. (1991). Marketing services: competing through quality. Academic Press.

Betriebsergebnis der Sparkassen in Deutschland in den Jahren von 1999 bis 2018 (in Millionen Euro) [Operating profit of savings banks in Germany in the years 1999 to 2018 (in millions of euros)]. (n.d.). https://de.statista.com/statistik/daten/studie/13622/umfrage/betriebsergebnis-deutscher-sparkassen-seit-dem-jahr-1999/

Bhagat, S., Cormode, G., & Muthukrishnan, S. (2011). Node Classification in Social Networks. In *Social Network Data Analytics* (pp. 115–148). Springer. doi:10.1007/978-1-4419-8462-3_5

Bhatt, C., Shah, T., & Ganatra, A. (2014). Business Analytics -Applications and Practices for Continuous Iterative Exploration. *CSI Communications, 38*, 10–13.

Bichindaritz, I. (1994). A case-based assistant for clinical psychiatry expertise. *Proceedings of the Annual Symposium on Computer Application in Medical Care.*

Bichler, M., Heinzl, A., & van der Aalst, W. M. P. (2017). Business Analytics and Data Science: Once Again? *Business & Information Systems Engineering, 59*(2), 77–79. doi:10.100712599-016-0461-1

Bignold, A., Cruz, F., Dazeley, R., Vamplew, P., & Foale, C. (2021). *Persistent Rule-based Interactive Reinforcement Learning.* arXiv preprint arXiv:2102.02441.

Blayney, P. J., & Sun, Z. (2019). Using Excel and Excel VBA for Preliminary Analysis in Big Data Research. In Z. Sun & Z. Sun (Eds.), *Managerial Perspectives on Intelligent Big Data Analytics* (pp. 110–136). IGI Global. doi:10.4018/978-1-5225-7277-0.ch007

Blei, D. M., Ng, A. Y., & Jordan, M. I. (2003). Latent Dirichlet allocation. *Journal of Machine Learning Research, 3*(Jan), 993–1022.

Blume, B. D., Ford, J. K., Baldwin, T. T., & Huang, J. L. (2010). Transfer of training: A meta-analytic review. *Journal of Management*, *36*(4), 1065–1105. doi:10.1177/0149206309352880

Boden, M. (1977). Artificial intelligence and natural man Basic Books. Academic Press.

Bodie, M. T., Cherry, M. A., McCormick, M. L., & Tang, J. (2017). *The law and policy of people analytics*. Academic Press.

Boehmke, B., Hazen, B., Boone, C. A., & Robinson, J. (2020). *A data science and open source software approach to analytics for strategic sourcing*. Academic Press.

Bonney, L., Plouffe, C. R., & Brady, M. (2016). Investigations of sales representatives' valuation of options. *Journal of the Academy of Marketing Science*, *44*(2), 135–150. doi:10.100711747-014-0412-7

Boost Labs. (2019, April 24). *Why Excel Is Still Essential to Data Analytics*. Retrieved June 12, 2021, from Boost Labs: https://boostlabs.com/blog/why-excel-is-still-essential-to-data-analytics/

Borgatti, S. P. (2009). Social Network Analysis, Two-Mode Concepts in. In *Encyclopedia of Complexity and Systems Science* (pp. 8279–8291). Springer New York. doi:10.1007/978-0-387-30440-3_491

Bossmann, J. (2016). Top 9 ethical issues in artificial intelligence. *World Economic Forum*. Retrieved from https://www.weforum.org/agenda/2016/10/top-10-ethical-issues-in-artificial-intelligence/

Bostrom, N., & Yudkowsky, E. (2018). The Ethics of Artificial Intelligence. In *Cambridge Handbook of Artificial Intelligence*. Cambridge University Press. doi:10.1201/9781351251389-4

Bouguettaya, A., Zarzour, H., Kechida, A., & Taberkit, A. M. (2021a). Vehicle Detection From UAV Imagery With Deep Learning: A Review. *IEEE Transactions on Neural Networks and Learning Systems*, 1–21. doi:10.1109/TNNLS.2021.3080276 PMID:34029200

Bouguettaya, A., Zarzour, H., Kechida, A., & Taberkit, A. M. (2021b). Recent Advances on UAV and Deep Learning for Early Crop Diseases Identification: A Short Review. In *2021 International Conference on Information Technology (ICIT)* (pp. 334-339). IEEE. 10.1109/ICIT52682.2021.9491661

Bouguettaya, A., Zarzour, H., Taberkit, A. M., & Kechida, A. (2022). A Review on Early Wildfire Detection from Unmanned Aerial Vehicles using Deep Learning-Based Computer Vision Algorithms. *Signal Processing*, *190*, 108309. doi:10.1016/j.sigpro.2021.108309

Bouslimi, R., Ayadi, M. G., & Akaichi, J. (2017). Semantic medical image retrieval in a medical social network. *Social Network Analysis and Mining*, *7*(1), 2. Advance online publication. doi:10.100713278-016-0420-3

Boutell, M., & Luo, J. (2005). Beyond pixels: Exploiting camera metadata for photo classification. *Pattern Recognition*, *38*(6), 935–946. doi:10.1016/j.patcog.2004.11.013

Božič, K., & Dimovski, V. (2019). Business intelligence and analytics for value creation: The role of absorptive capacity. *International Journal of Information Management*, *46*, 93-103. doi:10.1016/j.ijinfomgt.2018.11.020

Brandi. (2021). *How To Train Your Pixel To Fetch Better Results*. https://blog.embertribe.com/train-your-facebook-pixel-to-fetch-better-results

Brechter, S. (2012, March 28). *Process 101: The Case for Process Management in Business Aviation*. Retrieved June 12, 2021, from Gray Stone Advisors: https://www.graystoneadvisors.com/process-management-in-business-aviation/

Brechter, S. (2021). *Operating Partners in Business Aviation*. Retrieved June 12, 2021, from Gray Stone Advisors: https://www.graystoneadvisors.com/operating-partners-in-business-aviation-2/

Brown, M. (2014). *Transforming Unstructured Data into Useful Information, Big Data, Mining, and Analytics*. Auerbach Publication. doi:10.1201/b16666

Brown, T. B., Mann, B., Ryder, N., Subbiah, M., Kaplan, J., Dhariwal, P., . . . Amodei, D. (2020). *Language Models are Few-Shot Learners*. arXiv:2005.14165v4.

Brühl, V. (2019). Big Data, Data Mining, Machine Learning und Predictive Analytics: Ein konzeptioneller Überblick [Big Data, Data Mining, Machine Learning and Predictive Analytics: A Conceptual Overview]. *CFS Working Paper Series, 617*. https://ssrn.com/abstract=3321195

Brunetto, Y., Teo, S., Shacklock, K., & Farr-Wharton, R. (2012). Emotional intelligence, job satisfaction, well-being and engagement: Explaining organisational commitment and turnover intentions in policing. *Human Resource Management Journal, 22*(4), 428–441. doi:10.1111/j.1748-8583.2012.00198.x

Buckley, J. J. (1985). Fuzzy hierarchical analysis. *Fuzzy Sets and Systems, 17*(3), 233–247. doi:10.1016/0165-0114(85)90090-9

Burnes, A. (2021). NVIDIA DLSS available now in Nioh 2 - The complete edition and Mount & Blade II: Bannerlord. Plus, Unreal Engine 4 DLSS Plugin released. *Nvidia*. Retrieved from https://www.nvidia.com/en-us/geforce/news/february-2021-rtx-dlss-game-update/

Cao, L. J., & Tay, F. E. H. (2003). Support vector machine with adaptive parameters in financial time series forecasting. *IEEE Transactions on Neural Networks, 14*(6), 1506–1518. doi:10.1109/TNN.2003.820556 PMID:18244595

Carion, N., Massa, F., Synnaeve, G., Usunier, N., Kirillov, A., & Zagoruyko, S. (2020). End-to-End Object Detection with Transformers. Lect. Notes Comput. Sci., 12346, 213–229. doi:10.1007/978-3-030-58452-8_13

Carpineto, C., Osiski, S., Romano, G., & Weiss, D. (2009). A survey of web clustering engines. *ACM Computing Surveys, 41*(3), 1–38. doi:10.1145/1541880.1541884

Carreira-Perpinán, M. A. (2015). *A review of mean-shift algorithms for clustering*. arXiv preprint arXiv:1503.00687.

Casebeer, J., Vale, V., Isik, U., Valin, J.-M., Giri, R., & Krishnaswamy, A. (2021). Enhancing into the Codec: Noise Robust Speech Coding with Vector-Quantized Autoencoders. *ICASSP 2021 - 2021 IEEE International Conference on Acoustics, Speech and Signal Processing (ICASSP)*. 10.1109/ICASSP39728.2021.9414605

Chakraborty, S., Bhatt, V., Chakravorty, T. (2020). *Big-data, iot wearable and mhealth cloud platform integration triads-a logical way to patient-health monitoring*. Academic Press.

Chandra, V. (2012). Work–life balance: Eastern and western perspectives. *International Journal of Human Resource Management, 23*(5), 1040–1056. doi:10.1080/09585192.2012.651339

Chang, W. H., Li, B., & Fang, X. (2014). Data collection and analysis from social network – Profile Analyzer System (PAS). In Lecture Notes in Computer Science (including subseries Lecture Notes in Artificial Intelligence and Lecture Notes in Bioinformatics) (Vol. 8643, pp. 765–772). Springer International Publishing. doi:10.1007/978-3-319-13186-3_68

Chatfield, C. (1978). The Holt - winters forecasting procedure. *Journal of the Royal Statistical Society. Series C, Applied Statistics, 27*(3), 264–279.

Chatham, M. (2018). *Glassdoor-review-scraper*. Retrieved from GitHub: https://github.com/MatthewChatham/glassdoor-review-scraper

Chebli, A., Djebbar, A., Marouani, H. F., & Lounis, H. (2021). Case-Base Maintenance: An approach based on Active Semi-Supervised Learning. *International Journal of Pattern Recognition and Artificial Intelligence, 35*(11), 2151011. doi:10.1142/S0218001421510113

Chebli, A., Djebbar, A., & Merouani, H. F. D. (2020). Improving the performance of computer-aided diagnosis systems using semi-supervised learning: A survey and analysis. *International Journal of Intelligent Information and Database Systems, 13*(2-4), 454–478. doi:10.1504/IJIIDS.2020.109466

Chelmis, C., & Prasanna, V. K. (2011). Social networking analysis: A state of the art and the effect of semantics. *Proceedings - 2011 IEEE International Conference on Privacy, Security, Risk and Trust and IEEE International Conference on Social Computing, PASSAT/SocialCom 2011*, 531–536. 10.1109/PASSAT/SocialCom.2011.23

Chen, L. (2011). Education Forum: How to Become a Good Programmer. *ACM SIGACT News, 42*(2), 77-81.

Chen, C., Li, O., Tao, D., Barnett, A., Rudin, C., & Su, J. K. (2019). This looks like that: Deep learning for interpretable image recognition. *Advances in Neural Information Processing Systems, 32*, 8930–8941.

Chen, H., Chiang, R., & Storey, V. (2012, December). Business intelligence and analytics: From big data to big impact. *Management Information Systems Quarterly, 36*(4), 1165–1188. doi:10.2307/41703503

Chen, L. (2020). How Do We Write a Good Project Report? *ACM SIGACT News, 1*(51), 118–119. doi:10.1145/3388392.3388405

Chen, T., & Guestrin, C. (2016, August). Xgboost: A scalable tree boosting system. In: *Proceedings of the 22nd ACM SigKDD International Conference on Knowledge Discovery and Data Mining* (pp. 785-794). 10.1145/2939672.2939785

Chen, X.-W., & Lin, X. (2014). Big data deep learning: Challenges and perspectives. *IEEE Access: Practical Innovations, Open Solutions, 2*, 514–525. doi:10.1109/ACCESS.2014.2325029

Chen, Y., Chiu, D. K. W., & Ho, K. K. W. (2018). Facilitating the learning of the art of Chinese painting and calligraphy at Chao Shao-an Gallery. *Micronesian Educators, 26*, 45–58.

Che, W., Fan, X., Xiong, R., & Zhao, D. (2020). Visual Relationship Embedding Network for Image Paragraph Generation. *IEEE Transactions on Multimedia, 22*(9), 2307–2320. doi:10.1109/TMM.2019.2954750

Chiu, M. C., Huang, J. H., Gupta, S., & Akman, G. (2021). Developing a personalized recommendation system in a smart product service system based on unsupervised learning model. *Computers in Industry, 128*, 103421. doi:10.1016/j.compind.2021.103421

Choudhary, V. (n.d.). *Airport and Passenger Analytics – Innovation Driven by Growth*. Retrieved April 26, 2021, from IGT Solutions: https://www.igtsolutions.com/blog/airport-and-passenger-analytics-innovation-driven-by-growth/

Chung, J., Gulcehre, C., Cho, K., & Bengio, Y. (2014). *Empirical Evaluation of Gated Recurrent Neural Networks on Sequence Modeling*. arXiv:1412.3555v1.

CISION PR Newswire. (2021). *Big Data - Global Market Trajectory & Analytics*. https://www.prnewswire.com/news-releases/global-big-data-market-to-reach-234-6-billion-by-2026--301322252.html

Çıtlak, O., Dörterler, M., & Doğru, İ. A. (2019). A survey on detecting spam accounts on Twitter network. *Social Network Analysis and Mining, 9*(1), 35. Advance online publication. doi:10.100713278-019-0582-x

Clement, J. (2021). *Leading gaming markets worldwide in 2020, by gaming revenue*. Statista. Retrieved from https://www.statista.com/statistics/308454/gaming-revenue-countries/

Clemons, E. K., Barnett, S., & Appadurai, A. (2007). The future of advertising and the value of social network websites: Some preliminary examinations. *ACM International Conference Proceeding Series, 258*, 267–276. 10.1145/1282100.1282153

Cohen, J. B. (1997). Retrospect: A Hybrid Decision Support System in the Domain of Breast Cancer Treatment Planning. *Proceedings of the AMIA Annual Fall Symposium.*

Coleman, S. Y. (2016). *Data-mining opportunities for small and medium enterprises with official statistics in the UK.* Academic Press.

Collins, C. J. (2003). Strategic Human Resource Practices, Top Management Team Social Networks, and Firm Performance: The Role of Human Resource Practices in Creating Organizational Competitive Advantage. *Academy of Management Journal*, 740–751.

Compton, P., & Kang, B. H. (2021). *Ripple-down Rules: The Alternative to Machine Learning.* CRC Press. doi:10.1201/9781003126157

Conklin, M. S. (2006). *Beyond low-hanging fruit: Seeking the next generation in floss data mining.* Paper presented at the IFIP International Conference on Open Source Systems. 10.1007/0-387-34226-5_5

Corbat, L., Nauval, M., Henriet, J., & Lapayre, J.-C. (2020). A fusion method based on deep learning and case-based reasoning which improves the resulting medical image segmentations. *Expert Systems with Applications, 147*, 113200. doi:10.1016/j.eswa.2020.113200

Corbu, E. C., Edelhauser, E., & Lupu-Dima, L. (2019). *Analytic Dashboard, a Solution for Increasing Efficiency in Management of the Public Administration.* Academic Press.

Coronel, C., Morris, S., & Rob, P. (2020). *Database Systems: Design, Implementation, and Management* (14th ed.). Course Technology, Cengage Learning.

Côrte-Real, N., Oliveira, T., & Ruivo, P. (2017). Assessing business value of Big Data Analytics in European firms. *Journal of Business Research, 70*, 379–390. doi:10.1016/j.jbusres.2016.08.011

Coussement, K., & Van den Poel, D. (2008). *Churn prediction in subscription services: An application of support vector machines while comparing two parameter-selection techniques.* Academic Press.

Craven, M. W., & Shavlik, J. W. (1997). Using neural networks for data mining. *Future Generation Computer Systems, 13*(2–3), 211–229. doi:10.1016/S0167-739X(97)00022-8

Cronbach, L. J., & Meehl, P. E. (1955). Construct validity in psycho- logical tests. *Psychological Bulletin, 52*(4), 281–302. doi:10.1037/h0040957 PMID:13245896

Cryer, J. D., & Chan, K. S. (2008). *Time series analysis: with applications in R.* Springer Science & Business Media. doi:10.1007/978-0-387-75959-3

Cunningham, H., Tablan, V., Roberts, A., & Bontcheva, K. (2013). Getting More Out of Biomedical Documents with GATE's Full Lifecycle Open Source Text Analytics. *PLoS Computational Biology, 9*(2), e1002854. doi:10.1371/journal.pcbi.1002854 PMID:23408875

Cybenko, G. (2017). Parallel computing for machine learning in social network analysis. *Proceedings - 2017 IEEE 31st International Parallel and Distributed Processing Symposium Workshops, IPDPSW 2017*, 1464–1471. 10.1109/IPDPSW.2017.178

Damaschke, C. (2020). Data Analytics. Ein Blick hinter die Kulisse [Data Analytics. A look behind the scenes]. *SparkassenZeitung.* Retrieved from: https://sparkassenzeitung.de/vertrieb/sparkassen-data-analytics-ein-blick-hinter-die-kulisse

Damaschke, C., & Giebe, C. (2020), Sparkassen-DataAnalytics: Den Datenschatz der Sparkassen-Finanzgruppe heben [Sparkassen-DataAnalytics: Lifting the Data Treasure of the Savings Banks Finance Group]. In Digitalisierung - "the next challenge" für Sparkassen Handlungsfelder zur künftigen Gestaltung des Geschäftsmodells in Sparkassen (pp. 139-154). Deutscher Sparkassenverlag.

Davenport, S. A. S. (2014). *Three big benefits of big data analytics*. http://book.itep.ru/depository/big_data/AST-0147176_Three_Big_Benefits_of_Big_Data_Analytics.pdf

Davenport, T. (2014). How strategists use "big data" to support internal business decisions, discovery and production. *Strategy and Leadership*, *42*(4), 45–50. doi:10.1108/SL-05-2014-0034

Davenport, T. H. (2013, December). Analytics 3.0. *Harvard Business Review*, 65–72.

Davenport, T., & Harris, J. (2017). *Competing on analytics: Updated, with a new introduction: The new science of winning*. Harvard Business Press.

Davidson, J., Liebald, B., Liu, J., Nandy, P., & Van Vleet, T. (2010). The YouTube video recommendation system. *RecSys'10 - Proc. 4th ACM Conf. Recomm. Syst.*, 293–296. 10.1145/1864708.1864770

De Oliveira, E. L., Torres, J. M., Moreira, R. S., & de Lima, R. A. F. (2019). Absenteeism Prediction in Call Center Using Machine Learning Algorithms. *New Knowledge in Information Systems and Technologies*, 958–968. doi:10.1007/978-3-030-16181-1_90

De Paz, J. F., Rodríguez, S., Bajo, J., & Corchado, J. M. (2009). Case-based reasoning as a decision support system for cancer diagnosis: A case study. *International Journal of Hybrid Intelligent Systems*, *6*(2), 97–110. doi:10.3233/HIS-2009-0089

Deeken, M., & Specht, K. (2017). *Zukunftsfähigkeit Deutscher Sparkassen* [Sustainability of German Savings Banks]. Springer Fachmedien Wiesbaden. doi:10.1007/978-3-658-18700-2

DeKay, S. H. (2013). Peering through Glassdoor.com: What social media can tell us about employee satisfaction and engagement. In C. M Genest (Ed.), *Proceedings: CCI Conference on Corporate Communication 2013* (pp. 369-382). New York, NY: Corporate Communication International.

Delena, D., & Demirkanb, H. (2013). Data, information and analytics as services. *Decision Support Systems*, *55*(1), 359–363. doi:10.1016/j.dss.2012.05.044

Deloitte. (2021). *The Insights-to-Action journey Using data and analytics to make better people decisions and drive business outcomes*. https://www2.deloitte.com/content/dam/Deloitte/us/Documents/human-capital/us-insights-to-action-journey-2021.pdf

Delvaux, M. (2016). *Motion for a European Parliament resolution: with recommendation to the commission on civil law rules on robotics*. Technical Report (2015/2103 (INL)).

Dena, D., & Mamo, K. (2020). *An Interior Guidance System*. Unpublished Senior Project Report, UDC.

Devlin, J., Chang, M. W., Lee, K., & Toutanova, K. (2018). *Bert: Pre-training of deep bidirectional transformers for language understanding*. arXiv preprint arXiv:1810.04805.

Devlin, J., Chang, M. W., Lee, K., & Toutanova, K. (2019). BERT: Pre-training of deep bidirectional transformers for language understanding. *NAACL HLT 2019 - 2019 Conf. North Am. Chapter Assoc. Comput. Linguist. Hum. Lang. Technol. - Proc. Conf.*, *1*, 4171–4186.

Di Capua, M., Di Nardo, E., & Petrosino, A. (2016). Unsupervised cyber bullying detection in social networks. *Proceedings - International Conference on Pattern Recognition, 0*, 432–437. 10.1109/ICPR.2016.7899672

Díaz, F., Fdez-Riverola, F., & Corchado, J. M. (2006). gene-CBR: A case-based reasoning tool for cancer diagnosis using microarray data sets. *Computational Intelligence, 22*(3-4), 254–268. doi:10.1111/j.1467-8640.2006.00287.x

Dincer, H., Hacioglu, U., Tatoglu, E., & Delen, D. (2019). *Developing a hybrid analytics approach to measure the efficiency of deposit banks*. Academic Press.

Dixit, V. V., Chand, S., & Nair, D. J. (2016). Autonomous vehicles: Disengagements, accidents and reaction times. *PLoS One, 11*(12), e0168054. doi:10.1371/journal.pone.0168054 PMID:27997566

Dixon, M. (2020, April 10). *How airport data analytics is changing airport operations*. Retrieved April 26, 2021, from Selerity: https://seleritysas.com/blog/2020/04/10/how-airport-data-analytics-is-changing-airport-operations/

Dixon, M. (2020, September 17). *Passenger data analytics forging the way forward for the aviation industry*. Retrieved May 27, 2021, from Selerity: https://seleritysas.com/blog/2020/09/17/passenger-data-analytics-the-way-forward-for-aviation-industry/

Dong, W., Liao, S., & Zhang, Z. (2018). Leveraging financial social media data for corporate fraud detection. *Journal of Management Information Systems, 35*(2), 461–487. doi:10.1080/07421222.2018.1451954

Dorogush, A. V., Ershov, V., & Gulin, A. (2018). *CatBoost: gradient boosting with categorical features support*. arXiv preprint arXiv:1810.11363.

Doshi-Velez, F., Kortz, M., Budish, R., Bavitz, C., Gershman, S., O'Brien, D., . . . Wood, A. (2017). *Accountability of AI under the law: The role of explanation*. arXiv preprint arXiv:.01134.

Dosovitskiy, A., Beyer, L., Kolesnikov, A., Weissenborn, D., Zhai, X., Unterthiner, T., . . . Houlsby, N. (2021). *An Image is Worth 16x16 Words: Transformers for Image Recognition at Scale*. arXiv:2010.11929v2.

Dou, D., Wang, H., & Liu, H. (2015). Semantic data mining: A survey of ontology-based approaches. *Proceedings of the 2015 IEEE 9th International Conference on Semantic Computing, IEEE ICSC 2015*, 244–251. 10.1109/ICOSC.2015.7050814

Dredge, R., Gleeson, J., & De La Piedad Garcia, X. (2014). Cyberbullying in social networking sites: An adolescent victim's perspective. *Computers in Human Behavior, 36*, 13–20. doi:10.1016/j.chb.2014.03.026

Drivas, I. C., Sakas, D. P., & Reklitis, P. (2017). Improving Website Usability and Traffic Based on Users Perceptions and Suggestions – A User-Centered Digital Marketing Approach. Strategic Innovative Marketing, 255-266.

Drummer, D., Jerenz, A., Siebelt, P., & Thaten, M. (2016). *FinTech – Challenges and Opportunities How digitization is transforming the financial sector*. McKinsey & Company. https://www.mckinsey.com/industries/financial-services/our-insights/fintech-challenges-and-opportunities

Duan, J., & Jiao, F. (2021). Novel Case-Based Reasoning System for Public Health Emergencies. *Risk Management and Healthcare Policy, 14*, 541–553. doi:10.2147/RMHP.S291441 PMID:33603520

Dugan, R. F. Jr. (2011). A survey of computer science capstone course literature. *Computer Science Education, 21*(3), 201–267. doi:10.1080/08993408.2011.606118

Durbin, J., & Koopman, S. J. (2012). *Time series analysis by state space methods*. Oxford University Press. doi:10.1093/acprof:oso/9780199641178.001.0001

Dynasty Warriors. (n.d.). In *Wikipedia*. Retrieved from https://en.wikipedia.org/wiki/Dynasty_Warriors

Eigenkapitalrentabilität nach Steuern der Sparkassen in Deutschland in den Jahren von 1994 bis 2018 [Return on equity after taxes of savings banks in Germany in the years 1994 to 2018]. (n.d.). https://de.statista.com/statistik/daten/studie/242273/umfrage/eigenkapitalrentabilitaet-der-sparkassen-in-deutschland/

Eiloart, J. (2018, December 2). *Top five business analytics intelligence trends for 2019.* Retrieved from https://www.information-age.com/business-analytics-intelligence-123477004/

Eisenstadt, V., Langenhan, C., & Althoff, K.-D. (2019). *Generation of Floor Plan Variations with Convolutional Neural Networks and Case-based Reasoning-An approach for transformative adaptation of room configurations within a framework for support of early conceptual design phases.* Academic Press.

El Barachi, M., AlKhatib, M., Mathew, S., & Oroumchian, F. (2021). A novel sentiment analysis framework for monitoring the evolving public opinion in real-time: Case study on climate change. *Journal of Cleaner Production, 312,* 127820. doi:10.1016/j.jclepro.2021.127820

Elahi, M., Ricci, F., & Rubens, N. (2013). Active learning strategies for rating elicitation in collaborative filtering: A system-wide perspective. *ACM Transactions on Intelligent Systems and Technology, 5*(1), 1–33. doi:10.1145/2542182.2542195

El, F., & Gamal, A. (2013). An Educational Data Mining Model for Predicting Student Performance in Programming Course. *International Journal of Computers and Applications, 70*(17), 22–28. doi:10.5120/12160-8163

Ellul, J., Pace, G., & McCarthy, S. (2021). *Regulating Artificial Intelligence: A Technology Regulator's Perspective.* Paper presented at the ICAIL'21, ICAIL '21: Proceedings of the Eighteenth International Conference on Artificial Intelligence and LawJune 21–25, 2021, São Paulo, Brazil. 10.1145/3462757.3466093

Eltermann, F., Godoy, A., & Von Zuben, F. J. (2020). Effects of Social Ties in Knowledge Diffusion: case study on PLOS ONE. *Anais Do Brazilian Workshop on Social Network Analysis and Mining ({BraSNAM}),* 97–108. 10.5753/brasnam.2016.6448

EM360 Tech. (2020, September 18). *Top 10 Cloud Data Warehouse Solution Providers.* Retrieved August 25, 2021, from https://em360tech.com/data_management/tech-features-featuredtech-news/top-10-cloud-data-warehouse-solution-providers

Engelbart, D. C. (1962). *Augmenting human intellect: A conceptual framework.* Retrieved from http://www.dougengelbart.org/pubs/augment-3906.html

Entwicklung der Cost-Income-Ratio der Sparkassen in Deutschland in den Jahren von 1998 bis 2018 [Development of the cost-income ratio of savings banks in Germany in the years 1998 to 2018]. (n.d.). https://de.statista.com/statistik/daten/studie/197223/umfrage/cost-income-ratio-der-sparkassen-in-deutschland-seit-2007/

Erdélyi, O. J., & Goldsmith, J. (2018). Regulating artificial intelligence: Proposal for a global solution. *Proceedings of the 2018 AAAI/ACM Conference on AI, Ethics, and Society.* 10.1145/3278721.3278731

Ernst & Young Global Limited. (2015). *Becoming an analytics driven.* Retrieved September 17, 2021, from https://assets.ey.com/content/dam/ey-sites/ey-com/en_gl/topics/digital/ey-global-becoming-an-analytics-driven-organization.pdf

EuSpRIG. (2021). *Basic Research.* Retrieved 06 12, 2021, from European Spreadsheet Risk Interest Group (EuSpRIG): http://www.eusprig.org/basic-research.htm

Everton, S. F. (2012). Disrupting Dark Networks. In *Disrupting Dark Networks.* Cambridge University Press. doi:10.1017/CBO9781139136877

Fan, C.-Y., Chang, P.-C., Lin, J.-J., & Hsieh, J. (2011). A hybrid model combining case-based reasoning and fuzzy decision tree for medical data classification. *Applied Soft Computing, 11*(1), 632–644. doi:10.1016/j.asoc.2009.12.023

Fang, J., Chiu, D. K. W., & Ho, K. K. W. (2020). Exploring Cryptocurrency Sentimental with Clustering Text Mining on Social Media. In Z. Sun (Ed.), Handbook of Research on Intelligent Analytics with Multi-Industry Applications (pp. 157–171). Academic Press.

Fan, J., Zhang, K., Huang, Y., Zhu, Y., & Chen, B. (2021). Parallel spatio-temporal attention-based TCN for multivariate time series prediction. *Neural Computing & Applications*, 1–10. doi:10.100700521-021-05958-z

Fan, S., Lau, R. Y., & Zhao, J. L. (2015). Demystifying Big Data Analytics for Business Intelligence Through the Lens of Marketing Mix. *Big Data Research*, 2(1), 28–32. doi:10.1016/j.bdr.2015.02.006

Fan, W., & Gordon, M. D. (2014). The power of social media analytics. *Communications of the ACM*, 57(6), 74–81. doi:10.1145/2602574

Fatima, A., Nazir, N., & Khan, M. G. (2017). Data cleaning in data warehouse: A survey of data pre-processing techniques and tools. *IJ Information Technology and Computer Science*, 3(3), 50–61. doi:10.5815/ijitcs.2017.03.06

Fattah, A., Lock, H., Buller, W., & Kirby, S. (2009). Smart Airports: Transforming Passenger Experience To Thrive in the New Economy. *Cisco Internet Business Solutions Group (IBSG)*, 1-16. Retrieved April &, 2020, from https://pdfs.semanticscholar.org/b579/1c0c4db633817f7c81f1bb0214081f1d3aa3.pdf

Fenech, R., Baguant, P., & Ivanov, D. (2019). The changing role of human resource management in an era of digital transformation. *International Journal of Entrepreneurship*, 22(2). https://www.abacademies.org/articles/the-changing-role-of-human-resource-management-in-an-era-of-digital-transformation-8154.html

Financial Centre Futures. (2020). *The Global Financial Centres Index 28*. Long Finance.

Flach, P. A., & Lachiche, N. (2004). Naive Bayesian classification of structured data. *Machine Learning*, 57(3), 233–269. doi:10.1023/B:MACH.0000039778.69032.ab

Foy, M. (2020, December 12). *Management by Data*. Retrieved May 4, 2021, from Berkeley Haas: newsroom.haas.berkeley.edu/magazine/fall-winter-2020/management-by-data/

Franco, P. G., Matthews, J. L., & Matlock, T. (2016). Framing the past: How virtual experience affects bodily description artefacts. *Journal of Cultural Heritage*, 17, 179–187. doi:10.1016/j.culher.2015.04.006

Freberg, K. (2017). *United Airlines crisis: PR takeaways & social media insights*. https://karenfreberg.com/blog/united-airlines-crisis-pr-takeaways-social-media-insights/

Freeman, L. C. (1977). A Set of Measures of Centrality Based on Betweenness. *Sociometry*, 40(1), 35. doi:10.2307/3033543

Freeman, L. C. (1978). Centrality in social networks conceptual clarification. *Social Networks*, 1(3), 215–239. doi:10.1016/0378-8733(78)90021-7

Friedman, J. H. (2001). Greedy function approximation: A gradient boosting machine. *Annals of Statistics*, 29(5), 1189–1232. doi:10.1214/aos/1013203451

Fu, D., Ionescu, C. M., Aghezzaf, E.-H., De Keyser, R. (2014). *Decentralized and centralized model predictive control to reduce the bullwhip effect in supply chain management*. Academic Press.

Fu, X., Liu, W., Xu, Y., & Cui, L. (2017). Combine HowNet lexicon to train phrase recursive autoencoder for sentence-level sentiment analysis. *Neurocomputing*, 241, 18–27. doi:10.1016/j.neucom.2017.01.079

Gacanin, H., & Wagner, M. (2019). Artificial Intelligence Paradigm for Customer Experience Management in Next-Generation Networks: Challenges and Perspectives. *IEEE Network*, 33(2), 188–194. doi:10.1109/MNET.2019.1800015

Gal, Y., & Ghahramani, Z. (2016). A theoretically grounded application of dropout in recurrent neural networks. *Advances in Neural Information Processing Systems*, *29*, 1019–1027.

Ganai, A. F., & Khursheed, F. (2020). Predicting next Word using RNN and LSTM cells: Stastical Language Modeling. *2019 Fifth Int. Conf. Image Inf. Process.*, 469–474. 10.1109/ICIIP47207.2019.8985885

Gao, W., Lam, K. M., Chiu, D. K. W., & Ho, K. K. W. (2020). A Big data Analysis of the Factors Influencing Movie Box Office in China. In Z. Sun (Ed.), Handbook of Research on Intelligent Analytics with Multi-Industry Applications (pp. 232–249). Academic Press.

Gao, Y., Wang, F., Luan, H., & Chua, T. S. (2014). Brand data gathering from live social media streams. *ICMR 2014 - Proceedings of the ACM International Conference on Multimedia Retrieval 2014*, 169–176. 10.1145/2578726.2578748

Gao, X., Braden, B., Zhang, L., Taylor, S., Pang, W., & Petridis, M. (2019). Case-based reasoning of a deep learning network for prediction of early stage of oesophageal cancer. *Proceedings of the 24th UK Symposium on Case-Based Reasoning*.

García, S., Ramírez-Gallego, S., & Luengo, J. (2016). Big data preprocessing: methods and prospects. *Big Data Analytics*, *1*(9), 1-22. doi:10.1186/s41044-016-0014-0

Gardner, E. S. Jr. (1985). Exponential smoothing: The state of the art. *Journal of Forecasting*, *4*(1), 1–28. doi:10.1002/for.3980040103

Gartner. (2017). *Glossary. Information Technology Glossary. Augmented Analytics*. Retrieved from https://www.gartner.com/en/information-technology/glossary/augmented-analytics

Gartner. (2020). *Magic Quadrant for Data Integration Tools*. Retrieved from https://www.gartner.com/en/documents/3989223/magic-quadrant-for-data-integration-tools

Gartner. (2021). *Analytics and Business Intelligence Platforms Reviews and Ratings*. Retrieved from https://www.gartner.com/reviews/market/analytics-business-intelligence-platforms

Gartner. (n.d.). *Gartner Glossary for the term Business Analytics*. https://www.gartner.com/en/information-technology/glossary/business-analytics

Gartner-diagnostic analytics. (2020). *Diagnostic Analytics*. Retrieved August 12, 2020, from Gartner: https://www.gartner.com/en/information-technology/glossary/diagnostic-analytics

Gasmi, S., Djebbar, A., & Merouani, H. F. (2021). *Case-Based Reasoning in Medicine: A survey*. Paper presented at the First National Conference on Artificial Intelligence and Information Technologies (CNIATI'21), University El-Tarf.

Gasser, U., & Almeida, V. A. (2017). A layered model for AI governance. *IEEE Internet Computing*, *21*(6), 58–62. doi:10.1109/MIC.2017.4180835

Gek, D., Kukartsev, V., Tynchenko, V., Bondarev, A., Pokushko, M., & Dalisova, N. (2019). The Problem of SEO promotion for the organization's web representation. *SHS Web of Conferences*, *69*, 1-6.

Gelbard, R. R.-G., Ramon-Gonen, R., Carmeli, A., Bittmann, R. M., & Talyansky, R. (2018). Sentiment analysis in organizational work: Towards an ontology of people analytics. *Expert Systems: International Journal of Knowledge Engineering and Neural Networks*, *35*(5), e12289. Advance online publication. doi:10.1111/exsy.12289

Gharieb, M. E. (2021). The Effect of Online Marketing through Social Media Platforms on Saudi Public Libraries. *Journal of Information Technology Management*, (Special Issue), 238–262.

Ghasemaghaei, M., Ebrahimi, S., & Hassanein, K. (2018). Data analytics competency for improving firm decision making performance. *The Journal of Strategic Information Systems, 27*, 101–113.

Ghavami, P. (2020). Big Data Analytics Methods: Analytics Techniques in Data Mining, Deep Learning and Natural Language Processing (2nd ed.). de Gruyter.

Giachanou, A., & Crestani, F. (2016). Like it or not: A survey of Twitter sentiment analysis methods. *ACM Computing Surveys, 49*(2), 28. doi:10.1145/2938640

Gibbons, F. X. (1990). Self-attention and behavior: A review and theoretical update. *Advances in Experimental Social Psychology, 23*, 249–303. doi:10.1016/S0065-2601(08)60321-4

Giebe, C. (2019). The Chief Digital Officer – Savior for the Digitalization in German Banks? *Journal of Economic Development, Environment and People, 8*(3), 6–15. doi:10.26458/jedep.v8i3.633

Giebe, C., Hammerström, L., & Zwerenz, D. (2019). Big Data & Analytics as a sustainable Customer Loyalty Instrument in Banking and Finance. *Financial Markets, Institutions and Risks, 3*(4), 74–88. doi:10.21272/fmir.3(4).74-88.2019

Giebe, C., & Schulz, K. (2021). Economic effects of the digital transformation on the banking market using the example of savings banks and cooperative banks in Germany. *International Journal of Economics and Finance, 13*(6), 34. Advance online publication. doi:10.5539/ijef.v13n6p34

Globe Newswire. (2021, January 8). *Global Aviation Analytics Market Report 2020: COVID-19 Could Affect Aviation Analytics Services by 40-45% - Forecast to 2025*. Retrieved May 06, 2021, from Globe Newswire: globenewswire.com/fr/news-release/2021/01/08/2155631/0/en/Global-Aviation-Analytics-Market-Report-2020-COVID-19-Could-Affect-Aviation-Analytics-Services-by-40-45-Forecast-to-2025.html

Goga, O., Loiseau, P., Sommer, R., Teixeira, R., & Gummadi, K. P. (2015). On the reliability of profile matching across large online social networks. *Proceedings of the ACM SIGKDD International Conference on Knowledge Discovery and Data Mining, 2015-August*, 1799–1808. 10.1145/2783258.2788601

Gomez-Uribe, C. A., & Hunt, N. (2015). The netflix recommender system: Algorithms, business value, and innovation. *ACM Transactions on Management Information Systems, 6*(4), 1–19. Advance online publication. doi:10.1145/2843948

Gong, M., Li, G., Wang, Z., Ma, L., & Tian, D. (2016). An efficient shortest path approach for social networks based on community structure. *CAAI Transactions on Intelligence Technology, 1*(1), 114–123. doi:10.1016/j.trit.2016.03.011

Goodfellow, I., Pouget-Abadie, J., Mirza, M., Xu, B., Warde-Farley, D., Ozair, S., ... Bengio, Y. (2014). Generative adversarial nets. *Advances in Neural Information Processing Systems, 27*.

Gordon, C. A. K., Burnak, B., Onel, M., & Pistikopoulos, E. (2020). Data-Driven Prescriptive Maintenance. *Failure Prediction Using Ensemble Support Vector Classification for Optimal Process and Maintenance Scheduling, 59*(44), 19607–19622.

Goyal, A., Bonchi, F., & Lakshmanan, L. V. S. (2010). Learning influence probabilities in social networks. *WSDM 2010 - Proceedings of the 3rd ACM International Conference on Web Search and Data Mining*, 241–250. 10.1145/1718487.1718518

Grace, K., Maher, M. L., Wilson, D. C., & Najjar, N. A. (2016). *Combining CBR and deep learning to generate surprising recipe designs*. Paper presented at the International Conference on Case-Based Reasoning. 10.1007/978-3-319-47096-2_11

Graves, A., Jaitly, N., & Mohamed, A. R. (2013, December). Hybrid speech recognition with deep bidirectional LSTM. In *2013 IEEE workshop on automatic speech recognition and understanding* (pp. 273-278). IEEE.

Graves, A., & Schmidhuber, J. (2005). Framewise phoneme classification with bidirectional LSTM and other Neural Network Architectures. *Neural Networks: The Official Journal of the International Neural Network Society*, *18*(5–6), 602–610. doi:10.1016/j.neunet.2005.06.042 PMID:16112549

Gronau, N., Thim, C., & Fohrholz, C. (2016). Business Analytics in der deutschen Praxis [Business Analytics in der deutschen Praxis.]. *Controlling*, *28*(8–9), 472–479. doi:10.15358/0935-0381-2016-8-9-472

Gu, D., Liang, C., & Zhao, H. (2017). A case-based reasoning system based on weighted heterogeneous value distance metric for breast cancer diagnosis. *Artificial Intelligence in Medicine*, *77*, 31–47. doi:10.1016/j.artmed.2017.02.003 PMID:28545610

Guessoum, S., Laskri, M. T., & Lieber, J. (2014). RespiDiag: A case-based reasoning system for the diagnosis of chronic obstructive pulmonary disease. *Expert Systems with Applications*, *41*(2), 267–273. doi:10.1016/j.eswa.2013.05.065

Gupta, P. (2015). Human Resource Analytics in Indian Banking Sector. *IJISRT*.

Gupta, M., & George, J. F. (2016). Toward the development of a big data analytics capability. *Information & Management*, *53*(8), 1049–1064. doi:10.1016/j.im.2016.07.004

Hafaiedh, K., Rhouma, M. B., Chargui, F., Haouas, Y., & Kerkeni, A. (2020). AdRobot: a smart segmentation application for automated & personalized marketing campaigns. *Proceedings of the 2nd International Conference on Digital Tools & Uses Congress*. 10.1145/3423603.3424052

Hammerström, L. (2018). Organizational Design of Big Data and Analytics Teams. *European Journal of Social Science Education and Research*, *5*(3), 132–149. doi:10.2478/ejser-2018-0065

Han, K., Wang, Y., Chen, H., Chen, X., Guo, J., Liu, Z., . . . Tao, D. (2021). *A Survey on Visual Transformer*. arXiv:2012.12556v3.

Hare, J. S., Lewis, P. H., Enser, P. G. B., & Sandom, C. J. (2007). Semantic facets: An in-depth analysis of a semantic image retrieval system. *Proceedings of the 6th ACM International Conference on Image and Video Retrieval, CIVR 2007*, 250–257. 10.1145/1282280.1282320

Harvard Business Review. (2014). *What VUCA Really Means for You*. https://hbr.org/2014/01/what-vuca-really-means-for-you

Harvey, A., & DeFreitas, C. (2019). How long does it take to beat RDR2. *Imagine Games Network*. Retrieved from https://www.ign.com/wikis/red-dead-redemption-2/How_Long_Does_It_Take_to_Beat_RDR2

He, K., Zhang, X., Ren, S., & Sun, J. (2016). Deep residual learning for image recognition. *Proceedings of the IEEE Computer Society Conference on Computer Vision and Pattern Recognition*, 770–778. 10.1109/CVPR.2016.90

He, K., Zhang, X., Ren, S., & Sun, J. (2016). Deep residual learning for image recognition. *Proceedings of the IEEE conference on computer vision and pattern recognition*.

Helskyaho, H., Yu, J., & Yu, K. (2021). *Machine Learning for Oracle Database Professionals*. Apress. doi:10.1007/978-1-4842-7032-5

Henke, N., & Bughin, J. (2016, December). *The Age of Analytics: Competing in a Data-Driven World*. McKinsey Global Institute.

Henry, N., & Fekete, J. D. (2007). MatLink: Enhanced matrix visualization for analyzing social networks. In Lecture Notes in Computer Science (including subseries Lecture Notes in Artificial Intelligence and Lecture Notes in Bioinformatics): Vol. 4663 LNCS (Issue PART 2, pp. 288–302). Springer Berlin Heidelberg. doi:10.1007/978-3-540-74800-7_24

Hinton, G. E., Osindero, S., & Teh, Y.-W. (2006). A fast learning algorithm for deep belief nets. *Neural Computation, 18*(7), 1527–1554. doi:10.1162/neco.2006.18.7.1527 PMID:16764513

Hoang, K. (2018). *Neural Network in Natural Language Processing.* Unpublished Senior Project Report, UDC.

Hochreiter, S. (1998). The vanishing gradient problem during learning recurrent neural nets and problem solutions. *International Journal of Uncertainty, Fuzziness and Knowledge-based Systems, 6*(02), 107–116. doi:10.1142/S0218488598000094

Hochreiter, S., & Schmidhuber, J. (1997). Long Short-Term Memory. *Neural Computation, 9*(8), 1735–1780. doi:10.1162/neco.1997.9.8.1735 PMID:9377276

Holsapple, C., Lee-Postb, A., & Pakath, R. (2014). A unified foundation for business analytics. *Decision Support Systems, 64*, 130–141. doi:10.1016/j.dss.2014.05.013

Holst, A. (2021). *Volume of data/information created, captured, copied, and consumed worldwide from 2010 to 2025.* https://www.statista.com/statistics/871513/worldwide-data-created/

Hong, J., Oh, J., & Lee, H. (2019). Smart Airport and Next Generation Security Screening. *Electronics and Telecommunications Trend, 34*(2), 73–82. doi:10.22648/ETRI.2019.J.340208

Hopkins, J., & Hawking, P. (2018). *Big Data Analytics and IoT in logistics: a case study.* Academic Press.

Howard, A.G., Zhu, M., Chen, B., Kalenichenko, D., Wang, W., Weyand, T., Andreetto, M., & Adam, H. (2017). *MobileNets: Efficient Convolutional Neural Networks for Mobile Vision Applications.* Academic Press.

Howard, A., Sandler, M., Chen, B., Wang, W., Chen, L. C., Tan, M., Chu, G., Vasudevan, V., Zhu, Y., Pang, R., Le, Q., & Adam, H. (2019). Searching for mobileNetV3. *Proceedings of the IEEE International Conference on Computer Vision*, 1314–1324. 10.1109/ICCV.2019.00140

Howson, C., Richardson, J., Sallam, R., & Kronz, A. (2019). *Magic Quadrant for Analytics and Business Intelligence Platforms.* Retrieved 7 7, 2019, from Gartner: https://cadran-analytics.nl/wp-content/uploads/2019/02/2019-Gartner-Magic-Quadrant-for-Analytics-and-Business-Intelligence-Platforms.pdf

Howson, C., Sallam, R. L., & Richa, J. L. (2018, Feb 26). *Magic Quadrant for Analytics and Business Intelligence Platforms.* Retrieved Aug 16, 2018, from Gartner: www.gartner.com

Hu, D. (2018) *An Introductory Survey on Attention Mechanisms in NLP Problems.* arXiv:1811.05544

Hu, J., Liu, M., & Zhang, J. (2014). A semantic model for academic social network analysis. *ASONAM 2014 - Proceedings of the 2014 IEEE/ACM International Conference on Advances in Social Networks Analysis and Mining*, 310–313. 10.1109/ASONAM.2014.6921602

Huai, Z. (2018, December 28). *How big data and AI will transform Shenzhen Airport.* Retrieved May 19, 2020, from Huawei: https://www.huawei.com/en/about-huawei/publications/winwin-magazine/32/shenzhen-airport-digital-platform-and-ai

Huang, G., Liu, Z., Van Der Maaten, L., & Weinberger, K. Q. (2017). Densely Connected Convolutional Networks. *Proc. IEEE Conf. Comput. Vis. pattern Recognit.*, 4700–4708. 10.1109/CVPR.2017.243

Huang, M.-J., Chen, M.-Y., & Lee, S.-C. (2007). Integrating data mining with case-based reasoning for chronic diseases prognosis and diagnosis. *Expert Systems with Applications, 32*(3), 856–867. doi:10.1016/j.eswa.2006.01.038

Huang, P. S., Paulino, Y., So, S., Chiu, D. K. W., & Ho, K. K. W. (2021). Special Issue Editorial - COVID-19 Pandemic and Health Informatics (Part 1). *Library Hi Tech, 39*(3), 693–695. doi:10.1108/LHT-09-2021-324

Huselid, M. (1995). The Impact of Human Resource Management Practices on Turnover, Productivity, and Corporate Financial Performance. *Academy of Management Journal, 38*, 635–672.

Hyndman, R. J., Koehler, A. B., Snyder, R. D., & Grose, S. (2002). A state space framework for automatic forecasting using exponential smoothing methods. *International Journal of Forecasting, 18*(3), 439–454. doi:10.1016/S0169-2070(01)00110-8

Iansiti, M. (2021). *The Value of Data and Its Impact on Competition.* Academic Press.

IBM. (2018). *Cognitive computing. Preparing for the Future of Artificial Intelligence.* Retrieved from https://research.ibm.com/cognitive-computing/ostp/rfi-response.shtml

IDC. (2019). *IDC Forecasts Revenues for Big Data and Business Analytics Solutions will Reach $189.1 Billion This Year with Double-Digit Annual Growth Through 2022.* Retrieved 1 23, 2020, from IDC: https://www.idc.com/getdoc.jsp?containerId=prUS44998419

IDC. (2021). *IDC Forecasts Improved Growth for Global AI Market in 2021.* https://www.idc.com/getdoc.jsp?containerId=prUS47482321

Ilie, O.-M., Popescu, C., & Iacob, S. E. (2017). Transforming the Banking Organization in the Context of Digital Economy. *Proceedings RCE, 2017*, 284–292. doi:10.18662/lumproc.rce2017.1.24

INFORMS. (2015). *Best definition of analytics.* https://www.informs.org/About-INFORMS/News-Room/O.R.-and-Analytics-in-the-News/Best-definition-of-analytics

Inoue, H., & Ye, S. Y. (2020). University students' Twitter usage and subjective well-being. *IEICE Technical Report, 119*(394), 83–88.

ITmagazin. (2019). Data Analytics. 360 Grad – den Kunden im Blick [Data Analytics. 360 degrees - the customer in view]. *ITmagazin 3/2019.* https://www.f-i.de/News/ITmagazin/Archiv/2019/Einfach.-Machen/Titelthema/360-Grad-den-Kunden-im-Blick

ITmagazin. (2020). Sparkassen-DataAnalytics. Es geht weiter! [Savings Banks DataAnalytics. It goes on!]. *ITmagazin 2/2020.* https://www.f-i.de/News/ITmagazin/Archiv/2020/Mit-Abstand-gut-beraten/Loesungen-Praxis/Es-geht-weiter

Jaffer, S., & Timbrell, G. (2014). Digital Strategy in Airports. In *25 Australasian Conference on Information Systems-Digital Strategy in Airports* (pp. 1-11). Australasian Conference on Information Systems (ACIS).

Jain, R., & Nayyar, A. (2018). Predicting Employee Attrition using XGBoost Machine Learning Approach. *2018 International Conference on System Modeling & Advancement in Research Trends.* 10.1109/SYSMART.2018.8746940

Janani, P., Verma, S., Natarajan, S., & Sinha, A. K. (2019). Communication Using IoT. In Information and Communication Technology for Sustainable Development, Advances in Intelligent Systems and Computing. Springer Singapore. doi:10.1007/978-981-13-7166-0

Jan, B., Farman, H., Khan, M., Imran, M., Islam, I. U., Ahmad, A., Ali, S., & Jeon, G. (2019). Deep learning in big data Analytics: A comparative study. *Computers & Electrical Engineering, 75*, 275–287. doi:10.1016/j.compeleceng.2017.12.009

Janke, D., Staab, S., & Thimm, M. (2018). Impact analysis of data placement strategies on query efforts in distributed RDF stores. *Journal of Web Semantics, 50*, 21–48. doi:10.1016/j.websem.2018.02.002

Janssen, M., Matheus, R., Longo, J., & Weerakkody, V. (2017). Transparency-by-design as a foundation for open government. *Transforming Government: People, Process and Policy, 11*(1).

Janssen, M., Matheus, R., & Zuiderwijk, A. (2015). Big and Open Linked Data (BOLD) to Create Smart Cities and Citizens: Insights from Smart Energy and Mobility Cases. In E. Tambouris, M. Janssen, H. J. Scholl, M. A. Wimmer, K. Tarabanis, M. Gascó, B. Klievink, I. Lindgren, & P. Parycek (Eds.), *Electronic Government* (Vol. 9248, pp. 79–90). Springer International Publishing. doi:10.1007/978-3-319-22479-4_6

Jin, Y., Khan, L., Wang, L., & Awad, M. (2005). Image annotations by combining multiple evidence & WordNet. *Proceedings of the 13th ACM International Conference on Multimedia, MM 2005*, 706–715. 10.1145/1101149.1101305

Ji, S., Kim, J., & Im, H. (2019). A comparative study of bitcoin price prediction using deep learning. *Mathematics*, *7*(10), 898. doi:10.3390/math7100898

Ji, S., Li, W., Gong, N. Z., Mittal, P., & Beyah, R. (2015). On Your Social Network De-anonymizablity: Quantification and Large Scale Evaluation with Seed Knowledge. *Proceedings 2015 Network and Distributed System Security Symposium*. 10.14722/ndss.2015.23096

Johnson, K., Tanner, M., Lalla, N., & Kawalski, D. (2013). Social capital: The benefit of Facebook "Friends.". *Behaviour & Information Technology*, *32*(1), 24–36. doi:10.1080/0144929X.2010.550063

Jung, Y., Pawlowski, S. D., & Kim, H.-W. (2017). Exploring associations between young adults' Facebook use and psychological well-being: A goal hierarchy approach. *International Journal of Information Management*, *37*(1), 1391–1404.

Kabakus, A. T., & Kara, R. (2018). TwitterSentiDetector: A domain-independent Twitter sentiment analyser. *INFOR*, *56*(5), 137–162. doi:10.1080/03155986.2017.1340797

Kahya-Özyirmidokuz, E. (2016). Analyzing unstructured Facebook social network data through web text mining: A study of online shopping firms in Turkey. *Information Development*, *32*(1), 70–80. doi:10.1177/0266666914528523

Kamit, M. H., & Mulualem, K. (2020). *Hands-Free Signaling*. Unpublished Senior Project Report, UDC.

Kan, Z. J., & Sourin, A. (2020). Generation of Irregular Music Patterns with Deep Learning. *Proc. - 2020 Int. Conf. Cyberworlds, CW 2020*, 188–195. 10.1109/CW49994.2020.00038

Kantardzic, M. (2011). *Data Mining: Concepts, Models, Methods, and Algorithms*. Wiley & IEEE Press. doi:10.1002/9781118029145

Karabarbounis, M., & Pinto, S. (2018). What Can We Learn from Online Wage Postings? Evidence from Glassdoor. *Economic Quarterly*, 173-189.

Kasthuri, S., & Jebaseeli, A. N. (2020). Social Network Analysis in Data Processing. *Adalya Journal*, *9*(2), 260–264.

Kauffmann, E., Peral, J., Gil, D., Ferrández, A., Sellers, R., & Mora, H. (2019). *Managing marketing decision-making with sentiment analysis: An evaluation of the main product features using text data mining*. Academic Press.

KDnuggets. (2019). *Statistical Modelling vs Machine Learning*. https://www.kdnuggets.com/2019/08/statistical-modelling-vs-machine-learning.html

Keane, M. T., Kenny, E. M., Temraz, M., Greene, D., & Smyth, B. (2021). *Twin Systems for DeepCBR: A Menagerie of Deep Learning and Case-Based Reasoning Pairings for Explanation and Data Augmentation*. arXiv preprint arXiv:2104.14461.

Ke, G., Meng, Q., Finley, T., Wang, T., Chen, W., Ma, W., ... Liu, T. Y. (2017). Lightgbm: A highly efficient gradient boosting decision tree. *Advances in Neural Information Processing Systems*, *30*, 3146–3154.

Kempe, D., Kleinberg, J., & Tardos, É. (2003). Maximizing the spread of influence through a social network. *Proceedings of the ACM SIGKDD International Conference on Knowledge Discovery and Data Mining*, 137–146. 10.1145/956750.956769

Khan, S., Naseer, M., Hayat, M., Zamir, S. W., Khan, F. S., & Shah, M. (2021). Transformers in Vision. *Survey (London, England)*, 1–28. arXiv2101.01169v2

Kherbachi, S., Benkhider, N., & Keddari, N. (2020). Application of pagerank in virtual organization architecture. *Researchpedia Journal of Computing.*, *1*(1), 1–14.

Kiron, D., & Shockley, R. (2011). Creating business value with analytics. *MIT Sloan Management Review*, *53*(1), 57–63.

Kitamura, S., Kawai, D., & Sasaki, Y. (2017). Relationships between the use of emotional terms on social media, posting motives, and network structure: Focusing on positive and negative emotional terms in Twitter. *The Japanese Journal of Language in Society*, *20*(1), 16–28.

Kitchens, B., Dobolyi, D., Li, J., & Abbasi, A. (2018). Advanced customer analytics: Strategic value through integration of relationship-oriented big data. *Journal of Management Information Systems*, *35*(2), 540–574. doi:10.1080/0742122 2.2018.1451957

Kitchin, R. (2014). Big Data, new epistemologies and paradigm shifts. *Big Data & Society*, *1*(1), 1–12. doi:10.1177/2053951714528481

Kittler, J., Hatef, M., Duin, R. P., & Matas, J. (1998). On combining classifiers. *IEEE Transactions on Pattern Analysis and Machine Intelligence*, *20*(3), 226–239. doi:10.1109/34.667881

Knapp, J., Zeratsky, J., & Kowitz, B. (2016). *Sprint: How to solve big problems and test new ideas in just five days.* Simon and Schuster.

KnightW. (2017). *Paying with Your Face.* https://www.technologyreview.com/technology/paying-with-your-face/

Knoke, D. (2015). Emerging Trends in Social Network Analysis of Terrorism and Counterterrorism. In *Emerging Trends in the Social and Behavioral Sciences* (pp. 1–15). Wiley. doi:10.1002/9781118900772.etrds0106

Ko, E., Taylor, C. R., Sung, H., Lee, J., Wagner, U., Navarro, D. M.-C., & Wang, F. (2012). *Global marketing segmentation usefulness in the sportswear industry.* Academic Press.

Kohli, D. (2018, November 2). *Big data facilitating the working towards a smart future.* Retrieved August 4, 2020, from International Airport Review: https://www.internationalairportreview.com/article/77340/working-towards-smart-future/

Komorowski, P. (2020), Role of digitization for German saving banks, In Digitalisierung - "the next challenge" für Sparkassen Handlungsfelder zur künftigen Gestaltung des Geschäftsmodells in Sparkassen (pp. 329-345). Deutscher Sparkassenverlag.

Kooi, T., Litjens, G., Van Ginneken, B., Gubern-Mérida, A., Sánchez, C. I., Mann, R., den Heeten, A., & Karssemeijer, N. (2017). Large scale deep learning for computer aided detection of mammographic lesions. *Medical Image Analysis*, *35*, 303–312. doi:10.1016/j.media.2016.07.007 PMID:27497072

Kothari, R., & Dong, M. (2001). Decision trees for classification: A review and some new results. *Pattern recognition: From classical to modern approaches*, 169-184.

Kou, F., Du, J., He, Y., & Ye, L. (2016). Social network search based on semantic analysis and learning. *CAAI Transactions on Intelligence Technology*, *1*(4), 293–302. doi:10.1016/j.trit.2016.12.001

Kovach, S., & Ruggiero, W. V. (2011). Online banking fraud detection based on local and global behavior. *Proc. of the Fifth International Conference on Digital Society.*

Kovynyov, I., & Mikut, R. (2018). *Digital Transformation in Airport Ground Operations.* Cornell University. doi:10.1007/s11066-019-09132-5

Kraus, M., Feuerriegel, S., & Oztekin, A. (2020). Deep learning in business analytics and operations research: Models, applications and managerial implications. *European Journal of Operational Research*, *281*(3), 628–641. doi:10.1016/j.ejor.2019.09.018

Krizhevsky, A., Sutskever, I., & Hinton, G. E. (2012). Imagenet classification with deep convolutional neural networks. *Advances in Neural Information Processing Systems*, *25*, 1097–1105.

Krizhevsky, A., Sutskever, I., & Hinton, G. E. (2012). ImageNet classification with deep convolutional neural networks. *Communications of the ACM*, *1*, 1097–1105. doi:10.1145/3065386

Krstic, N., & Maslikovic, D. (2018). Pain points of cultural institutions in search visibility: The case of Serbia. *Library Hi Tech*, *37*, 496–512.

Kulcu, S., Dogdu, E., & Ozbayoglu, A. M. (2016). A survey on semantic Web and big data technologies for social network analysis. *Proceedings - 2016 IEEE International Conference on Big Data*, 1768–1777. doi:10.1109/BigData.2016.7840792

Kulkarni, N., & Wazalwar, N. (2018). A Study on Effect of Demographic Variables on Purchase Intentions through Online Advertising. *SSRG International Journal of Economics Management Studies*, *5*(12), 16–19.

Kumar, V., Rajan, B., Venkatesan, R., & Lecinski, J. (2019). *Understanding the role of artificial intelligence in personalized engagement marketing*. Academic Press.

Kumar, G. B. (2015). An encyclopedic overview of 'Big Data' Analytics. *International Journal of Applied Engineering Research: IJAER*, *10*(3), 5681–5705.

Kumar, K., & Haider, M. T. U. (2021). *Enhanced Prediction of Intra-day Stock Market Using Metaheuristic Optimization on RNN–LSTM Network, New Generation Computing*. Ohmsha. doi:10.100700354-020-00104-0

Kurbiel, T., & Khaleghian, S. (2017). *Training of deep neural networks based on distance measures using RMSProp*. arXiv preprint arXiv:1708.01911.

Kushwaha, A. K., Kar, A. K., & Dwivedi, Y. K. (2021). Applications of big data in emerging management disciplines: A literature review using text mining. *International Journal of Information Management Data Insights*, *1*(2). doi:10.1016/j.jjimei.2021.100017

Kwolek, B. (2005). *Face detection using convolutional neural networks and Gabor filters*. Paper presented at the International Conference on Artificial Neural Networks. 10.1007/11550822_86

L'Heureux, A., Grolinger, K., Elyamany, H. F., & Capretz, M. A. M. (2017). Machine Learning With Big Data: Challenges and Approaches. *IEEE Access: Practical Innovations, Open Solutions*, *5*, 7776–7797. doi:10.1109/ACCESS.2017.2696365

Lackey, N. R., & Sullivan, J. J. (2004). Culture, Leadership and Organization. *Sage (Atlanta, Ga.)*.

Lai, G., Chang, W. C., Yang, Y., & Liu, H. (2018, June). Modeling long-and short-term temporal patterns with deep neural networks. In *The 41st International ACM SIGIR Conference on Research & Development in Information Retrieval* (pp. 95-104). 10.1145/3209978.3210006

Lamy, J.-B., Sekar, B., Guezennec, G., Bouaud, J., & Séroussi, B. (2019). Explainable artificial intelligence for breast cancer: A visual case-based reasoning approach. *Artificial Intelligence in Medicine*, *94*, 42–53. doi:10.1016/j.artmed.2019.01.001 PMID:30871682

Landers, R. N., Brusso, R. C., & Auer, E. M. (2019). Crowdsourcing Job Satisfaction Data: Examining the Construct Validity of Glassdoor.com Ratings. *Personnel Assessment and Decisions*, *5*(3), 6. Advance online publication. doi:10.25035/pad.2019.03.006

Laney, D., & Jain, A. (2017, June 20). *100 Data and Analytics Predictions Through.* Retrieved August 04, 2018, from Gartner: https://www.gartner.com/events-na/data-analytics/wp-content/uploads/sites/5/2017/10/Data-and-Analytics-Predictions.pdf

Lange, M. (2020). Finanz Informatik: Optimiertes Kundenmanagement mit Data Analytics [Finanz Informatik (Data Center): Optimised customer management with data analytics]. *IT Finanzmagazin.* https://www.it-finanzmagazin.de/data-analytics-so-geht-optimiertes-kundenmanagement-108798/

Lansley, M., Polatidis, N., Kapetanakis, S., Amin, K., Samakovitis, G., & Petridis, M. (2019). *Seen the villains: Detecting Social Engineering Attacks using Case-based Reasoning and Deep Learning.* Paper presented at the ICCBR Workshops.

LaPlante, A. (2019). *What Is Augmented Analytics? Powering Your Data with AI.* Boston: O' Realy. Retrieved from https://go.oracle.com/LP=84622

Larsen, T. (2013). Cross-platform Aviation analytics using big data analytics. *2013 Integrated Communications Navigation and Surveillance (ICNS) Conference,* 1-10. Retrieved May 27, 2021, from http://masflightbigdata.com/uploads/1/9/5/4/19547003/cross-platform-aviation-analytics-using-big-data-methods-paper.pdf

Latora, V., & Marchiori, M. (2001). Efficient behavior of small-world networks. *Physical Review Letters, 87*(19), 198701–198704. doi:10.1103/PhysRevLett.87.198701 PMID:11690461

Laudon, K. G., & Laudon, K. C. (2020). *Management Information Systems: Managing the Digital Firm* (16th ed.). Pearson.

Lebedev, A. A., & Ryjov, A. P. (2009). Design team capability and project progress evaluation based on information monitoring technology. In *Proceedings of the 5th International Conference on Soft Computing, Computing with Words and Perceptions in System Analysis, Decision and Control.* IEEE. 10.1109/ICSCCW.2009.5379492

LeBozec, C., Jaulent, M.-C., Zapletal, E., & Degoulet, P. (1998). Unified modeling language and design of a case-based retrieval system in medical imaging. *Proceedings of the AMIA Symposium.*

LeCun, Y., Boser, B., Denker, J., Henderson, D., Howard, R., Hubbard, W., & Jackel, L. (1989). Handwritten digit recognition with a back-propagation network. *Advances in Neural Information Processing Systems, 2.*

LeCun, Y., Bottou, L., Bengio, Y., & Haffner, P. (1998). Gradient-based learning applied to document recognition. *Proceedings of the IEEE, 86*(11), 2278–2324. doi:10.1109/5.726791

Lee, J., & Kang, J. (2017). *A Study on Job Satisfaction Factors in Retention and Turnover Groups using Dominance Analysis and LDA Topic Modeling with Employee Reviews on Glassdoor.com. In International Conference on Information Systems (ICIS).* AIS.

Lee, M. K., Kusbit, D., Kahng, A., Kim, J. T., Yuan, X., Chan, A., ... Psomas, A. (2019). WeBuildAI: Participatory framework for algorithmic governance. *Proceedings of the ACM on Human-Computer Interaction, 3*(CSCW), 1-35.

Lees, E. (2016). *A Better Way to Manage Airports: Passenger Analytics.* ICF International, Inc.

Lee, V. H., Hew, J. J., Leong, L. Y., Tan, G. W. H., & Ooi, K. B. (2020). Wearable payment: A deep learning-based dual-stage SEM-ANN analysis. *Expert Systems with Applications, 157,* 113477. doi:10.1016/j.eswa.2020.113477

Leonard, J. J. (2007). Challenges for autonomous mobile robots. *International Machine Vision and Image Processing Conference, IMVIP 2007,* 4. 10.1109/IMVIP.2007.46

Lepenioti, K., Bousdekis, A., Apostolou, D., & Mentzas, G. (2020). *Prescriptive analytics: Literature review and research challenges.* Academic Press.

Lessig, L. (2009). *Code: And other laws of cyberspace*: ReadHowYouWant.com.

Li, J. (1999). *American West Cowboy and Cowboy Culture* [美国西部牛仔和牛仔文化] (Unpublished doctoral dissertation). Capital Normal University, Beijing, China.

Li, J., Zhao, R., Hu, H., & Gong, Y. (2019). Improving RNN Transducer Modeling for End-to-End Speech Recognition. *2019 IEEE Autom. Speech Recognit. Underst. Work.*, 114–121.

Licklider, J. C. R. (1960). Man-Computer Symbiosis. *IRE Transactions on Human Factors in Electronics, HFE-1*, 4-11. Retrieved from http://groups.csail.mit.edu/medg/people/psz/Licklider.html

Liew, A. (2013). DIKIW: Data, Information, Knowledge, Intelligence, Wisdom and their Interrelationships. *Psychology (Irvine, Calif.)*.

LiK.MaiF.ShenR.YanX. (2018). *Measuring Corporate Culture Using Machine Learning*. doi:10.2139/ssrn.3256608

Lim, B., Sercan, O., & Arik, N. (2019). *Temporal Fusion Transformers for Interpretable Multi-horizon Time Series Forecasting*. arXiv:1912.09363

Lim, Chen, & Chen. (2013). Business intelligence and analytics: Research directions. *ACM Transactions on Management Information Systems*, 3(4), 1-10. https://ink.library.smu.edu.sg/sis_research/1966

Lim, B., Arık, S. Ö., Loeff, N., & Pfister, T. (2021). Temporal fusion transformers for interpretable multi-horizon time series forecasting. *International Journal of Forecasting*, 37(4), 1748–1764. doi:10.1016/j.ijforecast.2021.03.012

Lin, L. T. (2021a). *Total number of game users in China from 2008 to 2020*. Statista. Retrieved from https://www.statista.com/statistics/870620/china-number-of-game-users/

Lin, L. T. (2021b). *Console and PC game sales revenue in China 2008-2019*. Statista. Retrieved from https://www.statista.com/statistics/445407/console-and-pc-game-revenue-in-china/

Lin, L. T. (2021c). *Annual revenue of eSports games market in China 2016-2020*. Statista. Retrieved from https://www.statista.com/statistics/1087541/china-esports-game-market-revenue/

Lin, T., Wang, Y., Liu, X., & Qiu, X. (2021). *A Survey of Transformers*. arXiv:2106.04554v11

Lingiardi, V., Carone, N., Semeraro, G., Musto, C., D'Amico, M., & Brena, S. (2020). Mapping Twitter hate speech towards social and sexual minorities: A lexicon-based approach to semantic content analysis. *Behaviour & Information Technology*, 39(7), 711–721. doi:10.1080/0144929X.2019.1607903

Li, O., Liu, H., Chen, C., & Rudin, C. (2018). Deep learning for case-based reasoning through prototypes: A neural network that explains its predictions. *Proceedings of the AAAI Conference on Artificial Intelligence*.

Liu, Q.X., & Qie, D.J. (2016). A comparative analysis of Chinese and Japanese cultures based on martial arts and ninjas [基于武侠与忍者的中日文化比较分析]. *Journal of the Ninbo Radio & TV University*, 14(51), 35-40.

Liu, X., & Burns, A. (2018). *Designing a marketing analytics course for the digital age*. Academic Press.

Liu, Y., Ott, M., Goyal, N., Du, J., Joshi, M., Chen, D., . . . Stoyanov, V. (2019). *RoBERTa: A Robustly Optimized BERT Pretraining Approach*. arXiv:1907.11692v1

Liu, D., Baumeister, R. F., Yang, C.-C., & Hu, B. (2019). Digital communication media use and psychological well-being: A meta-analysis. *Journal of Computer-Mediated Communication*, 24(5), 259–274. doi:10.1093/jcmc/zmz013

Liu, N., Wang, K., Jin, X., Gao, B., Dellandréa, E., & Chen, L. (2017). Visual affective classification by combining visual and text features. *PLoS One*, 12(8), e0183018. doi:10.1371/journal.pone.0183018 PMID:28850566

Liu, W., Wang, Z., Liu, X., Zeng, N., Liu, Y., & Alsaadi, F. E. (2017). A survey of deep neural network architectures and their applications. *Neurocomputing, 234,* 11–26. doi:10.1016/j.neucom.2016.12.038

Liu, Y., Zhang, D., Lu, G., & Ma, W. Y. (2007). A survey of content-based image retrieval with high-level semantics. *Pattern Recognition, 40*(1), 262–282. doi:10.1016/j.patcog.2006.04.045

Livieris, I. E., Pintelas, E., & Pintelas, P. (2020). A CNN-LSTM model for gold price time-series forecasting. *Neural Computing & Applications, 32*(23), 17351–17360. doi:10.100700521-020-04867-x

Li, X., Snoek, C. G. M., & Worring, M. (2009). Learning social tag relevance by neighbor voting. *IEEE Transactions on Multimedia, 11*(7), 1310–1322. doi:10.1109/TMM.2009.2030598

Lo, S.-Y. J., Wei, H., Chuang, C., & Yin, C.-Y., & Hsieh10, J. (2017). *Applying data science for social good in nonprofit organization with troubled family risk profiling r dashboard application.* Paper presented at the The R User Conference, useR!, Brussels, Belgium.

Lo, P., Chan, H. H. Y., Tang, A. W. M., Chiu, D. K. W., Cho, A., Ho, K. K. W., See-To, E., He, J., Kenderdine, S., & Shaw, J. (2019). Visualising and Revitalising Traditional Chinese Martial Arts – Visitors' Engagement and Learning Experience at the 300 Years of Hakka KungFu. *Library Hi Tech, 37*(2), 273–292. doi:10.1108/LHT-05-2018-0071

Lo, P., Cheuk, M. K., Ng, C. H., Lam, S. K., & Chiu, D. K. W. (2021). *The way of Arts and Kungfu* [文武之道:以拳入哲] (Vol. 2). Systech Publications.

López Ibáñez, B., Pous i Sabadí, C., Gay Sacristán, P., Pla Planas, A., Sanz, J. N., & Brunet, J. S. (2011). EXiT CBR: A framework for case-based medical diagnosis development and experimentation. *Artificial Intelligence in Medicine, 51*(2), 81-91.

López-Sánchez, D., Corchado, J. M., & Arrieta, A. G. (2017). *A CBR system for image-based webpage classification: case representation with convolutional neural networks.* Paper presented at the Thirtieth International Flairs Conference.

Louati, A., Louati, H., & Li, Z. (2021). Deep learning and case-based reasoning for predictive and adaptive traffic emergency management. *The Journal of Supercomputing, 77*(5), 4389–4418. doi:10.100711227-020-03435-3

Lu, J., Cairns, L., & Smith, L. (2020). *Data science in the business environment: customer analytics case studies in SMEs.* Academic Press.

Lünemann, J., & Müller-Hammerstein, C. (2021). *Finanzinstitute: Kundenansprache mit Data Analytics* [Financial institutions: Addressing customers with data analytics]. KINote – eine Marke der Bank-Verlag GmbH. https://www.ki-note.de/einzelansicht/finanzinstitute-kundenansprache-mit-data-analytics

Luo, N., Zhou, Y., & Shon, J. (2016). *Employee Satisfaction and Corporate Performance: Mining Employee Reviews on Glassdoor.com. In ICIS.* AIS.

Luong, M. T., Pham, H., & Manning, C. D. (2015). *Effective approaches to attention-based neural machine translation.* arXiv preprint arXiv:1508.04025. doi:10.18653/v1/D15-1166

Lütkepohl, H., & Xu, F. (2012). The role of the log transformation in forecasting economic variables. *Empirical Economics, 42*(3), 619–638. doi:10.100700181-010-0440-1

Lycett, M. (2013). *'Datafication': Making sense of (big) data in a complex world.* Taylor & Francis.

Mahbod, A., Schaefer, G., Wang, C., Ecker, R., & Ellinge, I. (2019). *Skin lesion classification using hybrid deep neural networks.* Paper presented at the ICASSP 2019-2019 IEEE International Conference on Acoustics, Speech and Signal Processing (ICASSP). 10.1109/ICASSP.2019.8683352

Mahmud, M. S., Huang, J. Z., Salloum, S., Emara, T. Z., & Sadatdiynov, K. (2020). A survey of data partitioning and sampling methods to support big data analysis. *Big Data Mining and Analytics*, *3*(2), 85–101. doi:10.26599/BDMA.2019.9020015

Mansoul, A., Atmani, B., & Benbelkacem, S. (2013). *A hybrid decision support system: application on healthcare.* arXiv preprint arXiv:1311.4086.

Margherita, A. (2021). *Human resources analytics: A systematization of research topics and directions for future research.* Academic Press.

Marketresearchfuture. (2020). *Data Analytics Market Research Report.* https://www.marketresearchfuture.com/reports/data-analytics-market-1689

Markets and markets. Big Data Market. (2021). https://www.marketsandmarkets.com/Market-Reports/big-data-market-1068.html

Marler, J. H., & Boudreau, J. W. (2017). An evidence-based review of HR Analytics. *International Journal of Human Resource Management*, *28*(1), 3–26. doi:10.1080/09585192.2016.1244699

Marling, C., & Whitehouse, P. (2001). *Case-based reasoning in the care of Alzheimer's disease patients.* Paper presented at the International Conference on Case-Based Reasoning. 10.1007/3-540-44593-5_50

Martínez-Cámara, E., Martín-Valdivia, M. T., Ureña-López, L. A., & Montejo-Ráez, A. R. (2014). Sentiment analysis in Twitter. *Natural Language Engineering*, *20*(1), 1–28. doi:10.1017/S1351324912000332

Martins, N., Martins, S., & Brandão, D. (2022). Design Principles in the Development of Dashboards for Business Management. In *Perspectives on Design II* (pp. 353–365). Springer. doi:10.1007/978-3-030-79879-6_26

Matheus, R., Janssen, M., & Janowski, T. (2021). *Design principles for creating digital transparency in government.* Academic Press.

Matheus, R., & Janssen, M. (2019). *A systematic literature study to unravel transparency enabled by open government data: The Window Theory. In Public Performance & Management Review.* PPMR.

Matheus, R., Janssen, M., & Maheshwari, D. (2018). Data science empowering the public: Data-driven dashboards for transparent and accountable decision-making in smart cities. *Government Information Quarterly.*

Matheus, R., Vaz, J. C., & Ribeiro, M. M. (2014). Open government data and the data usage for improvement of public services in the Rio de Janeiro City. *Proceedings of the 8th International Conference on Theory and Practice of Electronic Governance.* 10.1145/2691195.2691240

Matosevic, G., Dobsa, J., & Mladenic, D. (2021). Using machine learning for web page classification in search engine optimization. *Future Internet, 13*(9), 1-20.

Matošević, G., Dobša, J., & Mladenić, D. (2021). *Using Machine Learning for Web Page Classification in Search Engine Optimization. Academic Press.*

Matti, T., Zhu, Y., & Xu, K. (2015). Financial fraud detection using social media crowdsourcing. *2014 IEEE 33rd International Performance Computing and Communications Conference, IPCCC 2014.* 10.1109/PCCC.2014.7017023

Mavlutova, I., & Volkova, T. (2019). Digital Transformation of Financial Sector and Challenges for Competencies Development. In *2019 7th International Conference on Modeling, Development and Strategic Management of Economic System (MDSMES 2019).* Atlantis Press. 10.2991/mdsmes-19.2019.31

Ma, X. H. (2011). The long Viking ship carrying death [载着死神而来的维京长船]. *Ocean World, 2011*(12), 24–27.

Maynard, D., Roberts, I., Greenwood, M. A., Rout, D., & Bontcheva, K. (2017). A framework for real-time semantic social media analysis. *Journal of Web Semantics*, *44*, 75–88. doi:10.1016/j.websem.2017.05.002

Mayo, A. (2018). Applying HR analytics to talent management. *Strategic HR Review*, *17*(5), 247–254. Advance online publication. doi:10.1108/SHR-08-2018-0072

McAfee, A., Brynjolfsson, E., Davenport, T. H., Patil, D. J., & Barton, D. (2012). Big data: The management revolution. *Harvard Business Review*, *90*(10), 60–68. https://pubmed.ncbi.nlm.nih.gov/23074865/ PMID:23074865

McKinsey & Company. (2016, April 16). *How advanced analytics can drive productivity*. Retrieved June 20, 2021, from McKinsey: https://www.mckinsey.com/business-functions/mckinsey-analytics/our-insights/how-advanced-analytics-can-drive-productivity

McKinsey Global Institute. (2013). *Disruptive technologies: Advances that will transform life, business, and the global economy*. Retrieved from https://www.mckinsey.com/insights/business_technology/disruptive_technologies

McKinsey. (2011, May). *Big data: The next frontier for innovation, competition, and productivity*. Retrieved from McKinsey Global Institute: https://www.mckinsey.com/business-functions/business-technology/our-insights/big-data-the-next-frontier-for-innovation

McMurrer, D., & Bassi, L. (2007). Maximizing Your Return on People. *Harvard Business Review*. PMID:17348175

Medsker, L. R., & Jain, L. C. (2001). Recurrent neural networks. *Design and Applications*, *5*, 64–67.

Melo, P. N., & Machado, C. (2020). *Business Intelligence and Analytics in Small and Medium Enterprises*. Taylor & Francis.

Menrad, M. (2020). Systematic review of omni-channel banking and preview of upcoming developments in Germany. *Innovative Marketing*, *16*(2), 104–125. doi:10.21511/im.16(2).2020.09

Merler, M., Cao, L., & Smith, J. R. (2015). You are what you tweet···pic! gender prediction based on semantic analysis of social media images. *Proceedings - IEEE International Conference on Multimedia and Expo*. 10.1109/ICME.2015.7177499

Mesarovich, M. D., Macko, D., & Takahara, Y. (1970). *Theory of hierarchical multilevel systems*. Academic Press.

Metz, C. (2016). *Apple Is Bringing the AI Revolution to Your iPhone*. https://www.wired.com/2016/06/apple-bringing-ai-revolution-iphone/

MHR. (2021). *Augmented analytics: The new face of BI & Analytics. A Future with Augmented Analytics*. Retrieved from https://www.mhranalytics.com/blog/augmented-analytics-the-new-face-of-bi-analytics/

Mikołajczyk, A., & Grochowski, M. (2018). *Data augmentation for improving deep learning in image classification problem*. Paper presented at the 2018 international interdisciplinary PhD workshop (IIPhDW). 10.1109/IIPHDW.2018.8388338

Mille, A., Fuchs, B., & Herbeaux, O. (1996). *A unifying framework for Adaptation in Case-Based Reasoning*. Paper presented at the Workshop on Adaptation in Case-Based Reasoning, ECAI-96.

Mimno, D., Hoffman, M. D., & Blei, D. M. (2012). Sparse stochastic inference for latent Dirichlet allocation. *Proceedings of the 29th International Conference on Machine Learning*.

Minelli, M., Chambers, M., & Dhiraj, A. (2013). *Big Data, Big Analytics: Emerging Business Intelligence and Analytic Trends for Today's Businesses* (Chinese Edition 2014). Wiley & Sons. doi:10.1002/9781118562260

Miotto, R., Li, L., Kidd, B. A., & Dudley, J. T. (2016). Deep patient: An unsupervised representation to predict the future of patients from the electronic health records. *Scientific Reports*, *6*(1), 1–10. doi:10.1038rep26094 PMID:27185194

Miskolczi, M., Jászberényi, M., & Tóth, D. (2021, January 13). Technology-Enhanced Airport Services—Attractiveness from the Travelers' Perspective. *Sustainability*, *13*, 705.

Mislove, A., Marcon, M., Gummadi, K. P., Druschel, P., & Bhattacharjee, B. (2007). Measurement and analysis of online social networks. *Proceedings of the ACM SIGCOMM Internet Measurement Conference, IMC*, 29–42. 10.1145/1298306.1298311

Mitra, A., Soman, B., & Singh, G. (2021). *An Interactive Dashboard for Real-Time Analytics and Monitoring of COVID-19 Outbreak in India: A proof of Concept*. Academic Press.

Mohamad, S. K., & Tasir, Z. (2013). Educational Data Mining: A Review. *Procedia: Social and Behavioral Sciences*, *97*, 320–324. doi:10.1016/j.sbspro.2013.10.240

Mohri, M., Rostamizadeh, A., & Talwalkar, A. (2012). *Foundations of machine learning*. The MIT Press.

Moormann, J. (2000). Die Digitalisierung des Bankgeschäfts. In *Informationstechnologie in Banken* [The digitalization of banking. In Information Technology in Banks] (pp. 3–16). Springer. doi:10.1007/978-3-642-56991-3_1

Mosavi, N. S., & Santos, M. F. (2020). *How prescriptive analytics influences decision making in precision medicine*. Academic Press.

Mrvar, A., & Batagelj, V. (2016). Analysis and visualization of large networks with program package Pajek. In Complex Adaptive Systems Modeling (Vol. 4, Issue 1). Springer Science and Business Media LLC. doi:10.118640294-016-0017-8

Mullan, M. (2019). The data-driven airport: How daa created data and analytics capabilities to drive business growth improve the passenger experience and deliver operational efficiency. *Journal of Airport Management*, *13*(4), 361–379. Retrieved June 26, 2021, from https://www.ingentaconnect.com/content/hsp/cam/2019/00000013/00000004/art00007

Nagarajan, S. M., Deverajan, G. G., Chatterjee, P., Alnumay, W., & Ghosh, U. (2021). Effective task scheduling algorithm with deep learning for Internet of Health Things (IoHT) in sustainable smart cities. *Sustainable Cities and Society*, *71*, 102945. doi:10.1016/j.scs.2021.102945

Najafabadi, M. K., Mohamed, A. H., & Mahrin, M. N. (2019). A survey on data mining techniques in recommender systems. *Soft Computing*, *23*(2), 627–654. doi:10.100700500-017-2918-7

Najafabadi, M. M., Villanustre, F., Khoshgoftaar, T. M., Seliya, N., Wald, R., & Muharemagic, E. (2015). Deep learning applications and challenges in big data analytics. *Journal of Big Data*, *2*(1), 1. doi:10.118640537-014-0007-7

Narongou, D., & Sun, Z. (2021). Big Data Analytics for Smart Airport Management. In Z. Sun & Z. Sun (Eds.), *Intelligent Analytics With Advanced Multi-Industry Applications* (pp. 209–231). IGI Global. doi:10.4018/978-1-7998-4963-6.ch010

Nasiri, S., Helsper, J., Jung, M., & Fathi, M. (2018). Enriching a CBR recommender system by classification of skin lesions using deep neural networks. *Proceedings (CBRDL: Case-Based Reasoning and Deep Learning) of the 26th International Conference on Case-Based Reasoning (ICCBR 2018)*.

National Academies of Sciences, Engineering, and Medicine. (2012). *Guidebook for Developing General Aviation Airport Business*. Washington, DC: The National Academies Press. doi:10.17226/22694

Nau, J.-B., & Benoit, F. (2017). *Smart Airport: How Technology is shaping the future of airports*. Wavestone.

Nayak, J., Naik, B., & Behera, H. (2015). Fuzzy C-means (FCM) clustering algorithm: a decade review from 2000 to 2014. *Computational Intelligence in Data Mining*, *2*, 133-149.

Neshat, M., Sargolzaei, M., Nadjaran Toosi, A., & Masoumi, A. (2012). Hepatitis disease diagnosis using hybrid case based reasoning and particle swarm optimization. *International Scholarly Research Notices*.

Network, X. (2018). *Encyclopedia of Social Network Analysis and Mining*. Springer New York. doi:10.1007/978-1-4939-7131-2_100771

Neves, J., Vicente, H., Ferraz, F., Leite, A. C., Rodrigues, A. R., Cruz, M., & Sampaio, L. (2018). *A deep learning approach to case based reasoning to the evaluation and diagnosis of cervical carcinoma. In Modern Approaches for Intelligent Information and Database Systems*. Springer.

Nguyen, L. D., Lin, D., Lin, Z., & Cao, J. (2018). *Deep CNNs for microscopic image classification by exploiting transfer learning and feature concatenation*. Paper presented at the 2018 IEEE International Symposium on Circuits and Systems (ISCAS). 10.1109/ISCAS.2018.8351550

Nguyen, L., Stoové, M., Boyle, D., Callander, D., McManus, H., Asselin, J., ... El-Hayek, C. (2020). *Privacy-preserving record linkage of deidentified records within a public health surveillance system: evaluation study*. Academic Press.

Nielsen, C., & Lund, M. (2019, November 25). *Small data: data strategies that most companies can profit from*. Retrieved June 12, 2021, from California Management Review: https://cmr.berkeley.edu/2019/11/small-data/

Niemann, J., & Pisla, A. (2020). *Life-Cycle Management of Machines and Mechanisms*. Springer.

Nintendo. (n.d.). In *Wikipedia*. Retrieved from https://en.wikipedia.org/wiki/Nintendo

Nioh 2. (n.d.). In *Wikipedia*. Retrieved from https://en.wikipedia.org/wiki/Nioh_2

Nolle, T., Luettgen, S., Seeliger, A., & Mühlhäuser, M. (2018). Analyzing business process anomalies using autoencoders. *Machine Learning*, *107*(11), 1875–1893. doi:10.100710994-018-5702-8

Norusis, M. J. (1997). *SPSS: SPSS 7.5 Guide to Data Analytics*. Prentice Hall.

Obaid, H. S., Dheyab, S. A., & Sabry, S. S. (2019). *The impact of data pre-processing techniques and dimensionality reduction on the accuracy of machine learning*. Paper presented at the 2019 9th Annual Information Technology, Electromechanical Engineering and Microelectronics Conference (IEMECON). 10.1109/IEMECONX.2019.8877011

Oh, K. T., Lee, S., Lee, H., Yun, M., & Yoo, S. K. (2020). Semantic segmentation of white matter in FDG-PET using generative adversarial network. *Journal of Digital Imaging*, *33*(4), 816–825. doi:10.100710278-020-00321-5 PMID:32043177

Oldenburg, M. (2020, January 25). *The biggest benefits of airport analytics*. Retrieved April 26, 2021, from Targit: https://www.targit.com/blog/the-biggest-benefits-of-airport-analytics

Oord, A. V. D., Dieleman, S., Zen, H., Simonyan, K., Vinyals, O., Graves, A., ... Kavukcuoglu, K. (2016). *Wavenet: A generative model for raw audio*. arXiv preprint arXiv:1609.03499.

Oreshkin, B. N., Carpov, D., Chapados, N., & Bengio, Y. (2019). *N-BEATS: Neural basis expansion analysis for interpretable time series forecasting*. arXiv preprint arXiv:1905.10437.

Oxford. (2008). *Oxford Advanced Learner's English Dictionary* (7th ed.). Oxford University Press.

Oyelade, O. N., & Ezugwu, A. E. (2020). A case-based reasoning framework for early detection and diagnosis of novel coronavirus. *Informatics in Medicine Unlocked*, *20*, 100395. doi:10.1016/j.imu.2020.100395 PMID:32835080

Page, C. (2020). *Microsoft Will Let Employees Work From Home Permanently: Report*. Retrieved from Forbes: https://www.forbes.com/sites/carlypage/2020/10/09/microsoft-will-let-employees-work-from-home-permanently/#5f3efa14172a

Pang, S., & Yang, X. (2016). Deep convolutional extreme learning machine and its application in handwritten digit classification. *Computational Intelligence and Neuroscience*, *2016*, 2016. doi:10.1155/2016/3049632 PMID:27610128

Pannala, N. U., Nawarathna, C. P., Jayakody, J., Rupasinghe, L., & Krishnadeva, K. (2016). *Supervised learning based approach to aspect based sentiment analysis.* Paper presented at the 2016 IEEE International Conference on Computer and Information Technology (CIT). 10.1109/CIT.2016.107

Papagiannopoulos, N. (2021, April 7). *The value of data analytics for airports: Use cases and novel methods.* Retrieved June 2, 2021, from International Airport Review: https://www.internationalairportreview.com/article/155857/value-data-analytics-airports/

Park, H., Ko, H., Lee, Y.-T. T., Cho, H., & Witherell, P. (2019). *A Framework for Identifying and Prioritizing Data Analytics Opportunities in Additive Manufacturing.* Paper presented at the 2019 IEEE International Conference on Big Data (Big Data). 10.1109/BigData47090.2019.9006489

Payrovnaziri, S. N., Chen, Z., Rengifo-Moreno, P., Miller, T., Bian, J., Chen, J. H., Liu, X., & He, Z. (2020). Explainable artificial intelligence models using real-world electronic health record data: A systematic scoping review. *Journal of the American Medical Informatics Association: JAMIA, 27*(7), 1173–1185. doi:10.1093/jamia/ocaa053 PMID:32417928

Pell, R., & Blondel, M. (2018). *Airport Digital Transformation.* Arthur D Little.

Pereira, S., Pinto, A., Alves, V., & Silva, C. A. (2016). Brain tumor segmentation using convolutional neural networks in MRI images. *IEEE Transactions on Medical Imaging, 35*(5), 1240–1251. doi:10.1109/TMI.2016.2538465 PMID:26960222

Perumal, V. (2016). Performance evaluation and comparative analysis of various machine learning techniques for diagnosis of breast cancer. *Biomedical Research, 27*(3).

Peters, H.-W. (2018). Bankenverband rechnet mit kräftigem Abbau von Filialen [Banking association expects strong reduction of branches]. *Frankfurter Allgemeine.* https://www.faz.net/aktuell/wirtschaft/bankenverband-rechnet-mit-kraeftigem-abbau-von-filialen-15579480.html?GEPC=s81&GEPC=s5

Pettey, C., & van der Meulen, R. (2018, April 25). *Gartner Says Global Artificial Intelligence Business Value to Reach $1.2 Trillion in 2018.* Retrieved August 04, 2018, from Gartner: https://www.gartner.com/newsroom/id/3872933

Popovic, V., Kraal, B., & Kirk, P. (2009). Passenger Experience in an Airport: An Activity-centred Approach. *IASDR 2009 Proceedings*, 18-22. Retrieved 11 29, 2019, from https://www.researchgate.net/publication/42424464

Potter, A., Motik, B., Nenov, Y., & Horrocks, I. (2016). Distributed RDF query answering with dynamic data exchange. In Lecture Notes in Computer Science (including subseries Lecture Notes in Artificial Intelligence and Lecture Notes in Bioinformatics): Vol. 9981 LNCS (pp. 480–497). Springer International Publishing. doi:10.1007/978-3-319-46523-4_29

PowerPyx. (2020). Nioh 2 Length (Playtime). *PowerPyx.* Retrieved from https://www.powerpyx.com/nioh-2-length-playtime/

Prasad, U. D., & Madhavi, S. (2012). *Prediction of churn behavior of bank customers using data mining tools.* Academic Press.

Pressman, R., & Maxim, B. (2014). *Software Engineering: A Practitioner's Approach* (8th ed.). McGraw-Hill Education.

Priadana, A., Maarif, M. R., & Habibi, M. (2020). Gender Prediction for Instagram User Profiling using Deep Learning. *2020 Int. Conf. Decis. Aid Sci. Appl. DASA 2020*, 432–436. 10.1109/DASA51403.2020.9317143

Prinzie, A., & Van den Poel, D. (2008). Random forests for multiclass classification: Random multinomial logit. *Expert Systems with Applications, 34*(3), 1721–1732. doi:10.1016/j.eswa.2007.01.029

Proskurnikov, A. V., & Tempo, R. (2017). A tutorial on modeling and analysis of dynamic social networks. Part I. *Annual Reviews in Control, 43*, 65–79. doi:10.1016/j.arcontrol.2017.03.002

Purwandari, B., Otmen, B., & Kumaralalita, L. (2019). Adoption factors of e-marketplace and instagram for micro, small, and medium enterprises (MSMEs) in Indonesia. *Proceedings of the 2019 2nd International Conference on Data Science and Information Technology.* 10.1145/3352411.3352453

Pusztová, Ľ., Babič, F., & Paralič, J. (2021). Semi-Automatic Adaptation of Diagnostic Rules in the Case-Based Reasoning Process. *Applied Sciences (Basel, Switzerland), 11*(1), 292. doi:10.3390/app11010292

Qian, X., Hua, X. S., Tang, Y. Y., & Mei, T. (2014). Social image tagging with diverse semantics. *IEEE Transactions on Cybernetics, 44*(12), 2493–2508. doi:10.1109/TCYB.2014.2309593 PMID:25415950

Qin, H. (2019). *Comparison of deep learning models on time series forecasting: A case study of dissolved oxygen prediction.* arXiv preprint arXiv:1911.08414.

Qiu, M., Li, P., Pan, H., Wang, C., Wang, A., Chen, C., Li, Y., Gao, D., Huang, J., Li, Yong, Yang, J., Cai, D., & Lin, W. (2020). *EasyTransfer -- A Simple and Scalable Deep Transfer Learning Platform for NLP Applications.* Academic Press.

Qlik. (2021). Retrieved August 28, 2021, from https://www.qlik.com/us

Radford, A., Narasimhan, K., Salimans, T., & Sutskever, I. (2018). *Improving Language Understanding by Generative Pre-Training.* Academic Press.

Radford, A., Wu, J., Child, R., Luan, D., Amodei, D., & Sutskever, I. (2020). Language Models are Unsupervised Multitask Learners. *OpenAI Blog, 1*, 1–7.

Rafailidis, D., & Manolopoulos, Y. (2019). Can virtual assistants produce recommendations? *ACM Int. Conf. Proceeding Ser.* 10.1145/3326467.3326468

Rahman, M. M. (2012). Mining Social Data to Extract Intellectual Knowledge. *International Journal of Intelligent Systems and Applications, 4*(10), 15–24. doi:10.5815/ijisa.2012.10.02

Rahwan, I. (2018). Society-in-the-loop: Programming the algorithmic social contract. *Ethics and Information Technology, 20*(1), 5–14. doi:10.100710676-017-9430-8

Rai, R., Tiwari, M. K., Ivanov, D., & Dolgui, A. (2021). Machine learning in manufacturing and industry 4.0 applications. *International Journal of Production Research, 59*(16), 4773–4778. doi:10.1080/00207543.2021.1956675

Rajan, Q. (2020, May 11). *Big Data for Small Business.* Retrieved April 29, 2021, from Towards Data Science: https://towardsdatascience.com/big-data-for-small-business-ae851f34e5a5

Rama, J., Zhang, C., & Koronios, A. (2016). The implications of Big Data analytics on Business Intelligence: A qualitative study in China. *Fourth International Conference on Recent Trends in Computer Science & Engineering, 87*, 221-226. doi:10.1016/j.procs.2016.05.152

Ravi, V., & Kamaruddin, S. (2017). Big data analytics enabled smart financial services: Opportunities and challenges. *Lect. Notes Comput. Sci., 10721*, 15–39. doi:10.1007/978-3-319-72413-3_2

Ravì, D., Wong, C., Lo, B., & Yang, G. (2017). A Deep Learning Approach to on-Node Sensor Data Analytics for Mobile or Wearable Devices. *IEEE Journal of Biomedical and Health Informatics, 21*(1), 56–64. doi:10.1109/JBHI.2016.2633287 PMID:28026792

Raviteja, T. (2020). An introduction of autonomous vehicles and a brief survey. *Journal of Critical Reviews, 7*(13), 196–202.

Rawassizadeh, R., Sen, T., Kim, S. J., Meurisch, C., Keshavarz, H., Mühlhäuser, M., & Pazzani, M. (2019). Manifestation of virtual assistants and robots into daily life: Vision and challenges. *CCF Trans. Pervasive Comput. Interact., 1*(3), 163–174. doi:10.100742486-019-00014-1

Rebane, J., Karlsson, I., Papapetrou, P., & Denic, S. (2018, August). Seq2Seq RNNs and ARIMA models for cryptocurrency prediction: A comparative study. In SIGKDD Fintech 2018, London, UK.

Red Dead Redemption 2. (n.d.). In *Wikipedia*. Retrieved from https://en.wikipedia.org/wiki/Red_Dead_Redemption_2

Reddy, M., Pesl, P., Xenou, M., Toumazou, C., Johnston, D., Georgiou, P., Herrero, P., & Oliver, N. (2016). Clinical safety and feasibility of the advanced bolus calculator for type 1 diabetes based on case-based reasoning: A 6-week nonrandomized single-arm pilot study. *Diabetes Technology & Therapeutics*, *18*(8), 487–493. doi:10.1089/dia.2015.0413 PMID:27196358

Reich, Y. (1995). Measuring the value of knowledge. *International Journal of Human-Computer Studies*, *42*(1), 3–30. doi:10.1006/ijhc.1995.1002

Reinicke, C. (2020). *Tesla's recent rally has pushed the stock up more than 200% this year. Here are CEO Elon Musk's most controversial tweets about the market*. Retrieved from Business Insider: https://markets.businessinsider.com/news/stocks/tesla-stock-elon-musks-most-controversial-tweets-about-market-twitter-2020-7-1029372168#

Richardson, J., Schlegel, K., Sallam, R., Kronz, A., & Sun, J. (2021). *Magic Quadrant for Analytics and Business Intelligence Platforms*. Gartner. Retrieved from https://www.gartner.com/doc/reprints?id=1-254T1IQX&ct=210202&st=sb

Richardson, J., Schlegel, K., Sallam, R., Kronz, A., & Sun, J. (2021, February 15). *Magic Quadrant for Analytics and Business Intelligence Platforms*. Retrieved March 6, 2021, from Gartner: https://www.gartner.com/doc/reprints?id=1-254T1IQX&ct=210202&st=sb

Rittel, H. W., & Webber, M. M. (1974). Wicked problems. *Man-made Futures*, *26*(1), 272–280.

Robins, G., Pattison, P., Kalish, Y., & Lusher, D. (2007). An introduction to exponential random graph (p*) models for social networks. *Social Networks*, *29*(2), 173–191. doi:10.1016/j.socnet.2006.08.002

Robinson, P. M., & Sims, C. A. (1994). Time series with strong dependence. In *Advances in econometrics, sixth world congress* (Vol. 1, pp. 47-95). 10.1017/CCOL0521444594.002

Roe, D. (2021, March 24). *Many Organizations Put Big Data Aside To Focus on Small Data*. Retrieved April 22, 2021, from CMSWire: https://www.cmswire.com/information-management/many-organizations-put-big-data-aside-to-focus-on-small-data/

Romero, C., & Ventura, S. (2007). Educational data mining: A survey from 1995 to 2005. *Expert Systems with Applications*, *33*(1), 135–146. doi:10.1016/j.eswa.2006.04.005

Ross, S. (2020). *Financial Services: Sizing the Sector in the Global Economy*. Academic Press.

Rostamy, A. A. A., Meysam, S., Behnam, A., & Bakhshi, T. F. (2012). Using fuzzy analytical hierarchy process to evaluate main dimensions of business process reengineering. *Journal of Applied Operational Research*, *4*(2), 69–77.

Rowley, J. (2007). The wisdom hierarchy: Representations of the DIKW hierarchy. *Journal of Information and Communication Science*, *33*(2), 163–180. doi:10.1177/0165551506070706

Roy, A., Sun, J., Mahoney, R., Alonzi, L., Adams, S., & Beling, P. (2018). Deep learning detecting fraud in credit card transactions. 2018 Syst. *Inf. Eng. Des. Symp. SIEDS*, *2018*, 129–134. doi:10.1109/SIEDS.2018.8374722

Ruan, X. H., Hu, X., & Zhang, X. (2014). Research on application model of semantic web-based social network analysis. In Lecture Notes in Electrical Engineering: Vol. 271 LNEE (Vol. 2, pp. 455–460). Springer Berlin Heidelberg. doi:10.1007/978-3-642-40630-0_59

Rumelhart, D. E., Hinton, G. E., & Williams, R. J. (1985). *Learning internal representations by error propagation.* California Univ San Diego La Jolla Inst for Cognitive Science.

Rumelhart, D. E., Hinton, G. E., & Williams, R. J. (1986). Learning representations by back-propagating errors. *Nature, 323*(6088), 533-536.

Russell, C., Ward, A. C., Vezza, V., Hoskisson, P., Alcorn, D., Steenson, D. P., & Corrigan, D. K. (2019). Development of a needle shaped microelectrode for electrochemical detection of the sepsis biomarker interleukin-6 (IL-6) in real time. *Biosensors & Bioelectronics, 126,* 806–814. doi:10.1016/j.bios.2018.11.053 PMID:30602262

Russell, S., & Norvig, P. (2010). *Artificial Intelligence: A Modern Approach* (3rd ed.). Prentice Hall.

Ryjov, A., Belenki, A., Hooper, R., Pouchkarev, V., Fattah, A., & Zadeh, L. A. (1998). Development of an Intelligent System for Monitoring and Evaluation of Peaceful Nuclear Activities (DISNA), Vienna: IAEA, STR-310.

Ryjov, A. (1988). *The principles of fuzzy set theory and measurement of fuzziness.* Dialog-MSU Publishing.

Ryjov, A. (2001). On information aggregation in fuzzy hierarchical systems. *Intelligent Systems, 6,* 341–364.

Ryjov, A. (2003). Fuzzy Linguistic Scales: Definition, Properties and Applications. In L. Reznik & V. Kreinovich (Eds.), *Soft Computing in Measurement and Information Acquisition* (pp. 23–38). Springer. doi:10.1007/978-3-540-36216-6_3

Ryjov, A. (2004). Information Monitoring Systems as a Tool for Strategic Analysis and Simulation in Business. In *Proceeding of the International Conference on Fuzzy Sets and Soft Computing in Economics and Finance.* RFSA.

Ryjov, A. (2004). *Models of information retrieval in a fuzzy environment.* MSU Publishing.

Ryjov, A. (2012). Modeling and Optimization of Information Retrieval for Perception-Based Information. In F. Zanzotto, S. Tsumoto, N. Taatgen, & Y.Y. Yao (Eds), *Proceedings of the International Conference on Brain Informatics 2012 (Macau, China)* (pp. 140-149). Springer. 10.1007/978-3-642-35139-6_14

Ryjov, A. (2013). Systems for evaluation and monitoring of complex processes and their applications [in Russian]. *Intelligent Systems, 17*(1-4), 104–117.

Ryjov, A. (2014a). Human-centric systems for evaluating the status and monitoring the progress for socio-political processes. In *Proceedings of the 8th International Conference on Theory and Practice of Electronic Governance.* ACM Conference Publications. 10.1145/2691195.2691285

Ryjov, A. (2014b). Personalization of Social Networks: Adaptive Semantic Layer Approach. In W. Pedrycz & S.-M. Chen (Eds.), *Social Networks: A Framework of Computational Intelligence* (pp. 21–40). Springer International Publishing Switzerland. doi:10.1007/978-3-319-02993-1_2

Ryjov, A. (2015). Towards an optimal task-driven information granulation. In W. Pedrycz & S.-M. Chen (Eds.), *Information Granularity, Big Data, and Computational Intelligence* (pp. 191–208). Springer International Publishing Switzerland.

Saaty, T. L. (1980). *The analytic hierarchy process.* McGraw-Hill.

Sabherwal, R., & Becerra-Fernandez, I. (2011). *Business Intelligence: Practices, Technologies, and Management.* John Wiley & Sons, Inc.

Sadiq, S., Umer, M., Ullah, S., Mirjalili, S., Rupapara, V., & Nappi, M. (2021). Discrepancy detection between actual user reviews and numeric ratings of Google App store using deep learning. *Expert Systems with Applications, 181,* 115111. doi:10.1016/j.eswa.2021.115111

Sahu, N., & Chhabra, R. (2016). Review on Search Engine Optimization. *Journal of Network Communications and Emerging Technologies*, 6, 19–21.

Saiz-Rubio, V., & Rovira-Más, F. (2020). From smart farming towards agriculture 5.0: A review on crop data management. *Agronomy (Basel)*, *10*(2), 207. Advance online publication. doi:10.3390/agronomy10020207

Salakhutdinov, R., & Hinton, G. (2009). *Deep boltzmann machines*. Paper presented at the Artificial intelligence and statistics.

Salathé, M. (2016). *Digital pharmacovigilance and disease surveillance: combining traditional and big-data systems for better public health*. Academic Press.

Salathé, M., Vu, D. Q., Khandelwal, S., & Hunter, D. R. (2013). The dynamics of health behavior sentiments on a large online social network. *EPJ Data Science*, *2*(1), 1–12. doi:10.1140/epjds16

Salinas, D., Flunkert, V., Gasthaus, J., & Januschowski, T. (2020). DeepAR: Probabilistic forecasting with autoregressive recurrent networks. *International Journal of Forecasting*, *36*(3), 1181–1191. doi:10.1016/j.ijforecast.2019.07.001

Sallam, R., Richardson, J., Kronz, A., Sun, J., & Schlegel, K. (2021, February 15). *Magic Quadrant for Analytics and Business Intelligence Platforms*. doi: ID G00467317

Salloum, S. A., Al-Emran, M., Monem, A. A., & Shaalan, K. (2017). A survey of text mining in social media: Facebook and Twitter perspectives. *Advances in Science. Technology and Engineering Systems*, *2*(1), 127–133. doi:10.25046/aj020115

Samal, K. K. R., Babu, K. S., Das, S. K., & Acharaya, A. (2019, August). Time series based air pollution forecasting using SARIMA and prophet model. In *Proceedings of the 2019 international conference on information technology and computer communications* (pp. 80-85). 10.1145/3355402.3355417

Samuel, A. L. (2000). Some studies in machine learning using the game of checkers. *IBM Journal of Research and Development*, *44*(1.2), 206-226.

Sandler, M., Howard, A., Zhu, M., Zhmoginov, A., & Chen, L.C. (2018). MobileNetV2: Inverted Residuals and Linear Bottlenecks. *Proc. IEEE Comput. Soc. Conf. Comput. Vis. Pattern Recognit.*, 4510–4520. doi:10.1109/CVPR.2018.00474

Sands, E. G., & Bakthavachalam, V. (2019). *Ranking Countries and Industries by Tech, Data, and Business Skills*. Retrieved from Harvard Business Review: https://hbr.org/2019/05/ranking-countries-and-industries-by-tech-data-and-business-skills

Sani, S., Wiratunga, N., & Massie, S. (2017). *Learning deep features for kNN-based human activity recognition*. Academic Press.

Sarkar, M., & De Bruyn, A. (2021). LSTM Response Models for Direct Marketing Analytics: Replacing Feature Engineering with Deep Learning. *Journal of Interactive Marketing*, *53*, 80–95. doi:10.1016/j.intmar.2020.07.002

Sarker, I. H. (2021). Machine Learning: Algorithms, Real-World Applications and Research Directions. *SN Computer Science, 2*(3), 1-21. doi:10.1007/s42979-021-00592-x

Sarlis, A. S., Drivas, I. C., & Sakas, D. P. (2017). *Implementation and dynamic simulation modeling of search engine optimization processes Improvement of website ranking. In Springer Proceedings in Business and Economics*. Strategic Innovative Marketing.

Sarma, A. D. N. (2018). A Generic Functional Architecture for Operational BI System. *International Journal of Business Intelligence Research*, *9*, 64–77. doi:10.4018/IJBIR.2018010105

Sarma, A. D. N. (2021). The five key components for building an operational business intelligence ecosystem, *Int. J. Business Intelligence and Data Mining*, *19*(3), 343–370.

Sarraf, S., & Tofighi, G. (2016). *Classification of alzheimer's disease using fmri data and deep learning convolutional neural networks.* arXiv preprint arXiv:1603.08631.

Saura, J. R., Sanchez, P. P., & Suarez, L. M. C. (2017). Understanding the digital marketing environment with KPIS and web analytics. *Future Internet, 9*(4), 1-13.

Sawant, N., Li, J., & Wang, J. Z. (2011). Automatic image semantic interpretation using social action and tagging data. *Multimedia Tools and Applications, 51*(1), 213–246. doi:10.100711042-010-0650-8

Scherer, M. (2015). Regulating artificial intelligence systems: Risks, challenges, competencies, and strategies. *Harv. JL & Tech., 29*, 353. doi:10.2139srn.2609777

Scherer, M. U. (2016). Regulating Artificial Intelligence Systems: Risks, Challenges, Competencies, and Strategies. *Harvard Journal of Law & Technology, 29*(2), 354–400.

Schmidhuber, J. (2014). *Deep Learning in Neural Networks: An Overview.* arXiv:1404.7828

Schmidt, R., & Vorobieva, O. (2005). *Case-based reasoning investigation of therapy inefficacy.* Paper presented at the International Conference on Innovative Techniques and Applications of Artificial Intelligence.

Schniederjans, M. J., Schniederjans, D. G., & Starkey, C. M. (2014). *Business Analytics Principles, Concepts, and Applications What, Why, and How.* Pearson FT Press.

Schreyögg, G. (2016). *Grundlagen der Organisation. Basiswissen für Studium und Praxis* [Fundamentals of Organisation. Basic knowledge for study and practice]. Springer Verlag. doi:10.1007/978-3-658-13959-9

Seawright, S. (2017, October 17). *5 Elements of the Aviation Ecosystem that will Impact the Future of the Industry.* Retrieved June 19, 2021, from Connected Aviation Today: https://connectedaviationtoday.com/aviation-ecosystem/#.YM1yU1QzaUk

See-To, E. W. K., & Ho, K. K. W. (2014). Value co-creation and purchase intention in social network sites: The role of electronic Word-of-Mouth and trust – A theoretical analysis. *Computers in Human Behavior, 31*, 182–189. doi:10.1016/j.chb.2013.10.013

Sengupta, S., Basak, S., Saikia, P., Paul, S., Tsalavoutis, V., Atiah, F., Ravi, V., & Peters, A. (2020). A review of deep learning with special emphasis on architectures, applications and recent trends. *Knowledge-Based Systems, 194*, 105596. Advance online publication. doi:10.1016/j.knosys.2020.105596

Shambour, Q., & Lu, J. (2015). An effective recommender system by unifying user and item trust information for B2B applications. *Journal of Computer and System Sciences, 81*(7), 1110–1126. doi:10.1016/j.jcss.2014.12.029

Sharaf-El-Deen, D. A., Moawad, I. F., & Khalifa, M. (2014). A new hybrid case-based reasoning approach for medical diagnosis systems. *Journal of Medical Systems, 38*(2), 1–11. doi:10.100710916-014-0009-1 PMID:24469683

Sharda, R., Delen, D., & Turba, E. (2018). *Business Intelligence and Analytics: Systems for Decision Support* (10th ed.). Pearson.

Sharda, R., Delen, D., Turban, E., & King, D. (2018). *Business Intelligence, Analytics, and Data Science: A Managerial Perspective* (4th ed.). Pearson.

Shen, B. J. (1994). A probe into the concept of "Three Kingdoms Culture" ["三国文化" 概念初探]. *Journal of Chinese Culture, 1994*(3), 98–101.

Shikha, N., & Khera, D. (2018). Predictive Modelling of Employee Turnover in Indian IT Industry Using Machine Learning Techniques. *Journal for Decision Makers.*

Shimamoto, K., & Ishii, M. (2006). Development of a daily life skills scale for college students. *Japanese Journal of Educational Psychology, 54*(2), 211–221. doi:10.5926/jjep1953.54.2_211

Shumway, R. H., & Stoffer, D. S. (2017). ARIMA models. In *Time series analysis and its applications* (pp. 75–163). Springer. doi:10.1007/978-3-319-52452-8_3

Simonyan, K., & Zisserman, A. (2014). *Very deep convolutional networks for large-scale image recognition.* arXiv preprint arXiv:1409.1556.

Simonyan, K., & Zisserman, A. (2015). Very deep convolutional networks for large-scale image recognition. *3rd International Conference on Learning Representations, ICLR 2015 - Conference Track Proceedings.*

Şimşek, A., & Kara, R. (2018). Using swarm intelligence algorithms to detect influential individuals for influence maximization in social networks. *Expert Systems with Applications, 114*, 224–236. doi:10.1016/j.eswa.2018.07.038

Singh, V. K., Taram, M., Agrawal, V., & Baghel, B. S. (2018). A Literature Review on Hadoop Ecosystem and Various Techniques of Big Data Optimization. In *Lecture Notes in Networks and Systems* (Vol. 38, pp. 231–240). Springer Singapore., doi:10.1007/978-981-10-8360-0_22

Sinha, P., & Jain, R. (2008). Classification and annotation of digital photos using optical context data. *CIVR 2008 - Proceedings of the International Conference on Content-Based Image and Video Retrieval*, 309–317. 10.1145/1386352.1386394

Sivarajah, U., Kamal, M. M., Irani, Z., & Weerakkody, V. (2017). Critical analysis of Big Data challenges and analytical methods. *Journal of Business Research, 70*, 263–286. https://dx.doi.org/10.1016/j.jbusres.2016.08.001

Skues, J. L., Williams, B., & Wise, K. (2012). The effects of personality traits, self-esteem, loneliness, and narcissism on Facebook use among university students. *Computers in Human Behavior, 28*(6), 2414–2419. doi:10.1016/j.chb.2012.07.012

Smolinska, A., Hauschild, A.-C., Fijten, R., Dallinga, J., Baumbach, J., & Van Schooten, F. (2014). Current breathomics—A review on data pre-processing techniques and machine learning in metabolomics breath analysis. *Journal of Breath Research, 8*(2), 027105. doi:10.1088/1752-7155/8/2/027105 PMID:24713999

Social Media Marketing Tree Diagram. (2021). https://slidemodel.com/templates/digital-marketing-powerpoint-template/social-media-marketing-tree-diagram-ppt/

Song, H., Zmyslinski-Seeling, A., Kim, J., Drent, A., Victor, A., Omori, K., & Allen, M. (2014). Does Facebook make you lonely?: A meta analysis. *Computers in Human Behavior, 36*, 446–452. doi:10.1016/j.chb.2014.04.011

Song, J. L., & Guo, L. (2012). Talking about the development of China's electronic game industry [浅谈中国电子游戏产业发展]. *Business (Atlanta, Ga.), 2012*(07), 161.

Song, Z., Zou, S., Zhou, W., Huang, Y., Shao, L., Yuan, J., ... Chen, X. (2020). Clinically applicable histopathological diagnosis system for gastric cancer detection using deep learning. *Nature Communications, 11*(1), 1–9. doi:10.103841467-020-18147-8 PMID:32855423

Soukal, I., & Hedvicakova, M. (2011). *Retail core banking services e-banking client cluster identification.* Academic Press.

Sparkassengesetz Baden-Württemberg in der Fassung vom 19.07.2005 (GBl. S. 587) zuletzt geändert durch Gesetz vom 07.05.2020 (GBl. S. 259) mit Wirkung vom 13.05.2020 [Savings Banks Act of Baden-Württemberg, §6 (1), 2020)]. https://dejure.org/gesetze/SpG

Srinivasan, V. (2020). *Introducing the new Google Analytics.* https://blog.google/products/marketingplatform/analytics/new_google_analytics/

Srivastava, D., & Nair, P. (2017). Employee Attrition Analysis Using Predictive Techniques. *Smart Innovation, Systems and Technologies*, 293–300.

Srivastava, J. (2008). Data mining for social network analysis. *2008 IEEE International Conference on Intelligence and Security Informatics*, xxxiii–xxxiv. 10.1109/ISI.2008.4565015

Srivastava, S., & Tripathi, K. (2012). Artificial neural network and non-linear regression: A comparative study. *International Journal of Scientific and Research Publications*, 2(12), 740–744.

Statista. (2020). *Projected coronavirus (COVID-19) impact index by industry and dimension*. Author.

Statista. (2020a). *The Statistics Portal. Global social media ranking 2020*. Statista. https://www.statista.com/statistics/272014/global-social-networks-ranked-by-number-of-users/

Statista. (2020b). *The Statistics Portal. Twitter: number of active users 2010-2020*. Statista. https://www.statista.com/statistics/282087/number-of-monthly-active-twitter-users/

Staudt, C. L., Sazonovs, A., & Meyerhenke, H. (2016). NetworKit: A tool suite for large-scale complex network analysis. *Network Science*, 4(4), 508–530. doi:10.1017/nws.2016.20

Stieglitz, S., & Dang-Xuan, L. (2012). Political communication and influence through microblogging - An empirical analysis of sentiment in Twitter messages and retweet behavior. *Proceedings of the Annual Hawaii International Conference on System Sciences*, 3500–3509. 10.1109/HICSS.2012.476

Stieglitz, S., & Linh, D.-X. (2013). Emotions and information diffusion in social media— Sentiment of microblogs and sharing behavior. *Journal of Management Information Systems*, 29(4), 217–247. doi:10.2753/MIS0742-1222290408

Stobierski, T. (2019, August 26). *The Advantages of Data-Driven Decision-Making*. Retrieved September 23, 2021, from Harvard Business School: https://online.hbs.edu/blog/post/data-driven-decision-making

Stranieri, A., & Sun, Z. (2021). Only Can AI Understand Me?: Big Data Analytics, Decision Making, and Reasoning. In S. Zhaohao (Ed.), *Intelligent Analytics With Advanced Multi-Industry Applications* (pp. 46–66). IGI Global. doi:10.4018/978-1-7998-4963-6.ch003

Strawson, P. F. (1962). Freedom and Resentment in Free Will. Oxford UP.

Subasi, A., & Ercelebi, E. (2005). Classification of EEG signals using neural network and logistic regression. *Computer Methods and Programs in Biomedicine*, 78(2), 87–99. doi:10.1016/j.cmpb.2004.10.009 PMID:15848265

Suk, H.-I., Lee, S.-W., & Shen, D. (2014). Hierarchical feature representation and multimodal fusion with deep learning for AD/MCI diagnosis. *NeuroImage*, 101, 569–582. doi:10.1016/j.neuroimage.2014.06.077 PMID:25042445

Sumino, Z. (1995). Creating a subjective well-being scale for life (1). *Annual convention of the Japanese Association of Educational Psychology*, 37, 95.

Sun, Z. (2017). A framework for developing management intelligent systems. In Decision Management: Concepts, Methodologies, Tools, and Applications (pp. 503-521): IGI Global. doi:10.4018/978-1-5225-1837-2.ch024

Sun, Z. (2020). *Business Analytics Intelligence: An Emerging Frontier for Innovation and Productivity*. Retrieved February 3, 2021, from https://www.researchgate.net/profile/Zhaohao_Sun/publication/343876626_Business_Analytics_Intelligence_An_Emerging_Frontier_for_Innovation_and_Productivity

Sun, Z. (2021). *An Introduction to Intelligent Business Analytics*. doi:10.13140/RG.2.2.19361.94562

Sun, Z. (2021). Ten Challenges and Opportunities of Intelligent Big Data. *PNG UoT BAIS*, 6(5), 1-6.

Sun, Z., & Finnie, G. (2010). Intelligent Techniques in E-Commerce: A Case-based Reasoning Perspective. Springer-Verlag.

Sun, Z., & Huo, Y. (2019). A Managerial Framework for Intelligent Big Data Analytics. In *Proceedings of ICBDSC 2019*. Bali, Indonesia: ACM.

Sun, Z., & Huo, Y. (2021). The spectrum of big data analytics. *Journal of Computer Information Systems*. doi:10.1080 /08874417.2019.1571456

Sun, Z., & Wu, Z. (2021). A Strategic Perspective on Big Data Driven Socioeconomic Development. In *The 5th International Conference on Big Data Research (ICBDR)*. ACM.

Sun, Z., Strang, K., & Li, R. (2018). Big data with ten big characteristics. *Proceedings of 2018 The 2nd Intl Conf. on Big Data Research (ICBDR 2018)*. 10.1145/3291801.3291822

Sun, Z. (2017). *Intelligent Big Data Analytics*. Centre of Big Data Analytics and Intelligent Systems. doi:10.13140/ RG.2.2.15854.61763

Sun, Z. (2018). 10 Bigs: Big Data and Its Ten Big Characteristics. *PNG UoT BAIS*, *3*(1), 1–10.

Sun, Z. (2018). Intelligent Big Data Analytics: Foundations and Applications. *PNG UoT BAIS*, *3*(4), 1–8. doi:10.13140/ RG.2.2.11037.41441

Sun, Z. (2019a). Intelligent Big Data Analytics: A Managerial Perspective. In Z. Sun (Ed.), *Managerial Perspectives on Intelligent Big Data Analytics* (pp. 1–19). IGI-Global. doi:10.4018/978-1-5225-7277-0.ch001

Sun, Z. (2020). Business Analytics Intelligence. *An Emerging Frontier for Innovation and Productivity*. Academic Press.

Sun, Z. (2021). An Introduction to Intelligent Analytics Ecosystems. *PNG UoT BAIS*, *6*(3), 1–11.

Sun, Z. (2021). An Introduction to Intelligent Analytics. *PNG UoT BAIS*, *6*(1), 1–6.

Sun, Z. (2021). An Introduction to Intelligent Business Analytics. *PNG UoT BAIS*, *6*(2), 1–6.

Sun, Z. (2021). *Intelligent Analytics with Advanced Multi-Industry Applications*. IGI-Global. doi:10.4018/978-1-7998-4963-6

Sun, Z., Finnie, G., & Weber, K. (2005). Abductive case-based reasoning. *International Journal of Intelligent Systems*, *20*(9), 957–983. doi:10.1002/int.20101

Sun, Z., & Huo, Y. (2020). Intelligence without Data. *Global Journal of Computer Science and Technology C*, *20*(1), 25–35. doi:10.34257/GJCSTCVOL20IS1PG25

Sun, Z., Strang, K., & Firmin, S. (2017). Business Analytics-Based Enterprise Information Systems. *Journal of Computer Information Systems*, *57*(2), 169–178. doi:10.1080/08874417.2016.1183977

Sun, Z., Strang, K., & Li, R. (2018). Big data with ten big characteristics. In *Proceedings of 2018 The 2nd Intl Conf. on Big Data Research (ICBDR 2018)* (pp. 56-61). Weihai, China: ACM.

Sun, Z., Strang, K., & Li, R. (2018). Big data with ten big characteristics. *Proceedings of 2018 The 2nd Intl Conf. on Big Data Research (ICBDR 2018), October 27-29* (pp. 56-61). Weihai, China: ACM.

Sun, Z., & Stranieri, A. (2021). The Nature of Intelligent Analytics. In Z. Sun (Ed.), *Intelligent Analytics with Advanced Multi-industry Applications* (pp. 1–22). IGI-Global. doi:10.4018/978-1-7998-4963-6.ch001

Sun, Z., & Stranieri, A. (2021). The Nature of Intelligent Analytics. In Z. Sun & Z. Sun (Eds.), *Intelligent Analytics With Advanced Multi-Industry Applications* (pp. 1–21). IGI Global.

Sun, Z., Sun, L., & Strang, K. (2018). Big Data Analytics Services for Enhancing Business Intelligence. *Journal of Computer Information Systems*, *58*(2), 162–169. doi:10.1080/08874417.2016.1220239

Sun, Z., & Wang, P. P. (2017). A Mathematical Foundation of Big Data. *Journal of New Mathematics and Natural Computation*, *13*(2), 8–24.

Sun, Z., Zou, H., & Strang, K. (2015). *Big Data Analytics as a Service for Business Intelligence. In I3E2015, LNCS 9373*. Springer.

Sutskever, I., Vinyals, O., & Le, Q. V. (2014). Sequence to sequence learning with neural networks. *Advances in Neural Information Processing Systems*, *4*, 3104–3112.

Svozil, D., Kvasnicka, V., & Pospichal, J. (1997). Introduction to multi-layer feed-forward neural networks. *Chemometrics and Intelligent Laboratory Systems*, *39*(1), 43–62. doi:10.1016/S0169-7439(97)00061-0

Szabo, G., & Huberman, B. A. (2010). Predicting the popularity of online content. *Communications of the ACM*, *53*(8), 80–88. doi:10.1145/1787234.1787254

Szegedy, C., Liu, W., Jia, Y., Sermanet, P., Reed, S., Anguelov, D., Erhan, D., Vanhoucke, V., & Rabinovich, A. (2015). Going deeper with convolutions. *Proc. IEEE Comput. Soc. Conf. Comput. Vis. Pattern Recognit.* 10.1109/CVPR.2015.7298594

Szegedy, C., Liu, W., Jia, Y., Sermanet, P., Reed, S., Anguelov, D., ... Rabinovich, A. (2015). Going deeper with convolutions. *Proceedings of the IEEE conference on computer vision and pattern recognition.*

Tableau. (2021, August 25). Retrieved August 25, 2021, from https://www.tableau.com/

Taieb, S. B., Bontempi, G., Atiya, A. F., & Sorjamaa, A. (2012). A review and comparison of strategies for multi-step ahead time series forecasting based on the NN5 forecasting competition. *Expert Systems with Applications*, *39*(8), 7067–7083. doi:10.1016/j.eswa.2012.01.039

Tang, H., Chen, X., Liu, Y., Lu, Z., You, J., Yang, M., ... Chen, T. (2019). Clinically applicable deep learning framework for organs at risk delineation in CT images. *Nature Machine Intelligence*, *1*(10), 480–491. doi:10.103842256-019-0099-z

Taylor, S. J., & Letham, B. (2018). Forecasting at scale. *The American Statistician*, *72*(1), 37–45. doi:10.1080/00031305.2017.1380080

TechTarget. (n.d.). *Definition for Business Analytics*. https://searchbusinessanalytics.techtarget.com/definition/business-analytics-BA

The Economic Times. (2016). *Human-machine super-intelligence may tackle world's problems*. Retrieved from http://articles.economictimes.indiatimes.com/2016-01-01/news/69448299_1_systems-hci-problems

The Economist. (2017). *Finding a voice*. https://www.economist.com/technology-quarterly/2017-05-01/language

The Fantasy Westward Journey. (n.d.). In *Baidu Baike*. Retrieved from https://baike.baidu.com/item/%E6%A2%A6%E5%B9%BB%E8%A5%BF%E6%B8%B8/157573?fr=aladdin

The Legend of Sword and Fairy. (n.d.). In *Wikipedia*. Retrieved from https://en.wikipedia.org/wiki/The_Legend_of_Sword_and_Fairy

Thelwall, M., Buckley, K., Paltoglou, G., Cai, D., & Kappas, A. (2010). Sentiment strength detection in short informal text. *Journal of the American Society for Information Science and Technology*, *61*(12), 2544–2558. doi:10.1002/asi.21416

Thierer, A., Russell, R., & O'Sullivan, A. (2017). *Artificial Intelligence and Public Policy-research summary*. Academic Press.

Thompson, C. (2020). *What If Working From Home Goes on ... Forever?* https://www.nytimes.com/interactive/2020/06/09/magazine/remote-work-covid.html

Thompson, G. (2021). *Small Data, Big Opportunities.* Retrieved April 22, 2021, from Toptal: https://www.toptal.com/finance/data-analysis-consultants/big-data-vs-small-data

ThoughtSpot. (2021) *Gartner. Augmented Analytics is the Future of Analytics.* Retrieved from https://go.thoughtspot.com/analyst-report-gartner-augmented-analytics.html

Thovex, C., & Trichet, F. (2011). A semantic and multidisciplinary model for professional and social networks analysis. *Proceedings - 2011 International Conference on Advances in Social Networks Analysis and Mining, ASONAM 2011,* 45–52. 10.1109/ASONAM.2011.102

Tibshirani, R. (1996). Regression shrinkage and selection via the Lasso. *Journal of the Royal Statistical Society. Series B, Statistical Methodology, 58*(1), 267–288.

Tiwari, V. (2017). Analysis and detection of fake profile over social network. *Proceeding - IEEE International Conference on Computing, Communication and Automation, ICCCA 2017,* 175–179. 10.1109/CCAA.2017.8229795

Tiwari, A. K., Ramakrishna, G., Sharma, L. K., & Kashyap, S. K. (2019). Academic performance prediction algorithm based on fuzzy data mining. *IAES International Journal of Artificial Intelligence, 8*(1), 26–32. doi:10.11591/ijai.v8.i1.pp26-32

Today. (2019). *Singapore ranks 32 out of 40 for work-life balance, second most overworked city.* https://www.todayonline.com/singapore/singapore-ranks-32-out-40-work-life-balance-second-most-overworked-city

Torra, V. (2002). A review of the construction of hierarchical fuzzy systems. *International Journal of Intelligent Systems, 17*(5), 531–543. doi:10.1002/int.10036

Tsuei, H., Tsai, W., Pan, F., & Tzeng, G. (2018). Improving search engine optimization (SEO) by using hybrid modified MCDM models. *Artificial Intelligence Review, 53,* 1–16.

Turban, E., & Volonino, L. (2011). *Information Technology for Management: Improving Performance in the Digital Economy* (8th ed.). John Wiley & Sons.

Turek, M. (2020). *Explainable Artificial Intelligence (XAI).* DARPA. Retrieved from https://www.darpa.mil/program/explainable-artificial-intelligence

Turner, J., Floyd, M. W., Gupta, K., & Oates, T. (2019). *NOD-CC: A Hybrid CBR-CNN Architecture for Novel Object Discovery.* Paper presented at the International Conference on Case-Based Reasoning. 10.1007/978-3-030-29249-2_25

Tursunbayeva, A., Di Lauro, S., & Pagliari, C. (2018). *People analytics—A scoping review of conceptual boundaries and value propositions.* Academic Press.

Tuytelaars, T., & Mikolajczyk, K. (2007). Local Invariant Feature Detectors: A Survey. In Local Invariant Feature Detectors: A Survey. Now Publishers Inc. doi:10.1561/9781601981394

Tu, Z. (2015). *The Big Data Revolution 3.0.* Guanxi Normal University Press. (in Chinese)

Tylenda, T., Angelova, R., & Bedathur, S. (2009). Towards time-aware link prediction in evolving social networks. *Proceedings of the 3rd Workshop on Social Network Mining and Analysis, SNA-KDD '09.* 10.1145/1731011.1731020

UN IEAG. (2014). *A world that counts mobilizing the data revolution for sustainable development.* https://www.undatarevolution.org/wp-content/uploads/2014/11/A-World-That-Counts.pdf

Uyeno, L. (2019). *An Empirical Analysis of Company Culture: Using Glassdoor Data to Measure the Impact of Culture and Employee Satisfaction on Performance*. Retrieved from Claremont College Scholarship: https://scholarship.claremont.edu/cmc_theses/2293/

Vailaya, A., Figueiredo, M., Jain, A., & Zhang, H. (1999). Content-based hierarchical classification of vacation images. *International Conference on Multimedia Computing and Systems -Proceedings, 1*, 518–523. 10.1109/MMCS.1999.779255

Valipour, M. (2015). Long-term runoff study using SARIMA and ARIMA models in the United States. *Meteorological Applications*, *22*(3), 592–598. doi:10.1002/met.1491

Vashisth, S., Heizenberg, J., Lo, T., Herschel, G., & Radhakrishnan, D. (2021, February 15). *Magic Quadrant for Data and Analytics Service Providers*. Retrieved April 26, 2021, from Gartner: https://www.gartner.com/doc/reprints?id=1-2586H7WL&ct=210216&st=sb

Vassakis, K., Petrakis, E., & Kopanakis, I. (2018). Big data analytics: Applications, prospects and challenges. In *Mobile big data* (pp. 3–20). Springer. doi:10.1007/978-3-319-67925-9_1

Vaswani, A., Shazeer, N., Parmar, N., Uszkoreit, J., Jones, L., Gomez, A. N., . . . Polosukhin, I. (2017). *Attention is all you need*. arXiv preprint arXiv:1706.03762

Vaswani, A., Shazeer, N., Parmar, N., Uszkoreit, J., Jones, L., Gomez, A. N., . . . Polosukhin, I. (2017). Attention is all you need. In Advances in neural information processing systems (pp. 5998-6008). Academic Press.

Vaswani, A., Shazeer, N., Parmar, N., Uszkoreit, J., Jones, L., Gomez, A. N., Kaiser, Ł., & Polosukhin, I. (2017). Attention is all you need. Adv. Neural Inf. Process. Syst., 5999–6009.

Verma, S., Sharma, R., Deb, S., & Maitra, D. (2021). Artificial intelligence in marketing: Systematic review and future research direction. *International Journal of Information Management Data Insights, 1*(1). https://www.sciencedirect.com/science/article/pii/S2667096820300021

Vermeulen, E. P. (2017, December 24). *What is "Smart" in Our New Digital World?* Retrieved March 05, 2020, from Hacker Noon: https://hackernoon.com/what-is-smart-in-our-new-digital-world-87e6426398

Vesset, D., McDonough, B., Schubmehl, D., & Wardley, M. (2013). *Worldwide Business Analytics Software 2013–2017 Forecast and 2012 Vendor Shares* (Doc # 241689). Retrieved 6 28, 2014, from https://www.idc.com/getdoc.jsp?containerId=241689

Vinh, T. Q., & Tran Dac Thinh, P. (2019). Advertisement System Based on Facial Expression Recognition and Convolutional Neural Network. *Proc. - 2019 19th Int. Symp. Commun. Inf. Technol. Isc.*, 476–480. 10.1109/ISCIT.2019.8905134

Vinyals, O., Toshev, A., Bengio, S., & Erhan, D. (2015). Show and tell: A neural image caption generator. *Proc. IEEE Comput. Soc. Conf. Comput. Vis. Pattern Recognit.*, 3156–3164. doi:10.1109/CVPR.2015.7298935

Wadhwa, P., & Bhatia, M. P. S. (2012). Social networks analysis: Trends, techniques and future prospects. *IET Conference Publications, 2012*(CP652), 1–6. 10.1049/cp.2012.2481

Walford-Wright, G., & Scott-Jackson, W. (2018). Talent Rising; people analytics and technology driving talent acquisition strategy. *Strategic HR Review*, *17*(5), 226–233. Advance online publication. doi:10.1108/SHR-08-2018-0071

Wamba, S. F., Akter, S., Edwards, A., Chopin, G., & Gnanzou, D. (2015). How 'big data'can make big impact: Findings from a systematic review and a longitudinal case study. *International Journal of Production Economics*, *165*, 234–246. doi:10.1016/j.ijpe.2014.12.031

Wang, F.-Y. (2012). A big-data perspective on AI: Newton, Merton, and Analytics Intelligence. *IEEE Intelligent Systems, 27*(5), 2-4.

Wang, J., & Li, G. (2017). A Multimodal Hashing Learning Framework for Automatic Image Annotation. *Proceedings - 2017 IEEE 2nd International Conference on Data Science in Cyberspace, DSC 2017*, 14–21. 10.1109/DSC.2017.48

Wang, Y. (2015, June). Formal Cognitive Models of Data, Information, Knowledge, and Intelligence. *WSEAS Transactions on Computers, 14*, 770–781.

Wang, Z.-Z., & Yong, J.-H. (2008). Texture analysis and classification with linear regression model based on wavelet transform. *IEEE Transactions on Image Processing, 17*(8), 1421–1430. doi:10.1109/TIP.2008.926150 PMID:18632350

Waschbusch, G., Blaß, R., & Berg, S. C. (2016). Zukunft der Bankfiliale–Auslaufmodell oder Erlebniswelt [The future of the bank branch - a model to be discontinued or a world of experience]. *Bank und Markt, 5*, 30-33. https://www.kreditwesen.de/bank-markt/themenschwerpunkte/aufsaetze/zukunft-bankfiliale-auslaufmodell-erlebniswelt-id33007.html

Weber, H. (2020). Big Data and Artificial Intelligence: Complete Guide to Data Science, AI, Big Data, and Machine Learning. ICGtesting.

Weber, H. (2020b). Big Data and Artificial Intelligence: Complete Guide to Data Science, AI, Big Data, and Machine Learning. ICGtesting.

Weber, H. (2020a). *Big Data and Artificial Intelligence: Complete Guide to Data Science, AI, Big Data and Machine Learning*. Hans Weber.

Wei, Y. (2010). Chivalry culture and Chinese wushu. *Wushu Science, 7*(11), 17–19.

What is Business Analytics? (n.d.). https://www.oracle.com/in/business-analytics/what-is-business-analytics/

Wikipedia. (2021, April 25). *Management by objectives*. Retrieved May 05, 2021, from Wikipedia: https://en.wikipedia.org/wiki/Management_by_objectives

Williams, S. (2016). *Business Intelligence Strategy and Big Data Analytics: A General Management Perspective*. Morgan Kaufmann.

Wirtz, B. W., Weyerer, J. C., & Sturm, B. J. (2020). The Dark Sides of Artificial Intelligence: An Integrated AI Governance Framework for Public Administration. *International Journal of Public Administration, 43*(9), 818–829. doi:10.1080/01900692.2020.1749851

Wirtz, D., Tucker, A., Briggs, C., & Schoemann, A. M. (2021). How and why social media affect subjective well-being: Multi-site use and social comparison as predictors of change across time. *Journal of Happiness Studies, 22*(4), 1673–1691. doi:10.100710902-020-00291-z

Wolgast, M. (2016). Das gegenwärtige Niedrigzinsumfeld aus Sicht der Sparkassen [The current low interest rate environment from the point of view of savings banks]. *Vierteljahrshefte zur Wirtschaftsforschung, 85*(1), 11–29. doi:10.3790/vjh.85.1.11

Wright, P., Gardner, T., Moynihan, L., & Allen, M. (2005). The relationship between HR practices and firm performance: Examining causal order. *Personnel Psychology*, 409–446.

Wright, P. M., Gardner, T. M., & Moynihan, L. M. (2003). The impact of HR practices on the performance of business units. *Human Resource Management Journal, 13*(3), 409–446. doi:10.1111/j.1748-8583.2003.tb00096.x

Wu, J., Jiang, N., Wu, Z., & Jiang, H. (2021). Early warning of risks in cross-border mobile payments. *Procedia Computer Science, 183*, 724–732. doi:10.1016/j.procs.2021.02.121

Xiang, Z., Yan, J., & Demir, I. (2020). A rainfall-runoff model with LSTM-based sequence-to-sequence learning. *Water Resources Research*, *56*(1).

Xiao, C., Freeman, D. M., & Hwa, T. (2015). Detecting clusters of fake accounts in online social networks. *AISec 2015 - Proceedings of the 8th ACM Workshop on Artificial Intelligence and Security, Co-Located with CCS 2015*, 91–102. 10.1145/2808769.2808779

Xie, R., Chu, S. K. W., Chiu, D. K. W., & Wang, Y. (2021). Exploring public response to COVID-19 on Weibo with LDA topic modeling and sentiment analysis. *Data and Information Management*, *5*(1), 86–99. doi:10.2478/dim-2020-0023

Xu, H., Yu, Z., Yang, J., & Xiong, H. (2016). *Talent Circle Detection in Job Transition Networks*. ACM. doi:10.1145/2939672.2939732

Xu, T., Zhu, H., Zhu, C., Li, P., & Xiong, H. (2018). Measuring the Popularity of Job Skills in Recruitment Market: A Multi-Criteria Approach. In *The Thirty-Second AAAI Conference on Artificial Intelligence (AAAI-18)*. Association for the Advancement of Artificial Intelligence.

Yamagishi, T. (1998). *The Structure of Trust: The Evolutionary Games of Mind and Society*. Tokyo University Press.

Yamanaka, J., Kuwashima, S., & Kurita, T. (2017, November). Fast and accurate image super resolution by deep CNN with skip connection and network in network. In *International Conference on Neural Information Processing* (pp. 217-225). Springer. 10.1007/978-3-319-70096-0_23

Yang, L., Giua, A., & Li, Z. (2017). Minimizing the Influence Propagation in Social Networks for Linear Threshold Models. *IFAC*, *50*(1), 14465–14470. doi:10.1016/j.ifacol.2017.08.2293

Yang, R., Mentzer, F., Van Gool, L., & Timofte, R. (2021). Learning for Video Compression with Recurrent Auto-Encoder and Recurrent Probability Model. *IEEE Journal of Selected Topics in Signal Processing*, *15*(2), 388–401. doi:10.1109/JSTSP.2020.3043590

Ye, X., Zhao, Z., Leake, D., Wang, X., & Crandall, D. (2021). *Applying the Case Difference Heuristic to Learn Adaptations from Deep Network Features*. arXiv preprint arXiv:2107.07095.

Ye, J., Zhao, Z., & Wu, M. (2007). Discriminative k-means for clustering. *Advances in Neural Information Processing Systems*, *20*, 1649–1656.

Yermal, L., & Balasubramanian, P. (2017, December). Application of auto arima model for forecasting returns on minute wise amalgamated data in nse. In *2017 IEEE International Conference on Computational Intelligence and Computing Research (ICCIC)* (pp. 1-5). IEEE. 10.1109/ICCIC.2017.8524232

Ye, S. Y. (2019). The relationships between Twitter use, social comparison and satisfaction with friendship among university students. *Socio-Informatics*, *8*(2), 111–112.

Ye, S. Y., Ho, K. W. K., & Zerbe, A. (2021). The effects of social media usage on loneliness and well-being: Analysing friendship connections of Facebook, Twitter and Instagram. *Information Discovery and Delivery*, *49*(2), 136–150. doi:10.1108/IDD-08-2020-0091

Ye, S. Y., Toshimori, A., & Horita, T. (2017). Causal relationships between media/social media and Internet literacy among college students: Addressing the effects of social skills and gender differences. *Educational Technology Review*, *40*(1), 61–70.

Yin, J., & Fernandez, V. (2020). A systematic review on business analytics. *Journal of Industrial Engineering and Management*, *13*(2), 283–295. doi:10.3926/jiem.3030

Yoshitaka, A., & Ichikawa, T. (1999). A survey on content-based retrieval for multimedia databases. *IEEE Transactions on Knowledge and Data Engineering*, *11*(1), 81–93. doi:10.1109/69.755617

Yu, J. (2017, July 9). *The Complex Aviation Ecosystem*. Retrieved June 19, 2021, from LinkedIn: https://www.linkedin.com/pulse/complex-aviation-ecosystem-jack-yu/

Yu, Y., Lin, H., Meng, J., & Zhao, Z. (2016). Visual and textual sentiment analysis of a microblog using deep convolutional neural networks. *Algorithms*, *9*(2), 41. doi:10.3390/a9020041

Zadeh, L. A. (1975). The concept of a linguistic variable and its application to approximate reasoning. Part 1,2,3, Information Sciences, 8, 199-249. doi:10.1016/0020-0255(75)90036-5

Zadeh, L. A. (1965). Fuzzy set. *Information and Control*, *8*(3), 338–353. doi:10.1016/S0019-9958(65)90241-X

Zarezade, A., Jafarzadeh, S., & Rabiee, H. R. (2018). Recurrent spatio-temporal modeling of check-ins in location-based social networks. *PLoS One*, *13*(5), e0197683. doi:10.1371/journal.pone.0197683 PMID:29791463

Zeiler, M. D., & Fergus, R. (2014). *Visualizing and understanding convolutional networks*. Paper presented at the European conference on computer vision.

Zeroual, A., Harrou, F., Dairi, A., & Sun, Y. (2020). Deep learning methods for forecasting COVID-19 time-Series data: A Comparative study. *Chaos, Solitons, and Fractals*, *140*, 110121. doi:10.1016/j.chaos.2020.110121 PMID:32834633

Zhang, X., Xie, C., Wang, J., Zhang, W., & Fu, X. (2018). Towards memory friendly long-short term memory networks (LSTMs) on mobile GPUs. *Proc. Annu. Int. Symp. Microarchitecture, MICRO 2018*, 162–174. 10.1109/MICRO.2018.00022

Zhang, G. P. (2000). Neural networks for classification: A survey. *IEEE Transactions on Systems, Man and Cybernetics. Part C, Applications and Reviews*, *30*(4), 451–462. doi:10.1109/5326.897072

Zhang, G., & Zhao, J. L. (2017). A review of the research on Chinese martial arts culture [中国武侠文化研究述评]. *Journal of Jilin Sport University*, *33*(1), 7–11.

Zhao, S., Yao, H., Gao, Y., Ding, G., & Chua, T. S. (2018). Predicting Personalized Image Emotion Perceptions in Social Networks. *IEEE Transactions on Affective Computing*, *9*(4), 526–540. doi:10.1109/TAFFC.2016.2628787

Zhong, W., Liao, L., Guo, X., & Wang, G. (2019). Fetal electrocardiography extraction with residual convolutional encoder–decoder networks. *Australasian Physical & Engineering Sciences in Medicine*, *42*(4), 1081–1089. doi:10.100713246-019-00805-x PMID:31617154

Zhou, H., Zhang, S., Peng, J., Zhang, S., Li, J., Xiong, H., & Zhang, W. (2020). *Informer: Beyond Efficient Transformer for Long Sequence Time-Series Forecasting*. arXiv preprint arXiv:2012.07436.

Zhou, R., Khemmarat, S., & Gao, L. (2010). The impact of YouTube recommendation system on video views. *Proc. ACM SIGCOMM Internet Meas. Conf. IMC*, 404–410. 10.1145/1879141.1879193

Zhou, L., Pan, S., Wang, J., & Vasilakos, A. V. (2017). Machine learning on big data: Opportunities and challenges. *Neurocomputing*, *237*, 350–361. doi:10.1016/j.neucom.2017.01.026

About the Contributors

Zhaohao Sun is a full professor of IT, PNG University of Technology, Director of Research Centre of Big Data Analytics and Intelligent Systems (BAIS). He graduated from Bond U, U of Ballarat, Australia; Brandenburg Techn. U Cottbus (TU Cottbus), Germany and Hebei U, China with PhD, Graduate Cert. of Edu., MSc, MSc, and BSc respectively. He is also an adjunct professor of the Federation U Australia, chair professor of Hebei U of Science & Techn. He previously held academic positions at Hebei U, Hebei Normal U, China; RWTH Aachen, TU Cottbus; Bond U and UoW. Dr Sun is a world renowned scholar in many fields such as big data, data science, e-commerce, CBR, and intelligent systems. He has 10 books and 170+ referred research publications, completed 30+ research grants, supported from China, Germany, Australia, USA and PNG, and lectured 46+ different courses for UG and PG students of IT, IS, and CS in universities of Australia, China, and PNG. His current research interests include big data analytics, data science, AI, and business intelligence. He is a senior member of ACS, and a MAIS and MIEEE.

Zhiyou Wu is a full professor of Chongqing Normal University. She is also the director of Chongqing Key Lab of Intelligent Finance and Big Data Analysis, a Humboldt Research Fellow, the New Century Talent of the Ministry of Education, one of the One hundred leading talents in academic disciplines in Chongqing, etc. She is also the Executive director of Operations Research Society of China, the President of Chongqing Operational Research Society, etc. Her research area is on optimization theory and algorithms, especially on global optimization. She is the Principal Investigator of more than 15 projects including three National Natural Science Foundation of China and Australian National Project (ARC), etc. She has published more than 70 papers in journals such as SIAM, J and OPTIM, and has won 3 Chongqing Natural Science Awards. She has visited many universities in Hong Kong, Singapore, Australia, Germany and so on. She is an adjunct professor and adjunct doctoral supervisor at Shanghai University and Southwest Jiaotong University.

* * *

Selvakumar Anthonyraj has 9 years of teaching experience. He did his M.Phil. Computer Science from Periyar University, M.C.A. from Madurai Kamaraj University. His area of research interest is Machine Learning.

Sarma A. D. N. is working at Centre for Good Governance, Hyderabad, India. He received M.Sc., and M.S. degree from Acharya Nagarjuna University and BITS, Pilani respectively. He received Ph.D.

degree in Computer Science and Engineering from Acharya Nagarjuna University. His research interests include data analytics and intelligent analytics, artificial intelligence, business intelligence, IT Operations and Security, e-Governance, IoT and blockchain.

Markus Bick is a full Professor of Business Information Systems at ESCP Business School Campus Berlin, Germany. He earned a PhD in Business Information Systems from the University of Duisburg-Essen, and a Diploma (MSc equivalent) in business information systems from the University of Essen. He was the local academic director of ESCP's bachelor in management in Berlin. His current research interests include gamification, digital transformation including digital competencies and digital maturity models as well as global knowledge management, or blockchain. He published his work in renowned international journals (Journal of Business Logistics, Information Systems Frontiers, Electronic Markets, Information & Management, Business Information Systems Engineering, Decision Support Systems, International Journal of Information Management or Information Systems Management) and is an Associate Editor of Electronics Market and a Senior Editor of Information Systems Management.

Abdelmalek Bouguettaya received the master's and Ph.D. degrees in telecommunications from Badji Mokhtar University, Annaba, Algeria, in 2011 and 2017, respectively. He was a member of the "Embedded and Detection" Advanced Systems Division, Laboratoire d'Etude et de Recherche en Instrumentation et en Communication d'Annaba (LERICA Laboratory), Annaba, from 2009 to 2018. He is currently a Senior Researcher with the Research Center in Industrial Technologies (CRTI), Chéraga, Algeria. His current research interests include Artificial Intelligence, deep learning, computer vision, and intelligent embedded systems.

Li Chen is currently a professor of computer science at the University of the District of Columbia. He received his BS, MS, and PhD in CS from Wuhan University (1982), Utah State University (1995), and the University of Bedfordshire (2001), respectively. Chen has published more than 70 research papers in journals and conference proceedings and published several books including "Mathematical problems in data science" (Springer, 2016), "Digital and discrete geometry" (Springer, 2014), "Digital functions and data reconstruction" (Springer, 2012). Chen also writes articles for CS and applied math education. He was an ACM Distinguished Speaker for 6 years.

Dickson K. W. Chiu received the B.Sc. (Hons.) degree in Computer Studies from the University of Hong Kong in 1987. He received the M.Sc. (1994) and the Ph.D. (2000) degrees in Computer Science from the Hong Kong University of Science and Technology (HKUST). He started his own computer company while studying part-time. He has also taught at several universities in Hong Kong. His teaching and research interests are in Information Management, Service Computing, Library Science, and E-learning with a cross-disciplinary approach, involving workflows, software engineering, information technologies, agents, information system research, and databases. The results have been widely published in over 250 international publications (most of them indexed by SCI, SCI-E, EI, and SSCI), including many practical taught master and undergraduate project results. He received a best paper award in the 37th Hawaii International Conference on System Sciences in 2004. He is the founding Editor-in-chief of the International Journal on Systems and Service-Oriented Engineering, and serves on the editorial boards of several international journals. He is an editor(-in-chief) of Library Hi Tech indexed by SSCI (impact factor 2.325). He co-founded several international workshops and co-edited several journal special issues. He also served as a program committee member for around 250 international conferences and workshops. Dr. Chiu is a Senior Member of both the ACM and the IEEE, and a life member of the Hong Kong Computer Society. According to Google Scholar, he has over 4,500 citations, h-index 36, i-10 index 97; ranked worldwide 1st in the category of "e-services," and "LIS," and 2ndh in "m-learning."

Akila Djebbar is currently Associate Professor at the university of Badji Mokhtar-Annaba. She received her engineer in Computer Science in 2002 from Annaba University. She received a Magister in "Distributed Artificial Intelligence" in 2006. She has her Ph.D (2013) in Artificial Intelligence. Dr Akila Djebbar is one of the reviewers of International Journal of Business Intelligence and Data Mining (IJBIDM) and International Journal of Intelligent Information and Database Systems (IJIIDS). She is a doctor at computer science department of Badji Mokhtar Annaba University (Algeria) and member of LRI Laboatory. Her research interests are Machine Learning, Case Based Reasoning approach, Case Base maintenance, Supervised learning, Semi-supervised learning, CAD system.

Safa Gasmi is currently pursuing her PhD at the LRI Laboratory of the Department of Computer Science, University Badji Mokhtar, Annaba, University of Algeria. She obtained a bachelor's degree in computer science "information system" in 2018. She obtained a master degree in "Artificial Intelligence and Information Processing" in 2020. She is currently working on the research topic "A hybrid approach: Case Based Reasoning and Deep Learning applied to medical data". Her current research interests also include: case-based reasoning (CBR) applied in the medical domain, deep learning (DL) techniques, hybrid CBR-DL systems applied in the medical context, computer-aided diagnostic systems, machine learning techniques, medical image classification.

Carsten Giebe works in the heart of Berlin as a Senior Consultant Data Analytics. He is a certified sales trainer, NLP master and systemic business coach. In 2007, he received a Diploma (MSc equivalent) in Economics from the FOM - University of Applied Sciences, Berlin (Germany). Since 2017, the trained banker is a PhD candidate at the Doctoral School in Management & Organizational Sciences, at today's MATE Hungarian University of Agriculture and Life Sciences - Kaposvár Campus, Kaposvár (Hungary) in cooperation with the Hamburger Fernhochschule - University of Applied Sciences, Hamburg (Germany). Moreover, he is an associate researcher at the International Organization for Business Coaching (IOBC). His research focuses on digital transformation, big data analytics, coaching, sales, psychology, business ethics and sustainability. Since 2020 he has been a lecturer at Macromedia - University of Applied Sciences, Berlin Campus (Germany), as well.

Merouani Hayet Farida received her engineer degree at the University of Badji Mokhtar, Annaba, Algeria in 1984, followed by a Ph.D. Degree from Robert Gordon University, Aberdeen, UK. Currently, she is a full Professor at the Badji Mokhtar University, Annaba. She leads the Computer Laboratory at Badji Mokhtar University more than five years. She also leads Research Group of Pattern Recognition, as a National Program Research of Breast Cancer. She also leads several national projects. Prof. Hayet Farida Merouani has authored more than 100 research papers publication. She is a permanent reviewer member of Artificial Intelligence in medicine (Springer), in Scientific Research and Essays (academic journals), and in Journal of King Saud University - Computer and Information Sciences (Springer) and her current works focus on the computer vision, pattern recognition and data mining, medical imaging, CAD system, artificial Intelligence.

Zhixuam He received the M.Sc. degree in Library and Information Management from the University of Hong Kong (HKU) in 2021. This chapter was mainly derived from his graduation project research. His research interest is in data analytics, especially for sports and electronic games.

Kevin K. W. Ho is the Professor of Management Information Systems at the School of Business and Public Administration, University of Guam. Kevin's research interests include electronic service, information systems strategy, social media, and sustainability management. He is the Co-Editor(-in-Chief) of Library Hi Tech (an SSCI Journal) and the associate editor of the International Journal of Systems and Service-Oriented Engineering. His research has been published in Behaviour & Information Technology, Communications of the Association for Information Systems, Computers in Human Behavior, Decision Support Systems, Government Information Quarterly, Health Policy, Information Systems Frontier, Internet Research, Information & Management, Journal of Retailing and Consumer Services, and Online Information Review, among others.

Ahmed Kechida received his M. S degree in electronics from Polytechnic Military School in 2003, and the Ph.D. degree in Electronics from Saad Dahleb Blida 1 University, Blida, Algeria in 2016. He is currently a Senior Researcher with Research Center in Industrial Technologies (CRTI). His research interests include Signal Processing, Image analysis, embedded systems for drones, Nondestructive evaluation by ultrasound.

Muhammad Haseeb Khan is doing his Ph.D. from the University of Tsukuba in Informatics. He did his master's from the same University. Most of his research work is in the field of NLP. He is in the building phase of his research profile so he has published a few papers in the NLP domain. His research interests include text summarization, interactive NLP systems, and social media analysis. He is amazed by the progress of ML/AI in the field of computer vision so like to have knowledge about that well also.

Ricardo Matheus is a lecturer and researcher in the field of Open Government Data and Infrastructures at the Information and Communication Technology research group of the Technology, Policy and Management Faculty of Delft University of Technology. He was a lecturer at Rotterdam School of Management of Erasmus Rotterdam University (The Netherlands) teaching Data Science and Programming for Managers courses. He led WPs in the CAP4CITY Project (www.cap4city.eu/) and in the H2020 OpenGovIntelligence project (www.opengovintelligence.eu) which aims to create transparency using open government data in six international governmental pilots. Prior to joining TU Delft, Ricardo was a data scientist helping to improve Big Data processes of the IBM Operation Center in Rio de Janeiro, Brazil.

Desmond Narongou holds a Bachelor's Degree of Commerce in Information Technology (with merit) from PNG University of Technology. Desmond currently works with the Office of Strategy Management, National Airports Corporation (NAC) Limited of Papua New Guinea. He is a freelance researcher and a writer. His research areas and interests cover Smart Airport, Big Data Analytics, AI, Cloud Computing, IoT, and e-Commerce, e-Business, SMEs, informal market sector, and Christian events and stories. He has written a number of stories and articles both within PNG and abroad, including publishing two book chapters related to Big Data and Smart airports, and has contributed to scholarly reviews of articles.

Isakki Alias Devi Paramasivam has 18 years of teaching experience. She did her Ph.D. Computer Science in VELS University, Chennai, India, M.Phil from Bharathidasan University, M.C.A from Madurai Kamaraj University, India. Her area of research interest is Data Mining and Machine Learning. She has published 23 papers in International journals, 1 Book Chapter in IGI Global, 19 papers in National / International conferences etc., She guided for 8 M.Phil scholars.

Francisca Pambel has been a lecturer of Information Technology and Head of Section IT for DBS, PNG University of Technology. She has published a few quality research papers in the area of big data analytics. Her current research interests include Information Technology and Systems, Big data Technology, Social Computing.

Luiz Pinheiro is a PhD in Business with expertise research in Information Systems (IS), Eletronic Government (eGov) and Cloud Computing. Assistant Professor in Business School, Conferencist in Information Technology (IT) and IS. Reviser in Conferences and Journals in the Brazil, United States, Europe and Latin America.

Shivanand Rai is a student of ESCP's Master's in Big Data program and undertook research under Professor Markus Bick's tutelage.

Alexander Ryjov, a Professor, Doctor of Sciences, has 30+years of the combined business, advanced research, and teaching experience. Alexander has a Ph.D. in Mathematics, a D.Sc. in Engineering, Executive MBA from Bled School of Management. He is a professor at Lomonosov Moscow State University (mathematics) and head of the Chair at Russian Presidential Academy of National Economy and Public Administration (high-tech business), a member of two authorizing Ph.D. Boards. He has100+scientific publications, including 6 books and chapters in 14 books — more information on http://www.intsys. msu.ru/en/staff/ryzhov/.

Andrew Stranieri is a researcher in the Centre for Informatics and Applied Optimisation at Federation University Australia. His research in health informatics spans data mining in health, complementary and alternative medicine informatics, telemedicine, and intelligent decision support systems. He is the author of over 150 peer reviewed journal and conference articles and has published two books.

Amine Mohammed Taberkit is senior researcher at Research Center in Industrial Technologies, CRTI, Algeria. His research interests are machine learning, deep learning, computer vision, unmanned arial vehicle, and precision agriculture.

Kei Wakabayashi received his Ph.D. in Engineering from Hosei University in 2012. He was appointed to the Faculty of Library, Information and Media Science at the University of Tsukuba in 2012 as an assistant professor and promoted to associate professor in 2020. He has published over 50 peer-reviewed technical papers in computer science and its related fields. His research interests include machine learning algorithms, natural language dialog systems, and social media analysis.

Bingnan Wang received the M.Sc. degree in Library and Information Management from the University of Hong Kong (HKU) in 2021. This chapter was mainly derived from his graduation project research. His research interest is in data analytics, especially deep learning and time series forecasting.

Shaoyu Ye is currently serving as Associate Professor at the Faculty of Library, Information and Media Science, University of Tsukuba in Japan. She received her Ph.D. in Philosophy from Tokyo Institute of Technology in March 2015; and master of social psychology from Ochanomizu University (Japan) in March 2010. She was also a research fellow of the Japan Society for the Promotion of Science (JSPS) from 2014-15 (DC2 & PD). Her research mainly specializes in media (especially social media) usage's effects on interpersonal communication, social support networks and social adaption. She is a member of Asian Association of Social Psychology (AASP).

Hafed Zarzour received the Ph.D. degree in computer science from Annaba University, Annaba, Algeria, in 2013. He is currently an Associate Professor of computer science with the University of Souk Ahras, Souk-Ahras, Algeria. He has published several research articles in international journals and conferences of high repute, including IEEE, Springer, Elsevier, Wiley, ACM, Taylor and Francis, IGI Global, and Inderscience. His research focuses on deep learning, artificial intelligence, and educational technology.

Index

A

Additive Trend Components 319
airport analytics 216-219, 221-222, 225-227, 229, 233, 236
airport services chain 222, 224, 236
analytics 1-37, 39-48, 56, 64, 66, 68-69, 71-73, 75-76, 84-86, 89-94, 98, 108, 110-111, 142-147, 150-155, 159-167, 179, 181-183, 185-188, 196, 198, 208-209, 211, 216-222, 224-236, 238-241, 244, 246, 252-254, 276, 286, 295-297, 299, 315, 318-319, 321, 346-347, 350, 353-355, 361-371
and e-Society 96-97, 108-109
Applications of machine learning 179
Artificial Intelligence (AI) 1-2, 20, 22-23, 70, 73, 76, 96, 111, 113, 116, 225, 228, 236, 300
Augmented Analytics 13-14, 18, 47-48, 56, 68-69
Augmented Intelligence 49, 69-70
aviation analytics 216-219, 221, 225, 227, 232-233
aviation ecosystem 216, 219, 221-222, 225-226, 228-229, 231, 234-236

B

Backlinks 157, 159, 165
big data 1-7, 9-13, 15-22, 24, 27-29, 31, 33-41, 43-48, 64, 66, 69, 74-75, 81, 89-93, 98-99, 108, 110-111, 134, 142-147, 149-151, 153, 158, 160-168, 179, 181-182, 185-186, 188, 198, 211, 213, 216-222, 225-236, 286-287, 318, 321, 347, 350, 353-355, 362-370
big data analytics 1-7, 9-13, 15-17, 19-22, 33-34, 36, 39, 44, 64, 66, 90, 92-93, 108, 110-111, 142-147, 151, 153, 161, 163-165, 185-186, 216-222, 225-236, 321, 350, 353-355, 362-370
business analytics 1-3, 6-7, 9-17, 19, 21-22, 24-27, 33, 35, 41, 43-46, 71-73, 75-76, 85-86, 92-93, 165-167, 179, 182, 185, 221, 228-229, 234, 295-296, 362, 366

Business Analytics Projects (BAP) 71, 75
Business Intelligence 1-2, 16-23, 25, 27, 41, 44-45, 71-72, 90, 92-93, 110, 143, 153, 166-167, 179, 186, 220, 234-235, 296, 354, 365, 368
business question 76-78, 80-81, 83, 85, 87, 94, 355
business value 2, 18, 33, 92, 184, 216-220, 225-226, 228, 230-232, 365

C

capstone projects 273-274, 285
CBR cycle 113-115, 132-133
Chinese culture 320-323, 346, 348
Chinese Word Segmentation 349
Chronic Kidney Disease 134, 140
Chronically Obstructed Pulmonary Illness 140
cloud computing 22, 27, 30, 96, 220, 225, 228, 236, 287, 319, 349
Cloud Service Providers 287
cluster analysis 323, 340, 344-346, 349
clustering 12, 26, 32, 35, 43, 74, 83-84, 116, 134, 138, 140, 170, 199, 208, 299, 315, 320, 340, 349
competition 9, 18, 90, 159-160, 176, 233, 301, 304-305, 309, 317, 350-351, 353-354, 370
Computer Science 19, 45, 93, 135, 156, 163, 168, 187, 208, 210, 212, 234, 273-274, 285-286, 315
Computer-Aided Detection (CAD) 141
coronavirus 138, 141, 254
COVID-19 6, 75, 91, 116, 166, 180, 182, 217, 228, 232, 238, 241-242, 249-251, 254, 314, 316, 318, 348

D

dashboard 71, 73-74, 77-81, 84-91, 93-94
dashboards 6, 12-14, 25, 27, 71-78, 80-89, 91, 93-94
data analytics 1-7, 9-24, 26-28, 32-34, 36, 39, 43-45, 64, 66, 71, 73, 75, 84, 90-94, 108, 110-111, 142-147, 151, 153-155, 161-165, 185-186, 208, 216-222, 224-236, 321, 350, 353-355, 361-370

data mining 6, 11-12, 17-18, 20, 23-24, 27, 32, 45, 66, 83, 89-91, 111, 136, 138, 146, 165, 181, 189, 193, 195, 197-198, 206-207, 209-214, 232, 286, 305, 315, 354, 365

data mining techniques 83, 189, 193, 197-198, 207, 212

data processing 3, 7, 27, 29-30, 38, 142, 181, 189, 193-195, 197, 211

Data Science 1, 9, 16, 19-21, 23, 43-44, 47, 71, 74-75, 87-92, 111, 183, 212, 214, 234-236, 273-274, 283, 286-287, 354

data sources 28, 39, 71, 77, 80-82, 87, 94, 143, 145, 158, 162, 193, 225, 251

Data Visualization 11-13, 27, 30, 71, 77, 82-83, 87, 94, 145

data warehouse 11, 17, 23, 71, 77, 81-83, 87, 94, 135, 219, 221-222, 227, 362

decision making 3-5, 9, 11-13, 15-16, 21-22, 24-26, 31, 34-36, 74, 91, 94, 98, 110, 144, 147, 162, 182, 216-217, 220-222, 225, 227, 236, 296

Decision-system 21

deep learning 12, 17, 23, 29-30, 33, 36, 41, 102-103, 113-114, 116, 118-124, 126-127, 132-140, 166-168, 170, 172-176, 179-183, 185-187, 232, 301-305, 307-310, 312-314, 316-319, 323, 348, 367

deep learning models 118, 120-122, 126-127, 132, 172, 301-303, 305, 307-310, 312-313, 317

digital transformation 16, 27, 29, 31, 42, 143, 233-234, 350-351, 353, 362-363, 366-367, 369-371

digitalization 73, 180, 239, 350, 353-355, 360, 362-364, 366-367, 369, 371

DIKIW 1-2, 7-13, 15-16, 18, 20

direct forecasting strategy 306-307, 309, 319

E

e-Business 15, 96-97, 108-109, 164

Emotional Expression Topics 288

Endocrine System 141

e-Services 12, 96-97, 108-109

e-sports 320-321

ethic AI 96, 108

Ethical Artificial Intelligence 96, 111

ETL 71, 77, 81-82, 85, 87, 94

evaluation and monitoring 47, 56-58, 60-61, 64-68, 70

evaluation and monitoring of complex processes 47, 58, 61, 66, 68

Examples in Data Science 273

explainable AI 96-97, 107-109

F

finance 21, 24, 27, 36, 41, 43, 68, 72-73, 86, 101, 161, 167, 179, 193, 221, 228, 235, 238-239, 241-242, 250-252, 366, 369-370

Fuzzy Linguistic Scales 68

fuzzy logic 11, 49, 67, 70, 165

Fuzzy Sets 55, 57, 60, 62, 67-68, 70

G

German banking system 350-351, 365, 371

Glassdoor 238-242, 244-246, 250-254, 259-261, 267

H

Hierarchical Systems 68, 70

Hybrid DL-CBR Medical System 113

Hybrid Forecasting Strategy 307, 309, 319

Hybrid Intelligence 47-48, 50, 56, 67

I

Information Technology 19, 24, 68, 75, 91, 110, 135, 138, 162-163, 183, 273, 297, 299, 317, 367

Intelligent Analytics 1-2, 10, 14-16, 19-22, 26, 29, 32-33, 36-37, 42-43, 98, 110-111, 218, 221, 230, 233-234, 286, 299, 315, 318, 347

intelligent big data analytics 1-6, 9, 11, 15, 19-22, 34, 108, 216-222, 225-231, 234, 236

intelligent business 1-3, 6-7, 9-17, 21, 33, 35, 41, 43, 142, 165, 221, 228, 234, 295-296

intelligent business analytics 1-3, 6-7, 9-17, 21, 33, 35, 43, 221, 234, 295-296

Intelligent System 3, 5, 69, 104, 111, 236

Internet of Things (IoT) 27, 73, 220, 225, 228, 236

K

keywords 1, 21, 47, 71, 73, 96, 113, 142, 146, 151-152, 155-156, 158-161, 164-166, 189, 195, 201, 216, 218, 238, 273, 288, 301, 320, 324, 340, 350, 353

L

Liver Disorder 141

London 185, 238-239, 242, 245-251, 255-258, 317

M

Machine Learning (ML) 12, 22-23, 30, 38, 73, 76, 113, 116, 221, 228 management 5, 7, 9, 13, 16-20, 23-24, 27, 31, 36-37, 39-41, 44-48, 56, 70, 74-75, 89, 91-94, 98, 101, 109-110, 135, 137, 143, 147, 149, 151, 153, 159, 162-165, 184, 186-187, 192-193, 205, 216, 220-222, 224-226, 231-233, 235-236, 238-242, 245-254, 264, 297-299, 318, 348, 363-370

Measurement 25, 68, 70, 212

Medical CBR systems 113, 117

ML 12-13, 22-23, 26, 30-31, 33, 35-39, 43, 73-77, 88, 113, 116, 221, 228, 230, 238

Multiplicative Trend Components 319

N

NAC 216-217, 221, 227, 237

Natural Language Processing (NLP) 23, 74, 175-177, 179, 288-290, 300

O

open government data 75, 78, 86, 91, 94

optimization 13, 33, 36-37, 68, 74, 91, 138, 142, 144, 148, 150-151, 154-156, 161-165, 185, 207, 213, 303, 314, 319, 349, 354, 362

P

people analytics 73, 89, 92, 238-241, 244, 246, 252, 254

perception-based descriptions 49, 60-61

PMIA 221, 237

process-oriented paradigm 98, 101, 111

Public Health Emergencies 135, 141

R

ranking 14, 102, 104, 148, 151-153, 155-156, 158, 160-165, 200, 213, 253, 295

recursive forecasting strategy 306-307, 309, 319

regulating AI systems 96-103, 107-108, 112

regulation 74, 96-99, 102-109, 191, 249

research 1-3, 5, 13-19, 21, 24, 27, 31, 35, 42-43, 45, 57, 66-68, 72-73, 87-88, 90-93, 96, 98-101, 107-109, 111, 113-114, 118, 120, 122, 133-134, 138-139, 147-148, 157-159, 163-166, 177, 185, 191-193, 195-200, 203-207, 212, 216-219, 221, 230-232, 234-235, 240-242, 246, 248, 251, 253, 273-283, 285, 287, 289-290, 294-298, 301-303, 308, 314-316, 318, 320-321, 324, 346-350, 353-354, 361-366, 369-370

retrieval phase 113-115, 132-133

S

savings banks 350-355, 357-359, 361-369, 371-373

search engine 1, 74, 91, 142-144, 148-151, 153-156, 159, 161-165

semantic image analysis 189, 193, 200, 202

sentiment analysis 90, 138, 150-151, 177, 184, 204, 209, 214, 252, 289-291, 293, 297, 299-300, 348

SEO 74, 142-143, 145-146, 148-163, 165

Singapore 210, 213, 238-239, 241-242, 245-252, 254-257

SMACS Technology 20

smart airport 216-220, 222, 226-227, 230-233, 236-237

Smart Airport Management 233, 236

social media 22, 28, 34, 42, 74-75, 81, 85, 142-143, 146, 149-152, 157, 159-162, 167-168, 181-182, 189-190, 193-195, 198-199, 202, 204, 207-208, 210-213, 220, 252, 288-291, 294-300, 315

social media analysis 189, 195, 207, 211

social network analysis 189-193, 195, 197-199, 204, 206-213

social networking 8, 150, 189-191, 193-195, 197, 199, 206, 208-209

Sparkassen-DataAnalytics 350, 353, 355-356, 361-364, 366-367, 371

stare decisis 106-107, 112

statistical models 34, 76, 301-302, 305, 309, 312-313, 354

Stop Words 349

subjective well-being 288-295, 297-300

T

text mining 36, 45, 198-199, 207, 211, 213, 288-290, 296, 299-300, 315

time series forecasting 301-310, 312-313, 315-317, 319

Time Series Models 301, 304

Tools for Business Analytics 166

traffic 15, 27, 39, 97, 107, 137, 142, 144-145, 148, 151-163, 165, 199, 224-225, 301, 306, 308-310, 314

trust 150-152, 158, 180, 183, 206, 208, 213, 289-295, 297-300, 364

Twitter 34, 74, 85, 150, 181, 189-190, 193-194, 199-200, 202, 208, 210, 213, 288-291, 293-300

U

undergraduate students 273, 285, 289

V

video games 183, 190, 320-324, 346

W

web traffic 158, 165, 301, 308-310, 314

Web Traffic Prediction 301
Weibo 190, 320, 324, 346, 348
word cloud 320, 323, 340, 349

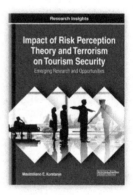

Become an Evaluator for IGI Global Authored Book Projects

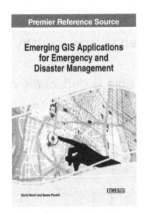

Premier Reference Source

Emerging GIS Applications for Emergency and Disaster Management

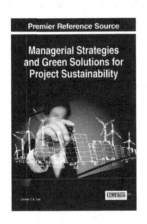

Premier Reference Source

Managerial Strategies and Green Solutions for Project Sustainability

Premier Reference Source

Comparative Approaches to Using R and Python for Statistical Data Analysis

Premier Reference Source

Solutions for High-Touch Communications in a High-Tech World

The overall success of an authored book project is dependent on quality and timely manuscript evaluations.

Applications and Inquiries may be sent to:
development@igi-global.com

Applicants must have a doctorate (or equivalent degree) as well as publishing, research, and reviewing experience. Authored Book Evaluators are appointed for one-year terms and are expected to complete at least three evaluations per term. Upon successful completion of this term, evaluators can be considered for an additional term.

If you have a colleague that may be interested in this opportunity, we encourage you to share this information with them.

www.igi-global.com

Publisher of Peer-Reviewed, Timely, and
Innovative Academic Research Since 1988

IGI Global's Transformative Open Access (OA) Model:
How to Turn Your University Library's Database Acquisitions Into a Source of OA Funding

Well in advance of Plan S, IGI Global unveiled their OA Fee Waiver (Read & Publish) Initiative. Under this initiative, librarians who invest in IGI Global's InfoSci-Books and/or InfoSci-Journals databases will be able to subsidize their patrons' OA article processing charges (APCs) when their work is submitted and accepted (after the peer review process) into an IGI Global journal.

How Does it Work?

Step 1: **Library Invests in the InfoSci-Databases:** A library perpetually purchases or subscribes to the InfoSci-Books, InfoSci-Journals, or discipline/subject databases.

Step 2: **IGI Global Matches the Library Investment with OA Subsidies Fund:** IGI Global provides a fund to go towards subsidizing the OA APCs for the library's patrons.

Step 3: **Patron of the Library is Accepted into IGI Global Journal (After Peer Review):** When a patron's paper is accepted into an IGI Global journal, they option to have their paper published under a traditional publishing model or as OA.

Step 4: **IGI Global Will Deduct APC Cost from OA Subsidies Fund:** If the author decides to publish under OA, the OA APC fee will be deducted from the OA subsidies fund.

Step 5: **Author's Work Becomes Freely Available:** The patron's work will be freely available under CC BY copyright license, enabling them to share it freely with the academic community.

Note: This fund will be offered on an annual basis and will renew as the subscription is renewed for each year thereafter. IGI Global will manage the fund and award the APC waivers unless the librarian has a preference as to how the funds should be managed.

Hear From the Experts on This Initiative:

"I'm very happy to have been able to make one of my recent research contributions *freely available* along with having access to the *valuable resources* found within IGI Global's InfoSci-Journals database."

– Prof. Stuart Palmer,
Deakin University, Australia

"Receiving the support from IGI Global's OA Fee Waiver Initiative *encourages me to continue my research work without any hesitation*."

– Prof. Wenlong Liu, College of Economics and Management at Nanjing University of Aeronautics & Astronautics, China

For More Information, Scan the QR Code or Contact:
IGI Global's Digital Resources Team at eresources@igi-global.com.

Printed in the United States
by Baker & Taylor Publisher Services